PRODUCTION: PLANNING, CONTROL, AND INTEGRATION

McGRAW-HILL SERIES IN INDUSTRIAL ENGINEERING AND MANAGEMENT SCIENCE

Consulting Editors

Kenneth E. Case, Department of Industrial Engineering and Management,
  Oklahoma State University
Philip M. Wolfe, Department of Industrial and Management Systems-Engineering,
  Arizona State University

PRODUCTION: PLANNING, CONTROL, AND INTEGRATION

Daniel Sipper

Department of Industrial Engineering
Tel Aviv University

Robert L. Bulfin, Jr.

Department of Industrial and Systems Engineering
Auburn University

The McGraw-Hill Companies, Inc.

New York   St. Louis   San Francisco   Auckland   Bogotá   Caracas   Lisbon
London   Madrid   Mexico City   Milan   Montreal   New Delhi
San Juan   Sydney   Tokyo   Toronto

McGraw-Hill

A Division of The **McGraw·Hill** *Companies*

PRODUCTION: PLANNING, CONTROL, AND INTEGRATION

Copyright©1997 by The McGraw-Hill Companies, Inc. All rights reserved. Printed in the United States of America. Except as permitted under the United States Copyright Act of 1976, no part of this publication may be reproduced or distributed in any form or by any means, or stored in a data base or retrieval system, without the prior written permission of the publisher.

This book is printed on acid-free paper.

1 2 3 4 5 6 7 8 9 0 DOC DOC 9 0 9 8 7 6

ISBN 0-07-057682-3

This book was set in Times Roman by Publication Services, Inc.
The editors were Eric M. Munson and John M. Morriss;
the production supervisor was Kathryn Porzio.
The cover was designed by Joan Greenfield.
Project supervision was done by Publication Services, Inc.
R. R. Donnelley & Sons Company was printer and binder.

Library of Congress Cataloging-in-Publication Data

Sipper, Daniel.
    Production : planning, control, and integration / Daniel Sipper,
Robert Bulfin.
       p.   cm.—(McGraw-Hill series in industrial engineering and
management science)
    Includes bibliographical references and index.
     ISBN 0-07-057682-3 (acid-free paper)
    1. Production planning. 2. Production control.   3. Inventory
control. I. Bulfin, Robert. II. Title. III. Series.
TS175.S559   1997
658.5—dc20   96-36137

http://www.mhcollege.com

ABOUT THE AUTHORS

Daniel Sipper is on the faculty of the department of Industrial Engineering at Tel Aviv University. He received his B.Sc. from Technion, Israel Institute of Technology, M.Sc. from Columbia University, and Ph.D. in Industrial Engineering from the Georgia Institute of Technology.

Prior to obtaining his Ph.D., Dr. Sipper spent 11 years in industry, both in Israel and the United States. He worked in different aspects of industrial systems, holding positions at various organizations and different levels—research engineer, production manager, and senior project manager. Among the topics he was involved in are manufacturing, production control, R&D, project control and strategic planning—in varied industries: process, metal, and defense.

Upon completing his Ph.D., Dr. Sipper stayed on the faculty of Georgia Tech. In 1972 he joined Tel Aviv University in Israel and established the program in Industrial Engineering, first as an undergraduate track, becoming a separate department granting all three degrees in 1980. He served as its first chairman until 1985. His teaching and research interests are in the various aspects of production systems. Over the years, Prof. Sipper served on numerous major university and national committees. He is a senior member of IIE, INFORMS, and ASME, and also serves on the editorial board of the *International Journal of Production Research*. Dr. Sipper is chairman of the Scientific Committee of ICTAF-Interdisciplinary Center for Technological Analysis and Forecasting at Tel Aviv University.

Robert L. Bulfin, Jr., received the B.I.E. from the Georgia Institute of Technology. Upon graduation, he accepted a position with Celanese Fibers Company as an industrial engineer. There he was involved in all phases of industrial engineering: job design, standards and methods, quality control, process optimization, layout, material flow, and inventory control.

After leaving Celanese, Bob returned to Georgia Tech and earned the M.S. and Ph.D. degrees from the School of Industrial & Systems Engineering. After completing the Ph.D., he accepted an appointment on the faculty of Systems and Industrial Engineering at the University of Arizona. There he was responsible for teaching undergraduate and graduate courses in industrial engineering and operations research. He left Arizona to accept a faculty position at Auburn University, where he is currently Professor of Industrial Engineering.

Dr. Bulfin's teaching and research interests are in production planning and control and operations reseach. He has worked with a number of private industries, including mining, electronics, agriculture, aerospace, plastics, textiles, and metal forming. His research has been primarily in production planning and control and sponsored NASA, DoD, USAID, and a number of private companies.

CONTENTS

PREFACE

1 INTRODUCTION

This preface describes the philosophy, approach and contents of *Production: Planning, Control, and Integration.* This book discusses production systems, the dynamic backbone of modern manufacturing and service. Without intelligent planning, control and integration of the production system, no business can be competitive in today's global marketplace.

We wrote this book for two reasons. First, the production environment is undergoing continual change. Second, the academic community is responding by changing curricula. After years of teaching and working in production systems, we wanted to be part of this exciting change.

The coverage of the text reflects our experience in teaching and working in production systems, combined with a study of current curricula in engineering and business programs and an assessment of future needs. We cover the evolution of production systems, problem solving, forecasting, aggregate planning, inventory, materials requirements planning, scheduling, project management, and integrated production planning and control. We assume the student is familiar with basic statistics and operations research. Detailed descriptions of the chapters are given later.

2 PHILOSOPHY

Most books present production control as a collection of models and algorithms. While we feel these are important and the student must master them, it is unlikely that any model will exactly fit situations encountered after graduation. Thus the emphasis is on understanding **how** to solve these problems. This means developing models, understanding underlying assumptions, identifying data needs, and knowing when and how to use them.

Learning certain skills is easy, all you need is to be told what to do and follow the "recipe." Learning the simplex algorithm is like that. These are things that a computer can do very well. Other skills, like becoming a good problem solver, are more difficult. Learning them is like learning to ride a bicycle—someone can tell you how, but the only way to really learn is by doing it. Ideally, we would learn these types of skills by serving an apprenticeship, but most companies want employees to be productive immediately. To aid the student, we have included a chapter on problem solving. While many think these skills are developed in earlier courses, we do not agree. Our problem driven approach further emphasizes more than plug-and-crank thinking.

3 APPROACH

The best term to describe our approach is "problem driven." Most chapters start with a comprehensive example of the problem environment, setting the stage for the subject matter discussion. Each chapter has ample examples demonstrating the specific technique or concept discussed. When appropriate, the chapter contains a summary and short overview of how the specific subject evolved. Also, as required, the discussion highlights computer aspects, and a separate section is devoted to the software available in the specific area.

The discussion includes a rigorous mathematical treatment where appropriate. However, the rigor builds gradually. For flexibility, each section ends with a set of homework problems. Our homework philosophy can be described as a "four-tier" approach, since problems belong to one of four types: drills, exercises, problems, or minicases. Drills are straightforward plug-and-crank assignments, exercises require the student to choose the one correct technique, problems may have several correct approaches depending on the assumptions made, and minicases require the student to recognize the appropriate need or opportunity. Some require the use of a computer. The book contains about 550 problems, plus mini-cases. Spreadsheets, STORM, QuickQuant, or other software ease the computational burden on the student. A reference list for further study appears at the end of each chapter.

4 IMPORTANT FEATURES

Certain important features of our text are unique. We summarize them as follows:

- A chapter on modeling and problem solving
- A chapter on integration
- Illustrative examples at the beginning of most sections, followed by a discussion of the theories and techniques
- A balance between breadth and depth
- Rigorous math—at the proper level
- A theoretically exact, but application-oriented approach that is in tune with today's problems and developments
- A problem-driven rather than tool-driven approach
- More than 100 examples
- More than 150 figures to enhance discussion
- Use of "boxes" (separate discussions) to highlight implementation and practice of the concepts

5 USING THE BOOK

The book is oriented toward upper level industrial engineering students and MBA programs that have a course focusing on production. The book can be used for a one- or two-quarter sequence or a one- or two-semester sequence, depending on coverage scope or depth. There is probably more material in the book than would be covered in a typical university offering.

This allows the instructor to choose topics to cover. We also view this book as more than a textbook—it should be a valuable resource for the **practitioner.** After all, learning does not stop when a student graduates.

When we wrote this book, we had flexibility in mind, both between chapters and within chapters. The sequence of topics is the one that looked most logical to us; however, we realize other instructors may do it differently. The embedded flexibility enables each instructor to construct a unique recipe without encountering too much difficulty. The only sequence-dependent chapters are Chapters 6 and 7.

Flexibility in terms of scope can be achieved by covering fewer topics. Flexibility in terms of depth is obtained by skipping sections within a chapter. Thus, if less mathematical rigor is desired, it is possible to omit the mathematical derivation and consider only the result.

The fact that homework appears after each section makes it easy for the instructor to assign homework if a section is omitted. The difficulty of each homework problem (the "four-tier" approach) can be judged from the Instructor's Manual.

6   SUMMARY AND UNIQUE ASPECTS

We give a brief summary and highlight unique aspects of each chapter of the book.

Chapter 1   The Production Paradigm

We begin by describing the world as an open trading system; global competition is a major factor. We identify four stages in the evolution of production systems: ancient systems, feudal systems, European factory systems, and American factory systems. All aspects of scientific management are discussed as part of production-driven systems. Discussions of product life cycle, high-tech and low-tech systems, and types of organization used and decisions made in production systems are also included.

Chapter 2   Market-Driven Systems

This chapter describes market-driven systems, a unique approach in production systems texts. From today's management practice, classical theories do not cover all aspects of the new environment. While future concepts are uncertain, we list major theories we believe will be applicable. We integrate these concepts in the "wheel of competitiveness," the hub of which is the customer. The transition from a culture of efficiency to one of effectiveness is presented. We elaborate on integration and show how it has generated a new manufacturing environment, the integrated production system. Finally, we discuss world-class manufacturing and its spin-offs, lean production and agile manufacturing.

Chapter 3   Problem Solving

Most production system textbooks do not have a chapter on problem solving, but we felt it necessary to include one. It begins with an outline of a problem-solving approach. The most important steps are identifying and understanding the problem. Once this is done, a model is usually constructed. Describing problem boundaries, objectives, relationships, and variables are part of model construction. Needed data are identified and a representation chosen.

The model is solved with an appropriate algorithm and the model's solution is interpreted considering the actual situation. Finally, a solution to the actual problem is implemented.

Chapter 4   Forecasting

We begin this chapter with a discussion of a forecasting system within a problem-solving framework. Most forecasting in a production system is based on identifying the pattern of the underlying process, using a correct model for the process and an appropriate forecasting method. We discuss several types of forecasting methods, including qualitative, causal, and time series methods. A brief discussion of nontraditional forecasting methods is given, along with appropriate references. We present ways to measure forecast accuracy, which is used to maintain control of the forecasting system. We conclude with a section devoted to forecasting in practice.

Chapter 5   Aggregate Planning

Aggregate planning focuses on intermediate range production planning. We discuss four factors affecting the decision: capacity, production costs, capacity change costs, and inventory costs. Two major approaches to aggregate planning are presented: spreadsheet methods and optimization methods. Spreadsheet methods can produce zero inventory, level production, and mixed strategies. Optimization approaches include linear programming and transportation models. Though not included in most texts, more advanced models for multiple products and multiple processes are presented here.

Chapter 6   Inventory: Independent Demand Systems

Rather than the common breakdown of inventory systems by deterministic and stochastic models, we discuss inventory models from a decision-based viewpoint. We divide the chapter by quantity, timing, and control decisions. Starting with a discussion of inventory policies and concepts, we present more than 20 models, most with rigorous mathematical and implementation aspects. A separate section discusses the relevance of inventory models in the era of inventory reduction and just-in-time production methods. Inventory as a service policy is emphasized both conceptually and quantitatively. Examples highlight the models. The section on control decisions is a unique addition to the book. It contains a mathematical analysis of the Pareto principle, followed by discussion of inventory-control system design in a multi-item environment. Each decision section ends with a summary table.

Chapter 7   Production, Capacity, and Material Planning

This chapter examines dependent demand systems. Within this framework, we discuss capacity, the master production schedule, and material requirements planning as they relate to three different product-market environments. Product structure, explosion, implosion, netting, and pegging are also covered. Lot sizing methods and their extension to multi-item hierarchical systems are presented. Multi-echelon inventory control in MRP systems follows. A touch telephone example is used to explain the models presented. Shop floor control and MRP as an information system conclude the chapter.

Chapter 8   Operations Scheduling

After defining the basic scheduling problem, we present single-machine models for various measures of performance. Parallel models follow, with worst-case results and list-based heuristics. Flow shops are defined and exact algorithms are given for special cases and heuristics for the general model. Job shops, the most difficult to schedule, are discussed last. Dispatch heuristics are provided, as is a discussion of several priority rules. Examples clarify the models and procedures, and a box on implementation adds real-world flavor.

Chapter 9   Project Planning, Scheduling, and Control

We discuss organizational, managerial, and quantitative aspects of projects. A section is devoted to product development, and a product development example is used throughout the chapter to illustrate concepts and methodologies. Basic planning, scheduling, and control of projects are discussed. A quantitative treatment of PERT, limited resources, and time/cost trade-offs follows. Again we use a box to discuss actual application issues.

Chapter 10   Integrated Production Planning and Control

We feel this chapter is unique in both its approach and structure. We focus on integration as a global approach to production planning and control. Integration describes both a concept and a technique. We begin by examining integration-related issues: interaction of the production function with the rest of the organization, control architecture, and interplant integration. Integrated production planning and control is an embracing concept with an underlying philosophy and a set of tools to implement it. We give the three major approaches to integrated production planning and control. These are push systems (MRP II and ERP), pull systems (JIT), and bottleneck systems (OPT and CONWIP). Detailed discussion of each approach is included; mathematical models and examples are used when appropriate. We conclude the chapter by comparing and contrasting the three approaches.

Daniel Sipper
Robert L. Bulfin, Jr.

ACKNOWLEDGMENTS

Writing a textbook is a long, intense effort. Fortunately, we had the assistance, advice, and encouragement of many people. We cannot list everyone who helped us here, but a few people must be thanked publicly. If we inadvertently omit anyone, we apologize in advance.

This book began while Dan was on sabbatical at Auburn University. Ed Unger, chairman of the department of industrial and systems engineering, provided encouragement, assistance, and material support throughout our efforts. Without his active support, we could not have completed the book.

The faculty and staff of the industrial engineering departments at Auburn and Tel Aviv and the senior staff of Telrad Corporation, Israel, sympathized with our problems, shared our joy, and provided advice and encouragement. In particular, we thank J Black, Russ Meller, Chan Park, and Chuck Sox.

Bob Inman, General Motors Research Labs, and Ed Mykytka, Air Force Institute of Technology, also made significant contributions to the book. Peter Purdue, the faculty and staff at the Naval Postgraduate School, John Jarvis, and the faculty and staff at Georgia Tech provided support for Bob while he visited them on sabbatical.

We thank our students at Auburn University and Tel Aviv University who read early drafts, worked problems, and provided valuable suggestions for improving the book. Cindi Perdue and Narayanan Venkatacha, Auburn University, and Avi Sless, Tel Aviv University, deserve special thanks for work on the text, graphics, homework problems, and solutions.

We are grateful to many reviewers who waded through several drafts of the manuscript. They provided excellent feedback and greatly improved the text. The reviewers include Ronald G. Askin, U. of Arizona, Diane E. Baily, USC, Catherine M. Harmonosky, Penn State, Timothy Ireland, Oklahoma State U., Hau L. Lee, Stanford, Surya D. Liman, Texas Tech, Jayant Rajgopal, U. of Pittsburgh, Nanua Singh, Wayne State U., G. Don Taylor, U. of Arkansas, and Wilbert Wilhelm, Texas A&M. Of course any mistakes in the text are entirely ours.

Eric Munson, Executive Editor-Engineering, McGraw-Hill, was our editor. He provided encouragement and helped us keep momentum through the tough times. We also thank the staffs at McGraw-Hill and Publication Services.

Last, but not least, we thank our families: Shosh, Moshe, and Yuval, and Lynn, Ben, and Matt. Without their support, inspiration, and sacrifices, this book would never have been published.

CHAPTER
1

THE PRODUCTION PARADIGM

Production systems are prominent in modern society. These systems form the base for building and improving the economic strength and vitality of a country. The task of developing and running production systems has become progressively complex. Major changes in products, processes, management technologies, concepts, and culture result in increasing challenges and demands. The information and techniques we present help meet these challenges. This chapter identifies and highlights some critical issues related to production systems. We start with a discussion of global production.

1   GLOBAL PRODUCTION

Spurred by the Renaissance in the 1600s and continuing with Britain's initiation of the first industrial revolution, Europe was the center of economic power in the nineteenth century; the United States, however, became the focus of the second industrial revolution, dominating twentieth century industry. Consequently, management theory and early techniques were the products of western developments. The concepts of the factory production line, division of labor, and functional management structure all matured in Europe and America. The post–World War II emergence of export-oriented southeast Asia, particularly Japan, as an industrial power has resulted in an open trading system in which we can no longer ignore international competition. The emergence of this global marketplace is the subject of this first section. We first present the evolution of production systems, followed by a discussion of the new competitive environment.

1.1   Evolution of Production Systems

We discuss two aspects of the evolution of production systems; its history and the management theories it created.

1

1.1.1   HISTORY. Four major types of production systems have evolved historically: ancient, feudal, European, and American.

We can trace the beginning of **ancient systems** to 5000 B.C. when Sumerian priests started keeping records of inventories, loans, and tax transactions. Around 4000 B.C. the Egyptians were using the basic management concepts of planning, organization, and control, as seen in their large construction projects such as the pyramids and similar structures. Other early developments included the ideas of a minimum wage and managerial responsibility stated in the Code of Hammurabi around 1800 B.C. Around 1500 B.C. the Hebrews were using the exception principle, choosing workers to suit tasks, and designating "staff" positions within the system.

In the Far East the Chinese had a fully developed government system in place by 1100 B.C. They were practicing specialization of labor and planning, organizing, and controlling production. Somewhat later, around 350 B.C., the Greeks were espousing specialization of labor and having workers use uniform motions and work at the same pace.

During the Middle Ages, the **feudal system** evolved, in which the emperor, king, or queen had total power over the country. Nobles were given power over regions in exchange for loyalty to the ruler. The nobles in turn might delegate lands and authority to lesser lords and so on, down to freemen and serfs. The production systems in existence at this time are best described as domestic. Typically, the family members were the owners as well as the workers, and they did the work at home. Land and labor were the major production factors of the time, which remained the case until the middle of the fifteenth century.

The **European system** started evolving during the Renaissance. Although we normally think of the Renaissance for cultural development, much was happening, particularly in Italy, that would affect industrialization and production systems. Double entry bookkeeping and cost accounting were practiced there in the 1300s. Of even more interest is the story of the Venice Arsenal, which was a sophisticated ship assembly facility (Box 1-1).

BOX 1-1: THE VENICE ARSENAL

As Venice prospered, it needed a strong navy to protect both the city and its commercial fleet. Initially the city commissioned warships from private builders and in emergencies, conscripted commercial vessels. However, by 1436 a government shipyard called the Arsenal was operational. This production system was the largest and most complex in the world at that time and would be considered as such even by today's standards. The Arsenal had 2000 workers and more than 60 acres of land and water. It built new ships, arms, and equipment and refurbished existing ships. All spare parts and naval supplies were stored there, and the entire facility was located on a canal. A ship hull was towed along the canal where workers installed various equipment at individual shops along the way. Shops were positioned in the order that tasks were performed, so a bare hull starting the process would emerge as a ship complete with crew at the end of the canal. If necessary, this process could be done in as little as one hour; the Arsenal once produced over 100 ships in less than two months.

The next major change, the Industrial Revolution, began in the British Isles in the early 1700s. More efficient farming methods requiring less land and fewer people to produce necessary foodstuffs was one cause. In addition, having the workers in a central location meant that someone, usually the owner, was in control, which meant that incentives for improving production methods were greater.

In 1776 Adam Smith publicized the division of labor concept in his book, *The Wealth of Nations.* Rather than have one person complete a product, he suggested each be responsible for only one part of the completed job. With specialization he increased the number of pins manufactured per person from 20 to 48,000 per day. About 50 years later, Charles Babbage published *On the Economy of Machinery and Manufactures* (1832), advocating specialization of labor.

Specialization of labor increased the market size in all areas. As people increasingly performed specialized tasks, they became increasingly dependent on others to make such items as clothing, shoes, and furniture, creating larger markets. The urbanization of society created large cities full of workers who needed to buy things and had money to spend, which, coupled with improved transportation, created mass markets that demanded mass production.

The beginning of the **American system** can be traced to the development of the modern lathe by Maudslay around 1800. The most important aspect of Maudslay's development was that now some machines were capable of reproducing themselves, which started the machine tool industry and had a great impact on later developments in production systems.

Across the Atlantic Ocean in America, other exciting events were happening. Eli Whitney, inventor of the cotton gin, promoted manufacturing with interchangeable parts. Widely credited as the first to use this idea, we note the Venice Arsenal used interchangeable parts in the 1400s. Whitney used jigs and fixtures to orient and hold the parts, which could be made by less-skilled machinists. This system of manufacture—called the *American system*—was adopted by many factories.

The convergence of interchangeable parts, specialization of labor, steam power, and machine tools resulted in the emergence of the American system, which was the precursor of mass production as we know it today.

In 1903 Oldsmobile Motors created a stationary assembly line to produce their cars. The potential number of cars produced per year increased by a factor of ten. In 1908 Cadillac demonstrated their parts were interchangeable. They shipped three cars to England and disassembled them. The parts were mixed, and the cars were then reassembled. In 1913 Ford expanded these ideas to a moving assembly line with interchangeable parts. A Model T rolled off the assembly line every two hours, with an affordable price of $400 that changed the automobile from a rich man's toy into a product for the masses.

The assembly line is the logical outgrowth of specialization of labor and the use of capital to replace labor. Not all manufacturing shops became mass production facilities. Plants that made a variety of parts with low demand or customized products remained the same.

1.1.2 MANAGEMENT THEORIES. Early management theories evolved in this environment because operating systems were needed to meet increased production demands. As in many other historical developments a beginning is hard to pinpoint. Many people contributed to the process, but Henry Towne was in the forefront. In 1886 he delivered a paper to the American Society of Mechanical Engineers in which he claimed shop management was as important as engineering management.

Frederick Taylor is often called the father of scientific management. Starting as a common laborer at Midvale Steel, he held a variety of jobs, working his way through the ranks until he became chief plant engineer. From his work experience, Taylor knew improvement must start with the workers. He felt the solution was not to make them work harder but to manage them better. Management should develop proper work methods, teach them to the workers, and see that they follow them.

Taylor later wrote a book, *The Principles of Scientific Management* (1911), about his theories. His stated purpose in writing was to provide simple examples of waste through inefficiency and to show that the remedy lies with better management, not extraordinary workers. In addition, he wrote that the best management is a true science, based on well defined laws, rules, and principles, applicable to all human endeavors and yielding astounding results.

The Eastern Rate Case in 1910 was instrumental in advancing the theory of scientific management. The Interstate Commerce Commission heard a case by the railroads asking for rate increases to defray increasing costs. Taylor and other proponents of scientific management (Towne, Gantt, Barth, F. Gilbreth, and Emmerson) testified for several days on the inefficiency of the railroads. They discussed ways to decrease costs and raise wages while maintaining rates at the present level. Louis Brandeis, the lawyer representing the shippers, and the expert witnesses coined the term *scientific management*. Through the publicity associated with the case, both the phrase and the theories gained wider acceptance.

As scientific management gained acceptance in the United States, Henri Fayol developed his own theories in France (Fayol, 1984). Fayol was an engineer who later became managing director of a large mining company. He viewed problems from the top down rather than from the shop floor, as Taylor did. Fayol believed a firm had six functions: technical (the actual production), commercial (buying and selling), financial (getting and allocating money), security (protection of people and property), accounting (keeping records), and managerial (planning, organizing, command, coordination, and control).

Academia's contribution to developing management theory came later. Between 1924 and 1927, production levels of a small group of workers at the Hawthorne Works of Western Electric were studied. The idea was to change working conditions one at a time and measure the workers' output. They first increased the lighting level, and as expected, production increased. The unexpected happened when production still increased as the lighting level was lowered. The increase continued, even when the available light was only as bright as moonlight. At this point, they judged the problem more complicated than originally thought and called in Elton Mayo, a Harvard professor and the first academic to make major contributions to production system management. The people discussed previously were all practitioners. Mayo concluded that logical factors are far less important than social factors in motivating workers. In essence, the *attention* the workers got made them feel special, and they worked harder. The lesson again is that the human factor is critical in production systems.

1.2   The Competitive Environment

The National Center for Manufacturing Sciences (NCMS, 1988) suggests:

> Competitiveness is the degree to which a nation can, under free and fair market conditions, produce goods and services that meet the tests of international markets, while simultaneously maintaining or expanding the real income of its citizens.

We adopt their definition. Today's global market has made competition more important than ever. Therefore, we review the development of the competitive environment since World War II.

1.2.1 THE STATUS. The consensus is that American competitiveness has declined in recent years. Now, instead of dominating world markets as they have since World War II, American firms are adjusting rather than leading (Cohen, Zysman, 1987). This situation is especially disheartening considering that the European and Japanese infrastructures were destroyed during World War II and American industry assumed a leading role.

1.2.2 THE DECLINE IN COMPETITIVENESS. The United States can re-establish its industrial competitive edge. First, however, we must understand the elements that led to this decline.

Following World War II, the United States helped the ruined Japanese and European economies recover. The Marshall Plan for economic aid in Europe and the MacArthur Plan in Japan helped rebuild the countries' industrial infrastructures. Not only did American manufacturers supply goods through these plans, the virtual lack of competition opened markets in the rest of the world to American products. Within the United States, a population weary of war and deprivation was all too ready to buy any product. By perfecting its manufacturing, America achieved awesome feats of production and innovation. This era was one of mass production, and management honed technology to provide cost-efficient production of high quality standardized goods. In turn, the customer bought what was offered; the market could be taken for granted. This market situation is a **production-driven system**. Whatever was manufactured would sell, allowing the customer little voice or influence. Efficiency of production was all important.

Due to marketing, economic, and political factors, some American companies began operating in foreign countries. These companies were called multinationals. The rising cost of U.S. labor caused American companies to move operations offshore, particularly to the Far East, where labor was cheaper and more productive. The cost advantage gained was used to sell those products in the home market. Subsequent to this offshore move, foreign countries were allowed on-site access to American production methods and management techniques, which would cost the United States later.

America entered the 1970s complacently and without recognizing the impact of the changes taking place in world markets. American companies continued to efficiently mass produce standardized goods, when products with different quality and price levels were now demanded. In the early 1980s some American companies began responding to the emerging global market. These responses gained momentum, and these companies entered the 1990s realizing that the importance of mass production had diminished. Although mass production is still used, production efficiency is no longer the only consideration. The philosophy of manufacturing excellence, or world class manufacturing, is replacing the philosophy of mass production.

1.2.3 THE CHANGING ENVIRONMENT. Of the many changes, the increase in customer sophistication has been most important. The customer is more demanding and seeks more variety, lower cost, and superb quality. The market economic structure switched from economy of scale (mass production) to economy of scope (variety). This economy of choice (Starr, 1988) has emphasized variety over mass standardized products. The idea of purchasing a car designed to suit individual taste in such things as power, color, and features has replaced the black Model T Ford syndrome. Industry has the difficult task of combining the efficiency of mass production with the variety and craftsmanship of pre-industrial revolution times. The customer dictates what is offered, and industry follows demands. The production-driven system of the mass production era has been replaced by a **market-driven system**.

In a market-driven system, the customer is the driving force, in contrast to production-driven systems, in which the customer had little voice. As a result of being responsive to customer demands, the market-driven system operates under swiftly changing dynamics, a direct contrast to the stable environment of earlier production-driven systems.

Foreign competition is a dominant factor in market-driven systems. The most significant development is that the world has become one global market, which is even more pronounced following developments in eastern Europe and the Far East. Beyond the regional or local competition of the 1970s, U.S. manufacturers must compete not only with European countries and Japan but also with countries in the Far East and South America. As competition grew from regional to global, so did the nature of the demand. A homogeneous market (as in the mass production era) has become a heterogeneous global market segmented by population dynamics. Changing from a market in which one product fits all, competition forced the manufacture of products that meet the needs and expectations of individual consumers. "Markets" do not buy anything, individuals do (Starr, 1988). These individuals demand high quality and custom design of products and services. A market of **consumers** has evolved into a market of **prosumers**—consumers integrated into the design process (Starr, 1988).

Other factors of the changing environment are summarized as follows (Skinner, copyright © 1985, John Wiley and Sons, Inc. Reprinted by permission.):

- The age of mass production is passing. The production-driven system of the past has been replaced by the market-driven system of the present and future.
- More sophisticated customers emphasize choice, quality, and lower cost—prosumers rather than consumers.
- Global competition and heterogeneous markets have evolved.
- Information technology has changed the business nature and the nature of the business.
- New materials, new manufacturing processes, and new product technologies are proliferating.
- Product life cycles are shorter.
- Product volumes are becoming smaller, and product variety is getting bigger.
- New product development cycles are shortening.
- Superb product quality combined with low cost is of utmost importance.
- The mix of costs is shifting, with overhead, material, and capital costs rising and direct labor declining.
- Worker culture, demographics, and the sociology of work are different now than they were in the 1960s.

In Section 2 we discuss production systems in more detail.

SECTION 1 PROBLEMS

1.1. Define ancient production system.
1.2. Define feudal production system.
1.3. Define European production system.
1.4. Define American production system.
1.5. Compare and contrast the four major types of production systems.

1.6. Suppose workers at the Venice Arsenal worked 14 hours a day, 6 days a week. Out of the 2000 workers, 1800 were direct labor. If 100 ships were produced in 8 weeks, how many man-hours were required to build a ship?

1.7. What is the new message Adam Smith had in his book *The Wealth of Nations?*

1.8. What is Whitney's contribution to production systems?

1.9. Describe the evolution of the assembly line.

1.10. What is the major finding of the Hawthorne experiments?

1.11. Summarize the evolution of the competitive environment.

1.12. What are the major components of market-driven systems?

1.13. Discuss how the market-driven system impacts the automotive industry.

2 PRODUCTION SYSTEMS

In the broadest sense a production system is anything that produces something. However, we will define it more formally to be anything that takes inputs and transforms them into outputs with inherent value. A good example of a production system is a firm that manufactures simple pencils. Raw materials such as wood, graphite, and paint are the inputs. The transformation consists of cutting the wood in sheets, sanding it, grooving the wood, adding the lead, joining the sheets, cutting the pencil shape, and finally painting the finished pencil. The pencil is the output. We think of large manufacturing operations as production systems, but many other examples are quite different. For example, your university is a production system. Freshmen are the input, acquisition of knowledge is the transformation, and the output is an educated person. We can break production systems into two classes: manufacturing and service. In manufacturing, the inputs and outputs are usually tangible, and the transformations are often physical. On the other hand, service-oriented production systems may have intangible inputs/outputs, such as information. Transformations may not be physical, as in education. Another difference is that manufacturing goods may be made in anticipation of customer need, which is often not possible for services. Education is a good example of this; students cannot be taught before they enroll. For simplicity, we limit our discussion to for-profit manufacturing production systems.

With production systems, we normally think of the portion we can see, usually the transformation processes. However, most modern production systems are like icebergs—the visible portion is a small part of the whole system. The study of production systems requires us to consider many of its components, which include the products, customers, raw materials, transformation processes, direct and indirect workers, and formal and informal systems that organize and control the entire process. These components lead to issues and decisions that must be addressed for the production system to operate properly.

We structure our discussion of production systems around four different components: production flow, building blocks of the system, technology, and system size.

2.1 The Flow Process

The backbone of any production system is the manufacturing process, a flow process with two major components: material and information. The physical flow of material can be seen, but information flow is intangible and more difficult to follow. Both types of flow have always existed; however, in the past, information flow was of little importance. As mentioned before,

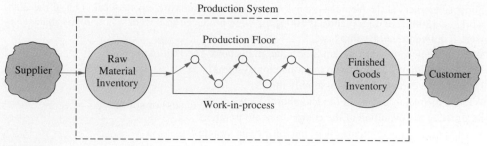

FIGURE 1-1
Generic physical flow

the emerging information technology reshaped production systems, so that information flow is critical.

In Figure 1-1 we show a generic model of physical flow in production systems. Material flows from the supplier to the production system, to become raw material inventory. It then moves to the production floor, where the material conversion process takes place. The material moves through different conversion processes performed at workstations but does not necessarily traverse the same route each time. Material on the production floor is called work-in-process inventory (WIP). From the production floor the material flows to a location where it becomes finished goods inventory. From there it flows to the customer, sometimes through intermediaries such as distribution centers or warehouses. Note that this discussion of physical production system flow includes both the supplier and customer. We elaborate on this concept in the following chapter.

Figure 1-2 shows a generic production information system. A common data base services all functions and activities of the production system, in whatever location. The leading principle is information integration. The outcome of information flow is seen on terminals throughout the production system.

To show the complexity of physical and information flows, we consider a television manufacturer. A TV is no longer just a TV; customer demands include a variety of sizes,

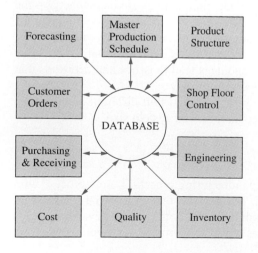

FIGURE 1-2
Generic production information system

styles, and features. Sizes range from the two-inch Watchman to 45-inch and larger projection screens. Styles include portables, table models, and consoles. Different features include picture-in-picture, cable readiness, sleep timer, a built-in VCR, and CD-ROM interactive systems. A plant must be able to make a range of the TVs demanded rather than just one standard model. The manufacturer must decide when and how many of each TV model to make. Once this decision is made the company must procure a variety of inputs, which may be the unprocessed raw materials (wood or plastic for the cases) or sophisticated components made separately (picture tubes). They must order the correct quantity and quality of these inputs and arrange for timely delivery and proper storage. People, processes, and materials are coordinated to ensure a quality product completed in a timely, cost-effective manner. Finally, the finished product is packed and shipped to the customer. Although giving a glimpse of system complexity, this simplified description ignores other functions of a production system, such as the choice of technology, maintenance of physical equipment, financial matters, advertising and marketing, and distribution.

2.2 Building Blocks

The goal of production systems is to manufacture and deliver products. The principal activity in meeting this goal is the manufacturing process, in which the material conversion of transforming raw material into a product takes place. The manufacturing process can be viewed as a value-adding process. In each phase the conversion performed (at a cost) adds value to the raw material. When this value-adding process is complete, the product is ready.

To be competitive the goal is that the material conversion has to meet, **concurrently**, the following objectives:

Quality: The product must have superb quality—equal to or better than its competitors.

Cost: The cost of the product must be lower than the competition.

Time: The product must be delivered to the customer on time, every time.

There are interactions among the three, e.g., customers accept higher cost for unique products and lower quality for cheap ones.

Later chapters elaborate on these objectives. We introduce them now because, in a way, they are the core of this book. A company meeting these objectives concurrently is, relative to production, in a very competitive position.

Although there are many elements that support the achievement of these objectives, we discuss only two here: the physical and organizational arrangements.

2.2.1 PHYSICAL ARRANGEMENTS. The material conversion process takes place on the production floor, which is arranged in a certain way to facilitate conversion. Production volume and product variety determine the type of arrangement, or **layout**. Consider, for example, a chair manufacturer. Intuitively, the manufacturing process to make 50 identical chairs would differ from one to produce 50,000 identical chairs. Also, producing the same number of five different types of chairs would compound the problem. To meet these varying needs, two fundamentally different types of physical layout have evolved: the **job shop** and the **flow shop**.

A **job shop** produces low-volume highly customized products, i.e., making 25 chairs each in three different styles. Job shops usually have several elements in common. Workers must be skilled enough to make a variety of products. Similarly, general purpose equipment,

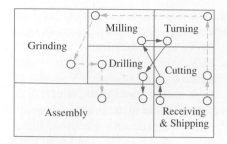

FIGURE 1-3
Process or functional layout

which can handle within limits different types of jobs, is normally used. A sewing machine, for example, is general purpose equipment for the garment industry. The final characteristic of a job shop is that each job follows its own path or route through the layout.

One typical job shop layout of manufacturing equipment is a **process layout**, in which similar machines are grouped. For example, in a machine shop (a classic job shop), lathes are located in one area and milling machines in another area, as shown in Figure 1-3. We also show the routing of two different jobs through this layout. Obviously, increasing product variety causes routing to be more complex. Even though managing a job shop can be a difficult task, a large portion of American production is done in a job shop setting.

A **flow shop** produces a high-volume standardized product. The automobile industry is a good example of a flow shop. An assembly line maintains the material flow, hundreds of thousands of a given model of car may be made, and production may last for a year. Workers use special purpose equipment, need little skill, and are able to do fewer tasks than job shop workers.

Each product in a flow shop follows the same sequence of operations. The manufacturing sequence or assembly operations required by the product determine the layout. A flow shop uses a **product layout**. Equipment is arranged so that the product always follows the same routing through the layout (Figure 1-4). In addition to the car industry, manufacturers of home appliances and electronic products use flow shops. Managing a flow shop differs from a job shop. Rather than daily scheduling, the critical problem is setting up and balancing tasks along the assembly line to ensure a smooth operation.

Between the extremes of job shops and flow shops is a hybrid of the two, the **batch shop**. A batch shop is not a high-volume producer; it produces in batches ranging in size from a few to several thousand units. Some degree of customization is possible, though not as much as in a job shop.

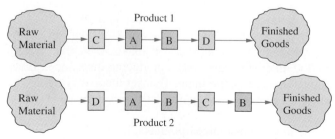

FIGURE 1-4
Product layout

Sometimes a single, customized product must be made. This production system is a **project shop**; its output is a one-time-only job. This layout is an extreme case of a job shop making a highly customized, unique product. A project shop uses a **fixed-position** layout. The product (ship, aircraft) stays in one place while the material and equipment are brought to it.

As the project shop is an extreme version of a job shop, the **continuous shop** is a radical extension of the flow shop. The continuous shop is characterized by continuous flow, as in petroleum and chemical industries. Discrete units are not produced, but liquids flowing through pipes are chemically transformed into the final products. Because we deal only with discrete production, continuous shops receive no further discussion.

The final physical layouts encountered are the **modern shops**. Modern shops fall into the class of Integrated Production Systems (IPS) and include three major types: Cellular Manufacturing Systems (CMS), Flexible Manufacturing Systems (FMS), and Computer Integrated Manufacturing (CIM). We discuss modern shops in Chapter 2.

2.2.2 ORGANIZATIONAL ARRANGEMENTS. The goal of organizations is to subdivide complex tasks into simpler components by division of labor. Designing a structure to do so requires addressing two primary issues: how to divide the labor and how to coordinate the resulting tasks (Hax and Majiluf, 1981). An industry's organization impacts its production system, so we must understand the organizational environment. There are three major types of organizational structures: functional, divisional, and matrix.

Functional and divisional are classic, though opposite, organizational structures. **Functional** structure is built around **inputs** used to achieve the tasks of an organization. These inputs are grouped according to the specialty of the functions performed, e.g., engineering, production, finance, marketing, human resources, quality, etc. A simplified functional organizational chart is shown in Figure 1-5. A more complex chart breaks each function into its sub-functions.

Divisional structure is built around the **outputs** generated by the organization. The most common is to structure the organization around its products. However, divisional structure could be built around projects, services, programs, clients, specific markets, or geographical locations. Today, a divisional structure is commonly called the *strategic business unit* (SBU). In Figure 1-6 we show a divisional organization by product. Each strategic business unit has separate engineering (including R&D), marketing, and control functions. The

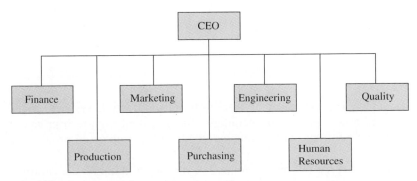

FIGURE 1-5
Functional organization

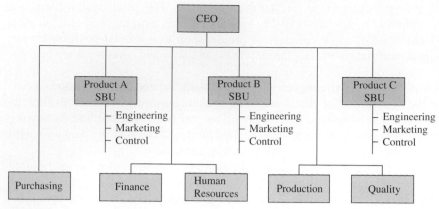

FIGURE 1-6
Product divisional organization (SBU)

control function is most important to a strategic business unit. Other functions such as production or purchasing may or may not be centralized.

Managers in a functional organization have authority commensurate with responsibility. In a strategic business unit structure, they tend to have more responsibility than authority. On the other hand a strategic business unit organization is more customer oriented, and therefore more popular in market-driven systems.

Both functional and divisional structures are designed around a single focus of either inputs or outputs, which maintains a "one person, one boss" hierarchy throughout the organization. A **matrix** organization is structured around two or more central design concepts. One person can have more than one boss, leading to ambiguity within the organization. In a matrix organization, a project or product manager is responsible for project completion or for successful development and sales of the product. The project manager does not directly control resources and must contract with other functions in the organization to complete project components. In Figure 1-7 we show a product matrix organization. It illustrates how a two-boss situation arises. An employee of a functional department also is responsible to the project manager; in effect, the employee has two bosses. Matrix organizations are difficult to manage and are commonly found in research and development (R&D) organizations.

These three organizational types are pure structures. In reality, an organization may be a hybrid of two or even all three. The dominant pattern of a hybrid can be traced back to one of the pure models.

2.3   Technology

In Section 1.2 we discussed the emergence of market-driven production systems. With these systems also appeared a new production paradigm: the so-called high-tech products or industries. In this section we further explore this paradigm and its impact on production systems.

Although it is difficult to agree on the definition of a high-tech industry, the continuously increasing rate of technological advancement is obvious. Just as clear is that this rate of advancement causes basic changes in products, processes, and managerial techniques. To

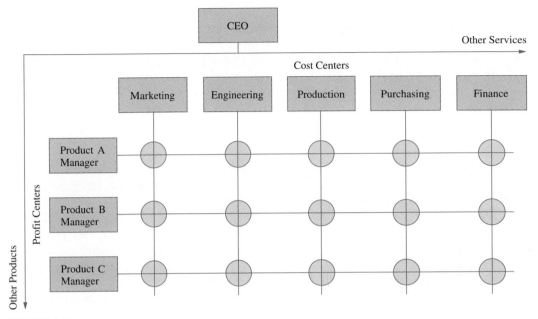

FIGURE 1-7
Matrix organization

incorporate and use these technological advances and enter the high-tech domain, industry must accept two realities:

- These advances are major and involve a shift in capital and complementary skills.
- These advances inherently involve a commitment to continuous change (Divan and Chakraborty, 1991).

Today certain products or industries are recognized as high-tech; e.g., aircraft and space industries, electronics, telecommunications, computers, pharmaceuticals, optics, and composite materials. Further study requires us to be more specific in our definition. Divan and Chakraborty (1991, p. 23) identify three criteria used to classify industries as high-tech.

- Research and development expenditures are above a minimum percentage of sales.
- The proportion of scientific and technological personnel to total employment is above a certain level.
- The product has a certain perceived degree of technological sophistication.

The third criterion is subjective and is the reason for including some industries on our earlier list. Numbers one and two are more objective. The Bureau of Labor Statistics (1982) offers definitions to get a more specific value for these ratios. Note that these two criteria do not depend on the product. The tacit assumption is that a high-tech product creates an environment that is independent of the product itself. Any industry not meeting these three criteria can be regarded as low-tech. Many industries traditionally perceived as low-tech are becoming increasingly high-tech. For example, the shoe industry is becoming more sophisticated, with high investment in R&D and automated production processes.

How does high-tech or low-tech impact a production system? As noted previously, a high-tech product impacts the entire production environment and requires constant change.

Therefore, production planning, management, and control cannot afford to lag. To produce a high-tech product, all supporting activities must themselves become as sophisticated as the high-tech environment.

The low-tech environment may not require sophisticated supporting activities, but they are not excluded. *Often, low-tech industries can benefit from sophisticated production planning and control techniques.* Approaches discussed in this book apply to both high- or low-tech industries.

2.4 Size of Organization

Organizations differ in size and scope, with these differences having an impact on the production systems. We examine three aspects of this impact: the physical process, the management process, and the production management decisions involved.

No matter the size of organizations, the physical process in each production system is similar in nature. The generic physical flow (Figure 1-1) and the ensuing layouts have much in common in any size industrial organization. The difference lies in relative complexity. Small organizations have straightforward material flow, as product volume and variety are limited. Large organizations, usually with a broader product mix, can have many flow routes through the production system. Although the physical locations may differ, each specific flow follows the general pattern described previously.

Before, we noted that organizational structures vary. The management process is different in large organizations as opposed to that of smaller ones. Each organization has a different managerial process, even though the physical flows are essentially the same. The major dissimilarity arises in the information flow and the related decision-making process. In a functional organization decisions are more centralized but are more decentralized in a strategic business unit. Because of size, decisions in a small organization are more centralized.

The production management decisions are another element of interest. In content, these decisions are virtually the same in any type of organization. Generating a forecast for future demand, preparing production plans, and purchasing material are generic decisions made in all size companies. Furthermore, the same types of production management tools are used. Again, the difference lies in complexity and scope. For a small organization a forecast or production plan can be generated by using a PC and simple software. A big organization may need sophisticated software and hardware for the same activities.

The major difference between small and large industrial organizations is not the nature of the physical flow, but the information flow and the decision-making processes used.

SECTION 2 PROBLEMS

1.14. Define production system.

1.15. Identify a production system of your choice, and define it.

1.16. What are the four major components of a production system?

1.17. Consider a production system that manufactures bicycles. Identify the material flow and information flow.

1.18. Explain the difficulties of concurrently meeting the three objectives of material conversion.

1.19. Discuss the interrelationships between flow shop, job shop, process layout, and product layout.

1.20. "In a divisional organizational arrangement we prefer market effectiveness at the 'cost' of some internal inefficiency." Agree with or dispute this statement, and explain why.

1.21. Why are matrix organizations common in research and development environments?

1.22. Propose an organizational chart for the Venice Arsenal.

1.23. Propose a possible layout for the Venice Arsenal.

1.24. State whether the following products are low-tech or high-tech industries, and discuss: furniture, dairy products, cosmetics, bicycles, soft drinks.

1.25. Elaborate on this statement: "The major difference between small and large industrial organizations is not the nature of the physical flow, but the information flow and the decision-making processes used."

3 PRODUCTION MANAGEMENT TECHNOLOGIES

By now we realize that production systems are complex and need managing. Production management technologies have many aspects; behavioral, process technology, quality, and production planning and control (PPC) are a few. We concentrate on PPC because it is a significant part of production management technology and the major topic of this book. We examine the evolution of PPC technology, define the vast area it represents, introduce the concept of product life cycle, and discuss appropriate technologies.

3.1 Evolution

Previously, we discussed the contributions of management pioneers such as Taylor and Fayol. Taylor laid the groundwork for operations-oriented analysis. Gantt, a contemporary and associate, added another dimension to Taylor's work by recognizing that a process is a combination of operations. He developed a rudimentary method of scheduling operations, the Gantt Chart. These charts are used today and deal with scheduling problems and project environments. Chapter 8 discusses Gantt Charts in more detail.

About the same time, Frank and Lillian Gilbreth (Gilbreth and Gilbreth, 1917) led a team that further developed the field of operations analysis. They originated the idea that operations are broken down into independent work components, such as grasp, search, and release. Putting these components together in different ways creates different operations. Their work is a basis for predetermined time standards used to estimate operation times, important data for production planning and control.

Shewhart proposed one of the first quantitative approaches to PPC. In the 1920s, he developed an organized theory of statistical quality control as applied to manufacturing operations. His rationale for dealing with variation was a breakthrough, replacing the deterministic approaches previously used.

The next breakthrough in quantitative PPC was Operations Research (OR). OR began in Britain during World War II as an outgrowth of Allied war efforts to develop more powerful methods of dealing with complex operational problems. After the war OR continued to develop and was increasingly applied in nonmilitary environments such as production systems. The computer gave additional impetus to this application, so today operations research and computer technology are important tools in production planning and control.

3.2 Production Planning and Control

Production planning and control technology combine the physical and information flows to manage the production system. As with any complex entity, PPC has several distinct elements. In Figure 1-8 we superimpose these elements on the physical flow of a production system.

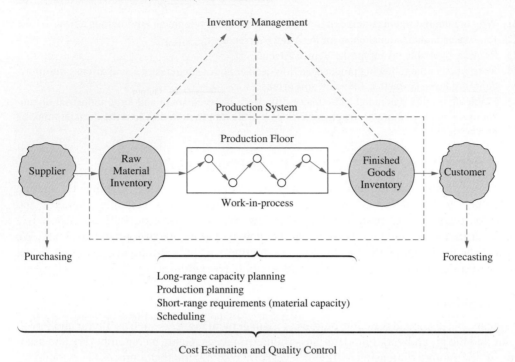

FIGURE 1-8
Elements of production planning and control

We position these elements at different places along the physical flow route. Interaction between the elements is not shown. The PPC function integrates material flow using the information system. Integration is achieved through a common data base (Figure 1-2).

Interaction with the external environment is accomplished by forecasting and purchasing. Forecasting customer demand starts the production planning and control activity. Purchasing connects the production system with its inputs provided by the external suppliers. Extending production planning and control to suppliers and customers is known as **supply chain management**.

Some elements are associated with the production floor itself. Long-range capacity planning guarantees that future capacity will be adequate to meet future demand, and it may include equipment, people, and even material. This decision is aided by a technique known as aggregate planning. Production planning transforms the demand forecasts into a master production plan, which considers overall availability of capacity and material. Detailed planning generates short-range requirements for material and capacity and performs short-term production scheduling. Additionally, inventory management maintains and controls raw material, work in process, and finished goods. Cost estimation and control and quality follow-up involve all parts of the production system.

Many of these elements relate to activities performed by other functions, e.g., the purchasing department or the production function. PPC does exactly what the name implies: planning and control of production. To understand how we do this, we use a feedback loop (Figure 1-9).

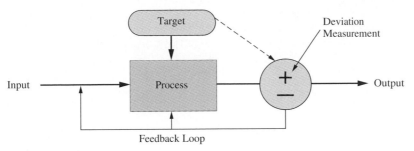

FIGURE 1-9
Feedback control loop

The core of the loop is a process; it could be purchasing, production, cost, inventory, etc. Each process has an input and an output specific to the individual process. In the inventory process, material flows in and out. The difference in flow rate determines the inventory level. Each process has a target, again process specific. Production's target might be a production plan, whereas cost's target could be operation within a certain cost level.

We measure the actual process output and compare it to the target. Any deviation feeds back to the process or its input. The deviation changes the process or input in order to control the deviation. The major functions of PPC are to set targets and measure deviations. Thus, the essence of production planning and control consists of **management of deviations** while maintaining targets consistent with those of the organization. System optimization, rather than optimization of only one element, is the goal.

3.3 Product Life Cycle

A product life cycle describes the evolution of the product as measured by sales over time. The five stages of a product life cycle are product planning, introduction, growth, maturity, and decline. Figure 1-10 shows sales in each of these stages.

Product planning is the development stage, in which both product design and production process are determined. There are no sales during this stage.

Introduction represents a period of low-volume sales. The product is refined, and marketing efforts are beginning.

The *growth* stage has rapid product growth and a fast increase in sales. This period is difficult for the manufacturing organization, which has to keep up with the increasing sales volume.

At *maturity,* we see a tapering off in the growth rate as the market becomes saturated. Demand is stable and may decline slowly.

A drop in product demand is seen in the *decline* phase. The product has been replaced by new products. Sales and profits decrease, and at some point, production is halted.

Neither life cycles nor the length of the individual stages are the same for all products. For some products the life cycle may be short—several years for high-tech products or a season for fashion goods. Other products may survive for years. By modifying a product, its life cycle may be extended. As we discuss in the next section, different stages in the product life cycle require varying management technology.

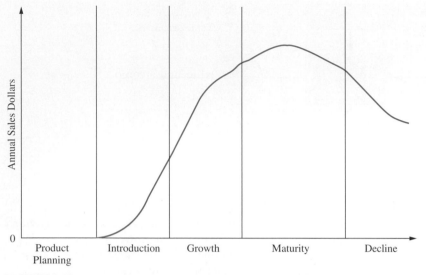

FIGURE 1-10
Product life cycle

3.4   Appropriate Technology

Let us reflect on what we have learned so far. Production systems are complex, have the same generic material flow but different information flow, can be low-tech or high-tech, and their decision-making process is impacted by their size. An added complication is seen when the product's life cycle is taken into account.

Production management technologies represent the body of knowledge developed over the years to manage this complex environment. This body of knowledge uses techniques that have evolved to solve different types of problems.

The issue is selecting the proper mix of production management technologies, which we discuss in later chapters, after separately presenting each technology. For example, we discuss forecasting in Chapter 4, tie it in with inventory in Chapter 6, and later integrate both in discussing material requirement planning in Chapter 7. These techniques embody the "scientific" approach to selecting management technology. In reality, successfully matching the proper technology with the problem is as much "art" as science. Some experience is necessary; however, there are certain guidelines that can help when faced with choices.

Initially, we must realize that different phases in the product life cycle may require varying techniques. Typically the product planning and introduction phases (Figure 1-10) are more project-type activities. As such, the project management approach (Chapter 9) is appropriate. Also, at this phase, long-range forecasts and capacity planning should be performed (Chapters 4 and 5). During the growth phase, models emphasizing dynamic changes should be used. At this phase it is proper to introduce, for example, MRP II (Chapters 7 and 10) and perform detailed production floor scheduling (Chapter 8) and inventory management (Chapters 6 and 7). The maturity phase requires the use of these same techniques but with more emphasis placed on static models than dynamic ones. The situation changes when we move into the decline stage; it becomes dynamic again, although this time decreasing.

The appropriate mix also depends on the type of organization with which we are dealing. As discussed earlier, both the physical and organizational arrangements and the degree of technical sophistication should be considered.

An essential guideline in designing a PPC system is the cliche "simple is beautiful." This statement is not as simple as it sounds; it is trivial to find a complicated solution to a simple problem. However, it takes more effort to find a simple solution to a complicated one. In most instances, the simpler solution will work better over time.

The price tag for implementing management technologies can be large or small, either in time invested or costs. For example, installing an MRP II system can cost anywhere between a few thousand dollars to several hundred thousand. The rule of thumb is not to spend any more than can be gained, which is another way of stating a more basic law of economics—that of diminishing returns. More precisely, we spend only up to the point where the marginal cost equals the marginal revenue. Having surveyed the aids to decision making, we now look at the decisions themselves.

SECTION 3 PROBLEMS

1.26. Consider pencil production as described in Section 2. Draw the physical flow for this production process, and identify how each PPC element interacts with the physical flow in this specific environment.

1.27. Use the feedback control loop to analyze the finished pencil inventory level for the pencil production process if the target for the inventory level is 1000 pencils.

1.28. Repeat Problem 1.27 for the production process, but assume weekly production is planned at 10,000 pencils.

1.29. Discuss the aspects of "management of deviations" from Problems 1.27 and 1.28.

1.30. Estimate the life cycle of the following products: personal computers, wristwatches, diamonds, cars, college textbooks, newspapers, magazines, Broadway shows.

4 DECISIONS IN PRODUCTION SYSTEMS

By now production systems, their evolution, organization, technology, and the tools required to manage them should be familiar. However, neither management tools nor computers run an organization. Organizations are run by people who make decisions that keep the organization moving toward its objectives. In the following section we address decision making in production systems. We discuss the notion of a planning horizon, present types of decisions, and introduce the implementation cycle.

4.1 Planning Horizon

The types of decisions to be made in a production system depend on the planning horizon, which is no different from everyday life. A decision to buy a house has long-term impact and takes a long time to prepare. On the other hand, deciding what to buy in the grocery store can be spontaneous, and its implications are short lived. For planning purposes, business and industry usually identify three types of planning horizons: long, medium, and short.

A **long planning horizon**, sometimes called strategic planning, covers a horizon of one to several years into the future. The decisions made for this horizon are called strategic

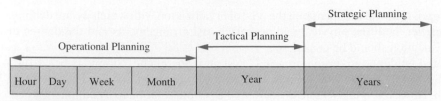

FIGURE 1-11
Planning horizons

decisions. They have a long-range impact on the direction of production systems and should be consistent with long-term organizational goals.

A **medium planning horizon** covers any period from one month to one year and is called tactical planning. Decisions made for this time frame, known as tactical decisions, are oriented towards achieving the annual goals set for the production system.

A time frame ranging from days (sometimes hours) to weeks or one month is the **short planning horizon**, also known as operational planning. Operational decisions are concerned with meeting the targets of the monthly production plan. In Figure 1-11 we show the three planning horizons on a time scale.

All planning is future oriented, implying that present decisions will determine future results. The three types of horizon planning are often interrelated. There is a hierarchical relationship among the three, in the sense that each planning phase has to be coordinated with that above or below. We further discuss this relationship in Chapter 5.

4.2   Types of Decisions

Even in a middle-sized industrial organization, there are hundreds of decisions made every day and at all management levels. The production system is part of this decision-making process, and some foundation is required to understand its decision-making environment. We identify three criteria for classifying production system decisions: organizational hierarchy, time, and topic.

Obviously the nature of decisions made by top management is different from those made by production line managers. Typically, strategic decisions are made by top management, tactical decisions are made by middle management, and operational decisions are made by operations managers. A strategic decision might involve capacity expansion. Its derived tactical decision would be the choice of equipment to increase capacity. How to install the equipment would be an operational decision.

Classification by time was covered in the discussion of planning horizons. A definite relationship exists between time and hierarchical classifications. Typical top management decisions are long term, whereas operational decisions are short term by nature.

Lastly, we include the topical content of different decisions. A decision might deal with production issues, a financial aspect, quality, or material. Some decisions will relate to more than one topical area.

In Table 1.1 we illustrate these decisions relative to production planning. As seen in the table the units used in defining production decisions may vary along the time/hierarchy axis.

TABLE 1.1
Production planning decisions

	Long (strategic) top management	Intermediate (tactical) middle management	Short (operational) operational management
Time	three to ten years	six months to three years	one week to six months
Unit	dollars; hours	dollars; hours; product line; product family	individual products; product family
Inputs	aggregate forecast; plant capacity	intermediate forecast; capacity and production levels taken from long range plan	short range forecast; work force levels, processes; inventory levels
Decisions	capacity; product; supplier needs; quality policy	work force levels; processes; production rates; inventory levels; contracts with suppliers; quality level; quality costs	allocation of jobs to machines; overtime; undertime; subcontracting; delivery dates for suppliers; product quality

SECTION 4 PROBLEMS

1.31. *The Daily Post* newspaper printed the following item in its industry and business section:

> TMC—Toy Manufacturing Company—increased its sales 20% in the third quarter. They will work two shifts in the fourth quarter to meet Christmas demand. They intend to increase their workforce during the next year, and plans for constructing a new building are underway to gear up for the increased demand.

Identify the planning horizons and types of decisions represented in the above quote.

5 SUMMARY

This chapter is an introduction to production systems. It sets the stage for the rest of the book. We described the world as an open trading system, with global competition being a major factor. Production systems have a place in this global market.

We next identified four major stages in the evolution of production systems. The ancient system can trace its beginnings to 5000 B.C. where Sumerian priests started recording inventories. A thousand years later the Egyptians introduced the basic management concepts of organization, management, and control. In 1500 B.C. the Hebrews were using the exception principle, and in 350 B.C. the Greeks were espousing the specialization of labor.

The Feudal system was a product of the Middle Ages, with its domestic production system.

The European factory system evolved during the Renaissance, as seen in the development of the Venice Arsenal. However, the most important development of this era was the Industrial Revolution in the British Isles in the 1700s. From it, production management theory emerged. Adam Smith, in his book *The Wealth of Nations*, developed the principle of division of labor.

The American factory system emerged with Eli Whitney's use of interchangeable parts, jigs, and fixtures. The assembly line and mass production were also products of this era.

Scientific management was a spin-off of the American factory system. By pushing the idea that management is a true science based on well-defined laws and principles, Frederick Taylor is regarded as the founder of scientific management. Fayol also made great contributions. Two milestones in its development are the Eastern Rate Case of 1910 and the Hawthorne experiments in the 1920s.

Dominant for two decades after World War II, the American system was a production-driven system that took the market for granted. American complacency led to its ignoring the rise of competitive industrial powers—mainly Japan. The market role in production systems was expanding, leading to market-driven systems. American competitiveness declined until the early 1980s when its resurgence began. The mass production era declined, and the market-driven system gained in importance. This change was a result of increasing customer sophistication.

Production systems were formally defined as "anything that takes inputs and transforms them into outputs with inherent value." This definition covers both manufacturing and service, although in this book we limit discussion to for-profit manufacturing production systems.

The backbone of the production system is the manufacturing process. It is a flow process composed of two major elements: material (physical) flow and information flow. A television manufacturing system demonstrates how complex physical and information flows can become. From this process we saw that most production systems are like icebergs; only a small part of the system is readily visible.

Any production system must concurrently meet three objectives: quality, cost, and time. Supporting these objectives are both physical and organizational arrangements. The physical arrangements deal with the production floor and can be a job shop, flow shop, batch shop, project shop, continuous shop, or the modern shop. The first two are more traditional, with the last gaining increasing acceptance.

Two classic and opposite organizational arrangements are functional and divisional (SBU). The matrix organization represents a hybrid of the two and breaks the rule of "one person, one boss." These three types of organizational structure are "pure" structures. In reality an organization's structure may result from a blend of two or all three.

Production systems can also be classified as high-tech or low-tech. We presented three criteria to distinguish a high-tech system. In high-tech systems, neither production planning, management, nor control may lag. Low-tech systems can often benefit from the use of more sophisticated production planning and control techniques.

Although organizations differ in size and scope, the generic physical flow and ensuing layouts differ only in relative complexity. Differences in information flow have an impact on the managerial decision-making processes.

Production management technologies are the tools needed to manage production systems. The major tool is production planning and control (PPC). PPC pioneers included Gantt, the Gilbreths, Shewhart, and the developers of Operations Research during and after World War II.

PPC is an integrated-material-flow-based information system. Some elements affect one part of the physical flow, but others affect the total process. The planning and control process is based on the feedback loop of control theory, and the essence of production planning and control is management of deviations.

Production management technologies consist of several techniques for solving different problems at varying depths. The "art" and the "science" lie in selecting the appropriate mix of these technologies. Different phases in the product life cycle may require varying technologies, with the organizational structure also having an impact. The general guideline that is most helpful is "simple is beautiful." We also need to remember that our efforts should not exceed the point of diminishing returns.

Production management technologies support decisions made in production systems. The nature of the decisions will vary for a long, intermediate, or short planning horizon, with corresponding decisions and planning horizons called strategic, tactical or operational. Production system decisions can be classified using three criteria: organizational hierarchy, time, and topic. Table 1.1 presents a decision scenario for production planning.

6 REFERENCES

Babbage, Charles, *On the Economy of Machinery and Manufactures,* R. Clay, Printer, London, 1832.

Cohen, S. S. and Zysman, J., *Manufacturing Matters: the Myth of the Post Industrial Economy,* Basic Books, New York, 1987.

Copely, F. B., *Fredrick W. Taylor: Father of Scientific Management,* vol I & II, Harper & Row, New York, 1923.

Divan, R. and Chakaborty, C., *High Technology and International Competitiveness,* Praeger, New York, 1991.

Duncan, W. J., *Great Ideas in Management,* Jossey-Bass Publishers, San Francisco, 1989.

Emmerson, H., *The Twelve Principles of Efficiency,* The Engineering Magazine Company, New York, 1924.

Fayol, H., *General and Industrial Management,* Institute of Electrical and Electronics Engineers, New York, 1984.

Gantt, H. L., (ed), *How Scientific Management Is Applied,* Hive Publishing Company, Easton, PA, 1911.

Gilbreth, F. B. and Gilbreth, L. M., *Applied Motion Study; A Collection of Papers on the Efficient Method to Industrial Preparedness,* Sturgis & Walton Company, New York, 1917.

Hax, A.C. and Majluf, N.S., "Organizational Design: A Survey and an Approach," *Operations Research,* 29, 3, 417–447, 1981.

Hayes, R. H., Wheelwright, S. C. and Clark, K. B., *Dynamic Manufacturing: Creating The Learning Organization,* Free Press, London, Collier Macmillan, 1988.

Lane, F. C., *Venetian Ships and Shipbuilders of the Renaissance,* The Johns Hopkins Press, Baltimore, 1934.

Sadler, P. and Hants, O., *Managerial Leadership in the Post-Industrial Society,* Gower, Brookfield, VT, 1988.

Skinner, W., *Manufacturing, the Formidable Competitive Weapon,* Wiley, New York, 1985.

Smith, A., *An Inquiry into the Nature and Causes of the Wealth of Nations,* Strahan, and Cadell Printers, London, 1776.

Starr, M. K., *Global Competitiveness: Getting the U.S. Back on Track,* W.W. Norton, New York, 1988.

Taylor, F. W., *Principles of Scientific Management,* Harper & Row, New York, 1911.

Taylor, F. W., *Shop Management,* Harper & Row, New York, 1903.

U.S. Department of Labor, Bureau of Labor Statistics, Washington, DC, 1982.

CHAPTER
2

MARKET-DRIVEN SYSTEMS

1 INTRODUCTION

The classical management theories described earlier brought ever increasing levels of achievement to the industrial process for many years. The American leadership position and its competitive edge started declining in the mid-1960s. However, it took some time to realize that different approaches were required to face the new industrial environment. This slow, uncoordinated process was carried out by individual companies, researchers, consultants, and professionals. Change occurred at two major sites: Japan and America. Now, these changes are converging into a single process.

The Japanese approach brought to light the weaknesses of American companies. It was natural for Americans to observe how Japan became a leading industrial power. Numbers of American industrialists and professionals visited Japan to study their systems, and large groups of Japanese consultants flooded western industries offering their services and advice. This phenomenon started in the early 1970s, reached its peak in the early 1980s, and to a certain extent is still occurring today. The extent of this phenomenon is indicated by the many Japanese production terms that have become part of the American jargon, e.g., *kanban, jidoka, poka yoka,* and *kaizen.* We will explain these terms in later chapters. Translated Japanese books on production matters are probably the most sought-after publications in this area. Westerners' trips to Japan included visits to Japanese "Masters" of various industries—metal cutting, automotive (Toyota being the leader), electronic, and optic (Matsushita, Sony).

Americans reacted to the Japanese resurgence in three phases. The first reaction was the surprise of finding an industry notorious for bad quality outselling American products. Also, Japan had more advanced facilities and more forward-looking management concepts. Then came admiration. In this phase was the feeling among many that Japan could do it better, and so the tendency was to *imitate* Japanese industry rather than *innovate* at home. Recently American industry moved to the third phase, sobriety, or to rephrase it, back to scale. Many of the Japanese successes are based on either American technology or management techniques. The latter were transferred to Japan in the early 1950s as part of the MacArthur Plan. Those techniques covered a spectrum of topics such as methods and quality and were championed by Deming, Juran, and others. The difference was that Japanese professionals listened and implemented but American industry ignored those ideas. For whatever reasons, today we see a resurgence of doing things "the American way," i.e., by innovation rather than imitation.

In America there was soul searching to identify the reasons for the decline, to suggest remedial action, and to develop techniques for regaining the competitive edge in the future. In the latter stages of this soul searching, Americans adapted and embedded the Japanese approach into traditional American production systems. As a result, an impressive array of research, books, and reports were generated by individuals or committees. There is no consensus in these results as to why things happened and what should be done in the future; however, a consensus is indicated on the following:

- Existing classical management theories (Chapter 1) are inadequate to cope with many problems of the present and future environment.
- Certain concepts exist that will be a part of any future theory.

We make a strong statement here by claiming that the management theories and techniques that have been used for a long time—over a century in some cases—need to be updated. The environment from which they emerged has been totally transformed. On the other hand, the substitute theories are in a state of flux. Many ideas, concepts, and techniques have been proposed but have yet to become a unified theory of production management. New industrial concepts are a mix; some are old concepts that were honed and re-emerged, some are concepts replacing the old ones, and some are totally new. We provide our view of the major emerging production management concepts. These ideas form the foundation for cutting edge management techniques. We embed these concepts in a platform we call the *wheel of competitiveness.* In the rest of this chapter, we discuss this platform, the new production environment that supports market driven systems, and finally world class manufacturing.

2   THE WHEEL OF COMPETITIVENESS

The wheel of competitiveness, shown in Figure 2-1, illustrates some of those concepts required to roll American industry back to its leadership position.

The wheel has four concentric circles; each represents different aspects of the emerging production management theory. We briefly define each circle and then follow with a more detailed discussion. The **hub** of the wheel is also the hub of all future systems: the **customer.** The **delivery circle** (Circle 2) shows what the production system should deliver to the customer. The **support circle** (Circle 3) indicates concepts needed to support what is delivered by the production system. The **impact circle** (Circle 4) shows the consequence of those concepts on the whole organization.

3   THE HUB

It is no coincidence that the customer is the hub of the "new industrial world" concepts. The customer is the engine that drives competitiveness. This concept itself is not new; it existed in the era of "classical" management theories—but the customer's importance, role, scope, and position have changed due to increasing customer sophistication. Education, technology, communication, and globalization are all elements that helped create the new customer.

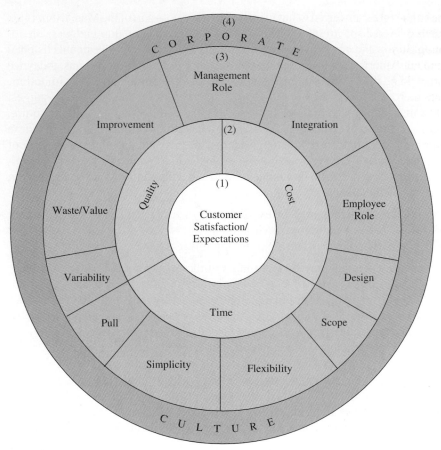

FIGURE 2-1
Wheel of competitiveness

Rather than operating to respond to and satisfy customer needs only, organizations must make an effort to achieve **customer satisfaction** as well. This term is a simple linguistic one, but it is a very complex industrial concept. Customer satisfaction is composed of many elements—needs, quality, cost, service, and more. Even the need satisfaction process of the past is totally different today. Emphasis is placed on satisfying the needs of the **individual** customer rather than those of the **average** customer (with the Ford Model T, for example). Remember, markets do not buy anything—people do (Chapter 1). Constantly changing customer expectations ensure that satisfaction is dynamic and increasingly complex. Customers have changing requirements, and they expect flexible reactions, which can be achieved only if the organization gets close to the customer. The customer should be made a part of the process rather than its terminal point. Securing a customer's allegiance has become more important than merely selling an item. Returning customers generate future sales.

By implication the "new" customer has an increasing say in running the organization, and new types of relationships have to be forged between the two. Changing and increasing customer expectations force management to raise their own expectations in terms of internal processes. Manufacturers have to meet customer expectations and even exceed them.

The scope of the term "customer" has also changed dramatically. Traditionally the customer was regarded as the end user of the product. Today we have the "internal customer" whose needs must also be addressed. Thus, manufacturing is purchasing's customer, assembly is manufacturing's customer, or in a general way, any operation is a customer of the previous operation. Any organization's activities can be viewed as a chain of interconnected customers. Each customer is the supplier of the next customer in the chain, and the whole production and business activity is governed by customer satisfaction.

If the customer is the engine driving the organization, expectation is the engine's fuel. Customer satisfaction with acceptable financial returns is the measure of business success (Macbeth, 1989).

SECTION 3   PROBLEMS

2.1. In production-driven systems products satisfied the needs of the market. In the "new industrial world" products satisfy the needs of a customer. Discuss the difference.

2.2. What is the difference between "internal customer" and "external customer" ?

4   THE DELIVERY CIRCLE[1]

In order to achieve customer satisfaction and meet its expectation, the whole business has to rise to the challenge. Each segment must contribute its share, and the manufacturing system is no different. Its role is to deliver a product of superb quality at the required time while keeping the cost as low as possible at every point in the supplier–customer chain. These goals are necessary, but not sufficient, for any business to become a leader in its market. As simple as these goals seem, achieving them is quite complicated. Although each independent goal is achievable, combining the three into one unified goal makes a complex and difficult mission. Manufacturing can always deliver superb quality by reworking and repairing until the desired quality is achieved, but the cost will skyrocket, and the delivery time will be long. The proper sequence of these goals is the subject of ongoing debate. One proposition is

$$\text{Quality} \longrightarrow \text{Time} \longrightarrow \text{Cost}$$

This is not a crucial issue as long as the combined result is achieved. Furthermore, the sequence may differ from one organization to another. We suggest arranging them in a circular fashion as shown in Figure 2-2.

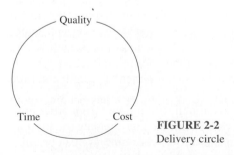

FIGURE 2-2
Delivery circle

[1]This section is influenced by Macbeth (1989) (used by permission of Springer-Verlag New York, Inc.).

4.1   Quality

Quality is a traditional concept whose scope has expanded and whose importance is enhanced in the modern production system. The common product-related definition of quality is **conformance to specifications.** But for the customer, quality is a more complex issue including individual perceptions of value for money, expectation of performance and appearance, presale and after-sale service offered, and warranty.

The new approach to quality recognizes all facets. From the product point of view one way to measure quality is by the number of products in a manufacturing batch not conforming to specifications, i.e., defective products. In the past a certain level of this measure was acceptable. Today we strive for perfection—allowing no defects at all. To put this change in perspective, not long ago three defectives per 100 units was considered good quality. Today some industries, especially electronics, consider more than one hundred defective *parts per million* (PPM) to be poor quality. This new attitude represents a big leap towards perfection and the kind of product quality a manufacturing system needs to deliver.

But quality includes more than product quality. All production, support (purchasing, accounting, etc.), engineering, research and development, and service activities need to be quality conscious. They must be aware of decisions affecting quality throughout the production chain, for both internal and external supplier and customer. Thus quality is an embracing concept, and each element in the production system strives for perfection. Quality has no "standard"; it is a moving target. From being quality expert-driven in the past, quality today is customer-driven. It provides a solid foundation for all aspects of the organization's activity. Contrary to the belief that increased quality means increased cost, in the new industrial world, improved quality reduces cost. IBM is a reinforcing example of this point. In 1990 they adopted a strategy of market-driven quality (MDQ). The essence of this strategy is represented by a statement made by J.F. Akers, CEO of IBM at that time.

Market-Driven Quality starts with making customers' satisfaction an obsession and empowering our people to use their creative energy to satisfy and delight their customer. It means our quality goals and objectives must be deployed throughout the company so that each person knows what their responsibility is, and also knows that they will be measured accordingly.

4.2   Time

Time is not a new concept, per se; it has always been with us. Also time has multiple meanings. It has a "point" meaning (What's the time now?), a "length" connotation (How much time does it take?), and a "punctuality" interpretation (Be there on time!). In addition it sometimes has an "opportunity" flavor (The time was right.), not to mention less scientific and more qualitative meanings, such as good time, interesting time, etc. In production systems we view time as two different but related entities: time as a measurement of length and time as an indication of goal.

Delivery or lead time is the length of time needed to deliver a product from order until the receipt by the customer. Delivery date is a goal, representing either the date the product is needed or the date promised for delivery. If we can shorten delivery time, we can promise sooner delivery dates, and vice versa. If the customer needs a shorter delivery date, we must find a way to shorten delivery time, keeping in mind that a shorter time may impact all components in the supplier–customer chain. Either we shorten raw material lead time, cut operations times (i.e., length), reduce set-up, or decrease time at some other point.

The importance of decreased time has become more important in the new industrial world because time is a major element in customer satisfaction. We refer here to all customers, both internal and external, in terms of both delivery time and delivery date. In the past, delivery eventually happened. Today, delivery is the driving force throughout the system that ensures the satisfaction of all customers.

In today's market, the concept of time is associated with time reliability or consistency. It is not enough to shorten delivery time and deliver on time once. We have to be able to do it repeatedly, i.e., reduce the time variability to zero. Furthermore, to exceed customer expectations, we have to keep improving our delivery length and punctuality.

Time affects not only the production system but also the whole business. Time-to-market and timing are especially crucial in new product development. Time-to-market is the length of time it takes from a product's inception until it goes to market. We have to shorten this period as much as possible, so as to have the right timing of market introduction. The U.S. car industry has a time-to-market of about five years for new models (down from seven) versus three years for Japanese cars—still a long way to go! The entire supplier–customer chain, including production, must participate in decreasing time-to-market. Quick response will create a competitive edge. If the 1980s were typified by quality-based competition, the 1990s add time-based competition.

4.3 Cost

Cost is a common term, but it has different meanings in different situations. Although the price of a product is a "cost" to the consumer, it is not the sum of the cost of all activities associated with generating the product. The price of the product should reflect profit the company intends to make above cost. Thus, cost and price are separate entities. For our purpose, cost is defined as *one measure of resource use,* and it is expressed in the same units used in that business. Thus, cost is an internal measure, and, conceptually at least, we can control its components. Price, however, is a matter of policy and is affected by the profit margin we want to have, the competition in the market, the product policy, and more. Price is of interest to the external customer, who does not care about the cost to the company (the internal cost). In contrast, quality and time are of great concern to the customer. Price policy is not totally detached from cost. The lower the cost is, the more flexibility marketing has in maneuvering the price policy to improve the competitive position.

The role cost plays has changed. Traditionally, cost has been the dominant measure of companies in running the production system, which is not surprising; a high proportion of the company's assets are tied up in manufacturing. The major responsibility of production management used to be **cost control.** That role still exists, but another major responsibility, **cost reduction,** is gaining more and more importance. To achieve cost reduction we must identify causes of unnecessary cost such as excess inventory and eliminate them. The shift has been from **cost control** to **cause control,** in which cost is a convenient measurement used to track cost reduction.

Cost reduction is a key "delivery" in the modern industrial world. In order to be competitive, cost can follow only one trend—down. The cost improvement required is in *orders of magnitudes*, not in small percentages. Cost, which was an input, has become an outcome of actions.

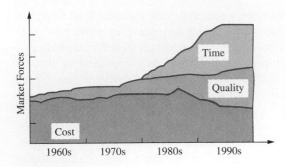

FIGURE 2-3
Evolution of cost, quality, and time (adapted from an IBM presentation)

4.4 Conclusions

The three goals of quality, time, and cost did not emerge and gain momentum at the same time. Figure 2-3 shows how the three evolved. Cost has always been an issue one way or another. In the late 1970s quality began playing a larger role, and it will continue to gain momentum throughout the 1990s. The combination of quality, time, and cost is the key to competitiveness in the new industrial world.

SECTION 4   PROBLEMS

2.3. What is the difference between product-related quality and the customer's perception of quality?

2.4. What is the new scope of quality?

2.5. Discuss the thought behind "quality is a moving target."

2.6. Discuss the two time entities as related to production cycle time and due date.

2.7. Repeat Problem 2.6 for set-up time and production start time.

2.8. Repeat Problem 2.6 for response time and time-to-market.

2.9. A company is developing a new product. They estimate their time-to-market to be 12 months. They realize that if development is delayed by three months, they are going to miss their timing. Explain.

2.10. What is the difference between cost and price?

2.11. Are cost control, cost reduction, and cause control related? Explain.

5   THE SUPPORT CIRCLE

We have stated the difficulty of combining the goals of the manufacturing system (quality, time, and cost) into one unified goal. Not surprisingly, many ways to achieve this larger goal have recently been suggested. Each of these suggestions, or combination of suggestions, represents a certain concept.

There is no consensus on the concepts, let alone on the relative importance of each. We do not believe this to be an impediment. Our list of the major emerging concepts is shown in the support circle of Figure 2-1. The location on the circle, the size of the segment, and its relation to the delivery circle are not significant. These concepts are discussed in a logical order. Any ordering will do, as long as we understand the meaning, importance, and contribution of each element. We reiterate that some of the concepts are old but may take on a new meaning. Others are altogether new. Each of these concepts has tools and techniques for implementation. Some of these tools are discussed in other sections of this book.

5.1 Scope

The scope of a business has been redefined to include both the customer on one hand and the external supplier on the other, which represents a direct contrast to the past, when the customer was "out there" and the supplier was considered more an adversary than a partner. We have already identified the concepts of consumer becoming prosumer. The same relationship develops on the supply side; the supplier is brought in as a member of the team, with the intention of a long-term association. This policy greatly reduces the number of suppliers. Xerox Corporation, for example, reduced its supplier base from 4500 to 400. Businesses no longer try to generate a price war among suppliers. Price is important, but the emphasis is on quality and consistency of delivery. As the external supplier becomes a part of the team, the producer–supplier relationship changes. Not only do you expect a product delivered to specifications, but you also expect the supplier to tell you if your quality expectations are high enough or can be increased. From a system of supplier, producer, and customer as three separate entities, we integrate the three as shown in Figure 2-4. This inclusion of all involved with the product is the basic philosophy of supply chain management.

5.2 Integration

Integration is used in many contexts: technical, organizational, behavioral, and more. It may be used to discuss a concept or a technique; consequently, confusion results. We consider integration as the process of looking at a system rather than a component, or to phrase it differently, the process of seeking global optimization rather than local optimization. We use

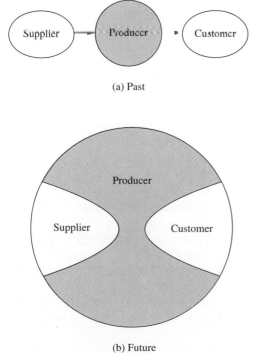

(a) Past

(b) Future

FIGURE 2-4
Supplier-producer-customer relationship

optimization not in its mathematical meaning but in the sense of obtaining good results. Both definitions imply recognizing the importance of interaction among components of the industrial organization. Examining each component separately, as was done in the past, is passé. The concept of scope discussed earlier represents one form of integration, in which both the supplier and customer were integrated into the system. Other examples help clarify this concept.

Product design and process design were done separately in the past. What looked like a perfect product on paper turned out to be a nightmare in terms of the manufacturing process, resulting in extremely high manufacturing costs. Today those two processes are integrated, and the customer (via the marketing function) is also included. When designing the product, the designers consider manufacturing issues and check with the marketing people about possible changes in specifications. This integration of processes achieves the goals of reducing cost and time and increasing quality. We have optimized the product design from a global perspective rather than from just the designers' point of view. Another integration example is found in the concept of total quality. In contrast to an emphasis on product quality only, we must integrate all activities to achieve total quality.

There are other aspects of integration in addition to the removal of barriers within an organization. On the production floor, instead of having clusters of machines of the same type (functional design) used to manufacture all kinds of products, we "integrate" a number of different machines to produce a group of similar products. Doing so facilitates the manufacturing process—again global rather than local optimization, with the integration being in terms of equipment.

Information integration occurs also because all information technology required to design, manufacture, and deliver the product is integrated. Information is moved directly among various components of the business, and the same information is accessible to different users, as required.

The concept of integration is often mistakenly associated with the advent of the computer. Integration, however, is a concept on its own, which can be applied without a computer, sometimes needing only simple communication among people. The role of the computer lies in increasing the speed, breadth, and depth of the information integration.

5.3   Flexibility

When discussing the hub, we mentioned that customers have changing requirements and expect flexible reactions. Those changing requirements include fluctuations in demand, greater product variety, and new products. To stay competitive, production systems are designed to cater to a changing market. Flexibility requires the production system to be able to rapidly design a new product and introduce it to the market place, cater to changing patterns of product volume required, and cater to greater product mix. In each case the production system should be able to perform those tasks in the context of the unified goal of quality, time, and cost. Flexibility places the major emphasis on the expediency with which each of the tasks is performed. This difficult mission forces a change in many practices on the production floor. Obviously the mass production line cannot adapt quickly and cheaply to changes in product mix. Recall that in Chapter 1 we claimed that the mass production era is diminishing, with one reason being the need for flexibility. The ultimate flexibility is achieved when the production system can produce a single item and still do it at a low cost.

Implementing flexibility caused tremendous changes in the organization and on the production floor. Time needed to change a production facility from one product to another has been slashed from hours to minutes; time-to-market of a new product has been cut from years to months; and flexible production facilities can concurrently manufacture many different products.

Flexible manufacturing is replacing the mass production concept of the past. As such, it is a key concept in achieving competitiveness. Some companies make flexibility a major goal of their manufacturing strategy.

5.4 Design

Design has undergone a major turnaround. We accept the belief that the major portion of product cost and quality are determined in the design phase. If we are to give the customer more variety faster and at a lower cost, it is impossible to use the same design approach as in the past. Design and product development are no longer isolated elements. Design now interacts with customers and manufacturing, tapping the expertise of other segments of the business. This integration, which fosters a team approach, helps achieve design for function (specifications), life (reliability), form (aesthetics), and effective manufacture. Although design has usually been a team effort, the composition of the team and its scope have changed.

5.5 Simplicity

At the beginning of the industrial age, simplicity was not a priority because things were simple by nature. In the new manufacturing environment we simplify for two important reasons.

- Simple things are understood by more people.
- Simple situations enable us to use simpler solutions, which are less expensive, less time consuming, implemented faster, and have a lower risk.

The new production environment is complex by nature. We have the technology, such as the computer and its derivatives, to deal with complex situations. It is tempting to rush into cutting edge technology to tackle the complex problem. Before implementing a complex solution to a complex problem, however, try to simplify the problem so that it becomes amenable to a less expensive solution. For example, in automation or computerization, a substantial share of the benefits (sometimes up to 80 percent) is achieved before automation was installed. In some cases this level of benefits may be sufficient and will be more cost effective. The same rationale applies to simplifying other manufacturing aspects—product and process design, control, information, etc. Although this simplicity was necessary in the previous industrial era, the concept is even more important today. We should not be so quick to use "coping-with-complexity" advanced technology unless it becomes necessary.

5.6 Variability

Variability has been a problem since society moved from craftsmanship to the industrial era. Everything varies—products, dimensions, manufacturing processes, delivery time, and quality levels. Variability, a universal enemy, is traditionally accepted as a fact of life. We have tried to define it and to use statistical methods to control or work around it. Now we try to eliminate it completely, reducing the need for a number of tools developed to control it. Note that this approach agrees with the concepts of simplicity and perfection introduced earlier.

Clearly, consistency of performance or reducing variability can reap great benefits. This idea was not ignored in the past; however, today we have the technology to implement this concept. For example, newer machine tools can have processes that have variability close to zero. These processes are referred to as deterministic manufacturing. In the case of hardware, low variability is a given technical characteristic of the machine. In other instances much effort is needed to achieve it.

5.7   Pull

The production process is basically a flow process. First there is physical flow; the raw material, later the semifinished product, moves from one machine workstation or assembly station to another. At each workstation some processing of the raw material is done, and the material moves to the next workstation in the manufacturing sequence. Other types of flows are nonphysical—the most important being information flow. Information flow can be either verbal, on paper, on a computer screen, or a combination of these.

Physical flow is the backbone of the system; without it there will be no output from the production system. Thus we want to maintain smooth flow of the product down the line with no delays. Note that a stop at a workstation for processing is not regarded as a delay, but it is part of the production process.

It is possible to compare the production flow to other types of flows, for example, flows in nature. Consider rivers, where the natural law of gravity dictates that the flow will be from high to low places. In contrast, production flow has man-made rules to govern it rather than natural laws. Traditionally the governing law was that of **push production: keep doing things regardless of what happens down the line—make to plan**. The information flows downstream, just as the physical flow, as shown in Figure 2-5(a). This rule worked well for production-driven systems in which we took the market (customer) for granted. Furthermore, upstream production was insensitive to what happened downstream. In case of a broken machine or other delay, upstream kept producing—the sorcerer's apprentice phenomenon. The result was congestion on the production floor and obstruction of flow.

Things changed for market-driven systems with the customer as the "hub." The governing law changed to the rule of **pull** or **pull production**. The essence of pull production is to **do things upstream only when requested from downstream**. The terminal point of the downstream is the customer. In a push production system, the physical and information flows are in the same direction. However, in the pull system the physical and information flows are in the opposite direction, as shown in Figure 2-5(b). In pull production nothing in the

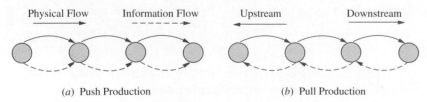

(*a*) Push Production   (*b*) Pull Production

FIGURE 2-5
Push and pull production

supplier–customer chain starts unless there is a request (information) from the downstream activities. This concept applies not only to production floor activities and flows, but also to the external supplier and external customer as well.

The pull concept is not simple to implement. A great amount of preparation is required, and a number of techniques are needed for successful implementation. In the dynamic environment of market-driven systems, it is a potent concept.

5.8 Waste/Value

In our daily lives we often receive counsel not to "waste" assets such as our time or our money. Upon reflection we see that we are really being advised not to use an important resource (i.e., time or money) if no **value** is gained. Because the major mission of the manufacturing process is to increase value for the final customer, this simple principle becomes an important concept in production systems. The customer is willing to pay for value but not for waste.

In the context of the manufacturing process, **waste** is defined as any resource expended over the amount required and valued by the customer. Although determining the minimum amount of resource required is not always easy, sometimes waste is obvious. The customer expects perfect quality in a product; we can achieve this quality by "doing it right the first time" (an important principle in itself) or by reworking the product until the desired quality level is achieved. From the customer's viewpoint, value must be obtained "in one pass," and additional rework and its resulting cost are waste. This example represents one measure of waste—in terms of cost. Reducing or eliminating waste amounts to reducing cost—a direct correlation to one of the major goals of the production system.

In general waste occurs in three forms: time, money, and effort. Time and effort may be expressed in a cost equivalent. Excess lead time and poor quality are waste, as are an over-engineered product design, excess inventory, and inflated overhead. Other activities whose contribution to the product value (and customer satisfaction) are questionable are also waste.

We classify production activities into two major categories: value-adding activities and cost-adding activities. **Value-adding activities** are those that by their nature are supposed to add value. Typically they are conversion activities where raw or purchased materials are transformed from their received state into the final product. Here waste would be the use of excess resources. **Cost-adding activities** are those that enable a smoother operation or make life easier in the production system. They support a conversion process, and although they may be important and even necessary, add no value—for example, materials handling. A third type of hybrid activities falls somewhere in between value adding and cost adding—for example, quality control.

Reducing waste should be approached differently for each of these activities. For value-adding activities, resource **optimization** is appropriate. For cost-adding activities, cost **elimination** is appropriate. Waste has always existed in production systems; its definition and recognition lead to devising ways to reduce it.

5.9 Improvement

The concept of improvement has been used in production systems since the days of Taylor and the Gilbreths. Initially improvement was attempted at the job level, basically through motion study (Chapter 1). As years went by, the concept of improvement expanded, and its scope included improvement in additional areas of manufacturing—processes, assembly, quality, time, and cost. Heretofore, the basis of the improvement approach included these three characteristics:

- A trade-off must be made; if you want better quality, you have to pay more for it.
- The outlook was local and not global; reduce the cost of an activity and not the total cost of the system.
- Typically, the improvement was of a project type (or ad hoc activity) to improve quality or reduce inventory.

Today's competitive market situation has made the important concept of improvement even more vital. To keep customers satisfied we must give them a good product now but also show that we are making efforts to give them a better product in the future. Thus, the "new" improvement process is based on the following two ideas:

- **Integrated Improvement:** the improvement process is a multidimensional process. It cannot touch on one goal at the expense of another. The goal of the production system has to be improved in all three dimensions: quality, time, and cost. We must provide better quality at lower cost and reduced delivery time, which means we have to take a global rather than local approach to ensure that we improve the total system.
- **Continuous Improvement:** improvement should be a continuous process; there is always room for future improvement. One improvement leads to another, establishing a cyclical process.

This process is sometimes called *kaizen*, the Japanese term for continuous improvement. The Japanese emphasize that *kaizen*, practiced in Japan for years, is a process involving everyone, from management to the lowest paid employee. They also make the subtle distinction between *kaizen* and innovation. *Kaizen* signifies small improvements made in the status quo as a result of on-going efforts. Innovation involves a drastic improvement in the status quo as a result of a large investment in new technology or equipment.

The biggest enemy of improvement is complacency. In Chapter 1 we saw the cost that American industry paid for being complacent. The concept of improvement is valid not only for more global, unified goals, but throughout the manufacturing system at all levels. Goal improvement can be achieved only through a series of mini-improvements, with constant adherence to the integration and continuity principles cited earlier.

5.10 Management Role

Because the human element is the most important resource a company possesses, it should not be surprising that the last two concepts to be discussed involve people. At opposite ends of the spectrum are management and employees. *Management* has an expanded role in the new production system. It transforms the system from its current mode into a new operational mode represented by the concepts described thus far. The manager is basically overseeing a change process, introduction of which is difficult due to the people in the system. Change represents a challenge to the individual worker because skills may become obsolete, status may be downgraded, work environment or location may be changed, or, even worse, the job may be eliminated. The manager's role is to facilitate change positively in three ways:

- **Commitment:** management must first and foremost show a commitment to the new concepts, which may be a major break from the status quo.
- **Participation:** management should become **part of the process** and not stay above the process. Change starts at the top, and management must undergo the elements of the change process throughout the organization.
- **Goals:** management should set **extraordinary goals**. Only then it is possible to obtain first rate results. In quality, for example, the goal is perfection, without an "acceptable" level of defects.

Drastic changes usually are not introduced voluntarily. Often some severe external threat to survival makes change necessary. The Harley Davidson Company is a well-known example of survival change. Studies (Hayes et al., 1988) show management can have 50 to 100 percent impact on manufacturing performance. The conclusion is that *management makes a great difference.*

5.11   Employee Role

Employees have always been part of the organization, but now they must become part of both the change process and mode of operation. In this context management has two goals for employees: involvement and development.

Employee involvement uses the creative energies of all employees to solve problems (Huge and Anderson, 1985). It requires a high degree of commitment to the company by all employees. This involvement takes many shapes and forms, but the basic idea is that employees involved in the process more readily accept the outcome. In addition, the company makes use of a huge brain trust to generate a host of good ideas.

Many new production systems have new technologies imbedded in them: new machines, processes, computers, and management technologies. Much preparation must be made within the organization for these new technologies. Employee development (Hayes et al., 1988)—upgrading the skills of the employees—is necessary for utilization of the new technologies. This system changes the traditional philosophy of employee control to a new concept of employee involvement and upgrade.

SECTION 5   PROBLEMS

2.12. What is the importance of increasing the scope of a business?

2.13. Compare and contrast physical integration and information integration.

2.14. Are flexibility and time reduction synonymous? Explain.

2.15. A common design jargon is known as KISS—"Keep it simple, stupid." Explain the rationale.

2.16. Two companies deliver the same product repeatedly. Company A delivers on time on the average but with high variability. Company B is consistently five days late. Which situation is preferable and why?

2.17. Consider the following three "solution scenarios":

  (a) A complex solution to a complex problem

  (b) A complex solution to a simple problem

  (c) A simple solution to a complex problem

Give an example for each of the above scenarios. Analyze if in your example to (a) and (b) the solution can be simplified.

2.18. For planning production, we use a parameter called lead time, which is the estimated time between the start and the finish of production. The real time between the start and the finish of production may be equal to the lead time or different, because of queues or other delays on the production floor. We call this real time flow time. Consider two different production processes. Both have lead time of 5; however, flow time is normally distributed. For the first process it is $N(5, 4)$ and for the second it is $N(5, 1)$. Analyze the situation and draw conclusions.

2.19. Consider product 1 in Figure 1-4, which represents a four-workstation serial production line. The line can be operated by using either push or pull production. Suppose the line can produce 400 units per week. For a certain month, the production plan was to manufacture 600 units. The actual demand per week during the month was the following:

Week	1	2	3	4
Demand	100	0	350	150

Evaluate the finished goods inventory level at the end of each week for push and pull production.

2.20. Identify whether each of the following elements is waste or not. Explain.

- Waiting time in an airport
- Two spare tires in a car
- Flight time
- A "lemon" car

2.21. Identify whether each of the following activities is value adding or cost adding. Explain.

- Set-up
- Bread baking
- Shipping
- Packaging
- Heat treating
- Material storage

2.22. Quality, especially for electronic components, is measured in parts per million (ppm), i.e., how many defective components per million produced. An electronic manufacturer has a quality level of 1000 ppm. Identify whether each of the following objectives is improvement or innovation. Explain.

(a) Quality improvement of 100 ppm a year
(b) Quality improvement of 15 percent a year
(c) Achieving 100 ppm in three years and 10 ppm in five years
(d) Achieving 100 ppm in three years and then 10 percent improvement every year

6   THE IMPACT CIRCLE

The concepts described in Section 5 have tremendous impact on an industrial organization adopting all or part of them. The bottom line of this impact is represented by a major cultural change in the organization.

What is organizational culture? Culture refers to the underlying values, beliefs, and principles that serve as a foundation for a management system. Also included are the set of management practices and behaviors that both exemplify and reinforce those basic principles (Schoenberger, 1986). For example, IBM's organizational culture includes the following set of beliefs:

- Respect for the individual
- The best customer service in the world
- The pursuit of excellence

It is not difficult to observe the change in some components of organizational culture required by these concepts. The net result of this change is that the organizational culture changes from pursuit of efficiency to pursuit of effectiveness, which has a much broader scope.

Efficiency—a local measure of performance—is defined as the ratio of output to input. The idea is to make things right.

Effectiveness, on the other hand, focuses on requirements of the total system, not subsets of it. The idea is to make the right things. Performance standards on the major parameters of the system are specified, and these become a framework within which efficiency measures still play a role (Macbeth, 1989).

Machine utilization—the percentage of the time a machine is operating and producing products—is an **efficiency measure.** A machine with 30 percent efficiency seems to be doing a poor job, whereas a machine with 90 percent efficiency is producing almost all the time. However, this analysis does not consider the **effectiveness** of the issue—in this case, whether the product is actually demanded by a customer. If customers are only willing to buy 30 percent of the capacity of the machine, running it at 90 percent efficiency only creates products that will sit in inventory.

The transition from a culture of efficiency to a culture of effectiveness is difficult. It usually takes several years to accomplish because the entire organization must be transformed. Adopting the concepts of the new industrial world is a commitment for the long haul; any quick fix or short cuts are doomed to fail.

SECTION 6   PROBLEMS

2.23. Is it possible to be efficient but not effective? Explain and give an example.
2.24. Is it possible to be effective but not efficient? Explain and give an example.

7   PRODUCTION SYSTEM OBJECTIVE

The major objective of a production system is to make maximum contribution towards **continuously increasing** customer satisfaction. Other parts of the organization contribute their share as well, but the production system is the pivotal point of this effort. It is the only place where ideas and material are transformed into a product delivered to the customer. Usually the objective of a system is defined as a prelude to the discussion. We waited until the reader is ready to appreciate this objective.

Derived from this major objective are the operational goals of the productions system: deliver a product of superb quality on time every time and at the lowest possible cost, or in short: quality, time, cost-combined. That is:

Quality (improved)

Time (on time all the time)

Cost (simultaneously) decreased

Combined

These are relatively simple goals to state but very difficult to achieve. An organization that can achieve them is on its way to becoming a World Class Manufacturer (WCM). Before discussing world class manufacturing, we illustrate several aspects of integrated production and relate them to the concepts in the wheel.

8 FROM CONCEPT TO IMPLEMENTATION

So far, we have presented a host of concepts for market-driven production systems. You may ask, "Does it really work that way in the real world, and if so, how?" It sure does, and in this section we present some examples and show their relevance to the concepts in the wheel of competitiveness.

In this section we focus on integration, a significant new concept. We first discuss its implementation in a production environment; then we give three specific implementations of integrated production systems, cellular manufacturing systems, flexible manufacturing systems, and computer-integrated manufacturing; and we conclude the section by presenting three integration processes that can be used within the production environment.

8.1 Overview: Integrated Production Systems

In Section 5.2 we discussed the general notion of integration. A legitimate question at this point may be "What is integrated manufacturing?" Is it a new manufacturing technology, a new management technique, a new computer product, or a new way of life for the industrial organization? Probably, it is a little of each. The ultimate goal of integration is to enable the manufacturing organization to gain a competitive edge in the market.

To obtain further insight into integration, we borrow an example from a different domain—music. Consider the case in which there is only one musician—a soloist. When playing, a soloist need only be concerned with the quality of his or her performance. The scene changes when we have a trio. Now every musician is a member of a team. If one ignores the others, we get noise rather than music. The music must be coordinated, or integrated, to be enjoyable (i.e., it has quality).

At the trio level, the musicians manage to do the integration themselves; this integration is **within** the group. If two groups of musicians play together, then we must worry about integration **between** the groups. In a symphonic orchestra integration is much more complex. Not only should each group of instruments (departments) start and finish together, but the proper emphasis should be employed for each piece of music. The job is so complex that we need a conductor (equivalent to a manager) to coordinate the music. The conductor uses music notes (algorithm) and a baton (decision-making tool) to run the orchestra. When is the music pleasant? When the integration works well and each musician is in harmony with the team (cell), and when each team is coordinated with the other teams (system integration).

In the real world, as in our music example, integration requires different approaches for different levels of the ensemble hierarchy. In the manufacturing environment, integrating the activities of a number of machines (into a cell) is different from integrating the activities of the whole enterprise (system). We briefly highlight three aspects of manufacturing systems integration: the integration niche, the integration essence, and the integration strategy, which are discussed in the next section.

8.2 Aspects of Integrated Production Systems

8.2.1 INTEGRATION NICHE. The integration niche is the situation in which integration will have the greatest benefit. Market-driven environments require that manufacturers have

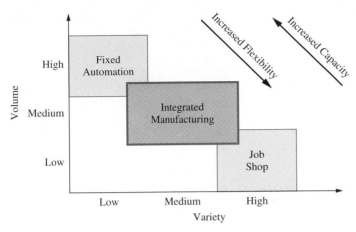

FIGURE 2-6
A volume variety plot

the **flexibility** to accommodate the frequently changing product variety demanded by customers. Figure 2-6, a volume variety plot, helps explain the integration niche.

The best potential improvement from applying integrated manufacturing is in the medium-variety, medium-volume zone where flexibility is required. The objective is to achieve economic production of a wide variety of parts, with many of the benefits previously associated only with mass production. The extreme regions are better served by other approaches—fixed automation for the high-volume, low-variety zone and a job shop for the low-volume, high-variety zone. However, new technologies and management techniques (such as just-in-time) have also penetrated these areas.

8.2.2 INTEGRATION ESSENCE. At the system level, two important elements of integration are **physical integration** and **information integration**.

Physical integration is achieved by properly arranging the equipment on the production floor (layout) and the material handling equipment servicing it. The integration novelty is not in the layout/material handling arrangement but in the design, operation, and control concepts that govern it.

Information integration is probably the most indicative single entity of integrated production systems. What truly integrates the system is not the closeness or remoteness of its entities, but the information flow between them. This is true of all aspects of information: technical information (say, between product/process design and production equipment), operational information (say, scheduling the production or controlling the material flow), and managerial information (say, monitoring the organization's policies). Thus, a free flow of information is *fundamental to the integration objective*.

8.2.3 INTEGRATION STRATEGY. Integration can be examined from two different perspectives: top down or bottom up. The two approaches are presented in Figure 2-7. A top down perspective views the enterprise as a complete system, i.e., it analyzes the system. A bottom up perspective looks at the components and actions of the system, as in synthesis.

Currently, there are three leading approaches to integrated production systems design— all focused on medium-variety and medium-volume production. They are as follows:

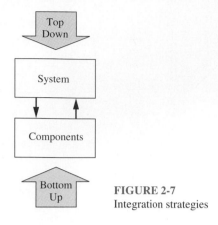

FIGURE 2-7
Integration strategies

- Cellular Manufacturing Systems (CMS)
- Flexible Manufacturing Systems (FMS)
- Computer Integrated Manufacturing (CIM)

CMS is a bottom up approach, CIM is a top down approach, and FMS falls somewhere between the two. These systems embed many of the concepts in the wheel of competitiveness in their design, including quality, time, cost, flexibility, integration, waste, pull, etc. The three systems are discussed next.

8.3   Integrated Production Systems Design

8.3.1   CELLULAR MANUFACTURING SYSTEMS (CMS). In cellular manufacturing systems production is organized around a manufacturing or assembly cell. What is a cell? A number of definitions exist, and we give two of them—one oriented more toward a manned cell, the other toward an unmanned cell.

A **manned cell** is dedicated to the manufacture or assembly of a family of parts that have similar processes. The operators in the cell are multifunctional, i.e., they can operate different kinds of machines. In an **unmanned cell,** the multifunctional worker is replaced by a robot (or other mechanical device) and a centralized cell controller.

The basis for cellular manufacturing is the process of grouping parts into families, which is is known as group technology. Group technology is a manufacturing concept or philosophy in which similar parts are grouped together in order to take advantage of their similarity in design, process, scheduling, and facilities planning. Thus, similar parts are arranged into families that possess similar manufacturing or design characteristics, and the processing of each member of the family is similar. This arrangement makes it possible to achieve the economies of scale of mass production, both in terms of cost and quality. Therefore, group technology has become one of the cornerstones of integrated production systems.

A manned cell is usually organized in a U-shaped layout, in which multifunctional workers perform the required operations. The U shape decreases walking time for multifunctional workers, contributing to cell flexibility, which can be further enhanced by reducing set-up times and employing pull control (discussed in Section 5.7). An example of a manned cell for assembling flexible computer disk drives is shown in Figure 2-8. (*kanban* squares will be discussed in Chapter 10.) In manned cells, physical integration is achieved by the

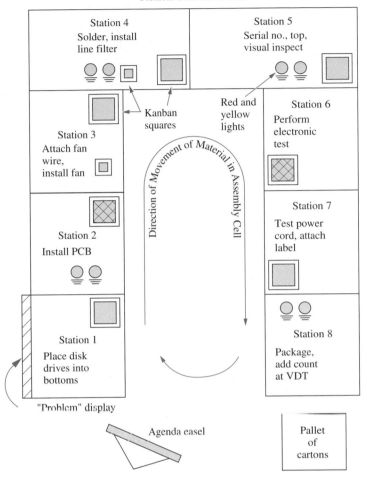

Flexible Disk Drive Line

FIGURE 2-8
Manned assembly cell (*Source:* Black, 1991) (reproduced by permission of the
McGraw-Hill Companies, Inc.)

U-shaped layout, and information integration is achieved by the multifunctional worker. Production control does not necessarily have to be computerized.

In an unmanned cell physical integration is again achieved through the layout—either U-shaped or circular. Information integration is achieved by the cell controller, usually a computer that drives the controllers of the machines and other cell equipment. A production plan can be downloaded to the cell controller and then monitored by it.

A cluster of independent cells forms a cellular manufacturing system (CMS). However, this integration is only partial, i.e., integration within the cells. If the cells are linked together by some material flow device, full integration is achieved. This is called a linked cellular manufacturing system (Black, 1991).

8.3.2   FLEXIBLE MANUFACTURING SYSTEM (FMS).   A flexible manufacturing system is another important technology for production floor operation and control. It also covers the

① Four Milacron T-30 CNC Machining Centers

② Four tool interchange stations, one per machine, for tool storage chain delivery via computer-controlled cart

③ Three computer-controlled carts, with wire-guided path

④ Cart maintenance station

⑤ Parts wash station, automatic handling

⑥ Automatic Workchanger (10 pallets) for online pallet queue

⑦ One inspection module — horizontal type coordinate measuring machine

⑧ Three queue stations for tool delivery chains

⑨ Tool delivery chain load/unload station

⑩ Four part load/unload stations

⑪ Pallet/fixture build station

⑫ Control center, computer room (elevated)

⑬ Centralized chip/coolant collection/recovery system (– – – flume path)

↻ Cart turnaround station (up to 360° around its own axis)

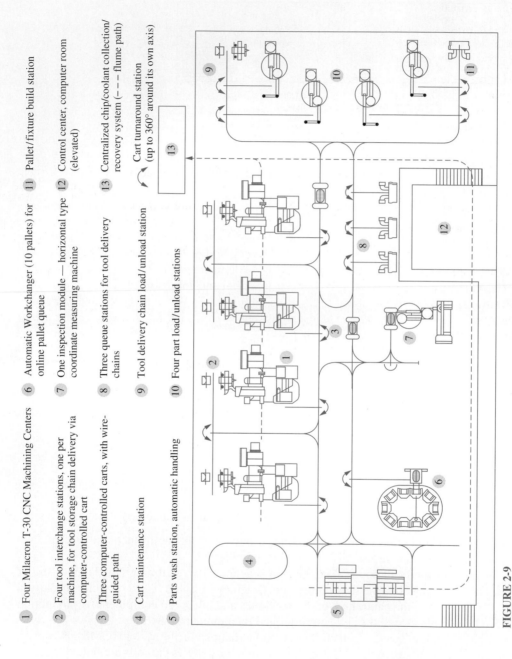

FIGURE 2-9

FMS at Millicron (*Source:* Miller and Walker, 1990) (reprinted by permission of Fairmount Press, Inc.)

middle ground of the volume variety plot, where flexibility is a major requirement. This feature is embedded in the following definition of flexible manufacturing system.

> A flexible manufacturing system is the integration of manufacturing or assembly processes, material flow and computer communication and control. The objective is to let the production floor respond rapidly and economically to changes in its operating environment.

Typical changes in the operating environment concern product mix, production volume, equipment breakdowns, etc. Note the wheel of competitiveness concepts embedded in the specification of a flexible manufacturing system.

The flexible manufacturing system would be impossible without certain technologies maturing: programmable automation, automated material handling, computer control, and communication systems. It should be emphasized that a flexible manufacturing system is not driven by the available technology but by the need for flexibility created by the market-driven environment.

Machining processes, especially in the metal industry, are currently the largest application areas in flexible manufacturing systems. However, many different applications are emerging, especially in assembly operations (e.g., electronic assembly). These systems are sometimes known as flexible assembly systems (FAS). Figure 2-9 is a typical FMS for metalworking. Three major components are production equipment (1, 2, and 7 in the figure), material handling equipment (3), and the computer control and communication network (12).

Computer control and communication network are likely the most important and the most complex aspects of any highly integrated system, including an FMS. Furthermore, it is the key element in implementing integrated production planning and control in a flexible manufacturing system, because one of the major functions of the computer control system is shop floor control, including such things as production control and scheduling, flow control, and machine control. Thus, any algorithm for integrated production planning and control has to be part of the control software of a flexible manufacturing system.

Information flow is an important element in the operation of an FMS. The success of a flexible manufacturing system usually depends on collecting and reacting to real-time status data in a timely manner. Based on this data, the control system must adjust when events do not occur according to plan.

8.3.3 COMPUTER INTEGRATED MANUFACTURING (CIM). Computer integrated manufacturing is a third approach to medium-volume, medium-variety manufacturing. Computer integrated manufacturing has a broader scope than cellular manufacturing systems or flexible manufacturing systems. Not only is it computer-based, but it implies a high degree of integration between all parts of the production system. All functions of production are tied into one large computer database, and access to the data is provided to various departments (users) in the organization. Theoretically, materials come in one end of the plant, and finished products come out the other end, all at the push of a button. In reality, this objective has rarely been achieved.

So what is CIM? There is no standard definition. Some view computer integrated manufacturing as a technology, but others look upon it as a management philosophy. In our opinion, both are correct; we view CIM as a management philosophy that has the required technology to implement it. We therefore propose the following definition:

> Computer integrated manufacturing is a management philosophy that uses computers, communication, and information technology to coordinate the business functions with product

development, design, and manufacturing. The objective is to obtain a better competitive position by achieving a high level of quality, on-time delivery and low cost.

It should be clear from this definition that the major integrating elements in computer integrated manufacturing are information and information technology. We want to carry the notion of computer integrated manufacturing one step further: it is a strategic goal that a firm strives to achieve over time. This definition is consistent with the wheel of competitiveness and the objectives of production systems we presented earlier.

There may be some confusion between flexible manufacturing systems and computer integrated manufacturing. One distinction is that FMS deals basically with the production floor, i.e., local integration, whereas CIM goes beyond the production floor toward global integration. Carrying this argument further, flexible manufacturing systems represent more of a bottom up approach to automation, but computer integrated manufacturing is top down. To phrase it differently, FMS creates islands of automation on the production floor, whereas CIM builds bridges between the islands to integrate them. In the long term, these two approaches will tend to merge. Flexible manufacturing systems will become just another aspect of a typical computer integrated manufacturing system. It will take some time before this happens on a wide scale, however. In order to get there, the system design must be part of a long-term automation strategy.

8.3.4   BENEFITS OF INTEGRATED PRODUCTION SYSTEMS.   Although achieved in different ways, certain benefits are common to the three types of integrated production systems. These benefits, corresponding to elements of the wheel of competitiveness, include quality, time, cost, integration, flexibility, and waste. A list is given in Table 2-1.

Numerous applications demonstrate the benefits of integrated production systems. For example, at a John Deere plant that produces hydraulic cylinders, a move to cellular manufacturing produced the following results (Martin, 1984):

- Part numbers reduced from 405 to 75
- Inventory reduced from 21 days to 10 days
- Set-up time cut by 75 percent
- Lead time cut by 42 percent
- Scrap reduced by 80 percent

TABLE 2-1
Benefits of integrated
production systems

Shorter lead time
Reliable delivery time
Flexibility in production scheduling
Reduced work in process
Reduced setup
Reduced floor space requirements
Better quality
Consistent quality
Improved management control

Of the three approaches to integrated production systems, cellular manufacturing is the most widely used. The reason is that cellular manufacturing integrates the manufacturing process without need of major capital investment.

There are certain integration processes that supplement and enhance the implementation of integrated production systems. We discuss some of them in the next section.

8.4 Integration Processes

Integration is a key element of market-driven production systems. The full benefits of an integrated production system will not be obtained unless certain integration processes take place. Some of these processes relate to designing the product and the system, but others relate to the operation of the system. We present an overview of three processes: teamwork, total quality management (TQM), and concurrent engineering. We first discuss teamwork, a part of the employee role in the wheel of competitiveness.

8.4.1 TEAMWORK. Machines do not run organizations, people do. People are the most important resource of an organization and in the final analysis make the difference. It is no wonder that the human element is the basis of many integration processes.

In our discussion of integrated production systems design, we noted the need for two aspects of integration: physical and information. The same philosophy applies, in a sense, to involving people in the integration process, which is achieved by building multifunctional teams to achieve a certain objective. Team meetings provide the physical integration. Information integration results from each member sharing different disciplinary knowledge with the team.

One outcome of teamwork is the elimination of functional barriers within the organization, those "walls" between departments that impede integration. Furthermore, by involving people from different disciplines, the outcomes will be more acceptable to everyone. In addition, a broad brain trust is put to work, which can generate a wide range of good ideas.

Teamwork itself is not a new idea. The novelty lies in the fact that it has become a company-wide approach and part of the management process aimed at achieving integration. Teamwork is the basis for two major integration processes: concurrent engineering and total quality management. We discuss them in the following sections.

8.4.2 CONCURRENT ENGINEERING. Concurrent engineering, also known as simultaneous engineering or life cycle engineering, is best described through the following definition:

> Concurrent Engineering is a systematic approach to the integrated, concurrent development of products and their related processes, including manufacture and support. This approach is intended to cause the developer, from the outset, to consider all elements of product life cycle, from conception through disposal, including quality, cost, schedule and user requirements. (Institute for Defense Analysis, 1988)

Concurrent engineering substitutes the sequential procedure of product and process design with a parallel one; product and process design are considered together, with an extended scope, which eliminates the functional barrier between product design and product manufacturing.

The process of concurrent engineering is implemented by using a team approach; cross functional teams are formed that include representatives of design and manufacturing,

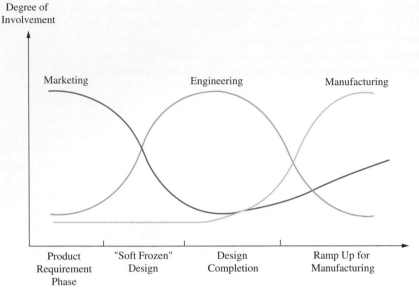

Degree of
Involvement

Marketing   Engineering   Manufacturing

Product   "Soft Frozen"   Design   Ramp Up for
Requirement   Design   Completion   Manufacturing
Phase

FIGURE 2-10
Team involvement by function (*Source:* Blackburn, 1991) (reprinted by permission of Irwin
Professional Publishing)

marketing, quality, and sometimes finance. Each team is responsible for a product or family
of products. Its mission is to shorten the time from product concept to market, often called
the time-to-market. In doing so, a product design yielding low manufacturing cost and high
quality is achieved.

Concurrent engineering organizes the team's work. It structures the flow of debate and
decisions so that people whose decisions come later in the process are involved in the decisions made earlier. The level of involvement of team members during the concurrent engineering process is dynamic, as shown schematically in Figure 2-10. Initially, marketing has
heavier involvement. Then, when requirements are defined, the product design has heavy input, to be followed by the process designer. The important fact is that the process is integrated;
each function is involved in every phase.

8.4.3   TOTAL QUALITY MANAGEMENT (TQM). Total quality management is a good example to demonstrate evolution of processes in market-driven systems. Some people feel
TQM is a different approach to quality, but others view it as simply a new buzzword. So,
what is it really? And what is its importance in the context of integrated production? These
issues and others are discussed in this section.

A number of different TQM definitions exist. We choose to define it as follows:

> TQM is an organization-wide quality focused culture. It is a journey to achieve excellence in all
> aspects of the organization's activity. It involves all members of the organization at all levels of
> operation.

Total quality management is a management philosophy rather than another quality technology. Its origin is attributed to Japanese industry, and it migrated to the West more than a

decade ago. Ironically, in Japan, TQM emerged in the early 1950s from the quality philosophy of Dr. W. Edwards Deming, a world-famous American quality expert.

In the West, an evolutionary process led to TQM, the three major phases of which are statistical quality control, total quality control, and total quality management.

Statistical quality control is the use of statistical methods to control quality. It originated in the United States in the mid-1930s by Shewhart. These methods were extended over the years, and they are still a major part of any quality program. An important technique in this context is statistical process control (SPC), a statistical tool used to control the variability of the process in order to achieve high product quality. Personal computers boosted statistical process control to widespread use on the production floor. Its organizational concept is that product quality is the responsibility of the quality control function. This philosophy is typical of the production-driven systems era.

Total quality control extends the organizational aspect of statistical quality control, but it does not change the basic tools. The total quality control philosophy recognizes that product quality is not just the responsibility of the quality control function. All parts of the organization, such as manufacturing, engineering, and marketing, must share this responsibility too; this process is an example of organizational integration. In retrospect, this concept was part of the transition from production-driven systems to market-driven systems.

Total quality management can be regarded as a spinoff of total quality control. It is a management philosophy with a set of tools to support it and is definitely a product of the market-driven system. Total quality management expands the scope of quality and the range of involvement in it. Quality no longer refers to just product quality; it is the quality of every activity in the organization, be it production or service. These activities include research and development, finance, maintenance, accounting, and sales. Furthermore, quality is the responsibility of every member of the organization, from the president to hourly employees.

SECTION 8   PROBLEMS

2.25. What are the various aspects of integration?

2.26. Integrated production is thought to be more suitable for a medium-variety, medium-volume production environment. Why?

2.27. What are the main approaches to integrated production?

2.28. What are the goals of integration?

2.29. Define five performance measures that are expected to improve as a result of integration.

2.30. Refer to integrated production systems benefits as noted in Table 2-1. Are these aspects interdependent or interrelated? Give a few examples of how improving one aspect can lead to an improvement of another.

2.31. What are the benefits of a "U shape" for manufacturing or assembly cells? How are they related to integration?

2.32. Explain how information and physical integration can be implemented in the following:

(a) Cellular manufacturing system

(b) Flexible manufacturing systems

2.33. What are the implications of partial integration—for example, implementing physical integration or information integration only?

2.34. Teddy Bear Inc. is a toy manufacturer who uses plastic and fibers as the main raw materials. Finished goods are sold through distributors to stores and customers. Company hierarchy and structure is illustrated in the following figure:

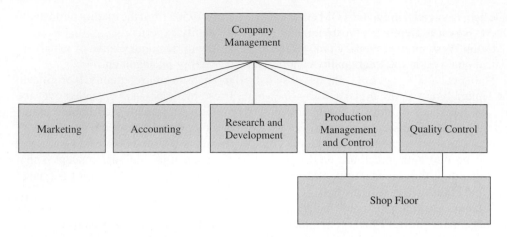

Marketing department is responsible for the distribution channels, order handling, and forecasted demand. Financial matters are handled by the accounting department. The research and development department develops new products and improves existing products and process plans. The production management and control department schedules batches for production and receives feedback from the shop floor. On-line inspection is performed by the quality control department.

(a) For each department in the block diagram, define at least five tasks that are typically performed by the department.

(b) For each task, define at least two information elements that are essential to complete the task. For example, production management and control releases batches to production and needs access to demand data and process plans.

(c) Try to locate information elements that are shared by more than one department. How are they related to information integration?

(d) What are the implications of running the various departments without a central database of shared information?

(e) What type of infrastructure is needed to implement information integration in this company?

9 WORLD CLASS MANUFACTURING (WCM)

The definition of **world class** is much discussed, as is the path to achieving it, and the term has recently become popular in the literature, mostly from Schoenberger's book, *World Class Manufacturing* (1986). Earlier, a common term, **manufacturing excellence,** was used. In both cases the goal is to achieve superior manufacturing capabilities. There is no standard definition of world class. However, this term represents the influence of the new market dynamics—the global market—and it nicely captures the breadth and essence of fundamental changes taking place in successful industrial enterprises. Some of the definitions that appear in the literature include only philosophies, but others include the philosophies and the means to achieve them. We present four definitions that appear in the literature and then propose our own.

Hayes et al. (1988) define world class manufacturing as follows:

• Become the best competitor; be better than almost every other company in your industry in at least one aspect of manufacturing.

• Be more profitable than competitors.

- Hire and retain the best people.
- Develop a top notch engineering staff.
- Be able to respond quickly and decisively to changing market conditions.
- Adopt a product and process engineering approach that maximizes the performance of both.
- Continually improve.

Huge and Anderson (1988) describe a new philosophy of manufacturing excellence that is based on the two fundamental principles of continuous improvement and elimination of waste.

Schoenberger (1986) identifies the turning point to world class manufacturing as 1980, the year North American companies began overhauling their manufacturing apparatus. As the overriding goal he suggests "continual and rapid improvement" in quality, cost, lead time, and customer service.

The National Center for Manufacturing Services (NCMS) Report (1988) presents eight areas of operating principles revolving around both customer and quality.

- Management approach
- Manufacturing strategy
- Quality and customer
- Manufacturing capabilities
- Performance measurement
- Organization
- Human assets
- Technology

Those areas are broken up into additional principles. The NCMS premise is that these principles, executed in concert, will increase the competitiveness of any manufacturer to that of a world class performer.

Obviously, these definitions are not contradictory, but rather complementary. Each emphasizes different aspects and provides a mix of concepts, principles, and tools.

Our definition of world class manufacturing is based on the objective of production systems defined in this chapter. *A world class manufacturing organization is one that subscribes to the objective of continuously increasing customer satisfaction; adopts the operational goals—quality, time, and cost-combined (QTCC); embraces the support concepts; and commits itself to the impact on the organization of the long-haul change process.* This definition is schematically represented in Figure 2-11.

There are two tendencies in the literature: one claims that all support concepts have to be adopted to succeed, but the other selects one or two "champions." We believe both approaches are wrong. Markets are different; organizations and cultures are different; so there is no one way to win this battle. Different situations, even in the same organization, may require a different **mix** of these concepts and their related tools. The **management art** of creating the proper mix will yield the best results. As Macbeth (1989) (used by permission of Springer-Verlag New York, Inc.) says,

> One of the features of the Western business world is that we are too easily persuaded of the merits of a particular "solution," and as a result, assume nothing else remains to be done. In this way companies move from one "panacea" to another as new "flavors of the month" are pushed by the latest "guru."

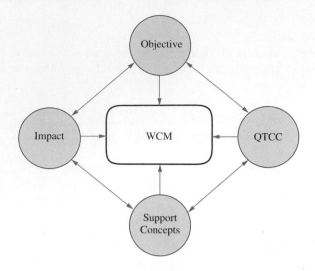

FIGURE 2-11
World class manufacturing

We cannot state too strongly that there is no "all or one" approach. A proper mix of these philosophies, concepts, and tools is determined by the particular situation.

Recently, two management philosophies elaborating on world class manufacturing have emerged: lean production and agile manufacturing. We discuss them next.

9.1   Lean Production

Lean production is a term coined by a research group at MIT (Womack et al., 1990). Their five-year study on the future of automobile production examined 90 plants in 19 countries. It promotes elimination of inventory and other forms of waste, greater flexibility in production scheduling, shorter lead times, and advanced levels of quality in both product and customer service. Lean production combines the advantages of craft and mass production without the high cost of the former or the rigidity of the latter. A cornerstone of lean production is the use of interdisciplinary teams at all levels of the organization.

Clearly, lean production employs many of the concepts and processes we described before. It is widely recognized that Japan was far ahead of the rest of the world in implementing lean production, which started in the 1950s at Toyota. It did not catch on in Western industry, however, until the 1980s.

The term was coined because it uses less of everything, compared to mass production—less human effort in the factory, less manufacturing space, and less engineering time to develop a new product.

Lean production differs from mass production in a number of ways, but the major difference is in the ultimate objectives. By implication, mass production set a limited goal—that of good enough. Operationally, there is an acceptable number of defects, an acceptable inventory level, and acceptable low product variety. The rationale was that to do better will be costly, and doing better was not required in the production-driven era.

Lean production sets its sights on performance, defining a path to perfection—zero defects, declining costs, higher flexibility, and more product variety. Thus lean production is a result of market-driven systems.

9.2   Agile Manufacturing

The concept of **agile manufacturing** started in a report titled "21ˢᵗ Century Manufacturing Enterprise Strategy," (Goldman et al, 1991). This study, done by the Iacocca Institute at Lehigh University, involved more than 150 industry executives. The report describes how U.S. industrial competitiveness will—or might—evolve in the next 15 years. An organization called the Agile Manufacturing Enterprise Forum (AMEF) was formed to continue this work. The Iacocca Institute effort was, to a certain degree, inspired by the Japanese study Manufacturing 21, which scripts scenarios for Japanese competitiveness in the twenty-first century.

The major thrust of agile manufacturing is an enterprise view (Sheridan, 1993), which, specifically, includes the following:

- Greater product customization—manufacturing to order but at a relatively low unit cost
- Rapid introduction of new or modified products, in some cases through quick formation of a temporary strategic partnership to take advantage of brief windows of opportunity in the marketplace, which is called a virtual enterprise or virtual organization
- Upgradeable products that are designed for disassembly, recyclability, and reconfigurability
- Interactive customer relationship
- Dynamic reconfiguration of production processes in order to accommodate swift changes in product design or entirely new products lines
- Commitment to environmentally benign operations and products

Examining these specifics, we see that agile manufacturing uses many of the concepts from the wheel of competitiveness.

On the production floor, reconfiguration is the main issue in agility. It is the ability to quickly gather necessary resources to meet a specific deadline, say a delivery date for a large order. Furthermore, the reconfiguration should be implemented at a reasonable cost.

The concept of agile manufacturing is still somewhat amorphous, and some of the support systems have yet to be developed. However, this approach appears to be the major thrust to create a vision for manufacturing enterprises in the next century.

9.3   Lean Versus Agile

At first glance, agile manufacturing might seem to be another way to describe lean production. There are similarities, but there are also differences.

The major difference is that agile manufacturing takes an enterprise view, whereas lean production is typically concerned with the production floor. Further, lean production is regarded by some as an enhancement of mass production methods. Agility implies breaking from the mass production mold so that a wider variety of custom products can be made.

We believe that subtle differences between lean production and agile manufacturing are not that important. What really counts is that both are based on similar concepts—those outlined in the wheel of competitiveness. Furthermore, we view each as a milestone on a path to develop new production theories.

SECTION 9 PROBLEMS

2.35. What is the common denominator of the various definitions of world class manufacturing?

2.36. What concepts of the wheel of competitiveness are part of lean production?

2.37. Identify three major elements of agile manufacturing. Explain your selection.

10 SUMMARY

American competitiveness declined in the mid-1960s. Since then, Japan has captured many markets in the United States and other countries because they could make products better, faster, and at less cost. It took time to realize that different approaches are required to deal with this new industrial environment. In seeking new approaches we look at production in Japan and America.

American companies were initially surprised by the Japanese success. This surprise quickly turned to admiration and then to the realization that the Americans needed to regain a competitive advantage. Some U.S. companies attempted to imitate Japanese companies, while others tried new approaches. From trial and error, the best concepts from both Japanese and American production systems have emerged: some classical, some Japanese, and some new American.

Looking at the status of management theories today, we conclude that the classical theories do not cover all aspects of the new environment. Although concepts of future theory may not be certain, we list the major ones. We integrate these concepts in the "wheel of competitiveness." We believe the concepts in the wheel are some of those required to return American industry to a leadership position.

The wheel has four concentric circles, each representing different aspects of the emerging production management theory. These circles are hub, delivery, support, and impact. The hub of the wheel is the customer. The delivery circle shows system deliverables to the customer: quality, time, and cost. The support circle shows eleven concepts needed to support the production system deliverables. The impact circle addresses a change in the organizational culture.

The chapter includes a detailed discussion of each of the circles. Customer satisfaction, time, cost, and quality are defined. The concepts of integration, flexibility, simplicity, pull, waste, improvement, and others are discussed. The impact on the organizational culture is reflected by the transition from a culture of efficiency to a culture of effectiveness. This transition takes years to accomplish; there is no quick fix.

In our definition, a production system's objective is to make maximum contribution towards continuously increasing customer satisfaction, from which the operational goals quality, time, and cost follow.

To further illustrate the concepts, we elaborate on integration, showing how it generated a new manufacturing environment—integrated production systems. We discuss three common implementations of integrated production—cellular, flexible, and computer-integrated systems. While presenting these, we point out their use of the concepts presented in the wheel of competitiveness. We further elaborate on three processes—teamwork, total quality management, and concurrent engineering—that enhance integration.

Next we discuss the concept of world class manufacturing and give our definition. We stress the need to evaluate each situation independently; none of the concepts we discuss solve every problem. However, a proper mix of these concepts and common sense will provide a good start.

We conclude with a discussion of lean production and agile manufacturing. These two emerging management philosophies grew out of world class manufacturing and will likely impact the direction of production in the twenty-first century.

11 REFERENCES

Black J T., *The Design of a Factory with a Future,* McGraw-Hill Publishing Company, New York, 1991.

Blackburn, J. D., *Time Based Competition,* Business One, Irwin, Homewood, IL, 1991.

Deming, W., *Out of the Crisis*, MIT Press, Cambridge, MA, 1986.

Hayes, R. H. Wheelwright, S. C., and Clark, K. B. *Dynamic Manufacturing, Creating the Learning Organization,* Free Press, New York, 1988.

Huge, E. L., and Anderson, A. D., *The Spirit of Manufacturing Excellence: An Executive Guide to the New Mind Set,* Dow Jones-Irwin, Homewood, IL, 1988.

Goldman, S. L., Preis, K., *21st Century Manufacturing Enterprise Strategy,* Iacocca Institute report, Lehigh University, 1991.

Institute for Defense Analysis, Report R-338, December 1988.

Macbeth, D. K., *Advanced Manufacturing Strategy and Management,* IFS Publications, Springer-Verlag, Berlin, 1989.

Martin, J. M., "Cells Drive Manufacturing Strategy," *Manufacturing Engineering,* 102, 49–54, January 1989.

Miller, R. K. and Walker, T. C., *FMS/CIM Systems Integration Handbook,* The Fairman Press, Lilburn, GA, 1990.

National Center for Manufacturing Sciences, *World Class Manufacturing: Operating Principles for the 1990's and Beyond,* NCMS, Washington, DC, 1988.

Schoenberger, R., *Building a Chain of Customers: Linking Business Functions to Create the World Class Company,* Free Press, New York, 1990.

Schoenberger, R., *World Class Manufacturing: the Lessons of Simplicity Applied,* Free Press, New York, 1986.

Sheridan, J. H., "Agile Manufacturing," *Industry Week,* April 19, 1993.

Womack, J. P., Jones, D. T., and Roos, D., *The Machine That Changed The World: The Story of Lean Production,* Rawson Associates, New York, 1990.

CHAPTER
3

PROBLEM SOLVING

1 INTRODUCTION

Blake planned a career in operations research, but a summer internship at the World Bank changed his mind. When asked why, he said, "I didn't see one application of OR at the World Bank last summer." The next summer, Tania interned at the World Bank and developed a linear programming model to allocate resources in the Egyptian agricultural sector. They hired her for another year to continue work on the model. Why was the experience of the two students different?

Blake expected someone to provide a well defined problem he could plug into a computer program and solve. This seldom happens. Tania examined issues important to the World Bank and modeled a problem solvable by linear programming. Tania was a problem solver; Blake was not.

Problem solving is difficult to teach; it is more art than science. To learn problem solving, you must do it. As in riding a bicycle, explanations are helpful, but eventually you must do it yourself. You may fall, but that is usually necessary in learning to ride a bike. Failure is also frequently part of learning to solve problems. There is no magic formula for problem solving.

Because it is difficult to teach problem solving, most textbooks focus on techniques for solving models. You must understand how to use the techniques, but just knowing how to plug and crank with them is not enough. You should focus on the problem-solving process as well.

This chapter contains suggestions on the art of problem solving. We give an overview of the problem solving approach in Section 2. Each of the next six sections covers a step in problem solving. We discuss identifying the problem in Section 3, understanding the problem in Section 4, and developing a model in Section 5. Solving models, interpreting the solution, and implementation are covered in Sections 6–8. A brief comment on using computers in problem solving (Section 9) is followed by Section 10, the evolution of formal problem-solving approaches. We summarize the chapter in Section 11 and provide references in Section 12.

Before we discuss the problem solving approach, we define problems, solutions, and problem solvers.

1.1   Problems

What is a problem? We face problems daily, but defining them is not so easy. A **problem** exists when what is happening differs from what should happen. What is happening is the current state, and what should happen is the goal state.

We know the current and goal states exactly in well structured problems. Finding the minimum of a quadratic function is an example. The current state is the function, and the goal state is its minimum. Other problems are ill-structured. Ill-structured problems may not have a clear goal state, nor even a well defined current state. Improving the quality of life is an ill-structured problem.

Problems may be one-time problems or recurring problems. Deciding how many widgets to produce each month is a recurring problem, but determining why a machine failed is a one-time problem. Many concepts for problem solving apply to both kinds of problems, but these problems have different situations. Recurring problems require continuing data collection, reports, and other infrastructure.

Every problem has a lifespan. Some problems must be solved quickly, but others are not as urgent. We cannot take too long to develop a schedule for programs run on a computer, because the time to run programs is usually short. On the other hand, we have more time to determine the location of departments in a plant to be built next year.

Problems also have different impact. Problems solved should be worthy of the resources required to solve them. Paraphrasing Gene Woolsey (Woolsey and Swanson, 1975), if it costs more to do the study than it will save, *don't do it.* The problem impact should determine the amount of effort we put into solving the problem.

Economic studies can justify solving some problems. Others are hard to justify solely on cost and profit; reducing lead times is an example. If lead times are not reduced, customers may buy from a competitor who can deliver on shorter notice. Estimating the cost of potential lost customers is difficult. Identifying all impacts, including those difficult to quantify, is critical to knowing which problems deserve effort.

1.2   Solutions

Problems typically do not go away unless we do something to resolve them. This intervention is **problem solving.** We look for easy and quick solutions, but complex problems often require complex solutions. Solving most well-structured problems is easy. To find the minimum of a quadratic function, we use first and second derivatives. Solving ill-structured problems is not obvious. How would you reduce world hunger? A large part of problem solving is transforming ill-structured problems into well structured problems.

Ackoff (1991) discusses four approaches to a problem. The first, **absolution,** ignores the problem and hopes it goes away, which is seldom a good approach. The second approach is resolution. **Resolution** finds an acceptable solution to the problem using common sense;

resolution is usually better than absolution, but the answer may not be a good one. **Solution** is his third approach. It uses quantitative and experimental methods to get the "best" answer under the current conditions. The fourth approach, **dissolution,** redesigns the system to eliminate the cause of the problem. This approach, if possible and not too costly, is the preferred one.

To solve a problem five conditions should exist (VanGundy, 1981). There must be the following:

1. A gap between the current state and the goal state, i.e., a problem exists
2. An awareness of the gap, in which we recognize the problem
3. Motivation to close the gap—the problem is important to someone and has impact, and resources will be committed to solve it
4. The ability to "measure" the size of the gap; we have an idea of the severity of the problem and know when improvement occurs
5. The ability and resources to close the gap; we have the methodology to solve the problem and the resources to carry out the solution

If one or more of these conditions is missing, successfully solving the problem is unlikely. If these conditions exist, we can proceed with problem solving. Although there is no one best way to solve ill-structured problems, we present a framework that may prove useful.

1.3   Problem Solvers

Who is the problem solver? The person who has the problem or someone paid to solve problems could be the **problem solver.** In the production arena, the problem solver may be a manager, analyst, or industrial engineer. Often there are several problem solvers working together; for ease of discussion, we will use the singular. In this book, you are the problem solver.

Because problem solvers are people, they are not infallible. Personal values, biases, and judgment all affect the problem-solving process. Whether a problem exists or not is affected by a person's point of view, but recognizing that bias exists should minimize its impact.

The knowledge and experience of a problem solver also comes into play. If a person has more tools, that person has a wider range of options for solving problems. Experience teaches which tools to use in certain situations and even helps in inventing new ones or adapting old tools to new situations. If a particular tool is not in your tool kit, you will not use it.

SECTION 1   PROBLEMS

3.1. What is a problem?
3.2. List Ackoff's four types of solutions.
3.3. What five conditions should exist to solve a problem?

2   PROBLEM-SOLVING APPROACH

There are many approaches to problem solving. A general one includes problem identification, generation of solutions, and choosing a solution. We present a six step process, outlined in Figure 3-1. An overview of the process follows, with details given in later sections.

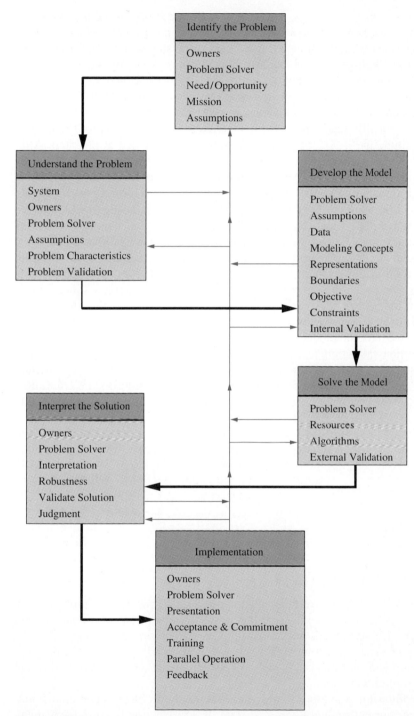

FIGURE 3-1
An overview of the problem-solving process

If all steps are successful, the process begins at *Identify the Problem* and then proceeds to *Understand the Problem, Develop the Model,* and so forth. This sequence is indicated by the heavy black lines. No step can be skipped. It is likely that a step will not be successfully completed; we must then return to a previous step. This return is shown by the blue lines. If we do not complete the *Solve the Model* step, we return to *Develop the Model, Understand the Model,* or *Identify the Model,* to be determined by the reason we could not solve the model. When we return to a step, the following steps must be done consecutively.

The first step is to identify the problem, which includes identifying the problem owners and, together, determining the problem mission. Assumptions are made at this step. After successfully identifying the problem, the problem solver and owners must understand the problem, which includes examining the system within which the problem occurs, specifying problem characteristics, including goals, and possibly making more assumptions. Validation ensures that the correct problem is solved at later steps. If this step is unsuccessful, a return to problem identification will be necessary. Once the problem solver and owners agree on the problem, a formal model is developed. Modeling concepts and data availability determine a representation for the model. Then, boundaries, constraints, objectives, and relationships are used to produce a formal model. Validate the model to make sure it does what the problem solver intended to do. Failure at this step may require a return to either problem identification or problem understanding. After constructing the formal model and collecting data, an appropriate algorithm is used to solve the model. Again, unsatisfactory results force a return to a previous step. Once we have the model solution, we interpret it considering the actual problem. Robustness, solution validation, and judgment lead to a problem solution. If necessary, return to a previous step to resolve differences. Finally, implement the solution. Implementation begins by proposing a solution. Once the solution is accepted, resources are committed to solve the problem. Appropriate people are trained and the new solution is implemented in parallel with the old procedure. Be sure to monitor progress for continued success.

We discuss each of these steps in some detail. Some topics, such as assumptions and owner involvement, appear in several steps. Unless there is something different about them in a particular step, we only discuss them the first time they occur.

SECTION 2   PROBLEMS

3.4. List the major steps in problem solving.
3.5. Discuss the nonsequential nature of problem solving.

3   PROBLEM IDENTIFICATION

Initially symptoms arise; from these we must make a problem diagnosis. The problem may arise from a need, an opportunity, or both. The problem solver and owners develop a problem mission, which determines what needs to be accomplished. To do so, assumptions are often necessary. Do not try to visualize a solution now; it will only restrict the ideas on problem identification. This step is a continuous interaction between owner and problem solver and results in an initial problem statement.

Problem identification converts a "mess" into a simple problem statement. Tentatively, we describe our current state and our goal state. If a production line produces many items rejected by the customer, the current state is a line that is producing poor quality items. The goal state would be a line that produces perfect items.

Identification is an important step in problem solving. A problem never recognized will never be solved. Ackoff (1991) believes it is better to get the wrong solution to the right problem than the right solution to the wrong problem. Solutions to the wrong problem are ignored, but wrong answers to the right problem create interest and are corrected and used.

Two sources of problems are need and opportunity. Problems can be driven by either or both. A broken machine is need driven; something undesirable has occurred that needs fixing. Often, complaints make us aware of these problems. Sometimes, need-driven problems are hard to recognize. In 1962, General Motors made 51 percent of all cars and light trucks sold in the United States. By 1991, their market share was only 35 percent. Their failure to respond to a changing market is a classic example of an unrecognized problem.

Even if there are no complaints, we may still have a problem. Satisfied customers are not enough; we may want to improve quality to increase our competitive edge. This situation is opportunity-driven. If it ain't broke, make it better! The Japanese insistence on continuous improvement is an example of opportunity-driven problem solving. To recognize opportunity-driven problems, we should follow the advice of Shaw, who said, "I dream things that never were, and say 'Why not?' "

3.1 Problem Mission

The most important phase of problem identification is to determine the **problem mission.** The mission is the overall purpose—what we want to accomplish. The mission will later be translated into goals, and then objectives. Different missions result in different solutions. For any problem, we could give many missions.

We may view missions as a pyramid with several levels. Each level represents a different mission, the most specific at the top and becoming more general as we move towards the base. Nadler and Hibino (1990) discuss a company that makes plastic bags. The bags are packaged in a cardboard box. One side of the box has a tab that can be pulled to create an opening. Individual bags are pulled out of the box through this hole. Currently, the company has problems cutting the perforations in the sheet of cardboard that becomes the box. Their list of missions is given in Figure 3-2.

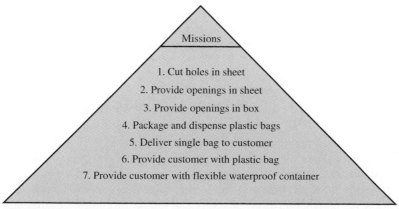

FIGURE 3-2
Hierarchy of problem missions

The first mission is quite different from the last. Cutting holes in the sheet restricts the possible solutions, while providing a customer with a flexible waterproof container places the problem in a new perspective. Pursuing a more general mission will probably result in greater change; in this case the company might change its entire product line.

It is not always best to pursue the most general mission. Time and resource constraints, or even policy decisions, may limit the mission. For example, to package and dispense plastic bags may be as far as we are willing to go. Choosing this mission eliminates the original problem because we may no longer need to cut holes in the sheet. Of course, we must now solve the problem of how to package and dispense bags.

Defining the correct mission will prevent confusing symptoms with problems. Problem identification has much in common with a doctor making a diagnosis. The problem solver looks at symptoms and determines the correct problem statement. A melt-spun extruder broke the key connecting a gear to the main drive shaft. After breaking twice, a mechanic assumed the mission was to keep the key from breaking, so he replaced it with a case-hardened steel key. Naturally, the key did not break again, but the shaft wound up looking like a pretzel.

The broken key was a symptom rather than the problem. In fact, the key did its job—it protected the shaft and gear. The true mission was finding out what caused the excess force applied to the key. Once the mission was known, a maintenance engineer found and fixed the problem. Often, identifying the right problem is more difficult than getting a solution.

To differentiate between symptoms and causes, Ohno (1988) recommends asking why?, five times. When the key broke, ask why. The answer would be that there was too much force applied. Now ask why there was too much force. When that is known, continue to ask why until the true problem is discovered. If the problem solver asks why at least five times, the real problem will probably be found.

Once the right mission has been chosen, identifying the problem is easier. Be careful to spend enough time on this phase. Do not try to incorporate solutions into problem identification—that will come later. Observing what is happening now will be very helpful. Also, brainstorming with a group of knowledgeable people can help clarify the problem.

3.2 Problem Owners

Problem owners are people who must live with the solution. It would be unusual in a production environment (or many other environments) to have a single owner. Often, different owners have different stakes in the problem and even different goals. Carefully review these stakes and goals and *continually* involve the owners in the solution process. Do not try to place blame for a problem. Make the problem a common enemy so that owners work with you rather than against you.

Failure to involve the owners continually may be disastrous. There are many horror stories of problem solvers developing an initial problem description and going back to the office to solve the problem. After spending time, effort, and resources, they present their solution to the owners, only to discover the problem they solved does not really exist. Turning in an assignment that was not what the professor wanted is a typical example.

Often owners only recognize symptoms and do not recognize the problem, which hampers problem identification. A good diagnosis is necessary and requires a continuous dialogue with the owners.

3.3 Assumptions

When identifying the problem, we seldom know all the facts, so we must make **assumptions.** If you work on well structured problems, assumptions may not be necessary. However, relationships between various parts of most problems are uncertain, which requires the problem solver to make assumptions about them.

It is very important to state assumptions *explicitly.* Then everyone can question and comment on them. Explicit assumptions remind us to check their influence on the solution. If an assumption is questionable and will have a large impact on the solution, try to use preliminary experiments to justify or change it.

Sometimes we must make questionable assumptions in spite of everything. It is better to make a questionable explicit assumption than not to state an assumption. Sensitivity analysis, discussed later, can determine the effect of assumptions. In any event, assumptions should be "reasonable," i.e., fit within the general problem environment. If possible, justify assumptions by observation, empirical data or evidence, or judgment of the owners.

3.4 Initial Problem Statement

Once you identify a problem, write down a "formal" problem statement. Include a one- or two-sentence description of the mission and a brief description of the current state and the goal state. Do not include restrictions, and do not go into great detail. List all assumptions, preferably in bold, capital letters. The next step is to understand the problem.

> **Example 3-1. Identify the MaTell problem.** MaTell makes telephones. Currently, they make three products; a desk phone, a wall phone, and an answering machine. All three products are made only at the Vinings plant. Many customers who want these products cannot buy them because they are unavailable. The production department at Vinings claims that it is making as many products as possible.
>
> Is there a problem? If so, is it need or opportunity driven? Being able to sell more products would benefit the company, so there is an opportunity here. Doing nothing may cause a need-driven problem later. If we have too many unsatisfied customers, they may switch to other brands, and MaTell's market share might slip.
>
> What is the problem mission? One mission might be to provide more products so that fewer sales are lost. Asking why we want fewer lost customers leads to a more general mission of increasing market share. Asking why we would like to increase market share may lead to a mission of making more money. Of course other missions are possible, but for illustration, we will only generate these. We need to address this problem quickly, so we will choose a mission of providing more products. The scope is smaller, more focused, and appropriate for the short term. We also might want to explore longer-term problems with increasing market share and making more money as missions.
>
> Who are the owners of this problem? First, we should think of the customers, because their dissatisfaction is creating the problem. We should be sure that there are customers who want products and are not getting them. Interviews and market surveys can answer this question. Marketing may have already done this step. Although customers are the most important owners of this problem, they do not care about the process of solving the problem, only the results. The natural bridge to the customer is marketing, which should be considered an owner at this stage. Someone in marketing should be designated to work with the problem solver on this effort.
>
> In solving this problem, there are several assumptions we must make. First, we assume an opportunity exists. Marketing and the customers can verify this assumption. We also must

assume demand for these products will remain constant or increase; if this assumption is not true, we do not need to provide more products. Finally, there is the assumption of an implied threat from our competitors; if we do not satisfy demand, someone else will. In brief,

- We can sell more products if they are available.
- Demand will continue at the present levels or increase.
- Competitors will sell products to customers who could not get our product.

This leads to an initial problem statement:

Current state: Some customers who want our product cannot get them.

Goal State: Deliver a product to all of our customers who want one.

Problem: How can we provide product to all our customers?

SECTION 3 PROBLEMS

3.6. Discuss symptoms versus problems.

3.7. Give two sources of problems.

3.8. How does the problem mission relate to Ackoff's four types of solutions?

3.9. What is the most important point in dealing with problem owners?

3.10. Why are assumptions necessary?

3.11. What is dangerous about assumptions?

3.12. Pizza from The Palace is the traditional game day meal in a small college town. Shoshana is one of sixteen students who delivers pizza on football weekends. This job is her only source of spending money. Because many alumni return for games, as soon as she returns from a delivery, another will be waiting for her. Her hourly wage is small, but tips average about $20/hour. Driving faster allows her to make more deliveries and more tips. However, the cost of operating her car increases as she goes faster. Experiments show that driving at 25 mph (miles per hour) costs $0.25/mile, at 30 mph costs $0.30/mile, and at 40 mph costs $0.40/mile.

(a) What are the possible missions?

(b) Which one would you choose? Explain.

(c) Who are the owners?

(d) Write an initial problem statement.

3.13. (The following problem is from Lumsdaine and Lumsdaine copyright © (1995) reproduced with permission of the McGraw-Hill Companies, Inc.) Seven passengers have just boarded a Boeing 747 aircraft for a transpacific flight. They find their assigned seats and sit down. The accompanying figure provides a sketch of the seats involved in this problem:

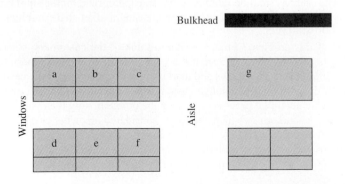

For this 14-hour flight, the people, their seat assignments, and their needs and wishes are the following:

(a) A Korean man who speaks some English has the bulkhead window seat (a).

(b) His wife who appears to be ill is in the bulkhead middle seat (b).

(c) A big English-speaking Filipino carrying a large bag that she refuses to stow in an overhead luggage bin is in the bulkhead aisle seat (c) but demands a seat farther back.

(d) A Korean woman who does not speak English has the window seat in the row behind the bulkhead (d). She carried on a large package that does not fit under the seat in front of her. She stows it in the leg space and covers it with a blanket and her purse. Of necessity, her legs extend into the space of the middle seat.

(e) A hunky U.S. serviceman is squeezed into the middle seat (e).

(f) A middle-aged American woman on crutches with a broken foot has the adjoining aisle seat (f). She finds it will be impossible for her to elevate her foot from this seat using the small folding camping seat she has brought along for this purpose.

(g) The woman's son, a six-foot-four-inch skinny guy with very long legs, has the bulkhead seat (g) across the aisle (behind the lavatory partition). He trades seats with his mother to give her more leg room. However, this is not sufficient to allow her to prop up her foot.

The stewardess has found a seat in the back of the crowded plane for the Filipino. The Korean couple is delighted at first, but then they find that the armrests in the bulkhead seats cannot be raised; thus the ill wife cannot lie down.

(a) What are the possible missions?

(b) Which one would you choose? Explain.

(c) Who are the owners?

(d) Write an initial problem statement.

4   UNDERSTAND THE PROBLEM

From the initial problem statement, we refine our understanding of the problem. Because problems do not exist in a vacuum, the problem solver must understand how the problem fits into its environment. We must describe the system within which it occurs. Once the boundaries of the problem are determined, the solver and owners identify problem characteristics. They also make the problem mission more specific by identifying solution goals. New assumptions may be needed in this step, leading to a deeper understanding of the problem. The problem must be validated to ensure the problem is the right one. Methods for problem understanding are similar to those used for problem identification, but at a more detailed level. We may need to redefine the system, make new assumptions, or even return to problem identification. A detailed problem statement is a result of problem understanding.

4.1   The Systems Perspective

A **system** is a collection of interacting components; its function cannot be done by any single component. Machines are one component of a production system. By itself, a machine cannot make a finished product, but correctly coupled with other machines, people, and raw material, it becomes a system capable of making a product. The machine is also a system made up of components, e.g., power supply, tools, etc. Thus, whether something is a system or a component depends on the particular problem. Problems often occur in the way parts of the system interact with each other. We must understand problems within the system's framework.

Analysis is one way to study a system. The system is taken apart and each component studied separately to see how it works. Then the knowledge of the components is combined to gain knowledge about the system, which can usually tell us *how* a system works.

Synthesis is another way to look at a system. Synthesis views the system as a component of a larger system, and we try to explain the behavior of the larger system. Then we can explain the original system as it functions within the larger system. Rather than tell us how the system operates, synthesis tells us *why* it operates as it does.

Figure 3-3 shows the difference between analysis and synthesis. Suppose the problem occurs within the system outlined in solid bold lines. Analysis is represented by the arrow pointing left. It looks within the system to see how the components interact, which tells how the system works. On the other hand, synthesis, represented by the arrow going out of the system, views the system as a component of a larger system, shown by the dashed lines. By considering its interaction with the components of the larger systems, we can discover why the system works as it does.

When examining a problem within the systems framework, important questions to ask are who, what, why, when, where, and how. Who does it; what do they do; why do they do

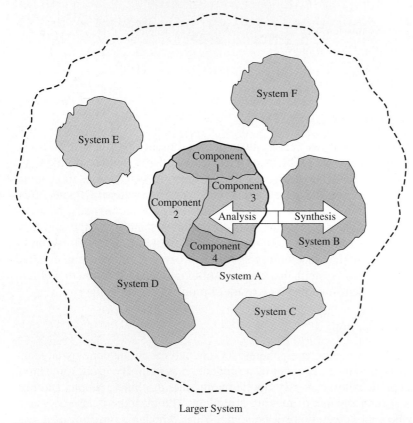

FIGURE 3-3
Analysis and synthesis of a system

it; when do they do it; where do they do it; and how do they do it? These questions further define the current state.

4.2   Goals

Given an initial problem statement and further understanding of the problem, we define the solution **goal.** The mission is our overall purpose, but the goal should be one or more accomplishments that will lead to fulfilling the mission. If our mission is to have satisfied customers, the goal might be to improve the quality of our product or service. Other common goals might be to reduce the time to carry out a task or provide a product or to reduce the associated cost. There is no need to describe the goals in minute detail, only to state them in a general way.

4.3   Problem Characteristics

The time frame in which the problem exists is important. If it is a one-time problem, the solution must be given before the problem disappears or changes. For example, we must determine the best way to lay out a production facility before using it. Similarly, if a manager needs to know how many employees to hire for next month, giving an answer two months from now does not help. Thus, the time available to solve a problem determines the approach we take to solve it.

Does the problem recur or is it a one-time situation? Recurring problems often require more resources. Reports, data collection, and other infrastructure needed for recurring problems are more elaborate than for one-time problems.

We also need to determine a proper level of detail for the problem. A dairy deciding how much skim, 2 percent, and whole milk to produce next week would not need to know the exact amount of milk an individual cow gives, only the total of all cows. Deciding which cows to breed requires knowing individual yields.

Next, try to determine if any physical laws control part of the problem. Conservation of matter and the law of gravity are typical physical laws. In production systems, physical laws are seldom problems. Company policy usually places far more restrictions on the way systems function. Do not include policy restrictions now; they are not absolute physical laws.

The characteristics and impact of the problem determine how much time and effort can be spent solving the problem. Important problems with a long time frame are worthy of time and effort. However, if the potential payoff is small, we should resort to "quick and dirty" solutions or not solve the problem at all. Quick and dirty methods may also be right for important problems with a short time horizon.

4.4   Validate Understanding

Our understanding of the problem is an abstraction of the real problem. If we understand the actual problem, our abstraction should capture its important features. We must make an effort to ensure this; i.e., we **validate** our problem understanding.

Validating understanding is not easy. Try describing the problem to the owners. If you cannot, it is unlikely you understand it. Critically question every part of the problem description. It helps to have someone else critically question your understanding of the problem. A model based on faulty understanding does not produce good solutions to the problem. If you cannot validate your understanding of the problem, return to the problem identification step.

4.5   Problem Statement

We can now write a more precise, detailed problem statement. After further study of the problem, we may have revised the mission or modified assumptions. Document all changes.

As before, involve the problem owners. It is helpful to have someone who is unfamiliar with the problem involved, which will help avoid the "can't see the forest for the trees" syndrome. Do not try to hurry through this phase to get to a solution. Time spent here saves wasted time and effort later.

Now make the problem statement more formal, usually done by developing a formal model. We discuss this step in the next section.

> **Example 3-2. Understand the MaTell problem.** There are a variety of ways to provide more products to our customers. We could build a new plant, expand the Vinings plant, or subcontract with another company to make our products. However, the first two approaches would take a long time, and the third could have serious ramifications for quality, sharing technology, etc. As a result, we can define our goal as increasing throughput in the Vinings plant.
>
> In understanding the MaTell problem, we must look at the problem from a systems perspective. One system is the entire MaTell operation. MaTell does many things in addition to making the three particular products at the Vinings plant. Because our goal is increasing throughput of the Vinings plant, we will concentrate on the actual production system.
>
> Physically, raw material is processed into components in a fabrication department and then assembled in another department. The finished products are then distributed to retail outlets, which sell them to the customers. We have had no sign of problems with suppliers, distribution, or sales, so we will concentrate on fabrication and assembly.
>
> Now, they are making 15,000 wall phones, 17,000 desk phones, and 5000 answering machines each week. The plant works three eight-hour shifts a day and operates seven days a week. Production records show fabrication is busy 135 hours per week, and assembly is busy 163 hours per week. Because there are 168 hours available per week (7 days $\times$ 24 hours/day), assembly appears to be the bottleneck.
>
> At this point, a new owner is identified—the production department. Discussions with them verify that assembly limits the number of units made. At this stage, it would be common to jump to the solution of adding capacity to assembly. However, this action might not be the best solution, because the telephone industry is very competitive and increasing costs could hurt sales. We should look at two other strategies: using capacity more effectively or reducing the time a product spends in assembly.
>
> Let's explore the idea of using capacity more effectively. Now, production is planned based on a projection of future demand. If it is not possible to produce all demand, a fixed percentage of the three products is produced. Because the three products use different amounts of assembly time, a different production plan could possibly make more products, resulting in more customers who buy our products. Using a new plan also brings the planning department into the picture as new owners.
>
> The impact of this problem is large. Marketing feels 10 to 15 percent of our sales are lost. Not only do we lose profit on those sales, but customer word-of-mouth may influence other customers not to buy our product.
>
> There are several important characteristics of this problem. Timing is important; we believe that if we cannot get more product to customers within two months, our competitors will eat into our market share. Reclaiming lost customers is much harder than keeping them. The problem is recurring because we must plan production each week. To get the correct level of detail, we must consider each of the three products; however, the assembly and fabrication areas do not need to be considered at the individual machine level. Natural laws are not important here.

To validate the problem understanding, we should ensure that our understanding agrees with all owners. Although this seems obvious, it is very important and often ignored.

There are several additional assumptions we have made here:

- The information we based our analysis on was correct.
- Not providing a solution within two months will have a negative effect on MaTell.
- We can use assembly capacity more effectively through better planning.

Further analysis at later steps will help validate these assumptions.

We now have a more detailed problem statement: How can we use capacity in assembly more effectively to provide more products for our customers?

SECTION 4   PROBLEMS

3.14. List steps to better understand a problem.

3.15. How do synthesis and analysis aid problem understanding?

3.16. What are the differences in the problem goals and mission?

3.17. List problem characteristics. Why are they important?

3.18. How is problem understanding validated?

3.19. Consider the Pizza Delivery problem.

(a) Validate your understanding, and describe how you did it.

(b) Write a detailed problem statement.

3.20. Consider the Airplane Seating problem.

(a) Validate your understanding, and describe how you did it.

(b) Write a detailed problem statement.

5   DEVELOP A MODEL

In this step, we turn a detailed problem statement into a formal model. A **model** is a representation of something. The problem solver uses available data, modeling concepts, and assumptions to choose a type of model. Then, specific data and the problem boundaries help generate an objective and constraints applicable to the model. Assumptions affect the model. A model is then proposed and structurally validated, which ensures the model works as it should. If unsuccessful, we return to any previous step. Eventually, we construct a formal model statement.

A model can be formal or possibly just in our minds. It is good practice to state the model explicitly. Its precise statement allows everyone involved a chance to agree on what is being done. We discuss various types of models, followed by sources and uses of data; then we discuss modeling itself. Again, involve the owners, and clearly state all assumptions. During this step, we may need to return to a prior step.

5.1   Model Representations

Models can be formal or informal, qualitative or quantitative. They are used to test an alternative, predict the behavior of a system, determine the best of many alternatives, or explore what-if questions. We can usually test more alternatives with a model than we could by direct experimentation. We briefly discuss iconic, analog, and symbolic models.

Iconic models are physical representations that usually have different scales than what they represent. Wind tunnel tests of scale model airplanes are less costly and time consuming than building actual planes to test. Traditionally, industrial engineers use iconic models of buildings and templates for machines to do layout studies. Iconic models are often used with computers—for example, CAD systems. These models are easy to explain, because they look like the real thing.

Analog models behave the same way the system does but do not look like the system. A flowchart showing the information flow in a production system is an analog model. We have used analog representation for the steps in problem solving. Historically, flows in systems were modeled by electrical circuits, because current flows in electrical circuits are easily calculated.

Symbolic models are an important class of models. As the name implies, the system is represented by symbols. This class includes graphical, tabular, and mathematical models.

For simple systems, a table or graph can be used as a model. Speed versus number of good products made could represent the output of a machine on the production floor. This relationship could be shown by a table or a graph or even as a mathematical equation. Spreadsheets are helpful for these types of models.

Systems too complicated for tables and graphs use more complicated models. Simulation models, which use relationships between components, are symbolic models. Often the relationships are stochastic, and they may not be defined as precisely as those used in mathematical models. Mathematical models capture relationships between components using mathematical equations. Linear programming formulations are typical mathematical models. Changes in input data usually do not affect the model structure, only the solution, which makes models easy to use repetitively.

5.2 Data

Data are often needed to identify and understand a problem. Specifically, data are used to validate assumptions, estimate model parameters, and validate models and are usually collected at every step of the problem-solving process. Availability of data may dictate the type of model used.

Data represent characteristics of people, objects, or events. Examples of data would be the number of machine hours available in the finishing department; the number of units a worker produced in one shift; the number of gallons of crude oil needed to produce one gallon of kerosene; and the cost to make one unit of product at the Salinas plant and ship it to Los Angeles. Some data may be functions of other data, but all data can be given values before solving the problem.

Data are not information; information describes or explains data. The number of units produced during a shift is data, and the average over many shifts is information. Be careful when extracting information from data; some information is unknowable exactly. Knowing the number of customers arriving at a restaurant between 11:00 AM and noon tomorrow is one example. Here we estimate, with limits on the accuracy of the estimate. The cost of overestimating may not equal the cost of underestimating, so make decisions accordingly.

Data are used to get information. *Do not collect data for the sake of collecting data.* Data collection is often the most expensive part of problem solving. If it does not provide information needed to solve the problem, do not collect it. Many projects start by trying to get all the data possible, usually at a large cost of time and money. At this point determine the data needed to solve the problem, and only collect this data.

A pessimistic view is that data are seldom available, and when they are, they are in the wrong form. If by chance data are in the right form, they are not accurate. More realistically, seldom will we have all the data we want, or even all we need. Availability of data may dictate the type of model used.

Where do we get data? The answer to this question depends on the data. Company records, people, government, and trade associations are all potential sources.

Company records are probably the best source of data. These records include accounting data, standards, sales and inventory reports, financial reports, engineering drawings and blueprints, or product brochures. Make sure you understand what these data are before they are used. For example, a cost accountant may have three or four ways to determine the value of one unit of product in inventory.

People are another source of data. Be careful to get facts rather than opinions when dealing with people. Problem owners are a source of data, as are customers, vendors, and even competitors. Interviews and questionnaires are two ways to elicit information from people, but the questions asked should be thought out so that the data will provide useful information.

Governments and trade associations often provide data; various industry reports produced by the government contain useful data. Research reports and regulatory publications are also sources of data. Magazine and journals published by trade associations may help.

The cost to get data will vary greatly depending on the source. Collecting data is expensive, but data from an existing database are relatively cheap. If the cost of the data is too high, the model may have to be changed so that the data are no longer needed. Also, if the data cannot be gotten before the problem must be solved, it will do little good to collect it.

Data must reflect the physical phenomenon, which we call data integrity. If data show a product needs two units of a particular component, it should use two, not one or three. Loss of data integrity occurs in several ways, but usually it is either an input problem or an accuracy problem. Control input by standard data processing techniques.

Data must be accurate, and the accuracy required should match the problem. To determine how many widgets to produce next month, you do not need to know the time to make one widget to six decimal places. Also, if there are several types of data, the least accurate data determine the model's accuracy. Once we develop a model, we can determine how variability of the data affects its solution.

Data may not be accurate enough. At a warehouse, bar code readers used to pull cases of yarn for shipping are 99.9 percent accurate. Each truck holds about 250 cases, so about one in four trucks has a wrong case on it—no longer considered good service.

No matter where data come from, do not trust the data without verifying it yourself. An industrial engineer's first job was to lay out a storage area. After getting floor plans for the area, a layout was drawn up, and a work order to paint lines on the floor was prepared. After painting, the engineer visited the area. Amazingly, there were columns right in the middle of the twelve-foot-wide aisles! The building had been renovated, and no one had updated the plans; they were completely wrong. If the engineer had measured the building and compared the measurements to the plans, the problem would have been avoided.

Be wary of single-source data. If not verified by observation or another source, consider the data questionable. Plan to use sensitivity analysis on the values of the data when you generate solutions. Also, the further removed from the shop floor the source of the data, the more you should question it.

5.3 Modeling Concepts

Modeling is an art; there is no recipe to tell how to do it. There are, however, some concepts that may help. We give some now.

It is impossible to completely understand most problems. There is too much uncertainty. Thus, several models of the problem may be valid. The modeler should develop the simplest correct model the owner understands.

Constructing a model is in itself a worthwhile task, even without a solution! Modeling requires a thorough understanding of the problem, which increases insight. Folklore insists that developing the model provides 90 percent of the value of a simulation project. In fact, when the model is "solved," the problem solvers often find the solution obvious because they now understand the problem so well.

In addition to using models to solve a particular problem, we also use them to gain insight into current operations. Ackoff (1962) discusses retrospective optimization, in which we use the model to impute data from a given situation. This model is similar to reverse engineering, in which a product is torn apart to deduce how it was made. In the classical price elasticity model, an estimated parameter gives the relationship between the price of a good and the number sold. This model is typically used to predict the sales, given a selling price. However, we could use it to determine an imputed parameter value by plugging in the actual price and number sold.

The modeler should ask if the problem fits a standard model, such as a project network. If so, the modeling task is much easier. We simply define needed data, collect them, and apply the right solution algorithm for that model. If the problem does not fit a standard model, we try simplifying assumptions so that it does. The assumptions must not hide important information about the problem.

Paraphrasing Einstein, "Models should be as simple as possible, but no simpler." Start with broad models and add detail as needed; simple models are more general and give more insight. More detail requires more data or assumptions, making the model more "accurate," but less general. Also, owners understand simple models more easily.

To determine key factors and important interactions between problem components, try rephrasing the problem to give a new perspective. If possible, draw diagrams or construct tables that highlight important aspects of the problem.

Break complicated problems into easier pieces. Try to recognize parts of the problem that are standard, and deal with them first. When you understand these parts, go back and include the unfamiliar parts into the model. It is often difficult for novice modelers to ignore parts of the problem. Remember that ignored parts will be included later.

Define notation, parameters, and variables carefully and precisely. Use them to express relationships that exist between parts of the problem, and discuss them with someone who can critically comment on them. Define any underlying physical laws that are appropriate. Also, search for empirical laws that may help simplify or provide understanding for the model.

We now discuss some common components of models.

5.3.1 BOUNDARIES.
The first step in describing the problem is to determine the important parts of the problem. Important information should be included, and irrelevant details should

be left out in order to determine appropriate **boundaries** that contain the problem. We do not necessarily exclude everything outside the boundaries, but treat anything outside as given input to the problem.

For example, if we are considering equipment and layout for a production facility, the boundary may be the building walls. The condition of the U.S. economy may affect hiring, but we would not include it in a plan to determine how many new employees to hire at a particular plant next month.

Be careful in defining boundaries. A problem solution for a particular department in a plant that ignores interaction with other departments could be disastrous. As an extreme case, suppose we schedule production of items in the sanding department to minimize idle time in the department. This schedule may cause the paint department trouble, causing lost profit for the entire company.

Boundary definition may be dynamic. As we proceed in the solution process, we may need to expand the boundaries. Conversely, something we initially thought important may not be, which changes the boundary.

5.3.2   OBJECTIVES. Once we tentatively set boundaries, we determine the **objectives.** An objective is a refinement of a goal. It must be measurable so that we can assess progress. If the goal is to improve the quality of a product, the objective might be to decrease the number of items defective to 10 in 1,000,000 or 10 PPM.

Be certain that the stated objectives accurately reflect the goals. People are quite adept at satisfying measures of performance, sometimes with undesirable results. One company decided to have all shipments on time. As the shipping date approached, a truck containing only one or two cases of goods was sent out rather than risk a late shipment. The company did not understand why their trucking costs increased dramatically. Although timeliness of deliveries is important, other factors, such as trucking costs, should be considered.

5.3.3   CONSTRAINTS. With unlimited resources, solving most problems is easy, but there are usually limitations or **constraints** on what we can do. These limits may be on people, time, knowledge, data, capacity, technology, money, or other resources. Constraints are inviolate—they must hold. Defining them is very important. Ignoring a constraint results in a problem solution that will not work, but including nonexistent constraints restricts the solution alternatives.

Question the validity of constraints. Often, people believe something done a particular way for a long time *must* be done that way. Thus, a policy is seen as a constraint rather than something that can change. One company stated that changeovers could only be done early in the morning. When questioned, the foreman admitted that they had always done them then. No one could give a reason why they could not be done anytime during the day, even on second and third shifts. Dropping this unnecessary "constraint" on changeovers resulted in a much more flexible production schedule.

Resources can be increased. If knowledge is a constraint, hiring experts may remove the constraint. Budget constraints are rarely absolute; showing that a small increase in budget saves money may increase the budget. The problem time frame also affects changes in resources. To increase capacity, working overtime is a short-term solution; increasing equipment is a longer-term solution.

5.3.4   RELATIONSHIPS. Once boundaries, objectives, constraints, and data are defined, we determine the **relationships** between them. First we define notation; it should be precise, with no ambiguity. Then, using this notation we describe relationships between various parts of the problem, which are linked by the variables.

Variables are the unknowns in the problem. Examples of variables are the number of workers to hire next month; the number of units to make at the Salinas plant next week; or the number of workers to have at the fast food counter from 10:00 AM until 11:00 AM. Properly defining variables is crucial to good problem solving, and the best way to do so is to imagine telling someone how to carry out the solution. A statement such as "Paul, put 30 pounds of nitrate, 60 pounds of ash, and 10 pounds of ammonia in a 100 pound bag of fertilizer" indicates three variables. Specify how many pounds of each ingredient to put into 100 pounds of fertilizer. When you can do this, you have taken a big step in specifying the solution variables.

5.4   Assumptions and Involvement

Although we may sound like a broken CD player, we again stress the need to explicitly state all assumptions made at this step. Involve the problem owners in modeling to ensure that the model is a reasonable representation of the problem. Depending on the results, we may need to return to a previous step to make revisions.

5.5   Internal Validation

Validation ensures that the solution will be relevant to the real problem, and it occurs throughout the problem-solving process. After constructing the model, we check to see if it is doing what we intended, which we call **internal validation.**

Internal validation begins with a careful evaluation of the logic of the model. This process should be done by someone familiar with the problem who knows modeling concepts but did not actually construct the model. If not possible, try going over the model with someone who is familiar with the problem. Explaining the model to them may uncover modeling flaws; flow charts are helpful tools in explaining logic to others. Dimensional analysis can also prove helpful; if parts of the model have inconsistent units of measurement, the model is incorrect. Logic in computer programs should be checked and the programs debugged. Data required by the model should be available. If not, either a plan to get the data or a change in the model is necessary.

> **Example 3-3.   Develop a model for MaTell.** We now develop a model for the MaTell problem. We would like a simple model that will help us increase throughput in the Vinings plant. The data available are the time it takes to make each product in the fabrication and assembly departments and an estimate of its maximum sales. Time estimates come from standards and sales data from marketing. Initially, we will choose a spreadsheet representation of the problem.
>
> Our model boundaries will be the same as the system boundaries—we will consider only the production floor. At this stage, we need to consider each product, but we will consider only the fabrication and assembly departments as entities and not break them up into specific equipment.
>
> To specify a solution to the problem, we would need to tell the departments how many desk telephones, wall telephones, and answering machines to make in a given week, which gives an initial definition of variables as the number of each product made each week. Let D, W, and A represent the number (in thousands) of desk telephones, wall telephones, and answering machines made each week.

Our objective should be measurable and reflect the goal of increasing throughput of the Vinings plant. We will use the total number of products made in a week as the measure. Mathematically, we have

$$W + D + A$$

There is a definite relationship between the number of products made and the amount of time needed in the fabrication and assembly departments. The more products we make, the more time we need. From the production department, we find that it takes 2.5 hours of fabrication time and 3 hours of assembly time to make 1000 desk phones. Times for wall phones are 4 and 3 hours/1000, and answering machines require 6 and 14 hours/1000. The total time needed in fabrication for wall telephones is 4 hours times the number of wall telephones made, W; thus the time to fabricate wall telephones is $4 \times W$. The total fabrication time for all products will be

$$4 \times W + 2.5 \times D + 6 \times A$$

Similarly, the time needed in assembly is

$$3 \times W + 3 \times D + 14 \times A$$

These are constraints on the number of products we may produce in a week.

Marketing feels there is a limit on how many of each product we can sell. These limits are 30 thousand for the two phones and 12 thousand for the answering machines.

The model representation will be a spreadsheet. Although there are many ways to develop a spreadsheet for this problem, we will have a column for each variable and each time to produce each product in each department. Then we can generate a column for the total number of products by summing the production columns, and we can generate a column for total time needed in each department. By placing values of the production level of each product in the proper cell, we can evaluate the time needed and the number produced.

To internally validate the model, we check the data in the spreadsheet, do a dimensional analysis, and plug in some numbers to ensure that we have set up the spreadsheet correctly. The data for production times should be verified by discussions with industrial engineering and shop floor personnel. Demand data should be checked with marketing and sales. The units of the objective value are products, which is correct. Each time column is in hours (units × hours/unit). Finally, we plug simple numbers, for example, $W = D = A = 1$, into the spreadsheet and verify that the total number of products is 3, the number of hours of fabrication is 12.5, and assembly is 20, which agree with hand calculations.

We have made several assumptions at this stage:

- Demand will continue at the same levels or higher for some time.
- The number of products made is a good measure for increasing throughput.
- The linear relationships between products and fabrication and assembly time are valid.
- Data are accurate.

During this part of problem solving we have kept the owners involved. Several discussions with marketing, production, and planning have taken place, which should help us keep on track in solving the right problem.

SECTION 5   PROBLEMS

3.21. List three types of models.

3.22. Why do we need data?

3.23 Where do we get data?

3.24. What is the main danger with data?

3.25. What is the major value of a model?

3.26. What are some other reasons to build a model?

3.27. What are some basic modeling concepts?

3.28. What are the common components of models?

3.29. What is internal validation?

3.30. Consider the Pizza Delivery problem (Problem 3.12).

(a) What are possible models for this problem?

(b) Develop one, and internally validate it.

(c) Why did you choose this model?

3.31. Consider the Airplane Seating problem (Problem 3.13).

(a) What are possible models for this problem?

(b) Develop one, and internally validate it.

(c) Why did you choose this model?

6 SOLVE THE MODEL

Starting with the model statement, the problem solver chooses an algorithm. This choice depends on the resources available to solve the problem, the available algorithms, and the precision of solution desired. Solve simplified problems to confirm that the model is appropriate for the problem. We may need to return to some previous step in the problem-solving process if our results are not satisfactory. When the model and solution algorithm are satisfactory, we solve the model and get a model solution.

6.1 External Validation

External validation tests the model solution. It finds inconsistencies in the model not found during internal validation and validates the solution procedure as well. Here, we are not transforming the model solution into the problem solution; we are just making sure that the solution to the model is correct. For simple models this may seem a waste of time, but for models with many variables it is sometimes difficult to know if they are being solved correctly. Model simplification and historical analysis are two basic strategies for external validation.

6.1.1 SIMPLIFICATION. Simplification changes the model or data so that we know the model solution. If it correctly solves the simplification, we have more confidence in its solution to the actual problem. If there is a difference between the model solution and the "known" solution, we reevaluate and change the model or problem statement.

The easiest simplification is to look at small instances of the problem. For very small instances, we can list all the possibilities and hence know the correct solution. We can examine the entire model for these small problems and do calculations by hand to check the logic.

Another approach is to make simplifying assumptions about the data and system configuration. Suppose that we are simulating a queuing system for which there is no analytical solution. By assuming exponential interarrival and service times and allowing only one server, we can get an analytical solution. Then we can run the simulation program under the same conditions and compare the results. If they are close, we have more confidence in the model.

We can force certain variables in the model to take on specific values, thus effectively removing them from the model. We can then examine the solution of the simplified model.

We also could combine variables by aggregating them. For example, suppose we have a production model with many products. A model with a single product having the characteristics of the average of all products would be one simplification.

6.1.2 HISTORICAL ANALYSIS. A second strategy for external validation is **historical perspective.** Its basis is the judgment of people familiar with the problem and environment; the problem solver applies the model to historical data, and experts examine the model solution to see if it is reasonable. We could solve problem instances with extreme data sets to make sure that the experts recognize unusual situations. Ackoff (1962) proposed "murder boards," a committee of people whose job is to find fault with the model. If the results are unacceptable, we return to a previous step.

Sometimes we cannot model our problem exactly. One course of action then is to use the model and ignore the fact that it does not fit the problem. Forgetting the model and taking a seat-of-the-pants approach is another choice. Both courses, however, are dangerous. Using the model while realizing the solution is flawed is probably the better alternative because doing so provides additional insight, which is always welcome. Always remember, however, that the model is flawed.

A model that "passes" validation tests is not guaranteed to be a good model. There is no way to ensure a good model; we can only weed out bad ones. Validation increases confidence in the model and hence the chance of using the results for the actual problem.

6.2 Solution Strategy

Although we discuss modeling and solution separately, they are intertwined. The solution procedure depends on the model, and the model depends on available solution procedures. Having a great model that cannot be solved is frustrating. We trade off the richness of the model with ease of solution. From the systems approach, we know that it is better to get a partial solution to the whole problem than a complete solution to each part.

Solving a model can be as simple as plugging a few numbers into a single equation or as complicated as collecting a lot of data, writing a matrix generator to put the data into proper formats, and solving a linear programming problem. Often, a computer is helpful—if not necessary—in solving problems.

Some models—for example, certain simulation models—only evaluate a given alternative. Generating alternatives is the problem solver's responsibility. But can we generate a good alternative to evaluate? Usually, we cannot guarantee that a single alternative generated is good, so, intuitively, the more alternatives we generate, the better our chance of finding a good one is. If it is inexpensive to evaluate them and they are easily generated, then we should look at many alternatives. Conversely, if it is hard to generate alternatives and costly to evaluate them, we cannot examine too many. Experimental design methods can help us trade off the expense of generating alternatives with the quality of the solution.

Other models can be solved by algorithms that generate alternatives as well as evaluate them. **Optimal,** or exact, algorithms look implicitly at all alternatives and choose the best; a critical path algorithm is an example. Other algorithms, called **heuristic** algorithms, generate alternatives that are not guaranteed to be optimal, but are, hopefully, close to the optimal solution. Choosing projects with the largest return until the budget is used up is an illustration of a heuristic algorithm.

Even if a model can theoretically be solved optimally, a solution may not be possible in practice. Total enumeration solves integer-programming problems, but for reasonably sized problems, it will take centuries on the fastest computer. To get solutions in a reasonable amount of time we may have to use heuristic algorithms for these problems.

Heuristic algorithms provide uncertain solutions; because they do not guarantee optimality, we do not know the **quality,** i.e., how good the solution is. Some heuristic algorithms have performance guarantees, in which, for any set of data, the algorithm guarantees a solution within a given percentage of the optimal solution. We also can generate bounds on the optimal solution for a particular data set. These bounds give an indication of how far from optimal the heuristic solution is. If the heuristic solution has a profit of $1000 and an upper bound on the profit is $1010, the heuristic solution is close enough. If the bound is $2000, we are uncertain about the quality of the heuristic solution. The solution could be far from optimal, or we could have a loose bound.

Even optimal algorithms have uncertainty. How well the model fits reality is one source of uncertainty, and data are another. If data estimates are not exact, what does an optimal solution mean? Data uncertainty may be greater than the uncertainty of a heuristic solution, so a heuristic algorithm may be as good as an optimal algorithm.

After we validate the model and determine an appropriate algorithm, we solve the model. The next step is to interpret the model solution.

Example 3-4. Solve the MaTell model. Once we have our MaTell model, we need to solve it. We will validate our model using historical analysis. We will plug in the current production figures ($D = 15, W = 17,$ and $A = 5$) and see if the results agree with what is actually happening. The time needed in fabrication is 132.5 hours and for assembly, 166 hours. These numbers are close to the actual values of 135 and 163, so we accept the model. Of course more complicated models would need more validation.

Because this spreadsheet model only evaluates solutions, we need to generate several alternatives. We could use a trial and error approach, but we will use a grid search algorithm instead.

TABLE 3-1
Spreadsheet for choosing product mix

Wall Phones (Units)	Desk Phones (Units)	Answering Machines (Units)	Fabrication Time (Hours)	Assembly Time (Hours)	Units Made (Units)
25	10	4	149	161	39
20	15	4	142	161	39
15	20	4	134	161	39
10	25	4	126	161	39
20	10	4	129	146	34
15	15	4	122	146	34
10	20	4	114	146	34
15	10	4	109	131	29
10	15	4	102	116	24
25	25	12	234	318	0
25	30	12	247	333	0
10	10	8	113	172	0
20	30	8	203	262	0
15	25	4	146	176	0
10	10	12	137	228	0

Let the production of desk phones vary from 5 to 30 by fives. Do the same for wall phones, and let answering machines vary from 4 to 12 by fours. This creates 74 combinations of the levels of the three products.

We create a row of the spreadsheet for each combination of the three products and evaluate each one. Modify the number of products made so that their values are zero if the plan needs more time in fabrication or assembly than is available. We sort the rows by putting the row with the maximum number produced at the top. The first 15 rows of the spreadsheet are shown in Table 3-1. Several model solutions make 39,000 units, more than the current 37,000. We discuss the model solution further when we translate it into the problem solution.

SECTION 6 PROBLEMS

3.32. What is external validation? How does it differ from validating problem understanding and internal validation?

3.33. What are two techniques that can be used in external validation?

3.34. What is an optimal algorithm? What is a heuristic algorithm?

3.35. Why do we use heuristic algorithms?

3.36. Consider the Pizza Delivery problem (Problem 3.12).

(a) Solve your model, and externally validate it.

(b) Is it sufficient to solve the problem?

(c) What are its strengths and weaknesses?

3.37. Consider the Airplane Seating problem (Problem 3.13).

(a) Solve your model, and externally validate it.

(b) Is it sufficient to solve the problem?

(c) What are its strengths and weaknesses?

7 INTERPRET THE SOLUTION

Model solutions are not necessarily problem solutions! If the model is a good representation of the problem, it may lead to a solution of the problem. Because it is difficult to include all interactions in a model and still solve it, be careful in applying the model solution to the actual problem. Together, the problem solver and problem owners must translate the model solution into a useful solution to the problem. Examining the stability of the solution to data inaccuracies and uncertainties would be discussed now. Also, they must determine the effects of the assumptions made earlier on the solution. The judgment of both solver and owner plays an important role here. Again, we may need to return to a previous step to change or refine the process; if not, we have a problem solution.

Check this solution for reasonableness. Give the solution to the people who will use it, and get their comments. If they think it is reasonable and would use the solution, we can have more confidence in our model and solution. If they believe the solution is unreasonable, the solution is not necessarily wrong, but their opinion indicates that there is more work to do. The problem solver must determine if there is a problem with the model or explain to the owner why the solution is correct.

Because the data used in the model may be inaccurate, we may question whether the solution will change as the data changes. Ideally, however, the solution does not change significantly with small changes in the data; such a solution is **robust**. If we solve the model by linear programming, we can use sensitivity analysis to resolve this question. Other models have similar ways to determine the sensitivity of the solution to the data. If such methods do not exist, we can solve the model multiple times with slightly different data sets and examine the solutions. If results at this step are not satisfactory, we need to modify the model and repeat the problem-solving process.

Robustness of assumptions also should be examined. Suppose we assumed a linear relationship for costs but were unsure about it. We might solve the model with the linear cost equation replaced by one having nonlinear costs. If the solutions to the two models are similar, our linearity assumption is robust. On the other hand, if the solutions are very different, the assumption is invalid. We must determine the true nature of the cost relationship so that the model more correctly represents the system.

Be wary of numbers produced by computers. When a computer produces 75.37542 some people assume that the number is exact. If the input data is not known to five decimals, the output cannot be that accurate. Also, unless they wrote the program themselves, they cannot be sure of the underlying assumptions made by the programmer. Even the programmer may make some assumptions without being aware of it.

Sometimes no matter what the effort is, acceptable results cannot be achieved. Some problems may defy solution using a modeling approach. In this case, the problem solver may have no choice but to give up and use a seat-of-the-pants approach. Not knowing when to quit is a common shortcoming of problem solvers.

Assuming we can derive the problem solution from the model solution, we are now ready for implementation.

Example 3-5. MaTell problem solution. The model solution is the beginning of problem solution. Discussion with owners in this stage is critical. There are several model solutions that allow MaTell to make 39 thousand products. The production people believe they could carry out any of these plans and get the desired production. This solution validates our assumption that we can make more products by better planning.

Marketing worries that the additional 2000 products will still leave some customers unable to buy the products they want. Because we have increased production, we might want to see if we can do better still. Given the coarse grid used in the spreadsheet, there may be other combinations that do even better. Thus, we will change our representation. A linear programming model will be similar to the spreadsheet but will evaluate all possible plans and choose the best one.

Marketing has another objection: the new mix of products may not be as profitable as the old mix. The profit of a plan has not been a consideration, but it should have been. Although maximizing profit may not be the most critical need in this situation, any plan that does not provide an acceptable profit should not be used. Marketing tells us that the margins on the three products are \$2.20, \$2.00, and \$7.00 for one desk phone, wall phone, and answering machine, respectively. Some quick calculations show producing (25, 10, 4) units returns \$103,000, slightly better than the current \$102,000. The other plans producing 39,000 units have no better profit than the current plan.

At this point, we return to the modeling stage and develop a more refined model, namely a linear program. Because it is very close to the spreadsheet model, we will simply state it here. However, we must resolve the conflict over the objective. Because profit must be considered, we should rethink the original mission statement. For brevity, we do not discuss it, but leave it to the student's imagination. Because the LP is simple, we will solve it twice, once maximizing the number of products made and once maximizing profit. The LP model for profit is as follows:

$$\text{Maximize} \quad 2.2D + 2W + 7A$$

s.t.
$$4D + 2.5W + 6A \leq 168$$
$$3D + 3W + 14A \leq 168$$
$$D \leq 30$$
$$W \leq 30$$
$$A \leq 12$$

Solving this LP using a standard solution package such as STORM or LINDO gives the solution (21.94, 30, 0.864) with total profit of $114,362. As soon as we see that it makes so few answering machines, we realize we have a problem. Producing so few answering machines could be a problem, even though this number is the most profitable according to our model. However, the model does not consider some people will buy phones and answering machines at the same time or will want to have the same brand. So we change our model by adding lower bounds of 10, 10, and 4 for the products. The new LP solution is (27.3, 10, 4) with profit $108,133. Calculating the number of products made, we find it is 41,333, which is a better solution than any considered so far. Changing the objective to $D + W + A$ and resolving the problem gives (10, 27.3, 4) with profit $104,600 and a total of 41,333 units produced. Because this solution produces the same number of units as the maximum profit plan, the maximum profit plan is superior. We should continue this discussion and look at various combinations of the plan until all owners are satisfied.

Using LP allows easy investigation of the stability of the model. Changes in data are easy to evaluate by standard LP sensitivity techniques. For the model with lower bounds, the objective is profit in dollars, and the assembly constraint is in hours, so we could only make an additional $0.73 (from the shadow price) by adding one hour of assembly time. Economically, adding more time prohibits adding more workers or machines, because their cost will exceed the increase in profit. This scenario validates the mission of better planning, because increasing capacity would be too expensive.

We could also evaluate other parts of the problem. Sensitivity analysis of the time to make one desk telephone in assembly could show that we need more accurate data, which might require time studies or other ways of estimating the problem parameters.

Once the owners are satisfied with the solution, we are ready to implement it.

SECTION 7 PROBLEMS

3.38. Why are we not finished when we have solved the model?

3.39. What is a robust solution?

3.40. What steps are taken to interpret a solution?

3.41. Consider the Pizza Delivery problem (Problem 3.12).

(a) How do you feel about your solution?

(b) What insight have you gained?

(c) If you had more time and resources, what would you do differently?

3.42. Consider the Airplane Seating problem (Problem 3.13).

(a) How do you feel about your solution?

(b) What insight have you gained?

(c) If you had more time and resources, what would you do differently?

8 IMPLEMENTATION

Once a problem solution is found, implementation begins. All concerned must accept the solution. Necessary resources are committed, and appropriate people are trained to carry out the new solution. It is good practice to have parallel operation of the new and old methods. Finally, the progress of the new solution must be monitored to make sure nothing goes wrong.

Recall that problems do not exist in a vacuum. To implement a solution, it is usually necessary to change some system. It is difficult to overcome the inertia of a well-established system. To be a successful problem solver, system change must be instituted.

People are notoriously resistant to change and accept change only when its need is clear and positive and they help plan the change. Unsatisfied owners will not accept a solution, so continually involving owners in the problem-solving process makes them more likely to understand and accept the final results.

Present your results with the enthusiasm of a salesperson, use simple language and give a clear statement of the importance of the problem, and use facts to back up your position. Present both the positive and negative aspects of your solution, stress key points, and try to anticipate questions. If possible, give several alternative solutions covering a range of benefits and costs, and include the "do nothing" alternative.

Successful implementation requires commitment, so the people who control the resources needed for implementation must be involved. People using the solution are the ones who will make it work. Even a great solution not supported by its users will fail.

Once implementation is underway, make sure that the solution is easy to use. User friendly software and appropriate reports are a must. People accept reports more readily if they are in familiar form, so examine current reports and try to make new ones as similar as possible, assuming that the owners were happy with the existing reports and the reports were effective.

Most systems will not run themselves so the people who carry out the solution must be properly trained. Time and money for training is usually well spent. Ill-trained users may cause the best system to give poor results. Be sure that the training is timely—neither too early nor too late.

Remember Murphy's law: Anything that can go wrong will go wrong. Before final implementation, try to anticipate and ask others what might go wrong; assume the worst, and examine the consequences; and develop contingency plans to be used if things go wrong. If you prepared for misfortune and everything went right, you wasted time, but if you did not prepare, you may be looking for a new job.

When running the new system, do not quit using the old one immediately. Rather, run both systems in parallel for some time. Invariably, unforeseen problems crop up, and if the old system is gone, chaos may result. Keeping it provides a fallback for these situations. Even if the new system works well, it can then be compared to the old one and its benefits more easily quantified.

A control system should be part of implementation. It monitors the system and gives feedback on its performance. The control system should also signal unexpected performance. This feedback should be used to change or adjust the solution.

Sometimes problem solving is not successful, and the most common cause of failure is not having the owners involved throughout the effort. As Gene Woolsey (Woolsey and Swanson, 1975) expresses it, "Managers would rather live with a problem they can't solve than accept a solution they can't understand." Upper management, therefore, should be committed to the project.

Getting the best solution to a part of the system rather than the whole system, called **suboptimization,** is another cause of failure. If this occurs, it is likely that either the problem boundaries or the problem mission were not correctly defined. If a worker wants to complete many jobs, shorter jobs should be done first. However, if the larger jobs were late and caused customers to cancel their orders, what was good for the worker was not good for the company.

Finally, people can cause failure. Incompetence, inexperience, and overconfidence of the problem solver and improper training of users can all cause failure. If people feel threatened by either the process or the solution, failure is likely.

> **Example 3-6. MaTell implementation.** In implementing a solution to the planning problem, we first need to present the solution. Though the spreadsheet model was not used to get the solution, it would be a good way to introduce the LP solution. Many people use spreadsheets in their work, so they are already familiar with them, and it is a small step to lead into the idea of automatic choice of the right levels of production.
>
> Because owners were involved in problem solving, acceptance should be relatively easy. Commitment may be more difficult, but the only resources needed are an LP package and training for the planners.
>
> It will be important to convince the planner that "automating" part of the planning decision will be a positive action. Sell this step as an increase in skills that will aid the planner's career.
>
> Remembering Murphy's Law, try to envision the worst that could happen in implementing the solution, and make sure that it does not cause failure.
>
> Initially, have the planner continue to develop the plan independently of the LP solution. Then, develop the actual plan as a combination of the two plans. If there are problems with the LP solution, a plan is available. As the planner gains confidence in the LP system, phase out the old way. Make sure reports are not too different from the old reports so that they are more readily accepted.
>
> Finally, check on the system from time to time. Make sure that as conditions change, the system is not outdated. Solutions that were fine under one set of conditions may become bad as the situation changes.

Most importantly, remember that there is seldom a single solution to any problem, even though solving a model may produce just one. The real purpose of constructing and solving a model is to produce insight into the problem. Ultimately, a person must decide; managers that let models decide are abdicating their responsibility.

SECTION 8   PROBLEMS

3.43. Why present alternative solutions to a problem?

3.44. What is most difficult about implementing a solution?

3.45. What is a control system, and why is it needed?

3.46. Outline an implementation plan for the Pizza Delivery problem (Problem 3.12).

3.47. Outline an implementation plan for the Airplane Seating problem (Problem 3.13).

9   SOFTWARE

Many software packages aid problem solving, and some problems cannot be solved without a computer. Spreadsheets (Excel, Lotus, Quattro) are easy to use and very helpful in problem solving. For more mathematical problems, computational algebra packages (Mathcad, Matlab, Mathematica), sometimes called electronic chalkboards, are useful. Statistical analysis packages (SAS, Minitab, SPSS) can extract information from data. Optimization solvers (LINDO, CPLEX, OSL) are readily available and provide optimal solutions to many models. Modeling languages (AMPL, GAMS) make creating optimization models easier, but at the expense of learning them. Simulation languages (GPSS, SIMAN) and packages (Promodel, Witness) can help provide insight into many problems.

There are also a number of software packages tailored especially to production planning and control courses. STORM (Emmons et al., 1989) was one of the first and is still a comprehensive, user-friendly package. QS (Chang, 1995) is similar, and Savage (1993) provides Lotus add-ins to solve production planning and control problems.

The software mentioned is typical, but by no means is this an inclusive list. As we discuss particular problems, specific software will be discussed.

10 EVOLUTION

People have studied problem solving for many years, and mathematicians have studied the subject formally for a century or so. The scientific method and scientific management are both precursors of the ideas we have presented. The seminal works for solving problems in production planning and control are most likely the books by Polya (1957) and Ackoff (1962) and the paper by Morris (1967). These sources made the subject more accessible to the production community.

For contemporary overviews of problem solving, the books by Ackoff (1991), Arnold (1992), and Keon (1985) are worth reading. For specific methods useful in problem solving, try Griver (1988), Murthy et al. (1990), Rubinstein (1986), Starfield et al. (1990), Van Gundy (1981), and Wilson (1984). Brown and Walter (1983) discuss problem identification thoroughly, and Eden et al. (1983) investigate the role of bias in problem solving. Also, the paper by Kimbrough et al. (1993) has several good examples of validation and sensitivity.

Creativity plays a large role in problem solving. Some good books on enhancing creativity are those of Adams (1986), Evans (1991), Flood and Jackson (1991), Lumsdaine and Lumsdaine (1995), and Nadler and Hibino (1990). More practically oriented books on problem solving in business situations are Lyles (1982), Plunkett and Hale (1982), and Woolsey and Swanson (1975). Although these books are older and may not exactly reflect the business world today, they contain much useful information, particularly Woolsey and Swanson.

Finally, it might be interesting to see a student perspective on problem solving. The paper by Pinker et al. (1993) discusses a student project done in the "real world." It reinforces many of the points of this chapter, so it should also be read.

11 SUMMARY

In this chapter we outline a problem-solving approach. The most important steps are in identifying and understanding the problem. Once these steps are taken, a model is usually constructed. Describing boundaries, objectives, relationships, and variables are part of model construction. Needed data are identified and a representation chosen. The model is solved with an appropriate algorithm, and the model solution is interpreted considering the actual situation. Finally, a solution to the actual problem is implemented.

To be successful, keep the problem owners involved throughout the process. If not, the chances for failure are high. Also, it is extremely important to recognize all assumptions.

The best way to do this is to write them out explicitly so that everyone involved knows what they are.

We present many models for production planning and control in this book. Our experience shows that rarely can you gather data and plug into one of these models to get a solution to an actual problem because the underlying assumptions of the model may not be right for your situation. Approach every problem independently.

Does this mean the models we present are useless? Certainly not! When solving real problems, start with a "standard" model and change it to fit the current problem, which means that you must not only know how to use the given models, but understand their assumptions and how they are developed. Doing so allows you to build new models and solve them as the situation requires.

MINICASE: WEIGHTY MATTERS

"That's the third order for 2PRs I've turned down this week," Doug said. "We could make a lot more money if we could sell to potential customers."

"It may become worse," Loretta replied. "Some of our customers may find other suppliers if we can't keep up with their demand. Maybe we need to build a new plant."

If you ever look closely at a table lamp, a weight is in the base to keep it from tipping over. Other products use weights too, including tractors. Several suppliers, including Heavyweight, Inc., make these weights. Their big seller is a two pound circular weight, the 2PR.

Heavyweight holds a patent on a special powder, called procrete, used to make the weights. They produce procrete in a small plant adjacent to the molding plant. Procrete is packaged in 100 lb bags, and some is sold to other weight makers, but most is sent to their own molding plant.

In the molding plant, procrete is put into a molding machine, where it is heated under pressure. This process gives procrete the consistency of mud, and the machine automatically squirts out a predetermined amount into a mold. One line is dedicated to 2PRs, with five 2-lb weights in each mold. After the procrete hardens, it is removed from the mold, packed in cartons, and shipped to the customer.

A diagram of the 2PR line is given below. There are six employees. One runs the machine; even though most of the operation is automatic, it must have an operator when running. Another employee feeds procrete to the machine. The machine hopper holds 1000 lbs, and it cannot be allowed to run dry. One worker takes the mold off the conveyor, removes the weights from the mold, and packs them in boxes. This process takes about one minute per mold. A different worker cleans the mold, sprays it with teflon, and puts it on the conveyor to return to the machine. These tasks take about 20 seconds per mold. The fifth employee sweeps, wipes up spills, etc. The sixth is a utility worker who can relieve other workers for personal time or breaks and lunch. The plant runs one eight-hour shift.

Loretta, the plant manager, feels that they could sell close to 9000 weights per day if they could produce that many. The molding machine is currently producing 60 molds per hour, but has capacity to produce 200 molds per hour. However, if the speed of the molding machine is increased, the weights will not be dry when taken out of the molds. Doug, the sales director, knows if the molds can be hardened faster, more product could be made. What recommendations do you have for Loretta?

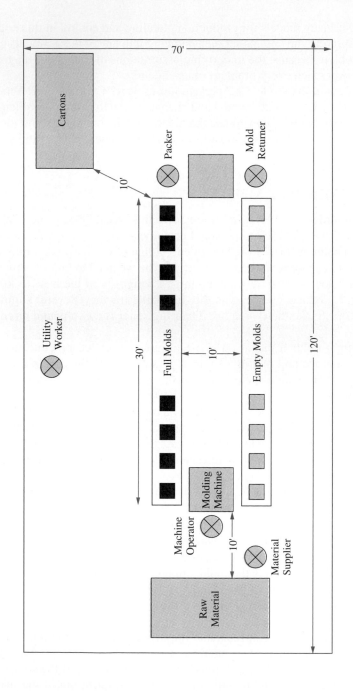

12 REFERENCES

Ackoff, R. L., *Scientific Method,* John Wiley & Sons, New York, 1962.

Ackoff, R. L., *Ackoff's Fables,* John Wiley & Sons, New York, 1991.

Adams, J. L., *Conceptual Blockbusting,* Addison-Wesley Publishing Company, Reading, MA, 1986.

Arnold, J. D., *The Complete Problem Solver,* John Wiley & Sons, New York, 1992.

Brown, S. I. and Walter, M. I., *The Art of Problem Posing,* Lawrence Erlbaum Associates, Hillsdale, NJ, 1983.

Chang, Y. L., *QS: Quantitative Systems,* Prentice Hall, Englewood Cliffs, NJ, 1995.

Eden, C., Jones, S., and Sims, D., *Messing About in Problems,* Pergamon Press, Oxford, UK, 1983.

Emmons, H., Flowers, A. D., Khot, C. M., and Mathur, K., *STORM: Quantitative Modeling for Decision Support,* Holden-Day, Inc., Oakland, CA, 1989.

Evans, J. R., *Creative Thinking in the Decision and Management Sciences,* South-Western Publishing Company, Cincinnati, OH, 1991.

Flood, R. L. and Jackson, M. C., *Creative Problem Solving,* John Wiley & Sons, Chichester, UK, 1991.

Griver, J. S., *Applied Problem Analysis Plus,* Compsych Systems, Inc., Publications Division, Marina del Rey, CA, 1988.

Kimbrough, S. O., Oliver, J. R., and Pritchett, C. W., "On Post-Evaluation Analysis: Candle-Lighting and Surrogate Models," *Interfaces,* 23, 17–28, 1993.

Koen, B. V., *Definition of the Engineering Method,* American Society for Engineering Education, Washington, DC, 1985.

Lyles, R. I., *Practical Management Problem Solving and Decision Making,* Van Nostrand Reinhold Company, New York, 1982.

Lumsdaine, E. and Lumsdaine, M., *Creative Problem Solving,* McGraw-Hill Publishing Company, New York, 1995.

Morris, W. T., "On the Art of Modeling," *Management Science,* 13, B707–B717, 1967.

Murthy, D. N. P., Page, N. W., and Rodin, E. Y., *Mathematical Modeling,* Pergamon Press, Elmsford, NY, 1990.

Nadler, G. and Hibino, S., *Breakthrough Thinking,* Prima Publishing, Rocklin, CA, 1990.

Ohno, T., *Toyota Production System: Beyond Large-Scale Production,* Productivity Press, Cambridge, MA, 1988.

Pinker, E. J., Shumsky, R. A., Malone, K. M., and Sungsu, A., "OR Theory and Practice: A Student Perspective," *OR/MS Today,* 20, 3, 56–58, 1993.

Plunkett, L. C. and Hale, G. A., *The Proactive Manager,* John Wiley & Sons, New York, 1982.

Polya, G., *How To Solve It,* Doubleday & Company, Garden City, NJ, 1957.

Rubinstein, M. F., *Tools for Thinking and Problem Solving,* Prentice-Hall, Incorporated, Englewood Cliffs, NJ, 1986.

Savage, S. L., *Fundamental Analytic Spreadsheet Tools for Quantitative Management,* McGraw-Hill Publishing Company, New York, 1993.

Starfield, A. M., Smith, K. A., and Bleloch, A. L., *How To Model It: Problem Solving for the Computer Age,* McGraw-Hill Publishing Company, New York, 1990.

VanGundy, A. B., *Techniques of Structured Problem Solving,* Van Nostrand Reinhold Company, New York, 1981.

Wilson, B., *Systems: Concepts, Methodologies and Applications,* John Wiley & Sons, New York, 1984.

Woolsey, R. E. D. and Swanson, H. S., *Operations Research for Immediate Application: A Quick & Dirty Manual,* Harper & Row, New York, 1975.

CHAPTER
4

FORECASTING

1 INTRODUCTION

"Twenty thousand tires? We'll never sell that many tires in June. The marketing people are crazy!" Carol exclaimed. Obviously, she did not agree with marketing's prediction of tire sales in June. How could you determine a better estimate?

There are several ways you could get an answer to this question. One is to simply guess. You could ask Pete, the molding room foreman. He has been here for 25 years, and his experience should give him a good feel for how many tires will be sold. Pete points out that automobile sales are expected to peak in August, so maybe the number is not so far off after all. Being a good problem solver, you might examine demand for previous months and try to estimate the demand for June.

Of course none of these methods are guaranteed to give good results. Your guess may be far off, and even Pete's experience may not be enough to get a good prediction. Car sales do affect tire sales—every new car needs tires—but maybe not in a straightforward way. Even sophisticated models may not always give accurate predictions; if you think otherwise, consider weather forecasting.

Determining what will happen in the future in order to make good decisions is a problem that must be faced quite often. This fact is true not only in our personal lives, but also in the business world. We use the term **forecast** to mean some definite method—rather than just a guess—of predicting future events.

In today's market-driven production system, forecasts are more important than ever. The rewards of good forecasts as well as the penalties for bad forecasts can be quite high. With the proliferation of personal computer packages, forecasting is easier and cheaper than ever. However, managers must beware of using canned packages without understanding their underlying principles. After all, the program will give an answer, even if it is bad. In this chapter we present a range of forecasting techniques, an idea of the situations in which to use them, and their underlying principles. This chapter also addresses how to monitor the forecasts and adjust both the forecast and the forecasting techniques.

We will discuss three classes of forecasting methods. The first class is composed of judgmental or qualitative methods. In their simplest form, they use "expert" opinion to get a forecast. Asking Pete is a simple example of this approach. The second class, causal methods, tries to relate the variable being forecast to something else. Relating automobile production to tire sales is one example. Time series methods use the past to try to determine the future and are based on statistical principles. Studying past tire sales to get a forecast of future tire sales could be done using a time series approach. Finally, an overall view of forecasting systems, control, methods, and practice is presented. First, we view forecasting from a systems perspective.

2   THE FORECASTING SYSTEM

As we noted in Chapter 3, problem solving involves a series of steps. When "standard" problems occur, we can often simplify the procedure. Forecasting has many standard models. We will discuss the stages of problem solving as they relate to forecasting in this section. The remainder of the chapter will elaborate on particular forecasting methodology.

2.1   Identify the Problem

Forecasts provide information to make better decisions. The first step is to identify the decision. If the decision will not be affected by the forecast, a forecast is unnecessary. The importance of the decision will dictate the effort that goes into producing a forecast. A one-time decision requires one forecast, whereas a recurring decision requires a forecast each time the decision is made. In either case, the decision will determine what to forecast, the level of detail needed, and how often the forecast will be made. Forecasts of sales, quality of raw materials, income, expenses, energy usage, or times customers arrive are commonly needed in business operations.

Suppose the decision is how many televisions to produce next year. This decision is important because it directly affects employment and raw material levels, marketing (advertising), distribution, and warehousing. The demand for the product itself will be forecast; at this stage, we may not care about the particular variations of the product. Because most plants operate on a monthly or four-week plan, we should forecast monthly demand. If some planning is done on a quarterly basis, monthly forecasts can be combined. On the other hand, a shorter-range forecast may need individual variations of the product, for example 13", 19", and 25" televisions.

The decision maker is the problem owner. The problem solver is the analyst or forecaster. Most forecasts are prepared by teams that include management, marketing, the forecaster, and possibly data processing. Problem identification determines the problem mission or purpose, which is shown as forecast need in Figure 4-1 and begins the design of a forecasting system.

2.2   Understand the Problem

The key to understanding forecasting problems is to understand the underlying **process**—for example, the process that creates demand for an item. We can never fully understand the

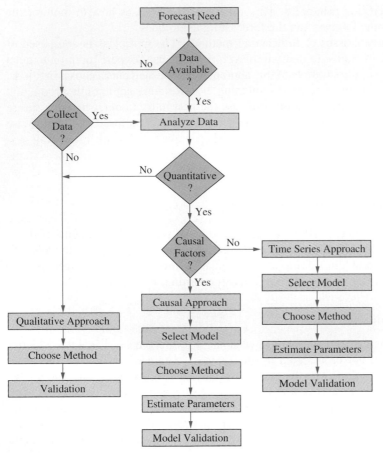

FIGURE 4-1
Designing a forecasting system

process, so we can only hope to gain insight and make necessary assumptions to create forecasts. To do so, we examine characteristics of the problem and analyze data, if they exist. We also state a forecast goal.

2.2.1 PROBLEM CHARACTERISTICS. The main characteristics of a forecasting problem are time frame, level of detail, accuracy needed, and number of items to forecast. We give examples of these by time frame.

In production systems, we are most often interested in forecasting demand for our product or services in order to decide how much to produce. Long-term decisions, such as opening new plants or adding capacity to existing plants, often depend on a forecast of demand. Here, we are not so much interested in individual products, but in overall volume. Therefore we might use dollars as an aggregate measure of sales. A typical time frame for these types of decisions would be three to five years. Long-term decisions do not require exact forecasts; the decision to build a new plant will be based on the trend of forecasts for several successive years rather than a single demand estimate. Thus very precise forecasts are unnecessary—a number in the ballpark will do. Typically, long-term forecasts are made for only one item. Causal and qualitative methods are often used for these forecasts.

A mid-range decision might be to allocate plant capacity to groups of products. Again, we might not need to know the demand for each individual item, but rather for groups of items that share certain production facilities. An example would be a monthly forecast of tires made in a plant; individual sizes are not important for determining gross capacity. Typical measures might be units, production hours, gallons, or pounds of an aggregate product. The time frame for these decisions is from three months to one or two years, and greater accuracy is required. Mid-range decisions typically require forecasts for only a few items. Quantitative methods, including causal and time series, are frequently used for mid-range forecasts.

The most common short-term decision is how much product we should produce. In this case, the actual number of units of the product are needed. This decision could be weekly, monthly, or possibly quarterly. Because short-term decisions are based on these forecasts, they need to be reasonably accurate. Time series methods are most often used for short-term forecasting, but in some situations, causal and qualitative methods are also useful. Short-term decisions may require forecasts of hundreds or thousands of items.

2.2.2 DATA. Examining data, when they exist, can provide much insight. Data may come from company records or commercial or government sources. Company records include sales and purchase information. Commercial services have access to such things as databases and surveys and can provide raw data or reports on specific topics; one example is *A Graphic Guide to Consumer Markets,* published yearly by the National Industrial Conference Board. The government also provides many types of data. Census data contains population and demographic information, and the Department of Commerce publishes *Survey of Business* monthly. Make sure, however, that the data reflects the true situation; for example, a record of actual sales may not include customers who wanted to buy the item but were unable because it was not available.

If no data exist, we must collect them or use a forecasting approach that does not use data. If data are unavailable or too costly to collect, we choose a qualitative approach. Qualitative methods, the left branch of Figure 4.1, are discussed in Section 3.

Data are affected by factors that are either external or internal. External factors are beyond our control, but we can influence internal factors.

A good example of an external factor is the economy. If the economy experiences a downturn, demand for goods and services usually declines too. A variety of economic indicators have been defined that may help us understand demand behavior. Other external factors include competitors' actions, complementary products, and consumer choices.

Internal factors include the product quality and price, delivery time, advertising, and rebates. If more advertising is done, demand will likely increase. Rebates are also used to increase demand. Poor quality, long waits for the item, or a high price will usually reduce demand.

Data should be analyzed to see if causal factors exist. A causal factor is something that influences the data in a known way and can be helpful in forecasting. Demand data for tires provide an example of a causal factor. If most tires are sold to an automobile manufacturer, knowing the number of cars to be produced will indicate the demand for tires; that is, the production of cars causes a demand for tires. Plotting tires sold versus cars produced will give an indication of the validity of this assumption. Of course tires are also sold to consumers as replacements on older cars. Causal forecasting is shown in the middle path in Figure 4-1; detailed discussion is given in Section 4. Selecting a model for a causal approach is similar to selecting a model for the time series approach, so we will combine the discussion. Time series approaches are discussed in Section 5.

If data are available, we plot them to see if there is a pattern. Figure 4-2 shows weekly demand for toothpaste for the last two years. We use this data to explain time series data analysis. Causal data analysis is similar, but rather than a plot of, say, demand versus time, we would plot demand versus the causal variable. When the plot is examined, it appears to be roughly level with some small variations, which is typical of a **constant process.** Because the population is relatively stable, at least in the short run, it seems reasonable that toothpaste sales would also be approximately constant. The weekly variation is caused by a **random** or **noise** component that we cannot control. For a constant underlying process, the noise component should have a mean of zero; if not, it is not noise, but part of the underlying process. Similarly, the likelihood of observing a value above the constant component should be the same as a value below it. If the variance changes over time, then our assumption of a constant process is not valid, so we will assume that the variance of the noise is constant. Thus it is reasonable to assume that the noise follows a symmetric probability distribution with mean zero and variance σ_ε^2. For now we assume the noise component is normally distributed; we see in Section 7.2 that this assumption is robust. Similar arguments can be made regarding the distribution of noise for underlying processes that are not constant.

We should have some reason to assume a process is constant. Demand for many items would seem to follow a constant process; toothpaste, milk, bread, and socks are mature items and are used regularly. Constant processes may be useful even for products that are not *always* used regularly. Over a short horizon, many things are approximately constant. In the

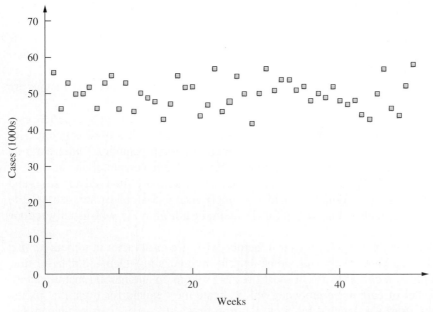

FIGURE 4-2
A constant process

mature stage of a product life cycle (see Chapter 1) many products exhibit stable sales. Also, models for constant processes are good introductions to more complicated models.

Some things are, by nature, not constant. During a product life cycle there is a growth stage in which sales increase. Similarly, there is a decline or phase-out stage when sales are decreasing. Assuming a constant process in either case can be disastrous. These processes are examples of a **trend process.** The rapid growth of personal computers and related equipment is a good example. The upper line of Figure 4-3 is an example of an increasing trend process. The lines connecting points have no meaning, but were added to emphasize the pattern in the data. This growth appears to be linear. As in the constant process, the line is not smooth but has many little jumps in it, which are caused by the random component. Again, just because the line appears to go up is not reason enough to assume a trend process; there should be some way to explain it. Trends could also be nonlinear, but for simplicity, we will restrict our discussion to linear trends.

Also plotted in Figure 4-3 is a **seasonal process.** Every four months, the pattern seems to repeat, but random fluctuations are still present. An example of this type of process would be passenger miles for an airline. The term seasonal is used because the weather is often an underlying cause; ice cream and soft drinks are more popular in summer than in winter. Sometimes cyclical processes are defined, a typical one being the number of telephone calls during a day; they peak at mid-morning and mid-afternoon. However, we will make no distinction between seasonal and cyclical. Again, there should be an underlying justification for assuming a seasonal process.

When data are plotted, the choice of scale is very important. If the wrong scale is chosen, data from a constant process may look seasonal due to the random fluctuations. When trend

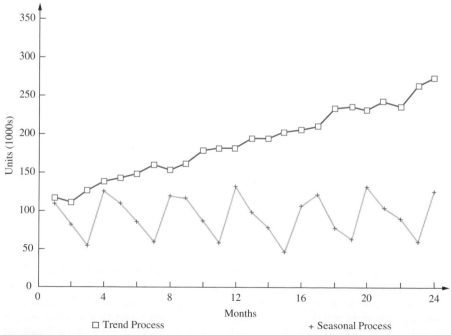

FIGURE 4-3
Typical demand patterns

and seasonality are present, the data must be decomposed to see the effects of each. Also, outliers should be removed before analyzing the data. An example would be sales that were extremely high or low due to an unusual occurrence such as a strike or earthquake. Retailers often remove special seasons, e.g., Christmas, from the time series data and handle them as exceptions.

The result of data analysis is to understand the process that causes demand. There will always be some part that is unexplainable—the random component. However, the model we use will be a direct result of the process we assume.

2.2.3   FORECAST GOAL.   The goal of any forecasting system is to provide forecasts of the appropriate accuracy in a timely manner and at a reasonable cost. A timely forecast is determined by its use. The basic tradeoff in forecasting is between response to a change and stability; that is, if we experience a demand that is abnormally high this week, we have to decide if we need to make more product next week. If the high demand reflected a change in the demand pattern, we should increase production, but if it was just a random fluctuation, we should not. A good forecasting system will react to actual changes but ignore chance variations.

2.3   Develop a Model

Once processes are identified, they determine the form of the model. Qualitative forecasting does not use easily stated models. Causal models depend on the particular situation but generally have the form

$$d_t = f(x_{t-k}) + \varepsilon_t$$

where d_t represents the dependent variable, e.g., demand, x_t the independent variable (or causal factor), and ε_t the noise component at time t. The dependent variable at time t is ideally a function of the independent variable at time $t - k$, $k \geq 1$. The k-period time lag allows us to know the value of the independent variable before we need to forecast the dependent variable; if there is no time lag, we must forecast the independent variable to get a forecast of the dependent variable. The functional relationship between d and x is represented by f and could be linear, quadratic, or some other mathematical relationship. There could be more than one causal factor.

For time series approaches, the common models discussed are constant, linear trend, and seasonal, or combinations of these. Mathematically, they are

$$d_t = a + \varepsilon_t \qquad \text{(Constant)}$$

$$d_t = a + bt + \varepsilon_t \qquad \text{(Linear trend)}$$

$$d_t = ac_t + \varepsilon_t \qquad \text{(Seasonal)}$$

where a represents the constant portion, b the trend, c_t the seasonal factor for period t, and ε_t the random or noise component. These are the most common models, but others are used.

Recall from Chapter 3 that models should be as simple as possible. In forecasting, try to use as few components in a model as possible. A complicated function may "fit" the data but also tends to obscure important relationships. If there are many components, the effect of each becomes small and may be indistinguishable from the noise. As an example, consider demand for CD players. Sales most of the year are relatively constant, but gifts during December cause sales to peak. Rather than using a complicated model to capture the December sales peak, use one simple model for all of the year but December and another just for December. In statistics, a simple model that captures the essence of the problem is called a **parsimonious** model.

2.4   Solve the Model

The first step in solving the model is to choose a method. If we have a causal model, the method will be regression. For time series models, there may be several methods available, even for the same process. For example, there are many methods to forecast a constant time series.

Given the model, if we know the coefficients, we could simply plug in the right numbers to get a forecast. Because we do not know the actual parameters of the model equation, we must estimate them. The method used determines how they are estimated; usually they are estimated to minimize the difference between the forecast and the actual value over some set of historical data. Once parameters are estimated, applying the model to the appropriate numbers provides a forecast.

2.5   Interpret and Implement the Solution

Interpreting the solution is the major task of operating the forecasting system. Figure 4-4 shows the steps involved. As new data become available, we update the forecast. Also, we compare the previous forecast to what actually happened to get feedback on the quality of the forecasting procedure. If the quality is acceptable, we say that the procedure is in control; control issues are discussed in Section 7. If the procedure is out of control, we need to return to the design phase; either we need to re-estimate the parameters of the current model or change the model itself. If the forecasting system is in control, we forecast for a future period. This

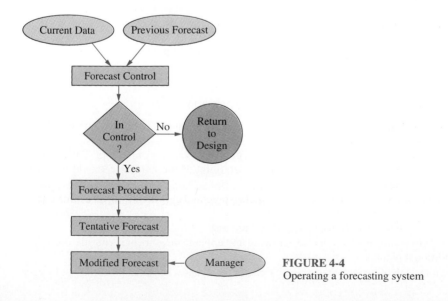

FIGURE 4-4
Operating a forecasting system

forecast is examined by a manager (owner) and judgment is used to accept, modify, or reject the forecast.

It is important to incorporate judgment into the system, especially when statistical methods are used. These methods have the underlying assumption that we are dealing in a stable environment, which is not always the case. For example, if a labor strike is forthcoming, the forecast should be modified to reflect this fact. It is important that any modification be done by the person making the decision and that it is done within the system. If no provision is made for modifications, either the forecast will not be used or at some point it will mislead the decision maker.

If a demand forecast is low, more units than expected are demanded and shortages, called stockouts, occur. On the other hand, a forecast higher than actual demand, which results in too many units, creates inventory that is marked down or scrapped. Fisher et al. (1994) point out that stockout plus markdown costs incurred for a particular product often exceed the manufacturing cost of the product. If the cost of an excess unit (inventory) is not equal to the cost of a unit short, then the decision maker will likely adjust the forecast accordingly—making the forecast larger if the shortage cost is higher or decreasing it if the inventory cost is higher.

2.6 Caveats

There are two very important facts to remember: forecasts almost never give the exact answer, and the farther into the future we look, the less accurate the forecast will be. It would be highly unlikely that the weekly sales forecast of doughnuts would be equal to the actual sales. Fortunately, exact forecasts are usually not required, we just need to be in the ballpark. A more reasonable approach might be to forecast a range of values or the probability of a group of values. We might forecast selling 250 dozen doughnuts next week but really mean sales should be between 230 and 270 dozen. The weather service does not say it will rain today, but that there is a 60 percent chance of rain. That the accuracy of a forecast depends on how far into the future we look can easily be seen from weather forecasts; the forecast for tomorrow is usually more accurate than the forecast for a week from today.

SECTION 2 PROBLEMS

4.1. Why is forecasting important? What role does it play in production planning and control?

4.2. What are the characteristics of a forecasting problem?

4.3. What are the differences in designing and operating a forecast system?

4.4. Identify the characteristics of the following forecasting scenarios:

  (a) You operate a newsstand in a metropolitan area, and you must tell your suppliers how many magazines to send you.

  (b) You work for a manufacturing organization that produces computer monitors. The planning department needs information to help them to determine if the company should hire new production employees.

  (c) You own a custom job shop and you must provide a potential customer with an estimate for a job.

  (d) Your company wishes to introduce a CD-ROM recorder.

  (e) Demand for your company's products is growing and upper management is considering building an additional plant.

4.5. Give one example each of a constant process, a trend process, and a seasonal process. Justify your reasoning.

4.6. What are some causal factors that might influence the following?

   (a) Sale of luxury cars
   (b) International air travel
   (c) Consumption of natural gas
   (d) Use of welding rods in a shipyard
   (e) Sale of computer software

4.7. Use a spreadsheet to generate 20 numbers for each of the following patterns. Plot them and note the differences.

   (a) $d_t = 100 + \varepsilon_t$, where $\varepsilon_t \sim N(0, 5^2)$
   (b) $d_t = 100 + \varepsilon_t$, where $\varepsilon_t \sim N(0, 30^2)$
   (c) $d_t = 100 + 2t + \varepsilon_t$, where $\varepsilon_t \sim N(0, 10^2)$
   (d) $d_t = 100 + 4t + \varepsilon_t$, where $\varepsilon_t \sim N(0, 10^2)$
   (e) $d_t = 100 + t^2 + \varepsilon_t$, where $\varepsilon_t \sim N(0, 10^2)$
   (f) $d_t = 100 + 20\sin(2\pi t/4) + \varepsilon_t$, where $\varepsilon_t \sim N(0, 10^2)$
   (g) $d_t = 100 + 20\sin(2\pi t/12) + \varepsilon_t$, where $\varepsilon_t \sim N(0, 10^2)$
   (h) $d_t = 100 + 40\sin(2\pi t/12) + \varepsilon_t$, where $\varepsilon_t \sim N(0, 10^2)$
   (i) $d_t = 100 + 20\sin(2\pi t/13) + \varepsilon_t$, where $\varepsilon_t \sim N(0, 10^2)$

4.8. Explain which model you would use to forecast each of the following time series. Also, tell why you would use that model.

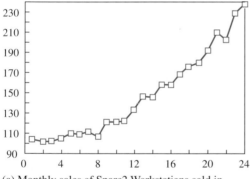

(a) Monthly sales of Sparc2 Workstations sold in Denver.

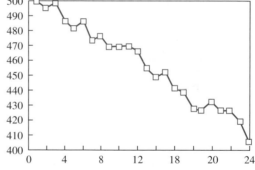

(b) Quarterly sales of audio tapes sold in Denver.

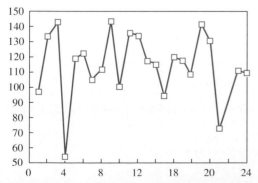

(c) Monthly sales of interior doors in Washington, D.C.

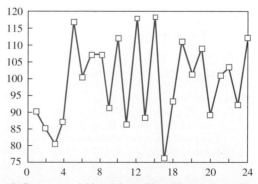

(d) Customers visiting Atlanta Pizza Huts each week.

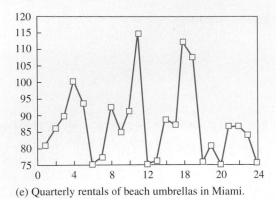

(e) Quarterly rentals of beach umbrellas in Miami.

4.9. Explain the role of the manager or decision maker in the forecasting system.

3 QUALITATIVE FORECASTING

DeVellia is responsible for the introduction of a new autofocus camera. Because the quality of pictures taken by autofocus cameras has increased significantly over the last few years, many owners of single lens reflex (SLR) cameras are switching. Historical demand will not reflect this increase. In this situation, she must use qualitative forecasting methods, which may include sending surveys to a number of potential customers and statistically analyzing the results, asking the opinion of a single expert, or asking many experts.

3.1 Market Survey

A market survey consists of several steps. First, a questionnaire must be developed that should contain questions whose answers provide the information needed to determine a forecast. This information about the customer might be things such as age and income as well as an indication of whether or not the customer will purchase the product. If the customer is a retail outlet, the information might include size of the store and the projected number of items that will be purchased. A survey to analyze demand for autofocus 35 mm cameras is given in Table 4-1. Along with survey design, a method to analyze the results must be determined.

The next step is carrying out the survey, which may be done by mail, FAX, e-mail, telephone, a tear-out postcard in a magazine, or in person. How the survey is carried out can

TABLE 4-1
A sample market survey form

Please check the appropriate boxes:
- ☐ I do not own a 35 mm camera.
- ☐ I own an SLR 35 mm camera.
- ☐ I own an autofocus 35 mm camera.
- ☐ I plan to purchase a new SLR 35 mm camera in the next two years.
- ☐ I plan to purchase a new autofocus 35 mm camera in the next two years.
- ☐ I do not plan to purchase a new 35 mm camera in the next two years.

affect the number as well as the quality of responses. The number, location, and individual customers to be surveyed should be carefully planned in conjunction with the purpose of the study.

After the survey is conducted, the results should be tabulated and analyzed. Care must be taken in interpreting these results. Response rates may be low, the questions answered incorrectly, or factors not considered in the questionnaire may affect the actual outcome of events. Statistical analysis can also be time consuming. Results of the camera survey might be that 75 percent of the respondents owned a 35 mm camera; 35 percent owned an SLR model and 50 percent owned an autofocus model. The percentages do not add up to 100 percent because some people own both. Of the 35 percent who own SLR cameras, 75 percent indicate that they will buy an autofocus camera within the next two years. Extrapolating the intentions of SLR and autofocus owners surveyed to the general population can give a forecast of the number of autofocus cameras demanded for the next two years. Of course other factors, e.g., the economy, may play a large role in actual purchases. For details in carrying out a market survey, see Kress and Snyder (1994).

Mastio (1994) discusses a survey based on 24 important needs and criteria to determine the factors blow molders use to select a machine supplier. Results indicate that machine dependability and spare parts availability are the most important needs to blow molders. Good technical service and machinery that is easy to operate are other key criteria when selecting a machine. Although important, price is not the most critical factor. About 65 percent of the blow molders said that they plan to purchase new equipment in the next year. A manufacturer of blow molding machinery can make aggressive expansion plans by providing these customers what they seek. Other examples of market surveys for forecasting purposes include demand for computer networks in industry (Smith, 1994) and demand for power transmission products, e.g., v-belts, gears, and transfer cases (Avery, 1993).

Recently, extensions and modifications of market survey techniques have been proposed. One is to use existing customer data base information to augment the survey (Ezop, 1994). Weerahandi et al. (1994) modify the procedure to account for cross effects on demand for similar products when a new product is made available. Using market surveys to provide insight for management to modify quantitative forecasts has been proposed by Cook (1995).

3.2   Expert Opinion and the Delphi Technique

A different method would be to ask an expert for an opinion on projected sales. This opinion is based on experience and knowledge of the particular situation. Sales and marketing personnel are prime examples of "experts" for forecasting a new product. A variation might be to ask several experts and use a combination of the results, say the median or average, as the forecast. This method is easy to implement but may be inaccurate.

A more formal variation of expert opinion is called the Delphi technique, named after the Oracle at Delphi of Greek mythology who predicted future events. A committee of "experts" corresponds to the Oracle in this technique, and a facilitator determines the participants, writes questionnaires, and analyzes the results. Committee members may be expert in quite different fields. For example, one may be sales oriented, but another may be an economist. They give a variety of views and consider many different factors in the process. The person from sales has a good idea of the company's history in selling other items, whereas the economist may have good information regarding the overall economic picture. Both of these factors affect the sale of a new product.

Committee members are asked to submit an anonymous forecast of specific events, and more importantly, their reasons why they picked that forecast. A simple example of an initial questionnaire is given in Table 4-2. Statements should be unambiguous and simple. Rather than the questionnaire asking if sales will be large, it should ask if they will be above a given value. Questions should have a single answer; if multiple responses are needed use a separate question for each.

Responses are summarized, and the questionnaire is modified and returned to committee members, who are then asked to repeat the process. The questionnaire for each round should reflect the results of previous rounds; summary statistics, e.g., mean, median, and range, are included in the updated questionnaire. Table 4-3 shows a questionnaire for intermediate rounds. The procedure continues until reasonable agreement among committee members is reached—usually three or four rounds are enough to reach consensus—and results are summarized, reported to the participants, and used to make decisions. Martino (1983) and Linstone and Turoff (1975) discuss conducting a Delphi study.

Delphi can be used to forecast demand for products. Vickers (1992) uses Delphi to examine the European automobile market, and Stocks (1990) forecasts CD-ROM demand in Australian libraries. Demand for services can also be forecast using Delphi. The number of families needing financial aid (Boehm et al., 1992) and tourists who visit a region (Kaynak and Leibold, 1994; Yong et al., 1989) are examples. Scala and McGrath (1993) use Delphi to identify advantages and disadvantages of electronic data interchange (EDI) in manufacturing companies, and Japan's Science and Technology Agency, a leading Delphi practitioner, has surveyed as many as 3000 scientists, engineers, and other experts on 1200 different topics (Maital, 1993).

Delphi has several advantages, among which are that it includes involving a variety of people, even those in different locations, and it prohibits domination by strong personalities,

TABLE 4-2
Sample initial Delphi questionnaire

(1a) At least 25% of the high schools in the midwest will have one or more self-paced, multimedia based courses by the year _____.
(1b) My reasons for this response are:

(2a) At least _____% of the high schools in the midwest will have one or more self-paced, multimedia based courses by the year 2000.
(2b) My reasons for this response are:

(3a) At least 80% of the high schools in the midwest will be able to pay $_____ for equipment to support multimedia based courses by the year 2000.
(3b) My reasons for this response are:

TABLE 4-3
Intermediate-round Delphi questionnaire

(1) Responses from the previous round indicate at least 25% of the high schools in the midwest will have one or more self-paced, multimedia based courses by the year **2001** (*median* response), with almost all responses falling between **1997** and **2006**. *Your* previous response was **2002**.
(1a) Given this information, at least 25% of the high school courses in the midwest will have one or more self-paced, multimedia based courses by the year _____.
(1b) My response varies from the median because:

(2) Responses from the previous round indicate at least **23%** (*median* response) of the high schools in the midwest will have one or more self-paced, multimedia based courses by the year 2000, with almost all responses between **20%** and **35%**.
(2a) Given this information, at least _____% of the high school courses in the midwest will have one or more self-paced, multimedia based courses by the year 2000.
(2b) My response varies from the median because:

(3) In the previous round, at least 80% of the high schools in the midwest will be able to pay **$10,500** (*median* response) for equipment to support multimedia based courses in the year 2000, with almost all responses between **$8,200** and **$13,600**.
(3a) Given this information, at least 80% of the high school courses in the midwest will be able to pay $_____for equipment to support multimedia based courses by the year 2000.
(3b) My response varies from the median because:

---

giving everyone an equal chance to participate; anonymity allows freer expression of ideas. It also keeps attention focused on the task; written responses are often better thought out than verbal ones. Probably its greatest advantage, however, is in generating and evaluating a large number of ideas for the forecast, many of which might be overlooked in face-to-face meetings.

The biggest disadvantage is the time needed to carry out a Delphi study, often more than a month; electronic methods (FAX and e-mail) may speed the process, however. It is also time consuming for the participants, and it may be difficult to keep them totally involved. Written ideas may need clarification or risk being misunderstood; a typical Delphi study has no mechanism for clarification. And because Delphi is a type of voting procedure, sometimes compromise agreements are not reached.

3.3 Comments on Qualitative Forecasting Methods

Qualitative methods are often used in industry. Sometimes, expert opinion is used because it is "close enough," fast, and easy to do, and it is particularly adept at quickly sensing trends in markets. On the other hand, market surveys and the Delphi method are both time consuming and costly. However, for new product introduction and forecasting technological advances, they may be the only choice. If all steps of the method are followed, the results are usually fairly accurate. One major benefit of judgmental forecasting may be that it forces a commitment from the responsible parties; that is, if the head of sales quotes a figure, he or she may work extra hard to see that sales are not less than the forecast. Market surveys give good results, but the time required to do them makes them less appropriate for short-term forecasting. With the growth of networks and customers with access to interactive computing, market surveys may become more timely and accurate. However, the cost must be weighed against the benefit the survey provides.

SECTION 3   PROBLEMS

4.10. What are the advantages and disadvantages of market surveys?

4.11. The city manager has hired you to investigate a curbside recycling program. Define this problem from a forecasting perspective and determine what type of data you could acquire and how.

4.12. Write a survey for the curbside recycling program forecasting problem.

4.13. What are the advantages and disadvantages of the Delphi method?

4.14. Give three examples of situations in which Delphi would be an appropriate way to forecast.

4.15. Design a Delphi procedure to determine the market potential of micromachines such as a machine injected into the human bloodstream to clean out arteries. The procedure should include an initial questionnaire, types of experts, and ways to communicate results.

4.16. What method would you use to forecast the following?

(a) Next year's sales of high definition TV
(b) Time until 95 percent of U.S. homes have Internet connections
(c) Number of subscribers to a new fashion magazine
(d) Next year's sales of a soft drink based on a Brazilian berry

4   CAUSAL FORECASTING WITH REGRESSION

Mary Carter is manager of the plumbing department for the Columbia store of HomeSales, a leading retailer of building supplies. Each month, she must place an order for bathroom plumbing fixtures. If she orders more than the number sold, the excess fixtures represent money the company cannot use elsewhere. If she orders too few, sales are lost to the store's competitors.

Mary has been thinking about how she might anticipate the demand for fixtures. She knows that most of the fixtures sold at her store are for new houses; replacement fixtures account for less than 6 percent of total sales. Plumbing fixtures are installed after the roof and walls of the house are on, typically about a month after the building permit is issued. Because each new house built requires a building permit, the number of building permits issued last month may help her determine the number of fixtures she should order this month.

This scenario is typical of many forecasting problems. We wish to forecast a dependent variable—sales of plumbing fixtures in our example—and the value of the dependent variable is related to an observable value of one or more independent variables—housing starts in the example. We call this process causal forecasting, because the value of the dependent variable is often caused by, or at least highly correlated with, the value of the independent variable(s).

The relationship between the dependent and independent variables, however, is not always clear-cut. For example, total sales for a company may vary in a pattern similar to that of some general economic indicators. In this case, aggregate sales could be the dependent variable and various economic indicators, such as the prime interest rate, would be the independent variables. To estimate the relationship, regression techniques are often useful. Let us examine Mary's problem more closely to see how this process is done.

4.1 Simple Linear Regression

The first thing Mary should do is make a scatter plot of her data. Table 4-4 gives the number of housing permits issued in the Columbia area and the number of plumbing fixtures sold in her store for each month of the last two years. Notice that the permits for a given month are aligned with the fixture sales for the following month because there is a one month lag between the permit and the sale; i.e., sales in February depend on permits from January. A scatter plot is given in Figure 4-5. This plot has housing permits, sorted in ascending order, as its x-axis and the corresponding fixture sales as its y-axis. The scatter plot seems to show a linear relationship between housing starts and fixture demand, so simple linear regression is appropriate. The underlying model is

$$d_t = a + bh_t + \varepsilon_t \qquad t = 1, 2, \ldots, n$$

where d_t = the number of fixtures sold in month t
h_t = the number of building permits issued in month $t - 1$

TABLE 4-4
Housing permits and plumbing fixture sales

Data point	Month of permit	Number of permits	Month of fixture sale	Number of fixtures
1	Jan. 94	22	Feb. 94	72
2	Feb. 94	16	Mar. 94	44
3	Mar. 94	24	Apr. 94	80
4	Apr. 94	95	May 94	191
5	May 94	84	Jun. 94	187
6	Jun. 94	13	Jul. 94	57
7	Jul. 94	114	Aug. 94	238
8	Aug. 94	147	Sep. 94	283
9	Sep. 94	96	Oct. 94	204
10	Oct. 94	59	Nov. 94	144
11	Nov. 94	35	Dec. 94	102
12	Dec. 94	41	Jan. 95	109
13	Jan. 95	28	Feb. 95	63
14	Feb. 95	21	Mar. 95	50
15	Mar. 95	18	Apr. 95	67
16	Apr. 95	46	May 95	109
17	May 95	145	Jun. 95	304
18	Jun. 95	122	Jul. 95	239
19	Jul. 95	108	Aug. 95	223
29	Aug. 95	85	Sep. 95	173
21	Sep. 95	107	Oct. 95	211
22	Oct. 95	53	Nov. 95	104
23	Nov. 95	17	Dec. 95	59
24	Dec. 95	12	Jan. 96	24

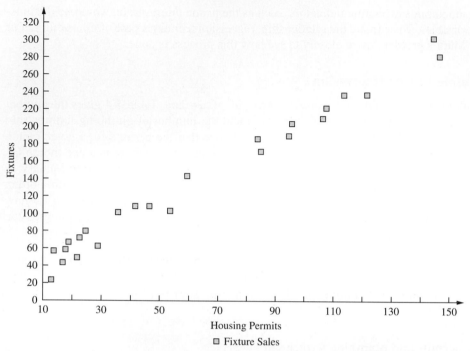

FIGURE 4-5
Scatter plot of permits and sales

ε_t = random error in the model
a = intercept of the straight line relating d_t and h_t
b = slope of the line
n = the total number of months of data available

We wish to choose estimates of a and b, say $\hat{a}$ and $\hat{b}$, so that a straight line fits the data as closely as possible. To do so, we minimize the sum of the squared differences between the actual sales and the sales indicated by the model. This difference is the "error" of the forecast. By squaring the difference we ensure that the value is nonnegative, penalizing both underestimates and overestimates. Squaring the difference also causes more weight to be placed on larger differences than on smaller differences. Thus we are minimizing the error in our prediction, with larger errors weighted more heavily.

From any basic statistics text, we find

$$\hat{b} = \frac{n\sum_{t=1}^{n} h_t d_t - \sum_{t=1}^{n} h_t \sum_{t=1}^{n} d_t}{n\sum_{t=1}^{n} h_t^2 - \left(\sum_{t=1}^{n} h_t\right)^2}$$

and

$$\hat{a} = \frac{1}{n}\sum_{t=1}^{n} d_t - \frac{\hat{b}}{n}\sum_{t=1}^{n} h_t$$

To calculate $\hat{b}$ we need $\sum h_t$, $\sum d_t$, $\sum (h_t \times d_t)$, and $\sum h_t^2$. Using a spreadsheet, we calculated these values (and $\sum d_t^2$, which is used later) for Mary's problem; they are given in Table 4-5. From these we compute

$$\hat{b} = \frac{(24 \times 294{,}095) - (1508 \times 3337)}{(24 \times 140{,}928) - (1508)^2} = 1.83$$

and

$$\hat{a} = \left(\frac{3337}{24}\right) - \left(\frac{1.83}{24}\right) 1508 = 24.17$$

This results in the regression equation

$$\hat{d} = 24.17 + 1.83h$$

where $\hat{d}$ is the estimate for the number of plumbing fixtures sold in a month given that there were h housing starts the previous month. If there are 23 housing starts in January of 1995, we would expect to sell about $24.17 + 1.83 \times 23 \approx 66$ fixtures in February.

In general, $\hat{b}$ can be positive or negative. A positive value implies that the dependent variable increases as the independent variable increases or that they are positively correlated. A negative $\hat{b}$ implies the opposite. The magnitude of $\hat{b}$ should reflect the amount of change in the dependent variable for a unit change in the independent variable. If either the sign or magnitude of $\hat{b}$ seems inappropriate for the situation, think carefully about the model.

TABLE 4.5
Regression computations for Mary's data

t	h_t	d_t	h_t^2	d_t^2	$h_t \times d_t$
1	22	72	484	5,184	1,584
2	16	44	256	1,936	704
3	24	80	576	6,400	1,920
4	95	191	9,025	36,481	18,145
5	84	187	7,056	34,969	15,708
6	13	57	169	3,249	741
7	114	238	12,996	56,644	27,132
8	147	283	21,609	80,089	41,601
9	96	204	9,216	41,616	19,584
10	59	144	3,481	20,736	8,496
11	35	102	1,225	10,404	3,570
12	41	109	1,681	11,881	4,469
13	28	63	784	3,969	1,764
14	21	50	441	2,500	1,050
15	18	67	324	4,489	1,206
16	46	109	2,116	11,881	5,041
17	145	304	21,025	92,416	44,080
18	122	239	14,884	57,121	29,158
19	108	223	11,664	49,729	24,084
20	85	173	7,225	29,929	14,705
21	107	211	11,449	44,521	22,577
22	53	104	2,809	10,816	5,512
23	17	59	289	3,481	1,003
24	12	24	144	576	288
Total	1,508	3,337	140,927	621,017	294,095

The value of $\hat{a}$ represents the value of the dependent variable when the independent variable is zero, which is not necessarily a meaningful number; if zero is not a possible value of the independent variable, $\hat{a}$ may still be positive. In this case, $\hat{a}$ calibrates the other values.

The coefficient of determination is defined as

$$r^2 = \frac{\sum\limits_{t=1}^{n}(\hat{d}_t - \bar{d})^2}{\sum\limits_{t=1}^{n}(d_t - \bar{d})^2}$$

For Mary's data, it is

$$r^2 = 0.98$$

An r^2 of 0.98 indicates an excellent fit, because the regression equation explains 98 percent of the variance, which should not be too surprising because these data are not real but were actually generated by a linear model with some random variation. In practice, a coefficient of determination of 0.85 is considered quite good.

4.2   Other Regression Models

In applications there may be several independent variables that affect the dependent variable. If there are n observations of the dependent variable and m independent variables, a linear model with noise would be

$$d_t = b_0 + b_1 x_{1t} + b_2 x_{2t} + \cdots + b_m x_{mt} + \varepsilon_t \qquad t = 1, 2, \ldots, n$$

We can estimate the values of the parameters $b_0, b_1, b_2, \ldots, b_m$ using a least squares approach. Even if the functional relationship between a dependent variable and the independent variables is not linear, the linear model for estimating coefficients is appropriate because the values of the independent variables, rather then their form, are used.

For demand forecasting, independent variables might include population of potential purchasers, price, and quality. We could postulate a model such as

$$d_t = b_0 + b_1 y_{1t} + b_2 y_{2t} + b_3 y_{3t}^2 + \varepsilon_t$$

where d_t = the demand in period t
y_{1t} = the number of potential customers in period t
y_{2t} = the price of the item in period t
y_{3t} = the number of defective products returned in period $t - 1$
ε_t = the noise term

In this model, b_0 represents the constant portion of the process, and b_1 could be viewed as the percentage of the potential customers who buy the product. Depending on the price, more or fewer customers will buy the product. The expected magnitude of b_2 will depend on the price units. The model has a quadratic effect for quality; twice as many returns will have a fourfold effect on demand. Because sales should decrease as the number of returns increases, b_3 should be less than zero. This model is nonlinear, but by letting $x_{1t} = y_{1t}$, $x_{2t} = y_{2t}$, and $x_{3t} = y_{2t}^2$ we can use the linear model.

Suppose we have n observations of the dependent and independent variables:

$$
\begin{array}{ccccc}
d_1 & x_{11} & x_{21} & \cdots & x_{m1} \\
d_2 & x_{12} & x_{22} & \cdots & x_{m2} \\
\cdots & \cdots & \cdots & \cdots & \cdots \\
d_n & x_{1n} & x_{2n} & \cdots & x_{mn}
\end{array}
$$

Let

$$
\mathbf{d} = \begin{vmatrix} d_1 \\ d_2 \\ \cdots \\ d_n \end{vmatrix}
\qquad
\boldsymbol{\varepsilon} = \begin{vmatrix} \varepsilon_1 \\ \varepsilon_2 \\ \cdots \\ \varepsilon_n \end{vmatrix}
\qquad
\mathbf{b} = \begin{vmatrix} b_0 \\ b_1 \\ b_2 \\ \cdots \\ b_m \end{vmatrix}
$$

$$
\mathbf{X} = \begin{vmatrix}
1 & x_{11} & x_{21} & \cdots & x_{m1} \\
1 & x_{12} & x_{22} & \cdots & x_{m2} \\
\cdots & \cdots & \cdots & \cdots & \cdots \\
1 & x_{1n} & x_{2n} & \cdots & x_{mn}
\end{vmatrix}
$$

Using matrix notation we can state the general model as

$$
\mathbf{d} = \mathbf{Xb} + \boldsymbol{\varepsilon}
$$

where $E(\boldsymbol{\varepsilon}) = \mathbf{0}$ and $\mathrm{cov}(\boldsymbol{\varepsilon}) = \sigma^2 \mathbf{I}$ and $\mathbf{I}$ is the identity matrix. To determine estimators of $\mathbf{b}$ we minimize the squared difference between a predicted value of demand and its actual value. The general solution for the least squares estimators is

$$
\hat{\mathbf{b}} = (\mathbf{X'X})^{-1}\mathbf{X'd}
$$

the covariance is

$$
\mathrm{cov}(\hat{\mathbf{b}}) = \sigma^2(\mathbf{X'X})^{-1}
$$

and an estimate of the error variance can be shown to be

$$
\hat{\sigma}^2 = \frac{\boldsymbol{\varepsilon'}\boldsymbol{\varepsilon}}{n - m}
$$

and it can further be shown that it is unbiased. If we assume the errors are normally distributed, e.g., $\varepsilon \sim \mathbf{N}(\mathbf{0}, \sigma^2\mathbf{I})$, then $\mathbf{d} \sim \mathbf{N}(\mathbf{Xb}, \sigma^2\mathbf{I})$. Given the point

$$
\mathbf{x}_t = (1, x_{1t}, x_{2t}, \ldots, x_{mt})
$$

a forecast would be

$$
F_t = \hat{d}_t = \mathbf{x}_t\hat{\mathbf{b}}
$$

The $100(1 - \alpha)$ percent prediction interval about the forecast is

$$
\hat{d}_t \pm t_{\alpha/2, n-m-1} \sqrt{\hat{\sigma}^2[1 + \mathbf{x}_t(\mathbf{X'X})^{-1}\mathbf{x}_t]}
$$

where $t_{\alpha/2, n-m-1}$ is the upper $\alpha/2$ percentage point of a t distribution with $n-m-1$ degrees of freedom. Statistical packages for multiple regression give tests similar to simple regression.

Example 4-1. Meller Sportswear. Meller Sportswear makes a variety of athletic clothing: T-shirts, sweatshirts, sweatpants, and replica uniform jerseys. Stephon is developing a capacity plan for next year and needs to know how many replica football jerseys Meller will need to make in each quarter of next year.

Solution. First Stephon collects data for the previous three years. These data, given in Table 4-6, indicate total sales by quarter with quarter 12 the last available data. The sales numbers are aggregate, so the jerseys are not differentiated by team. A plot of this data is given in Figure 4-6. As might be expected, sales appear to follow a seasonal pattern that repeats each year (four quarters).

TABLE 4-6
Football jersey sales

t	1	2	3	4	5	6	7	8	9	10	11	12
d_t	182	154	201	217	146	140	191	248	142	138	202	209

Stephon knows seasonal patterns can be represented by sine and cosine pairs. A sine wave has a period of 2π, so to adjust for the four-quarter period of jersey sales we use $\sin(2\pi t/4)$. The model Stephon uses has the form

$$d_t = b_0 + b_1 t + b_2 \sin(2\pi t/4) + b_3 \cos(2\pi t/4)$$

where d_t = the demand in quarter t

$\quad b_0$ = the constant term

$\quad b_1$ = the trend coefficient

$\quad b_2$ = the coefficient for the sine term

$\quad b_3$ = the coefficient for the cosine term

Stephon will estimate the coefficients for the model using multiple regression.

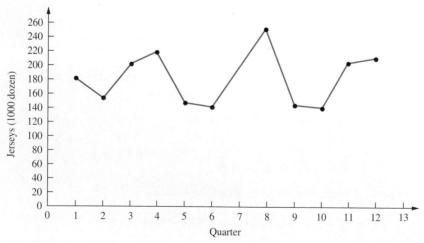

FIGURE 4-6
Football jersey sales

First the $\mathbf{X}$ matrix and $\mathbf{b}$ vector are formed:

$$\mathbf{X} = \begin{vmatrix} 1 & 1 & \sin(\pi/2) & \cos(\pi/2) \\ 1 & 2 & \sin(\pi) & \cos(\pi) \\ \cdots & \cdots & \cdots & \cdots \\ 1 & 12 & \sin(6\pi) & \cos(6\pi) \end{vmatrix} \qquad \mathbf{b} = \begin{vmatrix} b_0 \\ b_1 \\ b_2 \\ b_3 \end{vmatrix}$$

Plugging in numbers for the sine/cosine terms and using the demand figures gives

$$\mathbf{X} = \begin{vmatrix} 1 & 1 & 1 & 0 \\ 1 & 2 & 0 & -1 \\ 1 & 3 & -1 & 0 \\ 1 & 4 & 0 & 1 \\ 1 & 5 & 1 & 0 \\ 1 & 6 & 0 & -1 \\ 1 & 7 & -1 & 0 \\ 1 & 8 & 0 & 1 \\ 1 & 9 & 1 & 0 \\ 1 & 10 & 0 & -1 \\ 1 & 11 & -1 & 0 \\ 1 & 12 & 0 & 1 \end{vmatrix} \qquad \mathbf{d} = \begin{vmatrix} 182 \\ 154 \\ 201 \\ 217 \\ 146 \\ 140 \\ 191 \\ 248 \\ 142 \\ 138 \\ 202 \\ 209 \end{vmatrix}$$

Using a spreadsheet we calculate

$$\hat{\mathbf{b}} = (\mathbf{X}'\mathbf{X})^{-1}\mathbf{X}'\mathbf{b}$$

with result $b_0 = 192.30$, $b_1 = -1.76$, $b_2 = -22.43$, and $b_3 = 42.10$. The model is

$$d_t = 192.30 - 1.76t - 22.43\sin(2\pi t/4) + 42.10\cos(2\pi t/4)$$

Carrying out the regression using the spreadsheet Excel, the coefficient of determination is $r^2 = 0.88$, indicating that the model does a good job of explaining the variation. The t tests for all coefficients except b_2, the trend coefficient, are significant at the 0.01 level, so we can reject the hypothesis that they are zero. We cannot reject the hypothesis that the trend coefficient is zero. Including or ignoring the trend in the forecast should likely be based on judgment. With the trend included, the forecast for the next year (four quarters) would be 147 for quarter 13, 126 for quarter 14, 188 for quarter 15, and 206 for quarter 16. Not including the trend term would give the forecasts 170, 150, 215, and 234, respectively.

4.3 Comments on Regression

Regression models are very useful for forecasting when there is a strong relationship and a time lag between the dependent variable and the independent variable(s). If there is no time lag between dependent and independent variables, i.e., they occur in the same time period, we cannot forecast future values of the dependent value unless we use a forecast of the independent variable, which may introduce additional error in the forecast of the dependent variable. Consider Mary's problem: if permits and fixture sales occur at the same time, we cannot determine the number of fixtures demanded for next month without knowing the number of permits issued next month.

Extrapolating results of a regression equation can be dangerous. If 200 permits were issued in a particular month, this number is larger than any data point used to fit the regression equation. The resulting forecast from the equation is suspect, because statistically only values in the range of the data used to fit the equation should be used to forecast.

Be very careful using causal models. Often, the cause and effect relationship is not clear, but a causal model is used anyway. Barron and Targett (1985) discuss a case in Britain where passenger miles flown by a major airline were forecast by a causal model with U.K. manufacturing production as the independent value. Statistically the model "fit" well, but after several months of good forecasts, the results became unusable. There was no causal relationship; manufacturing production did not cause airmiles to be flown. The model fit because both variables increased during good economic times. The model failed when the economy worsened and manufacturing production dropped, which indicated a decrease in passenger miles flown. At the same time, the value of the dollar dropped relative to the pound, and many Britons flew to the United States for holidays, increasing the number of passenger miles flown.

If causal relationships do not exist, regression is not the best forecasting method. We will examine other forecasting approaches in the following sections.

SECTION 4 PROBLEMS

4.17. A regression equation has been developed for yield of four-nines (99.99 percent pure) copper per cubic acre of land as a function of soil acidity. The relationship is

$$y = 164 + 32.3x$$

where y is the number of tons/acre^3 of copper and x is the acidity of a soil sample.

(a) Give the forecast for a plot of land if its acidity is 2.2.
(b) Give the forecast for another plot of land with acidity 6.2.

4.18. Reno Shipyards repairs ocean-going vessels. Many large steel plates are welded together and to existing ship hulls. When a bid for a job is accepted, there is an estimate of the tons of steel needed to make the repair. The orders for the following month are added together and the steel is ordered from the mill. Welding rods are also ordered. It seems reasonable that the amount of welding rods used will be related to the amount of steel used. The following table shows data for the last two years of steel use (tons) and welding rod use (hundredweights).

(a) Create a scatter plot of the data.
(b) Using simple linear regression, write the equation for how many hundredweights of welding rods to order for a projected steel usage.
(c) Do you think that this is an accurate equation? Why or why not?
(d) Determine the amount of welding rods to order if Reno plans to use 175 tons of steel next month.
(e) Give confidence and prediction intervals for this forecast.

Month	1	2	3	4	5	6	7	8	9	10	11	12
Steel	116	104	119	96	79	78	104	103	114	92	97	110
Rods	229	234	272	196	161	189	226	209	262	179	204	234
Month	13	14	15	16	17	18	19	20	21	22	23	24
Steel	114	107	99	105	94	111	108	97	90	92	88	117
Rods	237	224	209	246	189	233	242	230	199	170	165	263

4.19. Trame Incorporated makes custom air conditioning systems. They take pride in getting orders to customers quickly; however, more important to them is being honest with customers about the delivery date of their order. The lead time is the time it will take from accepting the order until it is completed, and it is influenced by orders currently in process. To aid the sales force in setting realistic delivery dates and to improve scheduling (see Chapter 8), the production department wants to develop a model to predict leadtime. The following table contains 32 observations on the time (in hours) to complete a job, given the number of jobs currently in process. What model would you suggest? Justify your answer. If there are five jobs in the shop, what is your estimate for the lead time of an arriving job?

Obs	Jobs	Time	Obs	Jobs	Time
1	6	11.40	17	17	87.70
2	9	15.74	18	10	44.53
3	17	96.38	19	12	50.98
4	6	25.53	20	14	91.46
5	7	31.20	21	6	40.63
6	18	114.27	22	18	117.87
7	8	27.18	23	7	10.56
8	8	35.49	24	6	31.02
9	15	91.95	25	8	21.65
10	9	32.03	26	13	69.48
11	6	25.97	27	15	87.06
12	12	57.74	28	14	68.83
13	5	23.78	29	19	115.78
14	7	17.70	30	15	94.45
15	18	111.33	31	18	94.70
16	11	49.57	32	18	103.40

4.20. Ron owns the Popcorn and Movies store in a college town. On weekends, there are many requests for popular movies. He only has one opportunity to order videos so it is important that he get the right number. Too many tie up money, but if he orders too few, customers will go to other video rental locations. Suc, one of his employees is a business major and believes there is a relationship between the number of requests for a particular movie and the number of tickets sold for the movie when it played in theaters. She claims that the more tickets sold, the higher demand for rentals will be because it must have been a good movie. Ron feels that people who saw a movie at a theater will not rent it. To settle their argument, Sue recorded the number of requests for 20 movies on Friday night, the highest demand night. She also looked up ticket sales, in millions of dollars, for the movie. Use this information to help Ron decide how many videos of a particular movie to order.

Movie number	Tickets sold	Rental request	Movie number	Tickets sold	Rental request
1	13.06	14	11	13.67	14
2	12.15	11	12	14.08	14
3	10.67	6	13	10.58	8
4	10.47	5	14	15.45	16
5	11.37	10	15	14.26	13
6	17.76	15	16	18.30	14
7	15.00	17	17	13.61	14
8	18.57	11	18	17.79	16
9	17.51	13	19	19.86	12
10	18.88	10	20	12.76	11

4.21. Armando owns orange groves in Culican. He has collected data on total rainfall (inches), average high temperature, (degrees Fahrenheit), and yield (pounds/acre) for each of the last 20 growing seasons. The data are as follows:

Rain	11	22	20	22	13	23	23	10	24	21
Temp	91	80	88	85	94	83	82	87	84	89
Yield	1713	4439	5012	4741	2613	4436	4257	1520	4092	5040
Rain	21	19	19	25	14	24	24	22	12	18
Temp	92	82	93	86	84	90	94	81	93	88
Yield	5207	5075	4971	3794	4152	4585	4854	4497	2086	4918

The weather service has predicted a likelihood of rainfall of 17 in. and temperature of 88°F. They feel confident that rainfall will be between 15 in. and 20 in., and temperature between 85°F and 90°F. Oranges are processed in a one-week period at the end of the season. A worker can process 800 pounds per day. Armando has 100 acres of orange groves and currently has 100 workers contracted for the week after the current growing season. What advice would you give on his workforce level?

4.22. Standard simple linear regression techniques minimize the sum of squared deviations of the data points from the estimated line, i.e.,

$$\min \sum_{i=1}^{n} [y_i - (a + bx_i)]^2$$

If there are one or two outliers, the resulting line will be greatly affected, because the square of the difference is used. If we are forecasting a process with trend that has a lot of noise, we may want to decrease the "weight" of the difference. One way to do this is to minimize the sum of the absolute value of the differences, rather than the square. That is, $\min \sum_{i=1}^{n} |y_i - (a + bx_i)|$. Unfortunately, no closed form solution exists for this model, but the a and b can be obtained by solving a linear programming model. Develop an LP model to estimate the intercept and slope of a fitted line given n observations of both the dependent variable y_i and the independent variable x_i.

4.23. A tacit assumption of least squares is that an overestimate is equal to an underestimate, which is not always the case.

(a) Develop a method that will give proper estimates for a trend model for an inventory system if a stockout costs twice as much as an overage.

(b) Suppose a product has an expected life of one year. Early stockouts can likely be filled later, and overages can be used to satisfy future demand. Poor forecasts toward the end of the life of the product may be more expensive because there may be competing products and overages may have to be scrapped. Modify your solution in (a) to handle this problem.

5   TIME SERIES METHODS

For short-term forecasting, time series methods are favored. A time series is simply a time-ordered list of historical data, the underlying assumption of which is that history is a reasonable predictor of the future. There are several time series models and methods to choose from, including a constant, trend, or seasonal model, depending on the historical data and our understanding of the underlying process. For each model, there may be several forecasting methods available, including averages, moving averages, exponential smoothing, regression, and even combinations of all of them. Because we must recognize which model is appropriate for a given time series, we will discuss each model separately.

5.1 Constant Process

The Calgore Company is one of the largest producers of toothpaste in the United States. Almost 50 percent of their toothpaste is made at their New Jersey plant, with the rest of the production spread over five other plants dispersed across the country. As manager of toothpaste production, Ned Murphy is concerned about how much toothpaste he should produce next week. The actual sales figures (in cases) for the last 50 weeks, obtained from the marketing department, are given in Table 4-7. The first thing Ned does is plot the data; this plot is given in Figure 4-7

From the plot, sales appear to be basically constant with some random deviation. Therefore, we speculate that the underlying process is constant. Mathematically, demand in period t is represented by

$$d_t = a + \varepsilon_t$$

in which a represents the underlying constant of the process and ε_t the random noise, assumed to be normally distributed with mean zero and variance σ_ε^2.

Many methods are used to forecast a constant process. We will discuss using the last data point, an average of all data points, an average of the most recent data, and averages that count all data points but give more weight to the more recent points.

5.1.1 SIMPLE METHODS. One of the simplest forecasting methods is to use the last data point (LDP) as the forecast for the next period. Let T be the current time period, t be an arbitrary time period, d_t be the historical demand in period t, and F_{T+k} be the forecast made at time T for k periods ahead.

Using LDP, the forecast for the next period will be the demand in this period. Notationally, it is

$$F_{T+1} = d_T$$

TABLE 4-7
Weekly toothpaste sales (in thousands of cases)

Week	Demand	Week	Demand	Week	Demand
1	56	18	55	35	52
2	46	19	52	36	48
3	53	20	52	37	50
4	50	21	44	38	49
5	50	22	47	39	52
6	52	23	57	40	48
7	46	24	45	41	47
8	53	25	48	42	48
9	55	26	55	43	44
10	46	27	50	44	43
11	53	28	42	45	50
12	45	29	50	46	57
13	50	30	57	47	46
14	49	31	51	48	44
15	48	32	54	49	52
16	43	33	54	50	58
17	47	34	51		

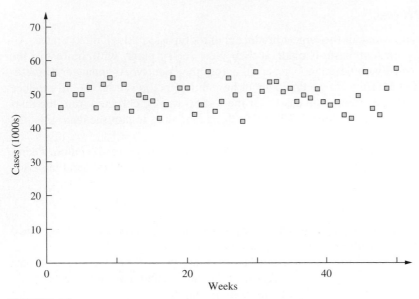

FIGURE 4-7
Weekly toothpaste sales plot

For Ned, the forecast for next week's demand would be 58, last week's demand. The forecast for k weeks in the future would also be

$$F_{T+k} = d_T$$

because constant processes should have a constant mean and estimates of future demand should be independent of how far in the future we look.

The problem with LDP is the inherent random variation. If last week's demand was on the high side, the forecast will be too. If the next demand is high, the forecast will be good. However, for a constant model, we assume a normally distributed random component, and the next demand is just as likely to be low. In this case, LDP will give a bad forecast.

To overcome this problem, we could use an average of the past data, which will make the forecast less sensitive to random variations. Given T periods of data, the average at time T is

$$\overline{D}_T = \frac{1}{T} \sum_{t=1}^{T} d_t$$

The forecast made in period T for next period is

$$F_{T+1} = \overline{D}_T$$

For the data in Table 4-7, we see that

$$\overline{D}_{50} = \frac{1}{50} \sum_{t=1}^{T} d_t = 49.88$$

Thus the forecast for the next week (51) will be

$$F_{51} = \overline{D}_{50} = 49.88$$

Because units are in thousands of cases, the forecast is 49,880 cases.

To forecast for more than one period in the future, we would still use this number because we are using a constant model. Thus, the forecast for k periods in the future calculated at time T is

$$F_{T+k} = \overline{D}_T$$

The last data point and average forecasting methods could be considered extreme methods. LDP ignores all but the last data point, whereas the average treats very old data the same as the most recent. If the process is truly constant, an average is preferred because it captures the essence of the time series and tends to damp out random fluctuations. However, very few processes are constant over a long period of time. If the underlying process changes, the last data point method will react to the change, but it will also react to random fluctuations. On the other hand, the average is slow to adjust to change but does not respond to random noise. Next we will examine some compromise methods.

5.1.2 MOVING AVERAGE. Rather than take an average of all data points, we might choose to average only some of the more recent data. This method, called a moving average, is a compromise between the last data point and average methods. It averages recent data to reduce the effect of random fluctuations. Because only recent data is used to forecast, a moving average responds to a change in the underlying process more quickly. Let N be the number of periods we wish to consider in the moving average and M_T be the value of the moving average. If we are currently at period T, the moving average is given by the sum of the last N data points, or mathematically,

$$M_T = \frac{1}{N}(d_{T-N+1} + d_{T-N+2} + \cdots + d_T) = \frac{1}{N}\sum_{t=T-N+1}^{T} d_t$$

The timing of the data points in a moving average can be illustrated by the following time line:

At time T, the points $T - N + 1, T - N + 2, \ldots, T$ are included in an N-period moving average. At time $T + 1$, the point $T + 1$ is added and the point $T - N + 1$ is dropped from the calculation, so the average will include $T - N + 2, T - N + 3, \ldots, t, T + 1$.

In week 50, the five-week moving average of Calgore's sales would be

$$M_{50} = \frac{d_{46} + d_{47} + d_{48} + d_{49} + d_{50}}{5} = \frac{57 + 46 + 44 + 52 + 58}{5} = 51.4$$

Thus Ned should plan to make 51,400 cases of toothpaste in week 51, as compared to the 49,880 cases forecast by the average. Again, because we are using a constant model, the forecast calculated at week 50 for any future period would be the same. Formally, we have

$$F_{T+k} = M_T$$

for all values of k.

The moving average is a "best" estimate of a constant process, because it minimizes the sum of squared errors for the data points $T - N + 1, T - N + 2, \ldots, t$. Let $\hat{a}$ be the minimum sum of squares estimator of the process. Then we wish to minimize

$$SS = \sum_{t=T-N+1}^{T} (d_t - \hat{a})^2$$

Taking the derivative, setting it to zero and solving gives

$$\frac{dSS}{d\hat{a}} = \sum_{t=T-N+1}^{T} 2(d_t - \hat{a})(-1) = 0 \Rightarrow \hat{a} = \frac{1}{N} \sum_{t=T-N+1}^{T} d_t$$

When a new data point is obtained, we calculate a new moving average. Suppose 45,000 cases were sold in week 51. The new five-week moving average would be the average of the sales for weeks 47, 48, 49, 50, and 51, i.e.,

$$M_{51} = \frac{d_{47} + d_{48} + d_{49} + d_{50} + d_{51}}{5} = \frac{46 + 44 + 52 + 58 + 45}{5} = 49.0$$

Recall that the general formula for the N-week moving average computed at time $T + 1$ is

$$M_{T+1} = \frac{d_{T-N+2} + d_{T-N+3} + \ldots + d_T + d_{T+1}}{N}$$

Suppose we add $(d_{T-N+1} - d_{T-N+1})/N$ (which is just zero) to the right-hand side of the equation for M_{T+1}. We then have

$$M_{T+1} = \frac{d_{T-N+2} + d_{T-N+3} + \ldots + d_T + d_{T+1}}{N} + \frac{d_{T-N+1} - d_{T-N+1}}{N}$$

Rearranging terms gives

$$M_{T+1} = \frac{d_{T-N+1} + d_{T-N+2} + d_{T-N+3} + \ldots + d_T}{N} + \frac{d_{T+1} - d_{T-N+1}}{N}$$

$$= M_T + \frac{d_{T+1} - d_{T-N+1}}{N}$$

which is a convenient way to update the moving average. Calculations for moving averages for weeks 41 through 50 are given in Table 4-8. Using the update formula, the five-week moving average computed at week 51 would be

$$M_{51} = M_{50} + \frac{(d_{51} - d_{46})}{5} = 51.4 + \frac{(45 - 57)}{5} = 49.0$$

The number of periods, N, used in a moving average affects how quickly the forecast will respond to a change in the process. For a constant process with mean 50 and no noise, the moving average will be 50 for any value of N. If the process mean suddenly shifts to 65, only after N periods will the moving average be 65. Of course noise, present in most processes, causes the moving average to only approximate the mean after this time lag. To illustrate this point, we add 15 to every observation of the data in Table 4-7 after week 10, corresponding to a change in process. Three-week and six-week moving averages of the first 25 weeks of

TABLE 4-8
Computations for a five-week moving average

t	d_t	M_t	d_{t+1}	d_{t-N}	M_{t+1}
41	47	49.20	48	50	48.80
42	48	48.80	44	49	47.80
43	44	47.80	43	52	46.00
44	43	46.00	50	48	46.40
45	50	46.40	57	47	48.40
46	57	48.40	46	48	48.00
47	46	48.00	44	44	48.00
48	44	48.00	52	43	49.80
49	52	49.80	58	50	51.40
50	58	51.40		57	

data are plotted in Figure 4-8. The three-week moving average has recovered by week 14, but the six-week average does not recover until week 18. Similar lags occur if the process changes from a constant to a growth or decline pattern.

Even if the mean stays constant, the moving average will change due to the noise. A large N is relatively unaffected by noise, but noise may change the forecast more dramatically if N is small, which is seen in Figure 4-8; during weeks 18 to 24, the three-week moving average changes due to the random noise more than the six-week moving average.

Choosing N is a trade-off between quick response to a process change and ignoring random fluctuations. If the process is relatively stable, choose a large N, although a smaller

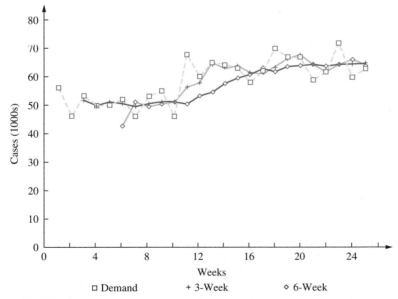

FIGURE 4-8
Comparing three- and six- week moving averages

N is better for a process that may be changing. For short-term forecasting, typical values of N are 5 to 7. Of course if you know the underlying process is not constant, a different model should be used.

5.1.3   SIMPLE EXPONENTIAL SMOOTHING. Suppose we want to calculate an N period moving average but no longer know d_{T-N+1}, which is needed in the update formula. Our only choice is to estimate it; using the moving average M_{T-1} as an estimate of d_{T-N+1} seems reasonable. Replacing d_{T-N+1} by M_{T-1}, the update equation becomes

$$M_T = M_{T-1} + \frac{(d_T - M_{T-1})}{N}$$

After collecting terms, we have

$$M_T = \frac{1}{N}d_T + (1 - \frac{1}{N})M_{T-1}$$

The advantage of this approach is that individual data points do not need to be kept; we calculate the forecast from the old forecast and the new data point.

This average is, strictly speaking, no longer a moving average. We can view it as a weighted average of the current data point and the previous estimate of the process mean. The weights do not have to be $1/N$ and $(1 - 1/N)$; to make the model general we will use $\alpha, 0 \le \alpha \le 1$, and $(1 - \alpha)$ as the weights and denote the estimate by S_T. This procedure is called **exponential smoothing.** The equation becomes

$$S_T = \alpha d_T + (1 - \alpha)S_{T-1}$$

As in other constant models, the forecast for period $T + k$ is

$$F_{T+k} = S_T$$

From the equation we see that α is the weight given to the most recent observation, so that a large weight will make the forecast more sensitive to the most recent data point. A smaller value will give more weight to an "average" value. To implement exponential smoothing at time T, we need a value for S_{T-1}. Although there are many ways to estimate S_{T-1}, the simplest is to average several past data points. Fortunately, the procedure is not very sensitive to this estimate.

Example 4-2. Simple exponential smoothing. Consider the data in Table 4-7. Averaging the demand from weeks 45 to 49 gives $S_{49} = 49.8$. Using d_{50} and $\alpha = 0.2$, we can compute S_{50} as

$$S_{50} = 0.2d_{50} + (1 - 0.2)S_{49} = 0.2 \times 58 + 0.8 \times 49.8 = 51.4$$

The forecast for the next week would be 51,400 cases of toothpaste. If the next weekly demand is 48, the new value of S would be

$$S_{51} = 0.2d_{51} + (1 - 0.2)S_{50} = 0.2 \times 48 + 0.8 \times 51.4 = 50.72$$

To gain some insight into exponential smoothing, expand S_T by substituting for S_{T-1}. This gives

$$S_T = \alpha d_T + (1 - \alpha)(\alpha d_{T-1} + (1 - \alpha)S_{T-2})$$

$$= \alpha d_T + \alpha(1 - \alpha)d_{T-1} + (1 - \alpha)^2 S_{T-2}$$

Now substituting for S_{T-2}, S_{T-3}, etc. gives

$$S_T = \alpha d_T + \alpha(1 - \alpha)d_{T-1} + \alpha(1 - \alpha)^2 d_{T-2} + \ldots + \alpha(1 - \alpha)^{T-1}d_1 + (1 - \alpha)^T S_0$$

$$= \alpha \sum_{t=0}^{T-1}(1 - \alpha)^t d_{T-t} + (1 - \alpha)^T S_0$$

We can view this equation as a "weighted" average of all the data points, but because $\alpha < 1$, the more recent data points count more towards the average. In fact, the weight is exponentially decreasing with the age of the data, hence the name exponential smoothing.

Figure 4-9 plots the weight given to a data point versus its age for four different values of α. Large values of α give greater weight to new data, and older data is quickly discounted. From Figure 4-9 we see that if $\alpha = 0.5$, the weight for a data point one period old is about 0.26, which is almost three times as large as the weight for the same data point if $\alpha = 0.1$. If we truly have a constant process, we would want a small value of α so that the random fluctuations are damped out. However, if we are unsure of the process, a larger value can be used. Typically, values of α between 0.1 and 0.3 are used; if larger values are needed, the assumption of a constant process is questionable, and more complex models should be considered.

The choice of α is a tradeoff between stability and response. We could conceivably determine "optimal" values for α if we can give "costs" of stability and responsiveness. A high cost of responding to random noise indicates that a smaller α should be used, whereas a high cost of not responding to a true change in the process would lead to a large α. Many forecasting programs will choose the smoothing parameter for the user. The data are divided into two groups; the first group is used to initialize the forecast procedure, and forecasts are made for the second group of data using a particular value of α. The results are tabulated and the experiment is repeated for a different α. The α that gave the most accurate results is chosen for the forecasting system.

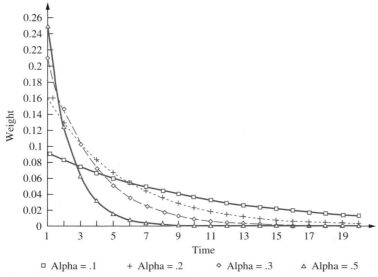

FIGURE 4-9
Exponential weights

To justify S_T as the forecast for a constant model, consider its expectation:

$$E[S_T] = E[\alpha \sum_{t=0}^{\infty} (1-\alpha)^t d_{T-t} + (1-\alpha)^T S_0]$$

$$= E[\alpha \sum_{t=0}^{\infty} (1-\alpha)^t d_{T-t}] + E[(1-\alpha)^T S_0]$$

The expectation of a constant is just the constant, giving

$$E[S_T] = \alpha \sum_{t=0}^{\infty} (1-\alpha)^t E[d_{T-t}] + (1-\alpha)^T S_0$$

As T gets large, $(1-\alpha)^T$ approaches zero, so the term with S_0 approaches zero and can be dropped, leaving

$$E[S_T] = \alpha \sum_{t=0}^{\infty} (1-\alpha)^t E[d_{T-t}]$$

Recall that, in our model, $d_t = a + \varepsilon_t$, where a is a constant and $E[\varepsilon_t] = 0$, so we have

$$E[d_{T-t}] = E[a + \varepsilon_{T-t}] = a + E[\varepsilon_{T-t}] = a$$

Because

$$\alpha \sum_{t=0}^{\infty} (1-\alpha)^t = \frac{\alpha}{1-(1-\alpha)} = 1$$

we have

$$E[S_T] = a$$

Thus, S_T is an estimate of the constant term of a constant model.

Define the weighted age of an observation as the weight given the observation in the forecast multiplied by the number of periods it is from the present. In a moving average, each of the N most recent observations is given equal weight $(1/N)$, and older observations are given no weight. Let the current observation be 0 periods old, let the previous observation be 1 period old, and so forth; the oldest observation that is counted in an N-period moving average is $N-1$ periods old. Thus the weighted average age of the data in an N-period moving average is

$$\bar{t} = \frac{0}{N} + \frac{1}{N} + \ldots + \frac{N-1}{N} = \frac{N-1}{2}$$

For exponential smoothing, define the age in the same way, but all data are counted in the estimate, albeit at different weights. The weight for the current observation is α, a one period old observation is $\alpha(1-\alpha)$, and so forth. For exponential smoothing, the weighted average age of an observation is

$$\bar{t} = 0\alpha + 1\alpha(1-\alpha) + 2\alpha(1-\alpha)^2 + \ldots$$

$$= \sum_{t=0}^{\infty} t(1-\alpha)^t$$

$$= \frac{(1-\alpha)}{\alpha}$$

TABLE 4-9
Equivalent N and α values

N	2	3	4	5	6	7	8
α	0.67	0.50	0.40	0.33	0.29	0.25	0.22
N	9	10	20	30	52	104	208
α	0.20	0.18	0.10	0.06	0.04	0.02	0.01

One way to equate moving average methods with exponential smoothing methods would be to have the same weighted average age. Set the two weighted average ages equal, and solve for α in terms of N. We have

$$\frac{1 - \alpha}{\alpha} = \frac{N - 1}{2}$$

which implies

$$\alpha = \frac{2}{N + 1}$$

Table 4-9 contains "equivalent" values of N and α. Using $N = \alpha = 1$ is the same as the last period demand (LPD) forecasting method. As N increases, α decreases.

If we need to have a large value of α or a small value of N, the assumption of a constant model may be questionable. Another common process, trend, can be modeled as a linear equation. We discuss this process, model, and associated solution methods in the next section.

5.2 Trend Process

Table 4-10 gives demand data for computer paper, and Figure 4-10 is a plot of the same data. Examining this data clearly indicates that the underlying process is not constant but is steadily increasing, which is not surprising, because more and more personal computers are in use. To accurately forecast this time series, a model that incorporates trend is necessary. The underlying model for a process with linear trend is given by

$$d_t = a + bt + \varepsilon_t$$

in which b is the slope of the trend and other notation is as previously defined. If b is positive,

TABLE 4-10
Computer paper sales (in cases)

Month	Sales	Month	Sales	Month	Sales
1	116	9	163	17	210
2	133	10	163	18	207
3	139	11	164	19	225
4	157	12	191	20	223
5	154	13	201	21	257
6	159	14	219	22	232
7	162	15	207	23	240
8	172	16	205	24	241

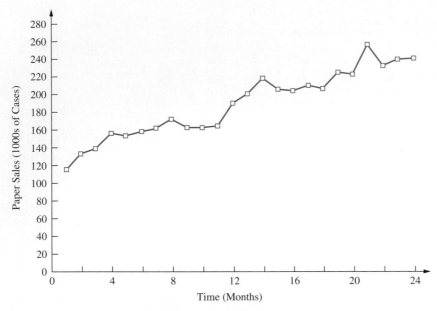

FIGURE 4-10
Computer paper sales

the process is increasing over time, but a negative b implies a decreasing process. We will discuss an increasing trend, but the methodology is also applicable to a decreasing trend.

To forecast when trend is present, we need to estimate the constant and the slope; there are many ways to do so, including regression and variations on moving averages and exponential smoothing. Here we discuss a modification of simple exponential smoothing for trend.

5.2.1   DOUBLE EXPONENTIAL SMOOTHING.   If we were to forecast a trend model using simple exponential smoothing, the forecast would be late reacting to the growth. Therefore, the forecast would tend to underestimate the actual demand. To correct this underestimate, we could estimate the slope and multiply this estimate by the number of periods in the future we wish to forecast. A simple estimate of the slope would be the difference between demands in two successive periods; however, the inherent random variation makes this estimate a poor one. To reduce the effect of randomness, we could use the difference of the averages computed at two successive periods. Using exponential smoothing, the estimate of the average at T is S_T, so the estimate of the slope at time T (see Figure 4-11) would be

$$B_T = (S_T - S_{T-1})$$

Taking this idea a step further, we could use exponential smoothing to update the trend estimate, which leads to double exponential smoothing, represented by the following set of equations:

$$S_T = \alpha d_T + (1 - \alpha)(S_{T-1} + B_{T-1})$$
$$B_T = \beta(S_T - S_{T-1}) + (1 - \beta)B_{T-1}$$
$$F_{T+k} = S_T + kB_T$$

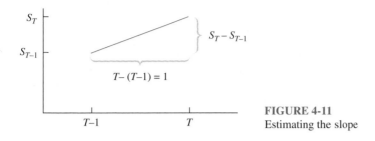

FIGURE 4-11
Estimating the slope

Note that the forecast for k periods in the future consists of the estimate for the constant plus a correction for the trend.

We must make a choice of two smoothing parameters, α and β, for double exponential smoothing. Comments regarding the choice of α for single smoothing are valid for both parameters here.

To implement double smoothing at time T, we need values of S_{T-1} and B_{T-1}. There are many ways to do this; we will discuss a simple one. First divide the data into two equal groups, and compute the average of each. This average is centered at the midpoint of the interval; if there were 12 points in the group, the average would be centered at 6.5. The difference in the two averages is the change in demand from the middle of each data set. To convert this difference to an estimate of the slope, divide it by the number of time periods separating the two averages. Then to get an estimate of the intercept, use the overall average plus the slope estimate per period times the number of periods from the midpoint to the current period. This process is easier to see by using an example.

Example 4-3. Double exponential smoothing. Develop a forecast of computer paper sales for months 25 and 30. If demand for month 25 is 259, update parameters and give forecasts for months 26 and 30.

Solution. Consider the data of Table 4-10. First, compute the averages of months 1 to 12, and 13 to 24. They are 156.08 and 222.25, respectively. The increase in average sales for the twelve-month period is $66.17 (= 222.25 - 156.08)$. Dividing this number by twelve gives 5.51, the average increase per month. Thus the estimate of the slope at time 24 will be $B_{24} = 5.51$. To get an estimate of the intercept, calculate the overall average of the 24 points, which is 189.16. This average is centered at month 12.5. To bring it up to the current time add the trend adjustment of 5.51 cases per month times $(24 - 12.5)$ months. Our estimate of the intercept is

$$S_{24} = 189.16 + 5.51(24 - 12.5) = 258.09$$

Once we have our initial values, we can forecast for future periods. The forecast for period 25 is

$$F_{25} = S_{24} + 1 \times B_{24} = 258.09 + 1 \times 5.51 = 263.60$$

Similarly, forecasting for period 30 gives

$$F_{30} = 258.09 + 6 \times 5.51 = 291.17$$

When actual demand for month 25 is known, we update our estimates. If the actual demand for month 25 is 259, and $\alpha = \beta = 0.1$, the new estimate of the intercept will be

$$S_T = \alpha d_T + (1 - \alpha)S_{T-1} = \alpha d_{25} + (1 - \alpha)(S_{24} + B_{24})$$

or $$S_{25} = 0.1 \times 259 + (1 - 0.1) \times (258.09 + 5.51) = 263.14$$

The new estimate of the slope will be

$$B_T = \beta(S_T - S_{T-1}) + (1 - \beta)B_{T-1} = \beta(S_{25} - S_{24}) + (1 - \beta)B_{24}$$

or $B_{25} = 0.1 \times (263.14 - 258.09) + (1 - 0.1) \times 5.51 = 5.46$

The forecast for period 26 would be given by

$$F_{26} = 263.14 + 1 \times 5.46 = 268.60$$

and the forecast for month 30 is now

$$F_{30} = 263.14 + 5 \times 5.46 = 290.46$$

Applications (see Section 9) often require forecasts for hundreds or even thousands of items. Generating thousands of forecasts for many different time series can require significant computer time. Double exponential smoothing is very simple to implement and requires little storage and time. The accuracy is acceptable for most short-term forecasting applications.

5.2.2 OTHER METHODS. There are other methods to forecast a process with trend. Typically, they differ in how estimates of the constant and slope are determined. For example, the double moving average method is similar to double exponential smoothing; it estimates the constant by a standard moving average and the slope by a moving average of the previous estimates of the slope, corrected for the constant.

Regression, with time as the independent variable, can also be used. Let d_t be the demand in period $t, t = 1, 2, \ldots, T$. Because the independent variable is a time index, the regression equations simplify, becoming

$$\hat{b} = \frac{\left(T \sum_{t=1}^{T} t d_t - \frac{1}{2}\big(T(T+1)\big) \sum_{t=1}^{T} d_t\right)}{\frac{1}{6}\big(T^2(T+1)(2T+1)\big) - \frac{1}{4}\big(T^2(T+1)^2\big)}$$

and $$\hat{a} = \left(\frac{1}{T} \sum_{t=1}^{T} d_t\right) - \left[\frac{\hat{b}}{2}(T+1)\right]$$

Because $\hat{a}$ is computed for time zero, to bring it to the current time T we have to add $\hat{b}T$ to it. Then the forecast made at time t for k periods ahead would be

$$F_{t+k} = \hat{a} + \hat{b}k$$

Care should be taken in using regression to forecast trend processes with time as the independent variable. There may not be an underlying cause and effect, or even correlation, between time and the dependent variable. Sales may be increasing over time, but time is not causing the increase; good economic conditions may cause the increase in sales. If the economy turns sour, sales likely will decrease, but a regression model with time as the independent variable will continue to predict an increase for some time. To forecast with time-based regression, we must extrapolate from our observed region, which is known to be dangerous. Even so, time-based regression is still used.

5.3 Seasonal Process

Outdoor Furniture makes swings. People typically buy more swings in the warmer months than they do in the cooler months, so sales change with the seasons. Suppose Outdoor

TABLE 4-11
Quarterly sales of Outdoor Furniture's swings

	Year		
Quarter	1	2	3
1	60	69	84
2	234	266	310
3	163	188	212
4	50	59	64
Yearly average	126.75	145.50	167.50
Overall average			146.58

Furniture's swings are very good, and word-of-mouth advertising is increasing the number of people who buy them. Their data, which reflect seasonality and trend is given in Table 4-11 and plotted in Figure 4-12.

Here, a year can be divided into four seasons, each three months or a quarter of a year. Many processes naturally have some number of seasons in a year. If the time periods are weeks, the year would have 52 seasons. Periods of months and quarters have 12 and 4 seasons in a year, respectively. Other processes may have a season that is not based on years, but there should be some underlying explanation for the seasonality. The methods presented here can be used for any season length.

To highlight the seasonality and trend, we plot by season in Figure 4-13. Demand for each quarter of the first year is below the demand of the same quarter for the second year, and the second year value is below the third year value, so demand appears to be growing. A good model must consider the constant portion of demand, the trend, and seasonality.

Several models consider all three factors; we will discuss a popular multiplicative model proposed by Winters (1960). Formally, the model is

$$d_t = (a + bt)c_t + \varepsilon_t$$

where a = the constant portion
b = the slope of the trend component

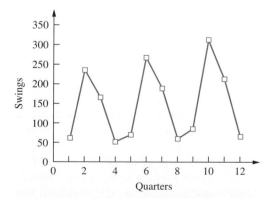

FIGURE 4-12
Seasonal data with trend

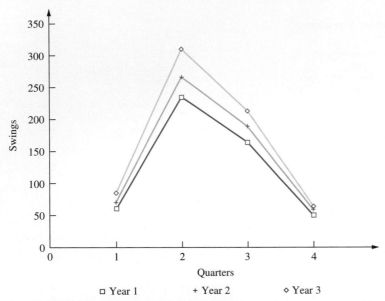

FIGURE 4-13
Seasonal data with trend plotted by season

c_t = the seasonal factor for period t
ε_t = the uncontrollable randomness

The forecasting method is to estimate the parameters of the model and use them to generate the forecast. We estimate the constant component independently of the trend and seasonal factors, so we call it the deseasonalized constant. Likewise, the trend factor should be independent of the seasonal factors. The seasonal factors can be viewed as a percentage of the constant and trend components for period t; if demand in a particular period of the season is lower than the constant/trend component, the seasonal factor will be less than one, and if demand is higher, it will be greater than one. The seasonal factors must sum to the number of seasons per year. To forecast, we get initial estimates of the components of the model and update them using exponential smoothing.

Let d_t = the demand in period t
$\quad L$ = the number of seasons in a year (or other time frame)
$\quad T$ = the number of periods of data available; $T = mL$ where m is the number of full years of data available
$\quad S_t$ = the estimate for the constant term a calculated at period t
$\quad B_t$ = the estimate for the trend term b calculated at time t
$\quad C_t$ = the estimate of the seasonal component for period t

To start the procedure, we need an initial value for S_T. A naive estimate is an average of one or more *complete* seasons of data. Partial seasons should not be used; using only the first 9 data points might give a poor estimate because larger or smaller demand in the first quarter does not reflect "average" demand. With trend, averaging one or more complete years of historical data values does not give an initial estimate of a. This average includes the "lower" demand at the beginning as well as the "higher" demand at the end of the historical data. The

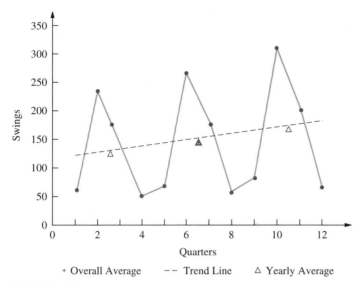

FIGURE 4-14
Fitting the trend in seasonal data

"+" in Figure 4-14 is the overall average of demand and is located at 6.5, the midpoint of the historical data. To determine the constant portion of the process at time T we must correct it for the trend. Therefore, to calculate S_T, the estimate of a, we need B_T, the estimate of b.

We need at least two complete years of data to calculate B_T; any less will not differentiate between trend and seasonal components. Compute the average demand for each of the last two years, and subtract the average of the older year from the average of the most recent year. The result is the "growth" over the two years, which should be converted to a growth per season by dividing by L, the number of seasons in a year. If there are more than two years of data, any two can be used to estimate the slope. If the first and last years are used, with m years of data available, divide by $(m - 1)L$ rather than L to convert to a per period growth.

Example 4-4. Initialize B_T and S_T for Outdoor Furniture. Determine the initial parameters for Winters' seasonal method using the data in Table 4-11.

Solution. The average of the third year (last four data points) is

$$\overline{d}_3 = \frac{d_9 + d_{10} + d_{11} + d_{12}}{L} = \frac{84 + 310 + 212 + 64}{4} = 167.5$$

The average for the second year is $\overline{d}_2 = 145.5$. Subtracting the year 2 average from the year 3 average gives the growth for one year. These averages are "centered" in the middle of the years, periods 6.5 and 10.5, respectively; so they are a year apart. Dividing by 4 converts to a growth per period. We have

$$B_T = \frac{\overline{d}_3 - \overline{d}_2}{L} = \frac{167.5 - 145.5}{4} = 5.5$$

Given an estimate of the trend, we can compute an estimate of the constant component. The average of all the data points is centered in the middle of the observations at $(T - 1)/2$,

(6.5 in Figure 4-14), or $(T - 1)/2$ periods from T, the present time. We can estimate the constant portion of the model at time T by multiplying the trend per period, B_T, by $(T - 1)/2$, the number of periods between the center and T. See Figure 4-14.

For our example, the overall average is

$$\overline{D} = \frac{1}{T} \sum_{t=1}^{T} d_t = \frac{1}{12} \sum_{t=1}^{12} d_t = 146.58$$

Because there are twelve periods of data, D is centered at period 6.5, so our initial estimate of the constant term, S_T, at period twelve would be

$$S_T = \overline{D} + \left(\frac{T-1}{2}\right) B_T = 146.58 + \left(\frac{11}{2}\right) 5.5 = 176.83$$

Once we have S_T and B_T, a naive estimate of the seasonal factor would seem to be the demand in a period divided by the constant term. However, we must correct for the trend part of the constant.

The estimate for the constant portion, S_T, was computed to reflect the process at time T. Intuitively, the constant portion of the process at $T - 1$ should be B_T smaller, and at $T - 2$ it should be $2B_T$ smaller. In general, an estimate of the constant portion of the process for period t ($t < T$) is the estimate of the constant at time T minus the estimate of trend times the number of periods, i.e., $S_T - B_T \times (T - t)$. Once adjusted for the trend, we can divide the actual demand by this adjusted value to get an estimate of the seasonal factor. We compute the seasonal factors using the formula

$$C_t = \frac{d_t}{S_T - B_T(T - t)}$$

in which C_t is the estimate of c_t. Seasonal factors for the same season of each year are averaged to damp out noise.

These seasonal factors, however, do not necessarily sum to L. To normalize them, first determine R, the ratio of the length of the season to the sum of the seasonal factors:

$$R = L \Big/ \sum_{t=T-L+1}^{T} C_t$$

Multiply this ratio by the old seasonal factors to get the new ones:

$$C'_t = R \times C_t \qquad t = T - L + 1, \ T - L + 2, \ldots, T$$

The new factors always sum to the number of periods in the season.

Example 4-5. Initializing the seasonal factors. Calculate the initial seasonal factors for the data in Table 4-11.

Solution. To compute an estimate of the seasonal factor for period 1 in our example, divide d_1 by the adjusted constant term for period 1. The adjusted constant term will be

$$S_T - B_T \times (12 - 1) = 176.83 - 5.5 \times 11 = 116.33$$

Dividing $d_1 = 60$ by 116.33 gives $C_1 = 0.52$. Thus, the first quarter sales are about 52 percent of the average value. We then compute the seasonal factors for the first quarter of years 2 and 3 and we set C_9 equal to the average of the three. Similar calculations, done on a spreadsheet, for the rest of the data are given in Table 4-12. The last column of the table normalizes the seasonal factors.

TABLE 4-12
Calculating initial seasonal factors

Quarter	Year 1	Year 2	Year 3	Average	Normalized
1	0.52	0.50	0.52	0.51	0.51
2	1.92	1.85	1.88	1.88	1.87
3	1.28	1.26	1.26	1.25	1.25
4	0.38	0.38	0.36	0.37	0.37
Sum				4.02	4.00

As new data become available, we can update our estimates with exponential smoothing. Let the smoothing constants for the constant term, the trend, and the seasonal factors be α, β, and γ, respectively. Given S_{T-1}, B_{T-1}, and $C_{T-L+1}, C_{T-L+2}, \ldots, C_{T-1}$, when we know d_T we can determine S_T, B_T, and C_T. The estimate for the constant term S_T will be

$$S_T = \alpha\left(\frac{d_T}{C_{T-L}}\right) + (1 - \alpha)(S_{T-1} + B_{T-1})$$

To update the estimate of the trend component, use the equation

$$B_T = \beta(S_T - S_{T-1}) + (1 - \beta)B_{T-1}$$

Finally, the updated seasonal factors will be estimated by

$$C_T = \gamma\left(\frac{d_T}{S_T}\right) + (1 - \gamma)C_{T-L}$$

The forecast for k periods from now ($k \leq L$) is given by

$$F_{T+k} = (S_T + kB_T)C_{T+k-L}$$

If we wish to forecast more than one season in the future, i.e., $k > L$, then $T + k - L$ is greater than T, and the specified estimate of the seasonal factor is unknown. Instead, we use the most recently calculated value for the corresponding period. Let g be the smallest integer greater than or equal to k/L; we last computed that seasonal estimate g seasons ago. Then the proper seasonal factor to use in the forecast equation is the one computed at time $T + k - gL$. The equation becomes

$$F_{T+k} = (S_T + kB_T)C_{T+k-gL}$$

Example 4-6. Forecasting with Winters method. If d_{13} is 97 and $\alpha = 0.15$, $\beta = 0.1$, and $\gamma = 0.2$, update the parameters and forecast for periods 14 and 17.

Solution. Set $S_{12} = 176.83$, $B_{12} = 5.5$, $C_9 = 0.51$, $C_{10} = 1.87$, $C_{11} = 1.25$, and $C_{12} = 0.37$. The new estimate for the constant is

$$S_{13} = \alpha\left(\frac{d_{13}}{C_9}\right) + (1 - \alpha)S_{12} = 0.15\left(\frac{97}{0.51}\right) + 0.85 \times 176.83 = 178.83$$

We can now update the trend component:

$$B_{13} = \beta(S_{13} - S_{12}) + (1 - \beta)B_{12} = 0.1(178.83 - 176.83) + 0.9 \times 5.5 = 5.15$$

Finally, we can compute a new seasonal estimate for period 13, which is the first period in the year. It is

$$C_{13} = \gamma\left(\frac{d_{13}}{S_{13}}\right) + (1 - \gamma)C_9 = 0.2\left(\frac{97}{178.83}\right) + 0.8 \times 0.51 = 0.516$$

Because rounding C_{13} to 0.52 gives a different value, we need to renormalize the seasonal factors. The new seasonal factors are 0.52, 1.86, 1.25, and 0.37.

To forecast for period 14, we would have

$$F_{14} = (S_{13} + 1 \times B_{13})C_{10} = (178.83 + 5.15)1.86 \approx 342.21$$

Similarly the forecast for period 17 would be

$$F_{17} = (S_{13} + 4 \times B_{13})C_{13} = (178.83 + 4 \times 5.15)0.52 \approx 103.71$$

In both forecasts, the seasonal factor for the corresponding period in the previous season was used. If we wish to forecast for period $20(k = 7)$, the smallest integer greater than 7/4 is 2, so we would use the seasonal factor for period $13 + 7 - 2 \times 4 = 12$.

We now summarize this forecasting procedure. Let L be the season length with m complete seasons of data available. There are $T = mL$ data points, $d_1, d_2, \ldots, d_T$.

Step 1. Calculate the average of each of the last two seasons of data, $\overline{d}_m$ and $\overline{d}_{m-1}$, from the formula

$$\overline{d}_i = \frac{\displaystyle\sum_{t=(i-1)L+1}^{iL} d_t}{L} \qquad i = m - 1, m$$

Now calculate B_T

$$B_T = \frac{\overline{d}_m - \overline{d}_{m-1}}{L}$$

Step 2. Calculate the overall average

$$\overline{D} = \frac{1}{T}\sum_{t=1}^{T} d_t$$

and use it and B_T to calculate S_T, the estimate of the constant as

$$S_T = \overline{D} + \frac{T-1}{2}B_T$$

Step 3. Calculate the seasonal factors using the equation

$$C_t = \frac{1}{m}\sum_{i=0}^{m-1} \frac{d_{t-iL}}{S_T - (T - [t - iL])B_T} \qquad t = T - L + 1, T - L + 2, \ldots, T$$

Step 4. To forecast k periods ahead, use

$$F_{T+k} = (S_T + kB_T)C_{T+k-gL}$$

where g is the smallest integer greater than or equal to k/L.

Step 5. When a new data point is obtained, set $T = T + 1$ and update the forecast parameters:

$$S_T = \alpha\left(\frac{d_T}{C_{T-L}}\right) + (1 - \alpha)(S_{T-1} + B_{T-1})$$

$$B_T = \beta(S_T - S_{T-1}) + (1 - \beta)B_{T-1}$$

$$C_T = \gamma\left(\frac{d_T}{S_T}\right) + (1 - \gamma)C_{T-L}$$

Other models are possible. If trend is not present, drop b from the model and B_T from all calculations. A drawback to the multiplicative model with trend is that the trend increases the amplitude of the seasonal pattern. Additive models,

$$d_t = a + bt + c_t + \varepsilon_t$$

do not have this limitation. Estimating the parameters and forecasting is very similar to the multiplicative models (see, e.g., Montgomery et al., 1990).

SECTION 5   PROBLEMS

4.24. Consider the data:

Period	1	2	3	4	5	6
Demand	107	93	106	98	100	96

Use the first five periods to forecast for period six using the following:

(a) LPD
(b) The average
(c) A three-period moving average
(d) Exponential smoothing with $\alpha = 0.2$
(e) Based on this prediction which method is better and why?
(f) What is the forecast for period 10 using each method?

4.25. Demand for an item is given below. Using simple exponential smoothing with $\alpha = 0.15$ and the forecast for period 13 is 255.

t	d_t	t	d_t	t	d_t	t	d_t
1	239	4	345	7	227	10	352
2	325	5	254	8	221	11	241
3	268	6	216	9	208	12	420

(a) Give a forecast for periods 14 and 20.
(b) What would an "equivalent" moving average be?
(c) Does a simple moving average seem appropriate for these data?

4.26. We are using Holt's method (double exponential smoothing) to forecast demand for an athletic shoe by month, with $\alpha = 0.1$ and $\beta = 0.2$. Our last estimates of the intercept and slope were 1067.2 and 21.6, respectively. This month's demand is 1100.

    (a) Give your forecast for next month.
    (b) Give your forecast for three months from now.

4.27. Heather Foods, Inc., makes snack foods, which sell mostly to convenient stores. The following table shows the monthly observation of sale of Heathers's corn nuts for 1992 and 1993 in thousands of bags. Heathers Foods has been selling corn nuts for 10 years, and the planning department treats the demand for corn nuts as a constant process. Determine the forecast for January of 1994 using the following methods:

    (a) LDP
    (b) Average of all data
    (c) Moving average with $N = 6$
    (d) Suppose the actual demand for January 1994 is 55.2 thousand bags. Compute the forecast for February using the update equation for the moving average with $N = 6$.

Observation	Month	Demand	Observation	Month	Demand
1	January	48.5	13	January	48.9
2	February	46.0	14	February	49.5
3	March	54.4	15	March	59.0
4	April	49.8	16	April	56.0
5	May	48.1	17	May	49.3
6	June	55.0	18	June	58.5
7	July	47.7	19	July	53.0
8	August	45.2	20	August	48.6
9	September	51.0	21	September	50.8
10	October	47.5	22	October	53.4
11	November	49.1	23	November	49.8
12	December	50.8	24	December	56.3

4.28. Suppose Heathers Foods wants to begin forecasting using simple exponential smoothing with a weighted average age of the data equal to that of their moving average forecasts. Calculate the January 1994 forecast using the overall average for S_{23}. Compute the February 1994 forecast if January 1994 demand is 55.2 thousand bags.

4.29. The demand for all-terrain bicycles had been steadily increasing since 1989. In the following table are the sales per quarter of mountain bikes produced by Canyon and Cactus Cycles since the second quarter of 1989.

    (a) Plot the data and verify that the model for linear trend is acceptable. Draw a line through the plotted data and obtain a visual estimate of a and b.
    (b) Estimate the parameters of the model in preparation for double exponential smoothing.
    (c) Forecast sales for the third quarter of 1996 using these initial estimates.
    (d) Forecast sales for the fourth quarter of 1996 using alpha $= 0.3$ and beta $= 0.25$ if sales in the third quarter of 1996 were equal to 234.
    (e) Use linear regression to estimate the parameters and forecast the third quarter of 1996.

Observation	Year	Quarter	Demand	Observation	Year	Quarter	Demand
1	1989	2	16	16	1993	1	147
2		3	73	17		2	142
3		4	61	18		3	134
4	1990	1	57	19		4	159
5		2	43	20	1994	1	181
6		3	44	21		2	168
7		4	68	22		3	168
8	1991	1	68	23		4	188
9		2	73	24	1995	1	186
10		3	84	25		2	189
11		4	93	26		3	184
12	1992	1	128	27		4	224
13		2	100	28	1996	1	207
14		3	130	29		2	223
15		4	148				

4.30. CompValu Corporation is a major manufacturer of computers and peripherals. Their sales (in millions of dollars) since 1980 are given below. When sales exceed $60 million, a new production facility must be built. When should a new plant be completed?

Year	1980	1981	1982	1983	1984	1985	1986	1987	1988
Demand	14.0	15.4	15.8	19.3	21.5	25.1	27.0	27.1	31.1

Year	1989	1990	1991	1992	1993	1994	1995	1996
Demand	33.9	34.9	36.2	39.3	44.8	45.3	46.8	48.3

4.31. The following are data from the Bureau of Labor Statistics on thousands of workers suffering from repetitive trauma disorders. Give a model and forecast for 1996.

Year	1982	1983	1984	1985	1986	1987	1988	1989	1990	1991	1992	1993
Number	22.6	26.7	34.7	37.0	45.5	72.9	115.3	146.9	185.4	223.6	281.8	302.0

4.32. Develop the equations to estimate the intercept and slope of a trend model by double moving averages. Apply them to the data of Problem 4.29.

4.33. Killian Corporation makes hot chocolate mix. Sales, in thousands of pounds, follow a seasonal pattern. Quarterly forecasts are made using exponential smoothing for a seasonal model without trend. Currently $S_4 = 186.5$, $c_1 = 1.4$, $c_2 = 0.6$, $c_3 = 0.3$, and $c_4 = 1.7$.

(a) Give forecasts for the next four quarters.
(b) Demand for the first quarter of the new year is 285. Update the parameters and give forecasts for the next four quarters if $\alpha = 0.25$ and $\gamma = 0.15$.

4.34. SafSeal extrudes plastic tamper-proof seals for consumer products. The extruders run best at a temperature of 68°. The plant is equipped with a gas furnace for cold weather and electric air conditioners for hot weather. For this reason, the electric usage is seasonal with a peak in the summer months and a drop in the winter months.
(a) Using a multiplicative model, estimate the parameters.
(b) Forecast the electric usage for each quarter of 1996.

Observation	Year	Season	Demand	Observation	Year	Season	Demand
1	1992	Winter	1752	9	1994	Winter	1783
2		Spring	3341	10		Spring	2324
3		Summer	4910	11		Summer	4377
4		Fall	3704	12		Fall	4042
5	1993	Winter	1738	13	1995	Winter	1741
6		Spring	2037	14		Spring	2712
7		Summer	4444	15		Summer	4972
8		Fall	3308	16		Fall	3839

4.35. Sue is a recently hired employee at the Southeast distribution center of Rash, Inc. She feels a better safety program is needed and has collected data of accidents per quarter. Give Sue a forecast of accidents by quarter for next year, and justify your model and numbers so Sue can effectively present her proposal to management.

		Accidents		
Quarter	1	2	3	4
Year 1	42	58	74	44
Year 2	48	70	95	50

4.36. Lily Pads Inc. makes swimming and water sport accessories for children. In 1992 they introduced their EZ Glide-On Flippers, and sales during the summer months have increased steadily since the summer of 1992.

Observation	Year	Season	Demand
1	1992	Spring	23
2		Summer	51
3		Fall	12
4	1993	Winter	7
5		Spring	30
6		Summer	67
7		Fall	18
8	1994	Winter	14
9		Spring	37
10		Summer	81
11		Fall	21
12	1995	Winter	12

(a) Plot all data and note seasonality. Plot each year's data separately and note increasing trend.
(b) Estimate S_T, B_T, and the seasonal factors.
(c) Forecast the sales for spring and summer of 1995.

4.37. If Lily Pad sales data for 1995/1996 are as given, forecast the sales for summer of 1996 and winter of 1997.

Quarter	Demand	Quarter	Demand
Spring 1995	46	Fall 1995	24
Summer 1995	99	Winter 1996	13

4.38. SnugFit is a Swedish company making ski boots from composite materials. After the boots had a slow start in the market, skiers have recognized that SnugFits's ski boots are excellent and the price is only about 15 percent higher than other brands. The binding department adds the bindings to the boot and last year had 25 workers. The worker efficiency was 83 percent last fall. Three of these workers have resigned. Given the last four years of demand data, how many workers would you recommend hiring for the coming winter? Would you recommend a different number for the spring, summer, and fall next year?

Quarter	Demand (boxes)			
	Year 1	Year 2	Year 3	Year 4
Winter	156	167	179	188
Spring	23	29	46	56
Summer	49	38	69	91
Fall	220	247	238	248

4.39. Bradley and Hillier make wooden baseball bats used primarily in professional baseball. The procurement department wants to sign a long-term contract with the supplier of varnish. This contract would specify the amount (in thousands of gallons) of varnish B& H would purchase each quarter for the next two years. Actual deliveries would be made weekly, but the total for the quarter must be close to the contracted figures. Varnish usage (in thousands of gallons) for the prior three years is given. Give procurement advice as to the amount of varnish to contract each quarter for the next two years.

Year	Quarter	Gallons	Year	Quarter	Gallons	Year	Quarter	Gallons
1	1	432	2	1	409	3	1	425
	2	323		2	406		2	343
	3	135		3	168		3	182
	4	2		4	38		4	8

6 OTHER FORECASTING METHODS

Many other forecasting methods have proven useful, and although the scope of this book prohibits us from discussing them all, we introduce several of them. Details can be found in the references.

6.1 Focus Forecasting Method

Focus forecasting, as defined by Smith (1978), is based on two fundamental ideas. One is that people prefer simple methods that they can understand, and another is that what worked well last time will likely work well this time. One way to combine these two ideas is to use several simple methods to generate a forecast and use the forecast that gave the best results in the prior period.

Often, the forecasting methods used are very intuitive. Some examples of generating forecasts would be last period's demand, the demand for the same period last year, 90 percent of last period's demand, average demand for the last three periods, simple exponential smoothing, or simply the manager's estimate. It is not difficult to come up with many other methods of this type.

The forecast actually used is the forecast of the method that did the best last period, and there are several ways to define the "best". A simple one is to calculate the absolute value of the difference between the forecast and the actual demand for last period. The forecasting procedure with the smallest difference becomes the champion, and its forecast is used for the next period. Of course the next period may have a new champion, depending on the performance of the forecasting methods this period.

Example 4-7. Focus forecasting. Use focus forecasting to determine a forecast for toothpaste in period 51 using data from Table 4-7.

Solution. Suppose we use five methods to forecast: last period's demand, 90 percent of last period's demand, 110 percent of last period's demand, a three-period moving average, and simple exponential smoothing. These forecasts for period 50 are given in Table 4-13, along with the actual demand for period 50 and the absolute difference of forecast and demand for each method. Because 110 percent of last period's demand would have given the forecast with the smallest error, we use it to forecast for period 51. That is

$$F_{51} = 1.1 \times 58 = 63.8 \approx 64$$

TABLE 4-13
Focus forecasting example

Method	F_{50}	d_{50}	$|F_{50} - d_{50}|$
LDP	52.0	58	6.0
90% LDP	46.8	58	11.2
110% LDP	57.2	58	0.8
3PMA	47.3	58	10.7
ES	49.8	58	8.2

Another way to implement this type of approach is to average all forecasts to get a single forecast. Using this approach with our previous example would give a forecast of 50.6 for period 51, which would be better for this period than the focus forecast.

The basic concept of focus forecasting is to use several simple methods. Newbold and Granger (1974) reinforce the concept, showing that better forecasts often result from using several techniques. Further justification is provided by Armstrong (1984), who cites literature indicating that simple forecasting techniques often give better forecasts than complicated methods in actual implementations.

6.2 Qualitative Methods

There are several qualitative methods that we did not discuss, including scenario writing and cross-impact analysis. A brief discussion of each follows.

Scenario writing is used to paint a picture of how the present will evolve into the future rather than to get a single number; it is often used in conjunction with Delphi. Scenario writing begins by trying to identify a set of possible future occurrences that are plausible. A set of scenarios, each based on a possible future occurrence, is written up. Each scenario is examined to determine its probability of occurrence, and contingency plans for the most likely ones are developed. Scenario writing is best suited for use in long-term, macro situations, typified by uncertainty, lack of data, and unquantifiable factors. It is especially useful to estimate future demand, technological innovations, or market position under a variety of economic and political conditions. Barron and Targett (1985), Huss (1988), and Schnaars (1987) provide more detail on scenario writing.

Georgia Power used scenarios to determine an expansion plan for its power generation capacity (Goldfarb and Huss, 1988). The study identified 14 major factors influencing electric consumption: GNP growth; productivity growth; T-bill rates; population; ratio of manufacturing to service employment; industrial electricity use; average electricity price; federal energy policy; acid rain legislation; nuclear power options; prices of oil, gas, and coal; and GPC return on common equity. Three scenarios—one each for high, moderate, and low economic growth—were developed. Likely values for each factor under the assumed economic conditions were determined and an expansion plan was developed for each of the three scenarios. Scenarios facilitated greater management involvement, integrated the separate planning functions within the company, and provided a forum for discussing the critical planning options in light of expert opinions.

An American company used scenarios to forecast demand for information technology in Europe (Millet, 1992), and 20 critical factors were identified by experts in the field. Assessment of these factors led to four scenarios, and after reviewing the scenarios, the company's management took a variety of actions, among them, making a commitment to maintain and expand its Brussels office.

A cross-impact analysis is often used to examine the results of a Delphi study. The cross-impact analysis indicates the scenarios to be written up. This procedure takes a broad view—like scenario writing—and assesses the probability of occurrences of certain future events that may interact and affect future decisions.

The first step is to determine critical events related to the subject of interest, which are narrowed down to a manageable number. A matrix is formed with each row representing some occurrence; a column represents the same occurrence as its corresponding row. Initially, the nature of the interaction between each event or factor is written in the matrix. An up arrow indicates a positive influence, and a down arrow indicates a negative influence. The probability of each event is estimated, and the probabilities of two events occurring together are estimated and become elements of the matrix.

> **Example 4-8. Cross-impact analysis.** A company producing solar panels to convert solar energy into electricity can purchase a new production process that will only be economical if demand increases by at least 30 percent in the next three years. How should they make this decision?

Solution. Time-series forecasting may not give a good indication of the increase because technological advancements, government regulations, and economic factors could totally change the picture; cross-impact analysis, on the other hand, is an appropriate forecasting method. For simplicity, we will only consider three events: a more efficient electric motor (MEM), government tax credits on solar power due to environmental concerns (GTC), and rising costs of alternative fuels (HCF).

	MEM	GTC	HCF
MEM	—	⇓	⇓
GTC	⇑	—	⇑
HCF	⇑	—	—

If a better motor is built, less of the alternative fuels will be demanded, lowering their cost. Reduced use of fossil fuels will help the environment, thus decreasing the chance the government offers tax credits for solar power. Other influences are determined to complete the influence portion of the cross-impact matrix.

The probability that a more efficient motor is developed is estimated to be 0.2. If the government institutes solar tax credits, more researchers will work on such a motor and the probability will increase to 0.3. Higher alternative fuel costs will stimulate this research, resulting in a probability of 0.4 that a more efficient motor will be developed. The remainder of the probabilities in the matrix are determined similarly.

	Prob	MEM	GTC	HCF
MEM	.2	—	.2	.6
GTC	.3	.3	—	.7
HCF	.8	.4	—	—

The matrix can be simulated to explore various outcomes. Using different values of the probabilities can determine the sensitivity of the result to the probability assessment. Insensitive factors can be dropped, and more effort can be spent on estimating the probability of sensitive factors. Scenarios for likely outcomes can be written, and contingency plans can be made.

Cross-impact analysis has been used in the European automobile industry (Vickers, 1992), the European information technology market (Millet, 1992), the demand for electric power (Goldfarb and Huss, 1988), and environmental protection legislation (Beasley, 1984). Schuler et al. (1991) present a typical cross-impact study. The Canadian lumber industry faced a declining quality of logs and feared a decline in sales. Several processing innovations and product innovations might help alleviate this problem, so a cross-impact matrix including factors for innovations, government regulations, and possible competitors' actions were developed. Technological investment strategies and comparisons were conducted for the resulting six scenarios. A mixed strategy of investment in both processing and product technologies was identified as the best approach to maintain and increase demand.

6.3 Causal Methods

Regression models are widely used in causal forecasting. Other methods are problem specific and would include simultaneous equation systems and simulation systems.

Simultaneous systems are like regression methods, but rather than a single equation, they are composed of several simultaneous equations. Econometric models, used to forecast and explain complicated economic phenomena, are simultaneous systems. Regression models have one dependent variable, which is a function of one or more independent variables. The independent variables are exogenous to the model; their values are known from other information. Simultaneous systems typically have several equations, and a dependent variable in one equation may be an independent variable in another. Thus variables are interdependent.

As an example, suppose we wish to forecast sales. Sales are determined by many factors, including the state of the economy, price, availability, and quality of the item and advertising. We may postulate a relationship using demand as the dependent variable and the other factors as independent variables. However, the independent variables may affect each other. For example, price is related to cost and cost may be related to production quantities. High demand may reduce the cost through economies of scale, thus reducing price and creating even higher demand. The model may consist of several equations relating the variables, and the equations may or may not be linear.

To construct a forecasting system from simultaneous equations, we must decide which variables are important and determine the form of the model. Estimating parameters is no longer a regression problem. If the equations can be manipulated so that one variable is a function of independent exogenous variables, regression can by applied to that equation. Once the dependent variable is expressed in terms of the exogenous variables, it can be substituted into another equation, and the procedure can be repeated. If such substitutions are not possible, all parameters must be estimated simultaneously. Sometimes, initial estimates are chosen, and several iterations of least squares are carried out, until the estimates do not change.

There have been many applications of simultaneous systems used in forecasting; for example, Goss (1990) developed a simultaneous equations model of the Australian wool market. The model contains functional relationships for inventories, consumption, and the activities of hedgers and speculators in wool futures. Coefficients are estimated by three-stage least squares, with correction for first-order serial correlation. The model provides good intra- and post-sample forecasts of most variables. A dynamic simultaneous-equations model to predict account balances gives better forecast accuracy than ARIMA models (Lin, 1992). Other examples include a macro model of Italy's economy using a nonlinear system of simultaneous equations (Calzolari and Panattoni, 1990) and a simultaneous equations model to predict prices for the Japanese, U.S., and U.K. stock markets, which incorporates the interaction of intermarket returns (Koch and Koch, 1994).

The major advantage of simultaneous systems is that the level of detail is controlled. If many factors need to be included, they can be. If interdependencies exist, this approach is necessary. As with many modeling efforts, developing the model produces much insight into the phenomena. Unfortunately, these models are technically challenging, both in construction and solution. They can be computationally expensive, and data collection costs may also be high. For details on this procedure, see Fildes (1985), Levenbach and Cleary (1984), or Makridakis and Wheelwright (1978).

Simulation methods mimic behavior of a system. These models can be based on a variety of relationships and usually consider stochastic elements of the problem. Like the equations in a simultaneous system, the interrelationships in a simulation model are highly dependent on the system under study. Great detail, and hence cost, is usually required for these approaches. These methods can be used when 'causes'can be determined and a proper model constructed. Toedter (1992) uses simulation to estimate the coefficients of a large, nonlinear, interdependent system to forecast for the Bundesbank. It considers uncertainty due to residuals, coefficient estimates, and exogenous variable forecasts. Empirical results suggest that the simulation is superior to forecasts obtained from deterministic simultaneous systems.

6.4 Time-Series Methods

There are three additional time-series methods that deserve mention: autoregressive integrated moving averages (ARIMA), Bayesian methods, and neural networks. Brief discussions follow.

AutoRegressive integrated moving average (ARIMA) methods relax the assumption of independence of the successive observations in the time series. Often, this assumption is unwarranted because successive observations can be highly dependent. Although exponential smoothing and moving averages may be adequate when observations are dependent, methods that exploit this fact should provide a better forecast. The best known ARIMA method is the Box–Jenkins method, named after the foremost proponents and developers of the methods.

ARIMA methods can be viewed as a combination of moving average or smoothing and regression. The forecast is based on a function of weighted historical data, which allows a wider range of patterns to be forecast. One Box–Jenkins model is the k-term autoregressive model. Mathematically, it is

$$x_t = a_0 + a_1 x_{t-1} + a_2 x_{t-2} + \cdots + a_k x_{t-k} + \varepsilon_t$$

Each observation depends on a constant term a_0, k previous observations, and the noise component. Estimates of the parameters $a_0, a_1, \ldots, a_k$ can be obtained through least-squares or other techniques. The choice of k depends on the time series to be forecast. Many other models for autoregressive time series also exist.

For good results, a large number of observations (more than 50) should be available. Determining the right model to use requires judgement, trial and error, and statistical analysis, which may make these methods unattractive if many time series are to be forecast. However, if autocorrelation does exist between observations, this approach may be the best one.

Madsen (1991) wanted to explain how production expectations in the manufacturing industry, and hence supply behavior, are affected by risk. He modeled the process by using leading indicators of manufacturing production in an autoregressive integrated moving average (ARIMA) model to forecast production. Data from manufacturing industries in nine countries are used in the model. Other ARIMA forecasting models have been used to predict corporate earnings (Jarrett, 1990), special telephone services (Grambsch and Stahel, 1990), membership growth of a Canadian labor union (Lin et al., 1992), weekly electricity consumption (Ringwood et al., 1993), and the price of farmland (Tegene and Kuchler, 1994).

For details of ARIMA methods, see the book by Box and Jenkins (1976). Many forecasting texts, e.g., Montgomery et al. (1990), Levenbach and Cleary (1984), and Makridakis and Wheelwright (1978), also cover this material.

Bayesian methods are especially useful when little data are available. Initially, a subjective estimate of parameters used in the forecast is made, and as data become available, Bayes Theorem is used to update the parameter estimates. Bradford and Sugrue (1990) present a model to forecast style goods demand for a firm that stocks many hundreds of distinctive items—unframed poster art with no demand history and demand patterns that can change rapidly. After initial forecasts, the model revises forecasts with a Bayesian procedure based on an aggregation-by-items scheme. The revised predictions of demands, seasonal profits, and service levels were, on average, within 1 percent to 5 percent of the comparable values obtained using the empirical data from the case study. Other applications of Bayesian methods include forecasting traffic on computer networks (Greis and Gilstein, 1991), bonus coupon redemption (Lenk, 1992), and income tax revenue for school districts (Duncan et al., 1993). Montgomery, Johnson, and Gardiner (1990) discuss Bayesian forecasting methods in detail.

Neural networks have recently had an impact in forecasting (Belt, 1993; Papalexopoulos et al., 1994; Sharda, 1994); for basic information on neural networks, see Chester (1993) or Fausett (1994). A neural network imitates a brain's structure and function. It represents knowledge implicitly within its structure and applies inductive reasoning to process knowledge. An artificial neural network is a number of small primitive processing units (neurons) linked by weighted, directed connections (a network). Each neuron receives input signals from either an input source or other neurons. The input signal is weighted by the connection through which it passes. If the total weight of all incoming signals is strong enough, the neuron responds by sending a signal on each of its outgoing connections to other neurons.

A neural network must be "trained." Presenting the network different sets of input data along with the corresponding output allows the network to associate an output to certain characteristics of the input. The exact form of the associations is unknown. When new input is given to the network, it forecasts an output based on the associations it has "learned." After-the-fact outputs are provided to the network so it can continue to learn. Learning allows neural networks to be adaptive and infer solutions from the data presented to them, often capturing subtle relationships. In addition, they can generalize, correctly processing data that only broadly resembles the data they were trained on originally. They can also handle imperfect or incomplete data, providing a measure of fault tolerance.

Because a neural network learns directly from data, it can perform classification, forecasting, data compression, and other similar tasks. A number of applications in forecasting have been published, which include retail sales, stock prices, results of a leadscrew grinding process, bank failures, and electric power requirements. A neural network can also select the proper forecast method; Chu and Widjaja (1994) developed a neural network that picked the correct model for time-series data 90 percent of the time and the correct smoothing method 70 percent of the time.

Neural networks do have limitations, however; the actual mathematics are not easily understood and may be mistrusted. Because "one size fits all," they are not parsimonious and can be influenced by irrelevant information. One important model validation was determining an underlying reason for the model; e.g., soft drink sales are seasonal because they are more refreshing in hot weather. Because neural networks do not explicitly state the form of the model, this validation is absent. Finally, statistical techniques can provide accuracy measures such as confidence intervals that are unavailable for neural networks. Still, these methods appear viable and are readily available, even as an add-on to a spreadsheet.

7 FORECAST CONTROL

The forecasting system needs feedback to ensure the best results. Forecast control is part of the feedback process (see Figure 4-3). It tries to determine if forecasts deviate from actual results because of randomness or an underlying process change. Random variations should be ignored, but nonrandom variations call for changes in the model parameters or even the model itself. The concepts discussed in this section can be used to control any forecasting system that produces a numerical forecast, even those based on qualitative forecasting techniques.

The forecast error is the basis for forecast control. First determine the forecast error and its variance. Then the variance can be used to make probability statements, such as that the error should exceed a certain value only one time in twenty. These statements are used to determine if the system is performing as expected; if it does not meet expectations, corrective action is in order.

7.1   Forecast Error

Forecast error is the difference between the actual demand and the forecast. Mathematically, we have

$$e_t = d_t - F_t$$

Recall that F_T is the forecast for period T calculated in an earlier period. For notational ease, we will assume that it is calculated in the previous period. There are times when we might not want to define the error based on the forecast calculated in the previous period. For example, suppose we forecast on a monthly basis with a three-month rolling horizon and use the forecasts to determine workforce levels and also to plan actual production. The workforce decision is usually made several months in advance, so the workforce for June would be determined, say, by the forecast calculated in March. We cannot calculate an error until we know the actual demand for June, at which time we have forecasts for June made in March, April, and May. Because the March forecast is used in the June workforce decision, it should also be used to calculate the forecast error in determining workforce, even though we have more recent forecasts for the same period. That is, to assess how well the forecast is doing for the workforce decision, we calculate the error for June by subtracting the June forecast made in March from the actual June demand. On the other hand, the production decision is likely made from the May forecast, so when evaluating that forecast, the most recent forecast should be used to calculate the error.

We cannot expect to forecast exactly; the random or noise component of the underlying process ensures error will occur. Recall that our model assumes that the noise is normally distributed, so e_t can be positive (an underestimate of demand) or negative (an overestimate). If noise is the only cause of error, it is just as likely to be positive as negative.

Looking at the error for an isolated period does not provide much useful information. Rather we will look at errors over the history of the forecasting system. There are several methods for this process, although each has different meaning.

Define the **sum of forecast errors** as

$$E_T = \sum_{t=1}^{T} e_t$$

Because we assume that the underlying process has a normally distributed random component ε_t with mean zero and variance σ_ε^2, then E_T should be close to zero if the forecast is behaving properly. That is, sometimes it overestimates and sometimes it underestimates, but in the long run these should cancel out.

Table 4-14 illustrates various error functions. For each period, column one contains the actual demand in that period. S_t (column 2) is an exponentially smoothed estimate ($\alpha = 0.2$) of the demand computed in period t. We initialized the procedure with an S_0 of 100. The error for period t (column 3) is the demand minus the forecast for that period. We will assume we are forecasting one period ahead, so

$$e_t = d_t - S_{t-1}$$

The sum of the errors E_t (column 4) fluctuates but does not get too large in either the positive or negative direction.

If E_t is consistently moving away from zero, then the forecast is said to be biased; it is wrong in some particular and consistent way. A forecast consistently larger than actual is called biased high, while a forecast consistently lower than actual is called biased low. When a bias occurs, there are likely problems with the forecasting system. Suppose E_t is getting larger. If it is increasing at an approximately constant rate, each forecast underestimates demand by approximately a constant amount, which would occur if the value of the constant portion of the process shifted. Adding this amount to the forecast should correct the bias and provide a reasonable forecast.

If E_t is increasing at an increasing rate, it is likely that we are using the wrong model. Either we did not choose the correct model for the underlying process, or the underlying process has changed. For example, the underlying process may have been constant, but now the product has matured, and new competitors have taken sales away, so the process now has a decreasing trend. The error will get larger for each successive forecast, and E_t will increase at an increasing rate. Anytime E_t does not hover around zero, you should search for reasons the process might have changed.

TABLE 4-14
Some error measures

	1	2	3	4	5	6	7
t	d_t	S_t	$e_t = d_t - S_{t-1}$	E_t	MAD	MSE	MAPE
1	105	101	5	5	5.00	25.00	4.76
2	97	100	−4	1	4.50	20.50	4.44
3	107	101	7	8	5.33	30.00	5.14
4	109	102	8	16	6.00	38.50	5.69
5	83	98	−19	−3	8.60	103.00	9.13
6	109	100	11	8	9.00	106.00	9.29
7	117	103	17	25	10.14	132.14	10.04
8	106	103	3	28	9.25	116.75	9.14
9	96	101	−7	21	9.00	109.22	8.93
10	103	101	2	23	8.30	98.70	8.23
11	99	100	−2	21	7.73	90.09	7.67
12	88	97	−12	9	8.08	94.58	8.17
13	103	98	6	15	7.92	90.08	7.99
14	91	96	−7	8	7.86	87.14	7.97
15	94	95	−2	6	7.47	81.60	7.58
16	90	94	−5	1	7.31	78.06	7.45
17	100	95	6	7	7.24	75.59	7.36
18	81	92	−14	−7	7.61	82.28	7.92
19	85	90	−7	−14	7.58	80.53	7.93
20	113	94	23	9	8.35	102.95	8.55

Even E_t being zero does not guarantee a good forecasting system. For example, if the error is $+10$ in odd periods and -10 in even periods, the errors would cancel out, and E_t would be zero even though the forecast is obviously bad. To counteract this, the **mean absolute deviation** (MAD) is often used. It is defined as

$$\text{MAD} = \frac{1}{T} \sum_{t=1}^{T} |e_t|$$

where $|e_t|$ is the absolute value of e_t. MAD measures the dispersion of the errors, and if MAD is small, the forecast should be close to actual demand. Large values of MAD may indicate problems with the forecasting system. Column five in Table 4-14 gives MAD for the data. Again, because MAD is relatively small compared to d_t, the forecasts seem reasonable.

A similar measure sometimes used is the **mean squared error,** MSE, defined as

$$\text{MSE} = \frac{1}{T} \sum_{t=1}^{T} e_t^2$$

By squaring the error terms, the "penalty" is increased for large errors. Thus a single large error greatly increases MSE. MSE is given in column six of Table 4-14. Note the lasting effect on MSE in following periods after the large error in period 5.

All of the previously defined measures depend on the magnitude of the numbers being forecast. If the numbers are large, the error tends to be large. It may be more meaningful to look at error relative to the magnitude of the forecasts, which is done by using the **mean absolute percentage** error, MAPE, where

$$\text{MAPE} = \frac{1}{T} \left(\sum_{t=1}^{T} \frac{|e_t|}{d_t} \times 100 \right)$$

If MAPE is 10, then, on average, the forecasts are off by 10 percent. This process may be a more natural way to measure error. Column seven in Table 4-14 gives MAPE for the data. It is fairly constant around 8 percent, so we are comfortable with the forecasts.

Example 4-9. Choosing a model based on forecast error. Suppose we wish to forecast based on the data in Table 4-14. Which model and what parameter values are best?

Solution. Error information is used in many software packages to choose a model and its parameters for a set of data. Applying STORM to the data in Table 4-14, it uses periods 1 to 8 to fit different models for the data. The results are

Initial conditions for series

Component	Level model	Trend model	Seasonal model	Trend-seasonal model
Level	104.48	103.61	104.12	103.91
Trend	N/A	−0.13	N/A	−0.18
Seasonal 1	N/A	N/A	0.82	0.82
Seasonal 2	N/A	N/A	1.04	1.04
Seasonal 3	N/A	N/A	1.12	1.12
Seasonal 4	N/A	N/A	1.02	1.02
Smoothing	$\alpha = 0.3$	$\alpha = 0.2, \beta = 0.2$	$\alpha = 0.1, \gamma = 1.0$	$\alpha = 0.1, \beta = 0.1, \gamma = 1.0$

Thus the best level model has $S_8 = 104.48$ and uses $\alpha = 0.3$. The constant does not change significantly from model to model, the trend components are very small, and two of the four seasonal factors are close to 1, so there does not appear to be a great deal of difference in these models for the short term.

Forecast values for periods 9 to 16 are obtained from the four models updating the parameters using the smoothing constants previously given. The following error measures are recorded.

Model fitting error statistics

Statistic	Level model	Trend model	Seasonal model	Trend-seasonal model
Mean error	−4.25	−3.12	−4.12	−3.25
Mean % error	−4.75	−3.53	−4.54	−3.60
Mean absolute error	6.00	4.87	10.12	9.75
Mean absolute % error	6.45	5.23	10.63	10.23
Root mean square error	6.96	5.99	11.50	11.22

Based on these results, STORM chose the trend model because it has the smallest root mean squared error. There does not seem to be great differences in any of the error measures for any model.

To further validate the model, the final four periods (17 to 20) are forecast and updated using all four models. The following error measurements are obtained:

Model validation error statistics

Statistic	Level model	Trend model	Seasonal model	Trend-seasonal model
Mean error	2.25	4.50	1.25	2.25
Mean % error	0.42	2.87	−0.41	0.66
Mean absolute error	12.75	12.50	11.25	10.75
Mean absolute % error	13.20	12.63	11.47	10.84
Root mean square error	14.77	15.00	14.08*	14.20

*Seasonal model performed best during validation

Here the seasonal model performed the best, but the differences are relatively small.

If strong trend or seasonal effects were present, the error differences would have been much higher. Trying to keep our model as simple as possible, we would choose the constant (level) model. Using the trend model gives forecasts of 92, 91, 91, and 90 for the next four quarters, which is close to constant.

An intuitive way to judge a forecasting method would be to compare its accuracy to a naive method, such as the last data point (LDP) method. A rough comparison is given by

$$U = \sqrt{\left[\sum_{t=2}^{T} \left(\frac{d_t - F_t}{d_t} \right)^2 \right] \bigg/ \left[\sum_{t=2}^{T} \left(\frac{d_t - d_{t-1}}{d_t} \right)^2 \right]}$$

The top sum is error (actual minus forecast) divided by actual demand squared; squaring weights larger errors more heavily. The bottom sum is the same as the top but assumes an

LPD forecast; i.e., $F_t = d_{t-1}$. This process is a variation of a method suggested by Theil (1966).

If $U = 1$, the forecast is doing as well as the naive LPD forecast. Hopefully it will do better, so we would expect U to be smaller than 1. The smaller U is, the better the forecast is relative to LPD. If $U > 1$, the forecast is not as accurate as LPD and should not be used.

A forecast of the data in Table 4.14 is made using simple exponential smoothing, so in the formula for U we can replace F_t by S_{t-1}. We calculate U at period T from the computations for U made in the previous period. The sum of squared relative error for exponential smoothing and LDP are needed; they are 0.18 and 0.33, respectively, for period 19. When we know d_{20}, the new value of U is

$$U = \sqrt{\left[\sum_{t=2}^{T-1}\left(\frac{d_t - S_{t-1}}{d_t}\right)^2 + \left(\frac{d_T - S_{T-1}}{d_T}\right)^2\right] \Big/ \left[\sum_{t=2}^{T-1}\left(\frac{d_t - d_{t-1}}{d_t}\right)^2 + \left(\frac{d_T - d_{T-1}}{d_T}\right)^2\right]}$$

$$= \sqrt{\left[0.18 + \left(\frac{113 - 90}{113}\right)^2\right] \Big/ \left[0.33 + \left(\frac{113 - 85}{113}\right)^2\right]} = 0.75$$

From this calculation, the sum of squared relative error $\{0.18 + ((113 - 90)/113)^2\} = 0.22$ for exponential smoothing and 0.39 for LDP. Because U is less than one, exponential smoothing is doing better than LDP.

The tracking signal, discussed in the next session, is a more formal method of evaluating the accuracy of forecasts and appropriateness of the method used.

7.2   Tracking Signals

The forecast is an estimate of a random variable. We would like to examine the value of the forecast and see if the probability that it is a chance occurrence is reasonable. Recall that the probability that a random variable x lies within a certain range, say $[\ell, u]$, is given by

$$\Pr\{\ell \le x \le u\} = p$$

Here, we are more interested in finding an acceptable interval, so we will choose a probability and use it to determine the appropriate limits, which is similar to quality control charts.

For a normal distribution with mean μ and standard deviation σ, we know

$$\Pr\{\mu - K\sigma \le x \le \mu + K\sigma\} = p$$

Thus if the forecast exceeds these limits, we are $(1 - p)$ percent certain that it is not due to chance but to an assignable cause; i.e., the error is *not* random. Corrective action, such as a change in model parameters or using a different model, is in order.

A tracking signal is a method to check the randomness of the forecast error. Intuitively, the randomness of the tracking signal should be related to the noise of the underlying process. That is, if there were no noise and the model used was a good fit for the actual process, the forecast error should be zero. If the process noise ε is normally distributed with mean zero and standard deviation σ_ε then e_t is also normally distributed with mean zero and standard deviation σ_e.

The tracking signal we will use is based on E_t, the cumulative error, which is a good way to assess the nature of the error. We need to find σ_E, its standard deviation. Under the normality assumption, σ_E is a function of σ_t and hence σ_ε and the parameters of the particular forecasting technique used. For simple exponential smoothing, Brown (1963) shows

$$\sigma_E \approx \sqrt{\frac{1}{2\alpha}}\sigma_\varepsilon$$

Given that E_t is $N(0, \sigma_E)$, we can choose a probability p and determine an interval as

$$\Pr\{-K\sigma_E \leq E_t \leq K\sigma_E\} = p$$

Although we do not know σ_ε, for a normal distribution the mean absolute deviation and the standard deviation are related by (Brown, 1963)

$$\text{MAD} = \sqrt{(2/\pi)}\sigma_\varepsilon$$

or, because the square root of $2/\pi$ is about 0.8, MAD is approximately $0.8\sigma_\varepsilon$. Thus,

$$\sigma_\varepsilon \approx \frac{\text{MAD}}{0.8}$$

Brown (1963) has shown that MAD/0.8 is a good estimate of standard deviation even for a nonnormal distribution. His empirical study showed that for uniform, exponential, or triangular distributions, the constant only varies between 0.74 and 0.86, so 0.8 is still a good approximation. Thus, the normality of the forecast errors is a robust assumption.

Using the estimate of forecast error standard deviation, we can estimate the standard deviation of the cumulative error:

$$\sigma_E \approx \sqrt{\frac{1}{2\alpha}}\left(\frac{\text{MAD}}{0.8}\right)$$

Because the normal distribution is symmetrical, we can simplify calculations somewhat. Recall that we wish to specify a probability that defines an interval such that E_T being outside the interval is probably not a chance event. We define the interval in terms of the standard deviation. That is

$$-K\sigma_E \leq E_T \leq K\sigma_E$$

The following algebra allows us to express the interval in terms of the ratio of absolute cumulative error to MAD:

$$|E_T| \leq K\sigma_E$$

$$|E_T| \leq K\left(\sqrt{\frac{1}{2\alpha}}\left(\frac{\text{MAD}}{0.8}\right)\right)$$

$$\frac{|E_T|}{\text{MAD}} \leq \frac{K}{0.8}\sqrt{\frac{1}{2\alpha}}$$

Rather than calculate MAD each period, we will estimate it using exponential smoothing. Let Δ_T be the initial estimate of MAD found by calculating the actual MAD for a known part of the time series. For subsequent periods, update the estimate by

$$\Delta_T = \beta|e_T| + (1 - \beta)\Delta_{T-1}$$

where β is an appropriate smoothing constant. Now define the left-hand side of the last inequality, the ratio of absolute value of the cumulative error to the estimate of MAD, as the tracking signal at time T:

$$\rho_T = \frac{|E_T|}{\Delta_T}$$

Denote the right-hand side of the inequality as η, and call it the critical number, defined as

$$\eta = \frac{K}{0.8}\sqrt{\frac{1}{2\alpha}}$$

where α is the smoothing constant from the forecasting model, and K is an appropriate number of standard deviations. If

$$\rho_T \leq \eta$$

we say the forecast is in control.

Recall that ±2 standard deviations of a normal distribution accounts for about 95 percent of the distribution, so with $K = 2$ a tracking signal larger than η would occur less than 5 percent of the time by chance. If we are using $\alpha = 0.2$, with $K = 2$, then η would be $3.95 \approx 4$. The calculations for the tracking signal, using a smoothed estimate of MAD with $\beta = 0.2$ are given in Table 4-15 and plotted in Figure 4-15. Because all values are below 4, the tracking signal indicates that the forecast is in control. Also, there is no apparent trend in the tracking signal, so we would continue to forecast with this model. Rather than just thinking of the forecast as in or out of control, it is better to watch for trends. Also, if successive observations are close to the out-of-control region, it is cause for worry.

TABLE 4-15
Calculations for a tracking signal

t	d_t	S_t	$e_t = d_t - S_{t-1}$	E_t	Δ_t	ρ_t
1	105	101	5	5	5.00	1.00
2	97	100	−4	1	4.80	0.21
3	107	101	7	8	5.24	1.53
4	109	102	8	16	5.79	2.76
5	83	98	−19	−3	8.43	0.36
6	109	100	11	8	8.95	0.89
7	117	103	17	25	10.56	2.37
8	106	103	3	28	9.05	3.10
9	96	101	−7	21	8.64	2.43
10	103	101	2	23	7.31	3.15
11	99	100	−2	21	6.25	3.36
12	88	97	−12	9	7.40	1.22
13	103	98	6	15	7.12	2.11
14	91	96	−7	8	7.09	1.13
15	94	95	−2	6	6.08	0.99
16	90	94	−5	1	5.86	0.17
17	100	95	6	7	5.89	1.19
18	81	92	−14	−7	7.51	0.93
19	85	90	−7	−14	7.41	1.89
20	113	94	23	9	10.53	0.85

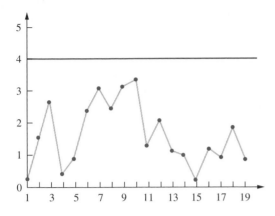

FIGURE 4-15
In-control tracking signal

Note that the critical number depends not only on the value of K, but also on α, the smoothing constant for simple exponential smoothing. If other models are used, η is no longer theoretically correct. However, in practice, picking values of η between 4 and 6 provides sufficient control for most situations. Brown shows that the cumulative error variance is approximately given by

$$\sigma_E^2 \approx \frac{1}{1 - (1 - \alpha)^{2n}} \sigma_\varepsilon^2$$

where n is the number of smoothing constants used. Thus, for double exponential smoothing, the relationship would be

$$\sigma_E^2 \approx \frac{1}{1 - (1 - \alpha)^4} \sigma_\varepsilon^2$$

7.3 Corrective Action

If the tracking signal exceeds the critical number, we should be concerned, but it may still be a random event rather than a change in process. If two consecutive observations are out of limits, we are fairly sure something is wrong. Suppose we take the data of Table 4-7 and add 20 to every demand after period 5. Recomputing the forecast and other relevant parameters gives us Table 4-16. The tracking signal is plotted in Figure 4-16.

The demand increase in period 6 causes the tracking signal to jump, but not above the control limit of 4. Even with the continued high demand, the period 7 tracking signal seems in control. However, the appearance of a trend in the tracking signal should warn management that a problem with the forecast may exist. Later periods are out of control; in practice, action should have been taken by period 9.

When the tracking signal exceeds the control limit, we need to look for assignable causes. If we find one, it will indicate the proper action. For example, suppose a heavy advertising campaign has caused a jump in sales, and we expect demand to remain at the new level. If simple exponential smoothing was used to forecast because the process is assumed to remain constant—but with a change in mean demand—we would set $E_t = 0$, reset the estimate of mean demand, and continue to use simple exponential smoothing. If growth is expected to continue, the model should be changed to one with a trend to reflect the changed conditions. If a trend model was already in use, the slope coefficient should be re-estimated.

TABLE 4-16
Calculations for out-of-control tracking signal

t	d_t	S_t	e_t	E_t	Δ_t	ρ_t
1	105	101	5	5	5.00	1.00
2	97	100	−4	1	4.80	0.21
3	107	101	7	8	5.24	1.53
4	109	102	8	16	5.79	2.76
5	83	98	−19	−3	8.43	0.36
6	129	104	31	28	12.95	2.16
7	137	110	33	61	16.96	3.60
8	126	113	16	77	16.77	4.59
9	116	113	3	80	14.01	5.71
10	123	115	10	90	13.21	6.81
11	119	115	4	94	11.37	8.27
12	108	113	−7	87	10.49	8.29
13	123	115	10	97	10.40	9.33
14	111	114	−4	93	9.12	10.20
15	114	114	0	93	7.29	12.75
16	110	113	−4	89	6.63	13.41
17	120	114	7	96	6.71	14.31
18	101	111	−13	83	7.97	10.42
19	105	109	−6	77	7.57	10.17
20	133	113	24	101	10.86	9.30

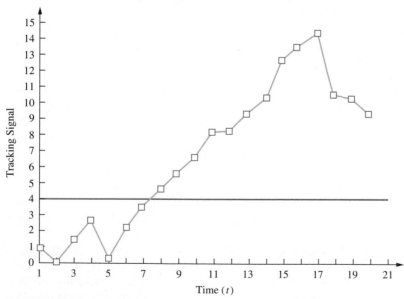

FIGURE 4-16
Out-of-control tracking signal

Even if the forecast catches up to the change in process mean, as happens by period 9, we must set $E_t = 0$ or continue to get an out-of-control indication.

If no assignable cause can be found, we assume something is wrong with the underlying model. A reasonable strategy, if exponential smoothing models are used, is to increase the value of the smoothing constant(s). Making N smaller in a moving average would have the same effect. This will more quickly discount older information, which seems appropriate if conditions are rapidly changing. Even if new terms are becoming relevant, such as seasonal variation, rapid discounting of older data will tend to follow these changes.

SECTION 7   PROBLEMS

4.40. Compute the error measures e, E, MAD, MSE, and MAPE for the given forecast.

t	1	2	3	4	5	6	7	8
d_t	375	348	373	337	314	332	283	257
F_t	385	382	373	373	363	349	344	327
t	9	10	11	12	13	14	15	16
d_t	269	238	231	225	201	189	219	191
F_t	307	297	280	267	255	240	226	224

4.41. Given the data, compute the forecast for June using a three-month moving average and simple exponential smoothing with an $\alpha = 0.1$ and $\alpha = 0.3$. Compute MAD for each based on February through May and tell which model you would use.

Month	Actual	Forecast
March	850	800
April	900	
May	975	
June	950	

4.42. Given the data for the monthly demand of a product, determine the forecasting method that would have provided the lowest mean absolute deviation for the last four months. (*Hint*: Plot the data first and make an assumption about the underlying model of the process.)

Observation	1	2	3	4	5	6	7	8	9	10
Sales	19	17	22	19	18	23	18	16	20	18

4.43. A company uses simple exponential smoothing with $\alpha = 0.1$ to forecast demand for boxes of rubber gloves. The forecast for this week was 237 boxes and the actual demand was 205.

(a) What is your forecast for next week?
(b) What is your forecast for three weeks from now?
(c) If the cumulative sum of the forecast errors before this week was 23 and the estimate of the mean absolute deviation was 10.6, do you feel that the forecasting system is doing a good job? Explain.

4.44. AutoCell uses Winters method to forecast quarterly demand for their automobile batteries. The forecast for this quarter was $F_T = 107$ batteries, and the actual demand was $d_T = 97$. The estimates of the intercept and trend were $S_T = 101$ and $B_T = 18$. Seasonal factors are $c_{T-3} = 0.9$, $c_{T-2} = 1.0$, $c_{T-1} = 1.2$ and $c_T = 0.9$. The smoothing constants are $\alpha = \beta = \gamma = 0.1$.

(a) What is the forecast for next quarter?
(b) What is the forecast for two quarters from now?
(c) If the smoothed estimate of forecast errors before this quarter was 2.0 and the smoothed estimate of the mean absolute deviation was 3.7, do you feel that the forecasting system is doing a good job? Explain.

8 SOFTWARE

There are hundreds of forecasting packages available for computer implementation today that range from simple Excel or Lotus macro commands to complex statistical packages such as SAS and SPSS. Packages exist for all of the quantitative methods, including Bayesian and neural networks, as well as some of the qualitative methods. Because the field is changing so rapidly, we will not give a comprehensive survey. Reilly (1990) and Fildes (1988) discuss requirements of a forecasting software package and illustrate it with a discussion of some particular packages. Other surveys that list packages and their features have been done by Compton and Compton (1990), Aghazadeh and Romal (1992), and Yurkiewicz (1993). Evaluations of specific packages are published in many journals and magazines. The reviews of two versions of SmartForecasts are typical and also show the dynamic nature of the software industry; see Perttula (1991) and Fuller (1993).

Probably the most important thing to look for in forecasting software is the number of forecasting methods supplied and how methods and parameters are chosen. Less expensive packages require the user to specify the method and the parameters. Choosing good ones manually is usually quite time consuming. Better packages will "optimally" choose both method and parameters for you, and most of these will also let the user specify them, which is a nice feature.

Communication with other software is another important feature. Often, the input comes from a data base and should be able to be read into the software easily. Also, output should be easily exported to report generators. For many users, spreadsheet compatibility is needed. Graphical output makes the results understandable to a wider audience, and advanced features, such as prediction intervals and tracking signals, should be available.

In any case, the package should be user friendly. If not, it will soon be neglected and ad hoc forecasts used instead. The user should also have a basic understanding of the methods the package uses, which will ensure that it is appropriate for the particular application and will give the user confidence in the result.

The needs of a particular situation will dictate what sort of package, if any, is warranted. An owner of a McDonald's franchise who wishes to forecast total sales (in dollars) for each month can likely get by with a simple microcomputer package or even a spreadsheet. However, a large company that will forecast weekly demand of thousands of items needs a more complex system. Corporate data bases supply the input, and quite a few people are likely to use the forecasts. In this case a team approach should be used to define needs and compare available packages against requirements and cost.

Most importantly, the package should be only one part of the forecasting system. Human judgment and intervention is necessary; if it is not used, poor performance will be the likely result.

9 FORECASTING IN PRACTICE

It has been said, and we agree, that forecasts are uncertain, imprecise, and unavoidable. Unavoidable implies that every company must forecast; the difference is in how formal their forecasting system is. As we saw in the software discussion, a simple spreadsheet may be all that is needed. A recent survey (Sanders and Manrodt, 1994) indicates that simple techniques are preferred in practice. However, many companies require a forecast manager and staff to develop forecasts.

Interviews with several forecasters are given in *The Journal of Business Forecasting*; see Cristo and Jain (1992) and Geesaman and Jain (1992) for examples. From these we can describe a typical forecasting situation. The number of items for which forecasts are needed is typically between 500 and 3000. Usually, forecasts are made for the next twelve months, both in units and dollars. The unit forecasts are used by production, and the dollar forecasts are used by financial planners. Teams made up of production, marketing, and sales representatives discuss the forecasts before they are finalized. Two years of data seems to be a common number of data points used in forecasting. Typical deviations of forecasts from actual values range from 5 percent to 40 percent. For more specific information on applications, *The Journal of Business Forecasting* is a good source; Meyer (1992) discusses forecasting at Schlegel Corporation, and Box 4-1 discusses forecasting at Howmedica (Anderson, 1991).

To reduce the large number of items that need to be forecast, items are categorized by importance. Typically, a small percentage (about 15 percent) of the items will account for a large dollar volume of sales (about 70 percent). A second group of items (20 percent) will account for another 15 percent. The remaining 60 percent of the items represent only about 15 percent of the sales dollars. Third-category items are forecast as groups having similar characteristics. Methods used on the first class of items may be very complex, because they are the most important items. This concept, called ABC analysis, is discussed in more detail in Chapter 6.

Fisher et al. (1994) propose the philosophy of **accurate response** forecasting, based on recognizing the difference in cost of stockouts and markdowns (Section 2.5) and categorizing products according to variance of the forecast. Forecast variance can be obtained by statistically analyzing multiple forecasts of the demand. Initially, the company produces a small percentage of the forecast of high-variance items and a large percentage of low-forecast-variance items, which frees capacity later to make high-variance items after more information is available, resulting in fewer stockouts and markdowns.

BOX 4-1: DEMAND FORECASTING AT HOWMEDICA

Demand forecasting at Howmedica is done first by grouping similar products into a family and then by establishing the phase of life cycle in which that family lies... customer base, customer usage rate, and repeat purchase are the key elements used in projecting the sales of newly introduced products... sales expectations of managers are often much higher than the forecaster.

BOX 4-1 (*continued*)

Howmedica is a division of the Pfizer Hospital Products Group with manufacturing and distribution centers throughout the world. The products that we manufacture and sell can be divided into three categories: (1) reconstructive products for total joint replacement, (2) trauma products to aid in healing bone fractures, and (3) system specific and generic type instrumentation. These three categories have over 6000 items (SKU's) in total, which indicates that we should forecast them as efficiently as possible.

Our competition is made up of divisions of many large drug companies including Bristol Myers and Johnson and Johnson. They compete with us in practically all the markets we serve. Our distribution network is composed of dealers (called customers) and agencies (called direct sales and inventory load).

WHY DO WE FORECAST?

Howmedica's policy is to ship orders from the stock; and this calls for sales forecasts, item by item. Our manufacturing department uses the forecasted sales unit (demand forecast) for short term inventory planning and long term resource planning. In the short term inventory planning, forecasts are used as an input to the MRP system. In the long run resource planning, they are used for determining manpower and requirements for plant and equipment. Demand forecasts are also used as an input to annual/interim sales and departmental budgets.

FORECASTING PROCESS

All sales forecasts originate from our forecasting department, which is solely responsible for this function. Sales (units) forecasts are input into the manufacturing planning system through our forecast data base. Sales (dollars) forecasts are provided to the finance department which serve as an input to the financial budgeting process.

Forecasts of unit sales (customer demand) for new products are developed by simulations. The simulations are based on the product launch plans. The launch plans are approved by the marketing senior management which we then quantify by utilizing inventory and customer usage relationships.

Forecasts of unit sales (customer demand) for existing products are prepared and approved exclusively by the forecasting department. Each month, all existing product forecasts are reviewed by reasonability, and are revised, if necessary. Additionally, even if the forecasts are tracking well, they must be revised at least every three months.

We have found that the selection of a forecasting model for a given product depends very much on the phase of life cycle (newly introduced products, mature products, products with declining demand, and obsolescent products) we consider, and their appropriate forecasting models are discussed below.

NEWLY INTRODUCED PRODUCTS

Simulation is used for preparing inventory demand forecasts for newly introduced products as it helps to specify the basic parameters needed to estimate their demand at the time of the product launch. The interaction of the basic input details, in turn, produces the product forecast at the item (SKU) level. In an industrial type of market such as ours, the following parameters are typical:

BOX 4-1 (*continued*)

1. Number of Customers: *This is determined by consensus within the marketing and sales groups. The total represents the number of customers to be activated from our current customers to be generated from the outside sources. If the new product is in the market that we have not participated in, its market size and share potential is estimated through primary/secondary market research. Most of the initial business for new products, however, comes from our own customers. The immediate surge of activity from our own customer file is followed by a conversion of our competitive accounts. The competitive conversion process usually occurs very slowly.*

2. Customer Use Rate: *The customer usage rate is the next most important parameter. Once the new product system is placed with the customer, usage starts almost immediately. The usage for our business is in terms of the number of surgical procedures per customer, per year. Each surgical procedure requires a specific quantity of different families of components. The number of surgical procedures per year is derived from our experience with other similar products introduced in the past.*

3. Size Distribution Within Family: *The individual item usage distribution within the product families is most often related to an anatomical size distribution. The anatomical distributions are directly determined by the frequency distribution(s) of physical sizes of the various parts of the human skeleton. Once the above parameters are estimated, the forecast by item for each period into the future (after the new product is launched) is calculated by determining the shelf inventory requirements for all that period's new customers (inventory load) and the projected usage for that period of all the customers that have been placed to date. In terms of a formula:*

$$\text{Item Level Forecast} = (A \times B) + (C \times D \times E \times F)$$

where A = *New customers per period*
B = *Inventory per customer*
C = *Cumulative customers to date*
D = *Usage rate per period*
E = *Size distribution within family*
F = *Period workday factor*

As an example, in June 1991, Howmedica intends to place 50 (A) new Total Hip systems into hospitals that are currently being serviced by the competition. The hip system has a range of 5 sizes (extra small to extra large), and the hospital will receive 2 (B) of each size for a total of 10 units. To date, Howmedica has accumulated 200 (C) new customers that use this Total Hip system, and the aggregate surgical procedure rate is 2 (D) per month. The medium size, which we will focus on, is used 35% (E) of the time. Since June has 24 workdays, the period workday factor is 1.166 (F). The workday factor is computed as: 1.166 = 24 (number of working days in a month)/20.58 (average working days per month). The average working days per month is computed as: 20.58 = 247 (number of working days in a year)/12 (number of months in a year).

The forecast of this item will come to:

$$256 \text{ (units)} = (50 \times 2) + (200 \times 2 \times 0.35 \times 1.166)$$

BOX 4-1 (*continued*)

More simply stated, the formula looks like this:

(new customers' inventory) + (usage from existing customers)

Since this is a simulation, the formulae are developed so that they utilize data from input fields, which can be easily changed.

This forecast produces item level quantity requirements. It should be analyzed for accuracy at the parameter input level, which is really what is being forecasted. Expost forecasts should be generated by inserting all known parameters (customer base, usage rates, etc.), and then comparing the actual item level demand with the forecast to check for validity.

MATURE PRODUCTS

The products that exhibit definable trends and solid seasonal patterns are called mature products. These products must have at least two years of demand history. The forecasts of such products are generated by forecasting the demand of one family of a product system. The family is defined as a group of products of the same line with similar demand patterns. Forecasts of such products are generated by forecasting the independent family of a product system. The independent family is defined as the group of product that actually determines the demand for the other members of the family. The other families (dependent) within the product system have consistent relationships with the independent family. In other words, each time a total hip surgical procedure is done, three components are used:

1. *A metal hip stem (independent family)*

2. *A metal hip cup shell (dependent family)*

3. *A plastic hip cup insert (dependent family)*

Since the same quantity (1) of each component is used, it is not necessary to forecast each one, just the component that is considered to be the system activity indicator (metal hip stem).

Depending upon a product, an independent family could have anywhere from zero to ten or more dependents. In addition, because of the sheer volume of products that we must forecast, we alternate between two sets of independent families and forecast each every other month. Our procedure for forecasting these families:

1. *Select the group of independent families to be forecasted.*

2. *Download from the main computer their demand history. The history is in terms of units per working day, per month. Number of working days in each month vary from year to year. January could have 10, 15, or 16 working days, depending upon a year.*

3. *Decompose the data into seasonality and trend. The quality of the trend is determined by the goodness of fit. The quality of seasonality is determined by the closeness of monthly indices of different years.*

4. *Select a forecasting model that best represents the characteristics of the data. For this group of products, models such as decomposition are used. The forecast of such*

BOX 4-1 (*continued*)

a model is not final. If the model gives results that are contradictory to that of the life cycle trend, the life cycle trend forecast may override the other. If the model projection looks reasonable, the results are saved on a Lotus spreadsheet file.

5. *Break down family unit forecasts into member unit forecasts by using their past relationships.*

6. *Upload the newly prepared forecasts to the main computer and save. The main computer is more a facility for data storage and manipulation than for preparing forecasts.*

7. *The independent and dependent family forecasts are then used to generate the item level forecast by a process that we call forcing. The forcing applies a previously computed factor that is derived by computing the item's historical demand contribution to the family demand for the last six months. This allocation percentage is applied to each of the month forecasts that were updated in the forecast file. All this is done on a PC. The results of the PC generated forecast are then adjusted for various marketing programs including upgrades and promotions.*

PRODUCTS WITH DECLINING DEMAND

These are the products that are still viable yet their demand is declining. Periodically, we test whether or not a given family of products or product is at the declining phase of its life cycle. For such products simple moving average and single exponential smoothing give the best forecasts. When we compare the forecasts produced by our standard PC forecasting software, the six-month moving average usually performs better than the other. When this occurs, the independent family and its dependent series are allowed to be forecasted with a simple moving average. Forecasts are updated automatically each month by the main computer. This forecasting technique is utilized until the product groups reach the obsolescent stage.

OBSOLESCENT PRODUCTS

The product that is at the very end of its life cycle is labeled as obsolescent. We periodically evaluate whether a given family of products or product should be labeled as obsolescent. This is done by studying the historical sales data, trend projections, and industry trends of similar products. The recommendations are then communicated to management for their approval.

FORECASTING ACCURACY

We often test models for their accuracy by preparing expost forecasts (forecasts for periods for which actuals are known). This helps us in selecting an appropriate model. Also, it tells us what kind of error to expect in the future. Our experience shows that the size of error depends very much on the phase of life cycle the product is in. In the introduction phase, the error rate may run anywhere between 25% and 30%. For mature products, the error rates run around 10%. Products with declining sales yield error rates around 20%.

> **BOX 4-1** (*continued*)
>
> **PROBLEMS, CHALLENGES, AND OPPORTUNITIES**
>
> *Often it is difficult to communicate to the users of the forecasts how the forecasts were developed. The job becomes even more difficult where the user has no background in statistics and forecasting. The more they understand how forecasts are prepared, the more they would know what forecasts can and cannot do. Often the user's expectations are much higher than the forecaster's. Also, because of lack of understanding, forecasts are often not used correctly. Forecasting is a combination of both art and science. But to the user's mind it is more an art than science. This perception has to be changed. This can be accomplished not by making what we do more difficult to understand, but by making it easier.*
>
> *Source:* Anderson (1991). Used by permission.

10   EVOLUTION

It is easy to imagine early man trying to predict the return of the game herds or the start of spring. Formal forecasting got its start with mathematicians and statisticians several hundred years ago. In terms of forecasting as we know it today, the seminal work is likely the book by R. G. Brown (1962), which is still a helpful reference. Also Box and Jenkins (1976) made a substantial contribution, moving forecasting into new territory. But more than any person, the personal computer has changed forecasting the most, and sophisticated forecasting packages that are inexpensive and easy to use have made forecasting available to everyone.

11   SUMMARY

In this chapter we discuss forecasting. We begin (Sections 1 and 2) with the forecasting system viewed in the problem-solving framework. First, we state the need for a forecast. Data availability often dictates the type of forecasting model/method used, but if data are unavailable and cannot be collected, qualitative models/methods—including market surveys, expert opinion, and Delphi methods—are appropriate (Section 3). We discuss these models/methods and point out the strengths and weaknesses of each. Practical applications are also provided.

If data are available or can be collected, we can use quantitative models. The approach to using these models is to identify the pattern of the underlying process, use an appropriate model for that pattern, and choose a correct method for the model. If a cause-and-effect relation between one or more independent variables and the quantity to be forecast exists and can be identified, we use casual methods (Section 4). Simple linear regression is a common way to forecast, and is discussed in detail. Here we estimate parameters by least-squares, and the resulting equation provides the forecast. We also include multiple regression.

If causal relations cannot be determined, time-series methods (Section 5) are used. Simple averages, moving averages, and exponential smoothing are the most popular methods. These are discussed for constant, trend, and seasonal process models. Table 4-17 summarizes various forecasting methods.

TABLE 4-17
Summary of forecasting methods

Process	Method	Data	Time	Cost	Complexity
Constant	Last data point	1	Short	Low	Low
	Average	> 5	Short, Medium	Low	Low
	Moving average	5–10	Short, Medium	Low	Low
	Exponential smoothing	> 3	Short, Medium	Low	Low
Trend	Double moving average	> 10	Short, Medium	Low	Moderate
	Double exponential smoothing	> 10	Short, Medium	Low	Moderate
	Regression	> 10	Short, Medium, Long	Modest	Moderate
Seasonal	Winters three-factor smoothing	2 seasons	Short, Medium	Modest	Moderate
Unknown	Market survey	None	Short, Medium, Long	High	Moderate
	Delphi method	None	Short, Medium, Long	High	Moderate

Data = minimum number of periods needed   Cost = expense of method
Time = horizon of the forecast   Complexity = ease of use/understanding

Some additional qualitative, causal, and time-series forecasting techniques are mentioned in Section 6. Although they are too specialized, too advanced, or not widely accepted for a detailed discussion, references provide links to more detailed information.

Forecast control (Section 7) is important for any forecasting system; we must have an indication of how well the system works. Forecast error, tracking signals, and corrective action are covered in detail.

Next we discuss computer packages to do forecasting, followed by some comments on forecasting in practice. Evolution of forecasting concludes the chapter.

MINICASE: BF SWINGS

Ben Floyd really enjoyed wood shop in high school, so he used an inheritance to buy some basic woodworking tools. He started out doing odd jobs, and then one day he made a porch swing for his house. Several people saw it and asked him to make one for them. Word of mouth brought him many customers. In June of 1991 he married Bobbie Ruth, a marketing graduate. Bobbie Ruth saw a chance to expand the swing business to similar products and eventually have hardware, building supply, and furniture stores. Thus, BF Swings was born. Due to his love of his work and Bobbie Ruth's marketing ability, the business prospered. Today, they make stools and rockers as well as swings. The company now employs about 35 people five days a week with sales close to $1.4 million dollars.

All is not peaches and cream at BFS, however. Due to growth and Ben's lack of knowledge, they feel that they are headed for serious trouble. To avoid this, they have decided to hire someone who knows production systems to help them. After interviewing many outstanding candidates they chose you to fill this position.

Other problems will be attacked later, but now Ben is concerned with production for the next month or so. Lupe, the accountant, tells him that overtime costs are a large part of his total operating costs and that they ought to hire more workers to reduce overtime. Samir, the shop foreman, reminds them that just adding people may not add capacity, because additional equipment may also be needed. Ben agrees, except that sanding, assembly, and finishing require little or no equipment.

The following table gives the standard processing time (in minutes) for each "operation" of the three products. It contains the expected time available in each department per week. This time is adjusted for preventative and unexpected maintenance and operator personal time. The number of employees currently working in the department is also provided.

| Department | Processing time (minutes) | | | Available | |
	Stool	Rocker	Swing	Hours	People
Drill	7	10	11	70	2
Lathe	15	0	0	35	1
Crosscut saw	3	16	10	105	3
Rip saw	0	3	4	35	1
Mortise	0	10	8	70	2
Tenon	0	22	11	105	3
Router/shaper	0	3	3	35	1
Plane	0	13	7	70	2
Sand	5	25	35	145	4
Assemble	12	30	45	150	4
Finish	5	15	22	80	2

Bobbie Ruth has kept some records on demand. A weekly demand history for each of the three products follows. Demand is in items, e.g., number of stools, rockers, or swings. These numbers include items sold plus orders not filled because of insufficient supply. Week 1 is the first week of January 1995, and week 117 is the fourth week of March 1997.

Week	Stool	Rocker	Swing	Week	Stool	Rocker	Swing	Week	Stool	Rocker	Swing
1	105	234	18	21	104	234	321	41	95	299	22
2	101	248	21	22	99	249	338	42	106	266	15
3	106	276	28	23	100	292	50	43	98	305	18
4	108	225	16	24	108	261	27	44	113	273	14
5	91	228	29	25	105	264	64	45	90	292	27
6	101	247	25	26	99	265	44	46	80	326	15
7	100	275	22	27	107	261	222	47	100	277	19
8	101	251	24	28	96	256	30	48	100	256	22
9	109	251	27	29	96	254	200	49	75	246	27
10	108	241	37	30	107	304	30	50	106	312	22
11	88	236	24	31	98	279	33	51	88	320	32
12	100	254	26	32	85	262	89	52	95	292	21
13	102	248	28	33	86	261	198	53	132	277	29
14	99	229	139	34	116	265	34	54	100	275	18
15	100	243	161	35	126	299	278	55	109	295	32
16	109	254	216	36	95	291	75	56	102	308	28
17	102	272	112	37	99	321	168	57	106	262	23
18	99	249	76	38	111	295	104	58	100	318	24
19	113	248	275	39	115	277	41	59	105	306	29
20	96	302	41	40	108	275	24	60	107	303	38

Week	Stool	Rocker	Swing	Week	Stool	Rocker	Swing	Week	Stool	Rocker	Swing
61	88	281	25	80	106	320	44	99	106	309	24
62	99	341	25	81	105	312	42	100	118	345	23
63	121	302	22	82	86	341	111	101	94	357	20
64	113	303	21	83	99	350	35	102	81	330	20
65	97	324	28	84	104	364	37	103	106	323	25
66	86	344	198	85	113	310	185	104	107	327	27
67	101	311	177	86	100	289	139	105	88	368	31
68	100	271	173	87	95	356	81	106	110	325	27
69	96	320	65	88	100	331	50	107	88	348	22
70	116	305	295	89	103	342	161	108	121	336	32
71	104	332	264	90	115	308	133	109	94	361	26
72	102	323	66	91	107	335	29	110	101	350	23
73	99	293	204	92	95	352	20	111	113	343	27
74	114	324	56	93	92	362	15	112	86	356	18
75	101	311	44	94	109	343	22	113	95	353	27
76	88	324	267	95	116	356	22	114	101	308	22
77	94	328	300	96	103	324	34	115	103	345	27
78	100	355	311	97	104	348	17	116	103	342	21
79	110	317	236	98	96	337	21				

Prepare a report for Ben recommending workforce levels for the next eight weeks. How confident are you of your results? Suppose the actual demands for products in the next four weeks are the following:

Week	Stools	Rockers	Swings
117	100	344	24
118	109	352	146
119	90	368	279
120	106	361	64

Does this change your recommendation for weeks 121–124? Explain.

12 REFERENCES

Aghazadeh, S. M. and Romal, J. B., "A Directory of 66 Packages for Forecasting and Statistical Analysis," *The Journal of Business Forecasting,* Summer 1992, pp. 14–20.

Anderson, T., "Demand Forecasting at Howmedica," *The Journal of Business Forecasting,* Summer 1991, pp. 14–20.

Armstrong, J. S., "Forecasting by Extrapolation: Conclusions from 25 Years of Research," *INTERFACES,* 14, 52–66, 1984.

Avery, S. "Power Transmission Recovers: Manufacturers Hike Prices," *Purchasing,* 114, 57–61, 1993.

Barron, M. and Targett, D., *The Manager's Guide to Business Forecasting,* Basil Blackwell, Ltd., Oxford, UK, 1985.

Beasley, J. E., "Forecasting Environmental Protection Legislation Using Cross-Impact Analysis," *Long Range Planning,* 17, 132–138, 1984.

Belt, D., "Neural Networks: Practical Retail Applications," *Discount Merchandiser,* 33, RT9–RT12, 1993.

Boehm, T. P., Mandy, D. M., and O Hara, M. D., "Modelling Aid to Families with Dependent Children," *Survey of Business,* 28, 2–9, 1992.

Box, G. E. P. and Jenkins, G. M., *Time Series Analysis—Forecasting and Control,* Holden-Day, Inc., San Francisco, 1976.

Bradford, J. W. and Sugrue, P. K., "A Bayesian Approach to the Two-Period Style-Goods Inventory Problem with Single Replenishment and Heterogeneous Poisson Demands," *Journal of the Operational Research Society,* 41, 211–218, 1990.

Brown, R. G., *Smoothing, Forecasting and Prediction of Discrete Time Series,* Prentice Hall, Inc., Englewood Cliffs, NJ, 1963.

Calzolari, G. and Panattoni, L., "Mode Predictors in Nonlinear Systems with Identities," *International Journal of Forecasting,* 6, 317–326, 1990.

Chester, M., *Neural Networks: A Tutorial,* Prentice-Hall, Englewood Cliffs, NJ, 1993.

Chu, C-H. and Widjaja, D., "Neural Network System for Forecasting Method Selection," *Decision Support Systems,* 12, 13–24, 1994.

Compton, J. C. and Compton S. B., *Successful Business Forecasting,* TAB Books, Blue Ridge Summit, PA, 1990.

Cook, T. "Understand Your Customer Before Preparing Forecasts," *Journal of Business Forecasting Methods & Systems,* 13, 27–29, 1994/1995.

Cristo, S. and Jain, C. L., "Forecasting at Colgate-Palmolive Company," *The Journal of Business Forecasting,* Spring 1992, pp. 14–20.

Duncan, G., Gorr, W., and Szczypula, J., "Bayesian Forecasting for Seemingly Unrelated Time Series: Application to Local Government Revenue Forecasting," *Management Science,* 39, 275–293, 1993.

Emmons, H., Flowers, A. D., Khot, C. M., and Mathur, K., *STORM: Quantitative Modeling for Decision Support,* Holden-Day, Oakland, CA, 1989.

Ezop, P. "Database Marketing Research," *Marketing Research: A Magazine of Management & Applications,* 6, 34–41, 1994.

Fausett, L. V., *Fundamentals of Neural Networks: Architectures, Algorithms, and Applications,* Prentice-Hall, Englewood Cliffs, NJ, 1994.

Fildes, R., "Quantitative Forecasting—the State of the Art: Econometric Models," *Journal of The Operational Research Society,* 36, 549–580, 1985.

Fildes, R., "Reviewing Forecasting Software—An Essay," *Journal of The Operational Research Society,* 39, 773–778, 1988.

Fisher, M. L., Hammond, J. H., Obermeyer, W. R., and Raman, A., "Making Supply Meet Demand in an Uncertain World," *Harvard Business Review,* 72, 83–92, 1994.

Fuller, M., "Software Review," *OR/MS Today,* December 1993, pp. 58–60.

Geesaman, T. A. and Jain, C. L., "Forecasting at McCormick & Company," *The Journal of Business Forecasting,* Winter 1991–1992, pp. 3–5.

Goldfarb, D. L. and Huss, W. R., "Building Scenarios for an Electric Utility," *Long Range Planning,* 21, 78–85, 1988.

Goss, B. A., "The Forecasting Approach to Efficiency in the Wool Market," *Applied Economics,* 22, 973–993, 1990.

Grambsch, P. and Stahel, W. A., "Forecasting Demand for Special Telephone Services—A Case Study," *International Journal of Forecasting,* 6, 53–64, 1990.

Greis, N. P. and Gilstein, C. Z., "Empirical Bayes Methods for Telecommunications Forecasting," *International Journal of Forecasting,* 7, 183–197, 1991.

Huss, W. R., "A Move Toward Scenario Analysis," *International Journal of Forecasting,* 4, 377–388, 1988.

Jarrett, J., "Forecasting Seasonal Time Series of Corporate Earnings: A Note," *Decision Sciences,* 21, 888–894, 1990.

Kaynak, E., Bloom, J., and Leibold, M., "Using the Delphi Technique to Predict Future Tourism Potential," *Marketing Intelligence & Planning,* 12, 18–29 1994.

Koch, P. D. and Koch, T. W., "Forecasting Stock Returns in the Japanese, UK and US Markets During the Crash of October 1987," *Managerial Finance,* 20, 68–89, 1994.

Kress, G. J. and Snyder, J., *Forecasting and Market Analysis Techniques,* Quorum Books, Westport, CT, 1994.

Lenk, P. J., "Hierarchical Bayes Forecasts of Multinomial Dirichlet Data Applied to Coupon Redemptions," *Journal of Forecasting,* 11, 603–619, 1992.

Levenbach, H. and Cleary, J. P., *The Modern Forecaster: The Forecasting Process Through Data Analysis,* Lifetime Learning Publications, Belmont, CA, 1984.

Lin, E. Y. H., Sharma, B., and Otuteye, E., "An ARIMA Model for Canadian Union Membership Growth, 1911–1985," *Applied Economics,* 24, 1035–1041, 1992.

Lin, W. T., "Analysis and Forecasting of Income Statement Account Balances: The Dynamic Interdependency and ARIMA Approaches," *Journal of Forecasting,* 11, 283–307, 1992.

Linstone, H. A. and Turoff, M., eds., *The Delphi Method, Techniques and Applications,* Addison-Wesley Publishing Company, Reading, MA, 1975.

Madsen, J. B., "Formation of Production Expectations Under Risk," *Journal of Economic Psychology,* 12, 101–119, 1991.

Maital, S., "Caution: Oracles at Work," *Across the Board,* 30, 52–53, 1993.

Makridakis, S. G. and Wheelwright, S. C., *Forecasting Methods and Applications,* John Wiley & Sons, New York, 1978.

Makridakis, S. G. and Wheelwright, S. C., eds., *The Handbook of Forecasting, A Manager's Guide,* John Wiley & Sons, New York, 1987.

Martino, J. P., *Technological Forecasting for Decision Making,* Elsevier Science Publishing Company, New York, 1983.

Mastio, R. C., "What Blow Molders Need from Their Machinery Suppliers," *Plastics World,* 52, 67, 1994.

Meyer, F., "Building Products Sales Forecasting at Schlegel," *The Journal of Business Forecasting,* Winter 1991–1992, 23–24.

Millet, S. M., "Battelle's Scenario Analysis of a European High-Tech Market," *Planning Review,* 20, 20–23, 1992.

Montgomery, D. C., Gardiner, J. S., and Johnson, L. A., *Forecasting and Time Series Analysis,* McGraw-Hill Book Company, New York, 1990.

Newbold, P., and Granger, C. W. J., "Experience with Forecasting Univariate Time Series and the Combination of Forecasts," *Journal of the Royal Statistical Society, Series A,* 137, 131–165, 1974.

Papalexopoulos, A. D., Hao, S., and Peng, T-M. "An Implementation of a Neural Network Based Load Forecasting Model for the EMS," *IEEE Transactions on Power Systems,* 9, 1956–1962, 1994.

Perttula, L. W., "SmartForecasts II," *The Journal of Business & Industrial Marketing,* 6, 74–75, 1991.

Reilly, P. K., "What to Look for in Selecting an Automatic Forecasting Package," *Journal of Business Forecasting,* 9, 27–29, 1990.

Ringwood, J. V., Austin, P. C., and Montieth, W., "Forecasting Weekly Electricity Consumption," *Energy Economics,* 15, 285–296, 1993.

Sanders, N. R. and Manrodt, K. B., "Forecasting Practices in U. S. Corporations: Survey Results," *INTERFACES,* 24, 92–100, 1994.

Scala, S. and McGrath, R., "Advantages and Disadvantages of Electronic Data Interchange—An Industry Perspective," *Information & Management,* 25, 85–91, 1993.

Schnaars, S. P., "How to Develop and Use Scenarios," *Long Range Planning,* 20, 105–114, 1987.

Schuler, A., Thompson, W. A., Vertinsky, I., and Ziv, Y., "Cross Impact Analysis of Technological Innovation and Development in the Softwood Lumber Industry in Canada: A Structural Modeling Approach," *IEEE Transactions on Engineering Management,* 38, 224–236, 1991.

Sharda, R., "Neural Networks for the MS/OR Analyst: An Application Bibliography," *INTERFACES,* 24, 116–130, 1994.

Smith, B., *Focus Forecasting: Computer Techniques for Inventory Control,* CBI Publishing, Incorporated, Boston, 1978.

Smith, T. "Explosive Demand Sparks Brisk Sales," *Computer Reseller News, Emerging Technologies Supplement,* December 12, 10-12, 1994.

Stocks, J., "CD-ROM Down Under: A Delphi Study of CD-ROM in Australian Academic and Special Libraries," *Laserdisk Professional,* 3, 18–22, 1990.

Tegene, A. and Kuchler, F., "Evaluating Forecasting Models of Farmland Prices," *International Journal of Forecasting,* 10, 65–80, 1994.

Theil, H., *Applied Economic Forecasting,* North Holland Publishing, Amsterdam, 1966.

Toedter, K.-H., "Structural Estimation and Stochastic Simulation of Large Non-Linear Models," *Economic Modelling,* 9, 121–128, 1992.

Vickers, B., "Using GDSS to Examine the Future European Automobile Industry," *Futures,* 24, 789–812, 1992.

Weerahandi, S., Hisiger, R. S., and Chien, V., "A Framework for Forecasting Demand for New Services and Their Cross Effects on Existing Services," *Information Economics & Policy,* 6, 143–162, 1994.

Winters, P. R., "Forecasting Sales by Exponentially Weighted Moving Averages," *Management Science,* 6, 324-342, 1960.

Yong, Y. W., Keng, K. A., and Leng, T. L., "A Delphi Forecast for the Singapore Tourism Industry: Future Scenario and Marketing Implications," *International Marketing Review,* 6, 35–46, 1989.

Yurkiewicz, J., "Forecasting Software: Clearing Up a Cloudy Picture," *OR/MS Today,* 20, 64–75, 1993.

CHAPTER
5

AGGREGATE PLANNING

1 INTRODUCTION

Chris owns and runs a small company that makes one product—plastic cases to hold computer diskettes. Making them is simple; raw plastic is fed into two injection molding machines. One machine makes the top of the case, the other makes the bottom. The two halves are manually put together, placed into boxes, and shipped. The injection molding machines are identical and can make 550 pieces per hour. A worker can fit the two halves together and put the finished case into a box at a rate of 55 per hour.

From forecasts, Chris anticipates steady sales of 80,000 cases per month for the next year. At four weeks per month, this is 20,000 cases per week. Assuming five days per week, the company can make 4000 cases a day. Working an eight hour shift and producing 500 cases per hour gives the desired quantity. Therefore, Chris should plan to have the injection molding machines running at 500 pieces per hour and should have 10 workers to assemble them.

This production plan is almost ideal. The constant production rate can be satisfied with constant capacity; capacity is defined as how much a production system can produce. For Chris, it is easy to design the facility to make 4000 cases per day. The work force will be constant, and the production rate is slightly less than the capacity of people and machines, which gives good utilization without overloading the facilities. Because of the constant production rate, raw material usage is also constant, and because suppliers and customers are close, frequent deliveries of raw materials and finished goods will keep inventory low.

Unfortunately, constant demand is rare, and when demand is not constant, determining production levels is more complicated. There are several strategies to cope with fluctuating demand. We can change the demand, produce at a constant rate anyway, vary the production rate, or use a combination. This strategy is a production plan and is the subject of this chapter.

164

2   INFLUENCING DEMAND

Rather than plan for fluctuating demand, it is better to make demand constant. There are three approaches to doing so:

- Do not satisfy demand during peak periods.
- Shift demand from peak periods to nonpeak periods or create new demand for nonpeak periods.
- Produce several products with peak demand in different periods.

The first strategy has capacity less than peak demand and maintains a constant production rate within capacity. This strategy will not satisfy all demand and some sales will be lost. Japanese car manufacturers often take this stance. They determine a percentage of the market share and produce at that level. Sales personnel are then expected to sell that amount. Often, supply is short. The ease of planning must be compared to lost revenue.

Creating new demand for nonpeak periods is usually done through advertising or incentive programs. U.S. automobile manufacturers offer rebates during nonpeak periods hoping new customers are attracted to the car. A nonmanufacturing example is a telephone company's differential pricing system to encourage customers to place calls in nonpeak periods. These strategies are helpful in smoothing demand.

Finally, we can make several products with offsetting demand patterns. To be successful, the products should be similar, so that manufacturing them is not too different. An example is snowmobiles and jetskis. Their technology is similar, so they could use the same engines and the body work would be similar; these are complementary products. Other examples are lawn mowers and snowblowers, coats and swim wear, boots and sandals, and baseball and football equipment.

3   PLANNING PRODUCTION

When demand varies, the desired production levels are not obvious. We must determine a **production plan**—how much and when to make each product. The goal is to match the production rate and the demand rate, so that products are made when needed.

As in forecasting, production is planned over several different time horizons through a hierarchical approach. Typically, three plans over different time horizons are developed sequentially. These are long-, intermediate-, and short-range plans. In a top-down approach, the long-range plan is developed first, and its decisions become input to an intermediate-range plan. This plan provides input to a short-range plan. A bottom-up approach starts with a short-range plan and works toward a long-range plan.

Whether a top-down or bottom-up approach is used, all three plans operate on a **rolling horizon**. A plan is made for all periods in the horizon, but in the next period a new plan is made. The first period of a plan is frozen; i.e., the decisions for that period are based on the current plan. However, decisions made in the second period depend more heavily on the new plan developed in the first period. For a six-month horizon, the first plan includes decisions for January through June. The January decisions are frozen, but the February through June decisions are finalized later. In January, the plan is redone for February through July. The decisions for February may differ from the original plan but are based on more current information. Because uncertainty increases the further into the future we look, the rolling horizon allows changes in later periods as new plans are constructed.

A **long-range plan** might cover a three-to-ten year period and is usually updated yearly. It is a corporate level plan and considers all plants and products. Inputs are the long-term aggregate forecast and current plant capacity. The units of measurement for both forecast and capacity are aggregates, likely dollars or standard hours. Decisions relate to capacity or products. A capacity decision might be whether to build a new plant or expand an existing plant. A product example would be whether a company expands, contracts, or deletes existing product lines or creates a new one. The plan would determine gross levels of production for each plant and product line and long-term supplier needs.

Next, an **intermediate-range plan** is made. An intermediate horizon is from six months to two years with monthly or quarterly updates. Typical plans are for one year with monthly updates. Inputs include capacity and product decisions from the long-range plan. Again, units of measurements are aggregate, but possibly by product line or family and plant department. Changes in the work force, additional machines, subcontracting, and overtime are typical decisions. Determining the process to use for each product family, the production rates, and the inventory levels could also be part of the plan. These decisions identify the amount of raw material needed, allowing contracts for capacity of various suppliers to be signed.

Finally, a **short-term plan** is developed. This plan may cover one week to six months, with updates made daily or weekly. A one-month horizon with a weekly update is common. It determines the time a particular product is made on a specific machine. Units might be a particular product and capacity might be the available hours of a particular machine. This plan determines overtime and undertime, as well as the possibility of not fulfilling all demand. Details are given to suppliers to deliver specific quantities on specific dates. Recall that the time frame, units, inputs, and decisions for the three different plans were given in Table 1-1.

The production planning function can be quite complex. Several factors affect this complexity, including the number of products, the demand pattern and uncertainty, the number of periods in the horizon, alternative processes to make products, subcontracting, overtime, and inventory.

In this chapter, we focus on intermediate-range planning. Different products are aggregated into a common unit, which is usually called **aggregate planning**. The approach is similar for the long- and short-range problems.

4   ASPECTS OF AGGREGATE PLANNING

The three aspects of aggregate planning that are most important are capacity, aggregate units, and costs. A brief discussion of each follows.

4.1   Capacity

Capacity is how much a production system can make. The definition of capacity depends upon the system: The capacity of a university is different from the capacity of a General Motors plant—but both indicate how much the system can produce.

Capacity is measured in many different ways, but there is usually a natural measure. For the General Motors plant, it might be the number of cars produced per hour. For a university, it could be the number of students graduated per term. The level of detail needed may dictate the measure used. We may be more concerned with the capacity of the fabrication shop than the entire plant, or with the capacity of one marketing course. However measured, capacity and demand must be in the same units.

To satisfy demand, system capacity should exceed demand, at least over the long run. However, excess capacity is costly. A plant that can produce 1000 units per day when only 500 are needed has idle capacity, representing wasted investment. Short-term changes in capacity can be made but are usually small changes. For example, overtime can be used. Larger changes in capacity require a longer time and are added in discrete increments, such as building a plant or adding a machine or shift.

4.2 Aggregate Units

Production usually involves many products made in a variety of ways. Intermediate- and long-term plans do not need this level of detail, so products are lumped together to form one product. Long-range plans are called **capacity plans**, and medium-range plans are called **aggregate plans**.

Often an aggregate product is expressed in terms of time or money. By doing so, different products can be aggregated using the same unit of measurement. For simplicity, assume products A, B, and C require 5, 2.5 and 0.75 hours, respectively, to produce. To convert the monthly demand for products to monthly demand for production hours, multiply the time required to produce each product by the number needed, and sum them. This process gives a monthly demand for an aggregate product in production hours. If demand for A is 200 units, demand for B is 100, and demand for C is 1000, an equivalent demand for production hours is

$$5 \times 200 + 2.5 \times 100 + 0.75 \times 1000 = 2000 \text{ hours}$$

An aggregate product in dollars is defined analogously by using production cost instead of production time.

Capacity must be measured in the same units as the aggregate product. Hours are natural; the capacity is the hours available per unit time. With 50 full-time workers, there are $50 \times 168 = 8400$ hours of production time available per month. Time can be converted to dollars by using the standard labor rates and cost of equipment.

4.3 Costs

Many costs affect the production plan. Broadly speaking, they are production costs, inventory costs, and capacity change costs.

Production costs include materials, direct labor, and other costs attributed to producing a unit, e.g., overtime or subcontracting costs. Costs that are constant with respect to the decision being made should be ignored. Overhead costs might be constant because they may be incurred regardless of the production plan used. Other process-related, overhead costs may affect the decisions and should be included. The particular situation determines which costs to consider.

Inventory-related costs are holding and shortage costs. The inventory holding cost coefficient is the actual cost to keep one unit in inventory for one period. It includes costs for lost opportunity, insurance, taxes, breakage, spoilage, pilferage, equipment and people to handle the inventory, and possibly physical space. Include only those costs affected by the decisions

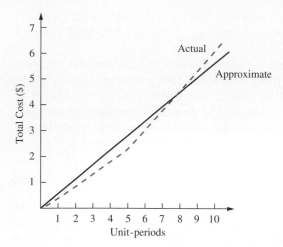

FIGURE 5-1
Typical holding costs

being made. A unit that is sold but not delivered because of a shortage is called a backorder. The shortage cost coefficient is for one unit short for one period. It includes special record keeping and handling of backordered items as well as loss of revenue and goodwill. In a manufacturing situation, if the next stage of the process is the "customer" and a shortage occurs, the whole plant might shut down, which would result in a very large shortage cost. Chapter 6 gives a more detailed discussion of inventory costs.

Often, both holding and shortage costs are assumed to be linear. Thus, holding two units in inventory is twice as costly as holding one. In actuality, neither cost is linear. For example, if all demand is backordered, customers will likely find other suppliers, resulting in a large cost. Similarly, the cost to keep 1000 units in inventory for one period is not likely to be 1000 times the cost of one unit in inventory for the same time. We assume that the linear approximation is reasonable within the range of likely values. Sensitivity analysis can help validate the assumption. A graph of holding costs are given in Figure 5-1. Both the actual cost curve and a linear approximation are shown. A graph of shortage costs would be similar.

Capacity-change costs include hiring and training workers, and can include a cost for lost capacity until a worker is fully trained. Laying off workers incurs direct separation costs and costs similar to loss of goodwill. A company that lays off workers frequently finds it difficult to hire workers. Hiring and layoff costs are similar to inventory and shortage costs.

After discussing capacity, aggregation, and costs, we look at methods for generating an aggregate production plan. The approaches for aggregate planning can be used for specific products. If there are many products, the complexity increases greatly. There are two types of approaches: spreadsheet methods and quantitative methods. We start with spreadsheet methods.

SECTION 4 PROBLEMS

5.1. Give complementary products for the following:
   (a) Sunscreen
   (b) Ski boots

   (c) Lawn mowers

   (d) Porch swings

   (e) Hockey helmets

   (f) Aluminum canoes

5.2. Explain how you would measure capacity for each of the following:

   (a) A fast-food hamburger restaurant

   (b) Your academic department

   (c) A pick-up truck

   (d) Your kitchen

   (e) A pizza delivery operation

   (f) A post office

   (g) A pencil manufacturer

5.3. What costs should be considered in aggregate planning?

5.4. What could you do if a cost, say shortage cost, is not linear?

5.5. Why forecast and plan for more than one period?

5   SPREADSHEET METHODS

There are many ways to develop a production plan. We examine a simple method that may not give the best solution but often provides good solutions. This method is a trial-and-error approach, easily implemented with a spreadsheet. A simple example illustrates the approach.

   There are two opposite strategies. The first, a **zero inventory** strategy, produces exactly the demand for each period, which requires a fluctuating work force. The second, a **level production** strategy, produces a constant amount each period. Variations in demand are accounted for by holding inventory. Also, a mixed strategy, in which both inventory and changing work force are used, is available.

   Precision Transfer, Inc., makes more than 300 different products, all precision gears. The operations to make them are similar, but the time and materials required are different. Because all gears made by Precision are similar, the aggregation unit is a gear. An aggregate gear is defined from the standards of the gears to be made in the next six months. Forecasts for the aggregate demand are given in Table 5-1.

   Last year, Precision made 41,383 gears of various kinds. There were 260 working days and an average of 40 workers. Thus Precision made 41,383 gears in 10,400 worker-days. On average, a worker can make

$$\frac{41,383 \ \text{gears/year}}{10,400 \ \text{worker-days/year}} = 3.98 \approx 4 \ \text{gears/worker-day}$$

TABLE 5-1
Aggregate demand forecast for precision gear

Month	January	February	March	April	May	June	Total
Demand (cases)	2760	3320	3970	3540	3180	2900	19,670

Production costs, excluding labor, do not change over the planning horizon and thus are ignored. A unit produced but not sold in a month is counted as inventory for that entire month (end-of-month inventory). Average monthly inventory could also be used. End-of-month inventory holding cost is $5 per gear per month. At the beginning of each month, new workers can be hired at a cost of $450 per worker. Existing workers can be laid off at a cost of $600 per worker. Wages and benefits for a worker are $15 per hour, all workers are paid for eight hours per day, and there are currently 35 workers at Precision.

5.1 Zero-Inventory Plan

First, we develop a zero inventory plan (also called a lot for lot plan) for Precision. Each month we produce exactly the amount demanded, and no inventory is carried. Workers are added when demand increases and are laid off when demand decreases. We wish to find the number of workers needed each month. Table 5-2 shows calculations for the zero inventory plan, given in a spreadsheet format. Parts of the spreadsheet table are not used for the zero inventory plan; we keep them to preserve consistency among the table format used for all plans.

The number of gears a worker can make per month is equal to the number one worker produces per day multiplied by the number of days in the month. The number of workers needed for that month is the demand for the month divided by the number of gears per month one worker can make. That is,

$$\text{workers needed} = \frac{\text{demand/month}}{\text{days/month} \times \text{units/worker/day}}$$

TABLE 5-2
Zero inventory plan

		January	February	March	April	May	June	Total
1	Days	21	20	23	21	22	22	129
2	Units/worker	84	80	92	84	88	88	516
3	Demand	2,760	3,320	3,970	3,540	3,180	2,900	19,670
4	Workers needed	33	42	44	43	37	33	232
5	Workers available	35	33	42	44	43	37	na
6	Workers hired	0	9	2	0	0	0	11
7	Hiring cost	0	4,050	900	0	0	0	4,950
8	Workers laid off	2	0	0	1	6	4	13
9	Lay-off cost	1,200	0	0	600	3,600	2,400	7,800
10	Workers used	33	42	44	43	37	33	232
11	Labor cost	83,160	100,800	121,440	108,360	97,680	87,120	598,560
12	Units produced	2,760	3,320	3,970	3,540	3,180	2,900	19,670
13	Net inventory	0	0	0	0	0	0	na
14	Holding cost	0	0	0	0	0	0	0
15	Backorder cost	0	0	0	0	0	0	0
16	Total cost	84,360	104,850	122,340	108,960	101,280	89,520	611,310

Production = four units/worker/day   Wages and benefits = $120/worker/day
Hiring cost = $450/worker   Firing cost = $600/worker
Holding cost = $5/unit/month   Backorder cost = $15/unit/month

A worker produces four gears a day, and there are 21 working days in January, so one worker can make 84 gears in January. Dividing 84 into 2760 gives 32.86 workers required to produce January's demand. If part-time workers and overtime are not allowed, we round up to 33 workers. Row 2 of the table is the number of units produced in the month by one worker. It is found by multiplying row 1 by 4, the number of gears a worker can make in one day. Row 4, obtained by dividing row 3 by row 2 and rounding up, indicates the workers needed for each of the remaining months.

Now adjust the number of workers available to the number needed. If we do not have enough, we hire more. If there are too many, we lay some off.

$$\text{workers hired} = \max\{0, \text{ workers needed} - \text{workers available}\}$$

$$\text{workers laid off} = \max\{0, \text{ workers available} - \text{workers needed}\}$$

In January, we have 35 workers available (row 5). We need 33 workers, so we lay off two workers (row 8). The cost to lay off the two workers is

$$\$600/\text{worker} \times 2 \text{ workers (row 8)} = \$1200 \text{ (row 9)}$$

Employees are paid for working eight hour/days each working day of the month, so the wages and benefits for January are

$$\$15/\text{hour} \times 8 \text{ hours/day} \times 21 \text{ days (row 1)} \times 33 \text{ workers (row 10)}$$

$$= \$83,160 \text{ (row 11)}$$

At the beginning of February, 33 workers are available (January, row 10). We need 42 (row 4), so hire nine (row 6) giving 42 (row 10) used in February. The cost to hire them is $4050 (row 7), obtained by multiplying the number hired (row 6) by $450. All rows containing costs are shaded. Results of the calculations for the remaining months can be found in Table 5-2.

We can produce

$$\text{capacity} = \text{workers} \times \text{days} \times \text{ units/worker/day}$$

gears per month. In January, the 33 workers (row 14) can produce four gears per day for 21 days (row 1), or 2772 gears, i.e.,

$$2772 = 33 \times 21 \times 4$$

Because January's demand is 2760, we plan to produce only that amount. That is,

$$\text{units produced} = \min\{\text{demand, capacity}\}$$

Capacity depends on the number of workers, which for our zero inventory plan was determined to satisfy demand. Thus capacity is always as big as demand.

Three worker days, the time to produce 12(2772 − 2760) gears, are unused. The labor cost includes all worker days, and therefore includes a cost of unused capacity.

The last column of Table 5-2 gives the totals over the six-month horizon. The plan ends with 33 workers employed and no inventory. The total cost is $611,310.

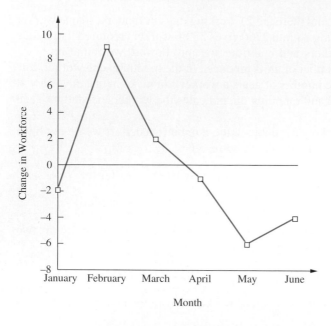

FIGURE 5-2
Zero inventory plan

A graph of the changes in work force is given in Figure 5-2. In January two workers are laid off, and in February nine workers are hired. More workers are laid off for the next three months, and in June, two workers are hired. There are a total of 11 workers hired and 13 laid off during the six months. We have 33 workers at the end of June. This graph emphasizes the variability in work force required by a zero inventory plan, an undesirable phenomenon.

5.2   Level Work Force Plan

Next, we see the other extreme, a level work force plan. It uses inventory produced in off-peak periods to satisfy demand in peak periods and is called a level production or constant work force plan because the same number of workers is used in each period.

Dividing demand over the horizon by the gears a worker can produce over the horizon gives the constant number of workers needed. A worker makes four gears per day, so in the planning horizon (129 days), 39 workers ($[19{,}670/(4 \times 129)] = 38.12$) are always needed. Always using 39 workers in our spreadsheet produces the results in Table 5-3.

We hire four workers in January and produce the maximum amount,

$$4 \times 21 \times 39 = 3276 \text{ gears}$$

In January, we produce more than demand so there will be inventory. For January it is

$$3276 \text{ produced (row 12)} - 2760 \text{ sold (row 3)} = 516 \text{ inventory (row 13)}$$

Holding one unit in inventory for one month costs \$5, so the inventory holding cost is

$$\$5 \times 516 = \$2580 \text{ (row 14)}$$

TABLE 5-3
Constant production: Backorders

		January	February	March	April	May	June	Total
1	Days	21	20	23	21	22	22	129
2	Units/worker	84	80	92	84	88	88	516
3	Demand	2,760	3,320	3,970	3,540	3,180	2,900	19,670
4	Workers needed	39	39	39	39	39	39	234
5	Workers available	35	39	39	39	39	39	na
6	Workers hired	4	0	0	0	0	0	4
7	Hiring cost	1,800	0	0	0	0	0	1,800
8	Workers laid off	0	0	0	0	0	0	0
9	Lay-off cost	0	0	0	0	0	0	0
10	Workers used	39	39	39	39	39	39	234
11	Labor cost	98,280	93,600	107,640	98,280	102,960	102,960	603,720
12	Units produced	3,276	3,120	3,588	3,276	3,432	2,978	19,670
13	Net inventory	516	316	−66	−330	−78	0	na
14	Holding cost	2,580	1,580	0	0	0	0	4,160
15	Backorder cost	0	0	990	4,950	1,170	0	7,110
16	Total cost	102,660	95,180	108,630	103,230	104,130	102,960	616,790

Production = four units/worker/day   Wages and benefits = $120/worker/day
Hiring cost = $450/worker   Firing cost = $600/worker
Holding cost = $5/unit/month   Backorder cost = $15/unit/month

February inventory is January inventory plus February production minus February demand:

$$516 + 4 \times 20 \times 39 - 3320 = 316$$

Note that we produce more than demand because we need more than 38 workers to make the 19,760 gears over the six months.

The timing of peak demands was not considered in this approach. In March, inventory (row 13) becomes −66. Cumulative production through March was less than cumulative demand; we sold more than we made. Negative inventory, called backorders, will be made and delivered at a later date. If there is a $15/unit/month backorder cost, the backorder cost for March is

$$\$15 \times 66 = \$990$$

June production is 2978, which covers the demand for June and backorders from May.

The plan finishes with no inventory, 39 workers, and a cost of $616,790. A graph of net inventory is given in Figure 5-3. Unlike the zero inventory plan, this plan has a constant work force and varying inventory. It minimizes the hiring and firing costs, but increases holding and backorder costs.

What should we do if backorders are not allowed? Dividing total demand by total working days times gears per day gives the number of workers to produce all units over the horizon, but we need to have enough workers for every month. Thus cumulative production must equal or exceed cumulative demand for every period. To get the number of workers needed for a cumulative period, divide cumulative production by cumulative units produced per worker:

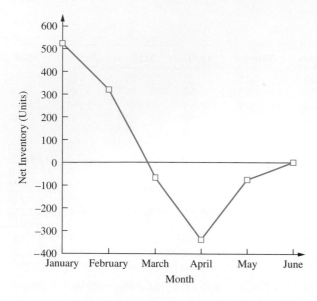

FIGURE 5-3

Constant production—backorders

$$\text{workers (cumulative)} = \frac{\text{cumulative demand}}{\text{cumulative days} \times \text{units/worker/day}}$$

For January, cumulative demand is 2760 and cumulative days are 21, so we need

$$32.86 \text{ workers} = 2760/(21 \times 4)$$

or 33 workers. For February we have

$$37.07 \text{ workers} = (2760 + 3320)/[(21 + 20) \times 4] = 6080/(41 \times 4)$$

or 38 workers needed in each of the first two months to ensure no backorders. Table 5-4 gives the results for the entire planning horizon. The maximum number of workers is 40 (January through April), so the level work force plan calls for 40 workers each month.

In January we produce to capacity, which is more than the demand. In February and March we produce to capacity, which is less than demand. The excess production from January covers demand in these months. In April, we produce only enough to satisfy demand, and inventory is zero. After April, producing to capacity builds inventory, so we produce to

TABLE 5-4

Constant number of workers needed for no backorders

	January	**February**	**March**	**April**	**May**	**June**
Days/month	21	20	23	21	22	22
Sum of days	21	41	64	85	107	129
Demand	2,760	3,320	3,970	3,540	3,180	2,900
Sum of demand	2,760	6,080	10,050	13,590	16,770	19,670
Workers	33	38	39	40	39	38

TABLE 5-5
Constant production: No backorders

		January	February	March	April	CMay	June	Total
1	Days	21	20	23	21	22	22	129
2	Units/worker	84	80	92	84	88	88	516
3	Demand	2,760	3,320	3,970	3,540	3,180	2,900	19,670
4	Workers needed	40	40	40	40	40	40	240
5	Workers available	35	40	40	40	40	40	na
6	Workers hired	5	0	0	0	0	0	5
7	Hiring cost	2,250	0	0	0	0	0	2,250
8	Workers laid off	0	0	0	0	0	0	0
9	Lay-off cost	0	0	0	0	0	0	0
10	Workers used	40	40	40	40	40	40	234
11	Labor cost	100,800	90,600	110,400	100,800	105,600	105,600	619,200
12	Units produced	3,360	3,200	3,680	3,350	3,180	2,900	19,670
13	Net inventory	600	480	190	0	0	0	na
14	Holding cost	3,000	2,400	950	0	0	0	6,350
15	Backorder cost	0	0	0	0	0	0	0
16	Total cost	106,050	98,400	111,350	100,800	105,600	105,600	627,800

Production = four units/worker/day Wages and benefits = $120/worker/day
Hiring cost = $450/worker Firing cost = $600/worker
Holding cost = $5/unit/month Backorder cost = $15/unit/month

demand. Any month requiring the maximum number of workers ends with zero inventory. We build inventory after that month if a following month needs the maximum number of workers. Table 5-5 shows calculations for the constant work force plan without backorders. At the end of June, there is no inventory, a work force of 40 people, and a six-month cost of $627,800. The plot of net inventory is given in Figure 5-4. The graph is always above zero, indicating no backorders.

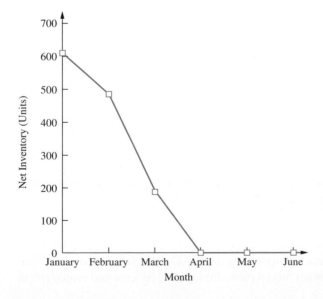

FIGURE 5-4
Constant production: No backorders

TABLE 5-6
A mixed plan

		January	February	March	April	May	June	Total
1	Days	21	20	23	21	22	22	129
2	Units/worker	84	80	92	84	88	88	516
3	Demand	2,760	3,320	3,970	3,540	3,180	2,900	19,670
4	Workers needed	38	38	42	42	35	35	230
5	Workers available	35	38	38	42	42	35	na
6	Workers hired	3	0	4	0	0	0	7
7	Hiring cost	1,350	0	1,800	0	0	0	3,150
8	Workers laid off	0	0	0	0	7	0	7
9	Lay-off cost	0	0	0	0	4,200	0	4,200
10	Workers used	38	38	42	42	35	35	230
11	Labor cost	95,760	91,200	115,920	105,840	92,400	92,400	593,520
12	Units produced	3,192	3,040	3,864	3,528	3,080	2,966	19,670
13	Net inventory	432	152	46	34	−66	0	na
14	Holding cost	2,160	760	230	170	0	0	3,320
15	Backorder cost	0	0	0	0	990	0	990
16	Total cost	99,270	91,960	117,950	106,010	97,590	92,400	605,180

Production = four units/worker/day   Wages and benefits = $120/worker/day
Hiring cost = $450/worker   Firing cost = $600/worker
Holding cost = $5/unit/month   Backorder cost = $15/unit/month

5.3 Mixed Plans

So far we have only considered pure strategies. Usually, mixed plans allowing inventory, backorders, and changing work force levels are superior to pure strategies.

Table 5-6 depicts an example of one mixed plan. The number of workers used in this plan is an educated guess based on the zero inventory and level work force plans. The zero inventory plan laid off two workers in January and hired nine in February. Rather than initially laying off workers, three workers were hired, giving us a total of 38 workers in January. As in the level work force plan, inventory satisfied demand in later months. In March, four more workers were hired to cover increased demand in March and April. In May, seven workers were laid off to account for reduced demand in May and June. The graph of net inventory on the left-hand side of Figure 5-5 shows that production matches demand more closely than the level plans. On the right-hand side of Figure 5-5, the change in work force is less drastic than in the zero inventory plan. This mixed plan costs $605,180 and ends with 35 employees and no inventory. Note that this plan has backorders; laying off six workers in May would prevent backorders but would increase cost.

With a spreadsheet, it is easy to change the number of workers to determine the costs of various plans. However, finding the cheapest plan by trial and error is a matter of both luck and the amount of time available to generate alternative plans.

5.4 Comparing Plans

So far, we have examined four plans: zero inventory, constant work force with backorders, constant work force without backorders, and a mixed plan. Table 5-7 gives cost and employment

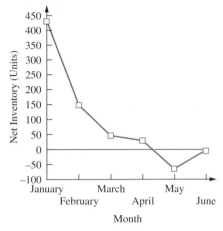
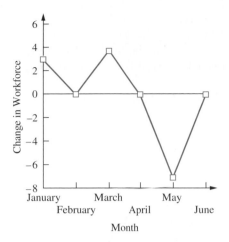

FIGURE 5-5
Production and demand for a mixed plan

information for each. The mixed plan is the least costly and will likely be preferred. However, different plans end with different work-force levels, so anticipated demand later may affect our choice of plan. If we have a desired work-force level at the end of June, we could add the cost of adjusting the number of workers in each plan to the total cost. To obtain 40 workers for July, we would need to hire seven, one, zero, and five workers for the four plans, respectively.

Changes in work-force levels may make hiring difficult. Higher cost may be an acceptable trade-off for stable employment. Also, on a rolling horizon, the decisions actually made for the last period are not as heavily influenced by the end-of-horizon effect.

5.5 Summary of Spreadsheet Methods

Spreadsheet methods for aggregate planning are quite useful because other factors can be considered; it is easy to add rows to represent overtime or subcontracting. The major drawback to spreadsheets is that they are trial-and-error methods. Thus, the quality of the plan depends on the creativity of the person using the spreadsheet. The advantage is that the planner can immediately see the impact of the plan and can easily change it.

TABLE 5-7
Comparing four plans

	Zero-inventory	Level/BO	Level/NBO	Mixed
Hiring cost	4,950	1,800	2,250	3,150
Lay-off cost	7,800	0	0	4,200
Labor cost	59,856	603,720	619,200	593,520
Holding cost	0	4,160	6,350	3,890
Backorder cost	0	7,110	0	990
Total cost	611,310	616,790	627,800	605,750
Workers	33	39	40	35

One alternative to trial-and-error approaches with a spreadsheet is to use linear programming. In fact, many spreadsheets have linear programming add-ins so that the spreadsheet sets up the data for the model. These methods determine a minimum cost plan. For larger problems, specialized linear programming solvers are used rather than spreadsheets.

SECTION 5 PROBLEMS

5.6. Name and explain the three basic strategies in aggregate planning.

5.7. What are the advantages of a spreadsheet-based production plan? What disadvantages does it have?

5.8. Consider the following production plan:

Month	Beginning inventory	Demand	Required production	Number of workers	Actual production
January	200	500	300	15	660
February	360	600	?	15	660
March	?	650	?	15	660

(a) How many units are produced by each worker?

(b) How many units must be produced in February if no shortages are allowed?

(c) What is the beginning inventory for March for the given plan?

(d) What is the total inventory cost incurred for this plan if it costs $12 per year to hold one unit in inventory?

(e) What would you call this plan?

(f) Is it optimal? Explain.

5.9. Poseidon Meter, Inc., makes a variety of water meters. Data for the past year indicate a worker can make, on average, 100 meters per four-week period. The inventory holding cost is computed to be $1 per meter per period. Backorders, if allowed, cost about $2 per meter per period. New workers can be hired, at a cost of $1000 per worker, and existing workers can be laid off at a cost of $2000 per worker. Workers are paid $1500 per period. There are currently 10 workers at Poseidon. The forecast for the next four periods is 1200, 1200, 1000, and 1000 meters, respectively.

(a) Develop a zero inventory plan for the next four periods.

(b) Develop a constant work force plan (no backorders) for the next four periods.

(c) Develop a constant work force plan (with no more than 50 backorders allowed) for the next four periods.

(d) Which plan would you recommend, and why?

5.10. X-Print Manufacturing makes laser printers. One plant assembles the PL-4000 model. Standards indicate that one worker can assemble five printers per day. This model costs about $350 to make, and the company figures it costs $5 to hold one printer in inventory for one month. Workers earn $1500 per month and can be hired for $500 each; firing a worker costs $750. Currently, there are 12 workers in the assembly department. If a printer is backordered, the cost is $35 per unit per month.

Month	July	August	September	October	November	December	Total
Working Days	21	22	21	23	19	20	126
Demand	1020	950	800	1000	1250	650	5670

(a) Develop a zero inventory plan for this problem.

(b) Develop a constant work force plan when no backorders are allowed.

(c) Because this plan does not consider backorders, your boss asks you to develop a constant work-force plan that allows backorders. Which is the better plan?

(d) Due to a long-range capacity plan, the assembly department will be relocated, which requires the department to shut down. There are two possible times for this to happen. One is to shut down for four days in October, and the other will necessitate an eight-day shutdown in December. Which plan would you recommend?

5.11. Jerry is production manager for the ProtoPlastics Company. They make two major items—widgets and gizmos. Demand history, by month, for the last two years is given. You have recently been hired at Proto, and Jerry has asked you to plan production for the next year. It takes a worker two days to make a widget and three days to make a gizmo. Currently, there are 32 workers at the plant. To hire a new worker costs $700, and to lay off an existing worker costs $1000. Workers are paid $2000 per month. A widget costs $250 to make, and a gizmo costs $380. The inventory-cost carrying rate for Proto is 36 percent per year. Backorders are not allowed. Develop a monthly aggregate production plan and work-force levels for months 25 through 30.

	Year 1			Year 2	
Month	Widgets	Gizmos	Month	Widgets	Gizmos
1	101	200	13	102	222
2	97	197	14	102	220
3	94	196	15	97	225
4	102	200	16	110	222
5	101	202	17	92	227
6	92	209	18	102	228
7	97	207	19	110	232
8	91	216	20	92	234
9	103	212	21	102	242
10	92	220	22	107	236
11	97	216	23	103	241
12	91	218	24	91	239

5.12. The SkAtZ company has forecast demand for in-line skates to be 56, 84, 108, and 59 thousand cases for the next four quarters. There is an initial inventory of 20,000 cases, and it costs $50 per month to hold a case in inventory. Customers will backorder, but there is a loss-of-goodwill cost of $250 per case. Production capacity and costs are as follows:

Period	1	2	3	4
Internal capacity (1000 cases)	60	70	60	55
Subcontracting capacity (1000 cases)	40	40	40	40
Internal costs ($100/case)	20	21	23	22
Subcontracting costs ($100/case)	22	28	30	28

Using a spreadsheet, determine a feasible aggregate production plan for next year. What are the advantages and disadvantages of your plan?

5.13. Eastern Electric makes washers and dryers. The production requirements for aggregate units are given in the table below. An employee can produce 20 units per month on regular time and can produce an additional two units per month on overtime. Currently, 25 people are employed with no overtime being used. New workers can be hired, but there is a $950 per employee cost; layoff costs are $1500 per employee. Regular-time salary is $1750 per employee per month with overtime costs of $180 per unit per employee. Carrying costs are $15 per unit per month, and backorder costs are $30 per unit per month. There is currently no inventory on hand. Develop an aggregate plan for the next five months.

Month	1	2	3	4	5
Demand	450	550	600	625	675

6 LINEAR PROGRAMMING APPROACHES TO AGGREGATE PLANNING

Linear programming is suitable to determine the best aggregate plan. Hanssmann and Hess (1960) first formulated aggregate planning as a linear programming model. To formalize the planning model of the previous section, we introduce some notation. For the parameters of the problem, let

$$T = \text{planning-horizon length, in periods}$$
$$t = \text{index of periods, } t = 1, 2, \ldots, T$$
$$D_t = \text{forecasted number of units demanded in period } t$$
$$n_t = \text{number of units that can be made by one worker in period } t$$
$$C_t^P = \text{cost to produce one unit in period } t$$
$$C_t^W = \text{cost of one worker in period } t$$
$$C_t^H = \text{cost to hire one worker in period } t$$
$$C_t^L = \text{cost to lay off one worker in period } t$$
$$C_t^I = \text{cost to hold one unit in inventory for period } t$$
$$C_t^B = \text{cost to backorder one unit for period } t$$

Again, the decision variables are the quantity to be produced, the number of workers to hire or lay off, and inventory and backorder levels. Formally, we have

$$P_t = \text{number of units produced in period } t$$
$$W_t = \text{number of workers available in period } t$$
$$H_t = \text{number of workers hired in period } t$$
$$L_t = \text{number of workers laid off in period } t$$
$$I_t = \text{number of units held in inventory at the end of period } t$$
$$B_t = \text{number of units backordered at the end of period } t$$

Recall that linear programming assumes all variables are continuously divisible. Thus, the solution may be to produce 2142.3 units next month. Although it may be impossible to produce 0.3 units, aggregate units are fictitious, so it probably does not matter. Also, rounding large numbers will likely be acceptable. If the solution is to hire 1.5 workers, however, we may have a problem. Satisfactory results can often be obtained by rounding and using common sense. Otherwise, integer programming software can be used. Unfortunately, integer programs are much more difficult to solve than linear programs and hence limit the size of the problems we can solve.

6.1 Constraints

We define several constraints for the linear programming model: constraints on capacity, work force, and material. Through the parameters, these constraints relate the decision variables to each other.

First, the size of the work force limits the number of units we can produce. In period t we have W_t workers, and each can produce n_t units in the period, meaning we can produce no more than $n_t W_t$ units in period t. Mathematically, we have

$$P_t \leq n_t W_t \qquad t = 1, 2, \ldots, T$$

The number of workers available is a function of the number we start with and how many we hire and lay off. Let W_0 be the initial number of workers. For later periods we have

$$W_t = W_{t-1} + H_t - L_t \qquad t = 1, 2, \ldots, T$$

Finally, we relate the units produced to net inventory:

net inventory this period $=$ net inventory last period $+$ production this period
$-$ demand this period

If the net inventory is positive, we physically have inventory, but if it is negative, we are in a backorder position. These two conditions cannot occur simultaneously. Let the net inventory at time t be $I_t - B_t$. Either $I_t \geq 0$ or $B_t \geq 0$, but at least one of them must be zero. The relationship, called the material or inventory balance equation, is

$$I_t - B_t = I_{t-1} - B_{t-1} + P_t - D_t \qquad t = 1, 2, \ldots, T$$

where I_0 and B_0 are the initial on-hand inventory and outstanding backorders, respectively.

6.2 Costs

The cost for any plan is the sum of production costs, hiring and lay-off costs, inventory holding costs, and backorder costs over all periods. Production costs are simply the number of units produced times the cost per unit to produce them and the cost per worker times the number of workers. Production costs per unit that do not change from period to period can be deleted from the model. The total cost for a plan is

$$\sum_{t=1}^{T} (C_t^P P_t + C_t^W W_t + C_t^H H_t + C_t^L L_t + C_t^I I_t + C_t^B B_t)$$

6.3 A Model

We are now ready to state a linear programming model. It is

$$\text{Minimize} \sum_{t=1}^{T} (C_t^P P_t + C_t^W W_t + C_t^H H_t + C_t^L L_t + C_t^I I_t + C_t^B B_t)$$

subject to
$$P_t \leq n_t W_t \qquad\qquad t = 1, 2, \ldots, T$$
$$W_t = W_{t-1} + H_t - L_t \qquad t = 1, 2, \ldots, T$$
$$I_t - B_t = I_{t-1} - B_{t-1} + P_t - D_t \quad t = 1, 2, \ldots, T$$
$$P_t, W_t, H_t, L_t, I_t \geq 0 \qquad t = 1, 2, \ldots, T$$

6.4   An Example Problem

Consider the Precision Transfer example in Section 5.5. The planning horizon is six periods, so $T = 6$. Costs do not vary over time, so $C_t^P = 0$, $C_t^W = \$120n_t$, $C_t^H = \$450$, $C_t^L = \$600$, and $C_t^I = \$5$. We assume that no backorders are allowed and delete the backorder costs and variables. Again, because production costs do not change over the horizon, we do not include them. Demand is given in Table 5-1, and we calculated the number of units a worker can produce in each month earlier. The linear programming equations for this problem are given in Table 5-8.

Using a linear programming software package, the optimal solution was obtained after 28 iterations. The total cost is \$600,191, and the values of the variables are given in Table 5-9.

TABLE 5-8
Linear programming model for Precision Transfer

Minimize	$2520W_1 + 2400W_2 + 2760W_3 + 2520W_4 + 2640W_5 + 2640W_6$
	$+ \; 450H_1 + \; 450H_2 + \; 450H_3 + \; 450H_4 + \; 450H_5 + \; 450H_6$
	$+ \; 600L_1 + \; 600L_2 + \; 600L_3 + \; 600L_4 + \; 600L_5 + \; 600L_6$
	$+ \quad 5I_1 + \quad 5I_2 + \quad 5I_3 + \quad 5I_4 + \quad 5I_5 + \quad 5I_6$

Subject to

Production-capacity constraints
$$P_1 \leq 84W_1$$
$$P_2 \leq 80W_2$$
$$P_3 \leq 92W_3$$
$$P_4 \leq 84W_4$$
$$P_5 \leq 88W_5$$
$$P_6 \leq 88W_6$$

Work-force constraints
$$W_1 = 35 + H_1 - L_1$$
$$W_2 = W_1 + H_2 - L_2$$
$$W_3 = W_2 + H_3 - L_3$$
$$W_4 = W_3 + H_4 - L_4$$
$$W_5 = W_4 + H_5 - L_5$$
$$W_6 = W_5 + H_6 - L_6$$

Inventory-balance constraints
$$I_1 = \quad\; + P_1 - 2760$$
$$I_2 = I_1 + P_2 - 3320$$
$$I_3 = I_2 + P_3 - 3970$$
$$I_4 = I_3 + P_4 - 3540$$
$$I_5 = I_4 + P_5 - 3180$$
$$I_6 = I_5 + P_6 - 2900$$

$$P_1, P_2, P_3, P_4, P_5, P_6, W_1, W_2, W_3, W_4, W_5, W_6,$$
$$H_1, H_2, H_3, H_4, H_5, H_6, L_1, L_2, L_3, L_4, L_5, L_6,$$
$$I_1, I_2, I_3, I_4, I_5, I_6 \geq 0.$$

TABLE 5-9
Linear programming solution

Month	Production	Inventory	Hired	Laid off	Workers
January	2940.00	180.0	0.00	0.00	35.00
February	3232.86	92.86	5.41	0.00	40.41
March	3877.14	0.00	1.73	0.00	42.14
April	3540.00	0.00	0.00	0.00	42.14
May	3180.00	0.00	0.00	6.00	36.14
June	2900.00	0.00	0.00	3.18	32.95

Total cost = $600,191.60

Recall the basic assumptions of linear programming: variables are linear and continuously divisible. Thus, the linear programming solution produces 3232.86 gears, carries 92.86 gears in inventory, and hires 5.41 workers for a work force of 40.41 in February. Because *gears* in this model are aggregates and do not represent actual gears, the fractional production and inventory figures are not too troubling. Also, 0.86 gears out of 3232 is miniscule and hence not a problem. The 5.41 workers hired is another matter, however. If we could hire part-time workers, the fraction would be unimportant. Because we assumed that only full-time workers were available, we must adjust the solution. Although the linear programming model does not optimally solve the actual problem, it will provide insight into a very good solution.

The linear programming solution produces to capacity in the first three months. In February, 5.41 workers were hired. Because we must hire six, there is about 0.6 worker-months more capacity available, which covers capacity needed for March and the following months. We use a spreadsheet (Table 5-10) with 35 workers in January, 41 in February, and 42 in both March and April. In May we drop to 36 and in June, 33. Capacity for February, March, April, and May is 170 units less than demand for the same months. To avoid backorders, these units must be produced in January. There is excess capacity of 180 units in January, so backorders can in fact be avoided. Using these numbers, we determine the production for each month. Changes in the number of workers might have been needed to get a feasible plan.

Using our standard spreadsheet with the workers and production levels from Table 5-10, the rounded plan has a total cost of $600,750 compared to the linear programming solution

TABLE 5-10
Rounding the linear programming solution

		January	February	March	April	May	June	Total
1	Units/worker	84	80	92	84	88	88	516
2	Workers	35	41	42	42	36	33	229
3	Capacity	2940	3280	3864	3528	3168	2904	19,684
4	Demand	2760	3320	3970	3540	3180	2900	19,670
5	Capacity − demand	180	−40	−106	−12	−12	4	14
6	Cumulative difference	180	140	34	22	10	14	14
7	Produced	2930	3280	3864	3528	3168	2900	19,670
8	Net inventory	170	130	24	12	0	0	336

of \$600,191.60. The rounded plan's cost thus is 0.09 percent above the linear programming solution; we could not do much better than that.

In addition to providing good starting solutions, linear programming can specify ending conditions. Suppose we want 36 workers and 100 units of inventory at the end of June. Setting $W_6 = 36$ and $I_6 = 100$ and solving the linear program gives the best plan satisfying those conditions.

Another advantage of linear programming is the use of dual-variable (or shadow-price) information. For the production capacity constraint in January, the dual variable is 25. If one more gear could be made in January, we could save \$25.00. It takes about two hours to make a gear, and a worker costs \$15 per hour. Thus, even on regular time it would cost \$30—more than the \$25 improvement in total cost—so using overtime would not help. Shadow prices for other constraints are interpreted in a similar way.

Reduced cost information can also provide valuable information. For I_3, the reduced cost is \$2.98. As long as the cost of carrying inventory in March is at least \$2.02(\$5.00 − \$2.98), we will have no inventory then. Even if the inventory holding cost for March is off by quite a bit, the solution will remain unchanged. Other costs can be validated using the reduced costs, or formal range-and-sensitivity analyses can be carried out.

6.5   Practical Issues Using Linear Programming

Large linear programming problems can be solved easily. Some production planning models with 100,000 variables and 40,000 constraints are solved weekly. Large corporations, such as AT&T and Delta Airlines, solve problems with several million variables. Solving huge problems requires more effort to generate the data required. Computer programs called matrix generators extract the appropriate data from a data base and generate the linear programming problem. Once the problem is solved, a report generator converts the output into a form that production planners and managers can use. Continued development in linear programming, modeling languages, and data technology will make even larger problems solvable. Thus, linear programming models will play a more important role in production planning in the future.

6.6   Extensions

Other constraints can be added to the linear programming problem to make the model more realistic. We now discuss a few simple modifications.

Direct bounds. If there is a space limitation, we impose an upper limit, say I_t^U, on the number of units in inventory during period t. This is done by adding the constraint

$$I_t \leq I_t^U$$

Lower bounds can also be included. Management policy might impose limits on hiring or laying off workers, which can be handled similarly. Terminal conditions can be handled by bounds. For example, to impose minimum and maximum final inventories add

$$I_T^L \leq I_T \leq I_T^U$$

Setting $B_T = 0$ assures that no outstanding backorders occur at the end of the horizon. Constraints of this type are called bounded variables. Adding them does not make solving the linear programming model much more difficult, because they are handled implicitly.

Percent Bounds. Rather than give a specific number as a limit on a variable, the bound can be a percentage of another variable. Suppose management imposes a constraint to lay off no more than 5 percent of the work force in any period. Mathematically, this can be stated as

$$L_t \leq .05W_t$$

Backorders restricted below a specified percentage of production provide another example. These constraints are called variable upper bounds. Although they are more complex than bounded variable constraints, they add less of a computational burden than constraints containing more than two variables.

Training. If workers must be trained before they are productive, we can change the work-force constraints to reflect the training period. If a worker hired in period t is trained for one period, the worker is not productive until period $t + 1$. The modified work-force balance equation has H_t replaced by H_{t-1}. The equation is

$$W_t = W_{t-1} + H_{t-1} - L_t$$

If trainees are paid at a different rate than regular employees, the labor component of the objective function is changed accordingly.

Multiple objectives. Sometimes it is difficult to determine shortage, hiring, and lay-off costs. Because plans that minimize shortages may hire and lay off many workers, a multiple-objective approach may be appropriate. Masud and Hwang (1980) give a multiple-objective model that tries to maximize profit while simultaneously minimizing shortages, inventory investment, and changes in the work force.

SECTION 6 PROBLEMS

5.14. Discuss linear programming for aggregate planning. Discuss the assumptions it requires and the possible problems associated with them. What are the strengths and weaknesses of the linear programming approach?

5.15. Develop and solve a linear program to determine an optimal plan for Poseidon Meter (Problem 5.9). Assume no more than 50 backorders are allowed in any period. How does it compare with the spreadsheet solution?

5.16. Consider X-Print Manufacturing (Problem 5.10).

    (a) Give the constraints for the first month of a linear programming formulation for this problem. Assume backorders are allowed and, in any month no more than a 25 percent change in work force is allowed.

    (b) Determine an optimal plan for X-Print. How does it compare with the spreadsheet plan?

    (c) Due to stiff competition in the laser printer market, X-Print wants to reexamine its backorder policy. What backorder cost would make the no-backorder case better than the backorder case?

    (d) Does the linear programming formulation answer the question of when to relocate the assembly department? If so, how? If not, can it be modified to do so?

5.17. Develop and solve a linear programming model for Eastern Electric's aggregate plan (Problem 5.13). Compare it with the spreadsheet solution.

5.18. Consumer Electronics makes a variety of small household appliances. Various models of toasters, coffee makers, and bread machines account for most of their production. The demand for each family for the next three months, the average number of each product a worker can produce in a month, and their average holding cost is as follows:

| | Month | | | | Holding |
	1	2	3	Output/worker	cost
Toaster	2000	2600	2000	70	$0.85
Coffee maker	2200	2400	2100	120	$1.25
Bread machine	900	1200	700	110	$2.10
Total	5100	6200	4800		

All workers are paid $2000 per month. Hiring a new worker costs $1200 and laying off a worker costs $2500. A new worker goes through one month of on-the-job training, during which he or she can only produce half of the output of a trained worker. For stability, Consumer Electrics wants no more than a 15 percent change in work force in any month; currently, there are 55 workers. Backorders are not allowed. Develop and solve a model to determine an aggregate production plan for Consumer Electronics.

7 TRANSPORTATION MODELS

A production planning problem with constant work force can be solved as a transportation problem (Bowman, 1956). Transportation algorithms are about 100 times faster than linear programming algorithms, and larger problems are more readily solved. A transportation problem minimizes the cost of shipping a single product from several plants to several customers. Plants are supply points with a given availability, whereas customers are demand points requiring a certain amount of the product. There is a cost of shipping a unit of product from each supply point to each demand point, and the total supply must equal the total demand. A dummy supply or demand point can be added as needed.

Suppose we consider only regular-time production with the possibility of carrying inventory. Let

$n_t W_t = $ the capacity (in units) during period t
$D_t = $ forecasted number of units demanded in period t
$C_t^P = $ the cost to produce one unit in period t
$C_t^I = $ the cost to hold one unit in inventory for period t

So that feasible solutions exist, assume total capacity over the horizon is at least as large as total demand.

7.1 The Production Planning Model

The transportation problem has one supply point (row) for each period. If there is initial inventory, it is another supply point. There is a demand point (column) for each period, plus one for final inventory if it is required. Finally, if there is excess capacity, we add a demand point for it. A problem with T periods has $T + 1$ rows and $T + 2$ columns. For each row, the capacity for that period is given. Likewise, each column has a demand. For the excess capacity column, demand is the difference in total capacity and total demand.

TABLE 5.11
Klean problem data

t	1	2	3
$n_t W_t$	350	300	350
D_t	200	300	400
C_t^P	10	11	12
C_t^I	2	2	2

Each cell in the transportation matrix has a cost. The cost for a unit made in period t and used to satisfy demand in period t is just the production cost C_t^P. Cost for a unit produced in period t and demanded in period $t+1$ is $C_t^P + C_t^I$. A unit made in period t and used two periods later has cost $C_t^P + C_t^I + C_{t+1}^I$. Other costs are calculated similarly. Because backlogging is not allowed, demand in period t cannot be satisfied from units produced in an earlier period; these cells have an infinite cost. Initial inventory has a zero cost for the first period, and later periods have the sum of the holding costs for all previous periods.

Example 5-1. A production plan for Klean, Inc. Klean, Inc., needs to plan production for the next three months. Expected demand for their degreaser is 200, 300, and 400 cases for the next three months. There is an initial inventory of 50 cases, and a final inventory of 75 cases is desired. Capacity for the next three months is 350, 300, and 350 cases. Total capacity is 1000 cases; adding the 50 cases of initial inventory gives 1050 cases available over the horizon. Total demand is 900 cases, but we need to add the final inventory for an effective demand of 975 cases. The excess capacity is 75 cases. Klean projects that it costs $1000, $1100, and $1200 to produce a case the next three months. Due to the volatile nature of he degreaser, it costs $200 per month to store a case. Data, with costs stated in multiples of $100, are summarized in Table 5.11.

Solution. The transportation tableau and the optimal solution for this problem are given in Table 5.12. The cost to produce one case in period 1 and use it to satisfy demand in period 1 is

TABLE 5.12
Transportation model: Klean, Inc.

	1		2		3		Ending inventory		Excess capacity		Available capacity
Beginning inventory		0		2		4		6		0	50
	50										
Period 1		10		12		14		16		0	350
	150				50		75		75		
Period 2		—		11		13		15		0	300
			300								
Period 3		—		—		12		14		0	350
					350						
Demand	200		300		400		75		75		1050

10, given in the upper right corner of cell (1,1). To make a case in period 1 and sell it in period 2 costs 10 to make plus 2 to store, so in cell (1,2) the cost is 12. Demands and availabilities are given in the respective column and row. Because backorders are not allowed the cost to satisfy demand in a period from production in a later period is not allowed, e.g., cell (3,1).

The optimal solution is represented in boldface in the table. We produce 275 cases in period 1; 150 are sold in period 1, 50 are sold in period 3, and the remainder make up the ending inventory. The total cost of this plan is $1,150,000. As with linear programming, shadow prices and reduced costs can provide more insight into the problem.

7.2 Extensions

Subcontracting and overtime. If other modes of obtaining products are available, they may be included in the transportation model. Two common alternatives are producing on overtime and subcontracting. Suppose 90 cases could be made on overtime in period 1 at a cost of $16 per case. Add a new row with supply 90 and costs equal to the overtime cost plus the proper carrying costs. The same idea models subcontracting.

Backorders. Suppose units are backordered at a cost of $5 per unit-month. Then production in period 2 can be used to satisfy demand in period 1. The cost for producing in period 2 is $11, so adding the $5 backorder cost results in a cost of $16 for cell (2,1). Similarly, the cost for cell (3,2) is 12 + 5 = 17, and for cell (3,1) it is 12 + 5 + 5 = $22. The appropriate model is easily constructed.

Suppose overtime costs per unit are $16, $18, and $20 for periods 1, 2, and 3, with overtime capacity of 90, 90, and 75 units in the three periods, respectively. If demand in period 1 is 400 units and all other parameters stay the same, the transportation tableau and optimal solution are given in Table 5.13. The optimal solution uses overtime in period 1 and has total cost of $1,370,000. It uses overtime in periods 1 and 3 rather than using inventory. There are no backorders, but with different costs they could have been used. Because parameters were changed, this plan cannot be compared to the Klean example.

SECTION 7 PROBLEMS

5.19. Goode Foods wishes to plan aggregate production at a single plant for the next three periods. An aggregate unit is thousands of gallons (k-gals) of food processed. The following data are relevant:

Period		1	2	3
Production capacity (k-gals)	Regular time	100	100	80
	Overtime	20	20	10
	Subcontracting	40	40	40
Production costs ($1000/k-gal)	Regular time	2.0	2.0	2.0
	Overtime	2.8	2.8	2.8
	Subcontracting	3.2	3.2	3.2
Demand (k-gals)		95	105	95

There is an initial inventory of 5000 gallons. The cost to carry 1000 gallons for one period is $60. Assuming all demand must be satisfied, formulate and solve a model to minimize total costs while satisfying all constraints.

TABLE 5.13
A Transportation Model with Overtime

	1	2	3	Ending inventory	Excess capacity	Available capacity
Beginning inventory	[0]	[2] **25**	[4] **25**	[6]	[0] **0**	50
Period 1 — Regular time	[10] **350**	[12]	[14]	[16]	[0] **0**	350
Period 1 — Overtime	[16] **50**	[18]	[20]	[22]	[0] **40**	90
Period 2 — Regular time	[16]	[11] **275**	[13]	[15] **75**	[0] **0**	350
Period 2 — Overtime	[23]	[18]	[20]	[22]	[0] **90**	90
Period 3 — Regular time	[22]	[17]	[12] **300**	[14]	[0] **0**	300
Period 3 — Overtime	[30]	[25]	[20] **75**	[22]	[0] **0**	75
Demand	400	300	400	75	130	1305

5.20. Develop and solve a model for the SkAtZ company planning problem (Problem 5.12). How does it compare with your spreadsheet solution? What drawbacks, if any, does it have?

5.21. Generic, Inc., produces a variety of generic prescription drugs, which are sold to chain pharmacies. All drugs are in tablet form and are made on the same production line. Currently, the plant is operating two shifts per day, five days per week, and demand for the next four months is 420, 350, 410, and 315 million tablets. Each shift can produce 200 million tablets per month at a cost of $0.50 per tablet. Overtime can be used to produce tablets at a 65 percent premium. Only two hours per day of overtime can be used, because of maintenance that must be performed on the production equipment. Current inventory is two million tablets, and Generic wants three million in inventory at the end of month 4. It costs $15,000 to hold one million tablets in inventory for one month. Because the pharmacies are ordering for their distribution centers, most orders can be backordered. Contracts specify a 30 percent penalty for late deliveries. Develop an optimal aggregate production plan for the next four months.

5.22. Suppose Generic (Problem 5.21) can modify their production line to get a 15 percent increase in capacity. How much could they afford to pay for the upgrade and recover the cost in one year? List all assumptions you make to answer the question.

8   DISAGGREGATING PLANS

An aggregate plan determines the production and inventory level for aggregate units in each period. Aggregate units are not actually produced, so the plan should consider individual products. This process is called disaggregation, and becomes the master production schedule.

Sometimes the master production schedule does not depend on the aggregate plan, so they are treated independently. An aggregate unit of dollars unrelated to actual capacity of the manufacturing processes is an example. Another situation is represented by different products sharing little or no machinery or processes. Complementary products, e.g., snowmobiles and jetskis, have an aggregate plan with little relation to the master production schedule. Some periods are devoted exclusively to one product because there is little or no demand for the other. Even when products are not complementary, if demand for one dominates in a given period, it is produced in that period.

Significant demand for two or more products sharing a process in the same period requires two decisions. How many of each product should be produced in the period, and when within the period should they be made? That is, what batch size and sequence should we use? If the choice involves machine set-ups, the resulting problems are much more difficult to solve.

We present two approaches to the disaggregation problem. Runout time is appropriate when capacity utilization is not too high and set-up times are small. When set-up cost or time is large and capacity constraints are tight, integer programming models are appropriate.

8.1   Runout Time

Runout time is probably the oldest, most widely used method to convert aggregate plans into plans for individual products. To compute the runout time R_i for product i, let

$$R_i = I_i/D_i$$

R_i is how long the current inventory of product i will last. Begin by producing the product with the smallest R_i. After producing i, produce the product with the next smallest runout time and continue this sequence until all products are produced. If set-up times are small and capacity is sufficiently larger than demand, this sequence will be feasible.

The amount of each product made in the runout sequence can affect feasibility of the plan. To avoid infeasibility, we use an aggregate runout time to determine the amount of each product to make in the sequence. The aggregate runout time is the number of periods it will take to use up all the available inventory plus new units produced during the current period (both in aggregate units) assuming they are used at the demand rate. Suppose an aggregate unit is in machine-hours, and letting R' be the aggregate runout time, we have

$$R' = \frac{\sum\limits_{i=1}^{n} r_i I_i + T}{\sum\limits_{i=1}^{n} r_i D_i}$$

where r_i is the production rate for product i and there are n products.

We produce in the smallest runout time sequence, but the amount of each product to produce is a proportion of the aggregate runout time R'. The batch size of product i, say Q_i, will be

$$Q_i = R' D_i - I_i$$

8.2   Integer Programming Models

It is not too difficult to formulate the disaggregation problem as an integer programming model. The particular form will depend on the aggregate model and the important characteristics needed from the detailed plan. We will illustrate with a typical scenario.

Suppose we produce n products on L lines or facilities. Both products and facilities have been aggregated in a quarterly plan by month. Thus for each of the next four months we have determined how much to produce in the aggregate and aggregate inventory levels. We wish to convert this information to a weekly production plan on an individual product and line basis. We must do so while keeping inventory at the level suggested by the aggregate plan to smooth production.

Consider the first month of the aggregate plan. Let

i = index of the products, $i = 1, 2, \ldots, n$

l = index of the production lines, $l = 1, 2, \ldots, L$

p = index of time subperiods within the month, say weeks, $p = 1, 2, 3, 4$

D_i = demand for product i in the month

I' = desired aggregate inventory at the end of the month

I_i^O = on-hand inventory of product i at the beginning of the month

I_i^E = on-hand inventory of product i at the end of the month

r_{il} = rate for product i to be produced on line l

k_i = factor to convert one unit of product i into an aggregate product

c_{il} = cost to produce the entire month's demand of product i on line l and

s_{ijl} = set-up cost for product j on line l if i is currently running on line l

The decision variables are x_{ilp} (the proportion of time in week p that product i is processed on line ℓ) and z_{ijlp} (a zero-or-one variable; it is one if product j follows product i on line ℓ in week p). The model is:

$$\text{Minimize} \sum_{i=1}^{n} \sum_{l=1}^{L} \sum_{p-1}^{4} \left(c_{il} x_{ilp} + \sum_{j=1}^{n} s_{ijl} z_{ijlp} \right)$$

subject to

$$I_i^0 - I_i^E + \sum_{i=1}^{n} \sum_{l=1}^{L} \sum_{p=1}^{4} r_{il} x_{ilp} = D_i \qquad i = 1, 2, \ldots, n$$

$$\sum_{i=1}^{n} k_i I_i^E = I'$$

$$\sum_{i=1}^{n} x_{ilp} = 1 \qquad l = 1, 2, \ldots, L; \ p = 1, 2, 3, 4$$

$$x_{ilp-1} - x_{ilp} = \sum_{q=1}^{n} z_{iqlp} - \sum_{q=1}^{n} z_{qjlp} \qquad \begin{matrix} i = 1, 2, \ldots, n; \ j = 1, 2, \ldots, n; \\ l = 1, 2, \ldots L; \ p = 1, 2, 3, 4 \end{matrix}$$

$$\sum_{i=1}^{n} \sum_{j=1}^{n} z_{ijlp} = 1 \qquad l = 1, 2, \ldots, L; \ p = 1, 2, 3, 4$$

$$x_{ilp} \geq 0 \qquad \begin{matrix} i = 1, 2, \ldots, n; \ l = 1, 2, \ldots, L; \\ p = 1, 2, 3, 4 \end{matrix}$$

$$z_{ijlp} \in \{0, 1\} \qquad \begin{matrix} i = 1, 2, \ldots, n; \ j = 1, 2, \ldots, n; \\ l = 1, 2, \ldots, L; \ p = 1, 2, 3, 4 \end{matrix}$$

The first constraint is a material balance constraint. The second requires inventory at the end of the month to conform to the aggregate plan. The third constraint forces production of the entire monthly demand during the four-week period. The next two constraints force the proper set-up to occur if a different product is made on the same line in the same week. The final two constraints are nonnegativity on the proportion of time a product is produced on a given line and the binary restriction on set-up variables.

It is easy to see that even for relativity small numbers of products, lines, and periods the resulting model can have a large number of variables and constraints. At one time this was a major drawback of integer programming models; however, as computers and algorithms have improved, it has posed less of a problem.

Other restrictions can be added. If set-up times use a significant part of capacity, a capacity constraint for each line can be added. It would add the production time for products made on the line that week to the set-up times and require them to be no greater than available time on the line, which may add further difficulty in solving the model.

SECTION 8 PROBLEMS

5.23. What are the main goals of disaggregation?
5.24. Discuss the difficulties of disaggregation.

5.25. Disaggregate the ProtoPlastic plan developed in Problem 5.11 so that both products can be feasibly produced.

    (a) What changes in the plan were needed?

    (b) How do the changes affect total cost?

5.26. State an "algorithm" to disaggregate an aggregate plan. Apply it to Goode Foods (Problem 5.19).

9 ADVANCED PRODUCTION PLANNING MODELS

You can use linear programming for more than a single aggregate product, although rapid growth in the size of the model can be a problem. If a few products or families of products need to be planned, linear programming is effective.

In this section, we examine models for multiple products. We start with a simple extension of the work force and inventory model. Backorders, overtime, and subcontracting are easily added to the model. Then we examine a model with resource constraints representing capacities in different production areas. We also consider alternative routings for the products. These models are not all-inclusive, but present a broad picture to enable the reader to recognize similar applications. Both Johnson and Montgomery (1974) and Lawrence and Zanakis (1984) present many mathematical models for production planning.

9.1 Multiple Products

We use the same notation as before but add the subscript i for product i. Formally, we have

$$
\begin{aligned}
T &= \text{horizon length, in periods}\\
N &= \text{number of products}\\
t &= \text{index of periods, } t = 1, 2, \ldots, T\\
i &= \text{index of products, } i = 1, 2, \ldots, N\\
D_{it} &= \text{forecasted number of units demanded for product } i \text{ in period } t\\
n_{it} &= \text{number of units of product } i \text{ that can be made by one worker in period } t\\
C_{it}^P &= \text{cost to produce one unit of product } i \text{ in period } t\\
C_t^W &= \text{cost of one worker in period } t\\
C_t^H &= \text{cost to hire one worker in period } t\\
C_t^L &= \text{cost to lay off one worker in period } t\\
C_{it}^I &= \text{cost to hold one unit of product } i \text{ in inventory for period } t
\end{aligned}
$$

The decision variables are

$$
\begin{aligned}
P_{it} &= \text{number of units of product } i \text{ produced in period } t\\
W_t &= \text{number of workers available in period } t\\
H_t &= \text{number of workers hired in period } t\\
L_t &= \text{number of workers laid off in period } t\\
I_{it} &= \text{number of units of product } i \text{ held in inventory at the end of period } t
\end{aligned}
$$

The linear programming formulation is

$$
\text{Minimize} \sum_{t=1}^{T} \sum_{i=1}^{N} (C_{it}^P P_{it} + C_t^W W_t + C_t^H H_t + C_t^L L_t + C_{it}^I I_{it})
$$

subject to
$$\sum_{i=1}^{N} \left(\frac{1}{n_{it}}\right) P_{it} \leq W_t \qquad t = 1, 2, \ldots, T$$

$$W_t = W_{t-1} + H_t - L_t \qquad t = 1, 2, \ldots, T$$

$$I_{it} = I_{it-1} + P_{it} - D_{it} \qquad t = 1, 2, \ldots, T; \quad i = 1, 2, \ldots, N$$

$$P_{it}, W_t, H_t, L_t, I_{it} \geq 0 \qquad t = 1, 2, \ldots, T; \quad i = 1, 2, \ldots, N$$

This model is similar to an aggregate planning model. However, we now have production and inventory variables for each product as well as for each period. Also, there are material balance constraints for every product and every period. The formulation has $3T + 2NT$ variables and $2T + NT$ constraints. A model with 10 products and a planning horizon of 12 periods would have 276 variables and 144 constraints. Increasing the size to $N = 100$ and $T = 12$ results in 2436 variables and 1224 constraints. These linear programming models are well within the range of current software packages. Stadtler (1986) discusses a model of this type applied to a large food-products manufacturer. Rather than for individual products, production levels for families of products were determined. The resulting linear program had 1100 variables and 830 constraints.

Example 5-2. Carolina Hardwood Product Mix. Carolina Hardwood produces three types of dining tables. There are currently 50 workers; new workers can be hired, and existing workers can be laid off. During the next four quarters, the cost of hiring one worker is 420, 410, 420, and 405, respectively. The cost to lay off one worker is 800, 790, 790, and 800. The cost of one worker per quarter is 600, 620, 620, and 610. The initial inventory is 100 units for table 1, 120 units for table 2, and 80 units for table 3. The number of units that can be made by one worker per quarter is 200, 220, 210, and 200 for table 1. They are 300, 310, 300, and 290 for table 2 and 260, 255, 250, and 265 for table 3. Forecasted demand, unit cost, and holding cost per unit are:

	Demand			Unit cost			Holding cost		
Quarter	Table 1	Table 2	Table 3	Table 1	Table 2	Table 3	Table 1	Table 2	Table 3
1	3500	5400	4500	120	150	200	10	12	12
2	3100	5000	4200	125	150	210	9	11	12
3	3000	5100	4100	120	145	205	10	12	11
4	3400	5500	4600	125	148	205	10	11	11

Solution. Using the above data, we can formulate the production planning problem as the following:

Minimize $\quad 600W_1 + 620W_2 + 620W_3 + 610W_4 + 420H_1 + 410H_2 + 420H_3$

$\qquad + 405H_4 + 800L_1 + 790L_2 + 790L_3 + 800L_4 + 120P_{11} + 150P_{21}$

$\qquad + 200P_{31} + 125P_{12} + 150P_{22} + 210P_{32} + 120P_{13} + 145P_{23} + 205P_{33}$

$\qquad + 125P_{14} + 148P_{24} + 205P_{34} + 10I_{11} + 12I_{21} + 12I_{31} + 9I_{12}$

$\qquad + 11I_{22} + 12I_{32} + 10I_{13} + 12I_{23} + 11I_{33} + 10I_{14} + 11I_{24} + 11I_{34}$

subject to

$$P_{11}/200 + P_{21}/300 + P_{31}/260 \leq W_1$$
$$P_{12}/220 + P_{22}/310 + P_{32}/255 \leq W_2$$
$$P_{13}/210 + P_{23}/300 + P_{33}/250 \leq W_3$$
$$P_{14}/200 + P_{24}/290 + P_{34}/265 \leq W_4$$

$$W_1 = 50 + H_1 - L_1$$
$$W_2 = W_1 + H_2 - L_2$$
$$W_3 = W_2 + H_3 - L_3$$
$$W_4 = W_3 + H_4 - L_4$$

$$I_{11} = 100 + P_{11} - 3500$$
$$I_{21} = 120 + P_{21} - 5400$$
$$I_{31} = 80 + P_{31} - 4500$$
$$I_{12} = I_{11} + P_{12} - 3100$$
$$I_{22} = I_{21} + P_{22} - 5000$$
$$I_{32} = I_{31} + P_{32} - 4200$$
$$I_{13} = I_{12} + P_{13} - 3000$$
$$I_{23} = I_{22} + P_{23} - 5100$$
$$I_{33} = I_{32} + P_{33} - 4100$$
$$I_{14} = I_{13} + P_{14} - 3400$$
$$I_{24} = I_{23} + P_{24} - 5500$$
$$I_{34} = I_{33} + P_{34} - 4600$$

$$P_{it}, I_{it}, W_t, H_t, L_t \geq 0 \qquad t = 1, \ldots, 4; \quad i = 1, \ldots, 3$$

Using a standard linear programming package, the optimal solution to the problem is

Quarter	Production			Inventory		
	Table 1	Table 2	Table 3	Table 1	Table 2	Table 3
1	3400	5280	4420	0	0	0
2	3100	5000	4200	0	0	0
3	3000	5100	4100	0	0	0
4	3400	5500	4600	0	0	0

Quarter	Workforce	Hired	Laid off
1	51.60	1.60	0.00
2	47.69	0.00	3.91
3	47.69	0.00	0.00
4	53.32	5.64	0.00

Objective function value = $8,354,166

The work-force variables are not integers, so a rounding procedure should be applied. Hiring two workers in the first quarter, laying off four in the second quarter, and hiring six in the fourth quarter and adjusting the total cost should give an acceptable solution. As with the other linear programming models discussed, sensitivity analysis provides insight into other possible solutions.

9.2 Multiple Products and Processes

Now consider multiple products, each of which may be manufactured in a different way, which could represent different processes with zero set-up times or possibly different plant locations. Suppose there are m_i ways, or processes, to make product i. Further, suppose there are K different resources available, and making one unit of product i by process j requires a_{ijk} units of resource k. In period t, there are A_{kt} units of resource k available. Resources could represent worker-hours or machine-hours in a particular department. Nebol (1987) provides a detailed model for planning cloth production. This model considers 300 cloth products to be made in 18 plants. Let

T = horizon length, in periods
N = number of products
K = number of resource types
t = index of periods, $t = 1, 2, \ldots, T$
i = index of products, $i = 1, 2, \ldots, N$
k = index of resource types, $k = 1, 2, \ldots, K$
D_{it} = forecasted number of units demanded for product i in period t
m_i = number of different processes available to make product i
A_{kt} = amount of resource k available in period t
a_{ijk} = amount of resource k required by one unit of product i if produced by process j
C_{ijt}^P = cost to produce one unit of product i using process j in period t
C_{it}^I = cost to hold one unit of product i in inventory for period t

The decision variables are

P_{ijt} = number of units of product i produced by process j in period t
I_{it} = number of units of product i held in inventory at the end of period t

The linear programming formulation is

$$\text{Minimize} \sum_{t=1}^{T} \sum_{i=1}^{N} \sum_{j=1}^{m_i} (C_{ijt}^P P_{ijt} + C_{it}^I I_{it})$$

subject to

$$\sum_{i=1}^{N} \sum_{j=1}^{m_i} a_{ijk} P_{ijt} \leq A_{kt} \qquad t = 1, 2, \ldots, T; \quad k = 1, 2, \ldots, K$$

$$I_{it} = I_{it-1} + \sum_{j=1}^{m_i} P_{ijt} - D_{it} \qquad t = 1, 2, \ldots, T; \quad i = 1, 2, \ldots, N$$

$$P_{ijt}, I_{it} \geq 0 \qquad t = 1, 2, \ldots, T; \quad i = 1, 2, \ldots, N; \\ j = 1, 2, \ldots, m_i$$

Example 5-3. Cactus Cycles process plan. Cactus Cycle produces two types of bicycles, street and road. Production is to be planned for the next three months. The estimated demand per month for street bicycles is 1000, 1050, and 1100 units and for road bicycles is 500, 600, and 550 units. The current inventory is 100 units for street bicycles and 50 units for road bicycles. Two resources, worker-hours and machine-hours, and two different processes are used to manufacture both bicycles. The additional information for available capacity of resources per unit, holding cost per unit, unit cost, and resource requirement per unit are the following:

	Capacity (hours)		Cost					
			Holding		Process 1		Process 2	
Month	Machine	Worker	Street	Road	Street	Road	Street	Road
1	8,600	17,000	5	6	72	85	80	90
2	8,500	16,600	6	7	74	88	78	95
3	8,800	17,200	5	7	75	84	78	92
	Machine hours required				5	8	4	6
	Worker hours required				10	12	8	9

Solution. Using the above data, the linear programming formulation is given by

Minimize
$$5I_{11} + 6I_{12} + 5I_{13} + 6I_{21} + 7I_{22} + 7I_{23} + 72P_{111} + 80P_{121}$$
$$+ 85P_{211} + 90P_{221} + 74P_{112} + 78P_{122} + 88P_{212} + 95P_{222}$$
$$+ 75P_{113} + 78P_{123} + 4P_{213} + 92P_{223}$$

subject to
$$5P_{111} + 4P_{121} + 8P_{211} + 6P_{221} \leq 8600$$
$$10P_{111} + 8P_{121} + 12P_{211} + 9P_{221} \leq 17{,}000$$
$$5P_{112} + 4P_{122} + 8P_{212} + 6P_{222} \leq 8500$$
$$10P_{112} + 8P_{122} + 12P_{212} + 9P_{222} \leq 16{,}600$$
$$5P_{113} + 4P_{123} + 8P_{213} + 6P_{223} \leq 8800$$
$$10P_{113} + 8P_{123} + 12P_{213} + 9P_{223} \leq 17{,}200$$

$$I_{11} = 100 + P_{111} + P_{121} - 1000$$
$$I_{12} = I_{11} + P_{112} + P_{122} - 1050$$
$$I_{13} = I_{12} + P_{113} + P_{123} - 1100$$
$$I_{21} = 50 + P_{211} + P_{221} - 500$$
$$I_{22} = I_{21} + P_{212} + P_{222} - 600$$
$$I_{23} = I_{22} + P_{213} + P_{223} - 550$$

$$P_{ijt}, I_{it} \geq 0 \qquad t = 1, 2, 3; \quad i = 1, 2; \quad j = 1, 2$$

The solution for this problem is

| | Street Bicycle | | | Road Bicycle | | |
| | Process | | | Process | | |
Month	1	2	Inventory	1	2	Inventory
1	900	0	0	118.75	525	193.75
2	1050	0	0	406.25	0	0.00
3	0	1100	0	550.00	0	0.00

Objective function value = $8,354,166

Resources are assumed to be fixed for the period, but hiring and lay-off constraints could easily be handled as in previous models. The same is true for overtime and subcontracting. Rounding the production and inventory of bicycle B should not be a problem. Sensitivity analysis can provide more insight into the linear programming solutions.

SECTION 9 PROBLEMS

5.27. Develop and solve a model for ProtoPlastic that explicitly considers both products. How does it compare to the aggregate plan of Problem 5.11 and the disaggregated plan of Problem 5.25?

5.28. Develop and solve a model for Goode Foods (Problem 5.19) that considers all three families of products. How does it compare to the aggregate plan?

5.29. Hardbody manufactures two fitness machines, the Flex (F) and the Crunch (C). Estimated demand for the Flex is 1500, 1200, and 1600 units, and for the Crunch it is 1000, 1200, and 900 units for the next three months. The current inventory is 550 units for the Flex and 250 units for the Crunch. Two resources, worker-hours and machine-hours, are used to manufacture both fitness machines. The additional information for available capacity of resources per unit, holding cost per unit, unit cost, and resource requirement per unit are as follows :

| | | | Cost ($) | | | |
| | Capacity (hours) | | Holding | | Process | |
Month	Machine	Worker	F	C	F	C
1	740	12,000	22	31	650	930
2	850	15,000	22	31	670	930
3	800	11,400	23	32	680	950
	Machine-hours required				0.45	0.75
	Worker-hours required				6	12

Develop a model and solution for the next three months' production at Hardbody.

5.30. Suppose Hardbody can use up to 20 percent of capacity on overtime in any month at a 60 percent higher cost. Give a modified model and solution.

5.31. Newnan Foundry makes nickel-based steel (Ni) and titanium (Ti) precision drop-forged rotors for the aircraft industry. The standard process is normally used to make both. However, another process using different raw material (billets) and operating characteristics at the forge changes the properties of the rotor, resulting in different machining requirements after forging. The data are as follows:

| | Capacity (Hours) | | Cost ($1000) | | | |
| | | | Standard process | | Other process | |
Month	Forge	Lathe	Ni	Ti	Ni	Ti
1	400	590	1.20	7.85	1.60	9.20
2	420	610	1.25	8.50	1.70	9.90
Hours required		Forge	5	12	3	8
		Lathe	5	5	9	12

Contracts for 50 nickel-based rotors and 18 titanium rotors have been signed for next month, with 55 and 20 expected the following month. It costs $1000 to hold a nickel-based rotor in inventory for one month. The holding cost for a titanium rotor is $4000 per rotor per month. Develop and solve a model to aid Newnan in production planning.

10 AGGREGATE PLANNING IN PRACTICE

Aggregate planning generates a production plan in aggregate units from forecasts (Chapter 4), and the aggregate plan is disaggregated into a plan for individual items. This plan becomes the master production schedule (Chapter 7). Box 5-1 gives an overview of aggregate planning at the Olean Tile Company. They generate aggregate plans with a transportation model similar to the one discussed in Section 5.7. This model has approximately 1660 variables and 570 constraints.

As computer capabilities and optimization algorithms improve, the need for aggregate planning lessens. Planning can be done at a more detailed level, similar to the models of Section 5.9. DeMatta and Miller (1993) discuss the evolution of the Olean Tile model. The new model considers inventory at the product level, and some models have 30,000 variables and 13,000 constraints.

Allen and Schuster (1994) discussed disaggregating plans at Welch's Foods. Increasing customer expectations for this make-to-stock manufacturer require that more attention be paid to safety stocks, dynamic demand, forecast error, manufacturing lead-time, product-quality hold time, and ABC classification (Chapter 6).Higher capacity utilization implies that the planning system needs to keep planned production within capacity limits, balance set-up costs and holding costs, and produce a wide variety of products. They report results for a manufacturing line with 14 end-items grouped into four families.

BOX 5-1: AGGREGATE PLANNING AT OLEAN TILE

Production planning can be seen as a hierarchy of managerial decision-making activities. The hierarchy ranges from strategic planning through tactical planning to operations control.

. . .

Such a hierarchical production planning system has been developed at American Olean Tile Company (AO) because of AO management's interest in using computer-based decision aids to integrate

BOX 5-1 (*continued*)

1. *The development of the annual production plan and source of supply,*
2. *Short-term production scheduling activities at each of the plants, and*
3. *Inventory control procedures at the sales distribution points (SDP).*

. . .

PRODUCTION PLANNING FRAMEWORK

The design of any product aggregation scheme depends on product structure, and consistency and feasibility are the principal objectives and constraints (Gelders and Van Wassenhove, 1982). The quarry tile product line was aggregated into 10 families, each of which comprises several hundred items or stock-keeping units (SKU's). Because the number of product families is small, demand seasonality is incorporated at the family level in our system. The Hax-Meal approach [1975] groups families into types having similar seasonality patterns. The level of aggregation employed at AC is appropriate to both the nature of the tile product and its manufacturing process.

In most general terms, tile can be classified into two product types: flat tile and trim tile. Flat tile constitutes approximately 90 percent of total quarry sales and is produced in approximately seven to 10 basic shapes (for example, 4″ × 8″ or 6″ × 6″). Trim tiles are pieces of tile specially shaped to form a border between the surface covered by flat tile and the surface next to the flat tile (for example, the border where a floor and a wall intersect).

The flat tile production process itself made it logical to further condense SKU's into major product families. In addition to a basic shape and color, flat tile is made in several different surfaces (for example regular and abrasive), and in several variations of the basic color (for example, Grey, and Grey Flash). However, tiles made from one basic flat shape in one color all require very similar raw materials and have virtually identical manufacturing cost and capacity constraints. Therefore, several major flat tile SKU's can be aggregated into one major product family with minimal impact on the accuracy of our model results. The aggregation process resulted in the formation of 10 major product families encompassing over 98 percent of total quarry sales.

. . .

IMPLEMENTATION

The process of implementing the revised plant, family, and SDP assignment patterns suggested by our modeling results has required at least as much effort as the model development process itself.

First and most importantly, we emphasized the potential savings resulting from model implementation. Management interest was heightened by the fact that the benefits would be ongoing. Second, the use of a staged process for implementation allowed changes to be made at an acceptable rate. Massive reassignments were not requested at the outset, nor would they have been approved by upper management. For example, the model suggested many changes in source of supply for the SDP's. However, only a few assignments were altered during each stage. This facilitated a smooth transition and avoided the turmoil and resistance which might otherwise have arisen.

. . .

BOX 5-1 (*continued*)

COSTS AND BENEFITS

The development costs fall into two basic categories: (1) man-months committed to data and model development, and (2) expenditures for computer software.

. . .

Development required approximately five man-months of an analyst's time distributed over a nine-month period. The computer model was developed and stored on a commercial time-sharing system at a cost of under $10,000.

. . .

An integrated hierarchical system for planning and scheduling production offers many benefits at both the individual component and the system-wide level of an organization. These benefits range from improved coordination and communication between departments to substantially reduced production and distribution costs. As a whole, the system significantly enhances American Olean's ability to position itself more competitively in the marketplace. AO has used the annual assignment model results in developing the production and distribution allocation plan for the quarry division. This plan saves between $400,000 and $750,000 per year. The suggested plan did not substantially alter the capacity loadings at the individual plants. However, it did suggest significant changes in their family mixes. Thus, the model uncovered comparative cost advantages in terms of delivered cost (variable production costs and freight) from each plant.

. . .

As an indirect benefit, the process of developing the model stimulated closer coordination between the marketing and manufacturing departments in meeting the needs of the sales territories. AO also derived several other indirect benefits, which are also difficult to quantify. Specifically, this methodology produces a general pattern of lower costs at AO's sales distribution points. This offers top management the marketing option of lowering product prices (or at least minimizing any price increases) while maintaining AO's required profit margins on an item-by-item basis.

The annual planning model can help AO management measure the financial impact of adjusting some medium-term manufacturing and distribution strategies. For example, a plant may have stopped making a particular product because the cost of a major raw material has become too high. The model can determine the system-wide change in annual manufacturing and distribution costs if a less costly alternative can be found. Other examples include determining what cost savings would result from such capital investment decisions as adding new production capacity to a plant, and what financial penalty would accompany controlling the usage rate of a scarce material at a producing location.

The annual assignment model also helps to reduce unplanned redistribution costs which occur every year. These "hidden" costs arise when one SDP transships a product to a second SDP which is out of stock. These costs are reduced because assignments are now tied more closely to demand patterns within each SDP's market area.

Source: Liberatore and Miller (1985), The Institute of Management Sciences and the Operations Research Society of America (currently INFORMS).Reprinted by permission.

11 EVOLUTION

The origins of formal aggregate planning can be traced to the early 1950s. In contrast to many other techniques for planning and controlling production, aggregate planning is a relative newcomer; the reason for its late arrival is that its scope is broader than other production planning techniques. Aggregate planning simultaneously considers several issues: planning, costs, inventory, work force, etc. Thus it is a forerunner of the systems approach to production planning and control.

We identify four aspects of the aggregate planning evolution:

- Initial introduction of the concept and its mathematical treatment
- Linear programming approaches
- Tabular and graphical methods
- Knowledge-based methods

Aggregate planning was likely introduced by Holt, Modigliani, Muth, and Simon in the mid-1950s. Their motivation was planning production for a local paint manufacturer, and the aggregate product was gallons of paint. A mathematical model was developed for the problem. An interesting element of their model is that they used quadratic rather than linear costs. To solve the model, the derivative of the objective was taken and set to zero. The resulting solution is a set of linear equations; hence the technique was called the linear-decision rule. For more information, see Holt, Modigliani, Muth, and Simon (1953).

Following the work of Holt, Modigliani, Muth, and Simon, Bowman (1963) proposed a different approach. Decisions for the current period are based on "good" decisions made in the past. This idea is similar to regression and can be regarded as a "mathematical behavioral" approach. Interestingly, Bowman's model includes all the familiar elements of aggregate planning except costs.

Sometime after the work of Holt, Modigliani, Muth, and Simon, linear programming models for aggregate planning were proposed, and Hanssmann and Hess (1960) were among the first to do so. The models presented in this chapter are continuations of this approach. Currently, attempts are being made to develop models that bypass the aggregate plan and directly plan for products. The advanced models presented in this chapter and the references on disaggregation are examples of this attempt.

Tabular and graphical methods—the precursors of the spreadsheet approach—appeared in the literature around 1960. These methods have been used in industry for many years, and personal computers and spreadsheets have increased their popularity. Their simplicity is both their strength and weakness; they do not guarantee an optimal solution, but they are easy to implement. With a little trial and error, good plans are usually found.

Artificial intelligence and expert systems have been applied to aggregate planning (Duchessi and O'Keefe, 1990). These approaches incorporate traditional planning rules in a heuristic manner. The model is less abstract than mathematical models, but at the cost of optimality. The aggregate plans obtained from these models indicate it is a credible approach to the aggregate planning problem.

The most widely used methods of aggregate planning are tabular. However, the importance of the other models should not be underestimated. Model solutions, coupled with sensitivity analysis, provide insight into the aggregate-planning problem environment. If properly constructed, these models require management to consider a broad scope in planning production.

12 SUMMARY

Aggregate planning focuses on intermediate-range production planning problems. At this level of planning, an aggregate unit rather than an individual product is considered. The aggregate unit is defined by some measure common to all products, such as production hours or dollars. Factors of aggregate planning include capacity, production costs, capacity change costs, and inventory costs.

Two major approaches are used to generate an aggregate production plan: spreadsheet methods and quantitative methods.

Spreadsheet methods are trial-and-error approaches. Typical strategies are zero inventory, level production (constant work force), and mixed strategies. The result is a feasible aggregate plan that usually projects a realistic cost.

The quantitative methods used in aggregate planning are variations of linear programming. Under given assumptions, these methods yield an optimal aggregate plan. The linear programming models can be extended to more general planning situations, including multiple products and multiple processes.

MINICASE: BF SWINGS II

Recall BF Swings from Chapter 4. Now Ben is concerned about his production for the next few months, and he assigns you to come up with a four-week production plan. Part of his motivation is that he thinks there is too much inventory. Samir, the foreman, contends that cannot be true, because the storage area is limited, and there can never be more than 500 total items in storage at any one time. Another motivation is that Lupe, the accountant, tells him that overtime costs are a large part of his total operating costs. Chan, from personnel, thinks they ought to hire more workers to alleviate overtime. When asked, Chan admits it will cost $1000 per worker to train them, and their wages are $400 per week. Bobbie Ruth points out that, by law, any worker laid off must be paid three weeks' separation pay, and overtime wages are time-and-one-half. Lupe quickly adds that adding fringe benefits and depreciation on equipment results in overtime being approximately double the cost of regular time in each department and that overtime work can be at most three hours a day, unless the employees work on Saturday. Samir also reminds them that adding people might not add capacity, because additional equipment may also be needed. Ben agrees with this except in the case of sanding, assembly, and finishing, which require little or no equipment.

Thanks to Bobbie Ruth's foresight, some data are available. The following table gives the cost per hour, including labor, for work done in each department. Inventory holding costs per week are $0.30, $0.80, and $0.90 per unit-week. Currently, there are 70 stools, 255 rockers, and 110 swings in inventory. Other information can be found in the Chapter 4 Minicase.

Department	Cost in $ per hour	Department	Cost in $ per hour
Drill	$12	Router	$15
Lathe	$15	Plane	$15
Crosscut	$12	Sand	$10
Rip	$12	Assemble	$10
Mortise	$20	Finish	$10
Tenon	$20		

Forecasted demand for products in the next four weeks are as follows:

Week	Stools	Rockers	Swings
117	100	344	24
118	109	352	146
119	90	368	279
120	106	361	64

Develop a four-week production plan for BFS. What important decisions need to be made? What level of detail is needed? If the plan is an aggregate plan, should products, processes, or both be aggregated? What solution method seems to be best?

13 REFERENCES

Allen, S. J. and Schuster, E. W., "Practical Production Scheduling with Capacity Constraints and Dynamic Demand: Family Planning and Disaggregation," *Production & Inventory Management Journal,* 35, 4, 15–21 (1994).

Bowman, E. H., "Consistency and Optimality in Managerial Decision Making," *Management Science*, 9, 310–321, 1963.

Bowman, E. H., "Production Scheduling by the Transportation Method of Linear Programming," *Operations Research*, 4, 100–103, 1956.

Duchessi, P. and O'Keefe, R. M., "A Knowledge Based Approach to Production Planning," *Journal of the Operational Research Society*, 41, 377–390, 1990.

DeMetta, R. and Miller, T. "A Note on the Growth of a Production Planning System: A Case Study in Evolution," *Interfaces*, 23,4, 116–122, 1993.

Hanssmann, F. and Hess, S.W., "A Linear Programming Approach to Production and Employment Scheduling," *Management Technology*, 1, 46–51, 1960.

Hax, A. C. and Meal, H. C., "Hierarchical Integration of Production Planning and Scheduling," in *Studies in Management Sciences, Volume 1, Logistics*, Geisler, M.A., ed., North Holland-American Elsevier, New York, 1975.

Holt, C. C., Modigliani, J. F., Muth, J. F., and Simon H., "A Linear Decision Rule for Production and Employment Scheduling," *Management Science*, 1, 1–30, 1953.

Johnson, L. A. and Montgomery, D. C., *Operations Research in Production Planning, Scheduling and Inventory Control*, John Wiley & Sons, New York, 1974.

Lawrence, K. D. and Zanakis, S. H., *Production Planning and Scheduling: Mathematical Programming Applications*, Industrial Engineering and Management Press, Norcross, GA, 1984.

Liberatore, M.J. and Miller, T. "A Hierarchical Production Planning System," *Interfaces*, 15, 4, 1–11, 1985.

Masud, A. S. M. and Hwang, C. L., "An Aggregate Production Planning Model and Application of Multiple Objective Decision Methods," *International Journal of Production Research*, 118, 115–127, 1980.

Nebol, E., "Macro Production Planning: An Applied Research Project," *Interfaces*, 17, 71–77, 1987.

Stadtler, H., "Tuning Aggregate Planning With Sequencing and Scheduling," in *Multi-Stage Production Planning and Inventory Control*, Axsater, S., Schneeweis, C. and Silver, E., eds., Springer-Verlag, Berlin, 1986.

Zoller, K., "Optimal Disaggregation of Aggregate Production Plan," *Management Science*, 17, B553–B549, 1971.

CHAPTER
6

INVENTORY:
INDEPENDENT
DEMAND
SYSTEMS

Inventory is used in most manufacturing, service, wholesale, and retail activities, and because it can enhance profitability and competitiveness, it is widely discussed within the manufacturing sector. What is inventory? What issues, problems, and complexities are associated with it? To understand these questions, we discuss a simple manufacturing-distribution system—a doughnut bakery store. Most people are familiar with this type of operation.

When you enter the store, you notice trays loaded with all kinds of doughnuts, which are the **finished goods** inventory of the store. Doughnuts are baked and put on trays so that when you enter the store, you can immediately be served. This inventory exists because of a temporary lull between two activities—in this case supply (the baking process) and demand (you, the customer). Another type of inventory in this system is **raw material**—the flour and ingredients needed to prepare a doughnut. It too represents a lull between supply (obtaining the raw material) and demand (cooking the doughnuts).

Let's look at the inventory decisions the shop owner has to make. The first decision is quantity—how many doughnuts of each type to prepare, or how much flour and other ingredients to order. The second decision concerns timing, i.e., when to place an order for the given quantity. Should doughnuts be made when a doughnut tray is empty, or when there are 10 left? Should flour be ordered once a week, or when it reaches a certain minimum quantity?

These two decisions are influenced by the demand for the finished product—how many doughnuts will be sold in the next few hours or days. This demand is uncertain. We do not know in advance when and how many customers will come into the store and how many doughnuts of each type they will purchase. At best, we can forecast this demand.

To account for the uncertainty, the owner may keep a large quantity of each doughnut available, thus being able to respond to any future demand. The penalty for doing so might be getting stuck with many unsold doughnuts, which are thrown away when they become stale. On the other hand, if customers want a certain doughnut that is unavailable, a different penalty, at least the revenue lost because of being short, will be incurred.

What is gradually unfolding is that even for this simple example, the inventory issue is not simple. It is a key element in the profitability of the doughnut store. In manufacturing organizations with hundreds of products, the inventory problem is even more complex and difficult to solve.

1 INVENTORY CONCEPTS

The doughnut example shows that inventory is an important and complex system and that we must understand its nature before analyzing it. We use this section to do just that. First, we expand the discussion of the role of inventory. Inventory systems have specific terminology, which we present next. We then identify inventory costs and present some measures of effectiveness for inventory systems. We conclude by discussing common inventory policies and the relevance of inventory models.

1.1 The Role of Inventory

So far, we have described inventory but have not defined it. From the many available definitions, we have selected the following one:

> A quantity of commodity in the control of an enterprise, held for some time to satisfy some future demand.

For the manufacturing sector, the commodity is principally materials: raw material, purchased items, semi-finished and finished products, spare parts, and supplies.

This definition reiterates what we noticed in the doughnut example. Inventory is a "buffer" between two processes—supply and demand. The supply process contributes commodity to the inventory, whereas demand depletes the same inventory. Inventory is necessary because of differences in rates and timing between supply and demand, and this difference can be attributed to both internal and exogenous factors. Internal factors are a matter of policy, but exogenous factors are uncontrollable. Among the internal factors are economies of scale, operation smoothing, and customer service. The most important exogenous factor is uncertainty.

Economies of scale may make inventory desirable, even if it is possible to balance supply and demand. There are certain fixed costs associated with production and purchasing; these are set-up cost and ordering cost, respectively. To recover this fixed cost and reduce the average unit cost, many units of an item may be purchased or produced. These large lot sizes will be ordered infrequently and placed in inventory to satisfy future demand.

Operation smoothing is used when demand varies over time. An example would be antifreeze or jet skis. Inventory, accumulated in periods of low demand, is used to satisfy higher demand in other periods, which enables the production facility to be operated at a relatively constant production rate, a desirable feature in manufacturing.

Customer service is another reason to carry an inventory. Inventory is built up so that customer demand can be met immediately from stock, yielding customer satisfaction.

Uncertainty was discussed in the doughnut store example. One way to hedge against uncertainty is to hold more inventory than the forecasted demand, which avoids the prospect of running out of stock if actual demand exceeds the forecast. This extra inventory is called safety stock. The resupply process is another source of uncertainty that may justify holding safety stock. The lead time is the time between issuing an order and receiving it. When the lead time is uncertain, we may not receive an order on the date we planned. The safety stock gives some protection from a production stoppage due to lead time uncertainty.

The roles of inventory described so far are operational. There is a totally different reason for carrying inventory—market exploitation. Often the vagaries of the market create an economic advantage of maintaining inventory. Price fluctuations in the market may justify acquiring more raw material than is required for estimated future demand. We emphasize that this is highly speculative and should be left to the financial function in the organization rather than operations management. Accordingly, this role of inventory will not be discussed further.

1.2   Inventory Terminology

In our doughnut store example, we identified the demand as being uncertain and mentioned two types of inventory—raw material and finished goods. We formally define the different demand environments and the various inventory types.

The **demand environment** can be classified into two major categories: deterministic or stochastic and independent or dependent.

Deterministic or stochastic.   Deterministic means that future demand for an inventory item is known with certainty; random future demand is called stochastic. Each of these cases requires different analysis. The stochastic case is more realistic but also more difficult to handle.

Independent or dependent demand.   Demand for an item not related to any other item and primarily influenced by market conditions is called independent demand. Examples include retail sales or finished goods in manufacturing. Dependent demand is very typical to manufacturing—the demand for one item is derived from the demand of another item. An example would be a car, wheels, and bolts. Each car requires four wheels, and each wheel requires bolts. The demand for cars is independent; wheels and bolts have dependent demand. There is a three-level hierarchy here, called product structure. Thus, one car generates demand for four wheels (excluding the spare) and 16 bolts. In our doughnut store example, the demand for doughnuts is independent, and the demand for flour is dependent. This chapter focuses on independent demand systems,whereas Chapter 7 examines dependent demand systems. We emphasize that some of the analysis is common to both systems.

Inventory types in production systems are classified according to the value added during the manufacturing process. The classifications are raw material, work in process (WIP), and finished goods; each type is defined below.

Raw materials include all items required for the manufacturing and assembly process. Typically, they are as follows:

- Material needing further processing (flour, wood, steel bars)
- Components that go into the product as is (computer chips, bolts)
- Supplies (welding electrodes, glue, screws)

Learning Resources
Centre

Work in process (WIP) is inventory in the production system waiting to be processed or assembled and may include semi-finished products (a bolt that has been threaded but not coated) or subassemblies (TV picture tubes).

Finished goods are the outputs of the production process, sometimes called end items—anything from cars to shirts to soft drink bottles. The demand for finished goods is usually independent. Also, finished goods of one manufacturing organization may be raw materials for another one, e.g., tires and cars.

1.3   Inventory Costs

We defined inventory as a "quantity of commodity"; as such it incurs costs. Purchasing cost is the obvious one. Other types of costs are ordering (set-up) cost, holding cost, shortage cost, and system operating cost. We elaborate on each of these.

Purchasing cost is the per-item cost paid to the supplier (sometimes called material cost). Let c be unit cost and Q be number of units purchased (lot size). Then the total purchasing cost is cQ—a linear function of Q. In some cases the supplier has a price schedule based on the quantity purchased. This unit cost is a function of Q, and the purchase cost is a more complex function (see Section 2.1.3).

If we manufacture the unit, c includes both material cost and the variable cost to manufacture a unit. The total manufacturing cost for a production lot is cQ.

An **ordering cost**—the cost of preparing and monitoring the order—is incurred each time an order is placed with a supplier. It is independent of the lot size purchased, and therefore it is a fixed cost denoted by A. However, the annual ordering cost, which we discuss later, depends on the lot size. For a manufactured lot, the fixed cost is dominated by the set-up cost, which includes the cost of preparing the machine for the production run (machine idle time and labor) and possibly some material start-up costs for rejects early in the run. The same notation, A, is used for the set-up cost.

The total cost for purchasing or producing a lot is

$$A + cQ$$

It consists of a fixed component A and a variable component cQ.

Inventory ties up capital, consumes space, and requires maintenance, which all cost money. This is called **holding cost** or carrying cost and includes the following costs:

- Opportunity cost
- Storage and handling costs
- Taxes and insurance
- Pilferage, damage, spoilage, obsolescence, etc.

The costs of carrying inventory begin with the investment in inventory. Money tied up in inventory cannot earn a return elsewhere. This cost is an opportunity cost, usually expressed as a percentage of the investment. The lowest value of this opportunity cost is the interest the money would earn in a savings account. Most companies have better opportunities than savings accounts, and most have a minimum rate of return used for evaluating investments, usually called the cost of capital. The same rate can be used as part of the inventory carrying cost.

We calculate costs as a percentage of the investment in inventory and add them to the opportunity cost, generating a total inventory holding cost. Thus, if the cost of capital is 25 percent annually and the other types of costs amount to an additional 10 percent, the total inventory holding cost is 35 percent. That is, for every dollar invested in inventory for one year, we pay 35 cents. Define

$$i = \text{total inventory holding cost (expressed as a percentage)}$$

It is the cost of carrying $1 of inventory for one unit of time. Because we usually measure inventory in units rather than dollars, and recalling that the cost of one unit is c, we obtain

$$h = ic$$

in which h is the cost to carry one **unit** of inventory for one unit of time—expressed in dollars. Typical annual values of i are 25 percent to 40 percent, but i can be as high as 60 percent.

In the doughnut store example we introduced the concept of **shortage cost.** A shortage occurs when there is demand for an out-of-stock item. A shortage can either be backlogged or lost; demand for durable goods is often backlogged. Thus, if the store does not have the TV you want, you may be willing to wait until they get it. On the other hand, demand may be lost if the doughnut store does not have the kind of doughnut you want. If you go elsewhere, it is called a lost sale.

In both cases we pay a penalty. If the demand is lost, the major penalty is lost profit and loss of goodwill. If the demand is backlogged, there are additional costs to expedite, costs to keep records, and a reputation for bad customer service. Material shortage for production is usually backlogged, and the penalty is production stoppage, expedition, and possible late delivery of the final product to the customer.

Two types of shortage costs are possible. One results just because a unit is short; the other considers the length of time the unit is short.

We define:

$$\pi = \text{shortage cost per unit short}$$

$$\hat{\pi} = \text{shortage cost per unit short per unit of time}$$

Typically, π is used for lost sales; backorders use both. Note that $\hat{\pi}$ is to backorders what h is to inventory. Shortage cost is often hard to estimate and may be an educated guess.

Finally, there are costs related to operating and controlling the inventory system, called **system operating cost.** This cost may be large; for example, there is the cost of computer hardware and software for inventory control. Ironically, most inventory models were developed before or in the early days of the computer era, and therefore this cost was often overlooked.

1.4   Measures of Effectiveness

Inventory is basically a service entity. If inventory satisfies demand as it occurs, then the service is perfect; otherwise there are problems with the service. Providing a high level of service is not free. The study of inventory systems is a **trade-off analysis** between the benefits and costs of carrying inventory. The goal is to maximize the benefits while minimizing the cost, a difficult mission. It is even more complex when there are many different items in inventory.

First we focus on costs, with benefits viewed as an opportunity cost. Later we examine models that address service benefits. There are two approaches to measures of effectiveness—a modeling approach or a managerial approach.

The **modeling approach** optimizes the inventory system. Cost minimization is the criterion used in most inventory models, although in principle, profit maximization could also be used. For most inventory systems these criteria are equivalent, because profit is the difference between price and cost. We focus on cost models because they are simpler to handle. Another reason is that cost is a *fact,* but price is a *policy.* Costs are known, but prices may differ due to management policy or market pressure.

A common measure of effectiveness for inventory models is *minimum average total cost per unit time.* A unit of time may be a day, week, month, or year. The total cost includes the cost elements previously discussed. We use the average because holding and shortage costs are proportional to the inventory level, which may vary during the period. To compute the average total cost we average the inventory or shortage over time and multiply it by h or $\hat{\pi}$.

The **managerial approach** is generally used for multi-item inventory systems. The immediate goal is to report the size of the inventory to management. One measure of inventory size is the total inventory investment at the reporting date. Multiply the on-hand quantity of each item by its cost, and sum the result for all items. To get a relative measure of whether we have "too much" or "too little" inventory or to compare our performance with our competitors' and "industry standards," two other measures are used:

$$\text{Months of supply} = \frac{\text{Total inventory investment}}{\text{Average forecasted demand (\$/month)}}$$

and $\quad$ $$\text{Annual inventory turnover} = \frac{12[\text{Average forecasted demand (\$/month)}]}{\text{Total inventory investment}}$$

The first measure indicates how long future demand can be met from on-hand inventory. The second measure indicates how fast the inventory is turned; the *higher* this value is, the *lower* the investment in inventory will be. These measures are changed slightly for different purposes and types of inventories (raw material, finished goods). To check future performance, use the forecast for demand, but use the actual demand to evaluate past performance. A quick way to calculate the inventory turnover from a company's balance sheet is

$$\text{Inventory turnover} = \frac{\text{Value of sales}}{\text{Value of inventory}}$$

Comparing this figure to turnover of other companies or industry standards gives an indication of the performance of the inventory operation.

1.5   Inventory Policies

The major element impacting inventory is demand. From the production control standpoint, we assume demand is an uncontrolled variable. There are three important factors in an inventory system—called decision variables—that can be controlled:

What to order?—Variety decision

When to order?—Timing decision

How much to order?—Quantity decision

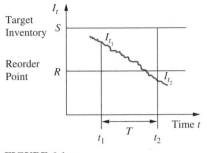

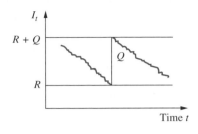

FIGURE 6-1
Periodic review policy

FIGURE 6-2
Continuous review policy

To gain an understanding of these inventory decisions, we examine a single-item system. The variety decision is irrelevant, and the other two decisions are made using two different inventory control policies—known as periodic review and continuous review.

Periodic review policy. At fixed time intervals—say a week, a month, or any time T, called the review period—check the inventory level I, and issue an order if I is below a certain predetermined level R, called the reorder point (timing decision). The size of the order Q is the amount required to bring the inventory to a predetermined level S (quantity decision). The size of Q varies from period to period. Figure 6-1 presents this policy assuming one unit is demanded at a time and orders are delivered instantaneously. At t_1 the inventory level is above the reorder point R, so no order is issued. At the next review time, t_2, T time periods after t_1, $I_{t_2} < R$ and an order for $Q = S - I_{t_2}$ units is issued. This policy is often referred to as a periodic policy or fixed order interval policy.

Continuous review policy. In this policy, the level of inventory is continuously monitored. When the inventory level reaches the reorder point R (timing decision), a fixed quantity Q is ordered (quantity decision). This is a continuous (Q, R) policy, or a fixed reorder quantity policy. Figure 6-2 presents this policy, assuming instantaneous delivery of the order, and demand of one unit at a time.

Before the computer era, periodic review systems were more popular, because they were easier to implement manually. With computers readily available, implementing a continuous review policy is easy. Continuous review has certain merits over periodic review; however, there is still a place for periodic review systems, as we discuss later under control decisions (Section 4.2).

1.6 Relevance of Inventory Models

Many of the "classical" inventory models were developed in the era of the classical theories of management. In Chapter 2 we discussed the emerging theory leading to world class manufacturing, which takes a totally different view of inventory: Reduce inventory as much as possible, rather than optimize it. So there is a dilemma in presenting many of the classical models. If, on the face of it, they are obsolete in the new theory of production, why teach them? Our answer is that we think that they are as relevant in the "new environment" as they were before.

We believe that even in the past, one of the biggest advantages of inventory models was the insight they provided. Of the hundreds of inventory models developed, the most widely used is the EOQ model, which was developed in 1915! A big benefit we get from using different models of inventory systems is in understanding the behavior of these systems, the relationships between the different parameters and variables, and the sensitivity to inaccuracies in data. This understanding was more prevalent in the past, and will be very important in the future. For example, in an actual inventory system with 100,000 items, it is difficult to calculate and update a shortage cost for each item. However, understanding the impact of shortage cost from shortage cost models helps us better manage inventory systems. Another example is set-up reduction; its implication can be studied and understood by using inventory models.

Even today inventory is not all evil. To illustrate, the GM Saturn plant runs one of the tightest just-in-time (inventoryless) systems in North America (Woodruff et al. 1992). Yet they found it necessary to add more inventory between departments as a buffer, so that snags will be less likely to delay final assembly.

As we have stated, classical inventory models are important not only for the results they yield, but also for enhanced understanding of the behavior of an inventory system. The future industrial engineer or operations manager should understand the classical models in order to help develop future models.

This chapter is decision oriented and divided into three major sections: quantity decisions, timing decisions, and control decisions. The next chapter discusses dependent demand systems.

SECTION 1 PROBLEMS

6.1. Use the inventory definition to classify the following entities as "inventory" or "noninventory." Explain.

- Merchandise in a store
- Water in a reservoir
- Money in a savings account
- Trees in a forest
- Cut tree in a pulp factory
- Bridge wire ropes
- Steel bar in a metal fabrication factory
- Iron ore
- Bourbon in a cask in a distillery
- Bottle of bourbon at home

6.2. List and explain a few exogenous factors that contribute to the need for inventory.

6.3. Suppose demand for a product is known with certainty. Is inventory still required? Why? Give an example.

6.4. Consider a product such as a bicycle that is being manufactured. Make a simple sketch of this product and identify the following:

(a) Independent and dependent demand items

(b) Raw materials inventory

(c) Work in process inventory

(d) Finished goods inventory

6.5. A soft drink bottler knows its cost breakdown to be as follows:

- Raw material cost for one gallon of soft drink, $1.80
- Bottling cost for one gallon of soft drink, $1.20
- Cost of one empty bottle of 1/12 gallon, 5¢
- Set-up cost for a bottling run, $5000
- Inventory holding cost, 35 percent per year

(a) Evaluate c—total unit production cost.

(b) What is the total production cost for lot sizes of 1000, 10,000, 50,000, and 100,000 bottles of 1/12 gallon?

(c) Let:

$$\frac{A}{A + cQ} = y$$

Plot $y = f(Q)$. What can you conclude?

(d) The company estimates demand to be 10,000 bottles per day. The policy is to have five days' demand in finished goods inventory. What is the investment in this inventory?

(e) Evaluate the inventory holding cost in dollars per year.

6.6. Company A has $10 million in inventory, and it is equivalent to three months of supply. Company B, which is in the same line of business, has $5 million in inventory, and it is equivalent to an inventory turnover of 4 (i.e., four inventory cycles per year). Analyze this situation.

6.7. In a balance sheet, there is always an entry of "current assets," which represents investment in inventory. The OPCABLE Company manufactures fiberoptic cables. Their balance sheet for 31-12-96 showed a total revenue of $50 million and current assets of $10 million.

(a) Give an approximation to months of supply and inventory turnover for this year.

(b) If the "industry standard" is six inventory turnovers per year, what can you tell the management of OPCABLE?

6.8. The OPCABLE Company ran a cost analysis of its material systems and came up with the following data for the past six months. Compute the average total cost per month.

Month	Ordering cost ($1000)	Holding cost ($1000)	Purchasing cost ($ million)
1	5	200	5
2	8	180	4
3	6	220	6
4	7	170	2
5	—	190	—
6	4	180	5

6.9. Three companies in the electronics industry have the following inventory cycles.

Company A   6
Company B   8
Company C   4

Which company will have the lowest inventory holding cost? Explain why.

6.10. Consider the three decision variables in inventory systems. Discuss the interrelationships among them.

6.11. Compare the two inventory review policies for the cases of deterministic and stochastic demand environments.

6.12. In addition to the two "pure" inventory review policies, there can be also a "hybrid" policy.

(a) Give an example in which a hybrid policy is useful

(b) Show the graph for a "hybrid" policy (such as Figures 6-1, 6-2).

6.13. The following items represent "inventory-like" environments we encounter in daily life. Classify whether, by implication, we use periodic review or continuous review policy for each. Explain.

- Car gasoline tank
- Money in checking account
- Food in a refrigerator
- Wine bottles in a cellar
- Car engine oil

6.14. You were hired by the METCUT Company to work in their costing department. They have just purchased a new inventory software package, and among other things they have to insert the value of A. Your first assignment is to obtain this value using past records, with the following data.

1.	Equipment set-up cost	$200
2.	Item loading/unloading cost	$1.80
3.	Initial test run per batch	$15/batch
4.	Cost of preparing production order per batch, time standard, and drawing	$120
5.	Cost of capital	25% annually
6.	Cost of handling one unit	$2/unit

2   QUANTITY DECISIONS

This section discusses one of the three major decisions related to inventory systems—the quantity decision (i.e., how much to order). This decision has a major impact on the level of inventory maintained, and, as such, it directly influences inventory costs.

We present the most common models developed over many years, and we discuss these models together to provide a comprehensive picture of what has been done. The common factor of these models is that they deal with known demand and a single item (except for the part of Section 2.1.4 covering resource-constrained multiple-item models) and they all can be extended to a multiple-item environment if there is no dependency among the items. Furthermore, they can be applied in a production environment as well as other environments such as retail sales. With some adjustments, they apply to raw material, finished goods, and in some cases WIP inventories.

Models for quantity decisions are usually called lot sizing models. There are many of them, and we group them under two headings:

- **Static lot sizing models** are used for uniform (constant) demand over the planning horizon.

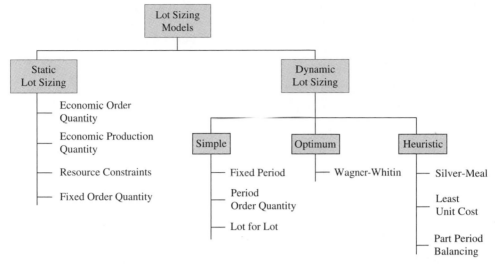

FIGURE 6-3
Classification of lot sizing models

> • **Dynamic lot sizing models** are models used for changing demand over the planning horizon. We assume demand is known with certainty, which is sometimes called *lumpy demand.*

Subclassification is possible; the general structure of this section and the models discussed appears in Figure 6-3.

2.1 Static Lot Sizing Models

A constant and uniform demand environment is not common in the real world. However, it is a convenient starting point for developing inventory models and gaining an understanding of the relationships within an inventory system. Four models in this category are developed (see Figure 6-3).

2.1.1 ECONOMIC ORDER QUANTITY (EOQ). This model is the most fundamental of all inventory models and was introduced in 1915 by Harris. It is also known as the Wilson formula, because Wilson advocated its use. The importance of this model is that it is still one of the most widely used inventory models in industry, and it serves as a basis for more sophisticated inventory models.

We assume the following decision environment:

- There is a single item inventory system.
- Demand is uniform and deterministic and amounts to D units per unit time—day, week, month, or year. We will use annual demand, but any other unit of time can be used, as long as the rest of the parameters are calculated for the same time unit.
- No shortages are allowed.
- There is no order lead time (time from ordering to receipt).
- All the quantity ordered arrives at the same time, which is called infinite replenishment rate.

This model is suitable for raw material purchase in production or for a retail environment. The decision variable for this model is Q, the number of units to be ordered, a positive real number. The cost parameters are all known with certainty and they are as follows:

c = unit cost (\$/unit)

i = total annual inventory holding cost (% per year)

$h = ic$ = total annual inventory holding cost (dollars per unit per year)

A = ordering cost (\$/order)

In addition, we define

D = demand per unit time

T = cycle length, the length of time between placement (or receipt) of replenishment orders

$K(Q)$ = total average annual cost as a function of the lot size Q

I_t = on-hand inventory at time t (quantity of material actually in stock)

The basic concept of this model is to create a balance between two opposing costs—ordering costs and holding costs. Ordering cost is a fixed cost; the more we order, the less the cost per unit will be. Holding cost is a variable cost that is lower the less inventory we have. This balance is achieved through minimizing $K(Q)$, the total average annual cost.

A helpful tool in analyzing inventory systems is the *inventory geometry*—a graphical description of I_t, shown in Figure 6-4.

We assume the inventory level is Q at time zero. As time moves, the inventory is depleted at a rate of D units per year (i.e., the slope of the inventory line is $-D$). When the inventory level reaches zero, we order Q units. Because we assume that lead time is zero and the replenishment rate is infinite, the inventory level will immediately rise to Q, and the process will repeat. Because of the shape of the inventory geometry, this model is sometimes called the sawtooth model.

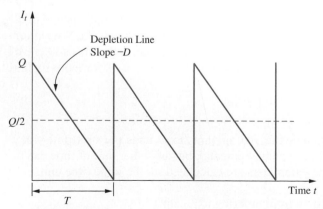

FIGURE 6-4
EOQ inventory geometry

This pattern is called a cycle, and during a year, there may be several cycles. Let T be the inventory cycle length. From the inventory geometry we note that

$$T = \frac{Q}{D}$$

Let $\overline{I}$ be the average inventory. From Figure 6-4 we see

$$\overline{I} = \frac{\text{Area under the inventory curve}}{T}$$

or
$$\overline{I} = \frac{\text{Inventory triangle area}}{T} = \frac{1}{T}\frac{QT}{2} = \frac{Q}{2}$$

This result can be obtained intuitively, as the inventory level fluctuates between 0 and Q, so the average is $Q/2$. The maximum inventory level is

$$I_{\max} = Q$$

There are three types of costs—purchasing cost, ordering cost, and inventory holding cost. For *each cycle,* the costs are

$$cQ = \text{purchasing cost}$$

$$A = \text{ordering (or set-up) cost}$$

$$icT\frac{Q}{2} = hT\frac{Q}{2} = \text{average inventory holding cost}$$

Thus, the average cost per *cycle* is

$$cQ + A + hT\frac{Q}{2}$$

Note that in the above, hT is the cost of carrying one unit in inventory for T time units.

To obtain the average annual cost $K(Q)$, we multiply the average cost per cycle by the number of cycles, which is $1/T$. We get

$$K(Q) = \frac{cQ}{T} + \frac{A}{T} + h\frac{Q}{2}$$

Because $1/T = D/Q$, the average total annual cost is

$$K(Q) = cD + \frac{AD}{Q} + h\frac{Q}{2}$$

We wish to find the value of the decision variable Q that minimizes $K(Q)$. This is achieved by solving the equation

$$K'(Q) = \frac{dk(Q)}{dQ} = -\frac{AD}{Q^2} + \frac{h}{2} = 0$$

Because the second derivative of $K(Q)$ is positive, $K(Q)$ is a convex function and achieves its minimum at the point where the derivative is zero. Solving the above equation yields

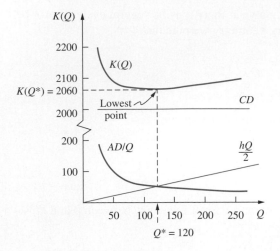

FIGURE 6-5
A plot of $K(Q)$ in Example 6-1

$$Q^* = \sqrt{\frac{2AD}{h}}$$

Q^* is known as the economic order quantity, or EOQ.

Figure 6-5 is a graphical description of $K(Q)$. The curve of $K(Q)$ is the summation of three individual curves, which represent the components of the function $K(Q)$. Q^* occurs where the curves for $hQ/2$ and AD/Q intersect; that is where we balance the two opposing costs—ordering cost and holding cost. (In general, the minimum of the sum of two functions does not have to occur at the intersection.) The annual purchasing cost cD does not affect the value of Q^*.

Substituting the value of Q^* in $K(Q)$, after some algebraic manipulations, we get the minimum total average annual cost:

$$K(Q^*) = cD + \sqrt{2ADh}$$

The annual ordering (set-up) cost is AD/Q^* and annual holding cost is $h(Q^*/2)$.

Example 6-1. Economic order quantity. A small welding shop uses welding rods at a uniform rate. Marvin, the owner, orders the rods from a local supplier. Marvin estimates the annual demand is about 1000 pounds. To place each order, he has to spend about \$3.60 for the phone call and paperwork. Marvin pays \$2 per pound of rods, and holding costs are based on a 25 percent annual rate. Analyze the system.

Solution. We first identify the various parameters.

$$A = \$3.60 \text{ per order}$$
$$D = 1000 \text{ pounds per year}$$
$$c = \$2 \text{ per pound}$$
$$i = 25 \text{ percent annually}$$
$$h = 0.25 \times \$2 = \$0.5 \text{ per pound per year}$$

The economic order quantity is

$$Q^* = \text{EOQ} = \sqrt{\frac{2AD}{h}} = \sqrt{\frac{(2)(3.6)(1000)}{0.5}} = 120$$

It is best for Marvin to place an order for 120 pounds. He should issue an order every $T = 120/1000 = 0.12$ year or 1.44 months. The total average annual cost is

$$K(Q^*) = cD + \sqrt{2ADh} = (2)(1000) + \sqrt{(2)(3.6)(1000)(0.5)} = \$2060$$

The annual ordering cost is $AD/Q^* = (3.6 \times 1000)/120 = \$30$. The annual inventory holding cost is $hQ^*/2 = (0.5 \times 120)/2 = \$30$.

The fact that annual inventory holding cost and annual ordering cost are equal should not be surprising. We showed that the optimum is at the intersection of the two curves. This problem could also be solved based on monthly or weekly quantities. We suggest the student try this as additional practice.

The assumption of zero lead time is limiting, and we relax it when we discuss timing decisions (Section 3). Further extensions of the EOQ formula usually include sensitivity of $K(Q^*)$ to errors in Q^* and relaxation of the no-shortage assumption.

Sensitivity of $K(Q^*)$. In the real world it is sometimes impractical to order exactly Q^* units. Assume, for example, that $Q^* = 1357$ and the item of interest comes in boxes of 1000 units each. Should we order one or two boxes? This question leads to examining the sensitivity of the function $K(Q)$ to deviations of Q from the optimum Q^*. This sensitivity is measured by the ratio

$$\frac{K(Q)}{K(Q^*)}$$

When there is no deviation ($Q = Q^*$), the value of this ratio is 1. For ease of computation, we ignore the purchasing cost cD in this ratio, because it does not change the general shape of the cost curve but simply moves it up by an amount cD. We obtain

$$\frac{K(Q)}{K(Q^*)} = \left(\frac{\frac{AD}{Q} + h\frac{Q}{2}}{\sqrt{2ADh}} \right) = \frac{1}{2Q}\sqrt{\frac{2AD}{h}} + \frac{Q}{2}\sqrt{\frac{h}{2AD}}$$

$$= \frac{Q^*}{2Q} + \frac{Q}{2Q^*} = \frac{1}{2}\left[\frac{Q^*}{Q} + \frac{Q}{Q^*} \right]$$

The graphical description of this function is given in Figure 6-6. The shape of this graph suggests that placing an order larger than Q^* (i.e., $Q/Q^* > 1$) will cost less than an order smaller by the same amount.

Example 6-2. Sensitivity of EOQ. Suppose the welding rods from Example 6-1 are ordered in packages of 75 pounds each. How many packages should Marvin order?

Solution. In Example 6-1, the economic order quantity is 120 pounds, and the new order quantity should be either one package (75 pounds) or two packages (150 pounds). We apply sensitivity analysis, giving

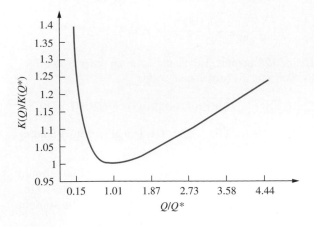

FIGURE 6-6
Sensitivity of the EOQ to values of Q

$$\frac{K(Q)}{K(Q^*)} = \frac{1}{2}\left[\frac{Q}{Q^*} + \frac{Q^*}{Q}\right]$$

1. Set $Q = 75$; then

$$K(75)/K(120) = (1/2)(75/120 + 120/75) = 1.1125$$

2. Set $Q = 150$; then

$$K(150)/K(120) = (1/2)(150/120 + 120/150) = 1.025$$

Marvin will be better off by ordering two packages each time. In Figure 6-6 we show the graphical description of $K(Q)/K(Q^*)$, assuming rods can be purchased one at a time.

2.1.2 ECONOMIC PRODUCTION QUANTITY (EPQ) WITH EXTENSIONS. This extension of the EOQ model relaxes the assumption of infinite replenishment rate. Instead there is a finite replenishment rate, which is typical of a manufactured item in which the lot is delivered over time according to the production rate.

We also allow shortages to occur and be backlogged, assuming there is a maximum level of backlog that management is willing to tolerate. Backlogs occur in productions systems because of either lack of material, lack of capacity, or both. Recall that shortage has two associated costs, π and $\hat{\pi}$ (Section 1.3). Because $\hat{\pi}$ is to shortage what h is to inventory, we evaluate it the same way—by considering the average shortage. Because π is the shortage (penalty) cost per unit short, we need the maximum shortage to evaluate it. Let

ψ = replenishment production rate, measured in the same units as the demand
Q = size of the production lot
A = set-up cost
c = unit production cost
B_t = shortage (backorder) level at time t
$\overline{B}$ = average shortage level
b = max B_t

The inventory geometry for this case is shown in Figure 6-7.

We assume that at time zero the inventory level is $-b$. At this point we issue a production order for Q units and because the lead time is zero, production starts immediately. The

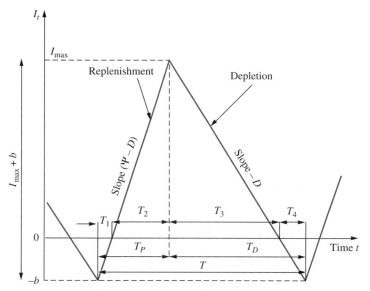

FIGURE 6-7
Inventory geometry: EPQ with backlog

production rate is ψ, but because there is demand at the same time, the net replenishment rate is $\psi - D$ and the replenishment line has a positive slope. When Q units have been manufactured, inventory reaches its maximum value, I_{max}, and production stops. The inventory is depleted at the demand rate D. When the inventory level reaches $-b$, production resumes and the cycle repeats.

Following a basically similar procedure as in the EOQ case:

$$T = \frac{Q}{D} \qquad \text{Cycle time}$$

$$T_P = \frac{Q}{\psi} \qquad \text{Time to produce } Q \text{ units}$$

$$T_D = \frac{I_{max}}{D} \qquad \text{Time to deplete maximum inventory}$$

From the inventory geometry:

$$I_{max} + b = T_p(\psi - D) = \frac{Q}{\psi}(\psi - D) = Q\left(1 - \frac{D}{\psi}\right)$$

or
$$I_{max} = Q\left(1 - \frac{D}{\psi}\right) - b$$

The on-hand inventory is positive during $T_2 + T_3$, whereas shortages are backlogged during T_1 and T_4. Production takes place during $T_p = T_1 + T_2$, whereas inventory depletion occurs during $T_D = T_3 + T_4$. From the inventory geometry we get

$$T_1 = \frac{b}{\psi - D} \qquad \text{Time to recover from the backlog}$$

$$T_2 = \frac{I_{max}}{\psi - D} \qquad \text{Time to generate } I_{max}$$

$$T_3 = \frac{I_{max}}{D} \qquad \text{Time to depelete } I_{max}$$

$$T_4 = \frac{b}{D} \qquad \text{Time to generate backlog of } b$$

To get the equation for $K(Q, b)$, we need $\overline{I}$ and $\overline{B}$. Both are obtained from the inventory geometry. Again these are averages per cycle.

$$\overline{I} = \frac{1}{2T} I_{max}(T_2 + T_3)$$

which, after introducing the terms for I_{max}, T_2, and T_3, yields

$$\overline{I} = \frac{\left[Q\left(1 - \dfrac{D}{\psi}\right) - b\right]^2}{2Q\left(1 - \dfrac{D}{\psi}\right)}$$

Also,

$$\overline{B} = \frac{1}{2T} b(T_1 + T_4)$$

and introducing the terms for T_1 and T_4 gives

$$\overline{B} = \frac{b^2}{2Q\left(1 - \dfrac{D}{\psi}\right)}$$

The average annual inventory holding cost is

$$\frac{1}{T}(hT\overline{I}) = h\overline{I} = \frac{h\left[Q\left(1 - \dfrac{D}{\psi}\right) - b\right]^2}{2Q\left(1 - \dfrac{D}{\psi}\right)}$$

The total shortage cost per cycle is

$$\pi b + \hat{\pi} T \overline{B}$$

and the average annual shortage cost is

$$\frac{1}{T}[\pi b + \hat{\pi} T \overline{B}] = \frac{\pi b D}{Q} + \frac{\hat{\pi} b^2}{2Q\left(1 - \dfrac{D}{\psi}\right)}$$

The total average annual cost is

$$K(Q, b) = cD + \frac{AD}{Q} + \frac{h\left[Q\left(1 - \frac{D}{\psi}\right) - b\right]^2}{2Q\left(1 - \frac{D}{\psi}\right)} + \frac{\pi b D}{Q} + \frac{\hat{\pi} b^2}{2Q\left(1 - \frac{D}{\psi}\right)}$$

To find Q^* and b^*, we simultaneously solve

$$\frac{\partial K}{\partial Q} = 0 \qquad \text{and} \qquad \frac{\partial K}{\partial b} = 0$$

Solving these two equations yields, for $\hat{\pi} \neq 0$,

$$Q^* = \sqrt{\frac{2AD}{h\left(1 - \frac{D}{\psi}\right)} - \frac{(\pi D)^2}{h(h + \hat{\pi})}} \sqrt{\frac{h + \hat{\pi}}{\hat{\pi}}}$$

and

$$b^* = \frac{(hQ^* - \pi D)\left(1 - \frac{D}{\psi}\right)}{(h + \hat{\pi})}$$

To get $K(Q^*, b^*)$, substitute Q^* and b^* into $K(Q, b)$.

If $\pi = 0$, Q^* and b^* will have finite positive values. If $\hat{\pi} > 0$ and π is sufficiently large, a negative value can be obtained under the radical for Q^*. In this case, no shortages should be allowed, i.e., $b^* = 0$. If $\hat{\pi} = 0$ and $\pi > 0$, it can be shown that the optimal policy is either to allow no shortages or to not inventory the item at all. In the latter case, all demand is backlogged before being satisfied. In manufacturing, this is called a produce-to-order policy.

> **Example 6-3. EPQ with backlog.** SuperSauce produces a certain salad dressing. The demand for this dressing is about 400 pounds per month, and SuperSauce can manufacture it at the rate of 2000 pounds per month. To initiate production, the machines have to be thoroughly checked and cleaned, and it costs the company $120 per set-up. The cost to produce this dressing is $3 a pound, and the inventory holding cost is estimated as 20 percent annually. If the demand for this dressing exceeds the available inventory, it is backlogged. Management estimates that a backlog accrues two types of cost—loss of goodwill and shortage penalty. The loss of goodwill is estimated to be $0.1 per pound short, and the shortage penalty is estimated to be $1.2 per pound short per month. Analyze the problem.
>
> *Solution.* The problem parameters are
>
> $A = \$120$ per set-up
>
> $i = 20\%$ annually
>
> $c = \$3$ per pound
>
> $h = 0.2 \times \$3 = \$0.6$ per pound per year
>
> $\pi = \$0.1$ per pound
>
> $\hat{\pi} = \$1.2$ per pound per month $= \$14.4$ per pound per year
>
> $D = 400/\text{month} = 4800/\text{year}$
>
> $\psi = 2000/\text{month} = 24{,}000/\text{year}$

The annual total inventory cost is

$$K(Q, b) = cD + \frac{AD}{Q} + \frac{h\left[Q\left(1 - \dfrac{D}{\psi}\right) - b\right]^2}{2Q\left(1 - \dfrac{D}{\psi}\right)} + \frac{\pi b D}{Q} + \frac{\hat{\pi} b^2}{2Q\left(1 - \dfrac{D}{\psi}\right)}$$

and the economic production quantity is

$$Q^* = \sqrt{\frac{2AD}{h\left(1 - \dfrac{D}{\psi}\right)} - \frac{(\pi D)^2}{h(h + \hat{\pi})}} \sqrt{\frac{h + \hat{\pi}}{\hat{\pi}}}$$

$$= \sqrt{\frac{(2)(120)(4800)}{(0.6)\left(1 - \dfrac{4800}{24{,}000}\right)} - \frac{[(0.1)(4800)]^2}{(0.6)(0.6 + 14.4)}} \sqrt{\frac{0.6 + 14.4}{14.4}}$$

$$= 1605$$

The optimal maximum backorder level is

$$b^* = \frac{(hQ^* - \pi D)\left(1 - \dfrac{D}{\psi}\right)}{(h + \hat{\pi})}$$

$$= \frac{[(0.6)(1605) - (0.1)(4800)]\left(1 - \dfrac{4800}{24{,}000}\right)}{(0.6 + 14.4)}$$

$$= 25.76 = 26$$

The economic order quantity is 1605 pounds, the maximum backorder level is 26 pounds, and production takes 4800/24,000 = 20 percent of the time. The annual total cost of inventory is

$$K(Q^*, b^*) = K(1605, 26) = (3)(4800) + \frac{(120)(4800)}{1605}$$

$$+ \frac{(0.6)\left[(1605)\left(1 - \dfrac{4800}{24{,}000}\right) - 26\right]^2}{(2)(1605)\left(1 - \dfrac{4800}{24{,}000}\right)} + \frac{(0.1)(25)(4800)}{1605}$$

$$+ \frac{(14.4)(26)^2}{(2)(1605)\left(1 - \dfrac{4800}{24{,}000}\right)} = \$15{,}136$$

From the EPQ with backlog model we obtain two special cases—EPQ without backlog and EOQ with backlog.

Economic production quantity (EPQ). In this case, we prohibit shortages by setting the shortage cost to be infinite. Obviously, no backlog is planned for this case, so $b = 0$.

The cost equation becomes

$$K(Q) = cD + \frac{AD}{Q} + \frac{hQ}{2}\left(1 - \frac{D}{\psi}\right)$$

by setting $b = 0$ in the previous cost equation. In the same way we obtain

$$Q^* = \sqrt{\frac{2AD}{h\left(1 - \dfrac{D}{\psi}\right)}}$$

In this case the value of Q^* is higher than in the EOQ case, because $(1 - D/\psi) < 1$. However, the value of $\bar{I}$ is lower than before, because of a period of combined replenishment and depletion. The term $(1 - D/\psi)$ is the *effective* replenishment rate. Note that when $\psi \to \infty$, we obtain the EOQ.

Example 6-4. Economic production quantity. The Rainbow Paint Manufacturing Company has a varied product line. One of their products is latex paint. Rainbow can manufacture the paint at an annual rate of 8000 gallons. The unit cost to produce one gallon of paint is $0.25, and the annual inventory holding cost is 40 percent. Prior to each production run, clean-up and check-out operations are performed, at a cost of $25. Analyze the problem.

Solution. The basic information for Rainbow's latex production is

$$A = \$25 \text{ per set-up}$$
$$i = 40 \text{ percent annually}$$
$$c = \$0.25 \text{ per gallon}$$
$$h = 0.40 \times \$0.25 = \$0.10 \text{ per gallon per year}$$
$$D = 4000 \text{ gallons per year}$$
$$\psi = 8000 \text{ gallons per year}$$

The annual average total inventory cost is given by

$$K(Q) = cD + \frac{AD}{Q} + \frac{hQ}{2}\left(1 - \frac{D}{\psi}\right)$$

and the economic production quantity is

$$\text{EPQ} = Q^* = \sqrt{\frac{2AD}{h(1 - D/\psi)}} = \sqrt{\frac{(2)(25)(4000)}{(0.1)(1 - 4000/8000)}} = 2000$$

Calculating,

$$T_P = \frac{Q}{\psi} = \frac{2000}{8000} = 0.25 \text{ year} = 3 \text{ months}$$

$$T = \frac{Q}{D} = \frac{2000}{4000} = 0.5 \text{ year} = 6 \text{ months}$$

i.e., there are two cycles per year. In each cycle, production takes place during T_p/T of the cycle, or half the time. We suggest you draw the inventory geometry for this example.

EOQ with backlog. This case is one of infinite replenishment rate in which shortages are allowed and backlogged. By setting $\psi \to \infty$ we obtain

$$K(Q, b) = cD + \frac{AD}{Q} + \frac{h(Q - b)^2}{2Q} + \frac{2\pi bD + \hat{\pi} b^2}{2Q}$$

yielding, for $\hat{\pi} \neq 0$,

$$Q^* = \sqrt{\frac{2AD}{h} - \frac{(\pi D)^2}{h(h + \hat{\pi})}} \sqrt{\frac{h + \hat{\pi}}{\hat{\pi}}}$$

$$b^* = \frac{hQ^* - \pi D}{(h + \hat{\pi})}$$

Example 6-5. EOQ with backlog. Jane sells, among other items, solvents. The demand is very steady at 500 gallons per year. The cost for placing an order is $50, and each gallon costs Jane $2. Inventory holding cost is 20 percent annually. If the demand exceeds the inventory, Jane estimates that there will be two types of penalty costs associated with the backorder. The loss of goodwill is $0.2 per unit short, and a "bookkeeping" cost of $0.2 per unit short per year. Analyze this problem.

Solution. The various parameters are

$$A = \$50$$
$$D = 500 \text{ gallons/year}$$
$$i = 20 \text{ percent}$$
$$c = \$2/\text{unit} \to h = ic = \$0.4 \text{ unit-year}$$
$$\pi = 0.2 \text{ per gallon}$$
$$\hat{\pi} = 0.2 \text{ per gallon per year}$$

Because Jane allows backorders, the average annual inventory cost is

$$K(Q, b) = \frac{AD}{Q} + cD + h\frac{(Q - b)^2}{2Q} + \frac{(2\pi Db + \hat{\pi} b^2)}{2Q}$$

and the economic order quantity and optimal maximum backorder level will be

$$Q^* = \sqrt{\frac{2AD}{h} - \frac{(\pi D)^2}{h(h + \hat{\pi})}} \sqrt{\frac{h + \hat{\pi}}{\hat{\pi}}}$$

$$= \sqrt{\frac{2 \times 50 \times 500}{0.4} - \frac{[0.2 \times 500]^2}{0.4 \times (0.4 + 0.2)}} \sqrt{\frac{0.4 + 0.2}{0.2}} = 500 \text{ gallons}$$

$$b^* = \frac{hQ^* - \pi D}{(h + \hat{\pi})} = \frac{(0.4)(500) - (0.2)(500)}{0.4 + 0.2} = 166.7 \approx 167$$

The minimal total annual average cost is

$$K(500, 167) = \frac{(50)(500)}{500} + (2)(500) + \frac{(0.4)(500 - 167)^2}{(2)(500)}$$

$$+ \frac{(2)(0.2)(500)(167) - (0.2)(167)^2}{(2)(500)}$$

$$= \$1133.33$$

Because $Q^* = 500$ is equal to D, the reorder cycle is one year. The percentage of time inventory is short can be found from the ratio

$$\frac{T_4}{T} = \frac{b}{TD} = \frac{167}{500} = 33.3 \text{ percent}$$

We suggest you draw the inventory geometry for this example.

2.1.3 QUANTITY DISCOUNTS. The EOQ model assumes that the unit cost is constant, no matter what quantity is purchased. In reality, suppliers may induce their customers to place larger orders by offering them quantity discounts. If the quantity purchased is greater than a specified "price break" quantity, the cost per unit is reduced. It is common practice to include this discount policy in the published price schedule.

The tendency of the buyer is to take advantage of this situation, especially if the item purchased is one that is used continuously. However, purchasing larger quantities means larger inventory, with higher inventory cost. So, the savings gained by purchasing at a lower unit cost may be lost by accruing higher inventory holding cost. We again see a need to balance opposing costs. Do we purchase more to take advantage of the cost breaks or purchase less to keep low inventory, resulting in lower inventory holding cost? This balance is obtained by modifying the basic EOQ model.

Two price break schedules are common. The **all-units discount** applies the discounted price to all units beginning with the first unit, if the quantity purchased exceeds the price break quantity. The other schedule applies the discounted price only to those units over the price break quantity—an **incremental discount** schedule. We introduce notation for quantity discounts. Unless otherwise stated, the notation is the same as the EOQ notation. Let

m = the number of price breaks
q_j = the upper limit of the jth price break interval
c_j = the cost of a unit in the jth price break interval $[q_{j-1}, q_j]$
Q_j = the EOQ quantity, calculated using c_j
Q_j^* = the best order quantity in interval j
Q^* = the optimal order quantity over all prices
$K_j(Q)$ = the cost of Q units in interval j
$K_j(Q_j)$ = the cost of EOQ units in interval j
$K_j(Q_j^*)$ = the minimum cost in interval j
$K^*(Q^*)$ = the minimum cost over all prices
$C_j(Q)$ = the cost to purchase Q units in interval j

By definition, $q_0 = 0$ and $q_{m+1} = \infty$, and logically, $c_j > c_{j+1}$. For all-units discount, the purchase price for buying Q units is

$$C_j(Q) = c_j Q \qquad \text{for } q_{j-1} \le Q < q_j$$

but an incremental discount has

$$C_j(Q) = \sum_{k=1}^{j-1} c_k q_k + c_j(Q - q_{j-1}) \qquad \text{for } q_{j-1} \le Q < q_j$$

We illustrate these two policies in Example 6-6.

Example 6-6. Quantity discounts. Coldpoint is a home appliance manufacturer. The company purchases a certain component for their products. Southern Electronics and ElectroTech are two companies that make the component, and their products and services are equal, so the component will be bought based solely on cost. Both companies offer a discount policy based on order quantity. However, these two companies post different price schedules. For Southern Electronics, if the order quantity is less than 500 (q_1) units, the price is \$0.60 per unit; if the quantity is 500 or more but less than 1000 (q_2), the unit price is \$0.58; any quantity 1000 units or over has a unit price of \$0.56. ElectroTech offers the same quantity range and prices. However, the discount rate applies only to the excess amount ordered. That is, if the order quantity is 500 units, the first 499 units cost \$0.60 and the 500th unit costs \$0.58. If 1000 units are ordered, the first 499 units cost \$0.60 and the next 500 [500, 999] cost \$0.58. Any unit beyond the 1000th costs \$0.56. Table 6-1 describes the two price schedules.

TABLE 6-1
$C(Q)$ for two price schedules

Quantity (Q)	Southern Electronics	ElectroTech
$0 \le Q < 500$	$0.60Q$	$0.6Q$
$500 \le Q < 1000$	$0.58Q$	$0.6 \times 500 + 0.58(Q - 500)$
$1000 \le Q < \infty$	$0.56Q$	$0.6 \times 500 + 0.58 \times 500 + 0.56(Q - 1000)$

The graphical description of the two different schedules is shown in Figures 6-8 and 6-9. The average cost per unit, $(C_j(Q))/Q$, is equal to c_j in the all-units discount and is larger than c_j in the case of incremental discounts (see Table 6-2).

All-units discounts. As before, our objective is to find Q that minimizes average total annual cost. Let

$$Q_j = \sqrt{\frac{2AD}{ic_j}}$$

$$K_j(Q_j) = c_jD + \sqrt{2ADic_j}$$

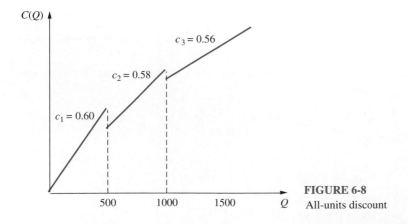

FIGURE 6-8
All-units discount

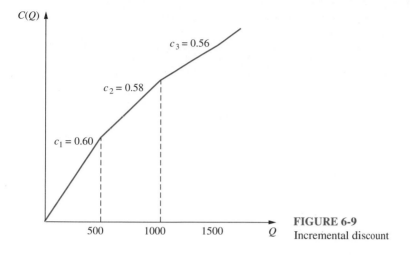

FIGURE 6-9
Incremental discount

These are the optimal order quantity and minimum cost, given a price of c_j. Because c_j changes, c_jD must be in the cost equation. If $q_{j-1} \leq Q_j < q_j$, the price c_j is valid, so Q_j is the best order quantity for the interval $[q_{j-1}, q_j]$. Let $Q_j^* = Q_j$ and $K_j^*(Q_j^*)$ be its cost.

However, Q_j may fall outside the price break interval. In this case, we need to find the best order quantity for the interval. Consider Figure 6-10, with two price break intervals. Three different cases for the location of Q_j relative to q_1 are shown. In case (a), Q_1^* is outside the valid region, $[0, q_1]$, and we cannot buy that quantity at c_1 per unit. The lowest cost for a quantity within $[0, q_1]$ is at q_1. Set $Q_1^* = q_1$ with $K_1(q_1)$ its cost. Case (a) has Q_2 in the interval $[q_1, \infty]$, so $Q_2^* = Q_2$ and its cost is $K_2(Q_2^*)$. $K_2(Q_2^*)$ is smaller than $K_1(q_1)$ because $c_2 < c_1$, so $Q^* = Q_2^*$ and $K^*(Q^*) = K_2(Q_2^*)$.

In (b), both Q_1^* and Q_2^* fall within their valid regions, but because $c_2 < c_1$, $K_2(Q) < K_1(Q)$ for all Q, so the optimal order quantity would be $Q^* = Q_2^*$ with minimum cost $K^*(Q^*) = K_2(Q_2^*)$. Case (c) has Q_1^* in $[0, q_1]$ while $Q_2^* < q_1$. Because $K_2(q_1) < K_1(Q_1^*)$, $Q^* = q_1$ with optimal cost $K^*(Q^*) = K_2(q_1)$.

Two conclusions come from this discussion:

- Because $c_j > c_{j+1}$, $K_j(Q) > K_{j+1}(Q)$ for all Q.
- The only quantities in the interval $[q_{j-1}, q_j]$ that could be optimal for the overall problem are Q_j and q_j. Because $K(Q)$ is a convex function, the only possibilities are Q_j, q_{j-1}, or q_j. Because $K_{j-1}(Q) > K_j(Q)$, q_j will have lower cost in the interval $[q_j, q_{j+1})$ and need not be considered in interval $[q_{j-1}, q_j)$.

TABLE 6-2
Average unit cost

Quantity (Q)	Southern Electronics	ElectroTech
$0 \leq Q < 500$	0.60	0.60
$500 \leq Q < 1000$	0.58	$10/Q + 0.58$
$1000 \leq Q \leq \infty$	0.56	$30/Q + 0.56$

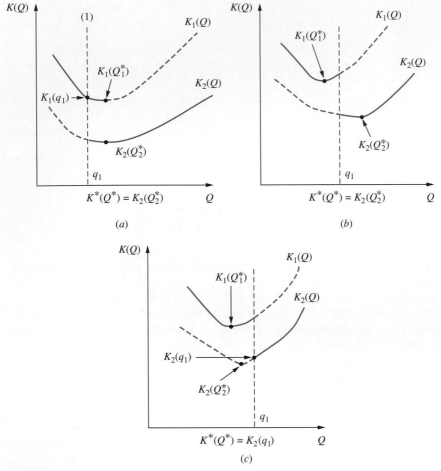

FIGURE 6-10
Cost curves for all-units discount

This is the basis for formulating the procedure for finding the optimum solution for the all-units discount policy. It is

Step 0: Set $Q^* = 0$, $K^*(Q^*) = \infty$, and $j = m$.

Step 1: Compute Q_j; if $q_{j-1} \leq Q_j \leq q_j$, go to step 3. Otherwise, set $Q_j^* = q_j$ and $K_j(Q_j^*) = K_j(q_j)$.

Step 2: If $K_j(Q_j^*) < K^*(Q^*)$, set $Q^* = Q_j$ and $K^*(Q^*) = K_j(Q_j^*)$. Set $j = j - 1$ and go to step 1.

Step 3: Set $K_j(Q_j^*) = c_j D + \sqrt{2ADic_j}$. If $K_j(Q_j^*) < K^*(Q^*)$, set $Q^* = Q_j^*$ and $K^*(Q^*) = K_j(Q_j^*)$. Stop; the optimal order quantity is Q^* with total cost $K^*(Q^*)$.

The following example demonstrates this procedure.

Example 6-7. All-units discount. We continue the Coldpoint example. The company estimates the cost of placing an order to be \$20, and the uniform annual demand for this subcomponent is 800 units. Inventory carrying cost is estimated to be 20 percent annually. We want to find the best purchasing policy if the subcomponent were to be ordered from Southern Electronics.

Solution. We note the basic parameters of this problem.

$$A = \$20$$
$$D = 800 \text{ units per year}$$
$$i = 20 \text{ percent annually}$$
$$m = 3$$

Step 0: Set $Q^* = 0$, $K^*(Q^*) = \infty$, and $j = m = 3$.

Step 1: Calculate the Q_3 with $c_3 = 0.56$:

$$Q_3 = \sqrt{\frac{(2)(20)(800)}{(0.2)(0.56)}} = 535$$

Because $Q_3 < 1000$, set $Q_3^* = 1000 = q_3$ and calculate

$$K_3(q_3) = c_3 D + \frac{AD}{q_3} + ic_3 \frac{q_3}{2}$$

$$= (0.56)(800) + \frac{(20)(800)}{1000} + (0.20)(0.56)\left(\frac{1000}{2}\right)$$

$$= 520$$

Step 2: $K_3(1000) < K^*(Q^*)$, so set $Q^* = 1000$ and $K^*(1000) = 520$. $j = 3 - 1 = 2$ and go to step 1.

Step 1: Calculate Q_2 with $c_2 = 0.58$:

$$Q_2 = \sqrt{\frac{(2)(20)(800)}{(0.2)(0.58)}} = 525$$

Because $500 \le 525 < 1000$, this is a feasible order quantity at the given price, so go to step 3.

Step 3: Calculate

$$K_2(Q_2^*) = c_2 D + \sqrt{2ADic_2}$$

$$= (0.58)800 + \sqrt{(2)(20)(800)(0.20)(0.56)}$$

$$\approx 525$$

Because $525 > 520$, the economic order quantity is 1000 units and the annual average inventory cost is $520 at the unit price of $0.56. We compare the three cost curves in Figure 6-11.

Incremental Discount. Now we examine the incremental discount option for ElectroTech presented in Example 6-6. As shown in Table 6-2, we can evaluate the average unit cost for each price break region. The unit cost used for evaluating the total average annual cost is the average unit cost in interval j, i.e., $C_j(Q)/Q$.

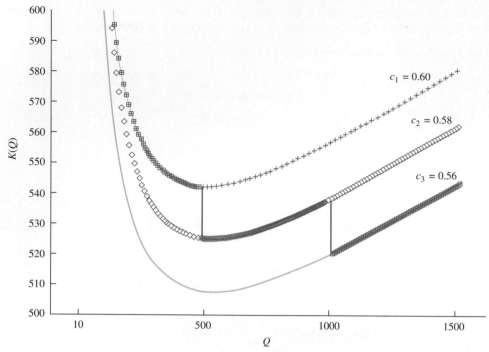

FIGURE 6-11
Cost curves for Southern Electronic

The average annual cost function for $q_{j-1} < Q < q_j$ is

$$K_j(Q) = \frac{C_j(Q)}{Q}D + \frac{AD}{Q} + i\left(\frac{C_j(Q)}{Q}\right)\left(\frac{Q}{2}\right)$$

$K_j(Q)$ is valid only between price break points $[q_{j-1}, q_j]$. It can be shown that the minimum cost point will never occur at a price break point (Hadley and Whitin, 1963). Further, if the optimal Q for an interval is in the interval, there is no guarantee that it is the best overall; we must compute the best Q for each price break, calculate the cost for any Q falling in its proper region, and choose the smallest cost. Differentiating $K_j(Q)$ and setting the result equal to zero gives the optimal Q for interval j as

$$Q_j = \sqrt{\frac{2D[A + C(q_{j-1}) - c_j q_{j-1}]}{ic_j}}$$

where $C(q_{j-1})$ is the total cost at breakpoint $j-1$.

The algorithm for the incremental discount problem is

Step 0: Set $Q^* = 0$, $K^*(Q^*) = \infty$, and $j = 1$.
Step 1: Compute Q_j; if $q_{j-1} < Q_j < q_j$, compute $K_j(Q_j)$. If Q_j is not in the interval, set $K_j(Q_j) = \infty$.

Step 2:   Set $j = j + 1$. If $j \leq m$, go to step 1.
Step 3:   Let $K_\ell(Q_\ell) = \text{Min}_{j=1,m} \ K_j(Q_j)$; then $Q^* = Q_\ell$ and $K^*(Q^*) = K_\ell(Q_\ell)$.

We demonstrate this procedure in Example 6-8.

> **Example 6-8. Incremental discount.** If Coldpoint considers purchasing from ElectroTech, what is the best purchasing policy?
>
> **Solution.** Recall that $A = \$20$, $D = 800$ units/year, and $i = 0.20$ annually. Other relevant data and calculations are given in Table 6-3. We follow the procedure for incremental discount to find Q^*.
>
> Step 0:   Set $Q^* = 0$, $K^*(Q^*) = \infty$, and $j = 1$.
> Step 1:   Compute
>
> $$Q_1 = \sqrt{\frac{2D[A + C(q_0) - c_1 q_0]}{ic_1}} = \sqrt{\frac{2 \times 800[20 + 0 - 0]}{0.2 \times 0.6}} \approx 516$$
>
> Because $Q_1 = 516 > 500$, it is not in the interval, so set $K_1(Q_1) = \infty$.
> Step 2:   Set $j = 1 + 1 = 2 < 3 = m$, so go to step 1.
> Step 1:   We find $Q_2 \approx 643$ (verify), which is in the interval (500, 1000]. Therefore, we calculate
>
> $$K_2(Q_2) = \frac{C_2(Q_2)}{Q_2}D + \frac{AD}{Q_2} + i\left(\frac{C_2(Q_2)}{Q_2}\right)\left(\frac{Q_2}{2}\right)$$
>
> $$K_2(643) = \left(0.58 + \frac{10}{643}\right)800 + \frac{20 \times 800}{643} + 0.2\left(0.58 + \frac{10}{643}\right)\left(\frac{643}{2}\right)$$
>
> $$= \$539.63$$
>
> Step 2:   Set $j = 2 + 1 = 3 \leq m$, so go to step 1.
> Step 1:   We find $Q_3 \approx 845$, which is not in the interval (1000, ∞], so we set $K_3(Q_3) = \infty$.
> Step 2:   Set $j = 3 + 1 = 4 > m$, so go to step 3.
> Step 3: $K_2(Q_2) = \text{Min}_{j=1,m} \ K_j(Q_j) = \text{Min}\{\infty, 539.62, \infty\}$; then $Q^* = Q_2 = 643$ and $K^*(Q^*) = K_2(Q_2) = \$539.62$.
>
> Therefore, if Coldpoint were to place an order with ElectroTech, each order would be 643 units, and the average annual cost is \$539.62. This cost is more expensive compared with 1000 units and an average annual cost of \$520 for purchasing from Southern Electronic. Obviously, Southern Electronic should be preferred, not only because of the cost advantage but also because of the convenience of placing fewer orders per year as a consequence of the larger order quantity. In Figure 6-12 we show the three cost curves of the incremental discount case. Compare it with Figure 6-11 for all-units discount.

TABLE 6-3
Calculations for ElectroTech

j	q_j	c_j	$C_j(Q)$	$C(q_j)$
1	500	0.60	$0.6Q$	300
2	1000	0.58	$300 + 0.58(Q - 500)$	590
3	>1000	0.56	$590 + 0.56(Q - 1000)$	—

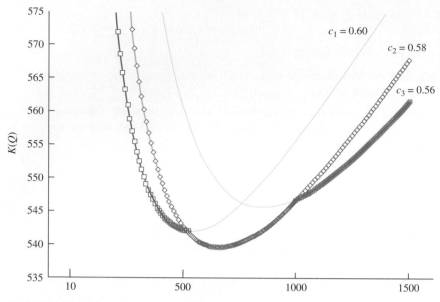

FIGURE 6-12
Cost curves for ElectroTech

2.1.4   RESOURCE-CONSTRAINED MULTIPLE-ITEM MODELS. The classic EOQ model is for a single item. What happens when we have more than one item?

The immediate and trivial answer is to calculate the EOQ for each item. To phrase it differently, we treat the one system with multiple items as multiple systems with one item. This procedure is adequate when there is no interaction among items, such as sharing common resources. Common resources can include, for example, budget, storage capacity, or both. Then the EOQ procedure is no longer adequate because these common resources are limited, and the result may violate the resource constraint. For that reason, a modification of the classic EOQ is needed.

We formulate the problem as a constrained optimization model and solve it using Lagrange multipliers. In many applications there are only one or two constraints. To introduce this approach, we will consider the case of one constraint—say the budget. We require that at any point in time the total investment in inventory should not exceed C dollars, i.e.,

$$\sum_{i=1}^{n} c_i Q_i \leq C$$

where n is the number of items. We do not consider the possibility of orders being phased so that the maximum inventory levels of all items do not occur simultaneously.

Our objective is still to minimize the total average annual cost,

$$K(Q) = \sum_{i=1}^{n} K_i(Q_i) = \sum_{i=1}^{n} \left(c_i D_i + \frac{A_i D_i}{Q_i} + h_i \frac{Q_i}{2} \right)$$

The Lagrangian equation considers both the objective and the constraint, and is

$$K(Q, \lambda) = K(Q) + \lambda \left\{ \sum_{i=1}^{n} c_i Q_i - C \right\}$$

where λ is the Lagrange multiplier. The multiplier acts as a penalty to reduce each Q_i^* to minimize cost while enforcing the constraint. We find the minimum value of K by taking partial derivatives of the function $K(Q, \lambda)$. The steps required to find an optimal solution are

1. Solve the unconstrained problem. If the constraint is satisfied, this solution is the optimal one.
2. If this is not the case, set the equation for $K(Q, \lambda)$.
3. Obtain Q_i^* by solving $(n + 1)$ equations given by

$$\frac{\partial K(Q, \lambda)}{\partial Q_i} = 0 \quad \text{for } i = 1, 2, \ldots, n$$

$$\frac{\partial K(Q, \lambda)}{\partial \lambda} = 0$$

We demonstrate this procedure in the following example.

> **Example 6-9. Multiple items—one constraint.** HiEnd, a small computer company, buys two types of floppy drives. Because of the small volume of this company, the manager limits the investment in inventory to a maximum of $5000. The price of these two floppy drives are $50 and $80, respectively, and the annual demand for these two drives is 250 and 484 units, respectively. The company has to spend $50 to process the order of either of these drives, and the manager uses 20 percent annually for financial evaluations.
>
> *Solution.* We analyze the problem by stating the basic parameters for this problem.
>
> $$A = \$50$$
> $$i = 20 \text{ percent annually}$$
> $$C = \$5000$$
> $$c_1 = \$50 \rightarrow h_1 = \$10 \text{ per unit per year}$$
> $$D_1 = 250 \text{ units per year}$$
> $$c_2 = \$80 \rightarrow h_2 = \$16 \text{ per unit per year}$$
> $$D_2 = 484 \text{ units per year}$$
>
> Step 1:   We compute the EOQ for each drive; i.e., we solve the unconstrained problem.
>
> $$Q_1 = \sqrt{\frac{(2)(50)(250)}{(0.2)(50)}} = 50 \text{ units}$$
>
> $$Q_2 = \sqrt{\frac{(2)(50)(484)}{(0.2)(80)}} = 55 \text{ units}$$

Using these two values we compute the investment in inventory:

$$(50)(50) + (80)(55) = 6900 > 5000$$

i.e., the budget constraint is violated, therefore the Lagrangian multiplier method is applied.

Step 2: The Lagrangian multiplier equation is

$$K(Q_1, Q_2, \lambda) = \sum_{i=1}^{2} \left(c_i D_i + \frac{A_i D_i}{Q_i} + \frac{h_i Q_i}{2} \right) + \left(\sum_{i=1}^{2} c_i Q_i - C \right)$$

We compute Q_1 and Q_2 using partial derivatives:

$$\frac{\partial K(Q_1, Q_2, \lambda)}{\partial Q_1} = 0$$

implies

$$Q_1^* = \sqrt{\frac{2A_1 D_1}{h_1 + 2\lambda c_1}}$$

$$= \sqrt{\frac{25,000}{10 + 100\lambda^*}}$$

$$= \frac{50}{\sqrt{1 + 10\lambda^*}}$$

and

$$\frac{\partial K(Q_1, Q_2, \lambda)}{\partial Q_2} = 0$$

implies

$$Q_2^* = \sqrt{\frac{48,400}{16 + 160\lambda^*}}$$

$$= \frac{55}{\sqrt{1 + 10\lambda^*}}$$

Finally,

$$\frac{\partial K(Q_1, Q_2, \lambda)}{\partial \lambda} = 0$$

implies

$$c_1 Q_1^* + c_2 Q_2^* = 5000$$

Set

$$X = \sqrt{1 + 10\lambda^*}$$

Then

$$c_1 Q_1^* + c_2 Q_2^* = (50)\{(50)/X\} + (80)\{(55)/X\} = 5000$$

Solving for $X = 6900/5000 = 1.38$ gives $\lambda^* = 0.09044$. Thus,

$$Q_1^* = 50/1.38 = 36.23 \approx 36$$
$$Q_2^* = 55/1.38 = 39.86 \approx 40$$

Then the Lagrangian function is

$$K(36, 40, 0.09044) = \left[(50)(250) + \frac{(50)(250)}{36} + \frac{(10)(36)}{2}\right]$$

$$+ \left[(80)(484) + \frac{(50)(484)}{40} + \frac{(16)(40)}{2}\right]$$

$$+ (0.09044)[(50)(36) + (80)(40) - 5000] = 52,672.22$$

(Note that the last term is zero—why?) The total investment in inventory is then

$$(36)(50) + (40)(80) = 5000$$

Resource-Constrained Multiple Items—Extension. We mentioned that the two most common constraints in inventory systems are space and budget. We extend our previous discussion to a two-constraint case. The general problem formulation is

minimize $\qquad K(Q) = \sum_{i=1}^{n} K_i(Q_i) = \sum_{i=1}^{n} \left(c_i D_i + \frac{A_i D_i}{Q_i} + h_i \frac{Q_i}{2}\right)$

subject to $\qquad \sum_{i=1}^{n} c_i Q_i \leq C \qquad$ (Budget constraint)

$$\sum_{i=1}^{n} f_i Q_i \leq F \qquad \text{(Space constraint)}$$

$$Q_i \geq 0 \qquad i = 1, 2, \ldots, n$$

f_i is the space required for a unit of item type i, and F is the total space available.

This problem is more complicated, because either or both of the constraints may be inactive. Therefore, the single-constraint procedure is changed as follows:

1. Solve the unconstrained problem. If both constraints are satisfied, this solution is the optimal one.
2. Otherwise include one of the constraints, say budget, and solve a one-constraint problem to find Q_i. If the space constraint is satisfied, this solution is the optimal one.
3. Otherwise repeat the process for only the space constraint.
4. If both single-constraint solutions do not yield the optimal solution, then both constraints are active, and the Lagrangian equation with both constraints must be solved:

$$K(Q_1, \lambda_1, \lambda_2) = \sum_{i=1}^{n} \left(c_i D_i + \frac{A_i D_i}{Q_i} + h \frac{Q_i}{2}\right) + \lambda_1 \left(\sum_{i=1}^{n} c_i Q_i - C\right) + \lambda_2 \left(\sum_{i=1}^{n} f_i Q_i - F\right)$$

To find the optimal $\{Q_i\}$, the following $(n + 2)$ equations are solved simultaneously:

$$\frac{\partial K}{\partial Q_i} = 0 \qquad i = 1, 2, \ldots, n$$

$$\frac{\partial K}{\partial \lambda_1} = 0 \qquad \frac{\partial K}{\partial \lambda_2} = 0$$

This procedure is demonstrated in the following example.

Example 6-10. Multiple items—two constraints. HiEnd does not have much space to store disk drives. Suppose each of these two kinds of drives requires 10 and 8 units of space, respectively, and there are a total of 500 units of space available. Will the previous result also satisfy the space constraint? Resolve this problem as necessary.

Solution. Recall the procedure in Example 6-9.

Step 1:   Because we know from Example 6-9 that the budget constraint is violated by the unconstrained solution, we skip to step 2.

Step 2:   We select one of the constraints and solve it as a single-constraint problem. In Example 6-9 we solved the problem with budget constraint. Therefore, we select budget as the only constraint, and we have the solution $Q'_1 = 36$ and $Q'_2 = 40$.

Step 3:   We check the budget constraint solution to see if it satisfies the space constraint:

$$(10)(36) + (8)(40) = 680 > 500$$

The space constraint is violated.

Step 4:   We solve the Lagrangian multiplier problem with only the space constraint.

$$K(Q_1, Q_2, \lambda_2) = \sum_{i=1}^{2} \left(C_i D_i + \frac{A_i D_i}{Q_i} + \frac{h_i Q_i}{2} \right) + \lambda_2 \left(\sum_{i=1}^{2} f_i Q_i - F \right)$$

We take the partial derivatives with respect to Q_1, Q_2, and λ_2, and set them to zero. We obtain

$$\frac{\partial K(Q_1, Q_2, \lambda_2)}{\partial Q_1} = 0 \Rightarrow Q_1^* = \sqrt{\frac{2A_1 D_1}{h_1 + 2\lambda_2^* f_1}} = \frac{50}{\sqrt{1 + 2\lambda_2^*}}$$

$$\frac{\partial K(Q_1, Q_2, \lambda_2)}{\partial Q_2} = 0 \Rightarrow Q_2^* = \sqrt{\frac{2A_2 D_2}{h_2 + 2\lambda_2^* f_2}} = \frac{55}{\sqrt{1 + \lambda_2^*}}$$

$$\frac{\partial K(Q_1, Q_2, \lambda_2)}{\partial \lambda_2} = 0 \Rightarrow f_1 Q_1^* + f_2 Q_2^* = 500$$

From the three equations, we have

$$10 \left(\frac{50}{\sqrt{1 + 2\lambda_2^*}} \right) + 8 \left(\frac{55}{\sqrt{1 + \lambda_2^*}} \right) = 500$$

and solving, we get $\lambda_2^* \approx 1.76$, and

$$Q_1^* = 23.51 \approx 23$$

$$Q_2^* = 33.11 \approx 33$$

We check this solution with the budget constraint.

$$(23)(50) + (33)(80) = 3790 < 5000$$

It does not violate the budget constraint. The optimal order quantities under both budget and space constraints are $Q_1^* = 26$, $Q_2^* = 33$.

Compare these results with Example 6-9.

2.1.5 MULTI-ITEM ORDERING.[1] A common trend in industry today is to reduce the number of suppliers and have each supplier deliver a higher number of items, both in terms of quantity and variety (Chapter 2). The logistics are that usually there is a long-term contract for all items incurring a certain initial cost, and then deliveries are made according to orders issued for each item (incurring an individual ordering cost). We analyze here this type of environment, i.e., a multi-item single-supplier system. In doing so, we follow closely the model presented by Goyal (1974).

Suppose n items are purchased from a single vendor. The ordering cost has two components—a major common ordering cost A incurred whenever an order is placed and a minor ordering cost a_i incurred if item i is included in the order. Demand for item i is assumed to be a constant rate of D_i units per period (year). Additional notations are

N = number of purchase orders in a planning period (a year)

N_i = number of replenishments for the ith item in the planning period (year)

h_i = total annual inventory holding cost for item i

Q_i = order quantity for item i

$K(N)$ = total average annual variable cost for all items (ordering and holding costs)

We assume the following decision environment:

- Procurement lead time is constant.
- No shortages are allowed (i.e., infinite shortage cost).
- There is an infinite replenishment rate.
- There is an infinite time horizon.
- Purchase orders are placed at constant time intervals.
- An item is replenished at equal time intervals.

Following the rationale of the EOQ formulation, we can express $K(N)$ as

$$K(N) = AN + \sum_{i=1}^{n} a_i N_i + \frac{1}{2} \sum_{i=1}^{n} \frac{h_i D_i}{N_i}$$

where

$$Q_i = \frac{D_i}{N_i}$$

Let the ith item be ordered in every k_ith purchase order. Then

$$k_i = \frac{N}{N_i}$$

---

[1]From Goyal (1974). Used by permission.

and it is the number of times item i is ordered. The reciprocal of k_i (i.e., N_i/N) is defined as the relative ordering frequency of the ith item. Thus, if the relative frequency of an item is known, its k value can be determined.

We let $N_i = N/k_i$, yielding

$$K(N) = N\left(A + \sum_{i=1}^{n}\frac{a_i}{k_i}\right) + \frac{1}{2N}\sum_{i=1}^{n}h_iD_ik_i$$

For n items, it is possible to specify the value of k for each item by a combination $\{k_1, k_2, \ldots, k_n\}$.

Suppose a particular combination of $\{k_i\}$ for $i = 1, 2, \ldots, n$ is given. Then, to get the optimum we take the first difference equations of $K(N)$, to obtain

$$K^*(k_i) = \sqrt{\left[2\left(A + \sum_{i=1}^{n}\frac{a_i}{k_i}\right)\sum h_iD_ik_i\right]} \qquad \text{Minimum average annual cost as a function of } \{k_i\}$$

$$N^*(k_i) = \sqrt{\left(\sum_{i=1}^{n}h_iD_ik_i\right)\bigg/\left[2\left(A + \sum_{i=1}^{n}\frac{a_i}{k_i}\right)\right]} \qquad \text{Economic number of purchase orders as a function of } \{k_i\}$$

$$Q_i^*(k_i) = \frac{D_ik_i}{N^*(k_i)} \qquad \text{Economic order quantity for item } i \text{ as a function of } \{k_i\}$$

The above values are optimal for a given set of $\{k_1, k_2, \ldots, k_l, \ldots, k_n\}$. Suppose we can consider changing k_l to k_{l_1} in order to reduce the minimum average annual variable cost as given by $K^*(k_i)$. The minimum average annual cost with the changed k value of the lth item is given by

$$K(k_{l_1}) =$$

$$\sqrt{\left[2\left(A + \sum_{i=1}^{l-1}\frac{a_i}{k_i} + \sum_{i=l+1}^{n}\frac{a_i}{k_i} + \frac{a_l}{k_{l_1}}\right)\left(\sum_{i=1}^{l-1}h_iD_ik_i + \sum_{i=l+1}^{n}h_iD_ik_i + k_lD_lk_{l_1}\right)\right]}$$

or

$$K(k_{l_1}) = \sqrt{\left[2\left(G_{l_1} + \frac{a_l}{k_{l_1}}\right)(W_{l_1} + h_lD_lk_{l_1})\right]} \qquad (1)$$

where

$$G_{l_1} = \sum_{i=1}^{l-1}\frac{a_i}{k_i} + \sum_{i=l+1}^{n}\frac{a_i}{k_i}$$

$$W_{l_1} = \sum_{i=1}^{l-1}h_iD_ik_i + \sum_{i=l+1}^{n}h_iD_ik_i$$

The local minimum of $K(k_{l_1})$ is obtained if both the following conditions are satisfied:

$$K(k_{l_1}) \leq K(k_{l_1} + 1) \tag{2}$$

$$K(k_{l_1}) < K(k_{l_1} - 1) \tag{3}$$

We substitute the value of $K(k_{l_1})$ obtained in (1) in (2). Simplifying, we get

$$\frac{W_{l_1}}{G_{l_1} H_l} \leq k_{l_1}(k_{l_1} + 1)$$

where, for the lth item

$$H_l = \frac{h_l D_l}{a_l}$$

We do the same for equation (3) to obtain

$$\frac{W_{l_1}}{G_{l_1} H_l} > k_{l_1}(k_{l_1} - 1)$$

Combining the last two equations yields the optimum conditions as

$$k_{l_1}(k_{l_1} - 1) < \frac{W_{l_1}}{G_{l_1} H_l} \leq k_{l_1}(k_{l_1} + 1)$$

If, for the lth item $k_{l_1} \neq k_l$, the new combination is given by $\{k_1, k_2, \ldots, k_{l_1}, \ldots, k_n\}$, and this has to be improved.

From the previous inequality, upper and lower bounds for the ratio $W_{l_1}/(G_{l_1} H_l)$ can be evaluated. Some values are given in Table 6-4.

Based upon the previous analysis, Goyal (1974) proposes the following algorithm for determining the optimum ordering policy:

1. Calculate $H_i = h_i D_i / a_i$ for each item.
2. Assume initial arbitrary values for k_i, say 1, i.e., $\{1, 1, \ldots, 1\}$ denoted as $\{k_{io}\}$.
3. For the first item in the list, determine k_{l_1} by comparing the ratio $W_{l_1}/G_{l_1} H_l$ with the values in Table 6-4. The new combination is $\{k_{l_1}, 1, 1, \ldots, 1\}$. Similarly, obtain the values of k_{i1} for $i = 1, 2, \ldots, n$. This completes the first set of computations, yielding $\{k_{i1}\}$ for $i = 1, 2, \ldots, n$.
4. Apply step 3 to $\{k_{i1}\}$ to obtain $\{k_{i2}\}$ for $i = 1, \ldots, n$. The optimum value is obtained when

$$\{k_{i(j+1)}\} = \{k_{ij}\} = \{k_i^*\} \quad \text{for all } i$$

Convergence is normally very rapid.

TABLE 6-4
Upper and lower bounds for W/GH

k	1	2	3	4	5	6	7	8	9	10
Lower bound	0	2	6	12	20	30	42	56	72	90
Upper bound	2	6	12	20	30	42	56	72	90	110

5. The optimum policy is as follows:

(a) Optimum number of purchase orders per year:

$$N^*(k_i^*) = \sqrt{\left(\sum_{i=1}^{n} h_i D_i k_i^*\right) \bigg/ \left[2\left(A + \sum_{i=1}^{n} \frac{a_i}{k_i^*}\right)\right]}$$

(b) Optimum number of replenishments for the ith item:

$$N_i^* = \frac{N^*(k_1^*)}{k_i^*} \quad \text{for all } i$$

(c) Optimum order quantity for the ith item:

$$Q_i^*(k_i^*) = \frac{D_i k_i^*}{N^*(k_i^*)} \quad \text{for all } i$$

We demonstrate this procedure in the following example.

Example 6-11. Multi-item ordering. Coldpoint decided to purchase all their electronic components from Electrotech. They negotiate an annual contract once a year, and the time and paperwork involved cost them $43.50. Annual values of D_i, h_i, and a_i are given in Table 6-5.

Solution. $A = \$43.50$. Values of $H_i = (h_i D_i)/a_i$ are also shown in Table 6-5. Steps 2, 3, and 4 of the algorithm are shown in Table 6-6, which can be generated by using a spreadsheet.

The rate of change in successive sets of computations can be judged by the following results:

Total average annual cost based on $\{k_{i0}\}$ = 11,920

Total average annual cost based on $\{k_{i1}\}$ = 11,454

TABLE 6-5
Data for Example 6-11

i (item)	D_i (units/year)	h_i ($/unit/year)	a_i ($)	$H_i = h_i D_i / a_i$
1	1,500	2	9	333
2	2,500	3	6	1,000
3	4,000	1.25	5	1,000
4	10,000	1	10	1,000
5	2,500	3	7	1,071
6	4,250	2	5	1,700
7	10,000	1.45	8	1,875
8	12,500	1.6	4.5	4,444
9	20,000	2	7	5,714
10	15,000	2	5	6,000
11	50,000	1	8	6,250
12	9,000	5	6	7,500
13	8,000	8	8	8,000
14	35,000	2	8	8,750
15	10,000	10	10	10,000

TABLE 6-6
Computations for determining the combination (k_i^*)

First set of computations:

When

$$k_{i0} = 1 \quad \text{for} \quad i = 1, 2, \ldots, 15$$

$$W_{i1} = \sum_{i=1}^{l-1} h_i D_i k_{i1} + \sum_{i=l+1}^{15} h_i D_i k_{i0}$$

and

$$G_{i1} = \sum_{i=1}^{l-1} a_i / k_{i1} + \sum_{i=l+1}^{15} a_i / k_{i0}$$

	$W_{i1}/G_{i1}H_i$	k_{i1}	k_{i2}	k_{i3}
1	$470{,}500/(141 \times 333) = 10.02$	3	4	4
2	$473{,}500/(138 \times 1000) = 3.43$	2	2	2
3	$480{,}500/(136 \times 1000) = 3.533$	2	2	2
4	$480{,}500/(128.5 \times 1000) = 3.739$	2	2	2
5	$493{,}000/(126.5 \times 1071) = 3.638$	2	2	2
6	$499{,}500/(125 \times 1700) = 2.3505$	2	2	2
7	$502{,}000/(119.5 \times 1812) = 2.318$	2	2	2
8	$511{,}000/(119 \times 4444) = 0.966$	1	1	1
9 to 15	k_{ij} remains 1 for these items			

Total average annual cost based on $\{k_{i2}\} = 11{,}450$
Total average annual cost based on $\{k_{i3}\} = 11{,}450$

$$\{k_{i3}\} = \{k_i^*\} = \{4, 2, 2, 2, 2, 2, 2, 1, 1, 1, 1, 1, 1, 1, 1\}$$

From step 5(a) of the algorithm we obtain

$$N^* = 46.6 = 47$$

Step 5(b) yields the following optimum number of replenishments per item (rounded-off numbers):

$$(12, 23, 23, 23, 23, 23, 23, 47, 47, 47, 47, 47, 47, 47, 47)$$

Step 5(c) yields the optimum order quantity per item (rounded-off numbers):

$$(129, 86, 172, 429, 107, 182, 429, 268, 429, 321, 1073, 193, 172, 751, 215)$$

The values for Q_i^* are lower than the ones obtained by using the EOQ formula for each item individually.

Extension of this anlaysis to the case where backlog is allowed can be found in Kumar and Arora (1990).

SECTION 2.1 PROBLEMS

6.15. A factory outlet sells 26 "Gizmos" per month. Ordering cost is $1.00 per order, and inventory holding cost is $0.3 per unit per month.

(a) Assuming no shortage is allowed, evaluate the order quantity (EOQ).

(b) Draw the inventory geometry for this case.

6.16. Harriet is the purchasing manager for High-Tech Company. She is faced now with the following dilemma. Her operation uses 10,000 units a year of copper cable connectors. She knows it can be manufactured internally at the rate of 100,000 units per year and at a cost of $40 per unit. However, associated with each production run there is a set-up cost of $5000, and the annual inventory holding cost is $i = 20$ percent.

Harriet is cost conscious and decided to get a price from two external suppliers. Electronic Hardware Company offered a price of $44 per unit, provided that the minimum quantity shipped is 1000 units; they could supply up to 6000 units per year. Metstamp Company fixed the price of $43.50 per unit, with a fixed cost of $200 per shipment, regardless of the quantity; they could supply up to 4000 units per year. What is the optimal policy Harriet should use, assuming no shortages are allowed?

6.17. Find the optimal turnover rate ((TR)*) for the following cases:

(a) EOQ model, no shortages

(b) EPQ model, with backlog (*Hint*: Consider the average inventory for the backorder case.)

6.18. Consider the EPQ case with backlog. Suppose that instead of ordering a quantity of Q^*, a quantity of βQ^* is ordered, where $\beta > 0$.
Let

$$\delta = \frac{K(Q) - K(Q^*)}{K(Q^*)}$$

Develop the equation for δ.

Show a graph of $\delta = f(\beta)$ and make observations about the sensitivity of the inventory system to nonoptimal order quantity. Can you draw a practical interpretation?

6.19. Consider an inventory system with infinite replenishment rate. Shortages are not backlogged, but lost. (This is the case of "lost sales.") Assume there is a loss of π dollars per unit short.

Develop the model for this case and show the optimal values. Show that it is never optimal to inventory the item and allow lost sales. (*Note*: Shortage cost is proportional to the number of units short, and *not* the elapsed time.)

6.20. The Agrichem Company is manufacturing a liquid chemical compound that is used in the fertilizer industry. The product is perishable in that it deteriorates in storage.

Based on past records, the company developed a nonlinear regression model and found that the cost of storing Q gallons for t time periods is cQt^m dollars, where c is a constant and $m > 1$.

The chemical compound is produced in batches of Q_0 gallons. The set-up cost is A dollars.

(a) Find Q_0^*, assuming no shortages and infinite replenishment rate.

(b) Evaluate the annual cost $K(Q_0^*)$.

(c) Analyze the result for $m = 1$ and $m \to \infty$.

6.21. The Bike Company has a special line of mountain bikes, for which 5000 handlebars are required annually. They can be purchased for $30 per unit or produced internally. The production cost is $20 per unit, and the production rate is 20,000 units per year. Set-up cost is $110, whereas issuing a purchase order costs $25. Inventory holding cost is 25 percent per annum.

(a) Should the Bike Company make or buy the item, assuming no shortages are allowed?

(b) Suppose shortages are allowed, with $\pi = \$0.15$ per unit, and $\hat{\pi} = \$7$ per unit per year. What should Bike do now?

6.22. A certain item has a daily demand of 1000 units. It is purchased in batches with unit cost of $5 and ordering cost of $80 per order. The annual inventory holding cost is 30 percent, and shortages are backlogged with shortage cost of $2 per unit per month. Purchase orders are scheduled so that every 30 days a batch arrives. Find Q^* and b^*.

6.23. Toys International has a number of manufacturing and assembly plants. One of the manufacturing plants has to supply 640 toy wheels per day to the assembly plant. No stockout is allowed, to ensure continuity of the assembly process. The plant has a capacity of 4200 wheels per day. Production set-up cost is $400, and inventory holding cost is $0.30 per unit per day, whereas production cost is $92 per wheel.

(a) Evaluate the minimum average daily cost.

(b) Evaluate T, T_p, T_D, I_{max}.

(c) What is the minimum average daily cost if set-up cost is $4000? Compare.

6.24. Consider the case of finite replenishment rate in which backlog is not allowed (Figure 6-7). During T_D, the machine is idle. Suppose the cost of idle time is c_d dollars per unit time (as the machine can be used to manufacture other products). Develop an equation for Q^* that yields minimum average total cost that includes idle time cost.

6.25. Use the results of Problem 6.24 and evaluate a ratio

$$\frac{c_d}{c}$$

Can you draw real-world conclusions?

6.26. Lou is the purchasing manager of a shoe manufacturer that has a line of heavy hiking boots. He purchases the laces for the boots from different suppliers. The demand is 30,000 pairs of laces a year, and no shortages are allowed. His major supplier gave him the following all-units discount price schedule:

Quantity	Unit price ($)
$Q < 1000$	1.00
$1000 \le Q < 3000$	0.98
$3000 \le Q < 5000$	0.96
$5000 \le Q < \infty$	0.94

Lou knows that issuing an order costs him $100, and the inventory holding cost is 35 percent annually.

(a) Compute Q^*.

(b) Plot the graph of $K(Q) = f(Q)$.

6.27. The Pine Garden souvenir store sells about 1000 keychains per year. They figure their inventory holding cost to be $1 per unit per year. Shortages are backlogged at the cost of $4 per item annually. The souvenir shop pays $2 per unit for quantities less than 2000 units and $1.97 per unit for any other quantity. They estimate their ordering cost to be $50.

(a) Find Q^* and b^*.

(b) Plot $K(Q) = f(Q)$.

6.28. Skatz Company is one of the leading manufacturers of roller blades. In their plant they do assembly only, and all components are purchased from external suppliers. They are unhappy now with their current supplier of rollers and decided to find a new source for their top-of-the-line model. The demand is 400,000 rollers per year, and they received different price schedules from three different suppliers.

Supplier A gave a flat rate of $3 per roller regardless of the quantity ordered.

Supplier B provided the following all units discount price schedule: $3.25 per roller if the order quantity is less than 5000, $3.00 per roller if the quantity is 5000 or more but less than 15,000, and $2.60 per unit for any quantity beyond 15,000.

Supplier C offered a price of $3.25 if the order quantity is less than 10,000 and $2.80 per roller for each unit purchased beyond 10,000, using incremental discount.

All three suppliers have the same roller quality. The order cost is $150, and inventory holding cost is taken to be 30 percent annually.

(a) Evaluate the optimal quantity to be ordered.

(b) Plot your results graphically.

6.29. The management policy of a certain company is to never run out of stock. The sales department carried out an analysis of a particular item to evaluate this policy. The demand is deterministic and constant over time at 625 units per year. The unit cost of the item is $50 independent of the quantity ordered. The cost of placing an order is $5.00, and the annual inventory carrying charge is $i = 0.20$. Units can be backordered at a cost of $0.20 per unit per week. Calculate the optimal operating doctrine under the assumption that no stockouts are allowed and also that units can be backordered at the cost indicated above. What is the dollar loss per year caused by the no-stockout policy if the sales department has correctly estimated the pertinent parameters?

6.30. A company produces two items, A and B, that are perishable and deteriorate in inventory. The pertinent data are

	A	B
Demand/year	2000	250
Item cost	50	60
Annual carrying cost rate	0.20	0.10
Set-up cost	100	480
Shortage costs/unit/year	∞	2

Management has established the policy that the total inventory turnover must be greater than or equal to 19 (recall that the inventory turnover is defined as the annual demand of all the items expressed in dollars divided by the average total investment in inventory).

Determine the optimal inventory policy and the cost to management of the inventory turnover policy.

6.31. A construction company requires 600 lb per year of special alloy welding rods. Each time an order for rods is placed, a cost of $8.00 is incurred. The purchase price depends on the amount purchased and is given by

Quantity	Price
$Q < 500$	$0.30
$500 \leq Q < 1000$	0.29
$Q \geq 1000$	0.28

This is an all-units discount. If the carrying rate per dollar-year of inventory is 0.20, how many units should be ordered each time an order is placed?

6.32. In the basic EOQ model, we assume a constant demand rate D. Suppose we find the optimal order quantity and follow this policy, but the demand is really $D'(D' > D)$. How will this affect the number of orders per year, average inventory per year, and number of shortages per year?

6.33. A company orders a component part from a supplier. The yearly demand is 6000 parts, and they order 1000 parts every 365/60 days. Stockouts are allowed.

    (a) Assuming the company acts optimally, what can you say about the relative values of holding and ordering costs?

    (b) If the production control manager told you that it costs $50 to place an order and each part costs $180, what comment would you make about the inventory holding cost?

    (c) What order quantity would you recommend?

6.34. A company orders two items. Item 1 costs $10, has a yearly demand of 100 units, and has an ordering cost of $40. Item 2 costs $40, has a yearly demand of 180, and costs $20 to order. The inventory carrying cost rate is 20 percent per year. Storage for the two items is limited, and because they are the same size, there can never be more than 40 total units in inventory at any time. Also, the total value of inventory must be within a budget of $400 at any time. What order quantity do you recommend?

6.35. A fruit stand stocks three products—apples, cantaloupes, and watermelons. The demands (for a season), unit costs, ordering costs, and size of the three items are: apples, 2500, 0.50, 25.00, 1; cantaloupes, 1000, 1.00, 20.00, 3; watermelons, 600, 3.50, 30.00, 10. Assume an inventory carrying cost rate of 10 percent per season. The economic order quantities for the three items are 1581, 632, and 321, respectively. However, the stand has only 6000 units of space, with one apple equal to one unit of space. Using a Lagrange multiplier approach, a student determines batch sizes for the constrained problem of 1392, 536, and 300, with $\lambda = 0.37$. A local carpenter will build 500 more units of space for $160.00. Should the vendor contract for the additional space?

6.36. Consider the deterministic EOQ model when backorders are allowed. As usual, let the demand be Q, the ordering cost A, and the holding cost per unit-year h. Suppose the backorder cost per unit-year is $\hat{\pi} = ah$, where a is a constant.

    (a) Determine Q^*, the optimal order quantity.

    (b) Determine b^*, the optimal backorder quantity.

    (c) Plot Q^*/b^* versus a.

6.37. The Bench Company is a small manufacturer of wooden benches. Their line includes four types of benches that differ in size, material, finish, and color. Pertinent production data are as follows:

	Bench Type			
	1	**2**	**3**	**4**
Annual demand (units)	1000	5000	10,000	8000
Set-up cost ($)	6	10	10	8
Unit cost ($)	10	3	5	2
Space per unit (ft^2)	5	1	1	1.5

Bench has a small warehouse for finished benches, which has an area of 1500 ft^2. Each bench has a fixed location. Assuming $i = 20$ percent annually, calculate the optimal quantities to be stored.

Bench has an offer to double the storage space, which will result in an increase of $200 in annual expenses. Should Bench do it?

6.38. Suppose that Bench, in addition to limited warehouse space, also has a budget limitation of $3800 for investment in inventory. Calculate the optimal quantities to be stored. Compare with the results of Problem 6.37.

6.39. For the case of incremental discount, show that the minimum-cost point will never occur at a price break point. (*Hint*: Evaluate the derivative of $K_j(Q)$ and $K_{j+1}(Q)$ at q_{j+1}, and show that the derivative of $K_{j+1}(Q)$ is less than the derviative of $K_j(Q)$.)

2.2 Dynamic Lot Sizing Models (DLS)

Dynamic lot sizing models come to bear when demand is lumpy, i.e., is not uniform during the planning horizon. We organize the discussion of "**lumpy demand**" models in four groups of solution techniques, as follows:

Simple rules are decision rules for the order quantity that are not based directly on "optimizing" the cost function but that have certain other merits. These simple methods are significant because they are widely used, especially in MRP systems (see Chapter 7).

Heuristic rules aim at achieving a low-cost solution that is not necessarily optimal.

Wagner-Whitin is an optimization approach to lumpy demand.

The Peterson-Silver rule is a test to tell when demand is lumpy.

2.2.1 SIMPLE RULES. There are three rules that are common—fixed period demand, period order quantity, and lot for lot (nicknamed "L4L").

Fixed period demand. This approach is equivalent to the simple rule of ordering "*m* months of future demand." For example, if we want to order "two months of demand," we sum the forecasted demand for the next two months, which is the quantity ordered. Weeks or days could be used instead of months. This rule is different from the "months of supply" measure of effectiveness presented in Section 1.4. The latter is an aggregate measure based on dollar value of **all** inventory items. Fixed period demand is for an individual item and is based on quantity.

Example 6-12. Fixed period demand. Consider the following two cases, where the forecasted demand is given in Table 6-7.

Solution. If we use a fixed period of six weeks, the order quantity is 60 for (a) and 72 for (b). The EOQ is preferred for constant demand.

TABLE 6-7
Fixed period demand

(a) Uniform demand					
Week	1	2	3	4	5	6
Demand	10	10	10	10	10	10

(b) Lumpy demand					
Week	1	2	3	4	5	6
Demand	10	15	11	18	8	10

Period order quantity (POQ). This is a modification of the previous rule, in which "structure" is used to select the fixed period. The average lot size desired (by whatever method) is divided by the average period demand, yielding the fixed period to be used. If the desired order quantity is 60, then the fixed period for (b) is five weeks, as the average weekly demand is 12.

Lot for lot (L4L). This is a special case of the fixed period rule; the order quantity is always the demand for one period. For Example 6-12(b) the order quantities will be 10, 15, 11, etc. This rule reduces the inventory level, and thus the inventory holding cost, but results in more orders and additional ordering cost. It is mostly used for expensive purchased items (in terms of annual dollar usage) and for items that have very lumpy demand.

2.2.2 HEURISTIC METHODS. A heuristic method is an approach that takes advantage of the structure of the problem. By using a set of "sensible" rules, it gets a solution that is "good"—i.e., close to optimal or sometimes even optimal. Heuristic methods are used when it is not possible or computationally feasible to solve for the optimum. We present three common heuristic approaches—Silver-Meal, least unit cost, and part period balancing, also known as least total cost. Their common denominator is that they all share the EOQ objective of minimizing the sum of set-up and inventory holding costs, but each employs a different method. Also, A and h are assumed constant for the entire planning horizon.

The Silver-Meal method (SM) (Silver and Meal, 1973). The principle of this heuristic is that it considers ordering for a number of periods ahead, say m. It tries to achieve the minimum average cost per period for the m-period span. The cost considered is the variable cost—i.e., ordering (set-up) cost plus inventory holding cost. The future demand for the next n periods is given and is

$$(D_1, D_2, \ldots, D_n)$$

Let $K(m)$ be average variable cost per period if the order covers m periods. We assume that the inventory holding cost occurs at the end of the period and the quantity needed for the period is used at the beginning of the period. If we order D_1 to meet the demand in period 1, we get

$$K(1) = A$$

If we order $D_1 + D_2$ in period 1 to meet the demand in periods 1 and 2, we get

$$K(2) = \tfrac{1}{2}(A + hD_2)$$

where h is the cost of holding one unit in inventory for one period. Because we hold D_2 an extra period, we multiply it by h, and to get the average cost for the two periods, we divide by 2. Similarly,

$$K(3) = \tfrac{1}{3}(A + hD_2 + 2hD_3)$$

and in general,

$$K(m) = \frac{1}{m}(A + hD_2 + 2hD_3 + \cdots + (m - 1)hD_m)$$

Compute $K(m)$, $m = 1, 2, \ldots, m$, and stop when

$$K(m + 1) > K(m)$$

i.e., the period in which the average cost per period starts increasing. We order in period 1 a quantity to meet the demand of the next m periods, i.e.,

$$Q_1 = D_1 + D_2 + \cdots + D_m$$

In general, Q_i is the quantity ordered in period i, and it covers m periods into the future. If no order is issued in period i, then Q_i is zero. The process repeats at period $(m + 1)$ and continues through the planning horizon.

Example 6-13. The Silver-Meal method. James, the manager of a local computer store, estimates the demand for 3.5" diskettes for the next five months to be 100, 100, 50, 50, and 210 boxes of 10 diskettes. Because the demand is lumpy, James applies the Silver-Meal method to order the correct quantity. To place an order for the diskettes costs James $50 regardless of the order size, and he estimates that holding a box for over a month will cost him $0.50. What can you suggest?

Solution. The basic data for this problem are

$A = \$50$

$h = \$0.50$ per box per month

The demand, D_i, for the next five months is

Month	1	2	3	4	5
Demand	100	100	50	50	210

We apply the Silver-Meal formula to compute $K(m)$:

$$K(m) = \frac{1}{m}(A + hD_2 + 2hD_3 + 3hD_4 + \cdots + (m - 1)hD_m)$$

1. $m = 1$

$$K(1) = 50$$

2. $m = 2$

$$K(2) = (1/2)(50 + (0.5)(100))$$
$$= 50 \le 50 = K(1), \quad \text{so continue}$$

3. $m = 3$

$$K(3) = (1/3)(50 + (0.5)(100) + (2)(0.5)(50))$$
$$= 50 \le 50 = K(2), \quad \text{so continue}$$

4. $m = 4$

$$K(4) = (1/4)(50 + (0.5)(100) + (2)(0.5)(50)$$
$$+ (3)(0.5)(50)$$
$$= 56.25 > K(3) = 50, \quad \text{STOP}$$

The first order quantity is

$$Q_1 = 100 + 100 + 50 = 250$$

We continue the procedure starting from the fourth month.

1. $m = 1$; starts from month 4.

$$K(1) = 50$$

2. $m = 2$

$$K(2) = (1/2)(50 + (0.5)(210))$$

$$= 72.50 > K(1), \quad \text{STOP}$$

The second order quantity $Q_4 = 50$, and we continue the procedure starting from the fifth month.

1. $m = 1$; starts from month 5.

$$K(1) = 50$$

Because there is no additional information, the procedure stops with $Q_5 = 210$.

According to the five months' demands, there will be three orders; they are at the beginning of the first, fourth, and fifth months. The order quantities are $Q_1 = 250, Q_4 = 50$, and $Q_5 = 210$. However, as each new forecast for a later period becomes available, quantities from month 5 onward should be recalculated.

Least unit cost (LUC). This procedure is similar to the Silver-Meal heuristic. The difference is that the decision is based on the average variable cost per unit rather than per period. Let

$K'(m)$ = average variable cost per unit if the order covers m periods

Following the same reasoning as in the Silver-Meal case,

$$K'(1) = \frac{A}{D_1}$$

$$K'(2) = \frac{A + hD_2}{D_1 + D_2}$$

$$K'(3) = \frac{A + hD_2 + 2hD_3}{D_1 + D_2 + D_3}$$

and in general

$$K'(m) = \frac{A + hD_2 + 2hD_3 + \cdots + (m-1)hD_m}{D_1 + D_2 + \cdots + D_m}$$

As before, the stopping rule is

$$K'(m + 1) > K(m)$$

and

$$Q_1 = D_1 + D_2 + \cdots + D_m$$

Again, the process repeats itself from period $(m + 1)$ on.

The limitation of both Silver-Meal and LUC approaches is that they consider one lot at a time, and the cost per period (or unit) can vary widely from period to period.

Example 6-14. Least unit cost. We repeat James's problem (Example 6-13) using the LUC method.

Solution. The basic data are as before.

1. $m = 1$; starts from month 1.

$$K'(1) = A/D_1 = 50/100 = 0.5$$

2. $m = 2$

$$K'(2) = (50 + (0.5)(100))/(100 + 100)$$
$$= 0.5 \leq K'(1) = 0.5, \quad \text{and we continue}$$

3. $m = 3$

$$K'(3) = \{50 + (0.5)(100) + (2)(0.5)(50)\}/(100 + 100 + 50)$$
$$= 0.6 > K'(2) = 0.5 \quad \text{STOP}$$

The first order is placed at the first month with

$$Q_1 = 100 + 100 = 200$$

Continue the procedure from the third month.

1. $m = 1$; starts from month 3.

$$K'(1) = (50)/(50) = 1$$

2. $m = 2$

$$K'(2) = (50 + (0.5)(50))/(50 + 50)$$
$$= 0.75 < K'(1) = 1, \quad \text{continue}$$

3. $m = 3$

$$K'(3) = (50 + (0.5)(50) + (2)(0.5)(210))/(50 + 50 + 210)$$
$$= 0.92 > K'(2) = 0.75 \quad \text{STOP}$$

The second order point is at the third month and

$$Q_3 = 50 + 50 + 210 = 310$$

Because no more information is available, we stop the procedure. There are two orders—one in the first month and one in the third month. The order quantities are 200 and 310, respectively.

Part period balancing (PPB). This method attempts to minimize the sum of the variable cost for all lots. Recall from the EOQ discussion that if demand is uniform, the ordering (set-up) cost is equal to the holding cost. Although this argument is correct for uniform demand, it is not true for lumpy demand in which the average inventory is not half the lot size. However, it may provide reasonable solutions for lumpy demand.

To get the inventory holding cost we introduce a part period, defined as one unit of the item carried in inventory for one period. Thus, 10 units carried in inventory for 1 period is equal to 10 part periods, which is equal to 5 units carried in inventory for 2 periods. Let

$$PP_m = \text{part period for } m \text{ periods.}$$

Thus
$$PP_1 = 0$$
$$PP_2 = D_2$$
$$PP_3 = D_2 + 2D_3$$
$$PP_m = D_2 + 2D_3 + \cdots + (m-1)D_m$$

The inventory holding cost is $h(PP_m)$, and we want to select the order horizon m that roughly covers the ordering cost A, i.e., choose m so that

$$A \cong h(PP_m)$$

or
$$PP_m \cong \frac{A}{h}$$

which is also the stopping rule. The ratio A/h is called "the economic part period factor." The order size is

$$Q_1 = D_1 + D_2 + \cdots + D_m$$

and the process repeats starting from period $m+1$. The PPB heuristic is also called least total cost (LTC). It is one of the most widely used heuristics in industry.

Example 6-15. Part period balancing. We repeat James's problem by applying the part period balancing method.

Solution. The part period factor $= A/h = 50/0.5 = 100 = $ PPF. We calculate the part period value by the formula

$$PP_m = D_2 + 2D_3 + 3D_4 + \cdots + (m-1)D_m$$

1. Starting from month 1:

$$PP_1 = 0$$
$$PP_2 = 100 \le 100 = \text{PPF}$$
$$PP_3 = 100 + (2)(50) = 200 > \text{PPF} \quad \text{STOP}$$

The first order point is in month 1, and the order quantity is

$$Q_1 = 100 + 100 = 200$$

which covers two months.

2. Starting from month 3:

$$PP_1 = 0$$
$$PP_2 = 50 < \text{PPF}$$
$$PP_3 = 50 + (2)(210) = 470 > \text{PPF} \quad \text{STOP}$$

The second order point is in month 3, and the order quantity is

$$Q_2 = 50 + 50 = 100$$

which again covers two months.

Because month 5 is the last month, we order month 5's demand at the beginning of that month. There are three orders in the five-month period, and they are in the first, the third, and the fifth month, with order quantities of 200, 100, and 210, respectively. Again, when data beyond month 5 become available, the remaining quantities should be recalculated.

2.2.3 WAGNER-WHITIN ALGORITHM (WW). This algorithm has the same objective as some of the heuristic approaches—minimizing the variable inventory cost, ordering (set-up), and holding cost over the planning horizon. The difference is that the Wagner-Whitin algorithm generates a minimum-cost solution yielding an optimum order quantity policy Q_i. The optimization procedure is based on dynamic programming. It evaluates all possible ways of ordering to cover demand in each period of the planning horizon. Its "elegance" is that it does not consider each of the policies possible; for an n-period horizon, the number of possible policies is 2^{n-1}. We have observed the fact that an order must satisfy all demand for some number of periods. That is, an optimal order quantity, say Q_i, satisfies

$$Q_i = \sum_{k=i}^{j} D_k \quad \text{for some } j \geq i$$

and
$$I_i Q_{i+1} = 0 \quad \text{for all } i = 0, 1, \ldots, n-1$$

Q_i is the number of units ordered in period i to cover demand through period j, with the next order placed at period $j + 1$. This notion, used in the heuristic methods, reduces the number of policies examined to the order of n^2, which means that many of the policies can be ignored by the algorithm.

Wagner-Whitin replaces EOQ for the case of lumpy demand. However, because it is somewhat cumbersome and difficult to understand, it is not widely applied in industry. Its major advantage is in serving as a standard to measure the effectiveness of the other dynamic lot sizing algorithms.

Using previously defined notation, we formally state the algorithm. Let $K_{t,l}$ be the cost to place an order to cover demand in periods $t, t + 1, \ldots, l$, assuming zero inventory at the beginning of period t and zero inventory at the end of period l. Mathematically, this cost is

$$K_{t,l} = A + h\left(\sum_{j=t+1}^{l} (j - t)D_j \right) \quad t = 1, 2, \ldots, n; \, l = t + 1, t + 2, \ldots, n$$

Now determine the minimum cost from the first period to period l assuming that there is to be no inventory remaining at the end of period l. The equation for this minimum can be found recursively. Let K_l^* denote this minimum, and it is given by

$$K_l^* = \min_{t = 1, 2, \ldots, l}\{K_{t-1}^* + K_{t,l}\}, \quad l = 1, 2, \ldots, N$$

K_0^* is defined as zero, and the least-cost solution value is given by K_N^*.

Consider James's problem (Example 6-13). For $l = 1$, we have

$$K_{1,1} = A + h\left(\sum_{j=1+1}^{1} (j - 1)D_j \right) = 50 + 0.5(0) = \$50$$

where a sum from a higher index to a smaller one (i.e., from 2 to 1) is defined as zero. The optimal cost if no inventory is held at the end of period 1 is

$$K_1^* = \min_{t=1}\{K_0^* + K_{1,1}\} = 0 + 50 = \$50$$

To compute $K_{1,2}$ and $K_{2,2}$ we have

$$K_{1,2} = A + h\left(\sum_{j=1+1}^{2}(j-1)D_j\right) = 50 + 0.5(100) = \$100$$

and

$$K_{2,2} = A + h\left(\sum_{j=2+1}^{2}(j-2)D_j\right) = 50 + 0 = \$50$$

To compute the minimum cost for the first two periods, we have

$$K_2^* = \min_{t=1,2}\{K_{t-1}^* + K_{t,2}\}$$

$$= \min\{K_0^* + K_{1,2}, K_1^* + K_{2,2}\}$$

$$= \min\{0 + 100, 50 + 50\}$$

$$= \$100$$

It is easy to do these calculations with a spreadsheet. The example calculations are completed in Table 6-8; problem data are repeated for clarity. Rather than calculate $K_{t,l}$, we calculate $K_{t-1} + K_{t,l}$ in the cells, and K_l^* is the minimum value in each column. The computations in a lower-indexed column must be completed before the next column is begun.

For the example, there are several alternative optimal solutions, all with total cost of $225. To find the order quantities, note that the row index represents the period in which the order that covers the demand in the period specified by the column index was placed. We start with the last period (5) and work backwards. Because the minimum cost ($225)

TABLE 6-8
Example problem solved by the Wagner-Whitin algorithm

Period, l	1	2	3	4	5
Forecasted demand, D_l	100	100	50	50	210
Fixed cost, A	50	50	50	50	50
Holding cost, h	0.5	0.5	0.5	0.5	0.5
t			$K_{t-1}^* + K_{t,l}$		
1	50	100	150	225	645
2		100	125	175	490
3			150	175	385
4				175	280
5					225
K_l^*	50	100	125	175	225

for period 5 occurs in row 5, we order in period 5 for period 5 only ($Q_5 = 210$). Because the demand for period 5 was satisfied by an order in period 5, we proceed to period 4. The minimum for column 4 ($175) is attained in rows 2, 3, and 4, so we have alternative optimal solutions; arbitrarily choose row 3. Thus we order in period 3 for periods 3 and 4 ($Q_3 = 100$). Because we placed an order in period 3, we next examine column 2, which also has alternative minima ($100) in rows 1 and 2. Arbitrarily choose row 1; order in period 1 for periods 1 and 2 ($Q_1 = 200$). The reader should verify that ($Q_1 = 100, Q_2 = 100, Q_3 = 100, Q_5 = 210$), ($Q_1 = 100, Q_2 = 150, Q_4 = 50, Q_5 = 210$), and ($Q_1 = 100, Q_2 = 200, Q_5 = 210$) are all optimal solutions.

Only the PPB heuristic got an optimal solution. The Silver-Meal heuristic was close, with a cost of $250, and the LUC heuristic was ineffective, yielding a total cost of $385, 71 percent higher than the optimal. Of course on a different data set, these results would likely be quite different.

It is possible now to compare the three heuristics and the optimal solution for James's problem, which is done in Table 6-9.

2.2.4   PETERSON-SILVER RULE. Dynamic lot sizing methods are used for lumpy demand. How do we know that demand is lumpy? By eyeballing it? There should be a better way. Peterson and Silver (1979) propose a useful measure of the variability of demand, called the variability coefficient. It is

$$V = \frac{\text{Variance of demand per period}}{\text{Square of average demand per period}}$$

They show that V can be evaluated by

$$V = \frac{n \sum\limits_{t=1}^{n} D_t^2}{\left(\sum\limits_{t=1}^{n} D_t \right)^2} - 1$$

where D_t is the discrete forecasted demand per period and n is the horizon length.

Peterson and Silver suggest the following "lumpiness test":

If $V < 0.25$, use the EOQ model with $\overline{D}$ as the demand estimate.

If $V \geq 0.25$, use a DLS method.

TABLE 6-9
Comparison of DLS methods

Method	Period					Cost
	1	**2**	**3**	**4**	**5**	
Silver-Meal	$Q_1 = 250$			$Q_4 = 50$	$Q_5 = 210$	$250
LUC	$Q_1 = 200$		$Q_3 = 310$			$385
PPB	$Q_1 = 200$		$Q_3 = 100$		$Q_5 = 100$	$225
Wagner-Whitin*	$Q_1 = 100$	$Q_2 = 200$			$Q_5 = 210$	$225

*One optimal solution

Applying this rule to the data of Example 6-13, we obtain

$$\sum_{t=1}^{5} D_t^2 = 69,100 \qquad \left(\sum_{t=1}^{5} D_t\right)^2 = 260,100$$

$$V = \frac{5 \times 69,100}{260,100} - 1 = 0.328 > 0.25$$

This result justifies the use of DLS methods on the example.

SECTION 2.2 PROBLEMS

6.40. Twelve-week demand forecasts are given in the following two tables:

Week	1	2	3	4	5	6	7	8	9	10	11	12
Demand	50	70	30	90	80	10	100	55	60	65	80	45

Week	1	2	3	4	5	6	7	8	9	10	11	12
Demand	120	80	—	40	—	—	75	85	—	60	—	90

(a) *Fixed period demand.* For both tables, evaluate the order quantity for 4, 8, and 12 weeks of demand.

(b) *Period order quantity.* For both tables, evaluate POQ for $Q = 100, 150, 250$, respectively.

(c) For both tables, evaluate the order quantity using the lot-for-lot rule.

(d) On the basis of your answers, make observations about the three methods.

6.41. The University Bookstore sells a variety of posters. One of them, the "Chief Huncho" poster, has the following 12-month demand forecast.

Month, i	1	2	3	4	5	6	7	8	9	10	11	12
Demand, D_i	55	70	105	120	115	95	100	75	120	75	60	45

It costs the store $20 to place an order, the cost of a poster is $2.00, and the annual inventory holding cost is 20 percent.

For each of the following methods develop the pattern of replenishments to cover the 12 months, and the associated total cost of each pattern.

(a) The Silver-Meal method

(b) Least unit cost

(c) Part period balancing

6.42. The University Bookstore also has the following 12-month forecast for a different poster, the "Garden of Eden Rose":

Month, i	1	2	3	4	5	6	7	8	9	10	11	12
Demand, D_i	580	440	288	202	150	102	68	50	38	24	15	12

It costs the store $20 to place an order, the cost of a poster is $2.00, and the annual inventory holding cost is 20 percent.

For each of the following methods develop the pattern of replenishments to cover the 12 months and the associated costs:

(a) The Silver-Meal method

(b) Least unit cost

(c) Part period balancing

6.43. Use the results of Problems 6.41 and 6.42 to analyze how the three methods behave in different demand patterns.

6.44. The demand forecast for calipers produced at Lagrange Foundry is given for the next six weeks. The molding machine that makes calipers is used for other products and must be set up each time calipers are made. It takes two mechanics one hour to set up the machine. Including fringe benefits, a mechanic costs the company $25 an hour. Calipers are worth $3.00 each. Handling costs for one caliper are computed to be about $0.40 per week. Paperwork costs add about $0.07 per unit-week, and lost opportunity cost, insurance, etc. is figured at a rate of 50 percent per year of the value of the item.

Week, l	1	2	3	4	5	6
Demand, D_l	100	100	200	100	120	80

(a) What lot sizes do you recommend?

(b) Suppose we could invest $3000 and reduce the set-up cost by 50 percent. If the company uses a payback period of one year, should it invest in set-up reduction? List any assumptions you made.

6.45. Rocky Mountain Wire has firm orders for rolls of 12 gauge copper wire for the next six planning periods. Each time this wire is made, a set-up is performed, which costs $150. A set-up reduction team has worked on decreasing the set-up time and will implement their results in three periods; set-up cost is to be reduced to $100. Currently, a roll costs $5.00 to make, but an increase in the price of copper will increase costs by 20 percent in period 3. A new labor contract will go into effect in period 5, adding another $1 per roll to the cost. The cost to hold a roll in inventory is $1 in the first two periods and $2 thereafter. Give an optimal lot sizing policy for Rocky Mountain.

Period, l	1	2	3	4	5	6
Demand, D_l	60	100	10	200	120	15

6.46. Tydown makes anchoring systems for storage buildings, mobile homes, etc. They have a contract with the local power company to supply anchors for utility poles. The power company has ordered anchors for the next six months. The quantity, set-up cost, variable cost, and holding costs are:

Month, l	1	2	3	4	5	6
Demand, D_l	1500	100	700	1200	200	1700
Fixed cost, A_l	150	150	150	200	200	200
Variable cost, c_l	10.0	10.5	10.0	11.0	11.0	11.0
Holding cost, h_l	1.0	1.0	1.0	1.5	1.5	1.5

How many anchors should Tydown make in each of the next six months to minimize their total cost?

6.47. Use the Peterson-Silver rule to verify whether the demand patterns in Problems 6.40–6.42 are lumpy.

2.3 Summary

In Table 6-10 we give a summary of the major quantity decision models presented in this section.

3 TIMING DECISIONS

This section discusses the second major decision in inventory systems—when to order. This decision impacts not only the inventory level and hence the inventory cost, but also the level of service provided to customers. Timing decisions play a major role in MDS philosophies; they impact the cost and on-time all-the-time elements, two major ingredients of customer satisfaction.

As with quantity decisions, we include "classic" models to help understand the behavior of inventory systems as related to timing decisions. We chose to include the general concept of inventory service strategies to further enhance the discussion of the different models.

We discuss models under three major headings:

- One-time decisions
- Continuous review systems, which are synonymous with continuous-time decisions
- Periodic review systems, which are synonymous with intermittent-time decisions

All models are single-item models but can be extended to multiple items, and many of them deal with stochastic demand. Figure 6-13 shows the detailed structure of this section.

3.1 One-Time Decisions

The one-time decision situation is common to both retail and manufacturing environments. Often the problem relates to seasonal goods, which are in demand during a short period only. The product value declines at the end of the season and may even be negative. The lead time may be longer than the selling season, so if demand is higher than the original order, we cannot rush an order for additional products. Thus, there is only one opportunity to order. A typical example is a newspaper stand. If the owner does not buy enough newspapers to meet demand, profit is lost. If too many are ordered, the excess is unsold, and a penalty to dispose of them is incurred. A similar situation is true for a Christmas tree or ornaments retailer. Hence this model is often called the "newsboy model" or "Christmas tree model." In manufacturing, the equivalent problem will be how much of the finished goods inventory should be held for this product?

We must decide the number of items to order before the sales period, which can be a day, a week, or any other time period. If demand is known (the deterministic case), the problem is trivial; order exactly the number of units that will be demanded. The practical situation, and therefore the one of interest, is when *exact* demand is unknown but can be described as a random variable. This is the *stochastic* case. To set the stage, consider Example 6-16.

TABLE 6-10
Quantity decisions—summary

Method	Demand	Solution	Objective	Quantity	Application	Remarks
Economic order quantity	Uniform	Optimal	Min total cost	$\sqrt{\dfrac{2AD}{h}}$	Raw material, finished goods, retail	First inventory model
Economic production quantity	Uniform	Optimal	Min total cost	$\sqrt{\dfrac{2AD}{h\left(1-\dfrac{D}{\psi}\right)}}$	Production	Finite production rate
Quantity discounts	Uniform	Optimal	Min total cost	$\sqrt{\dfrac{2AD}{h}}$	Raw material, finished goods, retail	Price discounts
Resource constrained	Uniform	Optimal	Min total cost	$\sqrt{\dfrac{2AD}{h+2c\lambda}}$	Raw material, finished goods, retail	Multiple items
Fixed period demand	Lumpy	Arbitrary	Convenience ordering	Arbitrary period demand	Raw material, in process, finished goods, retail	
Period order quantity	Lumpy	Arbitrary	Convenience ordering	Calculated period demand	Raw material, in process, finished goods, retail	
Lot for lot	Lumpy	Arbitrary	Holding cost	D_1	Raw material, in process, finished goods, retail	Wide application
Silver-Meal	Lumpy	Heuristic	Cost/period	$\sum D_t$	Raw material, in process, finished goods, retail	
Least unit cost	Lumpy	Heuristic	Cost/unit	$\sum D_t$	Raw material, in process, finished goods, retail	
Part period balancing	Lumpy	Heuristic	Balance cost	$\sum D_t$	Raw material, in process, finished goods, retail	Wide application
Wagner-Whitin	Lumpy	Optimal	Min total cost	$\sum D_t$	Raw material, in process, finished goods, retail	Comparison

All single item models can be repeated for an independent n-item population.

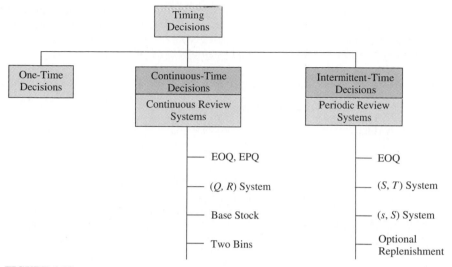

FIGURE 6-13
Structure of timing decisions

Example 6-16. One-time decisions. Mrs. Kandell has been in the Christmas tree business for years. She keeps track of sales volume each year and has made a table (Table 6-11) of the demand for the Christmas trees and its probability. It is obvious that demand was never below 22 trees or above 36 trees.

Solution. The demand is an uncontrollable variable, and the decision variable is Q—the one-time decision of the amount to be ordered. The solution approach is economic marginal analysis; overage and shortage costs are balanced. The optimal order quantity, Q^*, is found by optimizing expected cost, because we have a stochastic environment.

Let D = demand during the period—a random variable with probability density function $f(D)$

$F(D)$ = cumulative probability function of D, i.e., the probability that demand is less than or equal to D

π = shortage cost per unit short at the end of the period

c_0 = overage cost per unit of overage, at the end of the period

TABLE 6-11
Christmas tree demand

Demand, D	Probability, $f(D)$
22	0.05
24	0.10
26	0.15
28	0.20
30	0.20
32	0.15
34	0.10
36	0.05

The shortage cost may be the lost profit and loss of goodwill. The overage cost is the unit cost plus any additional cost to dispose of the overage, minus any revenue (salvage value) that might be obtained. We either ignore the purchase cost because it does not impact the optimal solution or implicitly consider it in the overage and shortage costs. We assume that there is no ordering cost.

Because Q is the decision variable, the expected overage cost is

$$F(Q)c_0$$

and the expected shortage cost is

$$[1 - F(Q)]\pi$$

The optimum value of Q in this case will be where these two costs are equal

$$F(Q^*)c_0 = [1 - F(Q^*)]\pi$$

yielding

$$F(Q^*) = \frac{\pi}{\pi + c_0}$$

The cost ratio in the above equation is called the **critical ratio** and is a number between 0 and 1. The critical ratio is the probability of satisfying the demand during the period if Q^* is purchased for the period, which is not the same as the proportion of satisfied demand.

To calculate Q^* we must use the cumulative probability distribution, which is typical of stochastic inventory models. We continue Example 6-16 to illustrate.

Example 6-16 (continued). One-time decisions. Mrs. Kandell estimates that if she buys more trees than she can sell, it costs about $40 for the tree and its disposal. If demand is higher than the number of trees she orders, she loses a profit of $40 per tree.

Solution. We determine Q^* by first calculating the cumulative probability of demand, given in Table 6-12. The critical value is

$$\frac{\pi}{c_0 + \pi} = \frac{40}{40 + 40} = 0.50$$

We must find the value of Q^* so that $F(Q^*) = 0.50$. From the table, we see that $Q^* = 28$, which is how many trees Mrs. Kandell should order.

TABLE 6-12
Cumulative probability

Demand, D	Probability, $F(D)$
22	0.05
24	0.15
26	0.30
28	0.50
30	0.70
32	0.85
34	0.95
36	1.00

Mathematical derivation. The critical ratio can also be derived mathematically. Let $f(D)$ be a continuous probability distribution function of demand. The amount sold during the period is

$$\min\{Q, D\}$$

and therefore the overage position is

$$Q - D \quad \text{if } D < Q$$

and the shortage position is

$$D - Q \quad \text{if } D > Q$$

We can rewrite these conditions as follows:

$$\text{Overage:} \quad \max\{Q - D, 0\} = \begin{cases} Q - D & \text{if } Q > D \\ 0 & \text{if } Q \leq D \end{cases}$$

$$\text{Shortage:} \quad \max\{D - Q, 0\} = \begin{cases} 0 & \text{if } Q \geq D \\ D - Q & \text{if } Q < D \end{cases}$$

This gives the following total cost function:

$$K(Q) = c_0 \max\{Q - D, 0\} + \pi \max\{D - Q, 0\}$$

The expected cost is

$$E\{K(Q)\} = c_0 \int_0^Q (Q - D) f(D) \, dD + \pi \int_Q^\infty (D - Q) f(D) \, dD$$

To get Q^*, we set

$$\frac{dE\{K(Q)\}}{dQ} = 0$$

This yields (using the Leibnitz rule for taking the derivative of the integrals),

$$c_0 \int_0^Q f(D) \, dD - \pi \int_Q^\infty f(D) \, dD = 0$$

or

$$c_0 F(Q) - \pi\{1 - F(Q)\} = 0$$

Rearranging terms gives

$$F(Q^*) = \frac{\pi}{c_0 + \pi}$$

This is the same result as obtained before. Taking the second derivative gives

$$\frac{d^2 E(K(Q))}{dQ^2} = (c_0 + \pi) f(Q)$$

If $c_0 + \pi \geq 0$, then the second derivative is always nonnegative, and $E\{K(Q)\}$ is convex with a minimum at Q^*.

The basic one-time decision model can be implemented in different environments. In the following example we consider the case in which demand is a continuous random variable.

Example 6-17. One-time decision: continuous version. Senior class students plan to sell T-shirts to raise money for the regional conference. Demand for the T-shirts is assumed to be equally likely for any number between 48 and 72. Each T-shirt costs $3.50 and will be sold for $5.00. If not enough shirts are purchased, the only cost will be the lost profit. Because these shirts will have the conference logo, it is felt that shirts not sold before the conference can only be sold for $2.50. Due to high set-up cost, only one order can be made.

Solution. We first set the parameters for this problem. We note that $f(D)$ is uniformly distributed, so

$$f(D) = \frac{1}{b - a} = \frac{1}{24}$$

$\pi = 5 - 3.50 = \$1.50$, which is equal to the lost profit.

$c_0 = 3.50 - 2.50 = \$1.00$, the difference between the unit cost and unit revenue.

This gives a critical ratio of

$$\frac{\pi}{c_0 + \pi} = \frac{1.5}{1 + 1.5} = 0.60$$

Therefore, the number of T-shirts to be ordered is

$$F(Q^*) = \int_{48}^{Q^*} \frac{1}{24} \, dx = 0.60$$

Integrating, we have

$$\frac{Q^* - 48}{24} = 0.60$$

and solving for Q^* gives

$$Q^* = 62.4 \approx 62$$

The number of unsold shirts the students expect to have after the conference is

$$\int_{48}^{Q^*} (Q^* - D) f(D) \, dD = \frac{1}{24} \int_{48}^{62} (62 - D) \, dD$$

$$= \frac{62}{24} D \bigg|_{48}^{62} - \frac{D^2}{24 \times 2} \bigg|_{48}^{62}$$

$$= 4.08 \approx 4$$

Similarly, the expected number of shirts short is

$$\int_{Q^*}^{72} (D - Q^*) f(D) \, dD = \frac{1}{24} \int_{62}^{72} (D - 62) \, dD$$

$$= \frac{D^2}{24 \times 2} \bigg|_{62}^{72} - \frac{72}{24} D \bigg|_{62}^{72}$$

$$= 2.08 \approx 2$$

Thus, the total expected cost is

$$E\{K(Q^*)\} = E\{K(62)\} = 1 \times 4 + 1.5 \times 2 = \$7.00$$

and the expected profit is

$$E\{\text{Profit}\} = 62 \times 1.5 - 7 = \$86.00$$

The case of starting inventory. The previous discussion assumed no on-hand inventory at the beginning of the period. If there are I units at the beginning of the period (say, Christmas ornaments left over from last year), then reduce the quantity order by that amount, i.e., order

$$\max\{(Q^* - I), 0\}$$

In this case, Q^* is the target inventory at the beginning of the period.

SECTION 3.1 PROBLEMS

6.48. The Lakeshore Restaurant plans to order pies for the 4th of July. It will cost \$3.50 to buy a pie, and they will sell for \$10.00. Any unsold pie can be sold to a local charity for \$2.00. The following table, using data from the last few holidays, gives potential demand and probabilities for them.

Demand, D	250	300	350	400	450	500
Probability, $f(D)$	0.25	0.20	0.20	0.15	0.10	0.10

(a) What value, if any, would you use for the cost of unsatisfied demand?

(b) If the restaurant buys 350 pies, what is its expected profit?

(c) How many pies would you recommend they buy?

(d) Show how an ordering cost can be handled in the newsboy problem.

6.49. Supermarket sells 2% milk, which is delivered daily. The daily demand is uniformly distributed between 100 and 200 gallons. The milk costs the store \$1.00 and sells for \$2.10. At the end of the day, unsold milk is sold to a chemical company for \$0.25 per gallon. If a shortage occurs, customers will buy skim milk instead. Profit on skim milk is \$0.50 per gallon. How much milk should be purchased?

6.50. A store in a remote village in Nepal serves as the last stocking point for Himalaya climbing missions. The climbing season is short, and the store builds inventory before the season starts. Because of its remoteness, no replenishment is possible during the season.

One of the items stocked is cracker boxes. Demand is estimated to be uniform between 200 and 400, i.e.,

$$f(D) = \frac{1}{200} \quad 200 \le D \le 400$$

$$f(D) = 0 \quad \text{otherwise}$$

The store purchases the crackers for \$2.00 a box and sells them for \$8.00 per box. Unsold boxes are given away to charity at the end of the season. The store owner estimates that a penalty of \$1.00 is accrued for every unsold box because of handling charges.

(a) Find the number of boxes the store should order to maximize profit.

(b) Find the expected number of boxes given away if optimal quantity is purchased.

(c) Find the expected profit for optimal quantity and the expected profit if a quantity equal to the expected demand were to be ordered. Explain the difference.

6.51. The Litengine Company manufactures piston engines for ultra-light aircraft. The company considers making a last production run of an old-model engine that is going to be eliminated within a year.

   The unit production cost is $1000, and the engine sells for $1800. Engines not sold will be moved to a faraway junkyard, at a transportation and handling cost of $180 per unit. The junkyard pays Litengine $110 for each engine. Litengine estimates a goodwill loss of $500 for any order short.

   The demand pattern for the engine is exponential, with pdf of

$$f(d) = \frac{1}{75}e^{-D/75} \quad D \geq 0$$

(a) Find the optimum production batch to maximize expected profit.
(b) Find the expected number of unsold engines.
(c) Find the expected profit for optimal quantity and the expected profit if a quantity equal to the expected demand were to be ordered.

6.52. Refer to Problem 6.51. Suppose there are 20 engines in finished goods inventory, and set-up cost for a production run is $2400. Reevaluate (a) and (b).

6.53. The Parker Flower Shop promises its customers delivery within four hours on all flower orders. All flowers are purchased on the prior day and delivered to Parker by 8:00 the next morning. Parker's daily demand for roses is as follows:

Dozens of roses	Probability
7	0.1
8	0.2
9	0.4
10	0.3

   Parker purchases roses for $5.00 per dozen and sells them for $15.00. All unsold roses are donated to a local hospital. Store policy is to purchase roses from a competitor for $15.00 a dozen if a customer orders roses and Parker does not have them. This costs $2.00 per dozen. What is Parker's expected stockout cost?

6.54. FunSki is a sporting goods shop on Leech Lake in Minnesota. Their major sales have been snowmobiles, ice skates, and cross-country skiing equipment. Recently, a decision to sell Jet Skis for use in the short summer was made. Jet Skis are purchased for $2000, including shipping, and sold for $2500. Due to the remoteness of the lake, only one shipment will be made. A market survey indicates that sales between 500 and 600 units are equally likely. If FunSki cannot satisfy a customer demand, a loss of goodwill of $250 will be incurred. At the end of June, it is unlikely that any more Jet Skis will be sold until next season, so a dealer in Fort Lauderdale has agreed to buy all unsold units for $1800 each. It costs $50 to ship each Jet Ski from Leech Lake to Fort Lauderdale.

(a) What is the optimal quantity to buy?
(b) What is the expected number of shortages?
(c) What is the total cost of this plan?

6.55. The Evergreen Company owns acreage of shrub trees to be harvested and sold each spring. The company estimates the costs of cutting and trimming the trees to be $2.50 per tree. The average cost of shipping the trees to the retailer is about $0.50 per tree, and the company receives about

$5.00 per tree ordered by the retailer. However, if the trees are cut and not sold to the retailer, they are a total loss. Shipping costs are not incurred if trees are not sold. The historical demand distribution is normal with mean 24,000 and standard deviation 1500.

(a) How many trees should be cut to maximize profit?

(b) What is the expected number of "lost" trees?

3.2   Continuous Review Systems

Continuous review systems were introduced in Section 1.5. To examine this system, we define two new inventory state variables:

X_t = inventory position at time t

O_t = on-order position at time t, sometimes called the "**pipeline**" inventory

Recall that I_t is the on-hand inventory at time t, and B_t is the shortage (backorder) level at time t. Then

$$X_t = I_t + O_t - B_t$$

Either I_t or B_t or both will be zero at any time. Basically, the difference between X_t and I_t is that X_t considers pipeline inventory. Let

R = reorder point, the level of X_t, when an order is placed

The timing decision, when to order, is

if $X_t \leq R$, then place an order for Q units

R determines the timing of the quantity decision. These systems are called (Q, R) systems; two decisions define the policy. The quantity decision was discussed in the previous section, and the reorder point is the subject of this section. Two things should be noted:

- The timing decision considers the total **inventory position,** and not only the on-hand inventory (*a very common error in practice*).
- The quantity ordered, Q, can be determined by any of the lot sizing methods.

We start by discussing continuous review systems in a deterministic environment and then move to the stochastic case.

3.2.1   EOQ, EPQ REVISITED. In Section 6.2.1 we derived the economic order quantity and the economic production quantity with zero order lead time. In this section we allow order lead time to be nonzero but assume it is a known constant, say τ. Order lead time—expressed in the same units as other data—is the elapsed time between placing an order and receiving it. We still assume that all units ordered arrive simultaneously τ units after the order is placed. Demand during lead time is known with certainty. As before, the annual demand is uniform and is denoted by D.

 We first examine the EOQ case. If we want the quantity Q to arrive when all inventory has been depleted, we set

$$R = D\tau$$

If no backlog is allowed and no other orders are in the pipeline, when placing an order, then

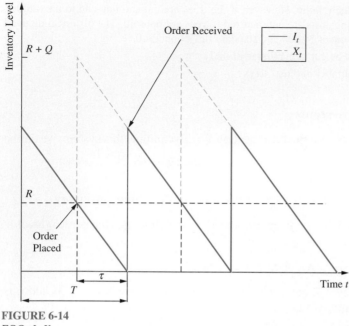

FIGURE 6-14
EOQ: I_t, X_t

$$X_t = I_t$$

and the timing decision is to place an order whenever

$$I_t \leq D\tau$$

Figure 6-14 depicts the behavior of I_t and X_t over time.

In this figure the tacit assumption is that $\tau < T$ (cycle time), i.e., there is at most one order outstanding. If $\tau > T$, the situation is somewhat more complex, as shown in Example 6-18.

Example 6-18. EOQ with lead time. Larry orders a certain fertilizer for his crop from a local company. The annual uniform usage of this fertilizer is about 3000 pounds, and each pound costs Larry $3.00. Larry spends about $12.50 to process each order. He usually has to wait one and a half months to receive the order. Larry estimates his inventory holding cost to be 40 percent annually. We show the inventory behavior for this case.

Solution

$$A = \$12.50$$

$$D = 3000 \text{ lb per year}$$

$$i = 40\% \text{ annually}$$

$$c = \$3.00 \rightarrow h = \$1.20 \text{ per pound per year}$$

$$\tau = 1.5 \text{ months} = 1.5/12 \text{ year} = 1/8 \text{ year}$$

$$\text{EOQ} = \sqrt{\frac{2AD}{h}} = \sqrt{\frac{(2)(12.5)(3000)}{1.2}} = 250$$

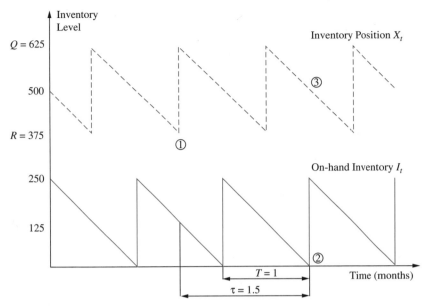

FIGURE 6-15
Inventory geometry

The cycle time T is equal to $250/3000 = 1/12$ year $= 1$ month. The reorder point is

$$R = (1.5/12)(3000) = 375 \text{ lb}$$

Note that the order lead time, 1.5 months, is greater than the cycle time. This is illustrated in Figure 6-15.

At point 1, $X_t = R$, and an order for $Q = 250$ units is issued, making $X_t = R + 250 = 625$. Note that I_t is not affected, as no change was made in the on-hand inventory. The order placed at point 1 arrives at point 2 after $\tau = 1.5$ months. Just as the on-hand inventory reaches 0, it is replenished to 250. At this point X_t does not change, because $I_t + O_t$ remain the same. Also, just before point 3 there are two outstanding orders in O_t, but after point 3 there is only one outstanding order. (Why?)

For the EPQ, the argument is similar. We set

$$R = D\tau$$

where τ is the lead time required to prepare for a new production run. When the inventory position is less than or equal to R, a new production order is initiated. However, due to the finite replenishment rate, X_t behaves differently, as shown in Figure 6-16.

For either EOQ or EPQ with a maximum backorder size of b, the timing decision is the same. The reorder point becomes

$$R = D\tau - b$$

Both cases assume that everything is known with certainty. In reality, both demand and lead time may vary. If an order arrives later than expected or demand during lead time is larger than expected, we may have shortages. To hedge against this, we can maintain a safety stock.

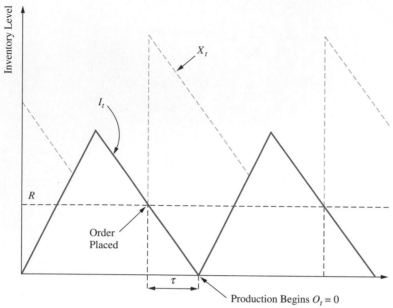

FIGURE 6-16
EPQ: I_t, X_t

3.2.2 SAFETY STOCK AND SERVICE LEVELS.

We have discussed (Section 1.1) the role of safety stock as hedging against uncertainties in demand and delivery time. We further explore this issue here.

Earlier we defined inventory to be a "buffer" between two processes—supply and demand. As such, inventory is a service function. The simplest notion of service is that whenever the customer needs an item from inventory, it is always there. In this case service is perfect, and we achieve our objective of customer satisfaction. Safety stock is additional inventory carried to ensure that the service objective is met. However, more inventory accrues more holding cost but decreases the chance that a customer faces a shortage. It boils down to a simple *trade-off*—how much service we can provide versus the cost. Later we develop tools that assist management in making this trade-off decision.

The "service test" for inventory is not when inventory is at its peak, but near the expected arrival of the lot ordered. Recall that there is uncertainty both in demand and in the length of the delivery time. Thus we will consider expected values. Let

$\overline{D}_\tau$ = the expected value of lead-time demand

We examine the infinite replenishment rate (EOQ) case. In the deterministic model we set the reorder point R equal to the lead-time demand D_τ. Similarly, for the stochastic model set $R = \overline{D}_\tau$. Figure 6-17 shows possible cases.

All three cases have the same reorder point. Because of the stochastic nature of the environment, the *placement* of the order occurs at the same inventory level but its arrival time varies. The order arrives when there is still on-hand inventory in case (a). In case (b) the order arrives just as the inventory is depleted. Finally, in case (c) we have shortages, and

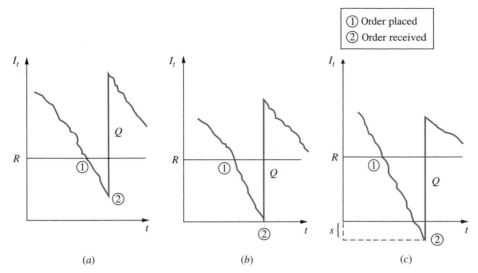

FIGURE 6-17
Inventory configurations

for a time the inventory does not fulfill its mission; carrying more inventory will prevent the shortages in case (c). To have more on-hand inventory, we set the reorder point to

$$R = \overline{D}_\tau + s$$

where s is the safety stock. The difference between the deterministic EOQ model and the stochastic model is in computing the reorder point, which includes safety stock.

D_τ is an uncontrollable variable, so basically a decision on R, the timing decision, is deciding the safety stock level s. The value of s determines the trade-off between service and investment. There are two approaches to finding the value of s: an optimization approach using a shortage cost π and a management approach, in which a service level policy is set. Before we pursue these issues, we need to further explore the method to evaluate $\overline{D}_\tau$.

Lead-time demand. Recall that both demand during lead time and the lead time itself are nondeterministic. To simplify derivations, we initially assume that lead time is deterministic. This gives a good approximation to the expected value of the stochastic case. Demand is a random variable, usually given over a certain period of time—a week, month, or year. Usually the value of the demand is obtained by a forecasting method (Chapter 4). We assume that the demand is a continuous random variable with probability density function $f(D)$ and cumulative distribution function $F(D)$. Let

$\overline{D} =$ expected value (or mean) of the demand distribution over a period of time

$\sigma =$ standard deviation of the demand distribution

$\tau =$ lead time, as in the deterministic case

The period over which demand is given may be different than the lead time. For example, demand may be given for one week, whereas lead time is four weeks. Therefore, we adjust the forecasted demand to the length of the lead time. We assume that demands for each period are independent random variables. Then, the lead-time distribution of demand has the following parameters:

$$\text{Expected value (mean)} = \overline{D}_\tau$$

$$\sigma_\tau^2 = \sigma^2 \tau$$

where σ_τ^2 is the lead-time demand variance, σ^2 is the variance of D, and τ is given in the same time units as D (day, week, etc.). We obtain

$$\sigma_\tau = \sigma \sqrt{\tau} \qquad \text{Standard deviation of lead-time demand}$$

and

$$\overline{D}_\tau = \overline{D}\tau$$

Example 6-19. Lead-time demand. The annual demand for sugar at a local soft drink manufacturer is normally distributed with $\overline{D} = 800$ tons and $\sigma = 25$ tons. The delivery time for sugar is 5 working days. We assume that there are 250 working days in a year.

Solution. The lead-time demand is also normally distributed with

$$\overline{D}_\tau = \overline{D}\tau = (800)\left(\frac{5}{250}\right) = 16$$

$$\sigma_\tau^2 = \sigma^2 \tau = (25)^2 \left(\frac{5}{250}\right) = 12.5$$

In reality, not only demand may vary, but lead time may, as well. This can be a case in which the supply source is not reliable—rail or air strike, weather conditions, etc. We therefore have to adjust our equations to consider lead-time variability. The general case is very complex, therefore we make two simplifying assumptions: successive lead times are independent random variables (a similar assumption to that of varying demand), and there are no order crossings; orders are received in the sequence they were issued. This phenomenon can happen if lead times vary. For a single supplier, order crossing is very unlikely.

Having made these two simultaneous assumptions, it is easy to incorporate lead-time variability into the analysis. Suppose lead time is randomly distributed with mean μ_L and variance σ_L^2. We know also that lead-time demand is a random variable with mean of $\overline{D}_\tau = \overline{D}\tau$ and variance $\sigma_\tau^2 = \sigma^2 \tau$. Hadley and Whitin (1963, p. 153) show that in this case, considering lead-time variability, lead-time demand mean and variance assume the following values:

$$\overline{D}_\tau = \overline{D}\mu_L$$

$$\sigma_\tau^2 = \mu_L \sigma^2 + \overline{D}^2 \sigma_L^2$$

We would like to comment that when in practice we fit a distribution to D_τ and do not fit to D and τ separately and convolute them, then it does not matter if τ is a random variable or not.

Example 6-20. We consider again the soft drink manufacturer of Example 6-19. Suppose that delivery time is no longer constant but varies with mean of 5 and standard deviation of 1.

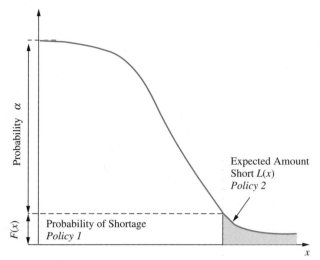

Probability α

$F(x)$

Expected Amount
Short $L(x)$
Policy 2

Probability of Shortage
Policy 1

x

FIGURE 6-18
Cumulative probability of demand

Solution. We notice that

$$\overline{D} = 800 \text{ tons annually} \qquad \sigma = 25 \qquad \mu_L = \frac{5}{250} \qquad \sigma_L = \frac{1}{250}$$

Lead-time demand has the following mean and variance.

$$\overline{D}_\tau = \overline{D}\mu_L = 800\left(\frac{5}{250}\right) = 16$$

$$\sigma_\tau^2 = \left(\frac{5}{250}\right)(25)^2 + (800)^2\left(\frac{1}{250}\right)^2 = 22.74$$

Note that due to lead-time variability, the variance of lead-time demand increased substantially.

Service level policies. There are two major service level policies, both related to shortage probabilities. Figure 6-18 will help us define these policies. It shows $F(x)$ as the *cumulative* distribution of a random variable x. The probability density function of x is $f(x)$. For any given value of x, the height of the curve $F(x)$ is the probability that the next observation will exceed x, i.e., fall into the interval $[x, \infty]$.

The two policies shown in the graph are as follows:

Policy 1: This policy specifies the probability of not running out of stock during a lead time, i.e., in any one inventory cycle. It is often called the "cycle service level." In Figure 6-18 this probability is equal to $1 - F(x)$, which we denote by α. Another way to view this policy is through the probability density function of lead-time demand D_τ. This is shown in Figure 6-19, assuming this distribution is normal with a mean of $\overline{D}_\tau$. This figure illustrates the influence of s on R and the shortage probability. α can also be viewed as the proportion of cycles in which no shortage occurs. This policy is most useful where the impact of a shortage does not depend on the number of units short.

Example 6-21. Policy 1. Again, consider the soft drink manufacturer of Example 6-19. Suppose they keep 5 extra tons in inventory as a safety stock. What is the service level obtained?

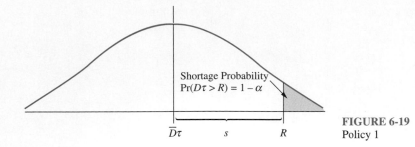

FIGURE 6-19
Policy 1

Solution. Recall that

$$R = \overline{D}_\tau + s = \overline{D}\tau + s = 16 + 5 = 21$$

and

$$F(R) = \alpha$$

To find $F(R)$ we evaluate the normal standard deviate z:

$$z = \frac{x - \mu}{\sigma} = \frac{R - \overline{D}\tau}{\sigma_\tau} = \frac{21 - 16}{3.54} = 1.41$$

From Table A-1,

$$F(z \le 1.41) \approx 0.92$$

or the service level is close to 92 percent. In other words, the shortage probability for each order cycle is about 8 percent, or 8 percent of the cycles per year will have one or more shortages.

Policy 2: In this policy we state the preferred proportion of annual demand (in units, customer orders, or dollars) that is instantaneously filled from stock. It is often known as the "fill rate," and we denote it by β. This measure determines the expected amount short during each lead time. The expected amount short is given by the shaded area of Figure 6-18, with a value of $(1 - \beta)\overline{D}$. This area is evaluated by taking partial expectations, denoted by $L(x)$. We used the same idea as in the newsboy problem. Formally, for any value z of x,

$$L(z) = \int_z^\infty (x - z)\phi(x)\,dx$$

where $\phi(x)$ is the density function for x. $L(z)$ can be tabulated for different distributions. Table A-2 in the appendix gives partial expectation values for the standard normal distribution, $\{N(0, 1)\}$, as a function of the normal standardized variate z. Because $L(z)$ is evaluated for $\sigma = 1$, to get the expected amount short during a lead time, we have to multiply it by σ_τ, i.e.,

$$\sigma_\tau L(z)$$

Recall that σ_τ is the standard deviation of lead-time demand. Because policy 2 is related to annual demand, the expected annual number of units short is given by

$$\sigma_\tau L(z)\left(\frac{\overline{D}}{Q}\right)$$

where Q is the order quantity, $\overline{D}/Q$ is the expected number of inventory cycles per year, and

$\overline{D}$ is annual average demand. Using the fill rate β, the desired number of units short per year is

$$(1 - \beta)\overline{D}$$

which we set equal to the previous value. Therefore, we get

$$(1 - \beta)\overline{D} = \sigma_\tau L(z)\left(\frac{\overline{D}}{Q}\right)$$

or

$$L(z) = \frac{(1 - \beta)Q}{\sigma_\tau}$$

Example 6-22. Policy 2. We return to our soft drink problem and evaluate the fill rate β for a safety stock of 5 tons. We assume the order quantity to be 20 tons.

Solution. The basic data on hand are

$$D \sim N(800, 625)$$
$$\{N(\mu, \sigma^2)\}\tau = 5/250 \text{ years}$$
$$D\tau \sim N(16, 12.5)$$
$$Q = 20 \text{ tons}$$
$$s = 5 \text{ tons}$$

To find β we evaluate $L(z)$.

$$\sigma_\tau = \sqrt{12.5} = 3.54$$

$$z = \frac{R - \overline{D}\tau}{\sigma_\tau} = \frac{21 - \left(800\dfrac{5}{250}\right)}{3.54} = 1.41$$

From Table A-2 in the appendix,

$$L(1.41) = 0.0359$$

so

$$L(z) = 0.0359 = \frac{(1 - \beta)Q}{\sigma_\tau}$$

or

$$\frac{(1 - \beta)20}{3.54} = 0.0359$$

Rearranging terms gives

$$\beta = 1 - \frac{(0.0359)3.54}{20} = 99.4\%$$

This is quite a different value than we got for policy 1. This result highlights the fact that the two policies measure different types of service.

The expected number of units short per year is

$$\sigma_\tau L(z)\frac{\overline{D}}{Q} = 3.54(0.0359)\frac{800}{20} = 5 \text{ tons}$$

Even with a safety stock of 5 tons the expected shortage is 5 tons of sugar per year.

We now compare the level of the safety stock s for each policy based on $\alpha = \beta = 0.95$.

Policy 1: From Table A-1 in the appendix,

$$F(z) = 0.95 \Rightarrow z = 1.65$$

and

$$z = \frac{R - \overline{D}\tau}{\sigma_\tau} = \frac{\overline{D}\tau + s - \overline{D}\tau}{\sigma_\tau} = \frac{s}{\sigma_\tau}$$

Then

$$s = z\sigma_\tau = (1.65)(3.54) = 5.84 \approx 6$$

Policy 2: Recall

$$L(z) = \frac{(1 - \beta)Q}{\sigma_\tau} = \frac{0.05 \times 20}{3.54} = 0.282$$

and from the $L(z)$ table,

$$L(0.26) = 0.282, \qquad \text{so } z = 0.26$$

This implies

$$s = z\sigma_\tau = (0.26)(3.54) = 0.92 \approx 1$$

Note that this s is much lower than the s determined from policy 1.

We emphasize that the two policies are totally different; policy 1 gives the proportion of annual cycles in which no shortage occurs, with no regard to the magnitude of the shortage, but policy 2 gives the proportion of annual demand filled from stock, unrelated to the number of cycles short. In industry, the fill rate is more common than policy 1.

3.2.3 (Q, R) MODEL. We now consider the core stochastic model for the continuous review system. We present a management approach, in which a service policy is set, and an optimization approach, which is the stochastic version of the deterministic EOQ. Recall that in the continuous review case (Section 1.5) R is a decision variable, in contrast to the deterministic case, in which R was derived from the demand and lead time. The two decision variables, Q and R, define the policy for this model.

The management approach—quantity decision. We evaluate the order quantity using the EOQ method, substituting the known demand by the expected value of the random demand:

$$Q = \sqrt{\frac{2A\overline{D}}{h}}$$

This value is not the value of Q used in the optimization approach.

The management approach—reorder point decision. The reorder point is given by

$$R = \overline{D}\tau + s$$

so that R is determined by the safety stock level. The safety stock copes with the variability of demand during lead time, which is measured by σ_τ. Therefore, the safety stock is measured in "standard deviation units," and is

$$\kappa \sigma_\tau$$

where κ is the safety factor chosen to yield the desired service level.

If lead-time demand is normally distributed, we gain further insight into the value of κ. Consider Figure 6-19. Due to the nature of the normal distribution,

$$s = z\sigma_\tau$$

where z is the normal standard deviate, and it measures the number of standard deviations from the mean. Note that in this case $\kappa = z$. For the rest of the discussion, we assume a normal distribution for lead-time demand; therefore

$$R = \overline{D}_\tau + z\sigma_\tau = \overline{D}\tau + z\sigma_\tau$$

This general structure of evaluating R is the same for both service level policies 1 and 2. The difference lies in the *value assigned to z*.

Reorder point—policy 1. The service level required is α. The procedure is

1. From Table A-1, find the value of z that corresponds to

$$F(z) = \alpha$$

2. Evaluate R using the value obtained for z.

Example 6-23. Reorder point—policy 1. We rework Example 6-21, but we reverse the order. We want to find R and s for a specified service level of $\alpha = 0.95$.

Solution. We recall that

$$D \sim N(800, 625)$$

and

$$D_\tau \sim N(16, 12.5)$$

Step 1:

$$F(z) = 0.95$$

and from the normal distribution table (Table A-1) we find

$$z = 1.65$$

Step 2:

$$R = \overline{D}_\tau + z\sigma_\tau = 16 + 1.65 \times 3.54 = 21.84$$

The larger safety stock, $s = 5.84$ tons, gives a better service level than $s = 5$ tons at a service level of 92 percent.

Reorder point—policy 2. The service level required is β (fill rate). The procedure is

1. Evaluate

$$L(z) = \frac{(1 - \beta)Q}{\sigma_\tau}$$

2. From Table A-2 use $L(z)$ to obtain z.
3. Evaluate R using the value of z.

Example 6-24. Reorder point—policy 2. We rework Example 6-22, calculating values of Q and s instead of arbitrarily setting them.

Solution. Again, we note that

$$D \sim N(800, 625)$$

$$D_\tau \sim N(16, 12.5)$$

Suppose a fill rate of $\beta = 95$ percent is required and

$A = \$50$
$c = \$4000$ per ton
$i = 20\%$
$h = 800$

Then

$$Q = \sqrt{\frac{2A\overline{D}}{h}} = \sqrt{\frac{2 \times 50 \times 800}{800}} = 10 \text{ tons}$$

Step 1:

$$L(z) = \frac{(1 - \beta)Q}{\sigma_\tau} = \frac{(1 - 0.95)10}{3.54} = 0.14$$

Step 2: From Table A-2 in the appendix,

$$z = 0.71$$

Step 3:

$$R = \overline{D}_\tau + z\sigma_\tau = 16 + 0.71 \times 3.54 = 18.51$$

Thus $s = 2.51$ tons for $Q = 10$ tons and $\beta = 95$ percent compared to the arbitrary values of $s = 5$ and $Q = 21$, yielding $\beta = 99.4$ percent.

Implied shortage cost. No matter what service level we select, a shortage can occur. If so, we pay a shortage penalty implied by the service level selected. To evaluate the implied shortage cost, we analyze the (Q, R) model using the marginal analysis approach used for the newsboy problem. In an inventory cycle, it is economical to hold an additional unit in safety stock as long as its holding cost is no greater than the expected shortage cost for one additional unit short. If we examine Figure 6-19, the general shortage probability is $F(z)$, where $[1 - F(z)] = \alpha$ is a specific value selected. Using familiar notation, let h be the annual unit holding cost, π the shortage cost per unit, and $\overline{D}/Q$ the number of inventory cycles per year. Then, *per cycle,* balancing holding and shortage costs gives

$$\frac{h}{\left(\dfrac{\overline{D}}{Q}\right)} = [1 - F(z)]\pi$$

or, rearranging terms,

$$\pi = \frac{hQ}{[1 - F(z)]\overline{D}}$$

The implied shortage cost is a useful way for management to judge whether the selection of a particular service level is appropriate. The equation for π holds for both service level policies. Again the difference is in evaluating the proper value of z. We show how in the following example.

Example 6-25. Implied shortage cost. We compute the implied shortage cost for the soft drink manufacturer in the previous examples.

Solution. Recall:

where $A = \$50$

$i = 20\%$

$c = \$4000$

$h = 800$

$D = N(800, 625)$

$Q = 10$

$D_\tau = N(16, 12.5)$

Policy 1:

$$\alpha = 95\% \quad \text{and} \quad F(z) = 0.95$$

$$\pi = \frac{hQ}{[1 - F(z)]\overline{D}} = \frac{800 \times 10}{[1 - 0.95]800} = \$20 \text{ per ton short}$$

Policy 2:

$$\beta = 95\% \quad \text{and} \quad L(z) = 0.14$$

From Table A-2 in the appendix,

$$z = 0.71$$

From the normal distribution table (Table A-1), for $z = 0.71$,

$$F(z) = 0.7611$$

$$\pi = \frac{hQ}{[1 - F(z)]\overline{D}} = \frac{800 \times 10}{(1 - 0.7611)800} = \$41.85 \text{ per ton short}$$

Why is π different for policy 1 and policy 2?

Service level exchange curve. An exchange curve, by its nature, shows a *trade-off* between two entities of interest. Here, we are interested in the trade-off between investment in safety stock and shortage. We will discuss this approach for a single item, but it can be extended to multiple items.

Consider policy 2—fill rate. For every value of β, two measures can be calculated. These are

- Expected number of units short per year, equal to

$$(1 - \beta)\overline{D}$$

- Investment in safety stock,

$$cz\sigma_\tau$$

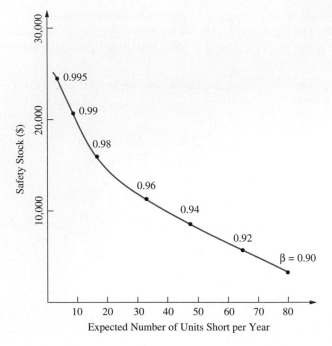

FIGURE 6-20
Exchange curve for policy 2

Each value of β generates a different value of z. The exchange curve obtained is shown in Figure 6-20. As the fill rate increases, the investment in safety stock increases and the number of units short decreases. This is a good way to assess the implications of a set service level policy. A similar exchange curve can be generated for policy 1.

Example 6-26. Service level exchange curve. We develop a policy 2 exchange curve for the soft drink manufacturer.

Solution. Recall

$$D_\tau \sim N(16, 12.5)$$
$$D \sim N(800, 625)$$

TABLE 6-13
Policy 2 exchange data

β, fill rate	0.90	0.92	0.94	0.96	0.98	0.99	0.995
$(1 - \beta)D$, number of units short	80	64	48	32	16	8	4
$L(z)$, partial expectation	0.282	0.225	0.169	0.113	0.056	0.028	0.014
z, normal standard deviate	0.26	0.41	0.60	0.83	1.20	1.51	1.80
$cz\sigma_\tau$, safety stock cost ($)	3682	5806	8496	11,753	16,992	21,382	25,488

TABLE 6-14
Policy 1 exchange data

α, percent	0.90	0.92	0.94	0.96	0.98	0.99	0.995
z, normal standard deviate	1.29	1.41	1.56	1.76	2.06	2.33	2.57
$D(1-\alpha)/Q$, number of cycles short	8	6.4	4.8	3.2	1.6	0.8	0.4
$cz\sigma_\tau$, safety stock (\$)	18,266	19,966	22,090	24,921	29,169	32,993	36,391

$$c = \$4000 \text{ per ton}$$

$$Q = 10 \text{ tons}$$

$$L(z) = \frac{(1-\beta)Q}{\sigma_\tau} = \frac{(1-\beta)10}{3.54} = 2.824(1-\beta)$$

Table 6-13 contains the data to generate the exchange curve given in Figure 6-20. We develop now a policy 1 exchange curve; recall the number of cycles short is

$$(1-\alpha)\frac{\overline{D}}{Q} = (1-\alpha)\frac{800}{10} = 80(1-\alpha)$$

Data for the exchange curve are given in Table 6-14; the plot of these data is Figure 6-21. Again, note that the safety stock investment for policy 1 is generally higher than that for policy 2.

The optimization approach. The optimization approach finds the optimum value for the two decision variables (Q^*, R^*) minimizing the expected annual total cost. Expected value is used because of the random nature of the demand. As before, the cost components are purchasing cost, ordering cost, inventory holding cost, and shortage cost. First, we develop these costs per inventory cycle and then transform them into an annual cost. The inventory geometry is shown in Figure 6-22.

The values of the cost components per cycle are

- Purchasing cost is equal to cQ, where c is the unit cost.
- Ordering cost is equal to A.
- Average holding cost is equal to $h\overline{I}$, where h is the holding cost per unit per unit time.

On the average, the inventory level fluctuates between $s+Q$ and s, so an approximation to the average inventory is

$$\overline{I} = \frac{1}{2}(s + Q + s) = \frac{Q}{2} + s$$

$$= \frac{Q}{2} + (R - \overline{D}\tau)$$

The expected cycle length is

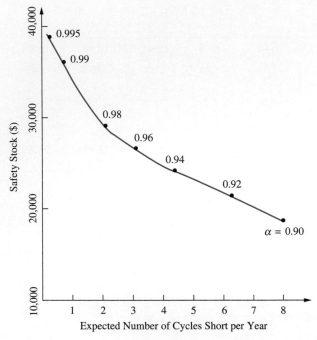

FIGURE 6-21
Exchange curve for policy 1

$$T = \frac{Q}{\overline{D}}$$

and the expected holding cost per cycle is

$$h\frac{Q}{\overline{D}}\left(\frac{Q}{2} + R - \overline{D}\tau\right)$$

Shortage cost is a function of the expected number of shortages. Shortages occur whenever

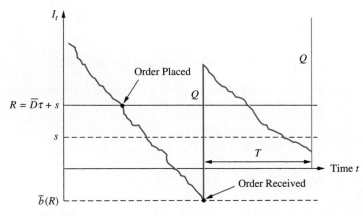

FIGURE 6-22
(Q, R) model geometry

demand during lead time exceeds the value of R. Therefore the expected number of units short is given by the partial expectation.

$$\overline{b}(R) = \int_R^\infty (D - R) f(D) \, dD$$

$b(R)$ is the shortage distribution as a function of R, $\overline{b}(R)$ is its expected value, and D, $f(D)$ are previously defined. If D is normally distributed, then

$$\overline{b}(R) = \sigma_\tau L(z)$$

The shortage cost per cycle is

$$\pi \overline{b}(R)$$

where π is the penalty per unit short.

The expected cost per cycle is given by

$$A + cQ + h\frac{Q}{\overline{D}}\left(\frac{Q}{2} + R - \overline{D}\tau\right) + \pi\overline{b}(R)$$

The expected number of cycles per year is $\overline{D}/Q$, and multiplying the cycle cost by this value yields the expected annual cost $K(Q, R)$.

$$K(Q, R) = \frac{A\overline{D}}{Q} + c\overline{D} + h\left(\frac{Q}{2} + R - \overline{D}\tau\right) + \frac{\pi\overline{D}\overline{b}(R)}{Q}$$

To get the minimum, we set

$$\frac{\partial K}{\partial Q} = \frac{\partial K}{\partial R} = 0$$

Now

$$\frac{\partial K}{\partial R} = h + \frac{\pi\overline{D}}{Q}\left(\frac{\partial\overline{b}(R)}{\partial R}\right)$$

First we find the partial of the backorder term.

$$\frac{\partial\overline{b}(R)}{\partial R} = \frac{\partial}{\partial R}\int_R^\infty (D - R) f(D) \, dD$$

$$= -\int_R^\infty Df(D) \, dD$$

$$= -[1 - F(R)]$$

This is a result of Leibnitz's rule for differentiating integrals.

Now substituting this result into the partial with respect to R, we have

$$\frac{\partial K}{\partial R} = h + \frac{\pi\overline{D}}{Q}\{-(1 - F(R)\} = 0$$

Rearranging terms gives

$$1 - F(R^*) = \frac{hQ}{\pi \overline{\overline{D}}}$$

Now we take the derivative with respect to Q and set it to zero:

$$\frac{\partial K}{\partial Q} = -\frac{A\overline{D}}{Q^2} + \frac{h}{2} - \frac{\pi \overline{D} \overline{b}(R)}{Q^2} = 0$$

Solving for Q gives

$$Q^* = \sqrt{\frac{2\overline{D}[A + \pi \overline{b}(R)]}{h}}$$

To find R^* we need Q^* and to find Q^* we need R^*. Fortunately, an iterative procedure can be used to find them. The procedure is

0. Set $j = 0$.
1. Assume $\overline{b}(R) = 0$. Solve the equation for Q^* to find Q_j.
2. Use Q_j to find R_j.
3. Evaluate $\overline{b}(R_j)$.
4. Use $\overline{b}(R_j)$ to find a new value for Q, say Q_{j+1}.
5. Use Q_{j+1} to find R_{j+1}.
6. If Q_{j+1} is about the same as Q_j or R_{j+1} is about the same as R_j, stop. Otherwise, set $j = j + 1$ and go to step 3.

It usually takes two to three iterations to obtain the optimal solution.

> **Example 6-27. (Q, R) model—the optimization approach.** Super-P is a peanut processing company. Past experience indicates that the annual demand is normally distributed with $\overline{D} = 25,000$ tons and a standard deviation of 36 tons. To order the peanuts, the company spends $50 to process the order. Each ton of peanuts costs $1000, and the annual interest rate for evaluating inventory holding cost is 25 percent. The penalty for a shortage is estimated to be $4 per ton. Ordering lead time is approximately one week. Calculate the economic order quantity and reorder point using the optimization approach.

> *Solution*

$$A = \$50$$
$$i = 25 \text{ percent annually}$$
$$c = \$1000 \text{ per ton} \rightarrow h = \$250 \text{ per ton per year}$$
$$D \sim N(25,000, 1296)$$
$$\pi = \$4 \text{ per ton}$$
$$\tau = 1 \text{ week} = 1/52 \text{ year}$$

> We can easily compute the lead-time distribution parameters:

$$\overline{D}_\tau = 25,000/52 \approx 481$$

$$\sigma_\tau^2 = 1296/52 \approx 25$$

so

$$D_\tau \sim N(481, 25.00)$$

We follow the stated procedure:

Step 0: Set $j = 0$.

Step 1: Assume $\bar{b}(R) = 0$ and compute the initial order quantity:

$$Q_0 = \sqrt{\frac{2A\bar{D}}{h}} = \sqrt{\frac{(2)(50)(25,000)}{(250)}} = 100$$

Step 2: Find the corresponding R_0 using the standardized normal distribution to find $F(z)$ and $R_0 = \bar{D}_\tau + z\sigma_\tau$.

$$1 - F(z) = \frac{hQ}{\pi\bar{D}} = \frac{(250)(100)}{(4)(25,000)} = 0.25$$

We have $F(z) = 0.75$. From Table A-1 in the appendix, we get $z = 0.67$ and

$$R_0 = 481 + (0.67)(5) = 484.4 \approx 484$$

Step 3: Compute the maximum backorder level; from the table, $L(0.67) = 0.1503$.

$$\bar{b}(R_0) = \sigma_\tau L(z) = (5)(0.1503) = 0.75$$

Step 4: Calculate the new order quantity:

$$Q_1 = \sqrt{\frac{2\bar{D}(A + \pi\bar{b}(R_0))}{h}} = \sqrt{\frac{(2)(25,000)(50 + (40)(0.75))}{(250)}} \approx 126$$

Step 5: Use Q_1 to find R_1.

$$1 - F(z) = \frac{(250)(126)}{(4)(25,000)} = 0.315$$

We have $F(z) = 0.685$, $z = 0.48$, and $L(z) = 0.204$. So

$$R_1 = 481 + (0.48)(5) \approx 484$$

Step 6: $Q_1 = 126 \neq Q_0 = 100$, but $R_1 = 484 = R_0 = 484$. We stop with $Q^* = 126$ and $R^* = 484$.

3.2.4 OTHER MODELS. We conclude continuous review systems with two variants of the previous models—the base stock system and the two-bin system. Both are easy to implement and commonly used in industry.

Base stock system. A base stock system is a special case of a (Q, R) model. In the system's simplest form, any time a withdrawal from inventory is made, a replenishment order equal to the amount withdrawn is issued. Only one decision variable is required, the reorder point R, which is equal to expected lead-time demand plus safety stock. The order quantity is planned to bring the inventory level back to R, so R is a target inventory. Thus, if $R = 100$ and 15 units were withdrawn from inventory at one time, the order quantity will be 15, to bring the inventory level back to 100. The inventory position (on hand plus on order) is always equal to R and is called the *base stock level*. The base stock level is the lowest inventory position needed to maintain a given service level. Base stock systems have lower inventory levels, but the number of orders issued is higher. This system is used where orders are infrequent and items are expensive. Examples are replacement engines for jet planes, heavy equipment, or furniture. The base stock system is often referred to as the "sell one, buy one" system.

Two-bin system. A two-bin system is a special case of the continuous review system. Its biggest advantage is that no record keeping is necessary. Inventory is usually stored in two bins; inventory is withdrawn from the first bin, which can contain Q = EOQ units. Once it is empty, a purchase order for EOQ units is issued, and the second bin is a backup until the order arrives. Thus, the second bin contains inventory to cover lead-time demand plus safety stock; that is, it is equal to R. When the new order arrives, the second bin is replenished first to restore it to its original value, and the balance of the order is placed in the first bin. The two-bin system is most suitable for cases of items of low value and fairly continuous use, i.e., nuts, bolts, and supplies.

SECTION 3.2 PROBLEMS

6.56. For a certain company, suppose the reorder point is 200, the on-hand inventory is 80, and pipeline inventory is 150. Should an order be placed if continuous review policy is used? What about pipeline inventory of 100?

6.57. Refer to Problem 6.15. Find R, and draw the inventory geometry for the following values of order lead time:

$$\tau = 1,3,6 \text{ months}$$

6.58. Refer to Problem 6.21. Assume Bike manufactures the handle bars, and shortages are allowed. Find R, and draw the inventory geometry, assuming $\tau = 6$ weeks.

6.59. A part of the manufacturing process in the textile industry is cloth sizing and dyeing. That is where the technical qualities of the cloth and its color are set.

A textile sizing and dyeing plant uses a continuous review system (Q, R) to manage its dye inventory. The ordering cost is $200, and a gallon of purple dye costs $5.00. Annual inventory holding cost is estimated at 20 percent. Expected annual demand is 10,000 gallons, and lead-time demand is normally distributed with $N(400, 900)$ ($= N(\mu, \sigma^2)$).

(a) Find the lead time τ.

(b) Find the reorder point for cycle service level of 90 percent, and the resulting safety stock.

(c) Because of delivery convenience, Q is set as 1000 gallons. Find R for minimum expected cost if shortage cost is estimated to be $4.00 per gallon.

6.60. In Problem 6.59, suppose $R = 400$ gallons.

(a) Find Q^*.

(b) What is the additional annual cost due to shortages?

(c) Find the percentage of time the inventory is going to be short.

6.61. A distributor sells electric can openers. Demand is 6000 units per year and is approximately constant throughout the year. These can openers cost $20 each, and the annual inventory carrying cost rate is 30 percent. It costs $150 to place an order. All shortages are backordered at a one-time cost of $50 per unit. Historically, demand during a lead time is uniformly distributed between 100 and 200 units. Because the distributor uses a bar-coding system, she believes that a (Q, R) system would be best to control ordering and stocking can openers.

(a) What value of Q and R would you recommend?

(b) Find the associated total cost.

6.62. Super Sound sells stereo equipment. Monthly demand for a particular CD player has historically been normally distributed with mean 28 and standard deviation 8. It takes about three months for a shipment of CD players to arrive, once an order has been placed. Each unit costs the store $60, and it costs $150 to place an order. The inventory carrying cost rate is 30 percent. Assume they use an order quantity based on the standard EOQ.

(a) What (Q,R) values would they use if they wish to apply policy 1 with 90 percent service level?

(b) What fill rate does this policy achieve?

6.63. Info Business Equipment (IBE) sells information-processing equipment. One item, the HDO80 800MB hard disk, has monthly demand that is normally distributed with mean 250 and standard deviation 100. IBE purchases the HDO80 for $360 a unit and sells it for $450. To place an order costs $209, and it takes one month from the time the order is placed until it arrives. Because the HDO80 is very popular and hard to get, customers who want one will wait as long as necessary to get one. The inventory cost carrying rate IBE uses is 20 percent.

(a) If the paperwork cost to backorder an item is estimated to be $5 per unit, what inventory policy would you recommend?

(b) The manager is reluctant to specify a backorder cost because she feels that substantial goodwill is also lost. She is willing to state that 98 percent of the customer demand should be satisfied immediately. What is your recommendation now?

6.64. Repeat Problem 6.63 for a demand that is exponentially distributed with a mean of 250 units per month.

6.65. In Problem 6.63, find the implied service level for policy 1 and policy 2.

6.66. Refer to Problem 6.16. Assume:

$\tau = 2$ weeks or 4 weeks for a production run

$\tau = 1$ week or 3 weeks for Electronic Hardware

$\tau = 2$ weeks or 5 weeks for Metstamp

(a) Evaluate R for each case.

(b) Evaluate O_t at R for each case.

(c) Draw the inventory geometry for each case.

6.67. Gregg is the marketing manager for the Aerocon Company, which manufactures a line of air conditioners. There are about 20 different models; however, over 70 percent of the subassemblies are common to all models. Therefore, the company is in a MTO (manufacture to order) mode; i.e., they assemble the final product only when they get an order. To expedite the final assembly, they stock the common subassemblies.

Gregg is responsible for the subassemblies inventory, and he decided to manage it using the continuous review approach. The weekly demand for fan subassembly is normally distributed with $N(500, 2500)$.

Gregg knows his ordering cost to be $300. Production cost of this subassembly is $40.00, and production lead time is two weeks. Inventory holding cost is 20 percent annually; shortages are backlogged at a penalty of $2.00 per unit.

(a) Find the average number of fan subassemblies if inventory were to be managed by the managerial approach.

(b) Find the service level for policy 1 and policy 2.

6.68. In Problem 6.67, suppose Aerocon shortened its assembly time, and delivery can now be made in one week. However, ordering cost was increased to $400. Recalculate (a) and (b), and compare the results.

6.69. Aerocon, the air conditioner manufacturer, also has a line of central air conditioners. They hold a stock of spare parts to service this product line. One of them is a subassembly for the compressor, which is purchased from an external supplier. It has a lead time of six weeks. The cost of this sub-assembly is $2000, and placing an order costs $100. Weekly demand is normal, with $N(50, 100)$. Inventory holding cost is estimated at 20 percent annually. Management set a service policy of shortage probability not being greater than 0.005. A continuous review approach is to be used.

    Interpret management's service policy and find Q and R. What are the size of the safety stock and the implied shortage cost?

6.70. Refer to Problem 6.59(b). Draw the exchange curve for policy 1 and policy 2 with $\beta = 0.90$. Compare the two policies.

6.71. Refer to Problem 6.62. Draw the exchange curve for policy 1 and policy 2. Compare the two policies.

6.72. Refer to Problem 6.63. Draw the exchange curve for policy 1 and policy 2. Compare the two policies.

6.73. Refer to the textile sizing and dyeing plant of Problem 6.59. Assume lead time to be as calculated in part (a), and shortage cost of $4.00 per gallon. Find the economic order quantity and reorder point using the optimization approach.

6.74. Refer to the Aerocon Company of Problem 6.67. Gregg decided to use an optimization approach. Find the economic order quantity and reorder point, and compare with the previous results. What is the resulting service level for policy 1 and policy 2, assuming safety stock is $\bar{b}(R^*)$?

6.75. Evaluate in Problem 6.74 Q^*, R^* if weekly demand has uniform distribution with $300 \le D \le 700$. Compare and analyze the results.

6.76. For the continuous review case, suppose there is also an annual inventory carrying cost that is proportional to the maximum on-hand inventory. Determine Q^* and R^* for both the service level approach and optimization approach.

6.77. Consider a continuous review system. Suppose orders can come in boxes and that each box contains n units. It is possible to order only whole boxes. Find Q^* and R^* for this case. Work out an example.

6.78. Teks is a multiplant textile manufacturing facility. In one of their plants they manufacture the cloth from cotton fibers. The manufacturing process is a weaving process, done in looms. One of the components of the loom is called a comb, as the fibers are directed by its "teeth" to the weaving area. Teks has over 50 looms. As the comb wears out, it needs replacement. Teks keeps stock of combs and manages it using base stock approach.

    Monthly demand for combs has a normal distribution with $N(10, 9)$. Delivery time is constant at six weeks. The cost of a comb is $3000, and shortage creates a cost of $7000 per inventory cycle, because of production stoppage. Annual inventory holding cost is estimated to be 20 percent, and ordering cost is $200.

(a) Find the reorder point for a cycle service level of 95 percent.

(b) What is the average number of combs held in inventory? Assume ordering once a week.

(c) What is the annual cost of the policy? (Include shortage cost.)

6.79. Suppose that Teks decides to use a policy of rush orders for combs in case of a shortage, to avoid production stoppage. The item will reach the plant within several hours, and a shortage will be avoided. A rush order costs $800 per order.

(a) Find the desired inventory level for this case, and the annual cost.

(b) Would you recommend using this policy?

6.80. To recap the notion of inventory being a service entity, we give a summary of a number of parameters that can measure service.

Expected number of shortages per cycle

Expected number of shortages per year

Probability of shortage during a cycle

Fraction of time the system is out of stock

Probability of one or more cycles having a shortage during a year

Fraction of demand satisfied immediately from inventory

(a) Write or develop a mathematical term for each.

(b) For a constant lead time, in which lead-time demand is $N(\mu,\sigma^2)$, develop an expression for each.

6.81. In Problem 6.80, suppose lead-time demand has a Poisson distribution with parameter λ. Develop an expression for each of the service parameters.

6.82. A regional service shop for a TV manufacturer keeps a stock of TV circuits. The purchasing lead time is three weeks, during which demand is normally distributed with $N(300, 1600)$. A circuit costs \$90 and sells for \$150. Annual inventory-holding cost is taken to be 25 percent. Shortages are backordered at a fixed cost of \$6.00 per unit short. The service shop uses the base stock approach to manage this item. Find the reorder point and the ordering policy.

6.83. Develop a model for the base stock system when purchasing lead time is constant, demand during lead time is normally distributed with $N(\mu,\sigma^2)$, and there is a shortage cost per unit (π) and shortage cost per unit per unit time $\hat{\pi}$. Make assumptions as necessary.

6.84. The distributor of can openers of Problem 6.61 decided to save some clerical work and manage her inventory using a two-bin system.

(a) Evaluate the required parameters.

(b) Explain how the system is going to work.

(c) Compare the average annual cost with the one obtained. What will be your recommendation to the distributor?

6.85. Suppose the service shop of Problem 6.82 were to use a two-bin system. Answer the same questions as in Problem 6.84.

3.3 Periodic Review Systems

A periodic review policy was introduced in Section 1.5. Here we expand on the timing decision of this policy. The inventory is reviewed every T periods. In each review, if $X_t > R$, do not order, but if $X_t \le R$, order up to inventory target level, S, where X_t is the inventory position. The behavior of this system is shown in Figure 6-23.

At the first review point, nothing happens. After the review period, T, inventory (assuming there are no on-order items) is below the reorder point (point 2), and an order of $Q = \{S - I_t\}$ is placed. This order arrives τ time units later (point 3) because of the lead time. The fact that the lot size varies draws our attention. It is not fixed as in the continuous case.

A special case of periodic review policy is when $R = S$ and an order is placed at *every* review point. The decision variable is the review period T. Similar to the approach taken for continuous review systems, we first look at a deterministic model and then at a stochastic model.

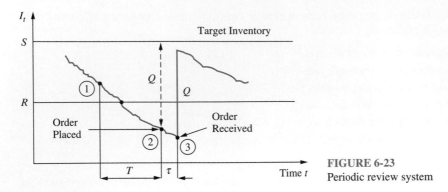

FIGURE 6-23
Periodic review system

3.3.1 EOQ REVISITED. The EOQ model can also be examined from a periodic review perspective. Recall that the assumption was that lead time is zero (Section 2.2.1). We could view EOQ as a periodic review system, in which the optimum value of the review period is

$$T^* = \frac{Q^*}{D} = \sqrt{\frac{2A}{hD}}$$

The target inventory level is Q^*, so the lot size ordered is Q^*. When the lead time is τ, T^* remains the same, but the target inventory is $R + Q^*$ with lot size Q^*.

Example 6-28. Periodic review systems. We refer to the small welding shop in Example 6-1.

Solution. We have

$$D = 1000 \text{ lb/year}$$
$$Q^* = \text{EOQ} = 120 \text{ lb}$$

Then

$$T^* = \frac{Q^*}{D} = \frac{120}{1000} = 0.12 \text{ years} = 6.24 \text{ weeks}$$

Let the delivery time be $\tau = 2$ weeks; the demand per week is $1000/52 = 19.25$ lb/week. This gives a reorder point of

$$R = D\tau = 38.50 \text{ lb}$$

The inventory geometry is shown in Figure 6-24.

3.3.2 (S, T) MODELS. Consider a periodic review system in which the target inventory is equal to S; in each review if $X_t \leq S$, we order up to the inventory target level S. This case is a special one in which $R = S$. There are two decision variables—the review interval T and the target inventory S. As in continuous review systems we still have a *trade-off* between service level and investment. Again there are two approaches—an optimization approach, based on a shortage cost π, and a management approach, in which a service level is set. We discuss the management approach.

We follow the same assumptions for the (Q, R) systems; there is infinite replenishment, demand is a random variable D, and the lead time is constant and equal to τ. The inventory geometry is shown in Figure 6-25.

Review period decision. The review period T can be convenience based, i.e., once a month, every Friday, etc., or according to the EOQ formula, i.e.,

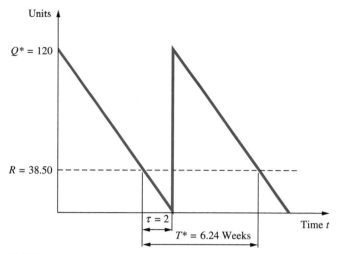

FIGURE 6-24
Periodic review geometry

$$T = \sqrt{\frac{2A}{h\overline{D}}}$$

Target inventory decision. The same argument that held for the (Q, R) system also holds here; choosing S is equivalent to deciding the safety stock level. The difference is in the length of the period for which safety stock protection is needed. In the (Q, R) system, safety stock was required to cover only the lead time τ, because orders can be placed any time. For (S, T) systems an order must be large enough to last until the next review, T periods away. Therefore S must be at least equal to the expected demand during $(T + \tau)$, which does not include safety stock. Considering safety stock and using the same notations as for the (Q, R) model, we get

$$S = \overline{D}(T + \tau) + s$$

For normally distributed lead-time demand,

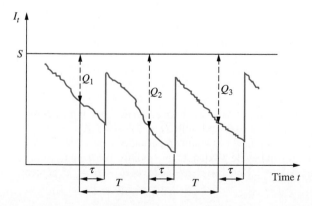

Time t **FIGURE 6-25**
(S, T) system geometry

$$s = z\sigma_{T+\tau}$$

yielding

$$S = \overline{D}(T + \tau) + z\sigma_{T+\tau}$$

where $\sigma_{T+\tau}$ is the standard deviation of demand during $(T + \tau)$. An (S, T) system requires more safety stock than a (Q, R) system because of the longer period that needs shortage protection.

The value of z determines the service level, and as before, we can use either policy 1 or policy 2.

Target inventory—policy 1: The service level required is α, and the procedure is the same as for a (Q, R) system.

1. From the normal distribution table (Table A-1), find the value of z that corresponds to

$$F(z) = \alpha$$

2. Evaluate S using the value obtained for z.

Target inventory—policy 2: The service level required is the fill rate β. The expected amount short during $(T + \tau)$ is

$$\sigma_{T+\tau}L(z)$$

The expected annual number of units short is

$$\frac{1}{(T + \tau)}(\sigma_{T+\tau}L(z))$$

because there are $1/(T + \tau)$ times per year when shortage protection is needed. This is equal to the desired number of units short per year obtained by the fill rate. Therefore,

$$(1 - \beta)\overline{D} = \frac{1}{(T + \tau)}\sigma_{T+\tau}L(z)$$

or, rearranging terms,

$$L(z) = \frac{(1 - \beta)\overline{D}(T + \tau)}{\sigma_{T+\tau}}$$

$\overline{D}(T + \tau)$ is the expected demand during the period that needs shortage protection. The procedure for policy 2 is

1. Evaluate $L(z)$.
2. Use $L(z)$ in Table A-2 to obtain z.
3. Calculate S using the value of z.

> **Example 6-29. (S, T) system.** Jones, the owner of a coffee shop, estimates that annual demand for a certain kind of coffee bean is normally distributed with $\overline{D} = 240$ lb and $\sigma = 32$. The order lead time for this coffee bean is 1/2 month. Jones adopts a periodic review policy, (S, T), to control the inventory and sets the reviewing cycle T equal to one month. We want to compute the reorder point for both policy 1 and policy 2. Both have service level $\alpha = \beta = 95$ percent.

Solution

$$D \sim N(240, 1024)$$
$$T = 1 \text{ month} = 1/12 \text{ year}$$
$$\tau = 1/2 \text{ month} = 1/24 \text{ year}$$
$$T + \tau = 1/12 + 1/24 \text{ year} = 1/8 \text{ year}$$
$$\overline{D}_{T+\tau} = \overline{D}(T + \tau) = 240 \times \tfrac{1}{8} = 30$$
$$\sigma^2_{T+\tau} = \frac{1024}{8} \to \sigma_{T+\tau} = 11.31$$

Therefore,

$$D_{T+\tau} \sim N(30, 128)$$

Policy 1:

$$\alpha = 95\%$$
$$F(z) = 0.95$$

Then from Table A-1,

$$z = 1.65$$

and
$$S = \overline{D}_{T+\tau} + z\sigma_{T+\tau} = 30 + (1.65)(11.31) = 48.6$$

Policy 2:

$$\beta = 95\%$$
$$L(z) = \frac{(1 - \beta)\overline{D}_{T+\tau}}{\sigma_{T+\tau}} = \frac{(1 - 0.95)(30)}{11.31} = 0.1326$$

From Table A-2, we find

$$z = 0.745$$

So
$$S = 30 + (0.745)(11.31) = 38.42$$

Again the same service level results in different reorder points for the two policies.

3.3.3 OPTIONAL REPLENISHMENT SYSTEMS.

Initially we discussed the general periodic review system and then the special case with $R = S$. We now examine a modification of the general case, the optional replenishment system, sometimes called optional review, min-max, or an (s, S) system.[2] The modification is that the reordering test is done using *on-hand inventory* rather than inventory position.

The system operates as follows. Two inventory levels are defined (s, S). The review interval is T, and at any review point the decision is that if $I_t \le s$, order $S - I_t$, but if $I_t > s$, do not order. I_t is the on-hand inventory at the review point. The advantage over (S, T) systems

---

[2]For this model we use s as the reorder level rather than safety stock to be consistent with existing literature.

is that a reasonable order quantity is placed. It is particularly useful when both review and ordering costs are significant.

This system has three decision variables—T, s, and S. We determine T using the method described earlier. Finding optimal values for s and S is very difficult. A good approximation can be obtained by computing a (Q, R) policy and letting

$$s = R \quad \text{and}$$
$$S = R + Q$$

The (s, S) policy is quite common in industry.

> **Example 6-30.** (s, S) **policy.** Consider the following (s, S) periodic inventory review policy, with $s = 50$, $S = 150$, and a review point at the end of every month. The monthly demands over the past few months are given in Table 6-15. Assuming that initial inventory is 123 units and zero lead time, we demonstrate the (s, S) policy.

TABLE 6-15
Demand data for Example 6-30

Month	t	1	2	3	4	5	6	7	8
Demand	D	30	54	50	62	55	50	66	30

> **Solution.** The first month's demand is 30 units and the initial inventory is 123 units, so the ending inventory for the first month is 93. The calculations are given in Table 6-16. Because 93 units is greater than the reorder point $s = 50$ units, no order is issued. The second month's demand is 54 units, resulting in an ending inventory of 39 units, which is below the reorder point. An order of 111 ($150 - 39$) units is issued, and the inventory is brought up to 150 units, the target inventory level. Calculations for months 3 through 8 are given in Table 6-16.

TABLE 6-16
Calculations for the (s, S) policy

Month	1	2	3	4	5	6	7	8
Inventory, beginning of month	123	93	150	100	150	95	150	84
D	30	54	50	62	55	50	66	30
I_t	93	39	100	48	95	45	84	54
Q	0	111	0	102	0	105	0	0

SECTION 3.3 PROBLEMS

6.86. Refer to Problem 6.29. Evaluate the optimal review period. State the periodic review policy. Evaluate R for τ of one month. Draw the inventory geometry.

6.87. Refer to Problem 6.33. Evaluate the optimal review period. State the periodic review policy. Evaluate R for τ of five weeks. Draw the inventory geometry.

6.88. Refer to the Toys International case of Problem 6.23. Evaluate the optimal review period. State the periodic review policy. Evaluate R for $\tau = 21$ days. Draw the inventory geometry.

6.89. A drug distributor has a certain prescription pain reliever that comes in containers of 100 pills each. The demand per container over any time period of length t is normal with mean $150t$ and variance of $300t$. Each container costs $20.00. Lead time is five weeks, and shortages are backlogged at a cost of goodwill loss of $15.00 per container. Purchase order cost is $100 and annual inventory holding cost is 25 percent. Suppose the inventory is reviewed every eight weeks. Find the optimum inventory target. (*Hint:* Convert shortage cost to service level.) What is the shortage probability? What is the annual expected inventory cost?

6.90. The drug distributor considers using a continuous review system with Q and $R = S$ obtained in Problem 6.89. What will be your recommendation? Justify.

6.91. In Problem 6.89, suppose the length of the review period T is also a decision variable. Find T^* if the cost of a review is $100. (*Hint:* Simulate a range of T values.)

6.92. A farmer raises chickens on an industrial basis. The chicken coops have a certain degree of automation. Specifically, the food distribution system is automated. To prevent chicken disease, the farmer adds nutritional additive to the chicken food.

He holds inventory for this additive and manages it using a periodic review system. Monthly demand is normally distributed with mean of 50 lb and standard deviation of 75 lb. Delivery time is four weeks, and the farmer estimates his inventory holding cost to be 20 percent annually. Ordering cost is $170 per order. A fill rate of 98 percent is required.

(a) Assume that inventory is reviewed every six weeks, and find the optimal inventory target.

(b) What is the annual expected cost of this policy to the farmer?

(c) What is the safety stock?

(d) What is the expected number of "pounds short" per year?

(e) What is the implied shortage cost?

6.93. Solve Problem 6.92 assuming monthly demand has a uniform distribution with $0 \le D \le 200$.

6.94. Sheri is a car distributor in a rural area. She has customers that own relatively old cars. To maintain good customer service, Sheri keeps a small inventory of spare parts for old-model cars. One item is brake boosters. It is a slow-moving item, and therefore she uses the periodic review policy with a review period of two months. The annual demand for booster sets has a normal distribution with mean of 15 and standard deviation of 5. Because this item is out of production, delivery lead time is five months. The cost of a set of boosters is $500. Sheri places high value on maintaining customer satisfaction. Therefore, she considers goodwill to be crucial, and estimates the shortage cost to be $5000. Shortages are backlogged, and annual inventory holding cost is 20 percent.

(a) Find the optimal target inventory.

(b) Find the implied service level for policy 1 and policy 2. Discuss.

(c) Find the safety stock for a set of brake boosters.

(d) Find the expected annual cost of the periodic review policy.

(e) Suppose a continuous review policy is used. Find the safety stock.

6.95. In Problem 6.94, suppose annual demand is 15 and deterministic. A periodic review policy is used. Find the average cost of uncertainty, defined as $K_s - K_D$

where K_S = expected annual cost of the stochastic case
K_D = average annual cost of the deterministic case

6.96. Consider a (s, S) system, with $s = 80$ and $S = 200$. The forecasted demand for the next 12 months is given in the following table. Initial inventory is 180, lead time is zero, and review is done at the end of every month. Find the order quantity.

Month, t	1	2	3	4	5	6	7	8	9	10	11	12
Demand, D	65	110	80	150	120	90	50	170	140	125	55	80

6.97. (a) Solve Problem 6.96 assuming lead time is $\tau = 2$ months.

(b) Repeat (a) when review is every 2 months. Compare.

6.98. Consider the subassembly inventory of the Aerocon Company described in Problem 6.69. Suppose, instead of continuous review, review is performed every two weeks, using an (s, S) policy.

(a) Set the (s, S) policy.

(b) For the next 12 weeks demand for the subassembly is forecasted to be as follows:

Month, t	1	2	3	4	5	6	7	8	9	10	11	12
Demand, D	20	32	16	28	35	42	38	28	18	34	40	18

Initial inventory is 45. Determine the number of subassemblies to be ordered following (s, S) policy.

6.99. The manager of Info Business Equipment (IBE) of Problem 6.63 considers using (s, S) policy to manage his hard disk inventory. To do so, he randomly selected demand values for the next 12 months from the normal distribution $N(250, 10,000)$.

(a) Set the (s, S) policy for IBE.

(b) Generate the demand value for IBE and determine the number of hard disks to be ordered in the next 12 months, assuming that initial inventory is 120.

3.4 Comparison of Timing Decisions

A comparison of the different models presented in this section appears in Table 6-17. The two major systems considered are continuous and periodic review systems. An important difference is that the safety stock required for continuous review systems is lower than the safety stock for periodic review systems. Implementation of both systems is discussed in the next section.

4 CONTROL DECISIONS

We have introduced a variety of models, policies, and approaches to various aspects of inventory systems. Now we focus on managing and controlling multi-item inventory systems. Multi-item systems may have 300, 3000, 30,000 or even 300,000 items! We still want to minimize cost and maximize service.

In Section 1.6, we discussed the relevance of inventory models. We stressed the importance of classical inventory models not only to get a solution but to enhance understanding of inventory systems. To aid understanding we discuss one managerial approach to inventory control under real-world conditions. To begin, we discuss Pareto analysis, an important tool to manage a multi-item system.

4.1 Pareto Analysis

Pareto analysis, a tool to separate "important" from "nonimportant," is a useful technique for allocating management effort. It is named after the Italian economist Villefredo Pareto, who

TABLE 6-17
Comparison of timing decisions

Model	Policy	Demand	Objective	Reorder point	Timing decision	Quantity decision	Application	Remarks
Newsboy	Single period	Stochastic	Minimum expected cost	R	Before period	$F(Q^*) = \dfrac{\pi}{\pi + c_0}$	One demand period Mainly retail	
EOQ	Continuous review	Uniform/deterministic	Minimum cost	$D\tau - b$	$X_t \le R$	$\sqrt{\dfrac{2A\overline{D}}{h}}$	Raw material or retail	
EPQ	Continuous review	Uniform/deterministic	Minimum cost	$D\tau - b$	$X_t \le R$	$\sqrt{\dfrac{2A\overline{D}}{h(1 - D/\psi)}}$	Production	Finite production rate
(Q, R)	Continuous review	Stochastic	Minimum expected cost	$\overline{D}\tau + z\sigma_\tau$	$X_t \le R$	$\sqrt{\dfrac{2A\overline{D}}{h}}$	Raw material or retail	Can fix z using policy 1 or policy 2
Base stock	Continuous review	Stochastic	Minimum expected cost	$\overline{D}\tau + z\sigma_\tau$	Each withdrawal	Up to R	Expensive items	
Two-bin	Continuous review	Stochastic	Minimum Cost	Bin 2: $\overline{D}\tau + z\sigma_\tau$	When bin 1 is empty	$\sqrt{\dfrac{2A\overline{D}}{h}}$	Cheap items	
EOQ	Periodic review	Uniform/deterministic	Minimum cost	—	$T = \sqrt{\dfrac{2A}{h\overline{D}}}$	—	Raw material or retail	
(S, T)	Periodic review	Stochastic	Minimum expected cost	$\overline{D}(T + \tau) + z\sigma_{T+\tau}$	$T = \sqrt{\dfrac{2A}{h\overline{D}}}$	Up to R		Can fix z using policy 1 or policy 2
Optional replenishment	Periodic review	Stochastic		s	$T = \sqrt{\dfrac{2A}{h\overline{D}}}$	Up to S		

Note: All models are single item, with known delivery time τ.

studied the distribution of wealth in Milan in the eighteenth century. He noted that a large portion of the wealth was owned by a small segment of the population. The same **Pareto** principle applies to many other situations; the few have great importance, and the many have little importance. Inventory systems typically have a few items that account for large annual dollar usage (or sales). This feature allows a trade-off between investment and control—an important element in maintaining low cost and high service.

The Pareto principle was first applied to inventory systems by Dickie (1951) of General Electric. He called it ABC analysis; A items are the few "important" items, and C items are the many "unimportant" items. B items fall between A and C items. In industry, Pareto analysis is known as the ABC analysis. For clarity, we call the tool ABC and the theory Pareto.

4.1.1 THE ABC CURVE. The ABC curve ranks the inventory items in descending order of annual dollar usage (or sales). This ranking in tabular form is called distribution by value; Table 6-18 is a typical example. We can plot the percentage of ranked items to total items

TABLE 6-18
Distribution by value

Rank	% of active items	Annual dollar usage	Cumulative annual dollar usage	Cumulative % of total usage
1	0.0034	292,150	292,150	1.43
2	0.0069	225,549	517,699	2.53
3	0.0103	153,418	671,117	3.28
4	0.0138	149,797	820,915	4.01
5	0.0172	146,697	967,614	4.73
6	0.0207	135,362	1,102,976	5.40
7	0.0241	131,011	1,233,987	6.04
8	0.0276	130,760	1,364,857	6.68
9	0.0310	124,702	1,489,559	7.29
10	0.0344	122,959	1,612,518	7.89
11–25	0.0861	63,672	2,907,815	14.23
26–77	0.265	28,900	5,113,576	25.03
78–119	0.410	21,205	6,144,048	30.08
120–248	0.854	12,387	8,170,675	40.00
249–461	1.59	7,418	10,214,450	50.00
462–820	2.82	4,464	12,254,380	60.00
821–1435	4.94	2,559	14,298,174	70.00
1436–2543	8.76	1,338	16,339,170	80.00
2544–5061	17.43	491	18,381,088	90.00
5062–8151	28.07	219	19,402,217	95.00
8152–9197	31.67	172	19,606,515	96.00
9198–10,565	36.38	129	19,810,651	97.00
10,566–12,496	43.03	86	20,014,900	98.00
12,497–15,650	53.89	47	20,219,132	99.00
15,651–16,279	56.06	42	20,247,133	99.13
16,280–18,001	61.99	30	20,307,996	99.43
18,002–20,443	70.40	18	20,364,329	99.71
20,444–24,009	82.68	7	20,407,231	99.92
24,010–29,037	1.00	0	20,423,347	100.00

Source: Herron (1976). Reprinted with the permission of the Institute of Industrial Engineers, 25 Technology Park/Atlanta, Norcross, GA, 30092, copyright © 1976.

against the corresponding cumulative percent of total dollar value represented by that percent of the ranked items. Plot 1 in Figure 6-26 is the plot corresponding to Table 6-18. In principle, we classify the ranked items into three groups:

A = "high dollar usage" items
B = "medium dollar usage" items
C = "low dollar usage" items

Typically, ABC curves show that group A items are about 20 percent of the ranked items and 80 percent of the total dollar usage. This is sometimes called the "20-80" rule. That these two numbers total 100 is coincidence.

In more detail, the procedure for preparing ABC curves is

Step 1:   Tabulate the inventory items in descending order of annual dollar usage per item. The annual dollar usage is the product of the unit cost and the annual number of units used.

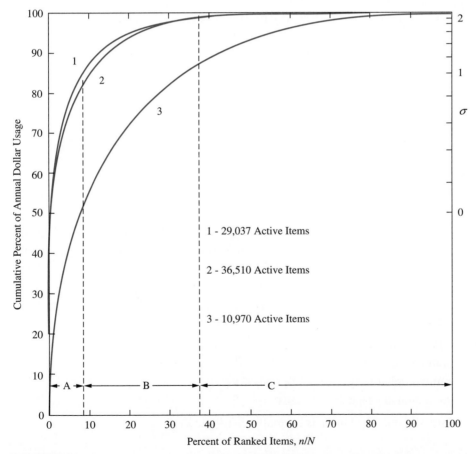

FIGURE 6-26
ABC curves for three companies (*Source:* Herron (1976). Reprinted with the permission of the Institute of Industrial Engineers, 25 Technology Park/Atlanta, Norcross, GA 30092, copyright © 1976.)

Step 2: Evaluate the cumulative activity by starting at the top of the list and accumulating item activity downwards.

Step 3: Work downwards and calculate:

- Cumulative percent of items based on the total number of items
- Cumulative percent of dollar usage, based on the annual total dollar usage

Step 4: Plot the ABC curve cumulative percent of dollar usage as a function of cumulative percent of items.

Table 6-18 shows the above steps for an inventory system with 29,073 items and annual usage of over $20,000,000. Obviously, it is impossible to show all items, so selected values are tabulated. The graphical description of the distribution by value—the ABC curve—is shown in Figure 6-26 (curve 1).

Some observations about ABC curve:

- There is no fixed convention as to which items are in the A, B, or C group. This is usually done by "eyeballing" the curve. Group A is roughly where the ABC curve starts bending, B is at the end of this bending, and C includes the rest of the items.
- Figure 6-26 shows two other curves (2,3). These curves are less "steep," and the distinction between A and B is more difficult.
- Typically, the steeper the ABC curve is, the more **separation power** it has. Separation power is the ability to differentiate between the groups. That is, fewer items will account for higher value; e.g., 15 percent of the items account for 90 percent of the value. For this example, about 1.5 percent of the items represent 50 percent of the value.
- In practice, it is easy to generate the distribution by value table and its associated ABC curve. Both the item's unit price and its annual usage are part of the inventory data base. A simple computer program can use these data to generate the table. A section of computer output is shown in Table 6-19.
- Unit cost is not the reason for placing an item in the A group. A cheap item with high annual usage can be classified as an A item, and vice versa.

This discussion shows how the Pareto principle helps allocate management efforts. Group A, which has most of the investment in inventory, is managed closely. Group C items get little management attention; they are worth less effort.

4.1.2 ANALYZING THE CURVE.[3] The distribution by value—the Pareto distribution—is approximated by the log-normal distribution. This distribution is one in which the probability density function of the natural logarithm of the random variable is normal. Let

n = nth *ranked* item

N = number of items

C_n = annual dollar usage of the nth ranked item

C = total annual usage for all items

C_n is the random variable; thus $\ln C_n$ is normally distributed.

[3] Adapted from Herron (1976)—Reprinted with the permission of the Institute of Industrial Engineers, 25 Technology Park/Atlanta, Norcross, GA 30092, copyright © 1976.

TABLE 6-19
Typical ABC computer output

#	Item no.	Description	Ann. units	Unit cost	Ann. $ usage	Cum $ usage	Cum% $ usage	Cum% items
1	850170	Plastic body	4945	49.50	24478	244778	13.50	0.90
2	615200	Motor	3965	47.50	188338	433116	23.90	1.80
3	425150	Handle	9750	17.30	168675	601791	33.20	2.70
4	530010	Cover assembly	6150	17.95	110393	712184	39.30	3.60
5	120211	Heating coil	9850	11.20	110320	822504	45.40	4.50
6	531110	Front cover	9000	7.25	65250	887754	49.00	5.40
7	470115	Cable	9419	5.40	50863	938617	51.80	6.30
8	770811	Hand grip	4875	8.30	40463	979080	54.00	7.10
9	615300	Motor	700	49.50	34650	1013730	55.90	8.00
10	530005	Cover assembly	4500	7.62	34295	1048025	57.80	8.90
11	850171	Plastic body	700	47.50	33250	1081275	59.70	9.80
12	532015	Back cover	3990	8.30	33117	1114392	61.50	10.70
13	110570	Grill	9800	3.05	29890	1144282	63.20	11.60
14	480001	Connector	5454	5.40	29452	1173734	64.80	12.50
15	425110	Handle	3190	8.30	26477	1200211	66.20	13.40
16	101050	Metal tag	6500	3.81	24765	1224976	67.60	14.30
17	120570	Box	6750	3.61	24368	1249344	68.90	15.20
18	615150	Motor	500	47.50	23750	1273094	70.30	16.10
19	770822	Hand grip	2825	8.30	23448	1296542	71.60	17.00
20	110580	Grill	7475	3.05	22799	1319341	72.80	17.90
21	470120	Cable shoe	13859	1.55	21481	1340822	74.00	18.80
22	531105	Front cover	5450	3.81	20765	1361587	75.10	19.60
23	850172	Plastic body	407	49.50	20147	1381734	76.30	20.50
24	252212	Tapered screw	13139	1.49	19577	1401311	77.30	21.40
25	532110	Back cover	4875	3.81	18574	1419885	78.40	22.30

Note: Only part of the output is shown.

The statistics of the log-normal distribution are as follows:

$$z_n = \frac{\ln C_n - \mu}{\sigma}$$

is the standard log-normal deviate similar to

$$\frac{x - \mu}{\sigma}$$

for the normal distribution. Also

μ = natural logarithm of annual dollar usage for the median ranked item

σ = standard deviation of the log-normal probability distribution

The variable σ is a helpful statistic for Pareto curves, with an interesting real-world interpretation, as we show later.

According to Herron (1976), the equation for the log-normal distribution applied to a multi-item population is

$$\frac{n}{N} = \int_{z_n}^{\infty} \phi(y)\, dy$$

where $\phi(y)$ is the probability density function of the normal distribution. It can be shown that

$$\frac{1}{C}\sum_{i=1}^{n} C_i = \int_{z_n-\sigma}^{\infty} \phi(y)\,dy$$

where

$$C = \sum_{i=1}^{N} C_i$$

By definition at $n/N = 0.50$, the median ranked item, $\ln C_n = \mu$ and therefore $z_n = 0$, and for the median ranked item we have

$$\frac{1}{C}\sum_{i=1}^{n} C_i = \int_{-\sigma}^{\infty} \phi(y)\,dy = \int_{-\infty}^{\sigma} \phi(y)\,dy$$

The left-hand side of this equation is the cumulative percent of dollar usage, and the right-hand side is the normal probability integral evaluated between $-\infty$ and σ. Figure 6-27 demonstrates this situation: the normal pdf, $N(0, 1)$, is shown with the normal probability integral being the shaded area.

If $\sigma = 1$, it represents 68.2 percent of the area under the curve. For σ equal to 2 or 3, it is 95.4 percent and 99.8 percent, respectively. Based on the previous equation, if we "translate" the cumulative percent of dollar value to its equivalent σ value using the normal probability distribution, the value of the ABC curve at $n/N = 0.50$ yields σ for the log-normal distribution. The σ scale is shown on the right-hand side in Figure 6-26. If we draw a vertical line at $n/N = 0.50$, its intersection with the curve gives the value of σ.

There is also an analytical way to get σ using the distribution by value (Table 6-18). Herron (1976) shows that

$$\sigma = \ln\left(\frac{C_{0.50}}{C_{0.8413}}\right)$$

where $C_{0.50}$ is the dollar usage of the item at $n/N = 0.50$, and $C_{0.8413}$ is the dollar usage of the item at $n/N = 0.8413$ (see Example 6-29).

Why is σ so important? We examine the three curves shown in Figure 6-26. As σ increases, the separation power of the ABC curve increases. Thus, σ is a measure of the separation power of the curve, and an inventory item population with higher σ is easier

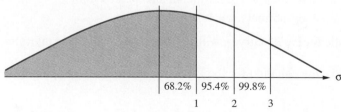

FIGURE 6-27
Normal pdf

to manage and control. Furthermore, similar types of products will have about the same values of σ. Some examples of representative values are:

$0.8 < \sigma < 2$ Wholesaler and retailers
$2.0 \leq \sigma < 2.6$ Spare parts inventories
$2.6 \leq \sigma < 3$ Electronic components, high-tech components

An example will illustrate ABC curves.

Example 6-31. Pareto analysis. Consider the data in Table 6-20. There are 2 items with annual usage over \$300,000, and their total annual usage is \$817,200. There are 17 items with annual usage over \$100,000 but below \$300,000; the total annual usage of these 17 items is \$2,273,867. Evaluate the standard deviation for the data listed in this table. Evaluate the separation power of the corresponding ABC curve.

Solution. Calculate the percentage of active items and annual usage; these are given in Table 6-21.
The standard deviation of this ABC curve is

$$\sigma = \ln\left(\frac{C_{0.5}}{C_{0.8413}}\right)$$

From the tables, $C_{0.5}$ is between groups 7 and 8; we apply linear interpolation to get the annual usage:

$$\frac{50 - 46.15}{64.84 - 46.15} = \frac{C_{0.5} - 525,768}{166,182 - 525,768} \Rightarrow C_{0.5} = 451,729$$

Using the same method to find $C_{0.8413}$ gives

$$\frac{84.13 - 81.64}{92.08 - 81.64} = \frac{C_{0.8413} - 48,232}{9613 - 48,232} \Rightarrow C_{0.8413} = 39,021.4$$

TABLE 6-20
Data for Example 6-31

Group	Value of annual usage	Number of items	Value of usage	Cumulative number of items	Cumulative annual usage
1	>300,000	2	817,200	2	817,200
2	100,000	17	2,273,857	19	3,091,057
3	30,000	70	3,902,394	89	6,993,451
4	10,000	193	3,262,217	282	10,255,668
5	3,000	399	2,112,391	681	12,368,059
6	1,000	666	1,161,808	1,347	13,529,867
7	300	908	525,768	2,255	14,055,635
8	100	913	166,182	3,168	14,221,817
9	30	821	48,232	3,989	14,270,094
10	10	510	9,613	4,499	14,279,662
11	3	262	1,678	4,761	14,281,340
12	1	89	183	4,850	14,281,523
13	0.3	31	21	4,881	14,281,544
14	0.1	5	1	4,886	14,281,545

TABLE 6-21
Percentage of items and usage

Group	% of active item	% of annual usage
1	0.04	5.72
2	0.39	21.64
3	1.82	48.97
4	5.77	71.81
5	13.93	86.60
6	27.57	94.94
7	46.15	98.42
8	64.84	99.58
9	81.64	99.92
10	92.08	99.99
11	97.44	99.99
12	99.26	99.99
13	99.90	99.99
14	100.00	100.00

So

$$\sigma = \ln\left(\frac{C_{0.5}}{C_{0.8413}}\right) = \ln\left(\frac{451,729}{39,021}\right) = 2.45$$

The ABC curve, given in Figure 6-28, has a relatively high separation power.

4.2   Inventory Control Systems: A Managerial Approach

We discuss a methodology for setting an inventory control system in a real-world environment. This system has the following characteristics:

- Multi-item
- Stochastic demand
- Stochastic lead time

We assume that a computer manages and controls the inventory system. This inventory control system can be used for independent or dependent demand or for raw material or finished goods inventories.

The objectives of this control system are

- Minimize cost—synonymous with minimizing investment in inventory
- Maximize customer satisfaction—synonymous with maximizing service level

It is not difficult to maximize service level at any cost. It is more difficult to do so at minimum cost.

An inventory control system must address the three basic inventory decisions:

- Variety decisions—what to order
- Quantity decisions—how much to order
- Timing decisions—when to order

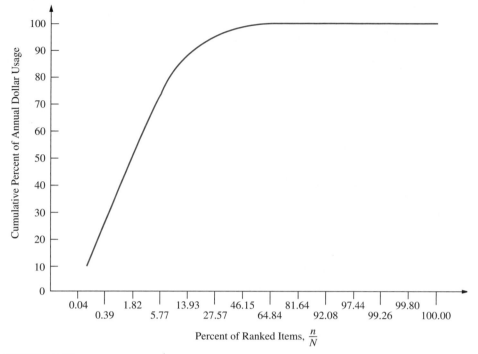

FIGURE 6-28
ABC curve (Example 6-31)

These decisions apply to single-item or multi-item systems. In multi-item systems we have to manage the decisions for many items. We first discuss the underlying principle of the control system and then describe its components and operation.

4.2.1 THE UNDERLYING PRINCIPLE. The underlying principle is a trade-off between **investment** and **control.** This is a result of combining the ABC concept with the fill rate and is demonstrated in Figure 6-29. The ABC classification is superimposed on the fill rate curve.

We use the following rationale. For low-value items (group C)

- Buying a high service level (fill rate) is cheap.
- Invest in safety stock.
- Relax control—items are mass controlled.

A "C" item can have a "low value" of annual dollar usage but may have a "high" shortage cost. As an example, suppose a $100,000 piece of equipment cannot be delivered because a $2 plate with the company's logo is missing.

For "high-value items" (group A)

- Buying high service level is expensive.
- Reduce investment in safety stock.
- Tighten control—individual item control.

Group B items fall somewhere in between and are controlled similarly to group C.

4.2.2 THE CONTROL SYSTEM DESIGN. After structuring the ABC classification, we first identify special items. These are group B and C items that need special attention. Examples are

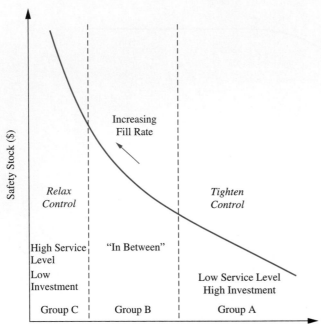

FIGURE 6-29
The leading principle

- Items that, if short, cause severe production problems (by implication—high shortage cost)
- Items that have incoming quality problems
- Items with short shelf life

These items need individual control and are included in group A.

The next step is developing the specific control structure for each group. Figure 6-30 shows the major control components, described in more detail later on.

4.2.3 CONTROL STRUCTURE. We describe the control structure separately for A, B, and C items. The group A control policy is *periodic review.* Its parameters are usually:

Review period: Typically one or two weeks

Order quantity: Lot for lot (Section 2.2.1)

Safety stock: Low—usually two to four weeks of forecasted demand

For group A we do not use the fill rate to set safety stock. By implication, low safety stock represents a low fill rate. We *compensate by individual control.*

For **planning** future inventory level for each item, use a material balance equation.

$$
\left\{ \begin{array}{c} \text{Period} \\ \text{beginning} \\ \text{inventory} \end{array} \right\} + \left\{ \begin{array}{c} \text{Period} \\ \text{scheduled} \\ \text{receipts} \end{array} \right\} - \left\{ \begin{array}{c} \text{Period} \\ \text{forecasted} \\ \text{demand} \end{array} \right\} = \left\{ \begin{array}{c} \text{Period} \\ \text{ending} \\ \text{inventory} \end{array} \right\}
$$

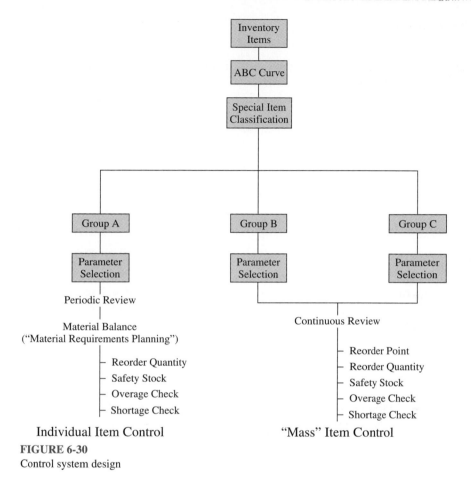

FIGURE 6-30
Control system design

For **monitoring,** use the same equation, but

- Instead of scheduled receipts we use **actual receipts.**
- Instead of forecasted demand we use **actual demand.**

The tool used for both cases is a material balance table for each item (similar to Table 7-12). At every review period the material balance table is updated, and each item is checked for shortage, overage, or reordering.

Groups B and C control. Groups B and C have the same control structure. The control policy used is **continuous review.** The difference between the two groups is the value assigned to the different parameters.

The approach is **mass control** with **management by exception.** Items are controlled as a group, not individually. The status of an item is continuously checked, and only when there is an exception is management notified. This approach enables us to manage and control a multi-item inventory system.

To set up the control structure for management by exception, four system parameters must be defined. They are the reorder point R, order quantity Q, safety stock s, and maximum inventory level, I_{max}.

The reorder point is set at

$$R = D\tau + s$$

The lead time, τ, is a random variable, and it is practically impossible to set and maintain individual lead times for thousands of items. Therefore, a group lead time is set. A group can consist of similar items, items from the same supplier, etc. The value of τ is assumed larger than the average value for the group.

For the timing decision, the inventory position X_t is used; if

$$X_t < R$$

issue an order.

Order quantity. Two different approaches are used for group B and group C.

Group B: In principle, we order quantities that have some economic measure. These might be EOQ, least unit cost, part period quantity, etc.

Group C: Group C items are ordered in large lots—fixed period requirements—usually for 6 or 12 months.

Safety stock. A high fill rate is used—higher for group C than for B. This will usually result in having 1.2 to 2.5 months of forecasted demand in inventory for group B items. C items will have about 3 months of forecasted demand in inventory. For these items we monitor the safety stock level, using the following test: if

$$I_t \leq s$$

then expedite.

Maximum inventory. Because of the mass control approach used here, there is a danger that the inventory level may get too high for some items. Therefore, a maximum inventory

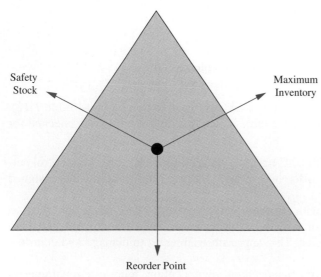

FIGURE 6-31
The control triangle

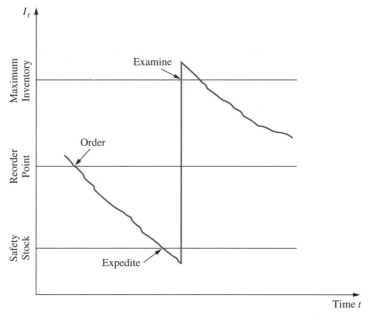

FIGURE 6-32
Managerial action

level, I_{max}, is set. It is measured by months of forecasted demand, and the overage check is

$$X_t \geq I_{max}$$

The control process (groups B and C). For each item in the inventory, the parameters reorder point, lead time, safety stock, and maximum inventory are defined and stored in the data base. For each inventory transaction, the computer checks that the item is contained within the control triangle shown in Figure 6-31. As long as the item remains in this triangle, (i.e., above the reorder point, above the safety stock, and below maximum inventory), nothing happens. An item that violates one of these limits is flagged as an exception. The inventory manager gets an exception report, usually arranged in descending order of urgency of the action to be taken. The order of urgency is

- Safety stock items
- To-order items
- Overage items

This report is typically generated once or twice a month. With today's on-line capabilities, this information is available anytime. The managerial action to be taken for each case is shown in Figure 6-32.

4.2.4 SUMMARY. Table 6-22 summarizes the complete structure of the control system. This methodology, of course, has to be computer based. It can be programmed, although many software packages available in the market have many features of the methodology presented here.

TABLE 6-22
Control decisions: summary

	Group A	Group B	Group C
Control principle	Individual item control	Mass control	Mass control
Inventory policy	Periodic review	Continuous review	Continuous review
Review period	1 or 2 weeks	None	None
Reorder point	None	$D\tau + s$ $(X_t \leq R)$	$D\tau + s$ $(X_t \leq R)$
Reorder quantity	Lot for lot	EOQ, LUC, PPB	FPD
Safety stock	0.5 to 1.5 months $(I_t \leq s)$	1.5 to 2.5 months $(I_t \leq s)$	≈ 3 months $(I_t \leq s)$
Maximum inventory	Low	More than group A $X_t \geq I_{max}$	More than group A $X_t \geq I_{max}$
Control method	Material balance equation	Control triangle	Control triangle
Control tool	Material balance chart	Exception report	Exception report

SECTION 4 PROBLEMS

6.100. Utilizing Pareto classification theory, classify the units according to whether they belong in class A, class B, or class C.

Item	Forecasted annual requirements	Item unit cost ($)
M 301	3000	0.20
M 764	3	1000.00
M 382	200	10.00
M 1216	500	10.00
M 870	50	250.00
M 387	1000	0.50
M 1242	1700	0.45

Also, plot the curve and from the curve and analytically find the value of σ. What can you conclude?

6.101. Plot to scale the Pareto curves that have the following values of the standard deviation:

$$\sigma = 0 \qquad \sigma = 2$$
$$\sigma = 1 \qquad \sigma = 2.5$$
$$\sigma = 1.5 \qquad \sigma = 2.8$$

Draw conclusions.

6.102. An inventory Pareto distribution has 100 items, $\sigma = 3$, and annual usage of the median item is $40.

(a) Find the annual usage of the 84th-ranked item.

(b) Comment on the separation power of this distribution.

6.103. Use the data of Table 6-18 and design an inventory control system for this company. Submit your plan in the form of a memo to the vice president of operations. Show all derivations and explain your rationale.

6.104. Repeat Problem 6.103 for the data of Table 6-19.

5 SOFTWARE

During the 1960s inventory software was developed solely to control inventory. In the early 1970s inventory control software became part of materials requirements planning systems, and the use of "stand-alone" systems diminished. Thus, inventory software per se is now more common in retail and service applications. Many commercial software packages exist; here we mention two early packages that set the standard for later software packages. The first package, IMPACT (Inventory Management Program and Control Techniques), was introduced by IBM in the early 1960s. It contained a forecasting system, inventory file, and logic of inventory control. The second package, INFOREM (Inventory Forecasting and Replenishment Modules), was introduced by IBM in 1978. It included an improved forecasting module and periodic review, reorder point, and fixed lot size system similar to the ones described in Section 3.3. Lot size was the EOQ. The reorder point was $\overline{D}(T + \tau) + s$, where $s = z\sigma_{T+\tau}$. z was based on the normal distribution and a policy 2 service level; backordering was allowed. Many of the inventory system elements described in this chapter are included. Newer packages include continuous review policies and most of the lot sizing methods described in Section 2. Some of these are Manufacturing PM (Software PM, Inc.), Vantage (DCD), Flow Manufacturing Technology (American Software), and Inventory Interface (Data Interface).

6 EVOLUTION

Inventory has been used for centuries. Recall the fifteenth-century Venice Arsenal (Chapter 1), where raw material inventory had to be maintained in order to keep boat production flowing.

The first quantitative treatment of inventory was the simple EOQ. It was developed in 1915 by Harris as part of an inventory system he marketed. Wilson (1934) created interest in the EOQ in academic circles, as well as in industries. Few additional papers were published until the early 1950s. However, work on mathematical theory of inventory systems was initiated during the Second World War. The war effort triggered research in both deterministic and stochastic inventory systems.

Since the early 1950s, research in inventory systems has exploded, and there are thousands of published works. The leading journals in the United States are *Operations Research, Management Science, IIE Transactions, Decision Sciences, Production and Inventory Management, Naval Research Logistics Quarterly,* and *Mathematics of Operations Research.* The three leading European journals are the *International Journal of Production Research, Operational Research Quarterly,* and *Omega.*

We highlight some milestone inventory work. The papers that laid the foundation for rigorous treatment of inventory models are those by Arrow, Harris, and Marschak (1951) and by Dvoretzky, Kiefer, and Wolfowitz (1952a, b). The quantity discount models are attributed to Churchman, Ackoff, and Arnoff (1957) and to Hadley and Whitin (1963). The last two authors were also among the first to consider budget and space constraints. Continuous review systems (Q, R) were discussed by Hadley and Whitin (1963) and later influenced the methodology of many commercial inventory systems. Dynamic programming was used to solve periodic review problems by Bellman, Elicksberg, and Gross (1955). A number of papers addressed (s, S) policies. Scarf (1960) and Iglehart (1963) proved (s, S) optimality, while Erhardt (1979) and later Freeland and Porteus (1980) developed approximation techniques for these policies.

In recent years inventory models have been extended to multi-echelon inventory systems, reparable inventory, perishable items, and even blood bank inventory.

Over the years, many books on inventory systems were published. We single out two that, in our opinion, influenced the thinking of a generation of researchers. The first is the book by Hadley and Whitin (1963), which gives a comprehensive treatment of inventory theory. The second book is by Brown (1967). It develops theory and applications through a real-world perspective and introduces exchange curves and service levels.

All in all, inventory is a very important and viable area, both in its research aspects and real-world applications.

Inventory is part of daily life in industry and business. No wonder some of the models and many of the concepts described in this chapter are widely used today; they were embedded in many software systems for inventory control. Unfortunately, documentation in the public literature of the extent of inventory models application is relatively sparse. However, some indications can be obtained.

From surveys, the most widely used inventory model is the EOQ. A study by Osteryoung et al. (1986) surveyed firms in manufacturing, retail, wholesale, and service. They found that 84 percent of the firms use EOQ, in spite of EOQ's shortcomings (Section 2.1.1).

The lot-for-lot model is also widely used. It became more widely used after the introduction of the JIT philosophy (Chapter 10). Fill rate as an indication of service level has received some attention in industry. Naturally, inventory control policies of periodic review and continuous review are part of any inventory system.

Many successful applications of inventory models appear in the literature. The common denominator is reduced inventory investment with maintained or increased customer service. Some highlights include Kleutghen and McGee (1985) reporting the use of an (s, S) system at Pfizer Pharmaceuticals for finished goods inventory. Lot size evaluation was based on EOQ, and the reorder point was computed based on service level. Since 1958, the Department of Defense directs all logistic agencies to use the EOQ model. Gardner (1987) reports the considerable cost savings in the Navy through the use of simple continuous review models and EOQ. Two journals, *Production and Inventory Management* (published by APICS, American Production and Inventory Control Society) and *Interfaces,* are a good source for inventory applications.

7 SUMMARY

This chapter focuses on inventory, a buffer between the two processes of supply and demand. Inventory is an important topic today, especially in the manufacturing sector. It can enhance both profitability and competitiveness.

Inventory is a broad area, and we view it from a decision-based approach. There are three decisions: quantity decisions, timing decisions, and control decisions. As a preamble we present general inventory concepts. We consider only independent demand systems where the demand for an item is not related to any other item.

Inventory is created because of a difference in rates and timing between supply and demand. This difference can be caused by four factors: economies of scale, operation smoothing, customer service, and uncertainty. There are three types of inventory: raw materials, work in process, and finished goods. Each can incur costs, including purchasing cost, ordering (set-up) cost, holding and storage cost, and system operating cost. These costs serve as a basis for analyzing inventory systems, where we trade off the benefits of carrying inventory with the costs associated with having it. Our measure of effectiveness for inventory is the average total cost per unit time.

Quantity decisions and timing decisions are governed by two inventory control policies: continuous review and periodic review. We use both to study and model inventory systems.

The relevance of inventory models is a much-debated issue. Although some of them are widely applied, we feel that the biggest benefit obtained from using them is a better understanding of the behavior of these systems.

In line with our decision-oriented approach, we first examine quantity decisions, i.e., how much to order. These models are typically called "lot sizing" models. They are either static models (uniform demand) or dynamic models (lumpy demand). In both cases demand is deterministic.

The primary model for static lot sizing is the classic economic order quantity (EOQ) model. Variants of this model include EOQ with backorders, economic production quantity (EPQ), and quantity discounts. Two quantity discount policies are presented: all-units discount and incremental discount. An extension of the single-item EOQ model to a multi-item case is given for a resource-constrained environment, such as budget, space, or both.

Discussion of dynamic lot sizing models is organized around four methods: simple rules, heuristic methods, the Wagner-Whitin algorithm, and the Peterson-Silver rule. Simple rules are not directly based on optimizing the cost function. They have other merits and are among the most widely used in industry. Included are period order quantity, and lot for lot. Heuristic methods try to find a low-cost solution that is not necessarily optimal. Heuristic methods are used when it is impossible to solve for the optimum or when the problem requires too much time or resources. The Silver-Meal heuristic finds the minimum average variable cost per period for an m-period span. The least unit cost (LUC) method finds the average variable cost per unit, whereas the part period balancing (PPB) heuristic minimizes the sum of the variable costs for all lots. The Wagner-Whitin algorithm is an optimization approach. Finally, the Peterson-Silver rule is a test to tell us when demand is lumpy.

The timing decision is the second major decision associated with inventory systems—when to order. This decision impacts not only the inventory level and hence the inventory cost, but also has a direct relation to the service level for our customer. As in the case of quantity decisions, we included those classic models. They are grouped under three major headings: one-time decisions, continuous-time decisions, and intermittent-time decisions. All models are single-item models but can be extended to multiple items. Most of them allow stochastic demand.

The one-time decision is to decide on the number of items to order before the demand period when demand is stochastic. Commonly known as the "newsboy model," the solution to this problem is indicative of stochastic inventory environments.

We launch continuous-time decisions by revisiting the single-item environment, in which lead time is taken to be a decision variable. We consider both the EOQ and EPQ cases and introduce the notion of reorder point, which is lead-time dependent. Determining the reorder point for the deterministic case is easy. However, when either demand or lead time (or both) vary, we need to introduce safety stock and service level.

Two service level policies are presented, policy 1 and policy 2. Policy 1 is a "cycle service level," whereas policy 2 uses a fill rate. Both policies are used to set safety stock and service levels.

We next consider the (Q, R) model. It is the core model for continuous review systems with stochastic demand. Both Q and R are decision variables, and two approaches are used to calculate them: a managerial approach and an optimization approach. The concepts of implied shortage cost and exchange curves are presented too. We conclude the continuous review system section with base stock and two-bin systems, which have widespread application in industry.

The discussion of periodic review systems is initiated by revisiting the EOQ model. Next, the leading periodic review model (S, T) is analyzed. There are two decision variables— the target inventory and review period—and demand is stochastic. For the analysis we use the managerial approach by setting a service level. The special case of optional replenishment concludes the section.

In the control decision section we present a practical methodology for controlling a multi-item inventory system. A major tool supporting the methodology for ABC analysis is Pareto analysis. Both theory and application are presented. Individual item control using a periodic review policy and material balance equations is appropriate for A items. Mass control is used for B and C items, where continuous review is applied along with the concept of the control triangle.

We conclude the chapter by discussing software for inventory systems and evolution of such systems.

ADDITIONAL PROBLEMS

6.105. In discussing the model for the infinite replenishment rate, we treated demand as a continuous variable. If Q^* is large, that approach is quite satisfactory, and we round Q^* to the nearest integer. However, it is instructive to examine the case where integrality of demand is directly accounted for. To do so, instead of equating $[dK(Q)/dQ] = 0$, we work with the first difference of K, i.e., $\Delta K(Q) = K(Q) - K(Q - 1)$. The value of Q^* is obtained by satisfying the following two difference equations:

$$\Delta K(Q^*) < 0 \qquad \Delta K(Q^* + 1) \geq 0$$

Show that if no shortages are allowed, then Q^* is the largest Q for which $Q(Q - 1) < 2AD/h$.

6.106. The one-time decision model was developed using a cost minimization approach. However, a profit maximization model can also be obtained. In addition to the notations in Section 3.1, let c be the unit cost, v be selling price per item, π_0 be the loss of goodwill in case of shortage in addition to lost profit, and w be the price obtained for any unit remaining at the end of the period ($w < c$). Show that the optimum value of Q is given by

$$F(Q^*) = \frac{c - w}{v + \pi_0 - w}$$

6.107. For the case of EOQ with backlog, discuss the impact on Q^* and b^* of the values of $h, \pi, \hat{\pi}$.

6.108. For the case of EOQ with backlog, show that for $\hat{\pi} = 0$ and $\pi > 0$ the optimal policy is either no shortages allowed, or the item is not stocked at all.

6.109. Repeat Problem 6.107 for the case of EPQ with backlog.

6.110. Repeat Problem 6.108 for the case of EPQ with backlog.

6.111. Presidential Electrical Co. (PEC) manufactures personal computer motherboards. The demand for T686 motherboards is constant and known to be 12,000 pieces for next year. A completed motherboard consists of the printed board, 4 SIMM modules, 16 type AIC chips, and 4 type BIC chips. The annual inventory holding cost rate is estimated at 20 percent. The basic inventory policy of PEC is that no shortages are allowed for any part.

    (a) PEC purchases SIMM modules from a supplier; the price is $30.00 per module. The cost to place an order for SIMM modules is $100.00. What is the economic order quantity? What is the average annual cost?

    (b) There is a production line to print the T686 motherboards. It is also used for other products. To set up for T686 boards costs $150.00, and its capacity is 30,000 pieces per year. What is the economic lot size? What will be the average inventory level for the printed motherboards?

    (c) Chip A is purchased from a distributor with an order cost of $50.00. The associated cost per unit is as follows (all-units discount).

Unit cost	$2.00	$2.80	$1.60	$1.50
Order quantity (Q)	$Q < 3000$	$3000 \le Q < 6000$	$6000 \le Q < 9000$	$9000 \le Q$

    Determine the optimal ordering policy. What is the average annual inventory cost?

    (d) The cost to place an order for chip B is $75.00, and the unit cost is $3.00. Determine the optimal inventory policy if no more than $20,000.00 can be invested in inventory at any point in time for those two types of IC chips. Determine the optimal lot size for each item. What is the average annual inventory cost for each item? (Assume chip A costs $1.60 regardless of the quantity ordered.)

6.112. Apex Stereo produces many different stereo units. The biggest seller is the MX-100 with 6000 units demanded constantly throughout the year. Each system has one CD component, which can be purchased from either of two suppliers. Supplier A offers an incremental discount policy; an order of 500 or less will cost $20.00 each, and units in excess of 500 cost $19.90. Supplier B offers an all-units discount with quantities up to 500 costing $20.00 each, but if the order is for more than 500 units, all units are $19.95. The cost to place an order to either supplier is $100, and the inventory carrying cost rate is 20 percent. Your boss asks you to make a recommendation as to which supplier should be used and what the order quantity should be. What is your recommendation?

6.113. Consider Problem 6.112, regarding Apex Stereo. Because of quality inspection of incoming parts, the order quantity must be one of the following: 125, 250, 375, 500, 62, 750, 875, 1000, 1125, 1250, 1375, or 1500. Determine which supplier should be chosen for each of these quantities.

6.114. In some cities in Europe there is a "day market." This is a channel to market fresh produce, fruit, and vegetables. The merchants assemble their stands in the morning, usually in one of the city squares. By 2:00 or 3:00 P.M. the stands are dismantled, the square is washed, and no trace of the market is left.

    To avoid traffic jams during the day, the city allows supply trucks to deliver their merchandise only once a day—early in the morning. No replenishment can be done during the day.

    One of the merchants in this market can order n items for her stand. Let the jth item have a cost of c_j dollars and selling price of v_j dollars per pound. The city is committed to buy any unsold quantity at the end of the day and give it to the food bank. The city will pay w_j dollars per pound (obviously, $w_j < c_j$). The demand for an item is stochastic with probability density function $f_j(D_j)$. The merchant has only M dollars to purchase merchandise.

Find the optimal quantity per item the merchant has to purchase.

MINICASE: THE VENUS MANUFACTURING COMPANY

Venus is a family-owned manufacturing company in the cosmetics business. It is located in a small town in southern France. The company was founded after the Second World War, when Pierre—the head of the family—returned from the war. He correctly predicted that cosmetics would again become a major French product.

Venus started as a "basement industry." It is still family owned but now employs 500 people and is run by the founder's children—Jeorge and Charlotte. Jeorge handles marketing and finance, and Charlotte is operations manager. They have a number of product lines; one, facial cream, is very successful and sells all over Europe. Sales have increased in recent years, as customs barriers fell due to the European Common Market.

One of their facial creams, Le-Jeune, is especially appealing to young women. A small jar sells for $15, and the production cost is $10. The jars are shipped in boxes of 25 each.

Charlotte is a very open-minded manager, and from time to time she challenges her own operation. In line with this, she invited Wilhelm, a Swiss consultant, to advise her on the inventory policy. As a starter, Wilhelm examined the inventory policy for Le-Jeune. The current policy is to have 40 boxes in stock. Inventory holding cost is $2 per jar per year. To smooth production, delivery time of Le-Jeune is 14 days. Wilhelm was told that demand during delivery time is normally distributed, with $N(40, 200)$. Annual demand is 1300 boxes (i.e., 32,500 jars). Wilhelm gave Charlotte a proposal based on a 90 percent fill rate, where set-up cost for a production run is $100.

Wilhelm's proposal encountered opposition from Morris, the plant manager. He claimed "I surely understand that sometimes, we cannot supply a customer's demand because of shortage. However, any inventory policy that assumes a priori shortage is unacceptable. This policy will cause lost customers and lost goodwill."

Wilhelm responded that his analysis revealed a shortage cost of $10 per jar, and his proposal based on a 90 percent fill rate is a good compromise. Morris would not accept this argument and asked Wilhelm to rework his analysis based on a 99.5 percent fill rate: "I don't care if it costs $50,000 per year."

Charlotte overruled Morris and accepted Wilhelm's proposal. However, after a while she felt the estimate of lead-time demand used in Wilhelm's inventory policy was wrong. The average looked right, but the standard deviation was apparently underestimated. As a consequence, service level was much lower than planned. Wilhelm was called back and asked to resubmit his proposal with service level of 99.5 percent.

Wilhelm analyzed the sales data and found that Le-Jeune sells mainly to 25 distributors spread across Western Europe. The weekly demand for each distributor has a normal distribution with an average of one box and variance of eight. Furthermore, orders from distributors arrive uniformly at Venus. Wilhelm worked out his numbers and identified the cause for the erroneous demand estimate on which he based his proposal. He prepared an updated proposal for inventory policy for Le-Jeune.

Venus purchases four of the ingredients that go into Le-Jeune from CHEMI, a company located in central France. Because of the secrecy of the Le-Jeune formula, these ingredients are labeled α, β, γ, and δ.

Venus sends a truck to pick up the material and bring it to its warehouse. One trip of the truck costs $490, and it can carry 4.5 tons. Inventory holding cost for these ingredients is 25 percent annually. The weekly demand for each ingredient and its cost per lb are as follows:

Ingredient	Weekly demand (lb)	Cost per pound
α	50	211
β	30	44
γ	102	63
δ	73	102

On one of the recent trips to CHEMI, Robert, the truck driver, overheard that CHEMI intends to raise the price of α by 10 percent.

By now, Charlotte is totally confused, and she needs your help.

(a) What is the original inventory policy submitted by Wilhelm (for 90 percent fill rate)?

(b) What is the extra cost incurred by accepting Morris's request for 99.5 percent fill rate?

(c) Analyze the cause that made Venus err in estimating demand.

(d) What is the updated inventory proposed by Wilhelm? What pdf did he use?

(e) How can Venus reduce inventory costs?

(f) Propose a purchase policy for the ingredients α, β, γ, and δ.

(g) There is a proposal "rolling around" Venus to send a smaller truck to CHEMI. Its payload is only 1 ton; however, the trip costs only $200. What is your recommendation?

(h) Due to the rumors of cost increase for α, how much should Venus purchase now?

Write a memo to Charlotte and respond to all of the above issues. Properly show all derivations.

8 REFERENCES

Arrow, K. A., Harris, T. E., and Marschak, J., "Optimal Inventory Policy," *Econometrica,* 19, 250–272, 1951.

Bellman, R. E., Elicksberg, I., Gross, O., "On the Optimal Inventory Equation," *Management Science,* 2, 83–104, 1955.

Brown, R. G., *Decision Rules for Inventory Management,* Dryden Press, Hinsdale, IL, 1967.

Churchman, C. W., Ackoff, R. L., and Arnoff, E. L., *Introduction to Operations Research,* John Wiley & Sons, New York, 1957.

Dickie, H. F., "ABC Inventory Analysis Shoots for Dollars," *Factory Management and Maintenance,* 1951.

Dvoretzky, A., Kiefer, J., and Wolfowitz, J., "The Inventory Problems: I. Case of Known Distributions of Demand," *Econometrica,* 20, 187–222, 1952a.

Dvoretzky, A., Kiefer, J., and Wolfowitz, J., "The Inventory Problem: II. Case of Unknown Distributions of Demand," *Econometrica,* 20, 450–466, 1952b.

Erhardt, R., "The Power Approximation for Computing (s, S) Inventory Policies," *Management Science,* 25, 777–786, 1979.

Freeland, J. R. and Porteus, E. L., "Evaluating the Effectiveness of a New Method of Computing Approximately Optimal (s, S) Inventory Policies," *Operations Research,* 28, 353–364, 1980.

Gardner, E. S., "A Top Down Approach to Modelling US Navy Inventories," *Interfaces,* 17, 4, 1–7, 1967.

Goyal, S. K., "Optimum Ordering Policy for a Multi Item Single Supplier System," *Operational Research Quarterly,* 25, 2, 293–298, 1974.

Hadley, G. and Whitin, T. M., *Analysis of Inventory Systems,* Prentice-Hall, Englewood Cliffs, NJ, 1963.

Harris, F. W., "How Many Parts to Make at Once, Factory," *The Magazine of Management,* 10, 2, 135–136, 152, 1913.

Harris, F., "Operations and Costs," *Factory Management Series,* Shaw, Chicago, 48–52, 1915.

Herron, D., "Industrial Engineering Application of ABC Curve," *AIIE Transactions,* 8, June 1976.

Iglehart, D. L., "Optimality of (s, S) Policies in the Infinite Horizon Dynamic Inventory Problem," *Management Science,* 9, 259–267, 1963.

Kleutghen, P. P. and McGee, J. C., "Development and Implementation of an Integrated Inventory Management Program at Pfizer Pharmaceuticals," *Interfaces,* 15, 1, 69–87, 1985.

Kumar, S. and Arora, S., "Optimal Ordering Policy for a Multi-item, Single Supplier System with Constant Demand Rates," *Journal of the Operational Research Society,* 41, 4, 345–349, 1990.

Osteryoung, J. A., McCarty, D. E., and Reinhart, W. J., "Use of the EOQ Model for Inventory Analysis," *Production and Inventory Management,* 27, 3, 39–45, 1986.

Peterson, R. and Silver, E. A., *Decision Systems for Inventory Management and Production Planning,* John Wiley & Sons, New York, 1979.

Scarf, H. E., "The Optimality of (s, S) Policies in the Dynamic Inventory Problem," in Arrow, K. D., Karlin, S., and Suppes, P., eds., *Mathematical Methods in the Social Sciences,* Stanford, CA, Stanford University Press, 1960.

Silver, E. A. and Meal, H. C., "A Heuristic for Selecting Lot Size Quantities for the Case of a Deterministic Time Varying Demand Rate and Discrete Opportunities for Replenishment," *Production and Inventory Management,* 14, 64–74, 1973.

Wagner, H. M. and Whitin, T. M., "Dynamic Version of the Economic Lot Size Model," *Management Science,* 5, 1, 89–96, 1958.

Wilson, R. H., "A Scientific Routine for Stock Control," *Harvard Business Review,* 13, 116–128, 1934.

Woodruff, D., Treece, J. E., Bhargava, S. W., and Miller, K. L., "Saturn," *Business Week,* 86–91, August 17, 1992.

CHAPTER
7

PRODUCTION, CAPACITY, AND MATERIAL PLANNING

In its simplest form, the relationship between the market (customer) and the production facility is iterative. Market demand prompts the production facility to manufacture the product, which is delivered to the market to satisfy the demand. When more demand is generated, the process repeats (Figure 7-1).

In some cases this cycle is performed almost instantaneously. Recall our doughnut shop example of Chapter 6. The doughnuts, in principle, can be made whenever a customer steps in. Changes in demand can be handled very easily as long as the raw material is available.

In other cases, the cycle takes much more time. Manufacturing cars, for instance, requires time for production to respond to changes in demand. A car is a complex product, and production is not immediate; components of the car must be manufactured, raw materials must be purchased, and the car has to be assembled. Much planning activity, among other efforts, is needed within the production component of Figure 7-1. In this chapter, we discuss planning of production, capacity, and material.

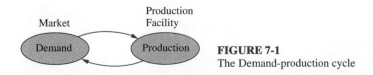

FIGURE 7-1
The Demand-production cycle

319

1 INTRODUCTION

Many products are not single entities. They are composed of subassemblies and parts, some purchased and some manufactured. One step in manufacturing a product is a production plan. A production plan specifies quantities of each final product (end item), subassemblies, and parts needed at distinct points in time. Two requirements for generating a production plan are estimates for end-product demand and a master production schedule (MPS) used to create a detailed production plan.

Estimates for end product demand are obtained using any of the forecasting approaches discussed in Chapter 4. Given a forecast, the required quantity of each component that makes up the end product is derived. Here we make a distinction between **dependent demand** and **independent demand** (see also Chapter 6, Section 1.2). Independent demand means no relationship exists between the need for an item and any other item. (This is not the same as statistical independence.) Typically, independent-demand items are end-items, where the demand is dependent on market conditions. On the other hand, dependent demand implies that the need for an item is created by the need for another item. Note that we *forecast* independent demand, but we *plan* dependent demand.

Manufacturing occurs only when dependent-demand items are needed. Therefore, the inventory models developed for independent-demand items (Chapter 6) should be modified for dependent demand.

The **master production schedule** (MPS) is a delivery plan for the manufacturing organization. It includes exact amounts and delivery timings for each end product. It is derived from the demand estimates, but is not necessarily equal to them. MPS must account for manufacturing constraints and finished-goods inventory. A major manufacturing constraint is *capacity*. Therefore, to check feasibility of the MPS, an initial capacity evaluation is made. This is known as **rough-cut capacity planning.** If available capacity is insufficient, the MPS is changed.

Breaking the MPS into a production schedule for each component of an end-item is achieved by the **material requirements planning** (MRP) system. The MRP system determines material requirements and timings for each phase of production. Material shortage is another major manufacturing constraint. Supplementing this process is detailed **capacity planning.**

The production planning process described above is shown in Figure 7-2. The production planning process has a hierarchical structure—from demand estimates to MRP. Another way to view this process is to consider it as having a "front end" and a "back end." The front end provides an interface with customer demand, and the back end interfaces with the execution of the production plan. MRP drives the back end: It generates the plan for meeting dependent demand.

The remainder of this chapter contains an in-depth discussion of the various phases and issues of the production planning process. We start with MPS, followed with capacity planning, and culminate with a discussion of the characteristics of MRP systems.

SECTION 1 PROBLEMS

7.1. What is a production plan and what are its inputs?

7.2. The Julo Company manufactures felt-tipped markers. Discuss the difference in the demand for their black felt-tipped pen (one of 126 products they produce) and their demand for felt.

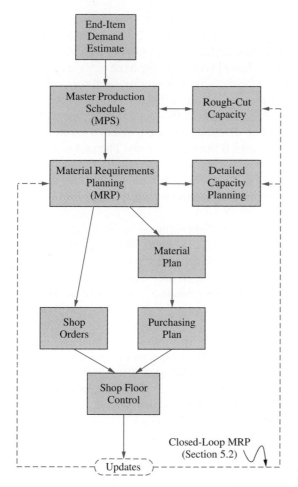

FIGURE 7-2
Production planning process

2   MASTER PRODUCTION SCHEDULING

2.1   Overview

A master production schedule is generated either from the aggregate plan, if available, or directly from demand estimates for individual end-items. If the MPS is generated from an aggregate plan, it must be disaggregated into individual products. An aggregate production plan represents a firm's aggregate measure of manufacturing output, whereas a master production schedule is a plan of production—how many finished products are to be produced and when they will be produced.

A master production schedule should not be confused with a forecast. A *forecast* represents an estimate of demand, whereas a *master production schedule* constitutes a plan of production. They are not necessarily the same, although their formats might look similar. The difference is that a production schedule considers existing inventory, capacity constraints, availability of material, and production lead time; therefore, production quantities will be shifted on the time axis as needed.

In developing an MPS, the nature of the product and the market should be considered. Three types of product–market environments are customarily identified as related to MPS: make-to-stock (MTS), make-to-order (MTO), and assemble-to-order (ATO). The MTS company produces in batches and carries finished-products inventories for most of its end-items. The small-appliance industry, in which manufacturers build inventories for future sales, is an example. The advantage is that customer delivery (delivery off the shelf) times are minimized at the expense of holding finished-goods inventory. In this environment, the MPS is performed at the end-item level. It is composed of demand forecasts, adjusted for finished-products inventory. Production begins before demand is known precisely. The make-to-stock environment is typical of companies that produce relatively few but standard items and have a relatively accurate demand forecast. Typically, make-to-stock companies produce a small number of end-items from a large number of raw-material items (including purchased items), as shown schematically in Figure 7-3.

At the other extreme is the make-to-order environment (Figure 7-3). No finished-goods inventory is carried, and customer orders are backlogged. A due date for each product is negotiated with the customer, and the end-item is then placed in the master schedule. Production does not begin until the order is in hand. The make-to-order environment usually has a relatively large number of product configurations, and the exact needs of a specific customer are difficult to anticipate. Jet engine manufacturing is a good example; jet engines are produced only in response to a customer order. Usually, the number of end-items and subassemblies exceeds the number of raw material items; the same raw materials are used for many products. The MPS consists of firm delivery dates to customers and can be regarded as order-driven. MRP plans the production, and demand forecasts are for the raw-materials level.

The assemble-to-order environment lies in a middle ground. A large number of end-items are assembled from a relatively small set of standard subassemblies, or modules. Automobile manufacture is an example. A dealer order specifies which options out of many are desired. The product structure has an hourglass shape (see Figure 7-3). The large number of end-items makes forecasting requirements extremely cumbersome. It makes more sense to develop the MPS at the module rather than at the end-item level. Modules are manufactured to stock, and final assembly is performed only when a customer order arrives. Thus, a

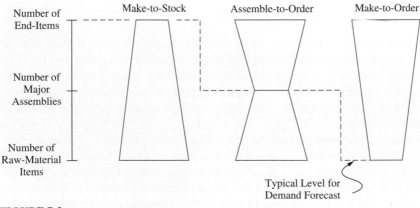

FIGURE 7-3
Product–market environments

fair compromise between inventory-holding cost and product flexibility and delivery time is achieved.

Assemble-to-order environments often have two master schedules. In addition to the MPS, there is also a final assembly schedule (FAS), performed at the end-item level. The MPS governs the production of modules, and as such it is forecast-driven. Final assembly scheduling governs end-item assembly and is order-driven. There are two manufacturing lead times: MPS lead time and FAS lead time. When a customer places an order, only the FAS lead time is noticed.

Example 7-1. MPS. As a hypothetical example for MPS, consider SIBUL Company. SIBUL manufactures a relatively large number of phones, which differ mainly in color and some features. Four specific phones are chosen, namely, three desktop models (labeled A, B, and C) and one wall telephone (D). A weekly MPS for this line of products is shown in Table 7-1. At this point, the MPS is equal to the demand forecast for each model.

According to this production schedule, model A is produced in uniform quantities of 1000 units per week in January and 2000 in February, whereas the quantities for the other models are lumpy. However, the monthly production quantity is stable at 12,200 units, which means that a stable work force is maintained—a very desirable feature. Note that the quantities for each week show the completion time for the units; i.e., the number in each cell is the quantity that should be completed by the end of the week associated with that cell.

TABLE 7-1
Weekly MPS

	January				February			
	Week				Week			
Product	**1**	**2**	**3**	**4**	**5**	**6**	**7**	**8**
Model A	1000	1000	1000	1000	2000	2000	2000	2000
Model B	—	500	500	—	350	—	—	350
Model C	1500	1500	1500	1500	1000	—	1000	1000
Model D	600	—	600	—	—	300	200	—
Weekly total	3100	3000	3600	2500	3350	2300	3200	3350
Monthly total	12,200				12,200			

2.2 MPS Planning

Time-phased records are used for MPS planning and maintenance. Product quantities are spread along time slots, usually called time buckets. Time buckets are usually one month or one week long. These records can be produced easily by a computer, and serve as an input to the MRP process. Planning the MPS resembles the process we used for inventory control (Chapter 6), where the material balance equation was the basic tool. The major difference for the MPS is that we are dealing with end-items, so that some modifications are necessary.

Recall that an MPS is a forecast adjusted for inventory, customer orders, production constraints, etc. Therefore, an MPS plan must have entries to break into a production plan. Typically, these entries include

Forecast—a time-phased delivery forecast for an end-item.

Customer orders—quantities for which there are firm customer orders and a promised delivery date.

End-of-period inventory—on-hand inventory at the end of the time bucket.

MPS—end-item quantity whose production has to be completed in a certain time bucket. Note that because of lead time, production of this quantity must start earlier.

Current inventory—inventory level at the beginning of the first period.

To obtain the MPS plan, a table format is used. The columns represent the time buckets and the rows include the entries. We demonstrate the MPS planning process and the required derivations in the following example.

Example 7-2. MPS Planning. Suppose we want to prepare the MPS plan for model A of the previous example. The nature of the product–market environment is such that this is a make-to-stock environment. (The same procedure is used for assemble-to-order.) We assume that no safety stock is held for the end-item. To show the impact of different production policies, two specific policies are considered: batch and lot-for-lot production. Table 7-2 shows the initial data. The time bucket is one week. All other entries are calculated; we discuss the method of calculation next.

To calculate the inventory and MPS entries, we use the following version of the material-balance equation:

$$I_t = I_{t-1} + Q_t - \max\{F_t, O_t\}$$

where I_t = end-item inventory at the end of week t

Q_t = manufactured quantity to be completed in week t (an element of the MPS)

F_t = forecast for week t

O_t = customer orders to be delivered in week t

We can verify that this equation represents a material balance: The current inventory level equals the previous one, plus the scheduled production, minus the amount expected to be delivered. Because this is a make-to-stock environment, we expect to deliver the forecasted amount, unless customer orders exceed the forecast, i.e., $\max\{F_t, O_t\}$. Q_t is the only decision variable in the equation; the rest are either given or calculated values.

Using the material-balance equation, we can evaluate the values of I_t and timing of Q_t. We start with a batch production policy.

TABLE 7-2
MPS planning—initial data

		Week							
Current inventory = 1600	**1**	**2**	**3**	**4**	**5**	**6**	**7**	**8**
F_t	1000	1000	1000	1000	2000	2000	2000	2000
O_t	1200	800	300	200	100	0	0	0

Batch production. Suppose that the batch size per time bucket is 2500. The procedure is as follows:

1. Use the material-balance equation to evaluate I_t, assuming $Q_t = 0$.

$$I_t = \max\{0, I_{t-1}\} - \max\{F_t, O_t\}$$

$$Q_t = \begin{cases} 0 & \text{if } I_t > 0 \\ 2500 & \text{otherwise} \end{cases}$$

2. If $Q_t > 0$, reevaluate I_t by $I_t = Q_t + I_{t-1} - \max\{F_t, O_t\}$.

As an example, consider the first two weeks:

Week 1:

$$I_1 = \max\{0, 1600\} - \max\{1000, 1200\} = 400 > 0$$

i.e., $Q_1 = 0$.

Week 2:

$$I_2 = \max\{0, 400\} - \max\{1000, 800\} = -600 < 0$$

i.e., schedule $Q_2 = 2500$ and reevaluate I_2.

$$I_2 = 2500 + 400 - \max\{1000, 800\} = 1900$$

Values for I_t and Q_t for the remaining weeks are shown in Table 7-3, where the decision values are boldfaced and the calculated values are underlined.

When the MPS is based on forecasts (e.g., in make-to-stock and assemble-to-order systems), a concept called **available-to-promise** (ATP) is important. Given a master schedule and end-item inventory, a certain amount can be assigned to customer orders, with the remainder *available* to meet future customer demand. Thus, when a new order arrives, ATP will tell whether the schedule contains enough available items to deliver the order on time. If not, the order has to be revised or forgone. We emphasize that MPS is generated using F_t, O_t, and I_t. However, ATP does not consider forecasts, but the MPS decision, initial inventory, and customer orders. The importance of ATP lies in the fact that it may give the sales staff the flexibility to promise more accurate delivery dates when new orders come in.

In principle, the ATP value is the difference between Q_t for a certain week and the cumulative value of customer orders between this week and the next week, for which $Q_t > 0$. For the first week, we add the value of the current inventory to Q_t. To illustrate, consider the first four weeks.

TABLE 7-3
MPS plan

				Week				
Current inventory = 1600	**1**	**2**	**3**	**4**	**5**	**6**	**7**	**8**
F_t	1000	1000	1000	1000	2000	2000	2000	2000
O_t	1200	800	300	200	100	0	0	0
I_t	<u>400</u>	<u>1900</u>	<u>900</u>	<u>2400</u>	<u>400</u>	<u>900</u>	<u>1400</u>	<u>1900</u>
MPS		**2500**		**2500**		**2500**	**2500**	**2500**

TABLE 7-4
Final MPS plan for batch production policy

Current inventory = 1600	Week							
	1	**2**	**3**	**4**	**5**	**6**	**7**	**8**
F_t	1000	1000	1000	1000	2000	2000	2000	2000
O_t	1200	800	300	200	100	0	0	0
I_t	400	1900	900	2400	400	900	1400	1900
MPS		2500		2500		2500	2500	2500
ATP	400	1400		2200		2500	2500	2500

1. ATP $= 1600 + 0 - 1200 = 400$
2. ATP $= 2500 - (800 + 300) = 1400$
3. Covered by the ATP of week 2
4. ATP $= 2500 - (200 + 100) = 2200$

ATP can have only positive values.

    The results are shown in Table 7-4. Whenever a new order comes in, ATP must be updated.

    Lot-for-lot production. Under this policy, the amount manufactured each week is exactly equal to the expected weekly demand, adjusted for inventory. The final MPS plan is shown in Table 7-5. Note that for this particular item, the lot-for-lot policy gives a smoother production than the batch policy. However, smoothing production should not be done at this level. This brings us back to the aggregate plan. The four different telephones require basically the same manufacturing resources. The production smoothing performed there will maintain work force and other resources at uniform levels, even though production for an individual product is not level.

2.3 MPS Modeling

Although the concept of master production scheduling is easily understood, there is little consensus on how to model the MPS problem. Furthermore, the nature of the problem is

TABLE 7-5
Final MPS for lot-for-lot production policy

Current inventory = 1600	Week							
	1	**2**	**3**	**4**	**5**	**6**	**7**	**8**
F_t	1000	1000	1000	1000	2000	2000	2000	2000
O_t	1200	800	300	200	100	0	0	0
I_t	400	0	0	0	0	0	0	0
MPS		600	1000	1000	2000	2000	2000	2000
ATP	400	0	700	800	1900	2000	2000	2000

different for make-to-stock, assemble-to-order, and make-to-order environments. In this section we show models of the master scheduling problem for make-to-stock and assemble-to-order.

2.3.1 MAKE-TO-STOCK MODELING. In MTS we have a forecast for the end-item, and we must choose the lot size for the last production step (usually the final assembly). Thus, it is a complex version of the lot-sizing problem discussed in Chapter 6. Here, too, we trade off set-up cost and finished-goods inventory cost. The multiproduct environment and limited production capacity increase the complexity of the problem. Because of the capacity constraint, there is dependency among the item's lot sizes: Therefore, solving independently for each item will not likely yield a feasible solution.

The mathematical formulation of this problem is as follows:

Let

Q_{it} = production quantity of product i in period t
I_{it} = inventory of product i at end of period t $(i = 1,\ldots,n; t = 1,\ldots,T)$
D_{it} = demand (requirements) for product i in time period t
a_i = production hours per unit of product i
h_i = inventory holding cost per unit of product i per time period
A_i = set-up cost for product i
G_t = production hours available in period t
y_{it} indicate whether a set-up cost must be incurred for product i in period t (i.e., $Q_{it} > 0$

implies that $y_{it} = 1$, and $Q_{it} = 0$ implies $y_{it} = 0$)

An integer programming formulation is

$$\text{Minimize} \sum_{i=1}^{n} \sum_{t=1}^{T} (A_i y_{it} + h_i I_{it})$$

subject to

$$I_{i,t-1} + Q_{it} - I_{it} = D_{it} \quad \text{for all } (i, t) \tag{1}$$

$$\sum_{i=1}^{n} a_i Q_{it} \leq G_t \quad \text{for all } t \tag{2}$$

$$Q_{it} - y_{it} \sum_{k=1}^{T} D_{it} \leq 0 \quad \text{for all } (i, t) \tag{3}$$

$$Q_{it} \geq 0, I_{it} \geq 0, y_{it} = 0, 1 \quad \text{for all } (i, t) \tag{4}$$

The objective function minimizes the sum of set-up cost and inventory-holding cost, which are all the relevant costs for this model.

The first constraint is a material-balance equation. The second is a capacity constraint, and the third guarantees that production from one period will not exceed total cumulative demand. The last constraint makes all variables nonnegative, which implies that no shortages are allowed.

The capacity constraint (2) can be determined by final assembly or any other bottleneck operation. Additional features such as overtime, subcontracting, and demand backlogging can be added to the model in a fashion similar to the LP models discussed in Chapter 5.

For many real-world problems, the number of variables and constraints explodes, which prohibits finding an optimum solution. For an efficient heuristic for solving this problem, see Maes and Van Wassenhove (1986).

2.3.2   ASSEMBLE-TO-ORDER MODELING.

In an ATO environment there are two master schedules: the MPS at the modules level and the final assembly schedule at the end-item level. The MPS is forecast-driven while the FAS is order-driven. This may cause a mismatch between the modules produced from the forecast and the modules actually required by customer orders. As a result, inventory is generated, and again we have to trade off overage cost and shortage cost. There are two types of shortage cost: lost sales and backorders. Baker[1] proposes a formulation for this problem under the following assumptions:

- A known MPS and initial inventory levels determine how much of each module will be available in each period for a T-period horizon.
- Customer demands are known throughout the planning horizon and backorders are permitted.

If there are m module types and n product types, the following information can be obtained from the MPS and product structure: Q_{kt} is the quantity of module k produced in period t, and g_{kj} is the number of modules of type k required to assemble order j, which includes one type of product.

There are two decision variables: I_{kt} (inventory of module k at the end of period t) and

$$y_{jt} = \begin{cases} 1 & \text{if order } j \text{ is assembled and delivered in period } t \\ 0 & \text{otherwise} \end{cases}$$

If multiple orders for a given product type were demanded, each one would be represented by a distinct index j.

Also, let h_k represent the inventory-holding cost per period for one unit of module k and π_{jt} represent the penalty cost if order j is satisfied in period t. Thus, if order j is due in period t' ($t' < t$) and satisfied in period t, it accrues a penalty π_{jt}.

The assumption is that assembly and delivery of an order occur in the same period. For the case of infinite capacity, this is a plausible assumption. If there is a shortage or capacity is limited, the order is delivered at a later period t, and accrues a penalty π_{jt}. Also, in case we hedge against capacity shortage in period t and manufacture order j in an earlier period to be delivered in t, we assess a penalty cost π_{jt} that reflects the holding cost for the order.

Let

G_t equal the number of assembly hours available in period t and let

a_j equal the number of hours required by order j

The mixed integer model is

$$\text{Minimize} \sum_{k=1}^{m} \sum_{t=1}^{L} h_k I_{kt} + \sum_{j=1}^{n} \sum_{t=1}^{L} \pi_{jt} y_{jt}$$

---

[1] Adapted from Baker (in Graves et al. (1993)) with the kind permission of Elsevier Science-NL, Sara Burgerhartstraat 25, 1055 KV Amsterdam, The Netherlands.

subject to

$$I_{kt} = I_{k,t-1} + Q_{kt} - \sum_{j=1}^{n} g_{kj} y_{jt} \quad \text{for all } (k, t)$$

$$\sum_{j=1}^{n} a_j y_{jt} \leq G_t \quad \text{for all } t$$

$$\sum_{t=1}^{L} y_{jt} = 1 \quad \text{for all } j$$

$$I_{kt} \geq 0 \qquad y_{j,t} = 0, 1 \quad \text{for all } j, k, t$$

The first two constraints are the familiar material-balance equations and capacity constraint, respectively. The last constraint guarantees that order j is made in only one period.

In this model we tacitly assume that the MPS is known for T periods and firm orders are known for L periods, where $L < T$. Allocation decisions are made for the first L periods, and when new orders come in, further allocation is made. L is called the accumulation period, and a longer L would lead to better decisions. Again, the number of variables and constraints grow explosively for real-world problems.

2.4   Capacity Planning

So far, MPS has not considered detailed capacity, a crucial element required for its implementation. The production facility, composed of work centers, machines, handling equipment, etc., has a finite capacity. Only a certain number of telephones can be assembled per week in an assembly station. Capacity can be measured in terms of units of product a facility can produce per unit of time. Another typical unit of measurement is the hour. If the MPS calls for higher production rates than are available, we have capacity shortages, resulting in late deliveries. We must either increase the capacity (if possible) or adjust the MPS. On the other hand, if the MPS calls for a lower production rate relative to the available capacity, we have idle capacity. Given that MPS reflects the market demand, we should avoid producing to stock just to increase the use of the facility. It is a very costly way to achieve high utilization. If the excess capacity will be long-term, a reduction in capacity is appropriate. The capacity of a production facility, in which the product flows through a number of workstations, is determined by its bottleneck operation. A bottleneck is an operation that limits output.

There are two levels at which capacity is evaluated: the MPS level and the MRP level (see Figure 7-2). At the MPS level we perform a quick check of the total capacity to find the aggregate feasibility of the MPS. This check can identify capacity violation but cannot guarantee implementation; it is usually performed at a department or workcenter level. We therefore call it rough-cut capacity planning (RCCP). However, a feasible schedule at the MPS level does not necessarily guarantee a feasible schedule at the MRP level. At this lower level subassemblies and components are considered, which reflects upon the use of individual machines or assembly operation. We therefore perform here another capacity check or *detailed* capacity planning, usually labeled CRP (for capacity requirement planning). The two processes are similar in nature.

The term *capacity planning* is somewhat misleading. Both RCCP and CRP are information tools rather than decision-making tools. They indicate which capacity constraints are violated, but they do not provide guidance for resolving the conflict. We use the following example to illustrate.

Example 7-3. Capacity planning. Consider the MPS of Example 7-1 for the month of January. The time-phased quantities for the four telephone models are given in Table 7-6.

TABLE 7-6
Capacity example

(a)

	MPS			
	Week			
	1	**2**	**3**	**4**
Model A	1000	1000	1000	1000
Model B		500	500	
Model C	1500	1500	1500	1500
Model D	600		600	

(b)

	Bill of capacity (min)	
	Assembly	**Inspection**
Model A	20	2.0
Model B	24	2.5
Model C	22	2.0
Model D	25	2.4

(c)

	Capacity required (hr)				
	Week				
	1	**2**	**3**	**4**	**Available capacity per week**
Assembly	1133	1083	1333	883	1200
Inspection	107	104	128	83	110

Production of the telephones requires an assembly workcenter and an inspection station. Table 7-6(b) shows the **bill of capacity,** i.e., the operation time per unit (in minutes) required in each workcenter. The bill of capacity allows us to convert the MPS quantities into a profile of capacity requirements. Weekly capacity requirements are shown for each week in part (c) of Table 7-6. For example, the required capacity for week 1 is calculated as follows:

Assembly: $1000 \times 20 + 1{,}500 \times 22 + 600 \times 25 = 68{,}000$ min $= 1133.33$ hr approximately 1133 hr.

Inspection: $1000 \times 2.0 + 1500 \times 2.0 + 600 \times 2.4 = 6440$ min $= 107.33$ hr approximately 107 hr.

      Capacity is measured in hours and not in units per hour. The available capacity per week is 1200 hours for the assembly work center and 110 hours for the inspection station. It can be immediately observed that capacity constraints are violated for week 3 for both assembly and inspection operations. Capacity planning provides a signal that some capacity restriction has been violated, but it does not show how to respond to this capacity problem.

      One response is to reschedule assembly quantities. For example, if we move 600 units from week 3 to week 4, we obtain the load profile shown in Table 7-7. Thus, the capacity violation has been removed. However, neither RCCP nor CRP indicates ways to do this.

TABLE 7-7
Load profiles

	Week			
	1	**2**	**3**	**4**
Assembly	1133	1083	1083	1133
Inspection	107	104	104	107

      Because capacity planning is an information tool only, it is regarded as **infinite capacity** planning. Capacity violations are ignored, and must be removed externally. This infinite capacity feature is often cited as a major shortcoming of MRP systems. Overcoming this shortcoming is difficult. The combinatorial nature of this *NP-hard* problem (see Box 8-1) makes any solution algorithm hard to implement in real-life situations. In recent years, however, progress has been made in overcoming this difficulty (see Chapter 10).

      When a detailed bill of capacity is not available, a method called **capacity planning using overall factors** (CPOF) is used. The input required for this method is MPS data and planning factors derived from standards or historical data. Typically, these planning factors are total standard hours of machines or direct labor required to complete the manufacture (or assembly) of the end product. Applying these standard times to the MPS yields an estimate of the total required labor or machine hours per period. The next step is to allocate the total number of hours to each workcenter. This allocation is done using historical data on shop workloads, in which the load for each workcenter (machine) is expressed in percentages. These percentages are the overall factors used for capacity planning. (For further details, see Vollman, Berry, and Whybark (1992)).

      The advantage of the capacity planning procedures discussed lies in their limited data requirements. However, they ignore actual lead times, which results in workloads that do not consider delays at various work centers. Rough-cut capacity planning (RCCP) identifies obvious capacity violations so that adjustments can be made prior to detailed MRP calculations. Capacity requirements planning (CRP) identifies more subtle violations created by detailed MRP calculations. In either case, the master schedule must be revised in order to make plans feasible.

2.5   Capacity Modeling

Rather than using exact methods to overcome the tacit infinite-capacity assumption of RCCP and CRP, we could use heuristics. While heuristics do not guarantee an optimal solution, they do not suffer from the combinatorial explosion of solution-effort of exact methods.

One heuristic for finite-capacity planning is based on input/output (I/O) analysis and was developed by Karni.[2] It considers the relationship between capacity and lead time. In the standard MRP process, lead time is taken as a constant parameter, disregarding capacity levels. I/O analysis links the two for a specific work center. Let

G = work center capacity
R_t = work released to the center in period t
Q_t = production (output) from the workcenter in period t
W_t = work in process in period t
U_t = queue at the workcenter measured at the beginning of period t, prior to the release of work
L_t = lead time at the workcenter in period t

All the above entities, except L_t, are measured in common units such as hours or physical units. L_t is measured in weeks (or months). For example, $R_2 = 20$ means that work release in week 2 will require 20 workcenter hours (or 20 units, depending on the unit of measurement).

The planned releases R_t are obtained from the MRP process. Capacity G is given, and the rest of the entities are obtained through the heuristic. The I/O analysis traces lead-time behavior over time using the following equations:

$$Q_t = \min\{G, U_{t-1} + R_t\} \qquad \text{production level is the minimum of work available or capacity}$$

$$U_t = U_{t-1} + R_t - Q_t \qquad \text{changes in queue size}$$

$$W_t = U_{t-1} + R_t = U_t + Q_t$$

$$L_t = \frac{W_t}{G}$$

This model suggests that lead time is not constant, but can vary depending on production levels. Thus, the I/O model provides a more realistic approach to lead-time representation.

This model has two tacit assumptions: The production rate is constant for any positive WIP level, and actual production time is small compared to the time period; i.e., as long as capacity exists, any order released in this period is completed in this period. As we move to shorter time periods, processing time and material transfer intervals may invalidate this assumption.

The I/O model can be implemented using a spreadsheet. The spreadsheet can perform two types of analyses: lead-time analysis for a given G and R_t, and capacity analysis for a given lead time (say from the MRP). We use the following spreadsheet example to demonstrate these two analyses.

---

[2]Adapted from Karni (1982) with the kind permission of Taylor & Francis.

TABLE 7-8
I/O analysis

			Period				
	0	**1**	**2**	**3**	**4**	**5**	**6**
G		36	36	36	36	36	36
R_t		20	30	60	20	40	40
Q_t		30	30	36	36	36	36
U_t	10	0	0	24	8	12	16
W_t		30	30	60	44	48	52
L_t		0.83	0.83	1.67	1.22	1.33	1.44

Example 7-4. Capacity modeling. In our telephone manufacturing facility, the final operation is packaging, in which each telephone is placed in a carton. This is done manually, at "packaging tables." Each workstation like this has a weekly capacity of 36 hours. The spreadsheet format depicted in Table 7-8 presents lead-time calculations. Entries for G are in hours per week, lead time is in weeks, and the others are in hours.

We can see that lead time is not a constant but fluctuates between 0.83 weeks and 1.67 weeks. If the production lead time specified in the MRP is 2 weeks, the above capacity is adequate. Furthermore, by searching over potential values of capacity, we find that 2-week lead time can be achieved with 32 weekly hours. Or even better, we could shorten the lead time to 1.5 weeks.

SECTION 2 PROBLEMS

7.3. Describe the difference between the demand forecasts and the MPS of the Julo Company's felt-tipped markers.

7.4. Give one example of a manufacturing process that would lend itself to:

(a) An MTS environment

(b) An MTO environment

(c) An ATO environment

7.5. Azure Mills, Inc., produces artists' oil paints in hundreds of colors and container sizes. They purchase pigments in primary colors in bulk amounts. With these, they mix and package their end-items. Which product-market environment would be best suited for Azure Mills's MPS?

7.6. What inputs are required to derive an MPS plan?

7.7. Given the forecasts, customer orders, and on-hand inventory shown for a product in an ATO environment, derive the MPS for

(a) Lot-for-lot production

(b) Batch production where batch size = 8000

			Week			
Current inventory = 7500	**1**	**2**	**3**	**4**	**5**	**6**
F_t	6000	6000	5600	5000	6000	5000
O_t	4600	4000	3500	500	0	0

7.8. Add the ATP values to the MPS plan in Problem 7.7.

7.9. For the data in Problem 7.7, derive the MPS if the product demand is met in an MTO environment.

7.10. Using the costs, requirements, and times as shown below for two products for a planning horizon of three weeks, with 1200 hours per week, formulate the MPS problem mathematically. This is an MTS environment.

	Demand (units)			Current		Cost ($)	
Week	1	2	3	inventory	Hours/unit	Set-up	Holding
P1	200	250	150	100	2.50	3.75	0.65
P2	560	590	700	50	1.20	5.50	0.32

7.11. Given the following data for an ATO environment, formulate the MPS problem mathematically. There are three modules that are assembled to produce two products. There are currently six orders to be filled over the next three time periods. There are 112 hours of production time available in each period.

	Customer orders		
Order j	Product i	Quantity Q_i	Week due t
1	1	15	1
2	2	30	1
3	1	20	2
4	2	30	2
5	1	10	3
6	2	20	3

	q_{ki}		
	k		
i	1	2	3
1	3	2	1
2	1	1	1

q_{ki} = number of modules of type k required to assemble product i

	g_{kj}						
	j						
k	1	2	3	4	5	6	Total
1	45	30	60	30	30	20	215
2	30	30	40	30	20	20	170
3	15	60	20	60	10	40	205

g_{kj} = number of modules of type k required for order j

			π_{jt}			
			j			
t	1	2	3	4	5	6
1	0	0	0.45	0.30	0.45	0.30
2	1	1	0	0	0.90	0.60
3	2	2	1	1	0	0

π_{jt} = penalty cost if order is satisfied in period t

	h_k	
h_1	h_2	h_3
0.120	0.010	0.085

h_k = holding cost per period for unit of module k

		a_j			
a_1	a_2	a_3	a_4	a_5	a_6
45	66	60	66	30	44

a_j = assembly hours per order j

7.12. What is a bottleneck, and what is the significance of a bottleneck operation in a production facility?

7.13. What is the difference between rough-cut capacity planning and detailed capacity planning? What is the major limitation of these procedures?

7.14. Pell Sons Boats manufactures three types of sailboats. Their final assembly operation consists of three workcenters: paint, mast fitting, and roping. Given the MPS and the bill of capacity for PSB, Inc., shown in the accompanying tables, create a capacity profile. If necessary, suggest an alternative MPS that would be feasible.

	MPS (units)							
Week	1	2	3	4	5	6	7	8
Boat 1	94	93	42	33	73	87	71	98
Boat 2	65	20	48	57	77	37	74	40
Boat 3	71	53	56	22	91	79	93	66

Bill of capacity (minutes)			
	Paint	Mast	Rope
Boat 1	43	22	17
Boat 2	57	30	23
Boat 3	90	50	41

7.15. The following data represent the planned releases to an assembly workcenter that has a capacity of 475 hr per week. Use Karni's (1982) I/O-analysis method to analyze the lead times, assuming $U_o = 0$.

		Week (t)				
	1	**2**	**3**	**4**	**5**	**6**
R_t	379	508	248	295	351	227

7.16. Using the data in Problem 7.15, determine the additional capacity that would be required to achieve a lead time of 0.5 weeks for this volume of work.

7.17. Rock Huggers, Inc., manufactures four types of contour sport sandals: the Chewy, the Tally, the Ammy, and the Grandy. Blick Carry, production planner for RHI received the following forecasts from the sales department:

Forecasts, in pairs × 1000

	September				**October**			
	1	**2**	**3**	**4**	**5**	**6**	**7**	**8**
Chewy	98	94	93	87	73	71	42	33
Tally	74	71	57	33	28	18	12	9
Ammy	50	48	21	13	11	9	4	2
Grandy	24	24	21	18	17	16	16	8

Blick also received the following quantities representing customer orders for those weeks:

Customer orders, in pairs × 1000

	September				**October**			
	1	**2**	**3**	**4**	**5**	**6**	**7**	**8**
Chewy	93	93	78	71	61	27	11	3
Tally	63	61	59	37	24	15	11	10
Ammy	44	34	19	18	17	14	8	7
Grandy	30	29	24	14	7	5	4	1

Inventory quantities for the Chewy, the Tally, the Ammy, and the Grandy are 129,000, 108,000, 79,000, and 43,000, respectively. The production departments like Blick to schedule in batch sizes that are multiples of 100,000. What would Blick's MPS quantities look like for the four types of sandals?

7.18. What forecast quantities were used to derive the following MPS?

			Week				
Current inventory = 890	**1**	**2**	**3**	**4**	**5**	**6**	**7**
F_t							
O_t	973	929	746	574	538	181	120
I_t	917	988	169	449	836	296	897
MPS	1000	1000	0	1000	1000	0	1000

7.19. A valued customer of Rock Huggers, Inc., (see Problem 7.17) calls the company in week 1 and requests a rush order of 14,000 pairs of Chewys and 25,000 pairs of Grandys. How soon can the customer expect to receive the sandals?

7.20. Why are inventory quantities not used to calculate available-to-promise quantities after the first period?

7.21. Rework the MPS calculations for Rock Huggers, Inc., using a lot-for-lot policy. Which is a better plan and why?

7.22. Find a feasible solution for the MPS model formulated in Problem 7.10.

7.23. Derive the mathematical relationship between Q_{kt} and g_{kj} in the MPS model for ATO environments.

3 MATERIAL REQUIREMENTS PLANNING

3.1 Overview

During the past two decades, many industrial companies changed their inventory systems from reorder point systems (i.e., independent-demand approach) to MRP systems (i.e., dependent-demand approach). Computer technology made this possible. This approach was developed in the early 1970s, and is attributed to a number of professionals, including Orlicky and Wight (see Chapter 10).

MRP is appropriate for considering complex products. We usually assume assembly of a discrete product from various components or subassemblies. As in MPS, time is viewed in discrete intervals or time buckets. The major objective of MRP is to determine **requirements**—discrete demand for each component in each time bucket. These requirements are used to generate information required for correct material purchasing or shop-floor production, by taking the time-phased quantities of the MPS and generating a resultant time-phased set of component or raw-material requirements. This procedure is followed by detailed capacity planning (CRP). We next discuss how an MRP plan is generated.

3.2 Essence of MRP

The major objective of MRP systems is to generate time-phased requirements for components or raw materials. This is a system output. In this section we discuss the required system input and elaborate more on the resulting output.

The three major inputs of an MRP system are **master production schedule, inventory status records,** and **bill of material** (product structure). We emphasize the importance of MPS as an input to MRP. It is the main input to the MRP system, because the major objective of this system is to translate end-product time-phased requirements into individual component requirements. Often, two additional inputs are used in generating the system output: orders for components originating from sources external to the plant, and forecasts for items subject to independent demand (such as maintenance material and soldering material).

Inventory status records contain the status of all items in inventory. The record is kept up to date by accounting for all inventory transactions—receipt, withdrawal, or disbursement of an item from or to inventory. By properly reporting each transaction, inventory-record integrity is achieved.

Inventory records also include planning factors, which typically are item lead time, safety stock, lot sizes, scrap allowance, etc. They are needed for determining the size and timing of planned purchase orders. Planning factors are determined by the system user according to inventory policy (safety stock, lot size) or exogenous constraints (supply lead time).

Bill of material (BOM) is sometimes also called the **product structure.** However, there is a subtle difference. Product structure is a diagram that shows the sequence in which raw material, purchased parts, and subassemblies are manufactured and assembled to form the end-item. The computer-product structure file is called BOM. We show a generic product structure in Figure 7-4. That specific example shows a product structure with four levels; we say it is four levels deep. The more levels the product structure has, the more complex the product is—the number of levels may be over ten. Each element of the product structure is numbered, and it is customary to show required quantities of each needed per end-item. In some cases, the lead time between each level of the product structure is included. Thus, for each quantity of the end-item it is possible to obtain **time-phased** requirements for each level.

The product structure hierarchy is commonly referred to as a **parent-child relationship.** Each element in the product structure has a parent—the item above it—and a child—the item below it. An end-item has only children, and RM and PP items have only parents.

A section of a BOM of a desk touch-phone is shown in Figure 7-5. Note that the product structure levels are shown, and therefore it is called **indented bill of material.**

The major **outputs** of an MRP system are **planned-order releases.** They are of two major types, purchase orders and workorders. **Purchase orders** are quantities of RM and PP items to be purchased, and the timing of their availability. Accordingly, the purchase order will be issued on its due date minus supply lead time. **Workorders** are quantities of MP

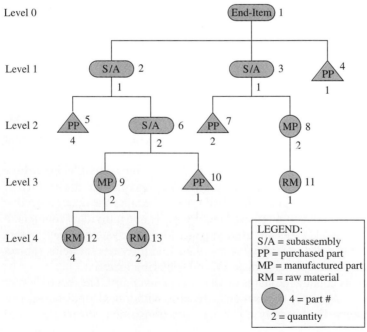

FIGURE 7-4
Generic product structure diagram

Indented Bill of Material

Review WU	Review Route	Review Bill	Add Struct	Stop		Printed Report	REV INDT BILL Both	EXIT	

Part number 638390015E

Indented Level	Part Number	CC	Qty Per	UM	LL	Description	Phan
0	638390015E			EA	4	RFI ALMON ZAMIR TEL W/O L. CORD	N
1	5110130022		1.0000	EA	10	BAG POLYETHYLENE 270 X 400	N
1	5110130116		1.0000	EA	6	POLYETHELENE BAG	N
1	6383100302		1.0000	EA	5	OPERATING INSTRUCTION SHEET	N
1	6383101252		1.0000	EA	5	COLOURED PACK. BOX-TEL. ZAMIR	N
1	638390207E		1.0000	EA	5	PACKING LABEL-TEL. 547/1 ALMOND	N
1	638390210E		1.0000	EA	5	COLORED LABEL-TEL. 547/1 ALMOND	N
1	638391015E		1.0000	EA	5	TEL 547-1 R-in ASSY. ALMOND	Y
2	2543824061		1.0000	EA	6	HANDSET CORD, RAL 1013, 12 FT., 4P	N
2	6383102141		1.0000	EA	6	CORK TO DTMF/PULSE SW.	N
2	638390115E		1.0000	EA	6	TEL 547-1 R-in ASSY NO H.S. ALM	Y
3	6383113001		1.0000	EA	7	BASE ASSEMBLY	Y
4	6383113015		1.0000	EA	8	BASE PLATE W/RINGER TRANSDUCE.	Y
5	6383113032		1.0000	EA	9	RINGER UNIT	N
5	6383113046		1.0000	EA	9	BASE FOR TELEPHONE	N
6	2526500319		.1075	KG	10	CYCOLAC TCA 333210 OXFORD GREY	N
6	5110120081		.0205	EA	10	PAKING FOR LOWER. UPPER COVER	N
6	5110130022		.5000	EA	10	BAG POLYETHYLENE 270 X 400	N
5	6383113050		.0012	LT	9	EPOXY GLUE	N
4	6383113029		4.0000	EA	8	FOOT	N
3	6383113094		1.0000	EA	7	SELECTING KNOB	N
3	6383113109		4.0000	EA	7	CAPTIVE TAPPING SCREW (BASE)	N
3	6383113206		1.0000	EA	7	WEIGHT, LARGE	N
3	6383113210		1.0000	EA	7	WEIGHT, SMALL	N
3	6383113223		1.0000	EA	7	COMPRESSION SPRING	N
4	3883113222		1.0000	EA	8	PRESING SORING	N
3	6383113237		1.0000	EA	7	LINE SWTCH PLUNGER	N
4	2526500291		.0050	KG	8		N
3	6383113241		1.0000	EA	7	ALERTER SWITCH ACTUATOR	N
4	2526500291		.0030	KG	8		N
3	638313010E		1.0000	EA	7	TEL 547-1 R-IN CARD ASSY	Y
4	638311610E		1.0000	EA	8	CARD ASSY. TEL. 547-1 E-6	N
5	2250428014		1.0000	EA	9	RES MET FILM 10M 1% 1/4W	N
5	2272400325		5.0000	EA	9	DIODAA SWITCHING 1N4148	N
5	2274122220		3.0000	EA	9	TRANSISTOR NPM PN2222A, T+R	N
5	2543906565		1.0000	EA	9	CONNECTOR RIBBON 10 CONT MALE	N
5	2543912403		1.0000	EA	9	JACK ASSY (HANDSET), 4 PIN, BLK	N
5	2543912417		1.0000	EA	9	JACK ASSY (LINE), 4 PIN/6WHITE	N
5	2545011136		1.0000	EA	9	SWITCH, SLIDE, DPDT, FOR PCB	N
5	2545012121		1.0000	EA	9	SLIDE SWITCH FOR ALERTER	N
5	2550230331		1.0000	EA	9	RES MET FILM 33.2 OHM 1% 1/2 W	N
5	2550230473		1.0000	EA	9	RES MET FILM 47.5 OHM 1% 1/2W	N
5	2550415587		1.0000	EA	9	RES METAL FILM 39.2K 1% 1/8W	N
5	2550416014		3.0000	EA	9	RES METAL FILM 100K 1% 1/8W	N
5	2550423388		1.0000	EA	9	RES MET FILM 243 OHM 1 % 1/4 W	N
5	2551311229		3.0000	EA	9	RES CRB FILM 220 OHM 5% 1/8W	N
5	2551311628		1.0000	EA	9	RES CARB FILM 620 OHM 5% 1/8W	N
5	2551312103		2.0000	EA	9	RES CRB FLM 1K 5% 1/8 W	N
5	2551312201		1.0000	EA	9	RES CRB FILM 2K 5% 0.125W	N
5	2551312360		1.0000	EA	9	RES CARBON FILM 3.6K 5% 1/8W	Y
6	2550414543		1.0000	EA	10	RES METAL FILM 3.57K 1% 1/8W	N

FIGURE 7-5

Touch-phone indented BOM (courtesy of Telrad Telecommunications and Electronic Industries Ltd, Lod, Israel) and S/A items to be manufactured and the timing of their delivery. Therefore, the workorder will be issued on its due date minus manufacturing lead time. Purchase orders constitute the **purchasing plan,** whereas workorders generate the **production plan** for the shop floor. Next, we discuss the logic of generating these two outputs.

3.3 MRP Process

The heart of an MRP system is the process that transforms input into output. The output of this process consists of **net requirements.** Net requirements form the basis for determining purchase orders and work orders. Transforming inputs to outputs is done systematically, using a sequence of steps called **explosion, netting, offsetting,** and **lot sizing** (see Figure 7-6).

In the **explosion process** we simulate the disassembly of the end product into its components. Using the MPS quantity and the BOM information, we descend through the product structure and evaluate for each parent its required quantity of children. This gives gross requirements for each element of the BOM. This process is demonstrated in the following example.

> **Example 7-5. The explosion process.** Consider the generic product structure diagram of Figure 7-4. Figure 7-7 shows the left branch of the diagram, along with the required quantities at each level. For simplicity, assume lead times are 0. Suppose the MPS requirement for the end-item is 100 units. The explosion process is shown in Table 7-9. The quantities at each level (parent) are the requirements for the lower level (children). To illustrate, at level 3, 400 units are needed for item 9, which has two children—12 and 13. The gross requirements are therefore 1600 for item 12 and 800 for item 13.

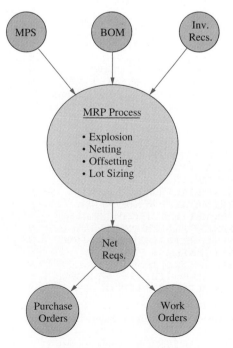

FIGURE 7-6
MRP process

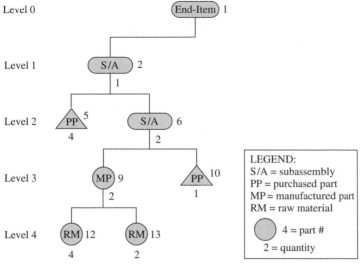

FIGURE 7-7
Segment of a generic product structure diagram

During the **netting** process, gross requirements are adjusted to account for on-hand inventory or quantity on order. Thus, net requirements are

Net requirements = Gross requirements − On-hand inventory − Quantity on order

This adjustment is done at every level of the BOM and for each time bucket. In other words, at each level of the BOM, gross requirements are netted before exploding into requirements at the next lower level. If there is no *on-hand inventory* and no *on-order quantity,* then net requirement is equal to gross requirement.

To present the explosion and netting process, along with the time phasing, a tabular form is used. This is called an **MRP record.** Its structure is similar to that of the MPS but its entries are different. We use a telephone product to illustrate the construction of an MRP record in the following example.

TABLE 7-9
Explosion process

	Item number	Gross requirement
Level 0 (MPS)	1	100
Level 1	2	×1 100
Level 2	5	×4 400 ×2
	6	200
Level 3	9	×2 400 ×1
	10	×4 200
Level 4	12	1600
	13	×2 800

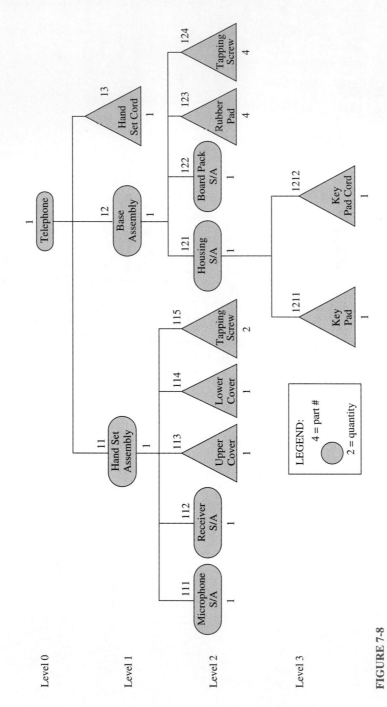

FIGURE 7-8
Touch-phone product structure diagram (simplified)

TABLE 7-10
MPS for a touch phone

				Week				
	1	2	3	4	5	6	7	8
MPS		600	1000	1000	2000	2000	2000	2000

Example 7-6. MRP record—net requirements. The product structure diagram of the desktop touch phone (model A) is shown in Figure 7-8. The MPS is given in Table 7-10. (See also Table 7-5.) Assuming there is no on-hand inventory of the telephone (part 1), the above MPS also contains gross requirements for the handset assembly (part 11). Those quantities of part 11 must be on hand at the beginning of each week to support the production plan at level 0. They are the first entry of the MRP record shown in Table 7-11. The final assembly is on a continuous basis and not on a batch basis, so we ignore lead time between level 0 and level 1.

The second row in the MRP record shows scheduled receipts. These are materials expected to arrive at the beginning of the week because of purchase orders or shop orders that have been previously released but not yet received because of supplier delivery time or production lead time. The next row shows the projected inventory balance (PIB) at the end of each week. The beginning inventory is shown under the heading *current* and is obtained from the inventory status record. Net requirements are shown in the last row.

The netting process proceeds from the first week into the future. We show it for weeks 2, 3, and 4:

$$(\text{Net requirements})_2 = 600 - (1600 + 700) = -1700$$

$$= \text{Gross requirements beginning of week 2}$$

$$- \{(\text{PIB end of week 1})$$

$$+ (\text{Scheduled receipts beginning of week 2})\}$$

The negative value means that net requirement at the beginning of week 2 is 0. The projected inventory balance at the end of week 2 is 1700.

$$(\text{Net requirements})_3 = 1000 - (1700 + 200) = -900$$

$$(\text{Net requirement} = 0, \quad \text{PIB} = 900)$$

$$(\text{Net requirements})_4 = 1000 - 900 = 100$$

The last two steps in the MRP process are offsetting and lot sizing. In **offsetting,** the timing of order release is determined. In order to meet net requirements, an order release is offset by the production lead time or supplier delivery time. Thus, in Table 7-11, if production lead time is two weeks, an order to the production floor has to be released in week 2 to meet net requirements for week 4.

Lot sizing is the step in which the batch size to be purchased or produced is determined. Lot sizing methods discussed in Chapter 6 can be used. We show the implementation of these two steps in the next example, where a complete MRP record is shown.

Example 7-7. Complete MRP record. We continue Example 7-6, and generate the complete MRP record (Table 7-12). There are two new entries in the MRP record: planned receipts and order release. *Planned receipts* shows the timing of new orders required to cover net requirements. *Planned order release* offsets the planned receipts by the appropriate lead time. The quantity in both is the selected lot size.

TABLE 7-11
Net requirements for part 11

	Current	1	2	3	4	5	6	7	8
					Week				
Gross requirements			600	1000	1000	2000	2000	2000	2000
Scheduled receipts		400	700	200	0	0	0	0	0
Projected inventory balance	1200	1600	1700	900	0	0	0	0	0
Net requirements					100	2000	2000	2000	2000

TABLE 7-12
MRP record for part 11

	Current	Week							
		1	2	3	4	5	6	7	8
Gross requirements			600	1000	1000	2000	2000	2000	2000
Scheduled receipts		400	700	200				0	0
Projected inventory balance*	1200	1600	1700	900	**2900**	**900**	**1900**	**2900**	**900**
Net requirements					100	2000	2000	2000	2000
Planned receipts					3000	3000	3000	3000	
Planned order release			3000		3000	3000			

*Projected inventory balance adjusted for planned receipts.

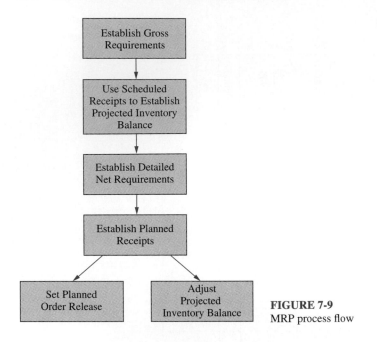

FIGURE 7-9
MRP process flow

Suppose the lot size for part 11 is 3000 and production lead time is two weeks. The first planned receipt is required in the beginning of week 4, so the planned order release will be two weeks earlier, i.e., in week 2.

The first planned receipt will cover net requirements for weeks 4 and 5, but there is not enough to cover week 6. Therefore, a new order is released in week 4.

Because of planned receipts, projected on-hand inventory is no longer zero. At the end of week 4, projected inventory will be $3000 - 100 = 2900$. At the end of week 5 it is $2900 - 2000 = 900$, and at the end of week 6 it is $900 + 3000 - 2000 = 1900$. If safety stock is to be maintained, the projected on-hand inventory should not be depleted below the safety stock.

There is an important difference between scheduled receipts, planned receipts, and planned order releases. Scheduled receipts are orders that have already been issued and are in the supply pipeline. The others are orders on paper. If a change in orders is required because of changes in the MPS, it is easier to change planned receipts than scheduled receipts.

We recap this section by showing the MRP process flow (Figure 7-9), and continue in the next section with multilevel explosion and MRP calculation.

3.4   Multilevel Explosion

In a complete MRP explosion process, the MRP record is generated for each component of the product structure diagram. This is a cascading process, where net requirements of one level explode into the gross requirements of the next level. We demonstrate this process using the touch-phone (refer to the product structure diagram in Figure 7-8). For clarity of presentation, we show only partial explosion using only part of the product structure components. The information for the partial explosion is given in Table 7-13. The last two

TABLE 7-13
Product structure data

Part number	Description	Quantity required per telephone
12	Base assembly	1
121	Housing S/A	1
123	Rubber pad	4
1211	Key pad	1

items are purchased; however, the structure of the MRP record is the same for all parts. We make the following assumptions:

- Purchasing lead time or production lead time is one week.
- Lot sizing policy is *lot for lot* except for part 12, which has a fixed lot size of 3000.
- Gross requirements for part 12 are the same as those for the finished telephone; i.e., there is no finished goods inventory.
- The final assembly is on a continuous basis and not on batch basis, so we ignore lead time between level 0 and level 1.
- Quantities of scheduled receipts and current on-hand inventory are given as shown.

The explosion process is shown in Table 7-14. The gross requirements of part 12 are the same as the MPS for product A (Table 7-5). We follow through the gross requirement of 2000 for part 12 in week 7.

Net requirements are the same as gross requirements, as the nonadjusted projected inventory balance is 0. Therefore, a planned receipt of size 3000 is required. At the end of week 6 projected inventory balance is 1400, so the balance at the end of week 7 is $1400 + 3000 - 2000 = 2400$.

Because of the one-week delivery time, planned order release is in week 6. It explodes into gross requirement in week 6 of 3000 for part 121 and 12,000 for part 123 (see the product structure diagram in Figure 7-10). The rest of the explosion process is performed in the same way. The student is encouraged to follow it through.

3.5   MRP Updating Methods

The calculation method is done in a static environment: For a given MPS we perform the explosion process and the required MRP calculation. However, MRP systems operate in a dynamic environment, in which forecasts (and hence MPS) change, product structures change, promised deliveries arrive late, and lead times change. The static solution becomes invalid, and an update process must be performed. This process can be done in two ways: the **regeneration method** and the **net change method.**

In the **regeneration method,** the entire material plan is recalculated, based on updating the MPS, actual deliveries, updated inventory, etc. Each item record is completely recalculated.

The **net change method** recalculates requirements only for those items affected by change; i.e., a partial explosion is performed. Furthermore, only additions and deletions from the master schedule are entered.

TABLE 7-14
Complete MRP explosion

Note: In the original, this table is printed rotated (landscape). The reconstruction below preserves the row/column structure. Underlined values denote given initial data; bold values denote projected inventory balance adjusted for planned receipts. Arrows with ×1 and ×4 indicate the quantity-per parent-to-component linkages.

Level	Item / Row	Current	1	2	3	4	5	6	7	8
1	**12 Base assembly:**									
	Gross requirements		400	600	1000	1000	2000	2000	2000	2000
	Scheduled receipts									
	Projected inventory balance	800	400	400	400	**2400**	**400**	**1400**	**2400**	**400**
	Net requirements					600	2000	2000	2000	2000
	Planned receipts			1200		3000		3000	3000	
	Planned order release		1200	1000	3000	3000	3000	3000		
2	**121 Housing S/A:**									
	Gross requirements				3000		3000	3000		
	Scheduled receipts									
	Projected inventory balance	500	500	500						
	Net requirements				2500		3000	3000		
	Planned receipts				2500		3000	3000		
	Planned order release			2500	3000		3000			
3	**123 Rubber pad:**									
	Gross requirements			10,000	12,000	12,000	12,000	12,000		
	Scheduled receipts									
	Projected inventory balance	15,000	15,000							
	Net requirements			25,000	13,000	13,000	11,000	11,000		
	Planned receipts				13,000	13,000	11,000	11,000		
	Planned order release			25,000	13,000	13,000	11,000			
3	**1211 Key pad:**									
	Gross requirements			2500		3000	3000			
	Scheduled receipts		1500							
	Projected inventory balance	1200	2700	200	200	2800	3000			
	Net requirements					2800	3000			
	Planned receipts					2800	3000			
	Planned order release				2800	3000				

Multiplier linkages shown by arrows: Base assembly planned order release ×1 → Housing S/A gross requirements, ×4 → Rubber pad; Housing S/A planned order release ×4 → Rubber pad gross requirements, ×1 → Key pad gross requirements.

Legend: Bold numbers denote projected inventory balance adjusted for planned receipts. __ denotes given initial data.

TABLE 7-15
MPS for February

| Product | February | | | |
| | Week | | | |
	5	6	7	8
Model A	2000	2000	2000	2000
Model B	350	—	—	350
Model C	1000	—	1000	1000
Model D	—	300	200	—

The net change method is quick to implement and requires relatively little computer time. It is performed daily or weekly. Its major drawback is that it is impossible to purge inaccurate requirements planning, so errors propagate.

This drawback is eliminated in the regeneration method, as all requirements planned are generated from scratch. However, the regeneration method is more cumbersome to implement and requires a relatively long computer time. Of course, in a very dynamic environment, MRP records become obsolete quickly.

Both methods are available and applied in conjunction with current software. Regeneration is performed once or twice a month, and between regenerations, the records are updated using the net change method.

Example 7-8. Net change method. Consider the MPS of Example 7-1. Table 7-15 gives the data for the month of February. Suppose that additional orders were accepted and some were canceled for weeks 7 and 8 for all models, resulting in the MPS given in Table 7-16. The difference between the current MPS and the previous one is the **net change.** The net change MPS is given in Table 7-17. Exploding the net change MPS will update all required records, but will not purge inaccurate requirements planning.

3.6 Additional Netting Procedures

Some special applications of the explosion and netting processes are often used, and we discuss three of them: **implosion, combining requirements,** and **pegging.**

TABLE 7-16
Updated MPS

| Product | February | | | |
| | Week | | | |
	5	6	7	8
Model A	2000	2000	2300	1900
Model B	500	—	200	150
Model C	1000	—	800	1000
Model D	—	300	200	—

TABLE 7-17
Net change

Product	February			
	Week			
	5	6	7	8
Model A			+300	−100
Model B			+200	−200
Model C			−200	
Model D				

The **implosion process** is the opposite of the explosion process. Explosion is a top-down procedure and implosion is a bottom-up one. We ascend along the product structure diagram and for each raw-material item find its parent end product. Thus, in the touch-phone product structure (Figure 7-8), an implosion process for item 1211 will ascend the diagram in the sequence: 1211 to 121 to 12 to 1, ending at item 1—the end-item. This procedure finds common items in the inventory holdings, i.e., items that are required for more than one end-item. Typically, demand for common items is less lumpy.

Combining requirements is the process of obtaining the gross requirements of a common item. Requirements for the same item originating from different products and BOM levels should be combined. The principles of this procedure are shown in Figure 7-10. For each week, the planned-order releases of the three products are combined to create the gross requirements of the common item.

Pegging is an important technique associated with combining requirements. Pegging relates all the gross requirements for a common item to all planned-order releases that created the requirement; i.e., each component of the gross requirement is "pegged" with the part number of its source. By pegging it is possible to ascend the BOM and identify the item's end product. Thus, pegging enables executing an implosion process for common items.

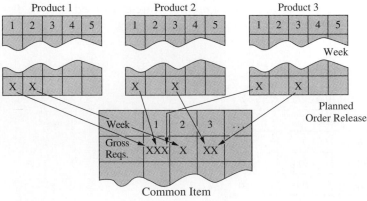

FIGURE 7-10
Combining requirements

One important use of pegging is when an item shortage occurs. It is then possible to use an implosion process to trace the impact of a material problem on all subassemblies and end products affected by this shortage. The drawback to introducing pegging is more complexity in the MRP information-storage requirements. However, knowledge of possible late deliveries is very important in today's markets.

3.7   Lot Sizing in MRP Systems

Single-item lot-sizing methods and their rationale are discussed in Chapter 6. MRP systems are multi-item and multilevel, encompassing the total product structure. In a multilevel system the lot size at one level will determine the requirements in the next-lowest level of the product structure. The problem is to find a set of lot sizes at each level that will minimize set-up cost and inventory-holding cost for the whole system. The simplest way to tackle the multilevel problem is to use any of the single-level lot-sizing methods and solve level by level. Descending through the product structure diagram, lot sizes for each item at all levels are determined. This approach, with lot sizes determined by EOQ or lot-for-lot, is common in industry. The problem can be formulated as a large integer-programming model, but it is difficult to solve; thus a variety of heuristic approaches are used.

3.8   Multi-Echelon Systems

In this section we present MRP as a multi-echelon system. We first discuss multi-echelon inventory and then treat MRP as a multi-echelon inventory-control system.

3.8.1   MULTI-ECHELON INVENTORY. Recall that a product structure has a number of levels (see, e.g., the one in Figure 7-4). In each level, inventory can be present to maintain safety stock, cycle inventory, etc. A similar situation exists in a distribution system, in which items are produced at a factory, shipped to warehouses for immediate storage, and subsequently shipped to retail outlets.

It is customary to refer to each level of such a system as an **echelon,** in which each echelon can be a stocking point—hence, the term **multi-echelon inventory.** In this section we show how the total inventory in the system varies with the number of stocking points. In doing so, we follow Freeland.[3]

We make the following assumptions:

- Demand is insensitive to the number of stocking points n.
- Demand is normally distributed and divided evenly among the stocking points. Furthermore, demands at the stocking points are independent of one another. Therefore, the variance of demand is divided evenly as well.
- A (Q, R) inventory policy is used. Q is determined from the EOQ formula. R is determined using policy 2 (Chapter 6). Thus, the safety stock is equal to

$$s = z\sigma_\tau$$

where σ_τ is the standard deviation of lead-time demand.

[3] Adapted from Freeland (1985) by permission of Darden Graduate School of Business Administration, University of Virginia. Copyright ©1984 by Darden Graduate Business School Foundation, Charlottesville, Virginia.

Based on the previous assumptions, the average inventory is

$$\bar{I}(1) = \frac{Q}{2} + s$$

where, in general, $\bar{I}(n)$ denotes the average inventory for n stocking points. Recall that

$$Q = \text{EOQ} = \sqrt{\frac{2A\bar{D}}{ic}}$$

$$s = z\sigma_\tau$$

Thus,

$$\bar{I}(1) = \frac{1}{2}\sqrt{\frac{2A\bar{D}}{ic}} + z\sigma_\tau$$

For two stocking points, the demand at each point is $D/2$, the variance of lead-time demand is $\sigma_\tau^2/2$, and the standard deviation is $\sigma_\tau/\sqrt{2}$. The average inventory at each stocking point is

$$\frac{1}{2}\sqrt{\frac{2A(\bar{D}/2)}{ic}} + \frac{z\sigma_\tau}{\sqrt{2}}$$

Simplifying gives

$$\frac{1}{2\sqrt{2}}\sqrt{\frac{2A\bar{D}}{ic}} + \frac{z\sigma_\tau}{\sqrt{2}} = \frac{1}{\sqrt{2}}\left(\frac{Q}{2} + s\right)$$

Therefore, the average inventory for two stocking points is

$$\bar{I}(2) = 2\left[\frac{1}{\sqrt{2}}\left(\frac{Q}{2} + s\right)\right] = \sqrt{2}\left(\frac{Q}{2} + s\right) = \sqrt{2}\bar{I}(1)$$

It should be easy to see how this would generalize to n stocking points, yielding

$$\bar{I}(n) = \sqrt{n}\bar{I}(1)$$

In an MRP system, if we consider each level as a possible stocking point, then, based on the above assumptions, for each level the safety stock is $s/\sqrt{n}$, rather than s/n as we may think intuitively. The total safety stock is $(\sqrt{n})s$.

It is customary in MRP systems to hold safety stock at only one level—raw materials, end-items, or major subassemblies (see Figure 7-3).

Example 7-9. Multi-echelon inventory. The packing department of a sugar refinery has a variety of end products: different grades of sugar packed in different carton sizes. One of their products is a very-high-grade powdered sugar that is packaged in 2-lb cartons. The product structure has two levels, as shown in the figure.

Cartons are purchased externally and delivered on a "just-in-time" basis; i.e., no inventory is necessary. Sugar-refining lead time is five days. Production lead time (filling time) can be regarded as negligible.

The annual demand for sugar is normally distributed with $\bar{D} = 800$ tons and $\sigma = 2.5$ tons. Lead-time demand is also normally distributed with $\bar{D}_\tau = 16$ tons and $\sigma_\tau = 3.54$ tons.

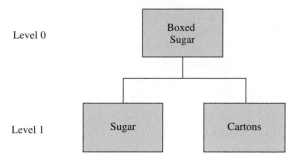

A fill rate of β = 95 percent is required, and A = \$50, c = \$4000 per ton, and i = 20 percent. Then

$$Q = \sqrt{\frac{2A\bar{D}}{ic}} = \sqrt{\frac{2 \times 50 \times 800}{800}} = 10 \text{ tons}$$

Using the method of Chapter 6 (Section 3.2.2), we obtain:

$$z = 0.71$$

$$s = z\sigma_\tau = 0.71 \times 3.54 = 2.51 \text{ tons}$$

Suppose we keep inventory in level 0 only, i.e., n = 1:

$$\bar{I}(1) = \frac{Q}{2} + s = \frac{10}{2} + 2.51 = 7.51 \text{ tons}$$

which are held in 2-lb cartons. Suppose inventory is maintained at both level 0 and level 1, i.e., n = 2. Then

$$\bar{I}(2) = \sqrt{2}\bar{I}(1) = 10.62 \text{ tons}$$

The safety stock in each level is going to be

$$\frac{s}{\sqrt{2}} = \frac{2.51}{\sqrt{2}} = 1.77 \text{ tons}$$

and not $2.51/2 = 1.2555$ tons, as we might intuitively think.

3.8.2 MRP AS MULTI-ECHELON INVENTORY CONTROL. An MRP system is essentially a multilevel system. As such, a multi-echelon inventory-control policy is appropriate here. In this section we present a continuous-review type policy (Q, R). In doing so, we follow Axsäter and Rosling.[4]

A multi-echelon inventory system is composed of a hierarchy of stocking points. Each stocking point (level) is called an installation. An installation-stock (Q, R) policy is based only on the installation-inventory position. An echelon-stock (Q, R) policy, on the other hand,

---

[4]Adapted from Axsäter and Rosling (1994) with kind permission of Elsevier Science-NL, Sara Burgerhatstraat 25, 1055 KV Amsterdam, The Netherlands.

is based on the echelon-inventory position, which is obtained by adding the usual installation-inventory position at the installation and all its downstream stock. MRP is conceived of as a rolling-horizon, level-by-level approach that bases ordering decisions on projected future installation-inventory levels. Lot-sizing rules, planning horizon, lead times, safety stock, and MPS are considered free-control parameters of an MRP system.

The model presented later is based on the following assumptions:

- All demands and orders (i.e., both demands for final products and orders of components) occur at the beginning of the time period.
- Orders are initiated immediately after the demands, first for the final items and then successively for the components.
- All demands and orders are for an integer number of units.

Let

T = Planning horizon, in periods
τ_i = Lead time for item i, in periods
s_i = Safety stock for item i, in units
Q_i = Fixed-order quantity of item i
D_{it} = External requirements of item i in period t (master schedule), in units

The production plan is generated by a level-by-level approach that begins with items demanded only by external customers. The external requirements over the planning horizon compose the MPS. A production order in a certain period is triggered if the installation-stock position minus safety stock is insufficient to cover the requirements over the next τ_i periods. Since the ordering takes place after the period's demand, the installation stock is already reduced by this demand when ordering. Thus, if $\tau_i = 0$ we do not have any future requirements, and an order will be initiated if and only if the installation inventory position is less than the safety stock. On the other hand, if, say, $\tau_i = 3$, we need to consider the requirements three periods ahead. If necessary, an order may consist of more than one order quantity Q_i.

The production schedule for the final-level items forms requirements for the preceding level, and so the procedure is simply repeated for all items (installations) in the whole system.

We consider now a serial (assembly) system with N installations. Installation 1 is the downstream installation producing the final product. Installation n represents the acquisition of raw material. We assume that the output of installation i, $1 < i \leq N$, is the input when producing one unit of item $i-1$ at the immediate downstream installation. Let w_i represent the installation-inventory position at installation i (at some moment) and let I_i represent echelon-inventory position at installation i (at some moment).

$$I_i = w_i + w_{i-1} + \cdots + w_1$$

A multi-echelon (Q, R) policy is denoted by (Q_i, R_i^e) for each installation i. Axsäter and Rosling (1994) use the following multi-echelon policy, and show that it is equivalent to a suitably designed MRP system:

$Q_i = j_i Q_{i-1}$ for some positive integer j_i (j_i can be a quantity multiplier descending along the BOM)

$I_i^o \leq R_i^e + Q_i$ for $1 \leq i \leq N - 1$ where I_i^o is the given initial-echelon inventory.

The equivalent MRP system has the following relationships, assuming that $D_{1t} = D$ for all t:

$$s_1 - 1 + D\tau_1 = R_1^e \qquad\qquad \text{for } i = 1$$

$$s_i - 1 + D\tau_i = R_i^e - R_{i-1}^e + Q_{i-1} \qquad \text{for all } i > 1$$

$$s_i - 1 = I_i^o - I_{i-1}^o + k_i Q_{i-1} \qquad \text{for all } i > 1$$

where k_i is an arbitrary integer, possibly negative.

The right-hand side of the first two equations can be interpreted as the installation-inventory reorder point when installation $(i - 1)$ has just ordered. The left-hand side can also be regarded as a reorder point, i.e., safety stock plus lead-time demand minus 1. The previous equations give an MRP system where the projected on-hand inventory τ_i periods ahead is always a single unit below s_i when an order is triggered.

We skip the proof of the previous relationship between the (Q, R^e) policy and an MRP system (see Axsäter and Rosling, 1994), and instead use an example to demonstrate the method.

Example 7-10. Multi-echelon inventory control. Consider a multi-echelon inventory (Q_i, R_i^e) policy for a two-stage assembly system. Suppose there are no outstanding orders, and

$$R_1^e = 20 \qquad R_2^e = 34 \qquad I_1^o = 18 \qquad I_2^o = 38 \qquad Q_1 = 10 \qquad Q_2 = 30$$

Then

$$s_1 - 1 + D\tau_1 = 20$$
$$s_2 - 1 + D\tau_2 = 4$$
$$s_2 - 1 = 20 + k_2 10$$

Suppose that we have the following solution:

$$k_2 = -2 \qquad D = 2 \qquad \tau_1 = 1 \qquad \tau_2 = 2 \qquad s_1 = 19 \qquad s_2 = 1$$

The MRP plan for the two items for six periods is presented in Table 7-18. For item 1 note that $w_1^o = I_1^o = 18$. Since $w_1^o < R_1^e$, a production order of $Q_1 = 10$ is initiated and at the same time, two units are deducted because of the demand. Therefore, beginning inventory in period 2 is 26. In period 5, inventory is $20 \le R_1^e = 20$, and therefore a production order is initiated and delivered in period 6, because $\tau_1 = 1$.

For item 2, $w_2^o = I_2^o - I_1^o = 20$. Since production was triggered for item 1, 10 units are withdrawn from item 2 stock, leaving it at 10 units. In period 3, $I_2 = 34 \le R_2^e = 34$, and a

TABLE 7-18
MRP for a two-level system

		1	2	3	4	5	6
	Period	1	2	3	4	5	6
	Demand	2	2	2	2	2	2
Item 1	Level w_1	18	26	24	22	20	28
	Production	10	0	0	0	10	0
Item 2	Level w_2	10	10	10	10	30	10
	Production	0	0	30	0	0	0

TABLE 7-19
MRP for period 2

		2	3	4	5	6	7
	Period	2	3	4	5	6	7
	Demand	5	2	2	2	2	2
Item 1	Level w_1	23	21	19	27	25	23
	Production	0	0	10	0	10	0
Item 2	Level w_2	10	10	30	30	30	30
	Production	30	0	0	0	0	0

production order of $Q_2 = 30$ is initiated to be delivered in period 5, as $\tau_2 = 2$. Note that in period 5, 10 units are withdrawn from item 2 stock because a production order is triggered for item 1.

Suppose now that five units (instead of two) were demanded in period 2. The echelon-inventory positions are $I_1 = 23$ and $I_2 = 33$. The new plan is depicted in Table 7-19. We leave it to the student to verify it.

3.9   Lot Size and Lead Time[5]

Lead time is affected by capacity constraints (Section 2.5). Lot size also affects lead time. These are the major reasons why the fixed-lead-time approach of the standard MRP system is often criticized. In this section we model the relationship between lot size and lead time. In doing so, we follow the exposition of Karmarkar, Kekre, and Freeman (1985), as summarized by Baker (Graves, Rinnooy Kan, and Zipkin, 1993). They identify two phenomena that should be present in any lead-time model; **batching effect** and **saturation effect.**

An increase in lot size should also increase lead time. This is called the **batching effect.** A batch of one unit can immediately move to the next operation as soon as its processing is complete. However, a batch of five units does not move until all five are completed. The first unit completed waits until the other four are completed before it moves to the next operation. Doubling the batch size to 10 requires the first unit to wait for the processing of nine units. Larger batches will cause longer delays of parts waiting for the rest of the batch to be completed (see Figure 10-23 in Chapter 10).

The **saturation effect** works in the opposite manner. When lot sizes decrease, and set-up is not reduced, lead time will eventually increase. The reason is that, if demand stays the same, as lot sizes are reduced there will be more lots in the shop. This results in more time spent on set-ups and less time available for processing. As a result, demand becomes a relatively larger proportion of available capacity, and congestion increases. Since the effects of the two phenomena are opposite, the aggregate behavior of lead time as a function of lot size should be U-shaped as shown in Figure 7-11.

Queueing theory can be used to model the above situation. Consider a single-server queueing system that serves n different products. Assuming Poisson arrivals and an arbitrary distribution of service time (M/G/1 service system), the standard formula for queueing delay (lead time) is

---

[5]Adapted from Baker (in Graves et al. (1993)) with the kind permission of Elsevier Science-NL, Sara Burgerhart straat 25, 1055 KV Amsterdam, The Netherlands.

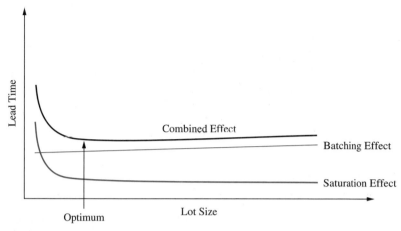

FIGURE 7-11
Lot size and lead time

$$L = \frac{(\lambda/\mu)^2 + \lambda^2\sigma^2}{2\lambda(1 - \lambda/\mu)} + \frac{1}{\mu}$$

where λ = Mean arrival rate
μ = Mean service time
σ^2 = Service-time variance

Let

D_j = Demand per period for product j
t_j = Unit-production time for product j
S_j = Set-up time for product j
Q_j = Lot size for product j (the decision variable)

A batch is a "customer," so the mean arrival rate of batches is

$$\lambda = \sum_{j=1}^{n} \lambda_j = \sum_{j=1}^{n} \frac{D_j}{Q_j}$$

where

$$\lambda_j = \frac{D_j}{Q_j}$$

is the mean arrival rate of batches of product j.

The mean service time is a weighted average given by

$$\mu = \frac{\displaystyle\sum_{j=1}^{n} \lambda_j(S_j + t_jQ_j)}{\displaystyle\sum_{j=1}^{n} \lambda_j}$$

and service-time variance is

$$
\sigma^2 = \left(\frac{\displaystyle\sum_{j=1}^{n} \lambda_j (S_j + t_j Q_j)^2}{\displaystyle\sum_{j=1}^{n} \lambda_j} \right) - \frac{1}{\mu^2}
$$

Substituting the values for λ, μ, and σ^2 into the equation for L, the lead time can be obtained. This equation is a multivariate version of the function described in Figure 7-11. We demonstrate the process in the next example.

> **Example 7-11. Lead time.** Consider a workcenter that manufactures four products. Weekly demand is obtained from the MPS, and set-up time and unit-production time are shown in Table 7-20. After setting up the formula for L in a spreadsheet, a trial-and-error search (try!) will yield close to a minimum value in a few iterations. The search yields $L^* = 1.29$ weeks, with $Q_1 = 60$, $Q_2 = 1300$, $Q_3 = 400$, and $Q_4 = 500$.

> **TABLE 7-20**
> **Product parameters**
>
> | Product | D_j (weekly) | S_j (hr) | t_j (hr per 1000) |
> |---------|------|------|-----------|
> | 1 | 100 | 3 | 30 |
> | 2 | 500 | 15 | 45 |
> | 3 | 50 | 6 | 75 |
> | 4 | 250 | 24 | 150 |

SECTION 3 PROBLEMS

7.24. What is the major objective of an MRP system?

7.25. Why did MRP systems replace reorder-point systems?

7.26. List and define the inputs to an MRP system.

7.27. List and define the outputs to an MRP system.

7.28. Create a product structure diagram for the following:

    (a) A hammock is made from a rope bed, two wooden ends, and two ring assemblies. A rope bed is constructed of 150 linear feet of rope. A wooden end is made of four linear feet of 2" × 1.5" wood. A ring assembly is made of an O-ring and a hook.

    (b) A silk daisy is made of a bloom and a stalk. A bloom consists of a plastic center and 15 petals. A stalk is made of a plastic stem and three leaves. A leaf is made of three square inches of green silk and 0.05 ounces of a hardening agent. A petal is made of one square inch of white silk and 0.01 ounces of hardening agent.

7.29. Write the indented BOM for part (a) of Problem 7.28.

7.30. Describe the MRP process.

7.31. For the generic product structure and the MPS shown below, perform the explosion part of the MRP process.

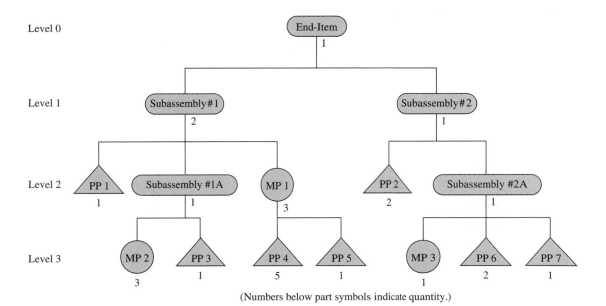

(Numbers below part symbols indicate quantity.)

Level	Item	Weekly quantity					
		1	**2**	**3**	**4**	**5**	**6**
0	End-item	150	200	240	190	140	100

7.32. Given the scheduled receipts shown below for the subassembly #1 in the generic product structure of Problem 7.31, perform the netting procedure if the on-hand inventory at time 0 is 75.

Scheduled receipts per week					
1	**2**	**3**	**4**	**5**	**6**
500	300	100	50	0	0

7.33. Perform the offsetting procedure for the net requirements in Problem 7.32 assuming a lead time of three weeks and a lot size of 500 units.

7.34. Complete the MRP record shown in the following table for subassembly #2 in the product structure of Problem 7.31. Use the following assumptions:

- Lead time for subassembly #2 = two weeks.
- Lead time for all other parts = 1 week.
- Lot size for subassembly #2 = 300 units.
- Lot-for-lot method is used to determine lot sizes for all other parts.

Problem 7.34 (*continued*)

Level	Item	Qty	Current	Week					
				1	**2**	**3**	**4**	**5**	**6**
1	S/A #2	1							
	Grs reqs			150	200	240	190	140	100
	Scd rcts			50	35	20	0	0	0
	PIB		500						
	Net reqs								
	Planned receipts								
	Planned releases								
2	PP 2	2							
	Grs reqs								
	Scd rcts			0	0	100	0	0	0
	PIB		230						
	Net reqs								
	Planned receipts								
	Planned releases								
2	S/A #2A	1							
	Grs reqs								
	Scd rcts			0	0	0	0	0	0
	PIB		90						
	Net reqs								
	Planned receipts								
	Planned releases								
3	MP 3	1							
	Grs reqs								
	Scd rcts			50	50	50	0	30	0
	PIB		175						
	Net reqs								
	Planned receipts								
	Planned releases								

Problem 7.34 (*continued*)

Level	Item	Qty	Current	Week 1	2	3	4	5	6
3	PP 6	2							
	Grs reqs								
	Scd rcts			0	0	0	500	0	0
	PIB		500						
	Net reqs								
	Planned receipts								
	Planned releases								
3	PP 7	1							
	Grs reqs			210	300	0	0	0	0
	Scd rcts			200	0	0	0	0	0
	PIB		350						
	Net reqs								
	Planned receipts								
	Planned releases								

7.35. Describe the differences between the regeneration method and the net-change method for updating the MRP record.

7.36. The Perez Plastics Company makes disposable dinnerware, including three sizes of plastic cups: large, medium, and small. The MPS for these products is shown below. Suppose the MPS changes as shown. What is the net change? Compare the number of records to be updated if the net-change method is used versus the regeneration method. (Quantities are in thousands of units.)

MPS for Perez Plastics Company's cups (in thousands of units)

	Week 1	2	3	4	5	6
Large	50	25	44	80	40	25
Medium	300	800	450	200	200	200
Small	100	250	100	300	100	100

New MPS for Perez Plastics Company's cups (in thousands of units)

	Week 1	2	3	4	5	6
Large	50	25	44	50	40	25
Medium	300	800	450	200	200	200
Small	100	250	100	100	50	50

7.37. Given the three product structures and MPS's below, obtain the gross requirements for all parts.

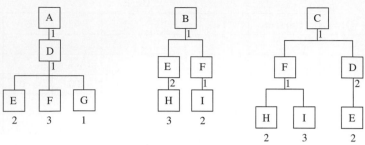

(Numbers below part symbols indicate quantity.)

		Period		
	1	**2**	**3**	**4**	**5**
Item A MPS	25	30	20	22	10
Item B MPS	100	80	70	70	60
Item C MPS	89	88	87	80	70

7.38. Suppose the combined requirements for one period in part F in the product structure above is 400 units and are pegged as follows:

180	Item A
100	Item B
120	Item C

Perform an implosion to determine requirements for all parts.

7.39. For the period described in Problem 7.38, a delivery of 300 units for part H has been canceled. Suggest an alternative MPS that would minimize the number of failed deliveries of the three items.

7.40. Explain the batching effect and the saturation effect.

7.41. Compute the mean arrival rate of batches for the following scenario:

		Product j		
	1	**2**	**3**	**4**	**5**
D_j	24	10	81	43	66
Q_j	50	50	100	50	75

7.42. Create a product-structure diagram for the following:

(a) A pair of in-line skates

(b) A filing cabinet

(c) A table lamp

7.43. Careta Darby, production planner for Kitsch Designs, Inc., performed a simple explosion of the product structure for a Kitsch coffee table to estimate the gross requirements for components at all levels for the upcoming week. Her explosion results are shown below. Complete the product-structure diagram by adding quantities as required.

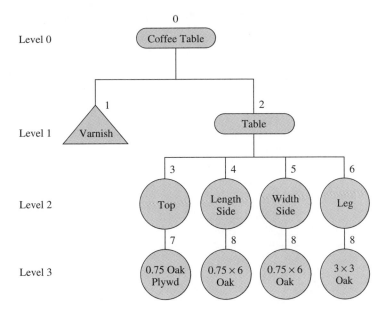

Level 0	0 Coffee Table
Level 1	1 Varnish 2 Table
Level 2	3 Top 4 Length Side 5 Width Side 6 Leg
Level 3	7 0.75 Oak Plywd 8 0.75 × 6 Oak 8 0.75 × 6 Oak 8 3 × 3 Oak

Level	Item number	Gross requirement
0	Table	400
1	1	800
2	2	800
2	3	2400
2	4	1600
2	5	800
3	6	4000
3	7	2400
3	8	3200

7.44. Perez Plastics (see Problem 7.36) must ship 300,000 medium-size cups per week for the next six weeks and 275,000 per week for three weeks afterwards. The shipping department is scheduled to receive 400,000 medium-size cups next week (week 1) and 350,000 in week 3. They currently have only 50,000 medium-size cups in stock. Compute the projected inventory balance and net requirements for each week.

7.45. Five ounces of plastic are used to produce each medium-size cup at Perez. Cups are produced in quantities to satisfy 1.5 weeks of demand. Generate the planned-order receipts and releases of plastic using a lot-for-lot policy. Perez currently has 2,800,000 ounces of plastic in stock. Assume a one-week lead time for cups and two weeks for plastic.

7.46. MPS's for the large and small cups at Perez Plastics for the next six weeks are given in Problem 7.36. For the three weeks following, there is no demand for the large cups, and 100,000 small cups per week are required. Eight ounces of plastic are required to produce one large cup and 3.5 ounces to produce one small cup. Using the MPS and receipts described in Problem 7.44 for the medium-size cup, create the MRP records for all three cups and for plastic. Perez has 70,000 large cups and 100,000 small cups in stock and are scheduled to receive 2,000,000 ounces of plastic in week 1 and 2,000,000 ounces in week 4.

7.47. Create a pegging record for the plastics in Problem 7.46 for week 4.

7.48. Using a spreadsheet model and a trial-and-error method, determine the lot sizes in the following table that will yield close-to-minimum lead time.

	Product				
	1	**2**	**3**	**4**	**5**
D_j (unit/week)	45	80	62	30	25
t_j (hr)	0.50	0.78	0.35	0.12	0.65
S_j (hr)	4.1	2.0	1.6	2.5	4.0

7.49. Plot lead time as a function of lot size for each product in Problem 7.48. At what lot size is the lead time for each product at a minimum?

7.50. Consider the following segment of a product-structure diagram (for legend, see Figure 7-7):

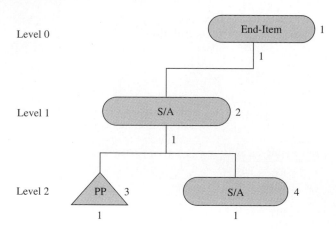

Lead time between level 2 and level 1 is one day, and lead time between level 1 and level 0 is 2 days. Demand for the end-item is constant at 100 units per day, and $A = \$500$, $i = 20$ percent. No set-up is required for the assembly operation in level 1.

(a) Evaluate inventory and safety stock if inventory is kept in level 0 only.
(b) Repeat (a) if inventory is maintained in level 0 and level 1.
(c) Repeat (a) if inventory is maintained at all three levels. Interpret your results.

7.51. Generate an MRP plan for a two-level system, using a multi-echelon-inventory approach, given that there are no outstanding orders, and

$$R_1^e = 30 \qquad R_2^e = 44 \qquad I_1^o = 28 \qquad I_2^o = 48 \qquad Q_1 = 20 \qquad Q_2 = 30$$

Assume a planning horizon of eight periods and make assumptions as necessary.

4 SHOP-FLOOR CONTROL

So far, we have emphasized the planning elements of MRP. Following the planning phase there is an execution phase, during which the plan is put into action. The execution has to be tracked and monitored by a set of procedures under the heading of **shop floor control** (SFC). SFC is a separate module in the MRP system (see Figure 7-2). SFC generally has four major procedures: **releasing, scheduling, monitoring,** and **updating.**

The **releasing** procedure checks the feasibility of planned releases generated by the MRP. It performs two functions: checking availability of raw material, parts, and subassemblies, and checking availability of capacity. It also checks the feasibility of the purchasing plan versus suppliers' capabilities.

The **scheduling** procedure details the order release of the MRP. Order release is performed in time buckets, usually weeks. The flow of jobs within the week, loading of machines, assigning operators to tasks, and sequencing priorities are handled by the scheduling routine. During the week, the scheduling routine adapts the schedule to the changing conditions on the production floor. We discuss scheduling models separately in Chapter 8.

The **monitoring** procedure tracks the workorders that are in the shop, the level of work in process, and work performed by outside vendors. As required, the procedure updates inventory and revises scheduled receipts.

Finally, the **updating** routine periodically revises MRP parameters to reflect the situation on the production floor. This includes lead time, capacity, yield, and similar data. Adequacy of these parameters is paramount to the MRP calculations.

SECTION 4 PROBLEMS

7.52. Describe shop-floor control.

7.53. The Zydecon Electronics Company produces portable radios and tape players. A radio is made of two identical electrical subassemblies and a case. Each electrical assembly requires two batteries. A tape player is made of two other identical electrical subassemmblies and one case (identical to the case for the radio). Each subassembly requires one battery. Hemente is their production planner, and he has derived the following MRP quantities:

	Planned-order receipts				
	Week				
Product	1	2	3	4	5
Tape	0	570	960	0	610
Radio	0	0	0	830	690

Hemente uses a one-week lead time to calculate release times. The items and subassemblies require the workcenters and times shown below. Workcenter capacities are shown as well. Perform a detailed capacity check to determine if Hemente's releases are feasible. If they are not, suggest releases to solve the capacity problem.

Part	Workcenter number	Time (min)
Tape	1	20
	2	17
Electrical S/A (tape player)	4	40
Case	3	36
Battery	5	10
Radio	2	55
Electrical S/A (radio)	4	37

	Workcenter				
	1	2	3	4	5
Capacity	10,000	30,000	33,000	50,000	28,000

5 OTHER ASPECTS OF MRP

5.1 MRP as an Information System

An MRP system is computer based. As such, we can describe it schematically in "computer terminology," essentially describing MRP in a different way. An MRP information system is shown in Figure 7-12. The purchase orders and workorders are the primary outputs of an MRP system. Rescheduling notices are issued to the production floor when a change is required. Other outputs can be obtained; two examples follow.

A purchasing budget can be obtained by multiplying the quantities appearing in the purchase orders by their respective unit costs. Since the orders are time-phased, a monthly, quarterly, and annual budget can be developed, depending on the planning horizon. This budget can be compared to the allocated budget, and adjustments can be made. The net result of this process is a **material plan** that shows required quantities and budget allocation over time.

Another possible output of the MRP system is **"what if" simulation,** by which the feasibility of changes in the MPS (because of arrival of a new customer order, for example) can be examined, and the proper delivery date can be promised. This is done by introducing the new quantity into the MPS and then using the net-change method to check availability of capacity and material. With the recent proliferation of workstations and PCs, the "what if" simulation has become very popular.

5.2 Additional MRP Aspects

Certain additional aspects of MRP are worth mentioning, namely, **closed-loop MRP** and **MRP in distribution systems.**

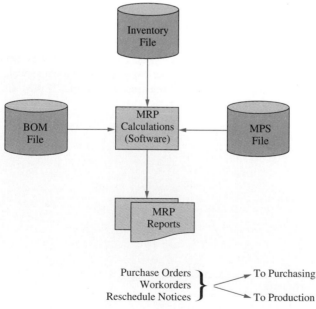

FIGURE 7-12
MRP information system

Closed-loop MRP. So far we have emphasized MRP during the planning phase. Obviously, during execution, things don't happen exactly as planned. Demand may change, deliveries may be late, and production interruptions may occur. The result is that over time the status on the production floor is different from the one planned. This new condition should be reflected in the MRP plan for the plan to be valid. This is achieved through closed-loop MRP, in which information about the execution of the plan is fed back to the MRP system. MRP records are then updated according to the actual status. The plan is kept valid and new MRP runs will launch realistic orders. We show this feedback loop in Figure 7-2.

MRP in distribution systems. A distribution system consists of a number of warehouses with a hierarchical relationship among them. There may be a local warehouse, a regional warehouse, a distribution center, etc. Each level in this system can be regarded as a level in the BOM. Orders generated at the local warehouse will generate requirements for the regional warehouse, which in turn generate requirements for the distribution center. The MRP procedure can be applied to distribution systems, and is often called **distribution-requirements planning (DRP).**

5.3 Benefits and Shortcomings of MRP

Certainly, MRP has many benefits as well as shortcomings, as do many other management tools. We examine this issue next. We reexamine this issue in a broader context when we discuss MRP II in Chapter 10.

Benefits. MRP benefits occur during the planning and execution phases of the production plan. The major benefit during the planning phase is the ability to evaluate the feasibility and requirements of different production plans. By doing so, a more reliable delivery date can be promised to the customer. In addition, one outcome of this phase is a "material plan" in terms of time-phased quantities, which can be transformed into a "time-phased budget." This can be checked and compared with the planned-material budget, and adjustments can be made. Thus, a management inventory policy can be implemented.

During the execution phase, MRP plays a major role in inventory control and inventory reduction. One of the major applications of MRP systems is in identifying future inventory shortages or overages. When a shortage situation is identified, a remedial action takes place in the form of **expediting** existing orders (scheduled receipts) that are in the pipeline. Similarly, in case of overages, existing orders are delayed or canceled.

Identifying a shortage requires, among other things, supply-lead-time follow-up. The MRP system may be used thus as a tool to classify suppliers in terms of their supply-time reliability.

Shortcomings. Most of the commercially available MRP systems tacitly assume **infinite production capacity** (see Section 2.3). The implication is that the production plan obtained often needs adjusting to consider the finite-capacity constraints. Some of the more recent MRP software applications try to address this issue. Infinite capacity can be considered to be an inherent shortcoming of the system. Other elements can cause problems unless properly addressed, namely, *uncertainty, production/supply lead time, yield, system nervousness,* and *data integrity.*

Uncertainty. The MRP system is a deterministic system. In reality, uncertainty affects each parameter of this system, including uncertainty about future production quantities, supply, and production lead time. We can hedge against uncertainty by generating safety stock at different levels of the production process or by building a certain amount of safety margin into the end-product quantities, which will automatically generate safety stock at all levels. In both cases, there is a danger of building excessive inventory levels. Another approach is to build safety stock at the raw-material level and use the Pareto concept to tighten control and allow for different safety-stock levels for A, B, and C items.

Production/supply lead time. Discrepancies between the actual and planned lead times will disrupt the production plan suggested by the MRP. If we consider that the system has to handle thousands of stock items, the lead-time distribution can present a major difficulty. Applying the methods for dealing with lead-time variability presented in Chapter 6 is impractical for that many items. The Pareto concept is also applicable here. B and C items are bundled into "lead time" groups where one lead time is given to each group. A items get an individual lead time, which is monitored and updated frequently.

Yield. In most production processes, some items are rejected because they do not meet quality standards. *Yield* is the ratio of the quantity of good products to the planned quantity. If the yield is 97 percent, out of a quantity of 100 only 97 will be delivered. Therefore, raw-material quantities have to be increased by the percentage of rejects (3 percent) in order to be able to meet the planned delivery. In this example, production should begin with raw material for 100/0.97 (approximately 103 units) to obtain 100 "good" products.

System nervousness. MRP is not used in a static environment. MRP is updated on a regular basis, and in an updating run the different MRP records are updated. The MPS is not only updated but also extended. If we have a 12-month planning horizon, an update after one month will require adding another month at the end of the remaining 11 months. (This is sometimes referred to as a 12-month **"rolling horizon."**) As a result of the changes introduced in an update run, changes may occur in the quantities of the planned-order release. Worse than that, scheduled receipts may require change. This phenomenon is known as **system nervousness.** To overcome system nervousness, many MRP systems introduce a **frozen horizon;** i.e., the MPS and planned-order release are kept constant for a number of time buckets into the future. This period is usually six weeks. In today's dynamic production world, frozen horizon is becoming difficult to cope with.

Data integrity. An MRP system, like many other systems, is very sensitive to data inaccuracies. Specifically, BOM and inventory files have to maintain high data integrity. The BOM must have the latest version of the product structure. Inventory records must be very accurate. Usually a level of accuracy higher than 92 percent is required for the MRP system to operate effectively. This is no simple task to achieve; nevertheless, there is no point in investing in an MRP system and, because of poor data integrity, failing to reap the benefits.

We are now ready to discuss how MRP is applied in the real world.

SECTION 5 PROBLEMS

7.54. What is distribution-requirements planning?

7.55. What are the advantages and disadvantages of using an MRP system?

7.56. Describe how an MRP system can be used to determine the number of new employees to hire.

7.57. BAM Chemical Company produces products that require a single manufacturing process. This process is very fast, and BAM maintains extra capacity to avoid lost sales. The lead times for the raw materials are very high and variable. Forecasting is difficult and is often inaccurate. BAM has one warehouse location in the facility from which it ships orders directly to customers. There is much finished-goods inventory. Is MRP appropriate? Why or why not?

6 APPLICATION AND EVOLUTION OF MRP

MRP is one of the most commonly applied production control systems; there are virtually thousands of applications. These occur in small and large organizations making a variety of products. It is difficult to make a distinction between an MRP application per se and MRP as part of a broader system called manufacturing resource planning (MRP II). The same reasoning applies also to MRP software. We therefore discuss both issues in Chapter 10, where MRP II systems are presented. In the meantime, to gain insight into MRP applications, we present Box 7-1, the case of Merit Brass Company, of Cleveland, Ohio. Use of MRP by Merit Brass resulted in lower investment in inventory and improved on-time delivery.

Evolution of MRP is also considered under a broader scope; MRP has evolved as part of the general evolution of integrated production planning and control systems. We discuss this issue also in Chapter 10.

BOX 7-1: MERIT BRASS COMPANY

People normally think of MRP systems primarily in conjunction with dependent demand inventory management, and the system did play that role at Merit Brass. However, an equally critical role for the system was capacity requirements planning (CRP); CRP is a more complex and demanding process for Merit Brass than material planning. The company manufactures primarily brass and stainless nipples, which have only brass and stainless steel pipe as material inputs. The primary operations consist of cutting the pipe to length, threading it to make nipples, degreasing the nipples, and packaging them to go into distribution inventories. Because the nipples have a wide variety of diameters and lengths (thus, the 2,000 plus part numbers), plant managers never knew whether a particular production schedule was feasible before MRP. They found this very frustrating, as did other managers in the company with whom they interact, particularly sales managers.

Since the plant was organized into manufacturing cells, we constructed a separate MRP data base for each cell. This provided the same advantages of modularity described for forecasting. The eight manufacturing cells vary in the number of part numbers and the volume of parts they produce. One small cell has less than 100 part numbers assigned to it, while a large one has over 600. Each large cell has its own day of the week for its weekly update run, but small cells are combined to allow more than one of them to be run on one day. The result is a five-day schedule that covers all eight cells. The PC on which MRP is run performs many other functions as well and is not dedicated to MRP alone. The only information not available on the PC that is needed to run the update is the current inventory level for each part or material item. The company's systems analyst developed a simple utility exactly analogous to the one described above for forecasting to download these data so that they can be imported into MRP's inventory status file. This utility allows the plant management personnel to add or delete part numbers from an MRP data base as needed without any additional programming support from the systems analyst.

BOX 7-1 *(continued)*

The forecasts that drive MRP are computed monthly, whereas MRP in the plant is run weekly. To accommodate these frequencies, the forecasts are imported into a spreadsheet program, converted to a weekly schedule, and then imported into the MRP system. The weekly conversion assumes a 4, 4, 5 pattern for weeks in each month of each quarter (so March always has five weeks). The monthly demand forecast is kept intact in this process because some part numbers have very low demand. This is done by making the last week of each month equal to the monthly forecast less the sum of the earlier weeks' forecasts. In the case in which demand is forecasted as one unit, the first three (or four) weeks' forecasts will be zero, and the last week will have a forecast of one unit. This system has worked out fairly well in practice since the demand patterns tend to be flat with random variations.

The company uses certain key capabilities of the STORM MRP module. For example, it plans capacity resources (CRP) through the bill of material (BOM) file. The users think of the BOM simply as a bill of resources and enter the material descendants of an item and the setup and operation times for each part number for each processing step. The resulting capacity load reports are critical to shop floor management and to planning overtime production when needed.

Another capability of the STORM MRP program is maintaining safety inventory levels. Providing the desired levels of safety stock for each item, the MRP program corrects planned orders according to the prevailing understock or overstock situation. This prevents inventory from building up if a part number is not selling and quickly rebuilds safety stocks if there is a run on an item.

By using the firm planned order capability, the plant management can override the MRP system's suggested planned orders. This is useful for smoothing capacity loads during the planning horizon.

The lot sizing procedures also proved useful, but in some interesting and unusual ways. Since the manufacturing cells are organized around part families, each time a part family is run we want to run every part in the family that has a net need. In this way, we spread the setup cost for the family over all the part numbers. Economic lot sizing procedures are generally designed for individual part numbers, however, not for part families. We needed to support a rolling schedule wherein all part numbers in a family called for production at about the same time.

To accomplish this task, we performed an independent economic lot sizing exercise using a spreadsheet. We sought to identify an economic production cycle for each part family by trading off the inventory carrying costs of both cycle stocks and safety stocks against the setup costs. If the family had a single class A high volume demand item, the family would have an economic production cycle of about one month regardless of the demand for other part numbers. If the family included no such high volume part, a cycle of about two months provided a reasonable trade-off. Since there is zero changeover time to go from one part number to another within a product family, we can run the low volume parts in the family on the same cycle as the high volume parts. It was easy to construct a master plan calling for high volume families to be produced once a month and low volume families every other month. We used STORM's fixed period lot-sizing rule to implement the results of our off-line economic analysis.

BOX 7-1 *(continued)*

After a few months of operation, we noticed a disturbing problem with parts for which there was very little demand. MRP would call for production of a one-month supply of two units. However, the packaging quantity for the part number might be five, 25, or more units per pack. We corrected this problem for these specific items by changing the lot-sizing rule to a fixed quantity rule and entering the minimal packaging quantity as the fixed quantity value. Once again, we found that meeting the user's needs required both ingenuity and software.

Preparing purchase orders for approximately 6,000 part numbers is an important task for Merit Brass acting as a master distributor. Prior to implementing MRP, the company made such purchases quarterly. Several problems were associated with this practice. First, extremely large shipments had to be received and put away. Many of these purchased parts had to be repackaged before they could be resold, and this created very lumpy demand on the packaging area. Second, the company was forced to make very large investments in inventory whenever it kept several months supply plus safety stock on hand. The vendors also had to build large inventories before shipping the orders since, in some cases, sales to Merit Brass represented large parts of their capacity. Finally, if the company ran out of an item, another shipment might not be due for months, during which the item would be backordered. Because each quarterly purchase order might contain several hundred items, each reviewed manually by the purchasing manager, the company was unable to support more frequent orders without modern management systems.

Now the company prepares forecasts for purchased items just as it does for manufactured ones. These forecasts drive an MRP process that allows for corrections to safety-stock inventories just as for manufactured products. Since the MRP data bases are by product group, the company now places monthly purchases with each vendor, resulting in more frequent and even shipments. It shares the bill-of-material explosion reports for several months into the future with its vendor partners to facilitate their capacity planning. This has resulted in shorter vendor lead times and more reliable vendor deliveries.

Source: Reprinted by permission, Flowers (1993), The Institute of Management Sciences and the Operations Research Society of America (currently INFORMS).

7 SUMMARY

This chapter focuses on three important planning activities. They are planning of production, capacity, and material.

We start by making a distinction between independent and dependent demand. Independent demand (e.g., end-items) is forecasted, whereas dependent demand is planned. Planning of dependent demand is the common thread of this chapter, and is presented through the production-planning process.

This production has a hierarchical structure, from demand estimates through master production schedule (MPS) to material requirement planning (MRP) to the execution phase—material plan, shop orders, and shop-floor control.

A master production plan is a plan of production—how many finished products are to be produced and when they will be produced. In developing the MPS the nature of the product and the market should be considered. Three types of product market environments are customarily identified as related to MPS: make-to-stock (MTS), make-to-order (MTO), and assemble-to-order (ATO).

Because of the nature of MPS, time-phased records are used for MPS planning and maintenance. Quantitative approaches to MTS and ATO models are discussed.

The feasibility of a production plan depends, among other things, on available capacity. Capacity is evaluated at the MPS and the MRP levels. At the MPS level the initial feasibility of the MPS is checked, which is called rough-cut capacity planning (RCCP). Detailed capacity planning, also called capacity-requirement planning (CRP), is performed at the MRP level. The two processes are similar in nature, and we demonstrate them through examples. Both RCCP and CRP are information tools rather than decision-making tools; hence they are regarded as infinite-capacity planning. To conclude the capacity discussion, an input/output-capacity model is presented.

MRP is the driving force of the production-planning system. The major objective of MRP is to determine requirements—discrete demand for each component in each time bucket. It requires three major inputs: a master production schedule, inventory status records, and a bill of material.

The major outputs of an MRP system are planned-order releases. Purchase orders make up the purchasing plan while work orders generate the production plan for the shop floor.

The MRP output is obtained through four steps: explosion, netting, offsetting, and lot sizing. A touch-phone example is used to demonstrate each of these steps. This example is carried further to demonstrate the process of multilevel explosion.

Once the MRP process is set in motion, it requires updating. Two updating methods, regeneration and net change, are presented. Net change is performed on a continuous basis, whereas regeneration is done once in a period.

An MRP system has supplemental netting procedures. They are implosion, combining requirements, and pegging. Pegging enables executing an implosion process for common items.

Essentially, an MRP system is a multilevel system. Therefore, two multilevel aspects are discussed: first, how multilevel inventory is built up, and second, how to incorporate multilevel inventory control in MRP systems.

An important spin-off of the lot-size issue is its impact on lead time. We present analyses of this relationship. In doing so, two phenomena are identified, the batching effect and the saturation effect. Striking a balance between the two yields an optimum value for the lead time. Queueing theory is used to model this situation.

When MRP plans are executed, they should be tracked and monitored. This is handled by a set of procedures under the heading of shop-floor control (SFC). SFC is a separate module in the MRP system. It generally has four major procedures: releasing, scheduling, monitoring, and updating.

To have a complete discussion of MRP systems, we examine MRP as an information system with its outputs and "what if" capability. The concept of "closed-loop MRP" is presented, followed by application of MRP to distribution systems.

Some of the benefits of an MRP system are its ability to plan ahead and simulate the feasibility of different production plans, identification of shortages or overages, and supply-time follow-up. Infinite capacity and fixed lead time are the two major shortcomings of such systems. Uncertainty and yield introduce "noise" into the system. Finally, MRP systems are very sensitive to data integrity.

Real-world application, software, and evolution of such systems are discussed in a later chapter.

ADDITIONAL PROBLEMS

7.58. Vered works in the planning department of Preston Brass Company, which manufactures brass bathroom and kitchen fixtures. She has derived the following MPS for PBC's Model 317 for the next six weeks.

	MPS					
Current =	**Week**					
750	**1**	**2**	**3**	**4**	**5**	**6**
F_t	550	540	540	540	540	540
O_t	600	400	500	150	100	0
I_t	150	710	170	730	190	750
MPS	0	1100	0	1100	0	1100
ATP	150	200		850		110

Vered uses a two-week moving average to forecast the next week's demand. PBC policy dictates a two-week frozen horizon for which projected production quantities cannot be changed. Holding cost for the 317 is $0.15 per unit per week. Set-up cost is $150 per batch. Production cost is $2.25 per unit. PBC sells the 317 for $3.00 per unit. Customers will tolerate a lead time of three weeks but will buy elsewhere if this cannot be met. The production department will produce in lots of any size, and Vered recognizes that changes to the lot size of the Model 317 could reduce costs.

Simulate Vered's job for the next six weeks with regard to the MPS for the Model 317 given the following occurrences during each week. Note that you must update the MPS six times, incorporating the new information one week at a time. Calculate the costs incurred each week, including a cost for lost sales, due to producing 317's from your MPS.

Week 1:	150 units ordered for Week 2
	200 units ordered for Week 6
	10 units ordered for Week 8
Week 2:	100 units canceled for Week 3
	100 units canceled for Week 4
	300 units ordered for Week 7
Week 3:	150 units ordered for Week 8
	75 units ordered for Week 9
	50 units ordered for Week 10
Week 4:	50 units canceled for Week 6
	300 units ordered for Week 11
Week 5:	100 units ordered for Week 6
Week 6:	300 units ordered for Week 12

7.59. Formulate an MPS model for an MTS environment that includes constraints for overtime, sub-contracting, and demand backlogging. (*Hint:* Refer to Chapter 5.)

7.60. Given the data below for an ATO environment, formulate the MPS problem mathematically. There are 70 hours available during period 1 and 80 hours available in period 2. A unit of module 1 incurs $0.20 per period in holding cost and requires 25 minutes of processing. A unit of module 2 costs $0.16 per period to hold and 10 minutes to process.

	Customer orders		
j	**Product**	**Quantity**	**Week due**
1	1	20	1
2	1	14	1
3	2	25	1
4	3	10	1
5	3	9	1
6	1	20	2
7	1	10	2
8	1	10	2
9	2	22	2
10	3	20	2

Final assembly schedule		
	Week 1	**Week 2**
Product 1	34	40
Product 2	25	22
Product 3	19	20

Module quantities per product		
	Module 1	**Module 2**
Product 1	2	1
Product 2	0	4
Product 3	2	2

					π_{jt}					
					j					
t	**1**	**2**	**3**	**4**	**5**	**6**	**7**	**8**	**9**	**10**
1	0	0	0	0	0	0.67	0.67	0.67	0.77	0.86
2	3	3	3	3	3	0	0	0	0	0

π_{jt} = penalty cost if order *j* is satisfied in period *t*

7.61. Janet Huang has just been given the job of deriving the MPS for her company's production for the next eight weeks. Her company, Saburg, Inc., produces closet storage systems and assembles the components to customer order. Ms. Huang remembers the integer-programming model for deriving the MPS for an ATO environment. Although she does not have the tools to solve her problem optimally, she believes that gathering the pertinent information and calculating the coefficients will be a good exercise for her and will give her insight as to deriving a low-cost solution. Shown below are customer orders for the next eight weeks, profits per unit for each product, and holding costs for products. The sales department at Saburg offers price breaks for late orders that increase for each week the order is late, as shown below. Saburg's customers will refuse shipment after three weeks, resulting in lost sales. Describe a general procedure for Janet to follow to calculate the penalty costs for her model. What would her π_{jt} matrix be?

Saburg, Inc., customer orders			
Order #	Product	Quantity	Week due
1	A	100	1
2	E	52	1
3	B	65	2
4	A	78	3
5	C	96	3
6	D	154	4
7	D	13	4
8	C	14	5
9	E	87	6
10	A	99	7
11	B	15	8
12	B	36	8

Product	Holding cost (dollars per unit-week)	Price break (dollars per order-week)	Profit (dollars per unit)
A	0.50	25.00	10.75
B	0.24	12.50	5.50
C	0.12	8.00	4.30
D	0.36	15.00	6.80
E	0.10	6.00	2.60

7.62. Cloudsox Industries produces appliquéd flags to sell in their beachfront store in Seabreeze, North Carolina. This fall season they are producing three new flags: a leaf flag, a Halloween flag, and a Thanksgiving flag. Each flag requires three operations processed in three of five workstations. At the first station, the material is cut. The pattern is stenciled and appliqués are attached at the second workstation. The flag is sewn and finished at the third. The routing for the three flags for the three operations is shown below.

Product	Operations		
	Cut	Attach	Sew
Leaf	WS100	WS400	WS300
Halloween	WS100	WS200	WS300
Thanksgiving	WS100	WS200	WS500

Darnell Walker, who began at Cloudsox as a cutter, became interested in computers and volunteered to write a set of spreadsheet programs to perform the functions of an MRP system. Rein Moore, owner of Cloudsox, asked Darnell to advise her about her production quantities for autumn. She believes, from historical data, that Cloudsox can sell a certain quantity of flags in their store this autumn (depicted in the accompanying table), and she planned to use these quantities to plan production. However, Rein has found a new market for flags that could increase these quantities by 40 percent for all three flag types. Rein now needs Darnell to determine if the manufacturing shop can handle the extra load.

| | Cloudsox master production schedule | | | | | | | | | | | | |
| | September | | | | October | | | | November | | | | |
Flag	1	2	3	4	1	2	3	4	1	2	3	4	5
L	15	15	15	17	20	20	20	22	20	20	15	15	15
H	10	10	12	12	20	20	20	15	5	5	5	5	5
T	8	8	8	8	10	10	10	15	20	25	25	25	10

Darnell has made the following projections about labor hours for the three new flags and the capacities available at each workstation to devote to fall flags. What should Darnell tell Rein about the capacity required this autumn with and without the 40 percent increase in demand? Identify one cause for inaccuracies in Darnell's rough-cut plan. What can Darnell do to reduce the number of calculations needed to check capacity requirements?

Cloudsox Industries' capacities by workstation

Workstation	Capacity (hr per week)
100	16
200	8
300	16
400	8
500	8

Cloudsox Industries' production requirements

Flag	Lot size	Workstation	Set-up (hr per batch)	Run (hr per unit)
Leaf	20	100	0.10	0.125
		400	0.25	0.050
		300	0.15	0.250
Halloween	25	100	0.10	0.105
		200	0.22	0.030
		300	0.20	0.200
Thanksgiving	25	100	0.15	0.120
		200	0.25	0.045
		500	0.25	0.320

7.63. The MPS for three products is shown below. Each product requires processing in three work-centers: WC100, WC200, and WC300. Product A requires 0.86 standard direct-labor hours. Product B requires 1.24 hours and product C requires 2.08 hours. Data from the last five years for total direct-labor hours worked at each workcenter are shown below. Devise a method of performing rough-cut capacity planning and determine if MPS is feasible. If it is not, suggest an alternative MPS that is feasible.

					Master production schedule (units)								
						Time period							
	1	**2**	**3**	**4**	**5**	**6**	**7**	**8**	**9**	**10**	**11**	**12**	**13**
A	35	35	35	42	42	42	32	32	32	40	40	40	40
B	15	15	15	12	12	12	12	20	20	20	20	25	25
C	8	8	8	8	8	14	14	20	20	22	22	22	22

	Direct-labor hours at each workcenter				
	Year				
WC	**1989**	**1990**	**1991**	**1992**	**1993**
100	1200	1050	990	1140	1250
200	560	1100	625	700	620
300	980	600	600	850	1000

7.64. You are an analyst in a manufacturing plant that produces exercise equipment. Quality problems with the model JX stationary bicycle has created a need for an additional operation in the manufacturing process for the JX frame. Currently the bicycle frame goes though three operations before entering final assembly: tube cutting, welding, and painting. The new operation, called post welding, will occur between the welding and painting operations. You have reviewed similar workstations in the plant and have estimated that each bicycle will require 15 minutes of processing by an operator at a workstation. For planning purposes, there are 6.8 hours per workday available for this operation.

Sarah Bunch of the facilities department says she has the equipment and the space to set up as many as three identical workstations to run this process. Jim Beck of the planning department tells you that the MRP system currently uses a lead time of zero for the bicycle end-item and a lead time of two weeks for the frame. The releases for the JX for the last two weeks were 150 (two weeks ago) and 200 (last week). The current processing times for the other operations are given below. Determine what you will tell Sarah and Jim about the new operation.

Operation	Processing time (min per unit)
Tube cutting	10
Welding	12
Painting	12

7.65. Complete the MRP record shown below. The set-up cost for WN is $85 per batch. Set-up for NL costs $168 per batch. Holding cost for the WN is $0.18 per unit for each week and is $0.07 for the NL per unit per week. Calculate the total cost (set-up plus holding costs) for your MRP record. Perturb lot sizes to achieve the best reduction you can in the total cost.

Level	Item	Qty	Current	Week					
				1	2	3	4	5	6
1	WN	1							
	Grs reqs			150	200	240	190	140	100
	Scd rcts			200	0	0	200	0	0
	PIB		100						
	Net reqs								
	Planned rcts								
	Planned rlse								
2	NL	2							
	Grs reqs								
	Scd rcts			0	0	200	0	0	0
	PIB		460						
	Net reqs								
	Planned rcts								
	Planned rlse								

7.66. Kudzukes, Inc., operates five department stores in Georgia and Alabama. They maintain a distribution center in Atlanta, Georgia, and regional warehouses in Birmingham, Alabama, and Macon, Georgia. The warehouse in Birmingham services stores in Auburn and Huntsville. The one in Macon services Thomaston and Savannah stores. The distribution center also services the department store in Atlanta. The following forecasts have been made for each store for an herb planter that is sold in the gardening department of Kudzukes.

Forecasts for herb planter

Store	Week						
	1	2	3	4	5	6	7
Atlanta	90	90	90	90	110	110	110
Huntsville	34	34	40	40	40	50	50
Auburn	33	33	33	35	35	35	35
Thomaston	20	20	20	20	22	22	22
Savannah	95	95	95	95	95	100	100

The following quantities represent shipments that are under way from some locations to others. It takes three days to process and deliver an order from the Atlanta distribution center to Birmingham or Macon. An order can be processed and delivered from the distribution center to the store in Atlanta on the same day. Shipments from the regional warehouses to stores are made once a week.

		To			
		Auburn	**Huntsville**	**Thomaston**	**Savannah**
From	Birmingham	50	55	—	—
	Macon	—	—	25	125

		To		
		Birmingham	**Macon**	**Atlanta store**
From	Atlanta distribution center	200	200	100

The Atlanta distribution center has 200 planters in inventory. Birmingham and Macon have 45 and 30, respectively. Using the logic of MRP, calculate the time-phased requirements at each location.

7.67. In Problem 7.49, you examined lead time as a function of lot size for each product in Problem 7.48. Develop a method of separating the function for each product and add graphs for the batching and saturation effects to your plots.

7.68. Describe a procedure for generating projected inventory turns from an MRP information system.

7.69. Given the MRP record that you created for Problem 7.46 for Perez Plastics' cups, simulate the planner's job for the next five weeks, accounting for the following occurrences. (Note that you must update the MRP record separately for each week.)

Week 1: Production is having trouble with set-up at the molder and requests lot sizes greater than or equal to 50 cups. Orders have arrived for the large cups to be delivered in weeks 7 and 8, changing the MPS for those weeks to 25,000 and 20,000 units, respectively. The MPS for week 10 is as follows: large cups = 0, medium-size cups = 200,000 and small cups = 100,000.

Week 2: Management is concerned about the erratic pattern of release quantities over the next three weeks and wants smoother production. MPS for week 11 is 150,000 for large cups, 200,000 for medium-sized cups, and 150,000 for small cups.

Week 3: A shipment of 400,000 ounces of plastic has arrived damaged. The shipping department can salvage 280,000 ounces for production. The MPS for week 12 is 10,000 for large cups, 150,000 for medium-sized cups, and 150,000 for small cups.

Week 4: The engineering department has made a change to the small cups and has created a new mold for producing them. They want to know how soon the new version can be shipped. The MPS for week 13 is 0 for large cups, 150,000 for medium-sized cups, and 100,000 for small cups.

Week 5: An order for 50,000 large cups has been received that was not planned for, and the sales department wants to know what delivery date they can promise the customer. The MPS for week 14 is 0 for large cups, 150,000 for medium-sized cups, and 75,000 for small cups.

MINICASE: ROCKVILLE PRODUCTS COMPANY

Rockville Products Company produces furniture. Their three top-selling products are a stereo cabinet, a television cabinet, and a large entertainment center. The facility has been in business for 15 years and was created as a job shop. There was a machine shop in which wooden component parts were manufactured; a finishing shop where the components were stained, painted, or laminated; and an assembly shop where the components were assembled and packaged for shipment to furniture stores. RPC now has a continuous improvement (CI) program, and the CI teams have made several changes in the plant to approach a more continuous-flow manufacturing process. The cost for new equipment was too high to place the machining and finishing tasks in assembly cells, but the remaining facilities were rearranged so that the assembly processes are cellular. The machine-room team is working on set-up reduction projects for all of their machines and has made progress. The planning department has coordinated a *kanban* system whereby lot sizes on many component parts have been reduced.

The production at RPC is seasonal and the customers require short lead times so RPC uses an MTS environment. Since the changes, the planning department has noticed that more shortages are occurring, so they have increased their forecasts to compensate. RPC uses an MRP system that also drives their costs-and-accounting system. The production teams are evaluated based on efficiencies, a percentage of actual time per unit versus standard time per unit.

You are a new employee at RPC, and your job is to analyze their problems and offer solutions to guide the company as they seek improvements. Toby, the accounting manager, has been in your office all morning complaining about the state of the company. She says, "None of these so-called improvements are showing up on our bottom-line costs! The inventory is too high, the machine room is way over budget on overtime costs, and our customers are not getting their orders on time! I believe that this 'team concept' that we are trying to enforce is making people take advantage of our company. People are talking too much about problems and working too little. How else can you explain the mess that we are in?" Ronnie, the machine-room supervisor, has another opinion when you go to see him. He says, "We have more active workorders now than we've ever had before. And we're getting these workorders for such small amounts! Why, just last week my people spent two hours setting up a machine to run 45 parts. As soon as they had completed the set-up for the next part on their list, I received a new workorder for 45 more of the first part! Of course we can't be profitable if the planning department is doing stupid things like that. What's more, our storage area is bursting at the seams! We've filled it up with partially filled pallets because our lot sizes are so small. It's those *kanban* things that are our downfall." The continuous-improvement facilitator, Arnold, has this to say: "We are using an antiquated measurement system to judge people. What good are efficiencies? We've proven that a part is only handled by a human being 3 percent of the time that it spends in this plant. Why aren't we looking at cycle times? Why aren't we making bigger improvements in set-up reduction? We are slaves to that MRP system, and nobody seems to recognize that the rules of the game have changed and the MRP numbers no longer make sense."

Below are data about three component parts that are used in Rockville Products Company's highest-volume products. Each of these components is produced in the machine room.

Part	Old set-up (hours)	New set-up (hours)	Old lot size (units)	New lot size (units)	Run time (hr per unit)
XB360	1.00	0.75	300	50	0.03
C044P	1.25	0.75	150	100	0.08
AM900	2.15	1.50	175	75	0.10

What would you recommend to the plant manager that RPC do? How do you respond to the comments made by Toby, Ronnie, and Arnold? Use mathematical methods when possible to justify your suggestions, making assumptions when necessary. Prepare a report to management.

8 REFERENCES

Axsäter, S. and Rosling, K., "Multi-Level Production-Inventory Control: Materials Requirements Planning or Reorder Point Policies?" *European Journal of Operations Research,* 75, 405–412, 1994.

Baker, K. R., "Requirements Planning," in Graves, S. C., Rinnooy Kan, A. H. G., and Zipkin, P. H., eds. *Logistics of Production and Inventory,* North Holland, Amsterdam, 1993.

Blackburn, J. D. and Millen, R. A., "The Impact of a Rolling Schedule in a Multi-Level MRP System," *Journal of Operations Management,* 2(2), 125–135, 1982.

Flowers, A. D. "The Modernization of Merit Brass," *Interfaces,* 23(1), 97–108, 1993.

Freeland, J. R., "A Note on the Relationship Between the Number of Stocking Points and Average Inventory," Darden Graduate School of Business Administration, University of Virginia, (UVA-OM-483), 1985.

Graves, S. C., Rinnooy Kan, A. H. G., and Zipkin, P. H., eds. *Logistics of Production and Inventory,* North Holland, Amsterdam, 1993.

Guerrero, H. H., "Demand Management Strategies for Assemble-to-Order Production Environments," *International Journal of Production Research,* 29(1), 39–51, 1991.

Karmarkar, U. S., Kekre, S., and Freeman, S., "Lot Sizing and Lead Time Performance in Manufacturing Cell," *Interfaces,* 15, 2, 1–9, 1985.

Karni, R., "Capacity Requirements Planning—Optimal Workstation Capacities," *International Journal of Production Research,* 19, 5, 595–611, 1981.

Karni, R., "Capacity Requirements Planning—A Systematization," *International Journal of Production Research,* 20, 6, 715–739, 1982.

King, B. E. and Benton, W. C., "Alternative Master Production Scheduling Techniques in an Assemble-to-Order Environment," *Journal of Operations Management,* 7(2), 179–201, 1987.

Maes, J. and Van Wassenhove, L., "A Simple Heuristic for the Multi Item Single Level Capacitated Lot Sizing Problem," *Operations Research Letters,* 4, 6, 265–273, 1986.

McClelland, M. K., "Order Promising and the Master Schedule," *Decision Sciences,* 19(4), 858–879, 1988.

McClelland, M. K. and Wagner, H. W., "Location of Inventories in the MRP Environment," *Decision Sciences,* 19(3), 535–553, 1988.

Vollman, T. E., Berry, W. L., and Whybark, D. C., *Manufacturing Planning and Control Systems,* Business One Irwin, Homewood, IL, 1992.

Wijngaard, J. and Wortmann, J. C., "MRP and Inventories," *European Journal of Operations Research,* 20, 283–293, 1985.

CHAPTER
8

OPERATIONS SCHEDULING

1 INTRODUCTION

Newnan Foundries makes a variety of metal castings used in the automotive industry. The basic process is sand casting, with the parts molded on automatic machines. The production process of a typical foundry consists of the operations shown in Figure 8-1. A furnace supplies molten metal to an automatic molding machine. The machine uses a pattern (stored in the pattern shop) to automatically make sand molds of one or more parts. As molten metal flows into the machine, it travels through gates and risers to fill the mold and form the part. If the part has a hollow space in its interior, cores are placed in the molds before they are filled. Cores are made from sand or other material in the core shop. The molding machine opens, ejects the parts and sand, then repeats the process.

The sand and molded parts are put into a shaker, which removes the sand for reuse, and also separates many parts from the gates and risers. If a part is still attached to a gate or riser, it is manually separated or degated. At this point, the part may be shipped to the customer. Usually, finishing operations are performed on the casting. These might include grinding; drilling; coating; heat treating; and various tests such as ultrasonic, gaging, and inspection.

The foundry produces more than one thousand different parts for several hundred customers. A customer order, or job, specifies the number of identical parts to be made and a delivery date for the job. Each part has a route sheet containing production information. Route sheets contain all information needed to produce the part, e.g., alloy content, pattern, route, and labor requirements. Because a job consists of some number of the same parts, the information for the job is easily derived from the part information.

As can be inferred from the production process, the foundry tries to minimize work-in-process and finished-goods inventory. Shipping a job to a customer by the delivery date is important, but the job should not be produced too far in advance. This gives a time window during which each order should be produced.

Jobs with similar windows are lumped together in the production plan. Every day, a schedule of the jobs is generated for a five-day rolling horizon. The plant was designed for

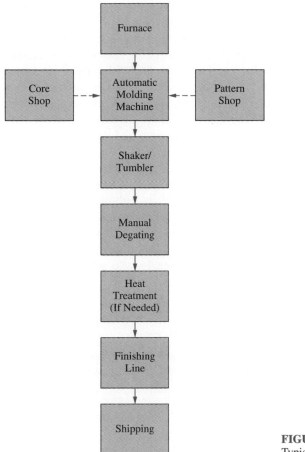

FIGURE 8-1
Typical foundry operations

products to flow smoothly through the process with no intermediate inventory, so the entire production line is treated as a single processor. The core shop has greater capacity than the line; its schedule is dictated by the foundry schedule. The foundry's problem is to determine which jobs are done at what time, i.e., to schedule the foundry.

Morton and Pentico (1993) state, "Scheduling is the process of organizing, choosing and timing resource usage to carry out all the activities necessary to produce the desired outputs at the desired times, while satisfying a large number of time and relationship constraints among the activities and the resources." This definition implies that, if resources are not limited, a scheduling problem does not exist.

In the foundry problem, jobs are activities and machines are resources. Thus a **schedule** specifies the time each job starts and completes on each machine, as well as any additional resources needed. A **sequence** is a simple ordering of the jobs; 3-1-2 implies job 3 is done first, job 1 is done second, and job 2 is done last. If every job starts as soon as possible and is processed without interruption for a given processing time, the sequence determines start and completion times, and hence, determines the schedule.

Determining a "best" sequence *seems* easy; just enumerate all the sequences and pick the one that optimizes some measure of performance. For 32 jobs, there are $32! \approx 2.6 \times 10^{35}$ possible sequences. Suppose a computer could examine one billion sequences per second. It would still take 8.4×10^{15} *centuries* to enumerate all of them! A computer one million times faster would still take 8.4×10^9 centuries to examine them all. With only 16 jobs there are over 20 trillion schedules, which, at one billion sequences per second, could be enumerated in about two-thirds of a year. Few real scheduling problems are that simple. Additional resources (manpower, raw materials, etc.) and dependencies between jobs (e.g., set-ups) further complicate the problem. For more about the complexity of scheduling problems, see Box 8-1.

This combinatorial explosion shows why some scheduling problems are difficult to solve and interesting to study. We begin the chapter by examining the scheduling environment, including jobs, machines, measures of performance, and algorithms. We then look at single-machine scheduling models; we categorize these models by measure of performance. After single-machine models, we examine parallel-machine models, followed by flow-shop models and job-shop models. Next we examine finite-capacity scheduling systems and comment on available software and the evolution of scheduling. We conclude with a summary of the chapter.

BOX 8-1: ALGORITHMIC COMPLEXITY

This is an intuitive discussion rather than a precise mathematical description. Although the following statements are not exact, they are close enough for practical considerations. For a more precise treatment, see Garey and Johnson (1979).

An efficient algorithm is one whose effort on any problem instance is bounded by a polynomial in the problem size, e.g., the number of jobs. An example would be the algorithm for the minimal spanning tree, which can be solved in at most n^2 iterations, where n is the number of edges. We say the algorithm is order of n-squared, or $O(n^2)$. If the effort is exponential (e.g., $O(2^n)$), the algorithm is not efficient. An example would be a branch-and-bound algorithm for 0/1 variables, which could require 2^n nodes to be explored.

The set NP is the set of all problems that can be solved by total enumeration. The set P is a subset of NP consisting of all problems for which efficient algorithms are known. Again, the minimal spanning tree is an example of a problem belonging to P. The set NP-hard is also a subset of NP, but these problems have been proven to be the hardest problems in NP. In fact, if anyone can find an efficient algorithm for any NP-hard problem, that algorithm can be modified to solve all problems in NP in polynomial time, thus making the inventor rich and famous. It seems unlikely that such an algorithm exists. The traveling-salesman problem is known to be NP-hard.

There are problems in NP that are not currently known to belong to P or NP-hard; i.e., they have unknown complexity and are called open problems.

If a problem is NP-hard, unless all problems in NP are polynomially solvable, we must resort to exponential (i.e., enumerative) algorithms to get optimal solutions. For small instances, or for some particular instances, enumerative algorithms may be acceptable. As instances get larger, the combinatorial explosion will make the problem

> **BOX 8-1:** (*continued*)
>
> *impossible to solve in a reasonable amount of time. Another approach is to use heuristic algorithms, which give usually good, but not necessarily optimal, solutions. Heuristics are usually polynomial algorithms tailored to the specific problem structure.*

SECTION 1 PROBLEMS

8.1. What is scheduling? How does it fit in with other production-planning and control tools?

2 BACKGROUND

This section provides a background for scheduling problems, models, and algorithms. We discuss the scheduling environment and define terminology and notation. The classic terminology of scheduling jobs on machines is used, but these are generic terms, and many nonmanufacturing applications exist.

2.1 Jobs

Jobs are activities to be done. In our introductory example, jobs were customer orders. In other situations, jobs could be patients to be x-rayed, customers to be served in a restaurant, programs to be run on a computer, or airplanes to land at an airport. We assume each job has a known processing time. Unless otherwise stated, once work on a job begins, it must be continuously processed until finished; i.e., preemption is not allowed. It may have a due time (or due date) by which it should be completed. A job may also have a ready time (or release date) before which processing cannot begin.

A job may depend on another job. One type of dependency occurs when one job must precede another; for example, a hole cannot be threaded before it is drilled. Another type of dependency occurs when the time needed for a job depends on the previous job processed. If job 1 needs one set of tooling on the machine and job 2 needs another, then after processing job 1 the machine tooling must be changed before processing job 2. If job 3 needs the same tooling as job 1, then the sequence 1-2-3 requires one more set-up than the sequence 1-3-2. This is typically called a **sequence-dependent set-up** time. If set-up times are not sequence-dependent they can be included in the processing time. Jobs are assumed to be independent unless otherwise stated. We also assume that, if a job must be processed by more than one machine, the job can only be processed by one machine at any given time; i.e., it cannot be done simultaneously with another job.

2.2 Machines

Machines process jobs. In manufacturing, a machine might be an automatic molding machine. In nonmanufacturing situations, a machine might represent an x-ray machine, a server in a restaurant, a computer, or a runway. We break the machine environment into several classes: single machine, parallel machines, flow shops, job shops, and open shops.

For **single-machine problems**, there is only one machine and all jobs must be processed on it. The machine can process at most one job at any time. Once a job has been processed by the machine, it is completed. Our introductory example views the production line as a single machine.

Several machines that can do the same process on jobs are called **parallel machines.** A job can be processed on any of the machines, and once processed by one machine, it is completed. Unless otherwise stated, we assume all parallel machines are identical. The time to process a job on one of several identical machines is independent of which machine does the work. A good example of parallel machines is a group of identical plastic-injection-molding machines, each of which can make a number of different plastic parts.

A **flow shop** consists of different machines. Each job must be processed by each machine exactly once. Furthermore, all jobs have the same routing; i.e., they must visit the machines in the same order. Without loss of generality, we can number the machines so machine 1 is first, machine 2 is second, and so forth. A job cannot begin processing on the second machine until it has completed processing on the first. Assembly lines and cells are typical examples of flow shops.

A **job shop** is more general than a flow shop; each job may have a unique routing. Metalworking shops are often job shops. One job must go to a lathe, then to a drill, and then to a mill, while another needs to be milled and then turned on the lathe, but is never drilled.

Open shops are job shops in which jobs have no specified routing. An example would be a car repair shop. Cars need multiple repairs requiring different equipment, but the order of the repairs may be unimportant. Because open shops are rare in the manufacturing world, we will not discuss them further.

2.3 Measures

A best schedule implies a measure of performance. Maximizing profit and minimizing cost are obvious measures. Unfortunately, it is difficult to estimate the financial parameters that relate a schedule to cost and profit. Also, efficient algorithms to optimize profit or cost for scheduling models are not known.

Proxy objectives are used to approximate some relevant costs. The proxy measures are normally functions of completion times for a given schedule. Most proxies are regular measures. A **regular measure** is a function of completion time in which the objective is to minimize the function, and in which the function only increases if at least one completion time in the schedule increases. Let

n = The number of jobs to be processed
m = The number of machines
p_{ik} = The time to process job i on machine k (p_i if $m = 1$)
r_i = The release time (or release date) of job i
d_i = The due time (or due date) of job i
w_i = The weight (importance or value) of job i relative to the other jobs

Given a particular schedule, define for each job i

C_i = The **completion time** of job i
$F_i = C_i - r_i$, the **flowtime** of job i ($F_i > 0$)
$L_i = C_i - d_i$, the **lateness** of job i ($L_i < 0$ denotes earliness)
$T_i = \max\{0, L_i\}$, the **tardiness** of job i
$E_i = \max\{0, -L_i\}$, the **earliness** of job i

$\delta_i = 1$ if job i is tardy (i.e., $T_I > 0$)
$\delta_i = 0$ if job i is on time or early (i.e., $T_i = 0$)
$C_{max} = \max_{i=1,n}\{C_i\}$, the maximum completion time of all jobs or **makespan**
$L_{max} = \max_{i=1,n}\{L_i\}$, the **maximum lateness** of all jobs
$T_{max} = \max_{i=1,n}\{T_i\}$, the **maximum tardiness** of all jobs

Common proxy objectives include minimizing total flowtime, total tardiness, maximum completion time, maximum tardiness, or the number of tardy jobs. All (except C_{max}, L_{max} and T_{max}) are simply the sum over all jobs of the respective quantity for each job. If all jobs are not equally important, an equivalent weighted measure can be calculated by multiplying the measure by the appropriate job weight.

Because the sum of processing times is constant, minimizing makespan (C_{max}) is equivalent to minimizing idle time or maximizing utilization of the machines. If holding costs dominate, weighted flowtime is an equivalent measure. Minimizing flowtime is equivalent to minimizing completion times, lateness, and job waiting times. Job waiting time is in-process inventory, so minimizing flowtime is equivalent to minimizing the number of jobs in process. Weighted flowtime corresponds to the value of in-process inventory. The number of tardy jobs, maximal tardiness, and total tardiness are measures of customer service. For more detail on costs and proxy measures, see Rinnooy Kan (1976).

Most scheduling problems assume data are known with certainty; set-up times are independent of the order of processing; all jobs are immediately available ($r_i = 0$); no precedence exists between jobs; and once a job starts processing, it cannot be interrupted.

2.4 Scheduling Algorithms

In Chapter 3 we briefly discussed algorithms. Here we discuss scheduling algorithms in greater detail. An algorithm is a "recipe" for obtaining a solution to a model. An **instance** is a particular set of data for the model. Exact algorithms give an optimal solution to every instance of the problem. Heuristic algorithms give solutions that are, we hope, optimal or close to optimal for any instance.

Why not always use an exact algorithm? For many scheduling models, the only known exact algorithms are based on enumeration, such as branch-and-bound algorithms or dynamic programming. For realistic instances, the combinatorial nature of the scheduling problem makes this computationally prohibitive.

Heuristic algorithms are judged by quality and efficacy. Quality is the difference between a heuristic solution and the optimal, while efficacy relates to the effort to obtain a solution. Both can be expressed theoretically or empirically. The best heuristics have guaranteed quality and efficacy (i.e., worst-case bounds on their performance).

A **worst-case bound** on efficacy determines the number of calculations the algorithm must perform for *any* problem instance of a particular size (hence the name "worst-case"). A good algorithm bounds the number of calculations by a function that is polynomial in the problem size. This has not been done for some heuristic algorithms, and they must be empirically evaluated.

To theoretically justify the quality of a heuristic algorithm, it must be mathematically proven to generate a solution within a certain percentage of optimality no matter what problem instance is solved. As with efficacy, if the quality of a heuristic algorithm cannot be theoretically justified, it must be empirically judged.

Empirical testing consists of generating and solving many problem instances and analyzing the results. Average time to solve the problems can be determined. The difference between heuristic and optimal solutions can be found for small instances. For instances that cannot be solved optimally, the heuristic solution is compared to a bound on the optimal solution. If there is a small difference, the quality of the heuristic appears good. A large difference could be caused by a loose bound or a poor heuristic. If the heuristic algorithm performs well on the test instances, we assume it performs as well on others. This may not be true for an instance that differs from the test instances. At implementation, compare the heuristic solution to the current solution.

All heuristics we discuss have worked well on test instances. Empirical tests are published and references are given in the various books on scheduling. This is not a guarantee of good or even usable solutions. Implementing a heuristic algorithm should always be preceded by testing on "typical" instances for the application.

2.5   Gantt Charts

In the early 1900s, Henry Gantt (1911) pioneered increased productivity through better scheduling. One of his primary tools was a pictorial representation of a schedule, now called a **Gantt Chart** in his honor. The purpose of the chart is to graphically display the state of each resource (usually a machine) at all times. The x axis represents time and the y axis consists of a horizontal bar for each machine. When a job is to be processed on a machine, a rectangle is placed on the horizontal bar, which begins at the job's start time and ends at its completion time. Gantt Charts also can be constructed placing jobs, instead of machines, on the y axis. The following example shows a Gantt Chart for a small scheduling problem.

Example 8-1. Gantt Chart. Table 8-1 gives data for a four-job, three-machine job-shop scheduling problem. The first operation of job 1 takes four minutes and is performed on machine 1; this is denoted by 4/1 in the row, job 1, and column, operation 1, of the table. All jobs are released at time zero, and their due-dates are given in the last column.

Solution.   Consider the sequence 2-1-4-3 on machine 1, the sequence 2-4-3-1 on machine 2, and the sequence 3-4-2-1 on machine 3. Figure 8-2 depicts this schedule in a Gantt Chart. Each block represents an operation of a job; the job number appears in the block. White blocks represent idle time, which occurs because no job is available for processing. Machine 1 is idle from time 0 to time 1, because job 2 was scheduled first on machine 1, but its first operation is on machine 2. Until job 2 finishes processing on machine 2, it cannot be processed on machine 1.

TABLE 8-1
Gantt Chart example data

| | Processing time/machine number | | | Release | |
Job	Operation 1	Operation 2	Operation 3	date	Due date
1	4/1	3/2	2/3	0	16
2	1/2	4/1	4/3	0	14
3	3/3	2/2	3/1	0	10
4	3/2	3/3	1/1	0	8

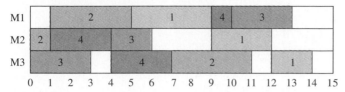

FIGURE 8-2
Gantt Chart

From Figure 8-2, note that the last operation of job 1 is on machine 3 and is completed at time 14; i.e.,

$$C_1 = 14 \qquad \text{(on machine 3)}$$

For the remaining jobs

$$C_2 = 11 \qquad \text{(machine 3)}$$
$$C_3 = 13 \qquad \text{(machine 1)}$$
$$C_4 = 10 \qquad \text{(machine 1)}$$

The makespan is

$$C_{\max} = \max\{C_1, C_2, C_3, C_4\} = \max\{14, 11, 13, 10\} = 14$$

Recall that $F_i = C_i - r_i$; in this example, $r_i = 0$ for all i, so flowtime and completion time are the same. The total flowtime (or sum of completion times) is

$$\sum_i F_i = \sum_i C_i = C_1 + C_2 + C_3 + C_4 = 14 + 11 + 13 + 10 = 48$$

The lateness of a job is its completion time minus its due-date; and its tardiness is the maximum of zero and its lateness. Thus

$$L_1 = C_1 - d_1 = 14 - 16 = -2 \quad \text{and} \quad T_1 = \max\{0, C_1 - d_1\} = \max\{0, -2\} = 0$$
$$L_2 = C_2 - d_2 = 11 - 14 = -3 \quad \text{and} \quad T_2 = \max\{0, C_2 - d_2\} = \max\{0, -3\} = 0$$
$$L_3 = C_3 - d_3 = 13 - 10 = 3 \quad \text{and} \quad T_3 = \max\{0, C_3 - d_3\} = \max\{0, 3\} = 3$$
$$L_4 = C_4 - d_4 = 10 - 8 = 2 \quad \text{and} \quad T_4 = \max\{0, C_4 - d_4\} = \max\{0, 2\} = 2$$

The total lateness is

$$\sum_i L_i = L_1 + L_2 + L_3 + L_4 = (-2) + (-3) + 3 + 2 = 0$$

and the total tardiness is

$$\sum_i T_i = T_1 + T_2 + T_3 + T_4 = 0 + 0 + 3 + 2 = 5$$

The maximum tardiness is

$$T_{\max} = \max\{T_1, T_2, T_3, T_4\} = \max\{0, 0, 3, 2\} = 3$$

Tardy jobs have $\delta_i = 1$, so

$$T_1 = 0 \Longrightarrow \delta_1 = 0$$
$$T_2 = 0 \Longrightarrow \delta_2 = 0$$
$$T_3 > 0 \Longrightarrow \delta_3 = 1$$
$$T_4 > 0 \Longrightarrow \delta_4 = 1$$

The number of tardy jobs is

$$N_T = \sum_i \delta_i = \delta_1 + \delta_2 + \delta_3 + \delta_4 = 0 + 0 + 1 + 1 = 2$$

SECTION 2 PROBLEMS

8.2. Using the schedule depicted in the following Gantt Chart and using (16,10,14,8) as the vector of due-dates, give the values of

(a) Makespan

(b) Total flowtime

(c) Total tardiness

(d) Total lateness

(e) Number of tardy jobs

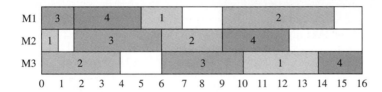

8.3. Find a feasible schedule for the following job shop data:

Job	Processing time Operation 1	2	3	Route Operation 1	2	3
1	5	10	12	A	B	C
2	4	3	8	A	C	B
3	9	6	7	C	B	A
4	7	5	11	B	C	A

Using a due-date of 27 for all jobs, determine

(a) Makespan

(b) Total flowtime

(c) Total tardiness

(d) Total lateness

(e) Number of tardy jobs

3 SINGLE-MACHINE SCHEDULING

In this section we study single-machine models and their solutions. These models are also useful for scheduling multiple machines. Our foundry example in the introduction to this chapter represents one situation. In that situation, several machines are considered to be an aggregate machine. Single-machine models also are appropriate for serial processes containing a bottleneck machine that constrains the entire system. It is important to generate a good schedule for the bottleneck machine, because its schedule determines the schedule for the machines before and after the bottleneck. This strategy is discussed more fully in Chapter 10.

The section is broken up by measure of performance. We first discuss simple algorithms for several models with flowtime, lateness, and weighted flowtime as the measure of performance. Simple algorithms for minimizing maximal lateness, maximal tardiness, and number of tardy jobs are given next. Unfortunately, minimizing the weighted number of tardy jobs has no elegant solution results, but we do present a heuristic algorithm. Minimizing tardiness on a single machine is a difficult problem. Simple algorithms for special cases and a heuristic algorithm for the general and weighted cases are provided. We then discuss solutions to a model with both earliness and tardiness penalties, followed by a framework for implementing these algorithms in a dynamic environment. Heuristic and branch-and-bound algorithms for sequence-dependent set-up times are discussed. Finally, search procedures are presented that may provide good solutions to most single-machine scheduling models and can be adapted to multiple-machine models as well.

3.1 Minimizing Flowtime

Suppose you are in charge of scheduling Newnan Foundry (see Section 1). Examining the costs affected by the schedule indicates in-process inventory costs dominate all others. The foundry is producing high-cost items that leave the factory as soon as they are completed. You also discover that the value of all products is about the same, so minimizing total flowtime tends to minimize the total holding costs. Now your question is, "How do I schedule the jobs to minimize total flowtime?"

We assume all jobs to be scheduled are available now, so release times are all zero, meaning that flowtime is equal to completion time. Starting with a particular instance of the scheduling problem may be helpful. Consider the one given in Table 8-2. Suppose we schedule job 1 to be done first, job 2 second, etc. (i.e., a "natural" sequence). This schedule is shown in Figure 8-3. Note that a job sequence specifies a schedule in this case. If job 2 follows job 1, it makes no sense to delay it, because doing so would only increase the flowtime. There is no idle time in the schedule.

To compute the total flowtime, we add up the completion times of all jobs. For the first job it is 4. The completion time of the second job is its processing time plus the processing

TABLE 8-2
Single-machine problem data

Job i	1	2	3	4	5
p_i	4	2	3	2	4

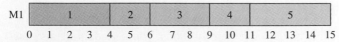

M1

0 1 2 3 4 5 6 7 8 9 10 11 12 13 14 15

FIGURE 8-3
Natural one-machine sequence

time of all jobs before it in the schedule, which is $4 + 2 = 6$. Continuing, we find the total flowtime is 45. In general, if we have n jobs scheduled 1-2-$\cdots$-$(n-1)$-n the total flowtime F is

$$F = p_1 + (p_1 + p_2) + (p_1 + p_2 + p_3) + \cdots + (p_1 + p_2 + \cdots + p_n)$$

Rearranging terms gives

$$F = np_1 + (n-1)p_2 + (n-2)p_3 + \cdots + p_n$$

From this it seems logical for the job in the first position to have the smallest processing time, because it gets counted n times. Similarly, we want the job in the second position to have the next smallest processing time, and continue placing them in order of nondecreasing processing times with the last job the largest. If there are ties, we break them arbitrarily. The sequence of jobs ordered from smallest to largest is the **shortest processing time** (SPT) sequence. This seems to minimize flowtime, but merely *seeming* is not good enough. Fortunately we can prove this result using a technique called adjacent pairwise interchange. This technique is useful for proving many scheduling results.

Theorem. SPT sequencing minimizes flowtime on a single machine with zero release times.

Proof. To prove this result we assume an optimal schedule is not an SPT sequence. We construct a better sequence that contradicts the assumption the optimal sequence is not an SPT sequence.

Assume schedule S minimizes flowtime and is not in SPT order. If S is not in SPT order, there must be a pair of jobs in S, say i and j, so i is scheduled immediately before j, and $p_i > p_j$. Now consider the schedule S' where S' is the same as S except jobs i and j have been interchanged so j is scheduled immediately before i. Figure 8-4 contains Gantt Charts of S and S'. Jobs in B and A are in the same position in both schedules. Let t be the completion time of the last job in B, $TF(B)$ be the total flowtime of the jobs scheduled before i and j, and $TF(A)$ the total flowtime for jobs after i and j. The total flowtime for S is

$$TF(S) = TF(B) + (t + p_i) + (t + p_i + p_j) + TF(A)$$

and the total flowtime for S' is

$$TF(S') = TF(B) + (t + p_j) + (t + p_j + p_i) + TF(A)$$

Subtracting, we get

$$TF(S) - TF(S') = p_i - p_j > 0$$

This implies the total flowtime of S' is smaller than S, which contradicts the assumption that S was optimal. Therefore, an optimal schedule must be in SPT order, which completes the proof.

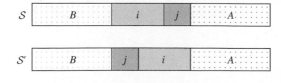

FIGURE 8-4
Schedules that differ by a pairwise interchange

Example 8-2. Flowtime on a single machine. Andre manages SpeedCopy, and has five jobs waiting to be done. The processing times are given in Table 8-2. When their jobs are finished, customers are notified by phone to come pick up the jobs. How should Andre sequence the jobs so total customer-waiting time is as small as possible?

Solution. Minimizing total wait is equivalent to minimizing flowtime, so Andre should use SPT. Applying SPT to the data gives the sequence 2-4-3-1-5. The completion times for the jobs are $C_2 = 2$, $C_4 = (2 + 2) = 4$, $C_3 = (2 + 2 + 3) = 7$, $C_1 = (2 + 2 + 3 + 4) = 11$, and $C_5 = (2 + 2 + 3 + 4 + 4) = 15$. Because release times are all zero, the total flowtime is the sum of the completion times, or $(2 + 4 + 7 + 11 + 15) = 39$. Note jobs 2 and 4 have the same processing times and could be interchanged without affecting the objective. This is also true for jobs 1 and 5.

The SPT sequence minimizes the total time all jobs spend in the system, because all release times are zero, and hence their total waiting time, because all processing times are constant. This would make customers happy if they were all waiting for their jobs to be completed. SPT also minimizes the mean number of jobs waiting to be processed, or, equivalently, the mean work-in-process inventory, measured in jobs.

3.1.1 LATENESS.

Recall that lateness of job i is defined as $L_i = C_i - d_i$. Total lateness is

$$\sum_i L_i = \sum_i (C_i - d_i) = \sum_i C_i - \sum_i d_i$$

Because $\sum d_i$ is constant for any schedule, minimizing total completion time also minimizes total lateness. So SPT minimizes total lateness. With lateness, earliness rewards offset tardiness penalties, which is uncommon. For example, many professors penalize work handed in late, but few give extra credit for handing it in early.

3.1.2 WEIGHTED FLOWTIME.

One problem with minimizing total flowtime is we must assume all jobs are equally important or valuable, which is not always true. It may be more important to finish a job on time for a regular customer than for an infrequent customer. Recall that minimizing flowtime is equivalent to minimizing the number of jobs in inventory. However, the value of inventory is usually more important than its size. Fortunately, we can handle this problem as well.

Let w_i be the weight or value of job i, where a larger weight means the job is more important or valuable. For inventory, the weight might be the value of the job. The value of inventory at any point in time is the value of jobs waiting to be processed. Let $[i]$ denote the index of the job scheduled in the ith position; if job 3 is scheduled first, $[1] = 3$. The completion time of the job scheduled in the ith position is the sum of the processing times of the jobs in positions 1 through i, or $C_{[i]} = p_{[1]} + p_{[2]} + \cdots + p_{[i]}$. If all jobs are released at time zero, the completion time is also the time they are in inventory. The total value of inventory for some schedule is

$$\sum w_i C_i = w_1 C_1 + w_2 C_2 + \cdots + w_n C_n$$

As we saw in Section 2.3, flowtime is related to customer waiting time, so if all customers or jobs are not equally important, the weighted measure is appropriate. For instance, the weight might be proportional to the yearly dollar-volume of business a customer does with our company.

If all jobs have the same weight, the SPT sequence is optimal. If all jobs have the same processing time, it seems natural to do the job with the largest weight first, the next largest second, and so forth. How can we combine these two ideas?

A job with a small processing time and a large weight should be scheduled toward the front, whereas one with a large processing time and a small weight should be scheduled toward the back. One way to do this is to look at the ratio of processing time to weight, and order the jobs in nondecreasing ratios. This is usually called the **weighted shortest processing time** (WSPT) sequence. Although we will not prove it, WSPT minimizes weighted flowtime, and the proof is analogous to the SPT proof.

> **Example 8-3. WSPT scheduling.** Suppose in Example 8-2 not all jobs were of equal value. In that case, minimizing flowtime does not minimize the value of service to the customer, so we want to use the WSPT schedule. We could use the actual dollar value of the jobs, or we could determine the relative values of the jobs. Suppose jobs 1 and 4 are of equal value, and jobs 3 and 5 are valued three times as much as 1 or 4. Finally, job 2 is worth four times as much as either job 1 or 4. The weights we would then use are $w_1 = 1$, $w_2 = 4$, $w_3 = 3$, $w_4 = 1$, and $w_5 = 3$. Calculating the processing-time-to-weight ratio gives 4/1, 2/4, 3/3, 2/1, and 4/3. Job 2 has the smallest ratio and should come first; the WSPT sequence is 2-3-5-4-1. This gives completion times $C_2 = 2$, $C_3 = 5$, $C_5 = 9$, $C_4 = 11$, and $C_1 = 15$. The value of weighted flowtime is
>
> $$\sum_{i=1}^{5} w_i F_i = 2 \times 4 + 5 \times 3 + 9 \times 3 + 11 \times 1 + 15 \times 1 = 76$$

3.2 Maximal Tardiness and Maximal Lateness

If customer satisfaction is the overriding measure of performance, we should consider due-dates. SPT sequencing does not consider due dates, so schedules that are good for flowtime may be bad for due date oriented measures. One due date oriented measure is maximal tardiness, T_{max}. Here we wish the most tardy job to have as little tardiness as possible. If the loudness of a customer's scream is proportional to how tardy the job is, minimizing maximum tardiness is making the loudest scream as quiet as possible Woolsey and Swanson, 1975).

How do we sequence jobs to minimize maximal tardiness? Surely the due dates must be involved, and from our discussion of flowtime it seems reasonable to put the job with the shortest due date first, the next shortest second, and so forth. This is called the **earliest due date** (EDD) sequence. Again, our intuition is correct and EDD minimizes T_{max}. The proof is similar to the proof that SPT minimizes the sum of completion times—assume a schedule in which EDD is not optimal, and use adjacent pairwise interchange to show the EDD schedule is better. The same argument shows the EDD sequence minimizes L_{max}.

> **Example 8-4. Minimizing T_{max}.** Suppose customers were given due dates of (16, 10, 7, 7, 5) for the five jobs in Example 8-2. The EDD sequence would be 5-3-4-2-1, and the tardiness of the jobs is (0, 0, 2, 1, 0), resulting in $T_{max} = 2$.

3.3 Number of Tardy Jobs

If it is possible to have all jobs on time, the EDD sequence has all jobs on time. However, if all jobs cannot be on time, one of the problems with using EDD is that, although no job is very tardy, many jobs (or even all of them) may be somewhat tardy. When the fixed-cost component of jobs being tardy dominates, we may wish to have as many jobs as possible on time or, equivalently, minimize the number of tardy jobs. To solve this model, Hodgson's algorithm is used. An intuitive discussion of the algorithm is followed by a more formal presentation.

First, put the jobs in EDD order and compute their tardiness. If all jobs are on time, quit; otherwise, find the first tardy job. From the set of jobs up to and including the first tardy job in the sequence, at least one *must* be tardy in any sequence. We need to determine which job in this set to move, and where in the sequence it should be placed. Since we are only trying to minimize the number of tardy jobs, any tardy job, no matter how tardy, might as well be put at the end of the schedule. This allows the other jobs to have smaller completion times and, we hope, be more nearly on time. Moving the job with the largest processing time from the set reduces the completion times of the remaining jobs as much as possible. Therefore, from the jobs in this set, remove the job with the longest processing time and place it at the end of the sequence. Ties can be broken arbitrarily.

Recall that $[i]$ is the index of the job scheduled in the ith position. The completion time for the job scheduled in the ith position is the sum of the processing times of the jobs in positions 1 through i, or $C_{[i]} = p_{[1]} + p_{[2]} + \cdots + p_{[i]}$. The tardiness is $T_{[i]} = \max\{0, C_{[i]} - d_{[i]}\}$. Formally, the algorithm is

Step 1. Compute the tardiness for each job in the EDD sequence. Set $N_T = 0$, and let k be the first position containing a tardy job. If no job is tardy, go to step 4.

Step 2. Find the job with the largest processing time in positions 1 to k. Let $p_{[j]} = \max_{i=1,k} p_{[i]}$; then $j^* = [j]$ is the index of the job with the largest processing time among the first k jobs.

Step 3. Remove job j^* from the sequence, set $N_T = N_T + 1$, and repeat step 1.

Step 4. Place the removed N_T jobs in any order at the end of the sequence. This sequence minimizes the number of tardy jobs.

The algorithm is intuitive, but the proof is quite complicated and therefore is not given here.

Example 8-5. Hodgson's algorithm. Consider our previous example. Recall that the EDD sequence was 5-3-4-2-1, so $[1] = 5$, $[2] = 3$, $[3] = 4$, $[4] = 2$, and $[5] = 1$.

Step 1. $N_T = 0$, the completion times are (4, 7, 9, 11, 15), and the tardiness is (0, 0, 2, 1, 0). There is a tardy job. Job 4, in the third position, is the first tardy job, so $k = 3$.

Step 2. The processing times of jobs 5, 3, and 4 (the jobs in the first three positions) are 4, 3, and 2, respectively. The largest processing time is 4, so $j^* = 5$.

Step 3. Remove job 5 from the sequence, set $N_T = 0 + 1 = 1$, and go to step 1.

Step 1. The new sequence is 3-4-2-1, with completion times (3, 5, 7, 11) and tardiness (0, 0, 0, 0). Because all jobs are on time, go to step 4.

Step 4. The schedule that minimizes the number of tardy jobs is 3-4-2-1-5, and because it has one tardy job $N_T = 1$.

3.3.1   WEIGHTED NUMBER OF TARDY JOBS. If all jobs are not equally important, we can give each job a weight, as we did with flowtime, and try to minimize the total weight of the tardy jobs. Because this problem is *NP-hard,* it seems unlikely that an efficient algorithm exists for this model. An obvious heuristic is to apply Hodgson's algorithm, removing the job with the largest processing-time-to-weight ratio from the first k jobs, rather than the job with the largest processing time.

> **Example 8-6.   Weighted number of tardy jobs.** Consider Example 8-5 with the weights of Example 8-3. Minimize the weighted number of tardy jobs.
>
> ***Solution.*** Recall that the EDD sequence was 5-3-4-2-1, so [1] = 5, [2] = 3, [3] = 4, [4] = 2, and [5] = 1.
>
> **Step 1.** The completion times are (4, 7, 9, 11, 15) and the tardiness is (0, 0, 2, 1, 0). There is a tardy job. Job 4, in the third position, is the first tardy job, so $k = 3$.
>
> **Step 2.** The processing-time-to-weight ratios of jobs 5, 3, and 4 (the jobs in the first three positions) are 4/3, 3/3, and 2/1, respectively. Job 4 has the largest (2/1), so $j^* = 4$.
>
> **Step 3.** Remove job 4 from the sequence and go to step 1.
>
> **Step 1.** The new sequence is 5-3-2-1, with completion times (4, 7, 9, 13) and tardiness (0, 0, 0, 0). All jobs are on time, so go to step 4.
>
> **Step 4.** The schedule 5-3-2-1-4 has one tardy job—job 4 with weight 1—so the weighted number of tardy jobs is $w_4 = 1$.
>
> This schedule does not, in general, minimize the weighted number of tardy jobs, but often gives good solutions (Villarreal and Bulfin, 1983).

3.3.2   MINIMIZE FLOWTIME WITH NO TARDY JOBS. Clearly, we would like to minimize in-process inventory and satisfy customer due-dates. If customer due-dates are more important, we would like to have flowtime as small as possible but keep all jobs on time. Remember, if it is possible to have all jobs on time, the EDD sequence will do so.

For all jobs to be on time, the last job must be on time. Let the **schedulable set** of jobs contain all jobs with due-dates greater than or equal to the sum of all processing times. If no such job exists, all jobs cannot be on time. From among the schedulable jobs, choose the job with the largest processing time and schedule it last. Remove the scheduled job from the problem and solve the scheduling problem over the remaining jobs in the same way. The result is the optimal schedule, constructed by first choosing the last job, second choosing the next to last job, and so forth. We illustrate with the following example.

> **Example 8-7.   Minimum flowtime with no tardy jobs.** In order to have all jobs on time, we must change the due-dates in Example 8-5. Suppose the new due-dates are (16, 11, 10, 9, 12). Recall that the processing times were (4, 2, 3, 2, 4) and the sum of the processing times is 15.
>
> ***Solution.*** Only job 1 has a due-date greater than or equal to 15 ($d_1 = 16$), so it is last in the schedule (x-x-x-x-1). Subtract its processing time ($p_1 = 4$) from 15 to get the sum of the remaining jobs' processing times, which is 11. Jobs 2 and 5 have due-dates at least as large as 11 ($d_2 = 11, d_5 = 12$), so choose job 5, which has a larger processing time ($p_5 = 4 > 2 = p_2$) to be scheduled last among the remaining jobs (x-x-x-5-1). Subtracting job 5's processing time, the total processing time of the unscheduled jobs is 7. All remaining jobs have due-dates at least

that big, so choose the one with the largest processing time, which is job 3, giving the partial sequence x-x-3-5-1. Continuing, we get the schedule 2-4-3-5-1, which has all jobs on time and gives a minimum flowtime of 39. Note that this schedule is an SPT schedule, which will not always happen.

It seems obvious that this procedure easily generalizes to weighted flowtime by scheduling last the job with the smallest weight-to-processing-time ratio. Even though this is a good heuristic, counterexamples can be generated that show the resulting schedule is not optimal.

3.4 Minimizing Tardiness

You probably have noticed that when we minimize the number of tardy jobs or maximal tardiness, the total tardiness of the schedule can be quite large. For $T_{\max}$, all jobs could be tardy, or minimizing N_T results in the tardy jobs being very tardy. An alternative measure might be to minimize total tardiness. If all jobs are not equally important, the appropriate measure would be to minimize weighted tardiness.

Special cases exist in which an optimal solution is easily found. Suppose all jobs have equal weights. If all jobs have a common due-date, the SPT sequence minimizes tardiness. Similarly, if all jobs have a common processing time, the EDD sequence is optimal. From these, if the SPT and EDD sequences are identical, they produce an optimal tardiness sequence. If the EDD sequence produces at most one tardy job, the sequence minimizes total tardiness. Finally, if all jobs must be tardy, tardiness is equivalent to flowtime and the SPT sequence is optimal. A pairwise interchange argument verifies these results.

Unfortunately, no *efficient* algorithm is known that can optimally solve the general single-machine tardiness problem. Furthermore, the problem can be shown to be *NP-hard,* even if all job weights are equal. Thus, we must resort to enumerative algorithms, such as branch-and-bound or dynamic-programming algorithms, or be content with heuristic solutions. We present a dispatch heuristic procedure (Rachamadugu and Morton, 1982) for the weighted problem that has performed well in empirical tests.

If all jobs are tardy, minimizing weighted tardiness is equivalent to minimizing weighted completion time, which is accomplished by the WSPT sequence. Here we use the **weight-to-processing-time ratio** (WTPTR), the reciprocal of the processing-time-to-weight ratio. Choosing the largest WTPTR is equivalent to choosing the smallest processing-time-to-weight ratio, and produces the WSPT sequence.

Define the slack of job i to be

$$S_i = d_i - p_i - t$$

where t is the current time. For static problems, $t = 0$, and S_i is the due-date minus the processing time. A job should not get full WTPTR "credit" if its slack is positive, because it could be delayed and still have zero tardiness. In fact, the more likely a job will be on time (i.e., the greater the slack) the less emphasis WTPTR should have. Figure 8-5 shows the characteristics of such a measure of importance.

Define

$$S_i^+ = \max\{0, S_i\}$$

S_i^+ is zero if slack is negative, and the job is tardy if scheduled now, so the importance of its WTPTR should be high. Jobs with small S_i^+ are close to being tardy, and their priority should

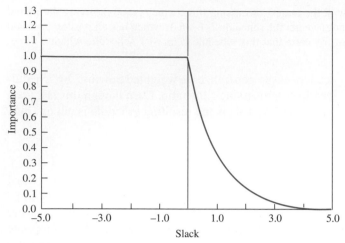

FIGURE 8-5
Importance of WTPTR as a function of slack

be close to the full value of WTPTR. If S_i^+ is very large, it will be a long time until it is tardy, so its WTPTR should not count much, if at all. The exponential function e^{-x} behaves this way if x is a function of S_i^+.

The exponential function gives the full value of WTPTR for a job with nonpositive slack, because $e^0 = 1$. The rate at which e^{-x} decreases (i.e., discounts the WTPTR) depends on the value of x. If a job has slack of 1, its weight would be $e^{-1} = 0.37$, and a slack of 3 gives $e^{-3} = 0.05$, which is not very large, so we need to replace the slack with a more meaningful measure. Define

$$p_{\text{av}} = \frac{1}{n} \sum_{i=1}^{n} p_i$$

to be the average processing time of the jobs. The ratio S_j^+ / p_{av} is the number of average job lengths until job j is tardy. This is a more meaningful quantity than slack. Now, if a job has $S_i^+ / p_{\text{av}} = 1$, it can be delayed for a period equal to an average job length and still be on time, which justifies a weight as small as $e^{-1} = 0.37$. As the slack increases, the multiplier decreases exponentially; slack that is twice the average processing time has the multiplier 0.14, and four times, 0.02.

These multipliers may not decrease quickly enough. Rachamadugu and Morton (1982) suggest multiplying the average job-processing time by the factor κ to hasten the reduction of importance given by WTPTR. Determine a value of κ by experimenting; Rachamadugu and Morton recommend $\kappa = 2$ for static single-machine problems.

Define the priority of job i by

$$\gamma_i = \left(\frac{w_i}{p_i}\right) e^{-[S_i^+ / (\kappa p_{\text{av}})]}$$

Compute the priority γ_i for each job and sequence the jobs in descending order of the priorities. The following example illustrates the procedure.

Example 8-8. R&M heuristic. Jamar Knight is the owner of Pensacola Boat Construction. He currently has 10 boats under contract. All customers are given projected delivery dates for their boats. If PBC delivers a boat after the delivery date, a penalty proportional to both the value of the boat and its tardiness must be paid to the customer. Given estimates of how long it takes to build each boat, how should Jamar schedule the work to minimize the penalty paid?

TABLE 8-3
Data for Pensacola Boat Construction

Job	1	2	3	4	5	6	7	8	9	10
p_i	8	12	6	10	3	11	9	11	13	7
w_i	4	1	6	5	1	4	5	9	8	1
d_i	26	28	32	35	38	48	50	51	53	64

Solution. We assume the penalty is weighted tardiness, where the weight is a measure of the value of the boat. All times are in weeks, and due-dates are in weeks from time zero (now). We choose $\kappa = 2$. The data are given in Table 8-3. The priority for the R&M heuristic for job 1 is

$$\gamma_1 = \left(\frac{w_1}{p_1}\right)e^{-[S_1^+/(\kappa p_{av})]} = \left(\frac{4}{8}\right)e^{-[(26-8)/(2\times 9)]} = 0.5e^{-1.0} = 0.18$$

Computations for the rest of the jobs are given in Table 8-4. Ordering the jobs by nonincreasing values of γ_i gives the schedule in Table 8-5. The weighted tardiness of this schedule is 230. To compare this schedule with other dispatching rules, see Table 8-6. The weighted tardiness is given for the SPT, EDD, BWF (biggest weight first), WSPT, and R&M rules. R&M is the clear winner for these data, but problem instances can be constructed so any of these dispatch procedures give a better schedule than the others.

Emmons (1969) developed conditions that must be satisfied by some optimal tardiness schedule. The most useful is that, if $p_i \leq p_j$, $d_i \leq d_j$, and $w_i \geq w_j$, then job i precedes job j in at least one optimal schedule. If we examine the data for PBC, we see job 1 has a smaller processing time and due-date but a larger weight than job 2, so job 1 precedes job 2 in some optimal schedule. Similarly, we see job 1 also precedes job 6; job 3 precedes jobs 4, 7, and 10; job 4 precedes job 6; job 5 precedes job 10; and job 8 precedes job 9. Even though the R&M schedule satisfies all precedence constraints for this particular problem, it does not always do so. (The reader can construct a problem for which R&M violates Emmons's conditions.)

TABLE 8-4
Calculating priorities for PBC

Job	1	2	3	4	5	6	7	8	9	10
p_i	8	12	6	10	3	11	9	11	13	7
w_i	4	1	6	5	1	4	5	9	8	1
d_i	26	28	32	35	38	48	50	51	53	64
w_i/p_i	0.5	0.08	1.00	0.50	0.33	0.36	0.56	0.82	0.62	0.14
S_i^+	18	16	26	25	35	37	41	40	40	57
$S_i^+/\kappa p_{av}$	1.00	0.89	1.44	1.39	1.94	2.06	2.28	2.22	2.22	3.17
γ_i	0.18	0.03	0.24	0.12	0.05	0.05	0.06	0.09	0.07	0.01

TABLE 8-5
The R&M sequence for PBC

Job	3	1	4	8	9	7	5	6	2	10	Sum
γ_i	0.24	0.18	0.125	0.09	0.07	0.06	0.05	0.047	0.03	0.01	
p_i	6	8	10	11	13	9	3	11	12	7	90
C_i	6	14	24	35	48	57	60	71	83	90	
d_i	32	26	35	51	53	50	38	48	28	64	
T_i	0	0	0	0	0	7	22	23	55	26	133
w_i	6	4	5	9	8	5	1	4	1	1	
w_iT_i	0	0	0	0	0	35	22	92	55	26	230

TABLE 8-6
Dispatch solutions to PBC

Rule	$\sum w_iT_i$
SPT	535
EDD	496
BWF	388
WSPT	299
R&M	230

3.5 Minimizing Earliness and Tardiness with a Common Due-Date

A job that completes before its due-date may be as costly as if it had completed after its due-date. In such a case an appropriate measure might be the sum of earliness and tardiness:

$$Z = \sum_{i=1}^{n}(E_i + T_i)$$

This is not a regular measure. Consequently, idle time may improve the objective and a sequence does not necessarily imply a schedule. We now examine the special case of a common due-date.

Suppose $d_j = D$ for all j, which occurs if all jobs are shipped on the same truck or if all jobs make up a single order. Number the jobs in LPT order, i.e., $p_1 \geq p_2 \geq \cdots \geq p_n$. There are two cases, unrestricted due-date and restricted due-date; we define these later. For the unrestricted case we know (Baker, 1995):

1. There is no inserted idle time between jobs, but there may be idle time at the beginning of the schedule.
2. A V-shaped schedule (on-time jobs in LPT, tardy jobs in SPT) dominates.
3. Some optimal schedule has a job, say j^*, with $C_{j*} = D$.
4. In some optimal schedule, j^* is the job whose position is the smallest integer greater than or equal to $n/2$; i.e., $[j^*] = \lfloor n/2 \rfloor$. If n is even there are the same number of jobs before and after the due-date. If n is odd there is one more job after the due-date than before it.

Let
$$\Delta = p_1 + p_3 + p_5 + \cdots + p_{j*}$$

If $D \geq \Delta$ the problem is unrestricted, schedule the jobs so that $C_{j*} = D$. The sequence

$$1\text{-}3\text{-}5\text{-}7\text{-}\ldots\text{-}n\text{-}\ldots\text{-}6\text{-}4\text{-}2$$

is one of many optimal sequences. The schedule may need idle time at the beginning to have $C_{j*} = D$.

> **Example 8-9. Earliness/tardiness at MetalFrame.** MetalFrame has 10 different jobs for a particular customer. As soon as all jobs are finished, they are placed on a truck and sent to the customer. The company tries to deliver orders in 10 working days. Finishing a job early causes problems, because there is little room to store the finished product before it is shipped. Finishing later than 10 working days after the order reduces customer service. Most people at MetalFrame believe the penalty for being early is about the same as the penalty for being late. The jobs and their processing times (in hours) are given in Table 8-7.

TABLE 8-7
MetalFrame earliness/tardiness data

Job	A	B	C	D	E	F	G	H	I	J
Processing time	8	18	11	4	15	5	23	25	10	17

> **Solution.** This problem can be modeled as a single machine with the objective to minimize the sum of earliness and tardiness. The common due-date for the jobs is 80 (working) hours from now. Table 8-8 contains the results of the calculations to optimally sequence the jobs.
>
> First, order the jobs so job 1 has the longest processing time, job 2 the second longest, etc. The ordered processing times are given in the first row of Table 8-8. Here,
>
> $$[j^*] = \lfloor 10/2 \rfloor = 5$$
>
> Job 9 is in the fifth position of the V-shaped sequence given in the second row, so $j^* = 9$ and
>
> $$\Delta = p_1 + p_3 + p_5 + p_7 + p_9 = 25 + 18 + 15 + 10 + 5 = 73$$
>
> This sum is also given in row 4. Since $D \geq \Delta$, it is an unrestricted problem and we wish to have $C_9 = 80$, so start the schedule at time 7, which gives the completion times in row 5. Finally, the earliness and tardiness of this optimal schedule are given in the last two rows. The total penalty is their sum, which is 240. Other schedules produce the same penalty.

From the discussion and the example, it should be intuitive that if we can set the due-date, the best choice is Δ.

TABLE 8-8
MetalFrame unrestricted due-date calculations

Job (LPT order)	1	2	3	4	5	6	7	8	9	10
Processing times	25	23	18	17	15	11	10	8	5	4
Sequence	1	3	5	7	9	10	8	6	4	2
Times	25	18	15	10	5	4	8	11	17	23
Sum of times	25	43	59	68	73	77	85	96	113	136
Completion	32	50	65	75	80	84	92	103	120	143
Earliness	48	30	15	5	0	0	0	0	0	0
Tardiness	0	0	0	0	0	4	12	23	40	63

Suppose $D \not\geq \Delta$; this is a restricted problem and is *NP-hard*. Facts 1 and 2 for the unrestricted case still hold, but 3 and 4 do not. One job can straddle the due-date, starting before D and completing after. An optimal schedule may begin with idle time.

A heuristic procedure has been developed and tested by Sundararaghavan and Ahmed (1984). It constructs a V-shaped schedule starting at time zero. The longest job is placed at the beginning of the schedule if there is more time between zero and the due-date than between the due-date and the sum of the processing times. Otherwise it is placed last. This procedure is repeated until all jobs are placed in sequence. Formally, we have

Step 0. Set $B = D$; $A = \sum_j p_j - D$; $k = b = 1; a = n$.

Step 1. If $B > A$

assign job k to position b

$b \longleftarrow b + 1$

$B \longleftarrow B - p_k$

else

assign job k to position a

$a \longleftarrow a - 1$

$A \longleftarrow A - p_k$

Step 2. Set $k \longleftarrow k + 1$. If $k \leq n$ go to step 1.

Baker (1995) shows that if more than half the jobs are early, the schedule can be improved by delaying the start of the schedule so that the last early job completes at time D.

Example 8-10. Restricted early/tardy at MetalFrame. Suppose the delivery policy at MetalFrame was seven working days; i.e., $D = 56$ hours. What is an appropriate schedule?

Solution. From the previous calculations, this problem has a restricted due-date. We use the S&A (Sundararaghavan and Ahmed, 1984) algorithm to solve the problem. Table 8-9 gives the calculations at each step. The resulting sequence is 2-5-7-9-10-8-6-4-3-1; if the first job starts at

TABLE 8-9
S&A heuristic steps

		B	b	A	a	Position
k	p_k	56	1	80	10	—
1	25	56	1	80	10	10
2	23	56	1	55	9	1
3	18	33	2	55	9	9
4	17	33	2	37	8	8
5	15	33	2	20	7	2
6	11	18	3	20	7	7
7	10	18	3	9	6	3
8	8	8	4	9	6	6
9	5	8	4	1	5	4
10	4	3	5	1	5	5

zero, the completion-time vector is (23, 38, 48, 53, 57, 65, 76, 93, 111, 136). The first four jobs are early; so the schedule can not be improved by delaying the start so the last early job (8, $C_8 = 53$) completes at the due-date 56. This sequence gives a schedule with earliness plus tardiness of 264. It is not necessarily the optimal schedule.

Heuristics exist for problems in which the cost of earliness is different from the cost of tardiness, where early/tardy penalties are job dependent, and for distinct due-dates. See Baker (1995) for more information.

3.6   Dynamic Scheduling

Most of this chapter deals with **static** problems; i.e., all data are initially known. If this is not the case, it is a **dynamic** scheduling problem. For example, a schedule is created for a set of jobs, but while they are processing, more jobs arrive. We begin by examining a static problem with nonzero release dates. We extend this approach to dynamic problems.

If release times are not all zero, SPT does not necessarily minimize flowtime. In fact, if the smallest job has a large release date, the machine would be idle while waiting to process that job first, whereas a longer job with earlier release date might be completed before the release date of the shortest job. Suppose the only available job has a large processing time, but several small jobs arrive one time period later. We would be better off not to schedule any job, leaving the machine idle, until the small jobs arrive. Then we could schedule the small jobs before the large job and reduce flowtime.

The best schedule for these problems is not apparent, and we must resort to heuristics or enumerative approaches for solutions. Let the **schedulable job set** be those jobs with release times less than or equal to the current time. An obvious heuristic is to schedule next the job in the schedulable set with the shortest processing time. This is a heuristic algorithm and does not guarantee an optimal solution. However, if preemption is allowed, scheduling the shortest available job and preempting the job currently in process if a job with processing time less than the remaining processing time of the in-process job does minimize flowtime.

This approach works for many other objectives. Calculate a priority for each job and choose the one with the best priority from the schedulable set. Most of the algorithms we have discussed can fit into this framework; e.g., use the R&M priority for tardiness. As with all heuristic algorithms, computational tests on typical problems should be used to validate the approach.

Suppose we have a dynamic situation. Each time a job completes, schedule the "best" job in the schedulable set. The schedulable set is updated when a new job arrives. One drawback to this approach is that a low-priority job is only scheduled when there are no other jobs to be done, so the job might never get done.

> **Example 8-11. Dynamic scheduling repairs for a city fleet.** Southwestern City has a fleet of about 2000 vehicles. These range from motorcycles to earth movers. As vehicles need repair, they are taken to the city garage and repair work is scheduled by a garage dispatcher. The schedule affects how long vehicles are unavailable, thus affecting the city's service. Develop a scheduling system to aid the garage dispatcher.

> **Solution.** It is more important to have some vehicles, say a fire truck or the mayor's car, operable than others, e.g., a street sweeper. Furthermore, the importance of some vehicles may depend on how many similar vehicles are in the shop. If one of 75 police cars is unavailable, the impact

is low, but if 10 of 75 are unavailable, it likely affects safety. Thus, all jobs are not of equal importance, and importance may change with the job mix. Because we want to return a vehicle to service as quickly as possible, weighted flowtime seems a logical measure of performance.

The tricky part is to come up with good weights. City personnel gave relative orderings of vehicles, such as, a police car is twice as important as a garbage truck. Some job weights are modified by the number of similar vehicles in the garage. An exponential function similar to the one used in the R&M heuristic is ideal. Thus, when a large percentage of the garbage trucks are not in service, their priority increases. To avoid low-priority vehicles going unrepaired, a job's weight is increased as a function of the time it waits for repair. Thus a street sweeper may initially have a low priority, but the longer it waits, the higher its priority grows.

Actually, there are a number of mechanics and bays to do repairs in parallel. To simplify discussion, treat the garage as a single processor. Once weights are determined, jobs are ordered by WSPT. An available mechanic takes the first job on the list. When a new job arrives, weights and priorities of all waiting jobs are recalculated and a new list formed. In Section 4, we see this is a good approach for parallel processors.

In the next section we examine single machine problems with sequence-dependent set-up times.

3.7   Minimizing Set-Up Times

Now consider a case with sequence-dependent set-up times. As an example, consider a manufacturer of plastic parts made by an injection molding machine. Plastic tops for shaving cream cans, hairspray, and other household products are made this way. If a different part is made, the die must be changed. If the type of plastic or the color changes, the machine must be thoroughly cleaned and the plastic brought to the right temperature, pressure, and humidity, resulting in a longer set-up. Other sequence-dependent processes are bottling soft drinks and making paint.

The time to change from one product to another may be significant and may depend on the previous part produced. We define p_{ij} to be the time to process job j if it immediately follows job i. Let $p_{ii} = \infty$ to keep a job from following itself. Makespan is a reasonable objective, because it finishes the jobs as quickly as possible. Processing times are sequence-dependent, so makespan is no longer independent of the sequence.

This problem is equivalent to the notorious **traveling salesman problem** (TSP), which is *NP-hard.* The TSP consists of a salesman who starts at some city, and must visit each city in a group of cities once and only once and then return to the original city. There is a cost to go from city to city, and it is desired to minimize the total cost of visiting all cities. The solution is called a tour; it is a cycle, and the initial city is immaterial. A tour is equivalent to a cyclic schedule where n jobs are done in a sequence and the sequence repeats. If this is not the case, a dummy job can be used as the initial and final job, with zero costs.

For the past century, hundreds of people have attempted to develop good heuristic algorithms for TSP. Complicated heuristics exist that give solutions to many test problems within 5 percent of optimal. This is quite good considering we may not know the data values within 5 percent. Branch-and-bound algorithms for TSP exist that can solve most instances with several hundred jobs in less than an hour.

We discuss a simple heuristic for the problem, and then a slightly more complicated one. Lower bounds on makespan are generated as part of the second heuristic. This leads directly to a branch-and-bound algorithm.

3.7.1 SHORTEST SET-UP TIME HEURISTIC. The shortest set-up time heuristic (SST) is a myopic way to build a schedule. Again, a sequence determines a schedule. Start by picking a job arbitrarily. Then choose the job not already in the sequence with the smallest set-up time when following the given job. Add it to the sequence and repeat this process until all jobs are sequenced. This procedure is best illustrated by an example.

Example 8-12. SST heuristic. Francisco Villarreal is the production control manager of the Lugowski Company, a metal products manufacturer. They have contracted to ship metal braces each day to four customers. Each brace requires a different set-up on the rolling mill, the bottleneck machine. Table 8-10 gives the time required to set up and process the required quantity of braces given the preceding brace. Denote the four customer orders as jobs A, B, C, and D. The rolling mill is currently set up to make job A, but since these four braces are made each day, we find a cyclic sequence. Because of quality problems, job C cannot follow job D; this is enforced by making the set-up time for job C following job D infinite. Francisco wants to finish the braces as soon as possible.

TABLE 8-10
Rolling mill set-up times

Job	A	B	C	D
A	∞	3	4	5
B	3	∞	4	6
C	1	6	∞	2
D	5	4	∞	∞

Solution. We start by arbitrarily choosing job A as the starting job. Find the smallest set-up time for a job that comes after A, i.e., the smallest number in the A row. It is job B (blue in Table 8-10), so our partial sequence is A-B. Find the smallest set-up time of any job in the B row not already in the partial sequence; it is C. Even though the entry in row A is smaller, B follows A, so A cannot follow B and be a cyclic schedule. Continuing, we find D follows C and hence A must follow D. This gives the sequence A-B-C-D-A with makespan of $3 + 4 + 2 + 5 = 14$. This is acceptable because they work two eight-hour shifts and it leaves some extra time for preventive maintenance, cleanup, etc.

Choosing the smallest set-up time in each row does not necessarily produce a cyclic schedule. Doing so in the example would give A-B, B-A, C-A, and D-B, which is not a possible sequence. SST avoids this by creating a cycle, but then the cycle depends on which job is chosen to start the cycle. Picking a different starting job may produce a different schedule; maybe better, maybe worse. Since SST is easy to do, it is wise to use each job as the starting job and take the best schedule generated. Another reason to choose more than one starting job is that a sequence generated by SST can be arbitrarily bad. If we start at job C we generate the sequence C-A-B-D-C. This sequence has job C following job D, even though it has infinite set-up time.

3.7.2 A REGRET-BASED ALGORITHM. An early TSP algorithm was proposed by Little et al. (1963). It is a branch-and-bound algorithm that uses the concept of **regret** to make decisions and compute bounds. In this context, regret is a penalty for a decision that was not made. The regret concept provides a good heuristic for the TSP, and is the basis for other scheduling algorithms, so we discuss it here. We also show how the exact solution can be obtained via branch and bound.

TABLE 8-11
Row reduction of rolling mill set-up times

Job	A	B	C	D	Min
A	∞	3	4	5	3
B	3	∞	4	6	3
C	1	6	∞	2	1
D	5	4	∞	∞	4
Sum					11

Any sequence must contain all n jobs, and since it is cyclic, must contain at least n elements of the matrix. Therefore, the makespan must be at least as big as the n smallest elements of the matrix. However, to be feasible, each job must be included once, so we know there must be at least one element from each row. This leads to a stronger lower bound; pick the smallest element in each row, and their sum is a lower bound on makespan. We can, without loss of generality, subtract the smallest element in each row from all other elements of that row, and the resulting matrix has the same optimal sequence as the original one. This is called **row reducing** the matrix. The smallest element in each row is called the **row reduction coefficient** for that row. The reduced matrix has at least one zero element in each row. The makespan for the new problem differs from the makespan of the original problem by the sum of the row reduction coefficients.

Consider the rolling mill set-up times of Example 8-12. Table 8-11 shows the row reduction of the matrix. The minimum element in each row is blue in the table and given in the right-hand column. The sum of the row reductions is 11, which implies the total set-up time must be at least 11. An equivalent problem is formed by subtracting the minimum from each row (Table 8-12) and adding 11 to its solution.

Furthermore, there must be one element from each column in the solution, so we can do **column reduction** on the row-reduced matrix to strengthen the bound. In Table 8-12, the minimum in each column is determined and shown in the bottom row. The sum of the column reduction coefficients is 2, giving a lower bound of $11 + 2 = 13$ for the original problem. Again, we can subtract the minimum in each column from each cell in the column to get an equivalent problem.

Column reduction followed by row reduction can give a different bound. The larger of the two bounds would be the stronger lower bound. Table 8-13 gives the results of column reduction followed by row reduction for the rolling mill data. Since the bound is $10 + 1 = 11$,

TABLE 8-12
Column reduction of the row-reduced set-up matrix

Job	A	B	C	D	Sum
A	∞	0	1	2	
B	0	∞	1	3	
C	0	5	∞	1	
D	1	0	∞	∞	
Min	0	0	1	1	2

TABLE 8-13
(a) Column reduction and (b) row reduction on the matrix

Job	A	B	C	D	Sum		Job	A	B	C	D	Min
A	∞	3	4	5			A	∞	0	0	3	0
B	3	∞	4	6			B	2	∞	0	4	0
C	1	6	∞	2			C	0	3	∞	0	0
D	5	4	∞	∞			D	4	1	∞	∞	1
Min	1	3	4	2	10		Sum					1
			(a)							(b)		

the first bound obtained is stronger, and we would use the matrix of Table 8-12, further re-duced by the column reduction as the problem to be solved.

The reduced matrix has a zero in every row and column. Let (i, j) be a zero element. If we choose j to follow i in a sequence, a "zero" set-up time is incurred; the actual set-up time is accounted for in the lower bound. What happens if we do not choose j to follow i? Then we must choose another job to follow i and another job to precede j. Which job should follow i? We do not know, but it must be a job whose set-up time is in the ith row. We know the smallest set-up time in that row, excluding j, is a lower bound on not choosing j to follow i. We can make a similar statement about the smallest element in the jth column. The sum of these two elements is a lower bound on not choosing job j to follow job i; i.e., it is how much we **regret** not making that decision.

Consider the reduced matrix of Table 8-14. If job B does not follow A, some other job must. Job C can follow it with no set-up time. Similarly, some other job must precede B; job D can do so with zero set-up time. Thus we have zero regret if we do not choose B to follow A. Another zero cell is C-D. If D does not follow C, the smallest set-up time of a job to follow C is 0 for job A. If C does not precede D, some other job must precede it; the one with the smallest set-up time is job A, with set-up time of 2. If we do not choose D to follow C, we must incur at least two more units of set-up time, or we regret not making that decision by two time units. It seems reasonable to make the decision C-D before we make the decision A-C, because C-D has the greater regret of the two.

It is reasonable to choose the zero cell with largest regret, say (i^*, j^*) and assign j^* to follow i^* in the sequence. We denote the assignment by i^*-j^*. Given this assignment, no other job can immediately follow job i^* nor immediately precede job j^*, so delete row i^* and column j^* from the matrix. The problem now has $n - 1$ rows and $n - 1$ columns. If

TABLE 8-14
Completely reduced matrix

Job	A	B	C	D
A	∞	0	0	2
B	0	∞	0	3
C	0	5	∞	0
D	1	0	∞	∞

necessary, reduce the coefficients of the $(n-1) \times (n-1)$ problem as we did the $n \times n$ problem, calculate regret, make an assignment, and delete a row and column. Each time the matrix is reduced, the makespan is increased by the sum of the reduction coefficients. After n steps, n assignments have been made and a cyclic sequence results.

All c_{ij} for the new matrix are unchanged except for one cell. In the simple case set $c_{j^*i^*} = \infty$ to prohibit the possible assignment i-j-i, which is a subcycle or subtour. If row j^* or column i^* were removed in a previous iteration, some other assignment exists that would form a subcycle. Suppose we previously assigned i-j and now assign j-k, giving the partial sequence i-j-k. Set $c_{ki} = \infty$ to prohibit assigning k-i, resulting in the subcycle i-j-k-i. Consider earlier iterations giving the assignments i_1-i_2-i_3 and j_1-j_2-j_3-j_4. Assigning i_3-j_1 creates the chain i_1-i_2-i_3-j_1-j_2-j_3-j_4, so prohibit the assignment j_4-i_1 by setting its cost to infinity. Each assignment requires another assignment to be prohibited. The resulting matrix should always have an infinity in every row and column.

Now we are ready to formalize the procedure. Let

p_{ij} = the ij element of the set-up time matrix, even if it has been reduced

R_{ij} = the regret for element ij, where $p_{ij} = 0$

$C_{\max}$ = the makespan of the partial sequence

Step 0. Set $C_{\max} = 0$ and $L = 1$.

Step 1. Reduce the matrix:
For $i = 1, n$
   Let $p_{ij^*} = \min_{j=1,n} p_{ij}$
   For $j = 1, n$
      $p_{ij} \leftarrow p_{ij} - p_{ij^*}$ and
      $C_{\max} \leftarrow C_{\max} + p_{ij}$
For $j = 1, n$
   Let $p_{i^*j} = \min_{i=1,n} p_{ij}$
   For $i = 1, n$
      $p_{ij} \leftarrow p_{ij} - p_{i^*j}$ and
      $C_{\max} \leftarrow C_{\max} + p_{i^*j}$

Step 2. Calculate regret:
For $i = 1, n$
For $j = 1, n$
   $R_{ij} = 0$
   If $p_{ij} = 0$
      $p_{ij^*} = \min_{k=1,n, k \neq j^*} p_{ik}$
      $p_{i^*j} = \min_{k=1,n, k \neq i^*} p_{kj}$
      $R_{ij} = p_{ij^*} + p_{i^*j}$

Step 3. Choose largest regret:

$$R_{i^*j^*} = \max_{i=1,n; j=1,n} R_{ij}$$

Step 4. Assign job pair:
Set i^*-j^* and $L = L + 1$.

If $L \not> n$, stop; the sequence is completed.
Prohibit a subcycle by setting some $p_{kl} = \infty$.
Remove row i^* and column j^* from the matrix.
Go to step 1.

Example 8-13. Regret heuristic. Janice Burton is the industrial engineer for an automobile manufacturer. She has been working on reducing set-up times for a group of products made on a large press. At this point, she feels there is little room for further reduction. She knows the set-ups are very dependent on the sequence of the products. The set-up times are given in Table 8-15. Since each of the products is made sequentially, she wants to find the cyclic sequence that minimizes the set-up time.

TABLE 8-15
Press set-up times

Job	1	2	3	4	5
1	∞	18	3	3	6
2	19	∞	9	10	5
3	9	18	∞	13	20
4	6	6	1	∞	2
5	17	1	13	17	∞

Solution. Janice knows this problem fits the TSP model. She will use the regret heuristic to solve the model.

   Step 0. Set $C_{max} = 0$ and $L = 1$.

   Step 1. Reduce the matrix. The minimum value in row 1 is 3, occurring in both columns 3 and 4. Thus, the makespan must be at least 3, so we set $C_{max} = 3$ and subtract 3 from each element of row 1. The minimum value for row 2 is 5 in column 5, and is given in the last column. Set $C_{max} = 3 + 5 = 8$ and subtract 5 from each element of row 2. Table 8-16 gives the row-reduced matrix; the cell in which the minimum occurred is in color. The total row reduction is 19, which is a lower bound on the makespan. There is a zero in every column, so there is no need to reduce by columns.

TABLE 8-16
The row-reduced press matrix

Job	1	2	3	4	5	Min
1	∞	15	0	0	6	3
2	14	∞	4	5	0	5
3	0	9	∞	4	11	9
4	5	5	0	∞	1	1
5	16	0	12	16	∞	1
						19

   Step 2. Calculate the regret. Cell (1, 3) has zero value, so we compute its regret. The smallest element in row 1, excluding (1, 3), is $p_{14} = 0$. The smallest element in column 3

TABLE 8-17
Regret calculations

Job	1	2	3	4	5
1	∞	15	0^0	0^4	3
2	14	∞	4	5	0^5
3	0^9	9	∞	4	11
4	5	5	0^1	∞	1
5	16	0^{17}	12	16	∞

TABLE 8-18
New press matrix

Job	1	3	4	5
1	∞	0	0	3
2	14	4	5	∞
3	0	∞	4	11
4	5	0	∞	1

(again excluding (1, 3)) is $p_{43} = 0$. The regret is $R_{13} = p_{14} + p_{43} = 0$. Similarly, the regret $R_{14} = p_{13} + p_{34} = 4$. Table 8-17 has the regret as a superscript for all zero cells.

Step 3. Choose the largest regret. The entry in the cell with maximum regret (5, 2) is in color in Table 8-17.

Step 4. Assign a job pair. Job 2 immediately follows job 5 (i.e., 5-2). Since the regret for cell (5, 2) is 17, any solution without 2 following 5 must have makespan of at least $19 + 17 = 36$. Set $L = 1 + 1 = 2$. $L \not> 5 = n$, so we do not stop. Cell (5, 2) has maximum regret, so we prohibit 2-5 by making $p_{25} = \infty$, and remove row 5 and column 2. Return to step 1 with the new matrix given in Table 8-18.

Step 1. Reduce the matrix. Row 2 is the only row without a zero in Table 8-18. The smallest element in row 2 is $p_{23} = 4$, so subtract 4 from every element in the row. After row reduction, column 5 still does not have a zero; the minimum element in column 5 is $p_{45} = 1$. Table 8-19 shows the cells with the nonzero minimums in color. Subtract 1 from all elements of column 5. Set $C_{\max} = 19 + 4 + 1 = 24$, so any schedule with 5-2 must have makespan of at least 24.

Step 2. Calculate the regret. Regret is calculated as before and is given in Table 8-20.

Step 3. Choose the largest regret. We find cell (3, 1) has the largest regret.

Step 4. Assign job pair. Choose job 1 to follow job 3. Remove row 3 and column 1; prohibit 1-3 by making its cost infinite. The lower bound on the best solution with 5-2 and 3-1 is still 24. The lower bound on the best solution with 2 immediately following 5 and 1 not immediately following 3 is $24 + 9 = 33$.

Step 1. Reduce the matrix. There is a zero in every row and column, so we do not need to reduce the coefficients. The resulting matrix is given in Table 8-21.

TABLE 8-19
Reduction coefficients

Job	1	3	4	5	Min
1	∞	0	0	3	0
2	14	4	5	∞	4
3	0	∞	4	11	0
4	5	0	∞	1	0
Min	0	0	0	1	5

TABLE 8-20
Regret for the second iteration

Job	1	3	4	5
1	∞	0^0	0^1	2
2	10	0^1	1	∞
3	0^9	∞	4	10
4	5	0^0	∞	0^2

TABLE 8-21
Reduced matrix: third iteration

Job	3	4	5
1	∞	0^3	2
2	0^1	1	∞
4	0^0	∞	0^2

TABLE 8-22
Final matrix

Job	3	5
2	0	∞
4	∞	0

Step 2. Calculate regret. The maximum regret of 3 is in cell (1, 4) of Table 8-21. We schedule job 4 immediately after job 1. Our partial sequence is now 5-2, 3-1-4. Remove row 1 and column 4. Prohibit 4-3 to keep 3-1-4-3 from being chosen. The bound on the partial schedule is 24. The bound for 5-2, 3-1, but with 4 not immediately after 1, is $24 + 3 = 27$.

The final matrix is shown in Table 8-22. At this point, we must choose 2-3 and 4-5, which gives the sequence 3-1-4-5-2. The total set-up time for this sequence is 24.

3.7.3 A BRANCH-AND-BOUND ALGORITHM.

The regret heuristic can easily be used in a branch-and-bound approach. Each assignment is a level in the branch-and-bound tree. If we assign job j to follow job i, i-j, this is one node in the tree. The alternative node is prohibiting the assignment of i-j, which we denote as $\overline{i\text{-}j}$. The bound on node i-j is the sum of the reductions, and the bound on $\overline{i\text{-}j}$ is the sum of the reductions plus the regret for not making the i-j assignment. The branch-and-bound tree for Example 8-13 is given in Figure 8-6.

For this problem, no branching is needed, because the regret heuristic produces a solution of value 24, and all alternative nodes have larger bounds. All nodes must be checked to

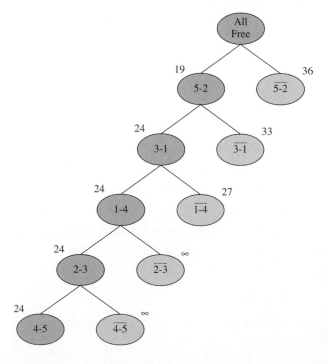

FIGURE 8-6
Branch-and-bound tree

assure optimality. If branching had been necessary, say from the node prohibiting the assignment i-j, the matrix from the parent node, adjusted by setting $p_{ij} = \infty$, would be used for the remainder of the branch.

3.8 Single-Machine Search Methods

Search procedures are used for a wide variety of optimization problems, including nonlinear optimization and combinatorial optimization. In scheduling, search procedures have been widely used. These include neighborhood search, simulated annealing, tabu search, genetic algorithms, and neural net approaches. For a more detailed discussion of search procedures for scheduling, see Morton and Pentico (1993). As an illustration, we describe a neighborhood search.

3.8.1 NEIGHBORHOOD SEARCH.
In **neighborhood search,** an initial schedule, called the **seed,** is selected. Then schedules "close" to the seed, called **neighbors,** are generated and evaluated, and a better neighbor is selected as the new seed. This is repeated until no neighbor is better, at which point the procedure terminates. The final schedule is at least a local optimum. Some problem-specific aspects of neighborhood search include which measure of performance to use, how to determine an initial seed, what constitutes a neighborhood, and which, if any, neighbor to choose as the new schedule.

Any of the previously defined measures of performance can be used in neighborhood search. One advantage of neighborhood search is that weighted combinations of measures can be used; this may reflect the cost or profit of a schedule more accurately. For ease of discussion, we refer to the cost of a schedule and assume it is a regular measure so a sequence defines the schedule.

Any heuristic can be used to produce an initial sequence. It is well known that a good initial seed is more likely to produce a better final solution. Therefore it is usually worthwhile to use a heuristic that gives a good starting sequence.

The simplest neighborhood is defined by **adjacent pairwise interchange** (API). Simply exchange two adjacent jobs, say i and j, in the sequence. For example, exchanging jobs 5 and 6 in the initial sequence

$$1\text{-}2\text{-}3\text{-}4\text{-}5\text{-}6\text{-}7\text{-}8\text{-}9$$

gives the sequence

$$1\text{-}2\text{-}3\text{-}4\text{-}6\text{-}5\text{-}7\text{-}8\text{-}9$$

API results in $n - 1$ neighbors of the initial sequence. **Pairwise interchange** (PI) defines a different neighborhood. PI does not require the interchanged jobs to be adjacent. For example,

$$1\text{-}2\text{-}8\text{-}4\text{-}5\text{-}6\text{-}7\text{-}3\text{-}9$$

is obtained from the initial sequence by interchanging jobs 3 and 8. Using PI, a sequence has $n(n - 1)/2$ neighbors. API is a special case of PI; its neighborhood is a subset of the PI neighborhood. A third neighborhood is formed by **insertion** (INS). Some job is inserted between two other jobs. The sequence

$$1\text{-}2\text{-}3\text{-}7\text{-}4\text{-}5\text{-}6\text{-}8\text{-}9$$

can be obtained from the initial sequence by choosing to insert job 7 between jobs 3 and 4. Each sequence has $(n - 1)^2$ INS neighbors.

Finally, we must choose which neighbor is to become the new seed sequence. One strategy is to evaluate the cost of all neighbors and choose the one with the lowest cost as the new seed. If the neighborhood is small and evaluating the cost of a sequence is easy, examining all neighbors is a reasonable task. If the neighborhood is large or it is relatively difficult to evaluate a sequence, a good strategy might be to take the first neighbor found with lower cost as the new seed. A compromise choice could be made; e.g., evaluate neighbors until one that is 10 percent better is found. If no neighbor is 10 percent better, select the best neighbor as the new seed. If no neighbor is better than the seed, stop. We illustrate a simple neighborhood search in Example 8-14.

Example 8-14. Neighborhood search. Consider the single-machine tardiness problem with data given in Table 8-23. Use the EDD sequence as the initial seed with an API neighborhood, taking the first improving sequence as the new seed.

TABLE 8-23
Data for neighborhood search

Job	1	2	3	4	5	6
Processing time	10	3	16	8	4	10
Due-date	15	16	24	30	35	37

Solution

Step 1. Construct the EDD sequence and evaluate its total tardiness. Denote the sequence by S^* and its tardiness by T^*. Set $i = 1$ and $j = 2$.

Step 2. Swap the jobs in the ith and jth position in sequence S^*; the sequence is S' with total tardiness T'. If $T' < T^*$, go to step 4.

Step 3. Set $j = j + 1$. If $j > n$, go to step 5. Otherwise, set $i = i + 1$ and go to step 2.

TABLE 8-24
Neighborhood search solution

Jobs		Schedule						Tardiness
i	j	1	2	3	4	5	6	32*
1	2	2	1	3	4	5	6	32
2	3	1	3	2	4	5	6	42
3	4	1	2	4	3	5	6	33
4	5	1	2	3	5	4	6	30†
1	2	2	1	3	5	4	6	30
2	3	1	3	2	5	4	6	40
3	5	1	2	5	3	4	6	34
5	4	1	2	3	4	5	6	32
4	6	1	2	3	5	6	4	32

*Initial seed

†New seed

Step 4. Replace S^* with S' and T^* with T'. Set $i = 1$ and $j = 2$. Go to step 2.

Step 5. Stop; S^* is a local optimal sequence.

The EDD sequence is 1-2-3-4-5-6 with tardiness vector $(0, 0, 5, 7, 6, 14)$ and total tardiness 32. The results of the neighborhood search are given in Table 8-24. The first interchange 2-1 (in color in the table) results in no change in tardiness. The second, 3-2, actually increases tardiness. The fourth neighbor examined (of five possible) decreases tardiness to 30, so it becomes the new seed and the procedure repeats. From Table 8-24, no API neighbor with tardiness less than 30 is found.

The best sequence for Example 8-14 is 1-2-4-5-6-3 with tardiness 27. The neighborhood search algorithm used does not find the best sequence starting with the EDD sequence. A different initial seed might have produced the best sequence. Recall that the R&M heuristic produces a sequence with tardiness 27, so it would have been an excellent starting seed. A different neighborhood could improve the quality of the sequence generated. For this problem, both PI and INS would have produced a sequence with tardiness 27. Evaluating all neighbors and choosing the best neighbor might also give better results. Accepting a neighbor with equal tardiness ($T' \leq T^*$ in step 2) may also produce better solutions. Running the neighborhood search from several different initial seeds and choosing the best result can also improve solutions. All of these changes require more computation, with no guarantee of better solutions. Computational effort is not an issue for a six-job problem, but it may be for large problems.

When possible, updating the value of a neighbor from the value of the seed, rather than completely evaluating a sequence from scratch reduces computational effort. Likewise, in step 4, we reset $i = 1$ and $j = 2$, which may not always be necessary. The structure of a particular problem also reduces effort; e.g., tardiness problems can prohibit a swap that violates Emmons's conditions.

If neighborhood search does not provide solutions close enough to optimal, other methods may be needed. We next discuss a variation called simulated annealing.

3.8.2 SIMULATED ANNEALING.

The major drawback of neighborhood search is, once a local optimum is found, the procedure stops. By allowing some moves to neighbors with worse solutions, **simulated annealing** explores more of the solution space, and, it is hoped, finds better solutions than neighborhood search.

Simulated annealing originated in the physical sciences; annealing is the process of controlled cooling of a liquid until it solidifies. By reducing the temperature slowly, the properties of the substance are enhanced. Initially, the material is at high temperature and can change states easily. As it cools, the material solidifies and it is more difficult to change states. Finally the material is frozen, and no further changes are possible. This gives us the terminology of simulated annealing. Accepting a neighbor as the new seed is a function of the temperature. We start with a high temperature, which allows many nonimproving neighbors to be accepted as the new seed. A cooling schedule decreases the temperature, reducing the number of nonimproving moves. Finally, the temperature is reduced enough to freeze the procedure, so that only improving solutions are accepted.

As in neighborhood search, there are many ways to implement simulated annealing; a variety of parameter values must be chosen. We present a straightforward approach following the ideas of Johnson et al. (1989). Let

$\mathcal{C}^* = $ the cost of the best sequence found so far (the incumbent)

$\mathcal{C} = $ the cost of the seed sequence

$\mathcal{C}' = $ the cost of the neighbor being examined

$\mathcal{T} = $ the initial temperature ($\mathcal{T} > 0$)

$\mathcal{R} = $ the cooling factor ($\mathcal{R} > 0$)

$\Delta = \mathcal{C}' - \mathcal{C} = $ the difference in cost of a neighbor and the seed

As in neighborhood search, if $\Delta < 0$, the neighbor is an improvement and it can become the new seed. However, if $\Delta \geq 0$, the neighbor may still replace the seed. A poorer solution is accepted with some probability. This probability depends on how much worse the neighbor is than the seed. If Δ is negative, a move is in order, but the larger Δ is, the less attractive changing the seed becomes. The probability should also depend on how long the search has been ongoing, as determined by the temperature. Early in the search we should be more willing to make "bad" moves, while later we should avoid them. The length of the search is determined by the temperature, which starts out at some positive value and decreases as the search goes along, until the search is finally frozen.

Consider the function $e^{-\Delta/\mathcal{T}}$; if $\Delta \leq 0$ and $\mathcal{T} > 0$ then $e^{-\Delta/\mathcal{T}} \geq 1$. If Δ is positive and $\mathcal{T} > 0$, $e^{-\Delta/\mathcal{T}} \in (0, 1)$. The larger Δ is and the smaller $\mathcal{T}$ is, the closer $e^{-\Delta/\mathcal{T}}$ is to zero. Let q be a random number generated from a uniform $(0, 1)$ distribution. If $q < e^{-\Delta/\mathcal{T}}$, replace the seed by its neighbor. This always accepts improving moves, and accepts worse moves if they are not "too" bad or if the temperature is high.

Simulated annealing algorithms also require a cooling schedule to control the temperature. We present a very simple one, the geometric cooling schedule (Collins, Eglese, and Golden, 1988). After a complete pass through the job set, the temperature is replaced by the old temperature multiplied by a constant. The constant, called the cooling ratio, is denoted by R and is less than 1. Each complete pass through the job set results in a decrease of the temperature. More complicated methods, such as the logarithmic schedule, have been proposed. The process is said to be "frozen" when the procedure has made K consecutive "passes" through the job set with no improvement in the cost.

Since the cost of the seed may increase, the algorithm saves the lowest cost discovered at any iteration. This is called the **incumbent sequence.** This ensures the lowest cost solution found is available, even if the process terminates with a higher cost seed.

We can state a simulated annealing algorithm for the single-machine tardiness problem. As before, we use API to generate neighbors, EDD as the initial seed, and choose the first neighbor accepted by the simulated annealing criteria previously discussed.

Step 1. Let $\mathcal{T} = 1$ be the initial temperature, $\mathcal{R} = 0.95$ be the cooling ratio, and $K = 5$ be the iteration limit. Let the seed sequence be the EDD sequence. Call this sequence $\mathcal{S}$, and calculate $\mathcal{C}$, the cost of $\mathcal{S}$, where $\mathcal{C}$ is the total tardiness of $\mathcal{S}$. Set the incumbent sequence and cost equal to the current sequence and cost: $\mathcal{S}^* = \mathcal{S}$ and $\mathcal{C}^* = \mathcal{C}$. Set $i = 1$, $j = 2$, and $k = 1$.

Step 2. Swap the jobs in the ith and jth positions of sequence $\mathcal{S}$ to form the neighbor sequence $\mathcal{S}'$. Let the tardiness of $\mathcal{S}'$ be $\mathcal{C}'$. Let $\Delta = \mathcal{C}' - \mathcal{C}$, and choose q randomly from $(0,1)$. If $q < e^{-\Delta/\mathcal{T}}$, go to step 4.

Step 3. Set $j = j + 1$. If $j > n$, go to step 5. Otherwise set $i = i + 1$ and go to step 2.

Step 4. Replace S with S' and $C = C'$. If $C < C^*$, set $C^* = C$, replace S^* with S, and set $k = 1$. Set $i = 1$, $j = 2$, and go to step 2.

Step 5. Reduce temperature by replacing T with $R \times T$. Set $k = k + 1$. If $k > K$, stop; the process is frozen and S^* is the lowest cost sequence found. Otherwise, go to step 2.

Most of the comments made about neighborhoods and selecting the next seed for neighborhood search are valid for simulated annealing. Simulated annealing appears to be much less dependent on the initial seed. To get a simulated annealing algorithm to perform well, experiments with the values of temperature, cooling ratios and schedules, and numbers of iterations without improvement to freeze the process should be carried out. Simulated annealing can be a powerful general purpose tool for scheduling problems.

Applying simulated annealing to Example 8-14 with API, a random seed, and a limit of 100 iterations gives the same sequence (1-2-3-5-4-6, $T = 30$) as does neighborhood search. Increasing the iteration limit to 500, or starting with the EDD seed, produces the sequence 1-2-4-6-5-3 with $T = 27$, which was also produced by the R&M heuristic. Branch and bound verifies this is the optimal sequence.

3.9 Single Machine Results

This section contains many basic results for single-machine problems. To summarize them, we constructed Table 8-25. For each measure discussed we give an appropriate algorithm and denote whether it is a heuristic or exact algorithm. Recall that branch-and-bound algorithms are exact, but the solution time for a problem is an exponential function of the problem's size.

TABLE 8-25
Summary of single-machine results

Model	Algorithm*
Flowtime	SPT (E)
Lateness	SPT (E)
Weighted flowtime	WSPT (E)
Maximal tardiness (lateness)	EDD (E)
Number of tardy jobs	Hodgson (E)
Weighted number of tardy jobs	Modified Hodgson (H)
No jobs tardy/flowtime	Modified SPT (E)
Tardiness ($d_j = D$)	SPT (E)
Tardiness ($p_j = P$)	EDD (E)
Tardiness	R&M (H)
Weighted tardiness	R&M (H)
Unrestricted earliness + tardiness	V-shape (E)
Restricted earliness + tardiness	S&A (H)
Dynamic dispatching (flowtime)	Dynamic WSPT (H)
Sequence dependent	Regret (H)
Sequence dependent	B&B (E)

*E = exact algorithm; H = heuristic algorithm

Search procedures are not included, because they could be used as a heuristic for any of the single-machine problems.

SECTION 3 PROBLEMS

8.4. Schedule the following jobs on one machine to minimize flowtime. Give the value of optimal flowtime.

Job j	1	2	3	4	5
p_j	3	6	1	2	4

8.5. A small auto-repair shop has six cars in for repair. The cars' owners are in the waiting area and will leave when their cars are finished. Only Gerry is available to do the repairs. He estimates the times needed to repair the cars are 115, 145, 40, 25, 70, and 30 minutes for cars 1 to 6, respectively. What schedule would you recommend?

8.6. Find the schedule that minimizes weighted flowtime for the following single-machine problem:

Job i	1	2	3	4	5	6	7	8	9	10
p_i	23	25	5	15	23	6	14	6	7	12
w_i	3	1	1	3	2	1	1	1	3	3

8.7. A company has a cell that can produce three parts: A, B, and C. The time required to produce each part is 25, 80, and 10 minutes for each, respectively. The value of the parts is $5, $20, and $1, respectively. How would you schedule the parts through the cell to minimize the value of work in process?

8.8. A contractor has orders to build five houses. The contractor has a reputation for excellence, so the customers will wait as long as necessary for their houses. The revenue to the contractor (in multiples of $1000) and time (in days) to build each house is

House	1	2	3	4	5
Cost	145	290	910	1150	2000
Time	15	20	40	45	100

Assuming they can only work on one house at a time, what would be an appropriate measure to schedule building the houses? Using this measure, what schedule should the contractor use?

8.9. Find the schedule that minimizes maximal tardiness for the following data.

Job i	1	2	3	4	5	6	7	8	9	10
p_i	17	22	12	6	11	17	9	15	10	9
d_i	67	75	37	59	67	88	61	48	79	57

8.10. Prove or give a counterexample to the following statement: SPT minimizes maximal lateness.

8.11. Let $S_j = d_j - p_j$ be the slack time for each job. Prove that MST (i.e., $S_{[1]} \leq S_{[2]} \leq \cdots \leq S_{[n]}$) *maximizes* $L_{min} = \min_{j=1,n}\{L_j\}$.

8.12. Using the data of Problem 8.9, find the schedule that minimizes flowtime with no tardy jobs.

8.13. Develop an algorithm to minimize flowtime while keeping T_{max} at a specified value. Is it an exact algorithm? Is it polynomial?

8.14. Seven jobs (see table; data are expressed in terms of days) are to be done by a small food-processing company. Management would like to deliver orders as quickly as possible to reduce space used for in-process jobs, but wants no job to be later than three days. What schedule do you recommend?

Job j	1	2	3	4	5	6	7
p_j	4	2	8	9	3	6	1
d_j	6	13	14	22	31	33	38

8.15. Give an algorithm to minimize the total flowtime on a single machine when there is precedence between the jobs. Is this a polynomial algorithm? Does it produce optimal schedules? (*Hint:* Think about minimizing flowtime with all jobs on time.)

8.16. Find a good flowtime schedule for the following jobs with release times:

Job i	1	2	3	4	5	6	7	8	9	10
p_i	16	11	6	18	2	20	19	20	8	16
r_i	22	6	0	6	21	7	29	121	64	48

8.17. Devonaire is supervisor of the core shop at Newnan Foundries. Four jobs that need cores are planned to be run on the molding line. Because there is uncertainty about the job actually running, a job cannot be started in the core shop until it is scheduled on the molding line. If job i needs cores and is scheduled to start on the molding line at time s_i, it cannot begin in the core shop until $s_i - p_i - 4$, where 4 hours is an arbitrary offset time. If cores are not ready when a job is scheduled to start on the molding line, the line must wait until the cores are ready. Data for the four jobs are given below, where all times are in hours and d_i is the time the job is due to start on the molding line.

Job i	1	2	3	4
p_i	5	8	2	10
d_i	16	30	38	44

(a) What is the proper objective for this problem?

(b) What schedule would you recommend to Devonaire?

(c) Suppose at time 10, job 2 is cancelled and replaced by jobs 5 and 6 with processing times 4 and 6 and due times 28 and 36. How would you change the schedule?

8.18. Find the tardiness of the EDD schedule and the R&M heuristic schedule for the following jobs:

Job i	1	2	3	4	5	6	7	8	9	10
p_i	7	12	2	6	11	15	9	3	9	14
d_i	67	75	37	59	67	88	61	48	79	57

8.19. Given a vector of processing times $p = (1, 5, 3, 4, 2, 2)$ and due-dates $d = (2, 7, 9, 8, 15, 18)$, find the optimal tardiness sequence.

8.20. Prove or give a counterexample to the following statement: EDD minimizes total tardiness if all jobs have the same processing times.

8.21. Prove that, if $p_i \leq p_j$ and $d_i \leq d_j$, then job i must come before job j in some optimal schedule for the single-machine tardiness problem.

8.22. Find the optimal total tardiness schedule for the following single-machine problem: (*Hint:* Use all information you can.)

Job j	1	2	3	4	5	6
p_j	79	96	102	121	130	147
d_j	255	683	580	260	337	269

8.23. Find the minimum number of tardy jobs on a single machine for the following data:

Job i	1	2	3	4	5	6	7	8	9	10
p_i	15	11	10	5	25	4	8	3	20	11
d_i	71	76	73	88	47	59	24	55	23	47

8.24. An auto repair shop gives a refund of $50 to each customer whose job is not ready by the promised date. Currently, the shop has five cars to repair, with the following processing times and due-dates (in days from now):

Job i	1	2	3	4	5
p_i	2	3	4	1	2
d_i	5	5	8	10	10

(a) Assuming only one car at a time can be repaired, in what order should the manager schedule the work?

(b) Suppose the garage does the work for free rather than giving a refund of $50. Comment on the resulting scheduling problem.

8.25. A student has four projects due in the next two weeks. She can earn a C on each with no additional effort, earning a B will require more time, and making an A on any of the projects seems impossible. Times (days of work) and due-dates (days from now) for the projects are

Project	1	2	3	4
Time	2	4	3	2
Due	5	8	8	10

How should she spend her time to get the best grades?

8.26. In Problem 8.24(b), suppose the charges (in dollars) to repair the jobs were 500, 1000, 2300, 400, and 600. What schedule would you recommend?

8.27. Give a branch-and-bound algorithm to minimize the weighted number of tardy jobs on one machine. Be as specific as possible; include starting solution, calculating bounds, branching, etc. Pictures may help you explain your methods.

8.28. Develop a mathematical programming model to solve the single-machine weighted number of tardy jobs problem.

8.29. Outline an algorithm to solve the single-machine weighted number of tardy jobs problem when all jobs have a common due-date D.

8.30. Consider the following job set:

Job i	1	2	3	4	5	6	7	8	9	10
p_i	5	11	18	8	20	4	14	9	10	16

(a) Find the minimum sum of earliness and tardiness if the common due-date is 90.

(b) Repeat if the due-date is 65.

8.31. Newnan Foundry has six jobs to do for a single customer. Because of extremely limited space, a job completed early costs about as much per hour as a job completed after its due-date. Today is Monday, and Newnan Foundry works two 10-hour shifts per day, six days per week. There are six jobs for a particular customer that were promised for first thing Friday: Their processing times are 7, 12, 3, 18, 10, and 8. When should the jobs be scheduled? What if they were promised for noon Wednesday?

8.32. Consider the following sequence-dependent processing times:

Job	1	2	3	4	5
1	—	22	15	24	15
2	35	—	24	29	1
3	19	23	—	30	13
4	39	18	0	—	9
5	11	0	2	12	—

(a) Give the sequence for the shortest set-up time heuristic.

(b) Give the sequence for the regret heuristic.

(c) Give the optimal sequence.

8.33. A drop forge makes four parts. After each part is completed, a changeover to the next scheduled part is performed. The time (in hours) to changeover is sequence dependent and given below. Actual processing of the parts may take as long as two days. Assuming the parts must be made one at a time in a rotational schedule, what sequence would you recommend?

Part	1	2	3	4
1	—	1	3	4
2	6	—	10	4
3	10	2	—	3
4	2	1	4	—

8.34. Prodigious Plastics, a small company, makes plastic parts for a variety of companies to use in consumer products. Currently they need to produce six batches of parts on one injection molding machine. When the machine is changed from one part to another there is a 10-minute delay to change the die (tool). The parts are either made of polystyrene (PST) or polypropylene (PPR). To change the set-up for the injection molding machine from one type of plastic to the other takes two hours. These times are independent of the parts. The batches have the following processing times and plastic base:

Job i	1	2	3	4	5	6
p_i	50	120	40	30	130	210
Plastic	PST	PST	PPR	PST	PPR	PST

What schedule would you recommend to minimize makespan?

8.35. Problem 8.34 is a typical group scheduling problem. We wish to schedule groups of jobs on a single machine. A group, i, consists of jobs $(i,1)$, $(i,2)$, ..., $(i,n(i))$, which share a common set-up. There are N groups of jobs that must be processed. Set-up for group i requires $s(i)$ time units and is independent of the order in which the groups are produced. Let $p(i, j)$ be the time required to process job j of group i. If two or more jobs from the same group are processed contiguously, only one set-up is incurred. However, if a job from group i is processed, followed by a job from group k, followed by another job from group i, two group i set-ups must be performed.

(a) Suppose the measure of performance is the sum of completion times of all jobs. Outline the approach you would take to solve this problem.

(b) There are N groups of n_i jobs with d_{ij} representing the due-date of job j in group i. All jobs in a group must be processed contiguously. Give an algorithm to minimize $T_{max} = \max_{ij}\{\max\{0, C_{ij} - d_{ij}\}\}$ for this problem. Assume that the batches have the following due-dates: 210, 240, 350, 600, 650, and 790. What schedule would you recommend to minimize maximal tardiness?

8.36. Consider the following tardiness problem data:

Job i	1	2	3	4	5	6	7	8	9	10
p_i	5	9	11	7	1	10	7	7	15	10
d_i	57	57	36	43	32	54	54	49	40	50

(a) Apply neighborhood search with adjacent pairwise interchange.

(b) Compare the result to using pairwise interchange.

8.37. Use a branch-and-bound method to determine the quality of the answer to Problem 8.36.

8.38. Apply neighborhood search to Problem 8.16.

8.39. Briefly discuss the difference in neighborhood search and simulated annealing.

8.40. Use simulated annealing to get a schedule for the data in Problem 8.36.

8.41. Consider the following one-machine scheduling problem with tardiness as the measure:

Job i	1	2	3	4	5
p_i	1	1	1	1	1
d_i	8	7	9	3	2

Starting from the seed sequence 1-2-4-5-3, do a neighborhood search using *adjacent* pairwise interchange. Is the resulting schedule optimal? Is the result surprising in light of Problem 8.20?

8.42. Consider neighborhood search using *adjacent* pairwise interchange. Draw the neighborhood for a three-job problem. Extend this to a four-job problem. Develop an instance of the single-machine tardiness problem with a local optimal schedule that is not a global optimum.

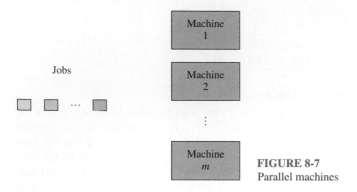

FIGURE 8-7
Parallel machines

4 PARALLEL MACHINES

Often, scheduling problems consider multiple machines. Multiple machines occur in parallel or in series. We discuss several models for parallel systems in this section.

Figure 8-7 depicts parallel machines. When multiple machines are used in parallel, we assume any job can be processed on any of the machines, and the time to process a job is the same on any machine; i.e., they are identical machines. Also, jobs consist of a single operation; once a job is processed by any one of the machines, it is completed. The scheduling decision is twofold; which machine processes the job and in what order.

Although identical parallel-machine problems are difficult to solve optimally, we know for any regular measure the optimal solution can be viewed as a **list schedule.** A list is a sequence of all the jobs. To create a schedule, assign the next job on the list to the machine with the smallest amount of work assigned; continue until all jobs on the list have been scheduled. The algorithm is

Step 0. Let $H_i = 0$, $i = 1, 2, \ldots, m$ be the assigned workload on machine i, $\mathcal{L} = ([1], [2], \ldots, [n])$ the ordered list sequence, $C_j = 0$, $j = 1, 2, \ldots, n$, and $k = 1$.

Step 1. Let $j^* = \mathcal{L}_k$ and $H_{i*} = \min_{i=1,m}\{H_i\}$; break ties arbitrarily. Assign job j^* to be processed on machine i^*, $C_{j^*} = H_{i^*} + p_{j^*}$, $H_{i^*} \longleftarrow H_{i^*} + p_{j^*}$.

Step 2. Set $k = k + 1$, If $k > n$, stop; the schedule is complete. Otherwise, go to step 1.

We examine some specific implementations of list schedules, again categorizing the models by measure of performance.

4.1 Flowtime

From our discussion of single-machine problems, we know that SPT minimizes flowtime on one machine, so the SPT list would probably be a good starting point. Schedule the job with smallest processing time on any processor, and the job with the next smallest processing time to start as soon as possible on the machine with the smallest total processing time. Continue until all jobs are scheduled. A straightforward proof shows that this procedure minimizes flowtime.

Example 8-15. Minimizing flowtime on parallel processors. Gerry Pratt owns Pratt Plastics, a small plastic injection molding facility. Currently Pratt has three identical injection molding machines and has 15 jobs that need to be done. All of the customers want their jobs now, so we want to minimize the total time all jobs spend waiting to be processed. The processing times are given in Table 8-26. Jobs have been numbered in SPT order.

TABLE 8-26
Pratt Plastics processing times

Job	1	2	3	4	5	6	7	8	9	10	11	12	13	14	15
Time	1	3	4	6	9	10	10	11	12	13	13	14	16	18	19

Solution. Minimizing waiting time is equivalent to minimizing flowtime, so apply the SPT list algorithm to the data in Table 8-26. Initially, no job is assigned to any machine, so the first job on the list can be assigned to any processor. We arbitrarily break ties by assigning the job to the machine with smallest identifying number, so job 1 is assigned to machine 1, and its processing time ($p_1 = 1$) is added to the total processing time on machine 1 ($H_1 = 0 + 1 = 1$). The second job is assigned to machine 2 ($H_2 = 3$) and the third to machine 3 ($H_3 = 4$). We assign the fourth job to the least loaded machine, which is machine 1 ($H_1 = \min\{1, 3, 4\}$). Add the processing time of job 4 ($p_4 = 6$) to the total workload on machine 1 ($H_1 = 1$), giving 7 time periods of processing on machine 1 ($H_1 = 1 + 6 = 7$).

Continuing in this manner leads to the optimal schedule summarized in Table 8-27. It is pictorially represented by the Gantt Chart given in Figure 8-8. This schedule has total flowtime of 372 time units.

TABLE 8-27
Minimum flowtime schedule for Pratt

	Machine 1			Machine 2			Machine 3	
j	p_j	C_j	j	p_j	C_j	j	p_j	C_j
1	1	1	2	3	3	3	4	4
4	6	7	5	9	12	6	10	14
7	10	17	8	11	23	9	12	26
10	13	30	11	13	36	12	14	40
13	16	46	14	18	54	15	19	59

4.2 Makespan

Suppose we wish to minimize the makespan rather than the flowtime. Unfortunately, no efficient algorithm is known to minimize makespan, even if there are only two machines. The list schedule, however, provides a good heuristic.

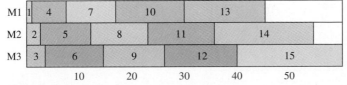

FIGURE 8-8
Gantt Chart for flowtime on parallel processors

TABLE 8-28
Makespan solution for Pratt

Machine 1			Machine 2			Machine 3		
j	p_j	C_j	j	p_j	C_j	j	p_j	C_j
15	19	19	14	18	18	13	16	16
10	13	32	11	13	31	12	14	30
7	10	42	8	11	42	9	12	42
6	10	52	5	9	51	4	6	48
1	1	53	2	3	54	3	4	52

If you have ever helped someone load a truck, you probably put the large items in first and used the smaller items to fill in available spaces. The same philosophy applies to constructing schedules to minimize makespan. Use a longest processing time (LPT) first list, and assign the next job on the list to the machine with the least total processing time assigned. As before, we can break ties arbitrarily, either for jobs on the list or machine assignments.

Using our previous example, the LPT list is just the opposite of the SPT list. First we assign job 15 to any of the three machines, say, to machine 1. Then, we assign job 14 to machine 2 and job 13 to machine 3. The three machines have workloads of 19, 18, and 16, respectively. Job 12, the next job on the list is assigned to machine 3, which has the least processing to do. Machine 3 now has 30 time units of processing assigned to it. Continuing in this manner, we assign the rest of the jobs. The results are given in Table 8-28 and the corresponding Gantt Chart in Figure 8-9. The makespan is 54, determined by machine 2.

The schedule given in Figure 8-9 may or may not be optimal; the LPT list algorithm is a heuristic and does not guarantee an optimal schedule. On most problems this heuristic gives answers within 5 percent of optimal, although there are instances where it does worse. Mathematically, we can bound how badly the LPT list algorithm will do. Let C^*_{max} be the optimal makespan and $C_{max}(LPT)$ be the makespan of the schedule constructed with the LPT list algorithm. It can be shown

$$C_{max}(LPT)/C^*_{max} \leq \frac{4}{3} - \frac{1}{3}m$$

where m is the number of machines (Graham, 1969). Thus, for a three-machine problem, no matter what the data, the LPT list algorithm never produces a makespan more than 23 percent above the optimal makespan. This is a pretty amazing result—a guarantee on a heuristic.

If we allow preemption (i.e., jobs to be split and one part worked on by one machine while the remainder is done by a different machine) we can easily obtain the minimum makespan schedule. McNaughton (1959) shows the minimum makespan when preemption

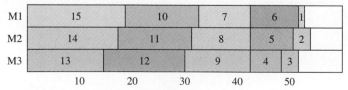

FIGURE 8-9
Gantt Chart for makespan on parallel processors

is allowed is

$$\underline{C}_{\max} = \max\left\{ \max_{i=1,n} p_i, \frac{1}{m} \sum_{i=1,n} p_i \right\}$$

Intuitively, if $\underline{C}_{\max} = \frac{1}{m}\sum_{i=1,n} p_i$ the jobs are assigned to machines as evenly as possible. To construct a schedule with this makespan, arbitrarily assign jobs to machine 1 until the total processing time exceeds $\underline{C}_{\max}$. Preempt the last job, moving the portion of it larger than $\underline{C}_{\max}$ to machine 2. Continue assigning jobs to each machine in this manner; a schedule is constructed with no idle time and makespan $\underline{C}_{\max}$. If $\underline{C}_{\max} = \max_{i=1,n} p_i$, schedule the longest job on a machine, remove the job and machine from the problem, and proceed as before.

To guarantee minimum makespan schedules without preemption, we must resort to enumerative algorithms such as branch and bound or dynamic programming. However, the preemptive makespan provides a lower bound on nonpreemptive makespan. For our example, $\underline{C}_{\max} = \max\{19, 53\}$. Since the LPT list algorithm constructed a schedule with makespan of 54, we are within 2 percent of optimal, which is close enough for most applications. There is a better schedule—swap job 11 on machine 2 with job 9 on machine 3, and all three machines have 53 units of processing, which is equal to the lower bound and hence must be optimal.

From Figure 8-8, the makespan for the minimum flowtime schedule was 59, whereas from Figure 8-9 the flowtime for the LPT schedule is 582. If both measures are important, which schedule should we choose? Actually, we can improve the flowtime of the minimum makespan schedule greatly just by reversing the order of the jobs on each machine, i.e., putting them in SPT order. This is not the same as the SPT list algorithm; we still assign by LPT and different assignments of jobs to machines result. For our example, reversing the order of the jobs on each machine reduces the flowtime to 372, which is equal to the flowtime of the SPT list algorithm schedule. For this example we can have our cake and eat it too, since we get a good makespan (54) and the optimal flowtime (372) in the same schedule. This is lucky and will not necessarily happen for other problem instances.

4.3 Other Models

If the measure is not makespan or flowtime, the identical parallel-machine scheduling problem is much more difficult. If the measure is $T_{\max}$, the EDD list would seem appropriate; for weighted flowtime, use WSPT. A generalization of Hodgson's algorithm is easily implemented to try to minimize the number of tardy jobs. If we are concerned with tardiness, a list formed by the R&M heuristic seems reasonable. Unfortunately, none of these are guaranteed to give optimal schedules. Adjacent pairwise interchange may improve the solution. Neighborhood search and simulated annealing procedures can easily be adapted to solve these problems. Specialized algorithms for other parallel-machine problems are found in Arkin and Roundy (1991), Cheng and Chen (1994), and So (1990).

If the processors are not identical, the problem may become even harder. Some parallel systems have proportional or uniform processors. Here the time to do job j on machine k is $p_{ik} = s_k p'_j$, where s_k reflects the speed of processor k and p'_j the size of job j. Thus, if job i takes more time on machine k than job j, it will take more time on any machine than job j. Unrelated processors have processing times p_{jk} that vary by job and machine with no apparent pattern. While optimal solutions for these models are difficult to obtain, good heuristics are available. See Morton and Pentico (1993) or Cheng and Sin (1990) for details.

SECTION 4 PROBLEMS

8.43. Determine the minimum flowtime schedule for the jobs described in the accompanying table, processed on three identical machines. How does flowtime compare to a single-machine solution?

Job i	1	2	3	4	5	6	7	8	9	10
p_i	16	9	10	8	5	11	15	6	3	19
Job i	11	12	13	14	15	16	17	18	19	20
p_i	8	4	3	11	5	1	11	10	6	5

8.44. Gerry, the mechanic in Problem 8.5, can hire another mechanic to help repair the six cars. The mechanic costs $10 an hour and must work a minimum of four hours. What cost per hour would Gerry have to assign to customer waiting time in order to justify hiring the mechanic?

8.45. AutoElectric produces automotive wiring and electrical parts. They have six outstanding orders for coated wire. The processing times (in hours) are

Job	1	2	3	4	5	6
Time	5	5	9	2	6	3

They have two identical wire-coating machines. What schedule would you recommend to minimize flowtime?

8.46. PowerTransfer makes large precision gears used in heavy equipment. These are made by drop forging, and they have two identical drop forges. Currently, there are five gears that must be finished by tomorrow morning. The company only has one shift of workers but will pay them overtime to finish the gears. All workers in the shift stay until all jobs are completed. The times to process the five jobs are 3, 7, 2, 15, and 4 hours, respectively. What schedule would you recommend for this problem? Explain.

8.47. Suppose PowerTransfer (Problem 8.46) receives payment as soon as the gears are delivered. What schedule would you recommend for this problem? Explain any assumptions you make and why you recommend the schedule.

5   FLOW SHOPS

When jobs are processed sequentially on multiple machines, it is called a flow shop. All jobs are processed in the same order, so we can number machines so machine 1 does the first operation and so on. Figure 8-10 depicts a flow shop. Dedicated cells are good examples of flow shops. A family, or group, of parts is produced in the cell. Each part visits the machines in the cell in the same order. We assume each part must be operated on by every machine; if not, the processing time for a machine not needed by the job is set to zero. We can solve very few of these models easily. We start with the two-machine makespan model.

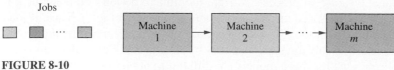

FIGURE 8-10
Typical flow shop

TABLE 8-29
Processing times for hinge upright operations

Machines	Jobs 1	2	3	4	Total time
1	5	4	3	2	14
2	2	5	2	6	15

5.1 Makespan on a Two-Machine Flow Shop: Johnson's Algorithm

MetalFrame makes metal door frames. Preparing the hinge upright is a two-step operation. First the upright is formed through a rolling mill (machine 1), then the hinge pattern is embossed using a press (machine 2). Four different types of hinge uprights are made for different MetalFrame customers. Processing times for the four current jobs (batches of the different types) on each machine are given in Table 8-29. The "natural" schedule (job 1 first, job 2 second, etc.) is depicted in the Gantt Chart of Figure 8-11. The makespan of this schedule is 22. Is this an optimal schedule?

Examining this schedule, we see there is quite a bit of idle time. Since minimizing makespan is equivalent to minimizing idle time in this case, if we had zero idle time the schedule would be optimal. However, in a flow shop it is impossible to have zero idle time. Since the first job scheduled on machine 2 cannot start until it is completed on machine 1, machine 2 must be idle during this time. Similarly, machine 1 must be idle while the last job is in process on machine 2. (Of course, if jobs other than the ones we are considering are available, they could be processed in these times.) Other idle time (e.g., the idle time between jobs 1 and 2 on machine 2 in Figure 8-11) may or may not be necessary.

Now consider the schedule 4-2-3-1 depicted in Figure 8-12. Its makespan is 17, so 1-2-3-4 is not optimal. Is 4-2-3-1 optimal? Clearly the makespan must be as large as the sum of the processing times on either machine, i.e.:

$$C_{max}^* \geq \max \left\{ \sum_{i=1}^{n} p_{i1}, \sum_{i=1}^{n} p_{i2} \right\}$$

Realizing that the idle time on machine 1 at the end of the schedule and the idle time at the beginning of the schedule are unavoidable, we can adjust the bound. We do not know which job should be first, and its processing time on machine 1 determines the unavoidable idle time on machine 2, so what should we use to augment the bound? That idle time must be at least as big as the smallest processing time on machine 1. Similarly, the unavoidable idle time on machine 1 must be at least as big as the smallest processing time on machine 2. This

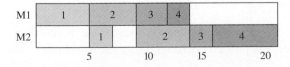

FIGURE 8-11
"Natural" schedule for MetalFrame

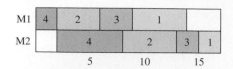

M1	4	2	3	1	

FIGURE 8-12
Another schedule for MetalFrame

leads to a better bound on makespan:

$$C^*_{\max} \geq \max\left\{ \left(\min_{i=1,n} p_{i2} + \sum_{i=1}^{n} p_{i1} \right), \left(\min_{i=1,n} p_{i1} + \sum_{i=1}^{n} p_{i2} \right) \right\}$$

Calculating this bound we see $C^*_{\max} \geq 17$, so the schedule 4-2-3-1 is optimal. From examining the bound on makespan, an idea for an algorithm evolves. If a job has a small processing time on machine 1, it seems we would like to schedule it at the beginning of the schedule, whereas one with a small processing time on the second machine should be scheduled toward the end of the schedule. This leads to Johnson's algorithm (Johnson, 1954):

Step 0. Let $U = \{1, 2, \ldots, n\}$ be the set of unscheduled jobs, $k = 1$, $\ell = n$, and $J_i = 0$, $i = 1, 2, \ldots, n$.

Step 1. If $U = \varnothing$, go to step 4. Let

$$p_{i^* j^*} = \min\left\{ \min_{i=1,n} p_{i1}, \min_{i=1,n} p_{i2} \right\}$$

If $j^* = 1$, go to step 2; otherwise go to step 3.

Step 2. Schedule job i^* in the earliest available position (k) of the sequence, update k, and remove the job from the schedulable set. Set $J_k = i^*$, $k = k + 1$ and $U = U - \{i^*\}$. Go to step 1.

Step 3. Schedule job i^* in the latest available position (ℓ) of the sequence, update ℓ, and remove the job from the schedulable set. Set $J_\ell = i^*$, $\ell = \ell - 1$, and $U = U - \{i^*\}$. Go to step 1.

Step 4. The sequence of the jobs is given by J_i, with J_1 the first job, and so forth.

To determine the actual schedule, we construct the Gantt Chart. Let H_j be the completion time of the last job scheduled on machine j and c_{ij} be the completion time of job i on machine j. To compute the completion times of each operation on each machine, we have the following:

Step 0. Set $k = 1$, $H_j = 0$, $j = 1, 2$, $c_{ij} = 0$, $i = 1, 2, \ldots, n$; $j = 1, 2$.

Step 1. Let $i = J_k$. Set $c_{i1} = H_1 + p_{j1}$, $c_{j2} = \max\{H_2, c_{i1}\} + p_{i2}$.

Step 2. Replace $H_j \longleftarrow c_{ij}$, $j = 1, 2$. Set $k = k + 1$; if $k \leq n$, go to step 1.

Johnson's algorithm always generates an optimal schedule. The start time of each job on each machine is its completion time minus the processing time. Using the start times, the Gantt Chart is easily constructed.

Example 8-16. Johnson's algorithm. Applying Johnson's algorithm to the MetalFrame data (Table 8-29), we have the following:

Step 0. $U = \{1, 2, 3, 4\}$, $k = 1$, $\ell = 4$, and $J_1 = J_2 = J_3 = J_4 = 0$.

Step 1. U is not empty. Job 1 has the smallest processing time ($p_{12} = 2$) of the jobs in U. (Ties are broken arbitrarily.) Therefore $i^* = 1$ and $j^* = 2$. Because $j^* = 2$, go to step 3.

Step 3. Set $J_4 = 1$, $\ell = 4 - 1 = 3$, and $U = \{2, 3, 4\}$ and go to step 1.

Step 1. U is not empty. Job 4 has the smallest processing time ($p_{41} = 2$) of the jobs in U. Therefore $i^* = 4$ and $j^* = 1$. Since $j^* = 1$, go to step 2.

Step 2. Set $J_1 = 4$, $k = 1 + 1 = 2$ and $U = \{2, 3\}$ and go to step 1.

Step 1. U is not empty. Job 3 has the smallest processing time ($p_{32} = 2$) of the jobs in U. Therefore $i^* = 3$ and $j^* = 2$. Since $j^* = 2$, go to step 3.

Step 3. Set $J_3 = 3$, $\ell = 3 - 1 = 2$ and $U = \{2\}$ and go to step 1.

Step 1. U is not empty. Job 2 has the smallest processing time ($p_{21} = 4$) of the jobs in U. Therefore $i^* = 2$ and $j^* = 1$. Since $j^* = 1$, go to step 2.

Step 2. Set $J_2 = 2$, $k = 2 + 1 = 3$ and $U = \varnothing$ and go to step 1.

Step 1. $U = \varnothing$, so go to step 4.

Step 4. The minimum makespan sequence is $J_1 = 4$, $J_2 = 2$, $J_3 = 3$, and $J_4 = 1$.

Constructing the Gantt Chart for this sequence (see Figure 8-12), we find that the makespan is 17.

5.2   Makespan with More Than Two Machines

If there are more than two machines, Johnson's algorithm does not work except in special cases. One special case occurs when the middle machine is dominated by either the first or third machine. A machine is dominated when its largest processing time is no larger than the smallest processing time on another machine, i.e., for the middle of three machines,

$$p_{i2} \leq \max\left\{ \min_i p_{i1}, \min_i p_{i3} \right\}$$

Form an equivalent two-machine problem with processing times

$$p'_{i1} = p_{i1} + p_{i2} \qquad \text{and} \qquad p'_{i2} = p_{i2} + p_{i3}$$

Solving this two-machine problem gives the optimal makespan sequence to the dominated three-machine problem. A job starts on a machine as soon as the previous job on that machine completes, or its operation on the previous machine completes. This works because in a dominated problem, machine 2 can never cause a delay in the schedule.

For two-machine problems and three-machine problems with machine 2 dominated, the optimal schedule is a **permutation schedule.** That is, the job sequence is the same on every machine. A nonpermutation schedule has different job sequences on at least two machines. Assume job i is scheduled before job j on machine k, but on machine $k + 1$, j is processed before i. Then job i could have been processed on $k + 1$ while j was on machine k, so there is inserted idle time on machine $k + 1$. If the objective is makespan, we can show some optimal schedule is a permutation schedule for three machines. However, for four or more machines, the optimal schedule may not be a permutation schedule. For other objectives, three-machine problems are not guaranteed to have optimal permutation schedules. If there is not a dominant machine in a three-machine problem, or if there are more than three machines, there is no simple way to get an optimal solution. We must resort to heuristics or enumerative algorithms to solve these problems.

5.2.1 HEURISTICS. A straightforward heuristic is to force the problem to look like a two-machine problem and use Johnson's algorithm. This sequence becomes a permutation schedule for the original problem. Different approaches to convert the m-machine problem into a two-machine problem produce different schedules. We can then choose the best of these.

Cambell, Dudek, and Smith (1970) proposed one approach to the conversion, the CDS heuristic. Let p'_{i1} and p'_{i2} be the processing times for the two-machine problem. Then for an m-machine problem, we have

$$p'_{i1} = \sum_{j=1}^{k} p_{ij} \qquad \text{and} \qquad p'_{i2} = \sum_{j=\ell}^{m} p_{ij}$$

They suggest starting with $k = 1$ and $\ell = m$ and generating a schedule with Johnson's algorithm. Then set $k = 2$ and $\ell = m - 1$ and repeat, continuing until $k = m - 1$ and $\ell = 2$. The best of the $m - 1$ schedules generated is used. Other ways to generate processing times for pseudomachines are possible.

Another heuristic algorithm was proposed by Gupta (1972). Let

$$e_i = \begin{cases} 1 & \text{if } p_{i1} < p_{im} \\ -1 & \text{if } p_{i1} \geq p_{im} \end{cases}$$

and define

$$s_i = \frac{e_i}{\min_{k=1,m-1}\{p_{ik} + p_{ik+1}\}}$$

A permutation sequence is determined by $s_{[1]} \geq s_{[2]} \geq \cdots \geq s_{[n]}$. Gupta based this rule on Johnson's algorithm for a dominated middle machine, because it is exact for that case.

Example 8-17. Flow-shop heuristics for Cincron. Chantel DeVillez is the supervisor for the blade cell at Cincron. There are five types of turbine blades processed in the cell. The cell consists of four machines that sequentially process each blade. Processing data are given in Table 8-30. Chantel wishes to complete all blades as soon as possible.

TABLE 8-30
Cincron cell data

Job	1	2	3	4	5
Machine 1	1	10	17	12	11
Machine 2	13	12	9	17	3
Machine 3	6	18	13	2	5
Machine 4	2	18	4	6	16

TABLE 8-31
Calculations for CDS heuristic for Cincron

j	1	2	3	4	5	1	2	3	4	5	1	2	3	4	5
p_1	1	10	17	12	11	14	22	26	29	14	20	40	39	31	19
p_2	2	18	4	6	16	8	36	17	8	21	21	48	26	25	24
$[j]$	1	2	5	4	3	4	2	3	5	1	2	3	4	5	1

1-2-5-4-3 $C_{max} = 88$	5-2-3-1-4 $C_{max} = 85$	5-1-2-3-4 $C_{max} = 85$

Solution. First, use the CDS heuristic to generate three schedules. Solve the problem using only the processing times of machines 1 and 4. The data for this problem are given in the first section of Table 8-31. Solving it with Johnson's algorithm gives the schedule 1-2-5-4-3 with makespan 88. Next, combine the processing times on machines 1 and 2 to get processing times for pseudomachine 1 and processing times on machines 3 and 4 to get processing times for the second pseudomachine. These times and the sequence produced by Johnson's algorithm are given in the second part of Table 8-31. Finally, combine processing times from machines 1, 2, and 3 for pseudomachine 1 and processing times 2, 3, and 4 for pseudomachine 2. This problem and sequence is given in the last section of Table 8-31. The sequences 5-2-3-1-4 and 5-1-2-3-4 both produce schedules with makespan 85. The Gantt Chart for 5-1-2-3-4, the best CDS sequence, is given in Figure 8-13. Processing times are given under the job number for each operation.

We solve the same problem using Gupta's heuristic. Table 8-32 gives the calculations and Figure 8-14 depicts the Gantt Chart. This schedule, with makespan 80, is better than any of the CDS schedules. Although the Gupta heuristic was better for this problem instance, CDS may be better for another instance. Total enumeration shows the Gupta schedule is the best permutation schedule.

5.2.2 BRANCH-AND-BOUND APPROACHES. Finding optimal makespan schedules for more than three machines is difficult. About the best we can hope for is finding the best permutation sequence. This can be done by the branch-and-bound method. We sketch a

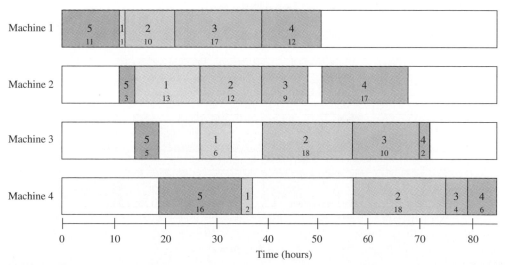

FIGURE 8-13
Gantt Chart for the CDS schedule

TABLE 8-32
Cincron's calculations for Gupta's heuristic

	Calculations						
Job	$p_1 + p_2$	$p_2 + p_3$	$p_3 + p_4$	min	e_i	s_i	$[i]$
1	14	19	8	8	1	0.12	1
2	22	30	36	22	1	0.05	3
3	26	22	17	17	−1	−0.06	4
4	29	19	8	8	−1	−0.12	5
5	14	8	21	8	1	0.12	2

branch-and-bound algorithm using simple machine-based and job-based bounds. More sophisticated approaches can be found in the scheduling literature.

For the two-machine flow shop,

$$C^*_{\max} \geq \max\left\{ \left(\min_{i=1,n} p_{i2} + \sum_{i=1}^{n} p_{i1} \right), \left(\min_{i=1,n} p_{1i} + \sum_{i=1}^{n} p_{i2} \right) \right\}$$

is a bound on makespan. Suppose we have a partial schedule with the set of unscheduled jobs U. Let H_j be the current completion time of the last job scheduled on machine j. If there are three machines, the makespan on machine 1 must be at least the current completion time plus the time to process the unscheduled jobs plus the time to do the last job on machines 2 and 3. Because we do not know which job will be last, we must use the minimum sum of the processing times over all unscheduled jobs on machines 2 and 3. Mathematically, we have

$$C^*_{\max} \geq H_1 + \sum_{i \in U} p_{i1} + \min_{i \in U}\{p_{i2} + p_{i3}\}$$

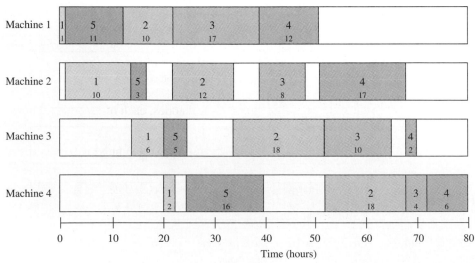

FIGURE 8-14
Gantt Chart of Gupta's heuristic schedule

For the second machine, we must process the jobs in U, and the last job scheduled on machine 2 must also be processed on machine 3. Because we do not know the order of jobs in U, we must use the smallest processing time on machine 3. Jobs in U cannot start on machine 2 until H_2, or until the first job scheduled from U completes on machine 1. Again, we do not know the order of jobs in U, so we use the smallest processing time on machine 1 plus H_1. The bound is

$$C^*_{\max} \geq \max\left\{\left[H_1 + \min_{i \in U}\{p_{i1}\}\right], H_2\right\} + \sum_{i \in U} p_{i2} + \min_{i \in U}\{p_{i3}\}$$

Similarly, for machine 3 we can use the bound

$$C^*_{\max} \geq \max\left\{\left[H_1 + \min_{i \in U}\{p_{i1} + p_{i2}\}\right], \left[H_2 + \min_{i \in U}\{p_{i2}\}\right], H_3\right\} + \sum_{i \in U} p_{i3}$$

These are machine-based bounds; i.e., they examine what might happen on each machine. Job-based bounds can also be derived. A trivial job-based bound is the sum of the processing times on all three machines for any unscheduled job. The maximum over all unscheduled jobs can be added to H_1:

$$C^*_{\max} \geq H_1 + \max_{i \in U}\left\{\sum_{j=1}^{m} p_{ij}\right\}$$

If U consists of more than one job and job k is scheduled first, the other jobs in U follow. If i is scheduled last, the other jobs precede it; otherwise some precede and others follow. A legitimate bound for job i is

$$C_{\max} \geq H_1 + \max_{i \in U}\left\{\sum_{j=1}^{m} p_{ij} + \sum_{k \in U, k \neq i} \min\{p_{k1}, p_{k3}\}\right\}$$

Similar job-based bounds for machines 2 and 3 can be developed. If there are more than three machines, both machine-based and job-based bounds are easily extended. Other bounds can be developed for the flow-shop model.

The branches of the tree correspond to jobs in a position of the sequence, starting with the first position. A heuristic solution, e.g., CDS or Gupta, provides an incumbent solution. Any node with a bound greater than or equal to the incumbent solution can be pruned. If a better solution than the incumbent is found, it replaces the incumbent. Ideally, the bounds will prune many of these, since the first level could have n nodes, each of which could have $n - 1$ nodes, etc. We illustrate with an example.

Example 8-18. Flow-shop branch and bound. Suppose we wish to find the best makespan permutation schedule for a three-machine flow shop. Table 8-33 contains the processing times.

Solution. We begin the branch-and-bound algorithm with no jobs scheduled. Thus, $H_1 = H_2 = H_3 = 0$ and $U = \{1, 2, 3, 4, 5\}$. We apply the CDS algorithm to obtain an incumbent sequence of 1-2-3-4-5 with makespan 65. We now calculate the initial lower bound.

M1 :
$$\begin{aligned}
C^*_{\max} &\geq H_1 + (p_{11} + p_{21} + p_{31} + p_{41} + p_{51}) \\
&\quad + \min\{p_{12} + p_{13}, p_{22} + p_{23}, p_{32} + p_{33}, p_{42} + p_{43}, p_{52} + p_{53}\} \\
&= 0 + (1 + 10 + 17 + 12 + 11) + \min\{19, 30, 22, 19, 8\} = 51 + 8 = 59
\end{aligned}$$

TABLE 8-33
Flow-shop branch-and-bound data

Machine j	Job i				
	1	2	3	4	5
1	1	10	17	12	11
2	13	12	9	17	3
3	6	18	13	2	5

M2 : $\begin{aligned} C_{\max}^* &\geq \max\{[H_1 + \min\{p_{11}, p_{21}, p_{31}, p_{41}, p_{51}\}], H_2\} \\ &\quad + (p_{12} + p_{22} + p_{32} + p_{42} + p_{52}) + \min\{p_{13}, p_{23}, p_{33}, p_{43}, p_{53}\} \\ &= \max\{[0 + \min\{1, 10, 17, 12, 11\}], 0\} \\ &\quad + (13 + 12 + 9 + 17 + 3) + \min\{6, 18, 13, 2, 5\} \\ &= 1 + 54 + 2 = 57 \end{aligned}$

M3 : $\begin{aligned} C_{\max}^* &\geq \max\{[H_1 + \min\{p_{11} + p_{12}, p_{21} + p_{22}, p_{31} + p_{32}, p_{41} + p_{42}, p_{51} + p_{52}\}], \\ &\quad [H_2 + \min\{p_{12}, p_{22}, p_{32}, p_{42}, p_{52}\}], H_3\} + (p_{13} + p_{23} + p_{33} + p_{43} + p_{53}) \\ &= \max\{[0 + \min\{14, 22, 26, 29, 14\}], \\ &\quad [0 + \min\{13, 12, 9, 17, 3\}], 0\} + (6 + 18 + 13 + 2 + 5) \\ &= \max\{14, 3, 0\} + 44 = 58 \end{aligned}$

Job-based bounds are the following:

$$ C_{\max} \geq H_1 + \sum_{j=1}^{3} p_{1j} + \sum_{k \in \{2,3,4,5\}} \min\{p_{k1}, p_{k3}\}. $$

J1 : $\begin{aligned} C_{\max}^* &\geq H_1 + (p_{11} + p_{12} + p_{13}) \\ &\quad + (\min\{p_{21}, p_{23}\} + \min\{p_{31}, p_{33}\} + \min\{p_{41}, p_{43}\} + \min\{p_{51}, p_{53}\}) \\ &= 0 + (1 + 13 + 6) + (\min\{10, 18\} + \min\{17, 13\} + \min\{12, 2\} + \min\{11, 5\}) \\ &= 0 + 20 + (10 + 13 + 2 + 5) = 50. \end{aligned}$

Similarly, we have

$$ \text{J2:} \qquad C_{\max}^* \geq 61 $$

$$ \text{J3:} \qquad C_{\max}^* \geq 57 $$

$$ \text{J4:} \qquad C_{\max}^* \geq 60 $$

$$ \text{J5:} \qquad C_{\max}^* \geq 45 $$

The best bound, 61, is given by J2. Because 61 < 65, the upper bound from CDS, we must branch. Form five nodes emanating from the all-free node, one with each job first.

For brevity, we only examine a few nodes of the tree in detail. In Figure 8-15, the value of the bound is followed by the machine or job that caused the node to be fathomed. Calculation of bounds was halted as soon as a bound exceeded or equaled the incumbent. Bounds were calculated in the order M1, M2, M3, J1, J2, J3, J4, and J5.

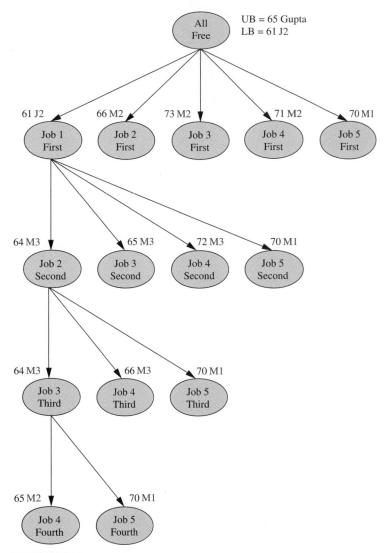

FIGURE 8-15
Branch-and-bound tree for flow shop

When job 2 is fixed as first in the sequence, we have $H_1 = 10$, $H_2 = 22$, $H_3 = 40$, and $U = \{1, 3, 4, 5\}$. The bounds are

$$\text{M1}: \qquad C^*_{\max} \geq 59$$

$$\text{M2}: \qquad C^*_{\max} \geq 66$$

This is greater than the upper bound, meaning we do not need to consider any schedule with job 2 first, so we fathom the node. All nodes with jobs other than 1 first can be fathomed in a similar fashion.

Now consider the node with job 1 first and job 3 second. Calculating completion times gives $H_1 = 18$, $H_2 = 27$, $H_3 = 40$, and $U = \{2, 4, 5\}$ with bounds:

$$M1: \quad C_{max}^* \geq 59$$

$$M2: \quad C_{max}^* \geq 62$$

$$M3: \quad C_{max}^* \geq 65$$

so fathom the node. Only the node representing job 1 first and job 2 second remains unfathomed.

Now examine the node with the sequence 1-2-3, with $H_1 = 28$, $H_2 = 37$, $H_3 = 57$, and $U = \{4, 5\}$. The bounds are

$$M1: \quad C_{max}^* \geq 59$$

$$M2: \quad C_{max}^* \geq 61$$

$$M3: \quad C_{max}^* \geq 64$$

The machine-based bounds did not fathom the node, so we calculate the job-based bounds. Job-based bounds are only calculated for unscheduled jobs.

$$J4: \quad C_{max}^* \geq 64$$

$$J5: \quad C_{max}^* \geq 49$$

The best bound for this node is 64 (M3 and J4), so we must continue by creating two nodes, one with job 4 fourth and the other with job 5 fourth. These nodes have only one unscheduled job and are easily evaluated.

More calculations will fathom these nodes, and the branch-and-bound algorithm is complete. It confirms that the optimal permutation schedule is 1-2-3-4-5 with makespan 65. Since permutation schedules are dominant for the three-machine makespan model, it is the best possible schedule. The partial schedule 1-3 has a bound of 65, and could produce an alternative optimal schedule.

5.3   Other Measures

Makespan focuses on machine utilization. Traditionally, utilization has been the most common measure of performance, but the changing production environment has made other measures more important, particularly measures of customer service. These include tardiness, number of tardy jobs, weighted flow time, and earliness. Few results exist for other measures. See Grabowski et al. (1983) and Kim (1993) for heuristics related to due dates.

General search procedures, such as neighborhood search and simulated annealing, are attractive heuristics for these models. It is relatively easy to extend the concepts of Section 3.8 to flow shops. Osman and Potts (1989) and Ogbu and Smith (1990) give details of simulated annealing algorithms for makespan on permutation flow shops, and Reeves (1995) provides a genetic algorithm for the same problem. These procedures can be modified to work for any measure for which a schedule can be evaluated. For permutation schedules, API, PI, and INS neighborhoods can be used. For computational effectiveness, ways to evaluate measures without generating schedules from scratch are necessary.

Two other approaches, dispatching and bottleneck procedures, are also useful for flow shops. They are often used to schedule job shops, so we defer their discussion. Since flow shops are special cases of job shops, it should be easy to use the job-shop algorithms to solve flow-shop models.

SECTION 5 PROBLEMS

8.48. Solve the following two-machine flow-shop problem.

Job i	1	2	3	4	5	6	7	8	9
p_{i1}	10	2	4	8	5	12	7	—	14
p_{i2}	2	4	5	8	6	9	—	15	—

8.49. Consider the schedule 3-2-1-4 with makespan 24 for the following three-machine flow-shop problem:

	Jobs			
Machine	1	2	3	4
A	3	2	1	8
B	5	1	8	7
C	7	4	2	2

(a) Draw the Gantt Chart for the problem.

(b) Show that the schedule is optimal.

8.50. A commercial film processor has 10 jobs that need to be processed through two operations. All jobs are done on operation 1 first and operation 2 next. The times depend on the particular film and desired result. Processing times (in minutes) for the jobs are:

Job i	1	2	3	4	5	6	7	8	9	10
p_{i1}	18	7	29	3	20	7	11	2	13	13
p_{i2}	19	8	11	14	15	6	28	17	16	10

The foreman can go home as soon as all jobs are completed. What schedule would you recommend?

8.51. Consider the following three-machine flow-shop data:

Job i	1	2	3	4	5	6
p_{i1}	2	23	25	5	15	10
p_{i2}	29	3	20	7	11	2
p_{i3}	19	8	11	14	7	4

(a) Apply the CDS heuristic and draw the Gantt Chart for the resulting schedule.

(b) Apply Gupta's heuristic and draw the Gantt Chart for the resulting schedule.

8.52. Data for a six-job four-machine flow shop are below:

Job i	1	2	3	4	5	6
p_{i1}	18	14	25	29	7	21
p_{i2}	2	23	25	5	15	6
p_{i3}	28	3	22	6	25	19
p_{i4}	16	11	26	1	16	21

(a) Give a good makespan schedule for the problem.

(b) What is the optimal makespan for this problem?

8.53. A cell consisting of three machines makes a family of parts. There are four parts in the family, and the set-up time to change from part to part is essentially zero. Each part has the same routing through the cell (assume A → B → C). Demand for each part is the same, so it is desired to use a cyclic schedule; that is, repeat the schedule for the four parts all day. The matrix of processing times for the four parts on the three machines is given below. What schedule would you recommend to have as many cycles as possible, i.e., to *maximize* the number of parts produced in an eight-hour shift?

	Machines		
Part	A	B	C
1	5	7	12
2	4	3	8
3	9	6	7
4	7	5	11

8.54. Show that permutation schedules are not always optimal for flow shops; i.e., give a counter-example.

8.55. Consider the NP-hard problem of minimizing flowtime in a two-machine flow shop. Develop two heuristics to solve this problem. Also, develop two bounds you could use in a branch-and-bound algorithm for this problem. Demonstrate the heuristics and bounds on the following problem:

Job	1	2	3	4	5	6	7	8
M1	21	47	2	79	30	83	96	88
M2	11	87	79	74	41	21	29	98

6 JOB SHOPS

Flow shops have identical routings for all jobs; if not, it is a job shop. Many metal fabrication plants are job shops. There are a number of products using the same machines, but perhaps in a different order. Figure 8-16 shows three jobs processed in a four-machine job shop. Job 1 consists of three operations, the first on machine B, the second on machine A, and the final operation on machine C. These operations must be done in this order (operation j precedes operation $j + 1$) for technological reasons, such as tapping a hole after it has been drilled. Job 2 is processed in the order A-B-D, while job 3 follows the route A-C-B-D.

Without loss of generality, assume each job is processed by each machine; if not, let the processing time on that machine be zero. Then, if there are m machines, each job consists of m operations, with operation j of job i having processing time p_{ij}. A route list specifies the machine to process each operation for every job. To simplify matters for job-shop data, we give a table of processing times for jobs and operations. The operation time is followed by a slash and the machine on which the operation occurs. For example, if operation 2 of job 6 has the entry 5/C, the second operation of job 6 is done on machine C and requires five minutes.

Job shops are difficult to schedule. There are $(n!)^m$ possible schedules for an n-job, m-machine job shop. Even for very small values of n and m, this number is immense. Even

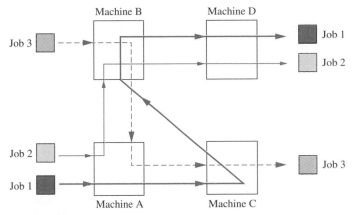

FIGURE 8-16
Typical job shop

our three-job, four-machine problem has more than 1000 schedules; a 10-job problem would have more than 10^{26}. We start with a solvable case of the problem, minimizing makespan on two machines. We discuss two heuristic approaches: dispatching and search procedures. We return to job shop scheduling in Chapter 10 when we discuss bottleneck heuristics.

6.1 Two-Machine Job Shops

Jackson (1956) extended Johnson's algorithm to minimize makespan for a two-machine flow shop to the two-machine job shop. Let the two machines be A and B. The basic concept is that a job shop with two machines has four possible job sets: jobs processed only by A, jobs processed only by B, jobs processed by A and then B, and jobs processed by B and then A. Denote these sets by {A}, {B}, {AB}, and {BA}, respectively. Intuitively, jobs in {AB} should come before jobs in {BA} on machine A, because we do not want machine A idle while waiting for the first operation of a {BA} job to complete on machine B before it can be processed on machine A. By the same argument, we want all {A} jobs to come before {BA} jobs on A. On the other hand, no {A} job should come before any {AB} job on machine A, because that could delay processing an {AB} job on machine B. This implies an ordering of the sets of jobs on machine A: {AB}{A}{BA}. Likewise, the order of the sets on B should be {BA}{B}{AB}. The order of jobs within the sets remains to be determined.

If we only had jobs {AB}, we could use Johnson's algorithm to schedule them. We could also use it to schedule jobs in {BA}, but with machine B first and A second. The order of jobs within {A} and {B} does not matter, so the minimal makespan schedule for a 2-machine job shop is

- Machine A: {AB} jobs ordered by Johnson's algorithm, then {A} jobs in any order, followed by {BA} jobs in reverse Johnson's order
- Machine B: {BA} jobs in reverse Johnson's order, {B} jobs in any order, and {AB} jobs in Johnson's order

This intuitive argument does not prove the optimality of the procedure. The interested student is referred to Jackson's paper (1956). An example illustrates the procedure.

TABLE 8-34
Header routings and processing times

Job	1	2	3	4	5	6	7	8	9	10
Route	BA	AB	BA	B	A	AB	B	BA	BA	AB
p_{i1}	3	1	11	0	3	9	0	8	13	2
p_{i2}	8	10	13	1	0	8	6	10	6	6

Example 8-19. Jackson's algorithm. MetalFrame makes metal door frames. The header is the top portion of the frame. There are two steps in preparing a header: notching and lancing. Some headers are only notched, and some are only lanced. Because of different header configurations, some headers must be lanced first and then notched, and others must be notched and then lanced. Given the routing (A represents lancing and B represents notching) and processing times of jobs to be done (Table 8-34), what schedule would finish all jobs as soon as possible?

Solution. First, we separate the jobs into the sets {A} = {5}, {B} = {4, 7}, {AB} = {2, 6, 10}, and {BA} = {1, 3, 8, 9}. We schedule {AB} by Johnson's algorithm; the results are given in Table 8-35. Colored numbers in the first part of the table pick the smaller of p_{i1} or p_{i2}. The second part of the table gives the proper sequence. Colored processing times on A are in SPT order. There is only one colored job on B; if there were more, they would be in LPT order.

Table 8-36 contains the same information for {BA}. Here, the colored times are nondecreasing for B and nonincreasing for A, since machine B is actually the first machine for these jobs.

Schedule the jobs on A in the order 2-10-6-5-9-3-8-1, with job 2 starting at time zero and jobs 10, 6, and 5 starting as soon as the previous job is completed on machine A. Schedule job 9 to start as soon as its first operation has completed on machine B, or when job 5 has finished on machine A, whichever is latest. The same holds true for jobs 3, 8, and 1. The sequence for B is 9-3-8-1-4-7-2-10-6; here, jobs in {AB} cannot be scheduled until their first operation is completed on A or the job sequenced immediately before it on B is completed. A Gantt Chart of the complete schedule is given in Figure 8-17. This schedule has no idle time between jobs, and the makespan is 67, as determined by machine B.

6.2 Dispatching

The most common scheduling approach to job shops is to use priority dispatching rules. The basic idea is to schedule an operation of a job as soon as possible; if there is more than one job waiting to be processed by the same machine, schedule the one with best priority. A schedule and a Gantt Chart can be easily constructed. Define

TABLE 8-35
Sequence for {AB}

Job	2	6	10		2	10	6
p_{i1}	1	9	2	$\implies$	1	2	9
p_{i2}	10	8	6		10	6	8

TABLE 8-36
Sequence for {BA}

Job	1	3	8	9		9	3	8	1
p_{i1}	3	11	8	13	$\implies$	13	11	8	3
p_{i2}	8	13	10	6		6	13	10	8

A = the set of idle machines

J_k = the index of the last job scheduled on machine k

U_k = the set of jobs that can be processed on machine k

H_k = the completion time of the job currently processed on machine k

u_{it} = the urgency, or priority, of job i at time t

Recall s_{ij} and c_{ij} are the start and completion times of operation j of job i, respectively. For now, we do not define priority, but assume smaller is better. Formally, the algorithm can be stated in the following manner:

Step 0. Initialize: $t = 0$; $H_k = 0$, $k = 1, 2, \ldots, m$; $A = \{1, 2, \ldots, m\}$; $U_k = \{i \mid$ operation 1 of i is on machine k, $i = 1, 2, \ldots, n\}$; $s_{ij} = c_{ij} = 0$, $i = 1, 2, \ldots, n$; $j = 1, 2, \ldots, m$. Go to step 4.

Step 1. Increment t; let $t = \min_{k=1,m; k \in A} H_k$, and $K = \{k \mid H_k = t\}$.

Step 2. Find the job or jobs that complete at time t and the machines released. Set $i^t = \{i \mid J_k = i, k \in K\}$ and $A = A \cup K$.

Step 3. Determine the jobs ready to be scheduled on each machine; let $U_k = \{i \mid$ job i uses machine k and all operations of job i before machine k are completed$\}$, $k = 1, 2, \ldots, m$. If $U_k = \emptyset$ for $k = 1, 2, \ldots, m$, stop; the schedule is complete. If $U_k = \emptyset$ for all $k \in A$, none of the waiting jobs has an available machine, so no job can be scheduled at this time. Go to Step 1.

Step 4. For each idle machine, try to schedule a job; for each $k \in A$ with $U_k \neq \emptyset$, let i^* be the job with the best priority, $u_{i^*t} = \min_{i \in U_k} u_{it}$. Schedule job i^* on machine k; set $J_k = i^*$, $s_{i^*k} = t$, $c_{i^*k} = t + p_{i^* j(k)}$, $H_k = c_{i^*k}$. Remove the scheduled job from U_k, $U_k \longleftarrow U_k - \{i^*\}$ and the machine from A, $A \longleftarrow A - \{k\}$. When all $k \in A$ with $U_k \neq \emptyset$ have been examined, go to step 1.

When the algorithm completes, the start and completion times on each machine can be used to construct a Gantt Chart.

Many priorities are possible. Some common priority measures are

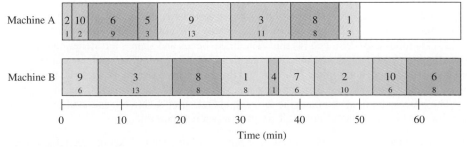

FIGURE 8-17
Minimal makespan schedule for two-machine job shop

SPT (shortest processing time):	Schedule the operation with the shortest processing time, $u_{it} = p_{ij}$ (WSPT, $u_{it} = p_{ij}/w_{ij}$, is also possible).
FCFS (first come, first served):	Schedule the operation that arrived first.
MWKR (most work remaining):	Schedule the operation of the job with the largest sum of processing times of unscheduled operations ($-u_{it} = p_i' = \sum_{k=j,m} p_{ik}$).
EDD (earliest due date):	Schedule the operation whose job has the smallest due date, $u_{it} = d_i$.
EDD/OP (earliest due date operation):	Schedule the operation with the smallest operation due date, $u_{it} = d_i - \sum_{k=j+1,m} p_{ik}$.
SLK (slack):	Schedule the operation with smallest slack. Slack is time until the job is due, $u_{it} = d_i - p_i' - t$, where t is the current time.
CR (critical ratio):	Schedule the operation with the smallest ratio of slack to remaining time until the job is due, $u_{it} = (d_i - p_i' - t)/(d_i - t)$.
SLK/OP (slack operation):	Schedule the operation with smallest ratio of slack to number of operations remaining, $u_{it} = (d_i - p_i' - t)/(m - j + 1)$.
R&M (Rachamadugu & Morton):	Schedule the operation with the smallest R &M ratio (see Section 3.4), using an average of processing times on the machine for this operation rather than averaging all processing times.

Other priorities are possible, and slight variations in the definitions occur in the literature. The priority used depends on the measure of schedule desirability. For example, you would expect SPT to be a reasonable priority rule for minimizing flowtime. Similarly, EDD would be reasonable for maximal tardiness. Morton and Pentico (1993) give computational results and more complicated dispatch rules for flow shops and job shops. WSPT does well for weighted flowtime (1 percent to 5 percent worse than the best heuristic solution found), and a weighted version of R&M does reasonably well (7 percent to 18 percent worse than the best heuristic solution found) for weighted tardiness. There have been many comparisons of dispatching rules for other performance measures published in the literature; e.g., Philipoom and Fry (1990).

Example 8-20. Quick Closures: job-shop dispatch heuristic. A small machine shop, Quick Closures, makes a variety of metal industrial fasteners. There are four machines in the shop: (1) brake, (2) emboss, (3) drill, and (4) mill. The brake bends and shapes a fastener, the emboss presses a pattern (e.g., an indentation where another object is connected, such as a hinge), the drill makes one or more holes in the fastener, and the mill is used to remove material and shape the part. Currently, they have orders for six parts, which use all the machines, but in different orders. The processing time and machine for each operation of each job (separated by a /) are given in Table 8-37. We wish to finish all six parts as soon as possible.

Solution. This is a classic job-shop scheduling problem. We wish to schedule the jobs so each operation is done in the proper order on the correct machine, so that makespan is kept to a minimum. We use a dispatch procedure with MWKR as the priority.

TABLE 8-37
Quick Closures data

Job	Operation 1	2	3	4
1	6/1	8/2	13/3	5/4
2	4/1	1/2	4/3	3/4
3	3/4	8/2	6/1	4/3
4	5/2	10/1	15/3	4/4
5	3/1	4/2	6/4	4/3
6	4/3	2/1	4/2	5/4

Step 0. Initialize: $t = 0$; $H_1 = H_2 = H_3 = H_4 = 0$, $A = \{1, 2, 3, 4\}$; $U_1 = \{1, 2, 5\}$, $U_2 = \{4\}$, $U_3 = \{6\}$, $U_4 = \{3\}$; $s_{ij} = c_{ij} = 0$, $i = 1, 2, 3, 4, 5, 6$; and $j = 1, 2, 3, 4$. Go to step 4.

Step 4. For each idle machine, try to schedule a job; for each $k \in A$ with $U_k \neq \emptyset$, let i^* be the job with the best priority, $u_{i^*t} = \min_{i \in U_k} u_{it}$. For $k = 1$, $u_{i^*0} = \min_{i \in \{1,2,5\}} u_{it}$. The priority is MWKR, so $u_{10} = -(6 + 8 + 13 + 5) = -32$, $u_{20} = -12$, and $u_{50} = -17$. Thus, $u_{i^*0} = \min \{-32, -12, -17\} = -32$ and $i^* = 1$. Schedule job 1 on machine 1; set $J_1 = 1$, $s_{11} = 0$, $c_{11} = 0 + 6 = 6$, $H_1 = 6$. Remove job 1 from U_1, $U_1 = \{2, 5\}$, and machine 1 from A, $A = \{2, 3, 4\}$. Now set $k = 2$; there is only one job in U_2 so we schedule it on machine 2; $i^* = 4$, $s_{41} = 0$, $c_{41} = 5$, $H_2 = 5$, $U_2 = \emptyset$, and $A = \{3, 4\}$. Similarly, we schedule jobs 6 and 3 on machines 3 and 4, respectively. The data are given in the $t = 0$ row of Table 8-38. Note for each U_k the chosen job is bold. Also, the blue values of H_k were computed at the time for the row. All $k \in A$ with $U_k \neq \emptyset$ have been examined, so go to step 1.

Step 1. Increment t; let $t = \min_{k = 1, m; k \in A} H_k = \min\{6, 5, 4, 3\} = 3$, and $K = \{k \mid H_k = 3\} = \{4\}$. The minimum value of H_k is bold in the table.

Step 2. Find the job(s) that complete at time t and the machines released. Only job 3 completes at time 3, and it is on machine 4, so $i^3 = \{i \mid J_k = i, k \in K\} = \{3\}$, $K = \{4\}$, and $A = \emptyset \cup \{4\} = \{4\}$. These values are given in the $t = 3$ row of Table 8-38.

Step 3. Determine the jobs ready to be scheduled on each machine. Job 3 completed, so its second operation, which is on machine 2, is ready to be scheduled. Now $U_1 = \{2, 5\}$, $U_2 = \{3\}$, $U_3 = \emptyset$, and $U_4 = \emptyset$. Since no jobs are waiting for machine 4 (which is the only idle machine), no job can be scheduled to start at time 3; therefore we return to step 1.

The algorithm continues, with the results given in Table 8-38. If no job is scheduled, the idle machine is not assigned a value for H_k. The value of H_k repeats in each row until k is idle or another job is scheduled on it. When $t = 5$, we schedule job 3 on machine 2. When $t = 6$ we again use MWKR to choose a job from U_1; it is job 4, which is bold in the table. At $t = 23$, we have two machines, 1 and 2, tied for minimum H_k, so when we advance t, there are two jobs ready to be scheduled on some machine. We also may be able to schedule two waiting jobs at $t = 25$. In that case, we schedule job 3 on machine 1 and job 6 on machine 2. When $t = 48$, there is a tie between jobs 3 and 5 for MWKR: we choose job 3 arbitrarily. At $t = 56$, job 5 finishes on machine 3, and all jobs are completed. The makespan for the schedule generated by the MWKR dispatch heuristic is 56, and is shown in Figure 8-18

TABLE 8-38
MWKR dispatch heuristic for Quick Closures

t	i^t	K	A	U_1	U_2	U_3	U_4	H_1	H_2	H_3	H_4
0	∅	∅	1, 2, 3, 4	**1**, 2, 5	**4**	6	3	6	5	4	3
3	3	4	4	2, 5	3			6	5	**4**	
4	6	3	3, 4	2, 5, 6	3			6	**5**		
5	4	2	2, 3, 4	2, 4, 5, 6	3			**6**	13		
6	1	1	1, 3, 4	2, **4**, 5, 6	1			16	**13**		
13	3	2	2, 3, 4	2, 3, 5, 6	**1**			**16**	21		
16	4	1	1, 3, 4	2, 3, **5**, 6		4		19	21	31	
19	5	1	1, 4	**2**, 3, 6	5			23	**21**	31	
21	1	2	2, 4	3, 6	**5**	1		**23**	25	31	
23	2	1	1, 4	3, **6**	2	1		25	**25**	31	
25	6, 5	1, 2	1, 2, 4	**3**	2, **6**	1	5	31	29	31	31
29	6	2	2		**2**	1	6	31	**30**	31	31
30	2	2	2			1, 2	6	**31**		31	31
31	3, 4	1, 3	1, 2, 3			**1**, 2, 3	4, **6**			44	36
36	6	4	1, 2, 4			2, 3, 5	**4**			44	**40**
40	4	4	1, 2, 4			2, 3, 5				**44**	
44	1	3	1, 2, 3, 4			**2**, 3, 5	1			48	49
48	2	3	1, 2, 3			**3**, 5	2			52	**49**
49	1	4	1, 2, 4			5	2			**52**	52
52	3, 2	3, 4	1, 2, 3, 4			**5**				56	
56	5	3	1, 2, 3, 4								

Other priorities would generate a different schedule; e.g., the least-work-remaining rule gives a makespan of 66.

Other methods can be used for scheduling job shops. Van Laarhoven et al. (1992) use a simulated annealing algorithm for the job shop. We discuss bottleneck heuristics, which are very useful for job shops, further in Chapter 10. Now we examine finite capacity scheduling systems.

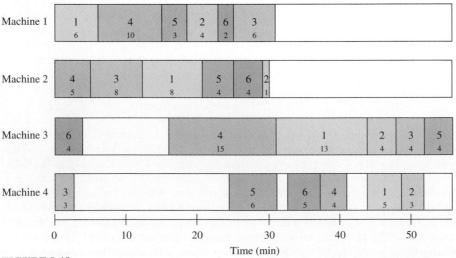

FIGURE 8-18
MWKR dispatch schedule for Quick Closures

SECTION 6 PROBLEMS

8.56. Determine the optimal makespan schedule for the following two-machine job-shop problem.

Job i	1	2	3	4	5	6	7	8	9
a_i	10	2	4	8	5	12	7	—	14
b_i	2	4	5	8	6	9	—	15	—
First machine	A	A	B	A	B	B	A	B	A

8.57. Give the schedule you would recommend to minimize makespan for the following three-machine, four-job job shop. Make as strong a comment as you can about how good the schedule might be.

	Processing Time			Route		
	Operation			Operation		
Job	1	2	3	1	2	3
1	5	10	12	A	B	C
2	4	3	8	A	C	B
3	9	6	7	C	B	A
4	7	5	11	B	C	A

8.58. Using the data below, give a Gantt Chart for the schedule of the five jobs through the drill (D), lathe (L), grinder (G), and mill (M) operations that you would recommend to minimize makespan. Discuss your solution method and optimality of the schedule.

Job 1		Job 2		Job 3		Job 4		Job 5	
Op	Time	Op	Time	Op	Time	Op	Time	Op	Time
D	1	L	2	G	2	D	1	M	2
L	2	M	2	D	2	G	2	D	2
M	2	D	2	G	1			G	1
				L	1				

7 FINITE-CAPACITY SCHEDULING SYSTEMS

The scheduling models discussed in this chapter are an integral part of a finite-capacity scheduling system. A finite-capacity scheduling system closes the gap between MRP capacity plans and detailed shop floor schedules. Since few MRP systems consider set-ups, and most assume constant lead times, their production goals may be unrealistic. Modern manufacturing requires product diversity, production in small lots, quick delivery, and adherence to promised delivery dates. Further, flexibility to respond to changes in customer orders, material availability, or capacity is necessary. Traditionally, inventory and excess capacity have hidden problems associated with these demands. Decreases in inventory levels and capacity have made finite-capacity scheduling a critical step in production planning and control.

There is a fundamental relationship between capacity and lead time. In many traditional plants, studies show that about 5 percent of the manufacturing lead time of a job is actual value-added processing. The rest is wait-and-move time. Wait time may be caused by other jobs in process, lack of materials or tools, or set-up time. Having excess capacity is one way to alleviate the problem. If there are dedicated machines for each job, then waiting for other jobs to process or set-ups to be carried out is unnecessary. On the other hand, inventory can allow instantaneous supply and decrease the number of set-ups needed. It decouples successive operations, and planning and scheduling can be done on a local scale, which is much easier to do. Unfortunately, this requires a high investment in capacity and inventory.

One approach is to simplify the production system. Cellular manufacturing converts job shops into dedicated flow shops for each product. Set-up reduction can eliminate lost time when changing production from one job to another. Although these concepts are sound, situations exist in which the cost of capacity prohibits dedicated equipment, or in which set-ups can be reduced no further. In such cases, proper scheduling can help by reducing lead time, resulting in better adherence to customer promise dates, and can create capacity by having less time devoted to set-ups or waiting for material. Scheduling can also smooth product flow. Computer-assisted scheduling frees managers to focus on important issues rather than spend time generating schedules.

Many companies have a manual scheduler or a committee to put together schedules. The resulting schedule determines order release and is used for shop-floor control. Often, change requires jobs to be placed on a hotlist that specifies important jobs, which take priority over other jobs. Expediters are people who make sure a hotlist job is rushed through; sales personnel, customer service representatives, and production managers may do likewise. These practices can do more harm than good.

Computer-assisted finite-capacity scheduling systems overcome many of these problems. Input from existing data bases is used to generate one or more schedules from an appropriate scheduling model, e.g., a bottleneck scheduling model. The schedule is reviewed by the scheduler and either accepted as-is or modified. It can be directly modified manually, or the scheduler may change priorities, times, or capacities and let the computer generate a new schedule. The schedule is implemented and jobs tracked on the shop floor. If production changes occur, the schedule is modified to account for them. Some details of this process are discussed in the software section (Section 8).

Some benefits of a finite capacity scheduling system are

- More on-time deliveries
- Reduced lead times
- Increased capacity
- Smoother production
- Increased management time for important problems

An improved shop-floor scheduling system at one company increased revenue by $844,000; another company reduced shortages from 60 percent to 13 percent; a third decreased WIP 70 percent; a fourth paid for the system in 21 days; and others have reduced late orders significantly. While such systems are not easy to develop, the gains are more than worth the effort. Box 8-2 discusses the implementation of a system at Eaton Corporation.

BOX 8-2: FINITE SCHEDULING HELPS EATON CUT LINE SETUPS AND INCREASE LINE THROUGHPUT

Switching from batch to just-in-time (JIT) operations affects more than inventory and the layout of machine tools. At Eaton Corporation Truck Components Operations North America (TCONA) in Shelbyville, Tenn., department supervisors needed a tool to eliminate hot lists caused by shortened customer lead times and to help them manage around a moving target.

That tool is the FACTOR finite capacity management system from Pritsker Corporation, Indianapolis, Indiana. "The system helps us recognize and plan around the bottlenecks that come from a production schedule that changes dramatically each day," explains Bill Dixon, plant manager, Eaton-Shelbyville.

The system schedules are driven by the customer order requirements generated by TCONA's manufacturing resource planning (MRP II) system. The MRP II system schedules the material into the TCONA manufacturing plants, the system then schedules the material through the plant.

The results include reduced setups and setup costs, increased gross utilization, orders completed on time, and the elimination of hot lists.

INCREASED THROUGHPUT ACHIEVED

TCONA manufactures transmission, axle and brake components and assemblies for the heavy- and medium-duty truck industry worldwide, particularly the original equipment manufacturer (OEM) and aftermarket industries. Headquartered in Galesburg, MI, TCONA encompasses seven manufacturing locations, several truck component marketing locations that support dealer fleets, several regional remanufacturing plants and two trim and sequencing facilities.

The Shelbyville plant manufactures parts ranging from metal shafts to entire transmission cases. The plant floor has more than 700 machine tools assigned to five departments, such as shaft, gear tuning, gray iron, and yoke and block. At any one time, about 75 parts numbers are being scheduled within each department; between 600 and 800 active part numbers are in production in any given month.

The division's mission, according to Bob DiRaimo, manager of information technologies, is to be "the world-class leader in our truck component market segments, measured by the highest level of customer satisfaction. TCONA's mission is to continuously meet its customers' needs with the highest quality, most competitive products in the world, and with a world-class design, manufacturing, and support organization.

Toward that goal, Shelbyville ten years ago replaced its batch operation, where parts were transferred by forklift between different areas in the plant, to cellular machining areas laid out in manufacturing flow lines.

Part throughput dramatically increased as a result, but so did the complexity of scheduling production.

At the time, department scheduling including part priorities and machines assignments, was done by the department's foreman based on gut feel. "Years ago, when we had as much as a 3-month lead time, it was easy to run a batch type operation

BOX 8-2 (*continued*)

through the factory," explains Dixon. "But as the marketplace changed over the last decade, so did Eaton's manufacturing philosophy. We began to operate JIT—reducing inventory at our customer sites and giving our customers what they want when they want it with shorter lead times. We were getting ourselves to the point to when a customer called, we could respond. But to do that, we had to handle thousands of small orders through the factory."

Meeting the increase in customer orders with shorter lead time was taking its toll on the plant. The shaft department, for example, was relying too much on hot lists—everything was a priority. Machinists found themselves tearing down and setting up new jobs of small lot numbers—maybe ten to fifteen parts—several times a day.

"In some areas where we developed machining cells or purchased brand new computer numerical control (CNC) machines, we had the capability of quick changeover. But it's impossible to take a 25-year-old factory like Shelbyville and have that throughput in all areas of the plant," continues Dixon.

Helping somewhat was TCONA's mainframe-based MRP II system, which consisted of material requirements planning (MRP), inventory control and accounting modules. The MRP II system provided some front-end shop floor scheduling. "All the schedules were created in Galesburg," explains Rob Conway, TCONA materials manager. "They would send us the part numbers and quantities to be manufactured, and we would manually schedule those by department through the plant."

Shelbyville soon realized it needed a better tool to schedule the shop floor. "We wanted more detail to help the foremen establish part priorities, group them, and reduce setups," continues Conway.

That tool was Pritsker's FACTOR finite capacity management system. TCONA first saw the system demonstrated at a trade show in 1989. Soon after, TCONA's Axle Brake Plant started using the software system. Shelbyville started working with it, and in February 1992, the plant's shaft department went "live" with it.

"It is the tool we use to match customer schedules with the capability of our factory and come up with the throughput that we can truly make," says Dixon.

INSTALLING THE SYSTEM

At installation, information had to be entered that reflected the plant's production capability and order requirements. This information included shift schedules, operating times for each shift, resource requirements (machine operational data), a list of all parts, process plans for individual parts, the shop calendar (including vacation schedules and planned shutdowns for inventory), setup matrices and order data.

With this information, the system now knows exactly what it takes to run a particular part through the plant.

Priority rules to schedule production were also entered into the system, which comes with about eighteen such rules. Shelbyville decided to use two of those rules and have Pritsker write a third that combined the other two. With one of the standard priority rules, earliest due date, the finite scheduling system generates a production schedule based strictly on the earliest due date of the customer orders in the plant, regardless of the number of setups required. In the second standard rule, minimize

BOX 8-2 (*continued*)

setup, the system generates a production schedule based strictly on minimizing the number of setups required to satisfy the customer orders, regardless of order due dates.

Shelbyville's third priority rule, the combination rule, divides a 30-day scheduling window into three categories: "hot," "warm," and 'cold." The system analyzes the due dates of customer orders and puts orders due in less than ten days in the "hot" category; orders due in ten to twenty days, the system puts in the "warm" category; and orders due in more than twenty days, the system puts in the "cold" category.

The system then schedules hot customer orders based on earliest due date; it schedules warm customer orders based on minimum setup, unless that causes the part to fall into the hot category, in which case it is scheduled based on earliest due date; and it schedules cold customer orders based on minimum setup alone.

This last scheduling rules gives us the best of all worlds: earliest due date, minimum setup, and the combination of both.

In operation, TCONA's MRP II system generates a planned assembly and build schedule for the customer orders in-house. Information associated with those orders within a 30-day window is downloaded to the system each week. The downloaded information includes the part numbers in each customer order, part quantities and due dates.

"Then we let the finite scheduling system do its thing," explains DiRaimo. "Based on the set of optimization rules we've established in system, we let it tell us what parts to run, in what quantities, and when."

Eaton runs three scheduling simulations and compares them. Schedules are compared based on the total number of hours that customer orders are late, the number of setups, total setup time, and the total run time. They take the best schedule, print reports, and then issue them to the shop foreman who uses the system-generated schedule.

"Within five minutes of getting a copy of the schedules, I know how our manufacturing area is doing," says Dixon. "Before, I would not have known how the flow of parts was going unless I went onto the floor and talked with each department supervisor."

REAL COST REDUCTIONS

Shelbyville's shaft department began running under the finite capacity scheduling system after almost seven months of system installation work, including data entry, entering and rewriting scheduling priorities, customizing reports, integrating the system with the MRP II system, and a week of training. The plant's gear department went live with the finite scheduling system in July 1992 after only three months of data entry work. Production schedules are now generated for the shaft department and for the gear department twice a week.

After six months of using the system, Shelbyville's shaft department has seen dramatic results: a 27 percent reduction in the number of set-ups, a 12 percent reduction in setup costs as a percent of direct labor, and a 29 percent increase in gross utilization—throughput. Just as important, hot lists are a thing of the past; orders are completed on time. The system also helps supervisors foresee manpower and overtime needs well in advance.

BOX 8-2 (*continued*)

Shelbyville's gear department also has been seeing benefits: late orders have been cut in half and the lateness of those orders has been reduced considerably. "We're talking thousands of dollars per month," says Dixon. "And there are the costs of meeting customer schedules, which translates into more sales and reduced overtime—-all of those things that we haven't yet got a handle on in terms of actual cost savings."

"This system helps us reach Eaton's philosophy of using JIT to satisfy our customers," explains DiRaimo. "It allows us to better schedule manufacturing capacity in the facility and to optimize that schedule based upon local management philosophies."

"Plus, as we develop team concepts, flow lines and machining centers at Shelbyville over the next twelve to eighteen months, the system will let us turn the responsibility of department scheduling over to the employees," says Rob Conway, materials manager, Eaton-Shelbyville. "Department supervisors can now be more managers than schedulers, and thereby facilitate work, solve bottleneck problems, and concentrate on the real problems in their respective departments."

8   SOFTWARE

There is an abundance of scheduling software available. Packages run the gamut from shareware PC programs to million-dollar customized applications. Be careful when purchasing a program, since capabilities vary widely. Tips for choosing a scheduling package are given in Voet and Dewilde (1994). Buyer's Guide (1995) provides information on more than 70 packages. For in-depth discussion of several packages, see Pinedo (1995).

The basic functions a scheduling package might perform are

- Schedule display
- Schedule evaluation
- Schedule adjustment
- Schedule generation
- Schedule simulation

Packages may contain one or more of these capabilities. A brief discussion of each follows.

A schedule display is a depiction of a given schedule. This can be done by a simple list of start and completion times for each job and machine combination. More often a Gantt Chart of the schedule is given. Gantt Charts range from crude bars of ASCII characters to many-colored, high-resolution graphics charts. It is important to make sure the schedule is easily understood by the user and to know where the displayed schedule comes from. Cheaper software requires the schedule to be generated by the user; more expensive packages contain schedule generators.

Schedule evaluation is also done by some packages. This provides measures of schedule "goodness," which may include measures such as makespan, flowtime, and tardiness, as well as resource usage, staffing, WIP levels, and other relevant information. As with schedule display, this information can be shown graphically or simply listed.

Some software provides the user the ability to change or adjust schedules. The high-end packages allow drag-and-insert operations on the Gantt Chart itself; these require very sophisticated graphical user interfaces. Less costly packages allow changes to be made in the start and completion times of the jobs. Coupled with schedule evaluation, schedule adjustment allows the user to perform some simple "what if" analysis.

To display, evaluate, or adjust a schedule, we must first generate one. This is the critical part of finite-capacity scheduling. Many packages leave schedule generation to the user and just display or evaluate it. If it is difficult to come up with good schedules by hand, which often is the case, these packages are not very helpful. More advanced packages generate schedules, but they may not be very good. The package may generate a single schedule, several schedules, or the "best" of a subset of schedules. Simple dispatch rules, such as "first come, first served" or SPT can produce a single schedule. Using a number of dispatching rules may generate several schedules; either the user can pick one, or only the "best" one is shown to the user. More advanced heuristics, or even branch-and-bound procedures, can be used to generate a schedule. Since scheduling is very difficult, the approach must be tailored to the problem at hand; the wrong sophisticated approach may be worse than simple dispatch rules.

If the production system is complicated (e.g., a large job shop), a simulation of a schedule may be needed. The schedule is tried out by simulation, and many factors not considered in the scheduling decision can be examined. This can be extremely helpful, particularly if heuristics use lead times, which can be better estimated by simulation. Packages that simulate the shop are relatively expensive, usually costing more than $30,000.

In our experience, few companies can get by with inexpensive, off-the-shelf software. Because of variations in scheduling environments, customized systems are often required. Usually, this involves purchasing a package and the consulting services of the vendor, which can become quite expensive.

There are "educational" scheduling packages available. Morton and Pentico (1993) bundle the software package, Parsifal, with their book. Parsifal solves most scheduling models. It has the ability to use a variety of heuristics for single machine, parallel, flow-shop, and job-shop models. Several general purpose algorithms are available, including simulated annealing. It does quite well on many small problems, and likely could be incorporated into a scheduling system. QS: Quantitative Systems (Chang, 1995) is a general software package that does flow-shop and job-shop scheduling. Many of the heuristics for flow shops can be used, and most dispatching rules are available for job shops.

9 EVOLUTION

Scheduling has always been done; certainly, constructing the pyramids required it. Gantt (1911) was perhaps the first to advocate a quantitative approach to scheduling. As an area of focus, scheduling really began in the mid-1950s. Classical models and solutions were developed by Johnson (1954), Smith (1956), Jackson (1956), and McNaughton (1959). These papers laid the foundation for the work that followed. Early results were consolidated by Muth & Thompson (1963). Many complicated scheduling problems were modeled as mixed-integer programming problems, but their combinatorial nature made them impossible to solve in reasonable amounts of time. This fostered emphasis on scheduling heuristics. Conway et al.

(1967) provided the first textbook on scheduling. A generation of researchers and practitioners learned scheduling from the rigorous but readable book by Baker (1974).

The 1970s produced more theoretical results. Seminal work on worst-case analysis of heuristics (Graham, 1969) and complexity of various scheduling models (Karp, 1972) led to many important results. These approaches were popularized by Rinnooy Kan (1976).

Scheduling research now appears to be focused on more applied results. Panwalker et al. (1973) and McKay et al. (1988) investigate scheduling in industry and identify relevant issues. The reorganization of manufacturing systems, particularly the move to reduce inventory and the need to reduce lead times, has made scheduling much more important. The exciting, if controversial, results of OPT scheduling systems (see Chapter 10) piqued the interest of many practitioners as well as researchers, which began the interest in bottleneck scheduling. General-purpose solution techniques, such as simulated annealing and genetic algorithms, have allowed more complex models to be solved. Current work on stochastic analysis and multiple-criteria scheduling holds promise for the future. A good starting point is the book by Pinedo (1995), which combines theoretical results with case studies.

Faster, readily available computers and user-friendly graphical interfaces have made scheduling easier to implement. *APICS: The Performance Advantage,* a journal oriented toward practitioners, has shifted its software evaluation from MRP II packages to finite-capacity scheduling packages. It has published several articles (e.g., Heuttel, 1993, and Gilman, 1994) on the growing interest in scheduling. As methodological advances occur, the distinction between planning and scheduling blurs (Lasserre, 1992), and a company that cannot schedule quickly and correctly will be at a tremendous disadvantage.

10   SUMMARY

This chapter has examined operations scheduling. Scheduling has become critical in today's low-inventory, short-lead-time manufacturing environment. Traditional MRP and MRP II systems do not emphasize true finite-capacity scheduling.

The chapter starts by defining basic scheduling problems. Jobs, machines, measures, and Gantt Charts are discussed. Single-machine models for various measures are presented. Many of them are easily solved, but for models with set-up times or tardiness, we find efficient algorithms are unlikely to exist. Finally, we discuss search methods that can be modified to solve most scheduling models.

Parallel-scheduling models are covered next. There are multiple machines that completely process any job. For identical machines, flowtime problems are easily solved. For other measures, list heuristics are good approaches. A worst-case bound is given for the makespan model.

Flow shops have multiple operations for each job, which are performed in the same order. Only two-machine and some three-machine makespan problems can be solved easily. Other models require heuristic solutions. Several heuristics are given, along with bounds that can be used in a branch-and-bound algorithm. Search methods can also be used to find good permutation schedules for flow shops.

Job shops, the most difficult scheduling models, are discussed next. Dispatch heuristics are discussed, and several reasonable priority rules are presented.

Scheduling software is now readily available. The rule of caveat emptor applies to its purchase; expensive systems may do no more than low-priced ones. Finally, we trace the evolution of scheduling. From its graphical beginning, a theoretical base for scheduling has developed. Lean production philosophies have made scheduling a top priority in current manufacturing systems.

MINICASE: ILANA DESIGNS

Ilana Designs, headquartered in Rotterdam, manufactures a variety of high-quality clothing items. The company was started by Ilana Bloem in 1954 and has rapidly become a major force in the Common Market. Men's dress shirts are a major product line of the company. Currently, the Dresden shirt plant is several weeks behind on deliveries, causing Joakim Valsta, head of marketing, to be concerned that current customers may buy elsewhere.

The Dresden plant produces shirts on a make-to-order basis. An order consists of quantities of different types (cloth, color, and style) of shirts. Each type of shirt becomes a separate job. Jobs from different orders consisting of the same type of shirt can be combined, or the same type shirts can be broken into more than one job. The latter occurs when there are more shirts in a job than can be layered on the cutting table. Once a job is defined, it goes through a sequence of operations that transform cloth into packaged shirts. All jobs go through the operations in the same order: spreading, marking, cutting, fitting, sewing, buttoning, and packaging.

There are many cells to make shirts, all following the described process. Each operation will now be discussed.

Spreading. Bolts of the appropriate cloth for the job are brought to the cutting tables and spread. One, two, or many layers of cloth may be spread on the table.

Marking. A pattern is "marked" on the cloth spread on the table, usually through NC machinery but occasionally with a paper pattern. A cutting pattern can have multiple shirts of the same or different sizes. All parts of each particular shirt must be cut from the same layer.

Cutting. The cloth is cut in the shape of the pattern with a laser knife. This cut actually cuts out many shirts, because there are usually many layers of cloth on the table and each layer contains multiple shirts. When cutting is complete, the table is transferred to fitting.

Fitting. Here, all components of each particular shirt are bundled together. All bundles are then sent to sewing.

Sewing. Skilled sewers put together the components to make an almost-finished shirt. There are 20 sewing machines and operators in the sewing room. When all shirts are sewn, they go to buttoning.

Buttoning. Here, buttons are sewn on the shirt. This is done using a special purpose machine called a "buttoner." It also makes the button hole. Once the buttons are in place, shirts are put in a bin. When a job is completed, the bin is taken to packaging.

Packaging. Shirts are folded around cardboard, pinned and packaged in clear plastic, and placed in totes. When all shirts are packaged, they are sent to shipping where they are recombined into orders and shipped to customers.

Teodor Boctor, the plant manager, believes there are several long-term solutions to the problem, all involving new technology to increase capacity. Lise Madsen, vice president of manufacturing, believes new technology and changes in procedures may help in the long term, but wants something done now. The superintendent of one cell, Amar Crainic, thinks too much cell time is wasted between jobs. However, he has not had time to verify this, or to come up with better schedules for his cell.

Lise has hired you as a consultant to do a preliminary study on the situation. Amar provides data for his cell in the following table:

Job	Operation times (minutes)						
	Spread	Mark	Cut	Fit	Sew	Button	Package
1	8	1	7	45	7	41	8
2	6	1	8	25	13	27	12
3	8	1	5	36	7	31	10
4	4	2	10	49	6	37	9
5	9	1	5	33	13	27	13
6	7	2	7	25	11	36	11
7	4	1	8	36	15	29	11
8	12	2	9	25	9	22	8
9	13	2	11	32	13	25	12
10	5	2	10	48	7	34	9
11	10	2	10	28	6	37	8
12	12	2	5	27	12	22	8
13	9	2	8	30	10	35	13
14	6	1	11	46	16	28	13
15	15	1	9	34	8	37	8

Give your recommended schedule for the data. Discuss your measure of schedule goodness. What would you propose to do as a full study? What additional data would be necessary? List all assumptions you make.

11   REFERENCES

Arkin, E. M. and Roundy, R. O., "Weighted-Tardiness Scheduling on Parallel Machines with Proportional Weights," *Operations Research,* 39, 64–81, 1991.

Baker, K. R., *Introduction to Sequencing and Scheduling,* John Wiley & Sons, New York, 1974.

Baker, K. R., *Elements of Sequencing and Scheduling,* Baker Press, Hanover, NH, 1995.

Buyer's Guide, "Scheduling Software," *IIE Solutions,* Sept. 1995, pp. 46–53.

Cambell, H. G., Dudek, R. A., and Smith, M. L., "A Heuristic Algorithm for the n Job, m Machine Sequencing Problem," *Management Science,* 16, B630–B637, 1970.

Chang, Y. L., *QS: Quantitative Systems Version 3.0,* Prentice Hall, Englewood Cliffs, NJ, 1995.

Cheng, T. C. E. and Chen, Z-L., "Parallel-Machine Scheduling Problems with Earliness and Tardiness Penalties," *Journal of the Operational Research Society,* 45, 685–695, 1994.

Cheng, T. C. E. and Sin, C. C. S., " A State-of-the-Art Review of Parallel-Machine Scheduling Research," *European Journal of Operational Research,* 47, 271–292, 1990.

Collins, N. E., Eglese, R. W., and Golden, B. L., "Simulated Annealing—An Annotated Bibliography," *American Journal of Mathematical and Management Science,* 8, 209–307, 1988.

Conway, R. W., Maxwell, W. L., and Miller, L. W., *Theory of Scheduling,* Addison-Wesley, Reading, MA, 1967.

Credle, R., "Finite Scheduling Helps Eaton Cut Line Setups and Increase Line Throughput," *Case History: Scheduling, APICS—The Performance Advantage,* Jan. 1993, pp. 30–32.

Emmons, H., "One-Machine Sequencing to Minimize Certain Functions of Job Tardiness," *Operations Research,* 17, 701–715, 1969.

French, S., *Sequencing and Scheduling,* John Wiley & Sons, New York, 1986.

Gantt, H. L., ed., *How Scientific Management Is Applied,* Hive Publishing Company, Easton, PA, 1911.

Garey, M. R., and Johnson, D. S., *Computers and Intractability,* Freeman, San Francisco, 1979.

Gilman, A., "Interest in Finite Scheduling Is Growing . . . Why?" *APICS: The Performance Advantage,* Aug., 1994, pp. 45–48.

Grabowski, J., Skubalska, E., and Smutnicki, C., "On Flow Shop Scheduling with Release and Due Dates to Minimize Maximum Lateness," *Journal of the Operational Research Society,* 34, 615–20, 1983.

Graham, R. L., "Bounds on Multiprocessing Timing Anomalies," *SIAM Journal on Applied Mathematics,* 17, 416–429, 1969.

Gupta, J. N. D., "Heuristic Algorithms for Multistage Flow Shop Problem," *AIIE Transactions,* 4, 11–18, 1972.

Huettle, J. "Finite Capacity Scheduling—Just a Luxury, Right?" *APICS: The Performance Advantage,* June 1993, pp. 37–39.

Jackson, J. R., "An Extension of Johnson's Results on Job-Lot Scheduling," *Naval Research Logistics Quarterly,* 3, 201–204, 1956.

Johnson, S. M., "Optimal Two- and Three-Stage Production Schedules with Setup Times Included," *Naval Research Logistics Quarterly,* 1, 61–68, 1954.

Johnson, D. S., Aragon, C. R., Mcgeoch, L. A., and Schevon, C., "Optimization by Simulated Annealing: An Experimental Evaluation; Part I, Graph Partitioning," *Operations Research,* 37, 865–892, 1989.

Karp, R. M., "Reducibility Among Combinatorial Problems," in Miller, R. E. and Thatcher, J. W., eds., *Complexity of Computer Computations,* Plennum Press, New York, 1972.

Kim, Y. D., "Heuristics for Flowshop Scheduling Problems Minimizing Mean Tardiness," *Journal of the Operational Research Society,* 44, 19–28, 1993.

Lasserre, J. B., "An Integrated Model for Job-Shop Planning and Scheduling," *Management Science,* 38, 1201–1211, 1992.

Little, J. D. C., Murty, K. G., Sweeney, D. W., and Karel, C., "An Algorithm for the Traveling Salesman Problem," *Operations Research,* 11, 979–989, 1963.

McKay, K. N., Safayeni, F. R., and Buzacott, J. A., "Job-Shop Scheduling Theory: What Is Relevant?" *Interfaces,* 18, 84–90, 1988.

McNaughton, R., "Sequencing with Deadlines and Loss Functions," *Management Science,* 6, 1–12, 1959.

Morton, T. E. and Pentico, D. W., *Heuristic Scheduling Systems,* John Wiley & Sons, New York, 1993.

Muth, J. F. and Thompson, G. L., *Industrial Scheduling,* Prentice-Hall, Englewood Cliffs, NJ, 1963.

Ogbu, F. A. and Smith, D. K., "The Application of the Simulated Annealing Algorithm to the Solution of the n/m/Cmax Flowshop Problem," *Computers & Operations Research,* 17, 243–253, 1990.

Osman, I. H. and Potts, C. N., "Simulated Annealing for Permutation Flow-Shop Scheduling," *OMEGA,* 17, 551–557, 1989.

Panwalkar, S. S., Dudek, R. K., and Smith, M. L., "Sequencing Research and the Industrial Scheduling Problem," in *Symposium on the Theory of Scheduling and Its Application,* Elmaghraby, S. E., ed., Springer Publishing, New York, 1973.

Philipoom, P. R. and Fry, T. D., "The Robustness of Selected Job-Shop Dispatching Rules with Respect to Load Balance and Work-Flow Structure," *Journal of the Operational Research Society,* 41, 897–906, 1990.

Pinedo, M., *Scheduling: Theory, Algorithms, and Systems,* Prentice-Hall, Englewood Cliffs, NJ, 1995.

Rachamadugu, R. V. and Morton, T. E., "Myopic Heuristics for the Single Machine Weighted Tardiness Problem," *GSIA Working Paper 30-82-83,* Carnegie Mellon University, Pittsburgh, PA, 1982.

Reeves, C. R., "A Genetic Algorithm for Flowshop Sequencing," *Computers & Operations Research,* 22, 5–14, 1995.

Rinnooy Kan, A. H. G., *Machine Scheduling Problems: Classification, Complexity and Computations,* Martinus Nijhoff, The Hague, Holland, 1976.

Smith, W. E., "Various Optimizers for Single Stage Production," *Naval Research Logistics Quarterly,* 3, 59–66, 1956.

So, K. C., "Some Heuristics for Scheduling Jobs on Parallel Machines with Setups," *Management Science,* 36, 467–475, 1990.

Sundararaghavan, P. and Ahmed, M., "Minimizing the Sum of Absolute Lateness in Single-Machine and Multi-machine Scheduling," *Naval Research Logistics Quarterly,* 31, 325–333, 1984.

Suresh, V. and Chaudhuri, D., "Dynamic Scheduling—A Survey of Research," *International Journal of Production Economics,* 32, 53–63, 1993.

Van Laarhoven, P. J. M., Aarts, E. H., and Lenstra, J. K., "Job Shop Scheduling by Simulated Annealing," *Operations Research,* 40, 113–125, 1992.

Villarreal, F. J. and Bulfin, R. L., "Scheduling a Single Machine to Minimize the Weighted Number of Tardy Jobs," *IIE Transactions,* 15, 337–343, 1983.

Voet, M. and Dewilde, P., "Choosing a Scheduling Package," *APICS—The Performance Advantage,* Nov. 1994, pp. 28–31.

Woolsey, R. E. D. and Swanson, H. S., *Operations Research for Immediate Application: A Quick & Dirty Manual,* Harper & Row, New York, 1975.

CHAPTER
9

PROJECT PLANNING, SCHEDULING, AND CONTROL

1 INTRODUCTION

Lynn walked out of the plant manager's office in shock. For the next year, she would be project manager for their new printer, the LJ9000. As project manager, she is responsible for specification and design, production methods, and initial marketing of the new product. The design, production methods, and time to market are critical factors affecting quality, cost, and market share of the final product. High technology projects of this type require increasingly large investment of up-front funds. At the same time, market pressures are forcing the time to market to be ever shorter. The project requires a high degree of interaction between experts in product design, production techniques, quality assurance, and marketing. This complexity makes the possibility of time delays and cost overruns more likely.

Many questions run through Lynn's mind as she thinks about her new assignment. How soon can the printer reach the market? Is there any way to reduce this time? Can she be sure there are no delays? What resources are needed to carry out the project? Is sufficient money allocated? Who should work with her, and how should she organize the team? These questions are answered by project planning, scheduling, and control.

1.1 Projects

Companies introduce new products infrequently, so why devote a chapter to project planning, scheduling, and control? The reason: Many other problems can be viewed as projects. Typical applications include moving from an old to a new plant, doing preventive maintenance on an important machine in a production line, building an apartment complex, paving a street, launching a space shuttle, planning a political campaign, and writing a textbook.

These examples have common characteristics. They are complex, consist of many activities, and have a specified goal. Formally, we define a **project** as a set of partially ordered, interrelated activities that must be completed to achieve a goal. All of the examples satisfy this definition. Usually, projects have a definite beginning and end. Typically, they happen only once or infrequently. However, recurring or cyclic projects, such as shipbuilding, do occur. The goal may be to complete the project as quickly as possible, as cheaply as possible, or a combination of the two. People with different backgrounds and skills work in teams to complete the project. Team members may be involved in the project on a part-time or temporary basis and return to their regular jobs upon completion of the project.

In the mid-1950s, several independent research teams developed similar approaches to project planning, scheduling, and control. All were highly successful, reducing both completion times and project costs 30 percent to 40 percent. One of the most publicized uses was the Polaris missile project for the U.S. Navy. After its success, some government projects were *required* to use some components of project planning, scheduling, and control. For more on its history, see Section 9.

1.2   Planning, Scheduling, and Control

Planning, scheduling, and control are fundamental concepts of management. **Planning** is an organized approach to accomplish some goal (in this case, the project). It begins by defining project objectives. Then component **activities** and how they interact are determined. Time and other resources required for each activity are estimated. Activities are often graphically represented on a **network.** Each activity corresponds to an arrow. If one activity precedes another, the arrows are connected by a node. **Scheduling** is the time-phased commitment of resources to do the project. Each activity is given a start time and a completion time. These times determine the project completion time and resource usage over time. The schedule identifies certain **critical activities,** which, if delayed, cause the project's completion to be delayed. Critical activities may warrant more effort in estimating time and resource requirements or even changes in the activity itself to reduce the project completion time or cost. **Control** monitors the progress of project activities and revises the plan accordingly.

Figure 9-1 shows the typical steps needed in a project planning, scheduling, and control study. The blocks above the top dashed line represent the planning phase. The project is defined and broken into activities or tasks. Interrelationships between the activities (i.e., precedence) are delineated and a corresponding network is created. Times and resources required for each activity are determined.

The next phase is scheduling and consists of the portion of Figure 9-1 between the dashed lines. Critical activities and project duration are found. If estimates for critical activities are not sufficiently accurate, better estimates are made. If the time to complete the project is too long, critical activity durations must be shortened by subcontracting, overtime, etc., until it is acceptable. The same is true of resources used by the activities.

Finally, control activities are shown below the bottom dashed line. As the project progresses, the status of each activity is updated. If activities take more time or use more resources than anticipated, replanning and scheduling is necessary. This continues until the project is completed.

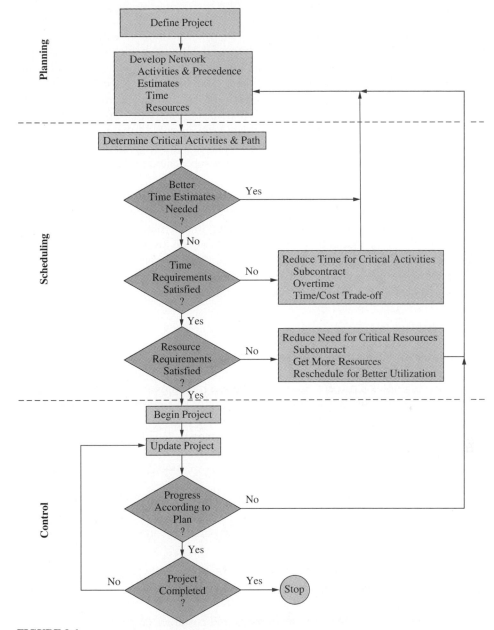

FIGURE 9-1
Steps for a project planning, scheduling, and control study

1.3 Benefits

Project planning, scheduling, and control provides many important advantages. The most important one is that it requires in-depth consideration of the project before anything is done. This gives greater knowledge of what to do and how to do it. A clear statement of project objectives is necessary. The plan specifies the activities that make up the project, as well as the time and resources required to do each activity. Furthermore, it delineates interrelationships between the activities. The procedure can be used to determine start and finish times of each activity and which activities are most critical to the overall success of the project. We focus on critical activities and tightly control them. This results in a master plan based on a global rather than local view, and the overall objectives are not subjugated to the objectives of one smaller part of the project.

This plan determines overall resource requirements throughout the life of the project. As the project proceeds, the expected results are compared to what actually happens, and plans are revised accordingly. It also allows "what if" planning to take place. This approach helps managers meet deadlines and budgets. It can be used at several levels of detail, and assigns responsibility for each activity to a specific person. Communication and coordination become easier, because all parties are working from a common base. More realistic expectations are obtained. Finally, it promotes a spirit of camaraderie among the participants of the project.

1.4 Product Development

Product development is a major application area of project planning, scheduling, and control. No wonder we opened this chapter with Lynn's task of developing a printer. Product development shows how complex a project can get, so we use it to demonstrate the scope, depth, and complexity of project planning, scheduling, and control. We rely heavily on Ulrich and Eppinger's (1995) discussion of product development.

Developing a new product takes a lot of time and money. Rarely is a new product developed in less than one year. A new automobile may take from three to five years and a new drug ten years or more to develop. The cost is roughly proportional to the duration and the number of people working on the project.

Attributes of development efforts for five products are given in Table 9-1. Even a simple screwdriver takes a year to develop, with a budget of $150,000. An airplane is at the other extreme, taking 4.5 years; $130,000,000; 130,000 parts; and during peak effort, 16,800 people to develop.

Product development has four major characteristics:

- Trade-offs between design parameters, cost, and performance, e.g., composite material versus metal
- Market dynamics, e.g., change in technology and customer needs
- Attention to detail, e.g., tolerances for each part
- Time to market

A large number of different types of decisions are made in product development.

To cope with this complex environment requires a step-by-step procedure. This procedure is a sequence of activities an organization follows to conceive, design, and commercialize a product. Some organizations define and follow a structured development process; others have difficulty defining the process. Furthermore, the definition of the process may vary from

TABLE 9-1
Development attributes and efforts

	Stanley Jobmaster screwdriver	Rollerblade Bravoblade in-line skates	H-P DeskJet 500 printer	Chrysler Concorde automobile	Boeing 777 airplane
Annual production volume	100,000 units/year	100,000 units/year	1,500,000 units/year	250,000 units/year	50 units/year
Sales lifetime	40 years	3 years	3 years	6 years	30 years
Sales price	$3	$200	$365	$19,000	$130 million
Number of unique parts (part numbers)	3 parts	35 parts	200 parts	10,000 parts	130,000 parts
Development time	1 year	2 years	1.5 years	3.5 years	4.5 years
Internal development team (peak size)	3 people	5 people	100 people	850 people	6,800 people
External development team (peak size)	3 people	10 people	100 people	1400 people	10,000 people
Development cost	$150,000	$750,000	$50 million	$1 billion	$3 billion
Production investment	$150,000	$1 million	$25 million	$600 million	$3 billion

Source: From Ulrich and Eppinger (1995). Used by permission of The McGraw-Hill Companies, Inc.

one organization to another. Many commonalities in the process exist, and it is possible to identify a generic product development process.

This process begins with a mission statement and ends with a product launch. There are five phases between these. They are

• Mission statement

1. Concept development
2. System level design
3. Detailed design
4. Testing and refining
5. Production ramp-up

• Product launch

The mission statement identifies the target market and provides a functional description for the product as well as the business goals of the effort. The product launch occurs when the product is available for purchase in the market. Table 9-2 shows activities within the five steps. It relates these to the organizational functions of marketing, design, and manufacturing.

Product development processes vary from organization to organization, so a generic process is adapted to the local environment. The specific process used by AMF Bowling is given in Figure 9-2. It shows the individual activities of the process and their roles in the different development functions. In the figure, alpha tests refer to internal testing of early prototypes. Beta prototypes are extensively evaluated internally, but are also tested by customers in their own environments.

An interesting addition to the generic process is including three major milestones, project approval, beginning tooling fabrication, and production release. Each milestone follows a major review.

As seen from Table 9-1, product development involves many people working on many different tasks. Successful product development projects result in high-quality, low-cost products while making efficient use of time and money. Project planning, scheduling, and control plays a major role in developing a successful product.

SECTION 1   PROBLEMS

9.1. What is a project?

9.2. List the steps used in project planning, scheduling, and control.

9.3. Describe the purposes of

    (a) Planning

    (b) Scheduling

    (c) Control

9.4. Give five situations in which project planning, scheduling, and control would be useful. Can you give one where it would not help? Explain.

9.5. Explain the AMF Bowling development process (Figure 9-2) in terms of the generic development process of Table 9-2.

9.6. Compare and contrast the steps of AMF development process with the steps given in Figure 9-1.

TABLE 9-2
Generic development process

	Concept development	System-level design	Detail design	Testing and refinement	Production ramp-up
Marketing	• Define market segments. • Identify lead users. • Identify competitive products.	• Develop plan for product options and extended product family.	• Develop marketing plan.	• Develop promotion and launch materials. • Facilitate field testing.	• Place early production with key customers.
Design	• Investigate feasibility of product concepts. • Develop industrial design concepts. • Build and test experimental prototypes.	• Generate alternative product architectures. • Define major subsystems and interfaces. • Refine industrial design.	• Define part geometry. • Choose materials. • Assign tolerances. • Complete industrial design control documentation.	• Do reliability testing, life testing, and performance testing. • Obtain regulatory approvals. • Implement design changes.	• Evaluate early production output.
Manufacturing	• Estimate manufacturing cost. • Assess production feasibility.	• Identify suppliers for key components. • Perform make-buy analysis. • Define final assembly scheme.	• Define piece-part production processes. • Design tooling. • Define quality assurance processes. • Begin procurement of long-lead tooling.	• Facilitate supplier ramp-up. • Refine fabrication and assembly processes. • Train work force. • Refine quality assurance processes.	• Begin operation of entire production system.
Other Functions	• Finance: Facilitate economic analysis. • Legal: Investigate patent issues.	• Finance: Facilitate make-buy anlysis. • Service: Identify service issues.		• Sales: Develop sales plan.	

Source: From Ulrich and Eppinger (1995). Used by permission of The McGraw-Hill Companies, Inc.

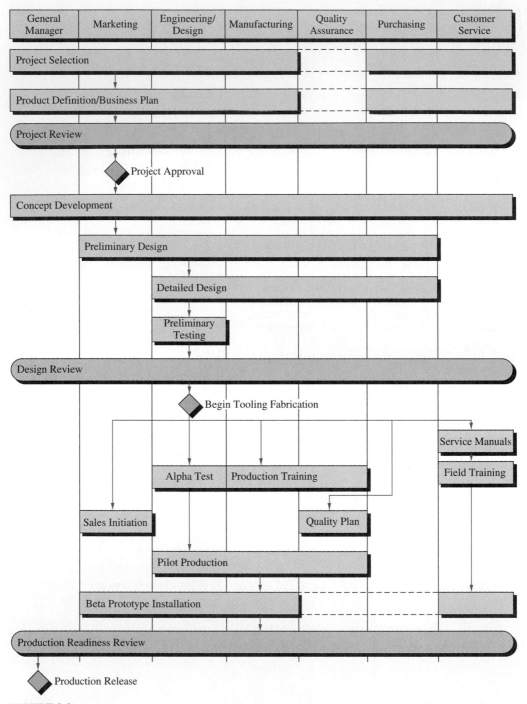

FIGURE 9-2
AMF Bowling development process from Ulrich and Eppinger (1995). Used by permission of The McGraw-Hill Companies, Inc.

2 PLANNING

We begin with planning. Planning includes selecting the right people to participate in the project and organizing them so the project is successful; defining the project goals; and determining the activities that make up the project, their interrelationships, and the time and resources required to do them.

2.1 Organizing the Project

The first step is to choose a project manager. A successful project manager should be goal oriented with good communication and interpersonal skills. Vision and the ability to foresee potential problems, along with the flexibility and creativity to overcome them, are also important qualities. Most important are leadership and sound organizational skills, particularly in goal setting, planning, and analyzing.

The project manager assembles a project team. Members are often experts in their respective areas. For many projects, team members work on the project part-time and continue their other duties. The project manager should have authority to pick and choose all team members.

In Chapter 1 we discussed organizational structures. A traditional functional organization with the project acting as the "company" is typically used for large projects. For small projects, divisional organization, with the project manager in a staff position, is often used. The project manager reports to the general manager, and team members report to functional managers rather than the project manager. For projects like Lynn's, a matrix organization is often used. The project manager has responsibility and accountability for the entire project, but delegates authority over the technical experts to the project representative from that department.

Communicating in projects is very important, especially in matrix organizations. The objective is to get the correct information to the proper people in time to make a difference. Regularly scheduled meetings are held at specified times or at the completion of important events in the project, called **milestones.** Meetings are also called when problems arise. Formal reports may be necessary. For example, an electrical designer may submit a weekly progress report to the head of the electrical engineering department, who in turn may submit a weekly progress report on all electrical activities to the project manager.

2.2 Project Definition

Once the team and organization are in place, planning begins. First, project objectives are determined. If there are several conflicting objectives, a compromise is reached through consensus. Next, responsibility for various areas of the project is assigned. This is followed by listing the resources available for the project. Finally, information requirements and availabilities are defined. Since these steps are application-dependent, we cannot go into great detail on them. This should not detract from their importance, however.

2.3 Defining Activities and the Network

After determining the project specifications, list all activities that make up the project. Each activity should have a definite beginning and ending point. Activities can be defined on many levels. For Lynn, a useful activity might be "design the printer." However, for the design team, this activity would be a complete project broken down into many subactivities. Choose the correct level of detail for each activity based on the ultimate user and purpose of the project. The level of detail should be no more than is needed to assign resources and manage the activity.

An activity is graphically represented by an arrow, with the tail of the arrow corresponding to the start of the activity and the head its completion. The arrows are called arcs, or edges. Figure 9-3 represents a typical activity. The duration of the activity and possibly a short description is sometimes written over or under the arrow. The length and angle of the arrow has no particular meaning.

We call the beginning and end of an activity **events.** Unlike activities, there is no time duration associated with an event. Graphically, we represent events by circles, called **nodes,** and give each event a unique number to specify it. In Figure 9-3, node 1 represents the beginning of the activity "design printer." We use the beginning and end nodes to "name" activities. In Figure 9-3, design printer is activity 1-2, or in general, activity i-j.

Activities may be related. One relationship between two activities is **precedence;** one activity cannot begin before another is completed. For example, a new product cannot be manufactured until its design is completed. All precedence relations between activities should be spelled out. Only include precedence that *must* be followed. If you feel one activity should be done before another but there is no technological reason to do so, do not include precedence between the two. Figure 9-4 shows two activities, with activity 1-2 preceding activity 2-3. Events actually represent several points in time. In Figure 9-4, event 2 represents the completion of activity 1-2 and the beginning of activity 2-3. Activity 2-3 does not have to start at the same time 1-2 finishes, but rather anytime after 1-2 finishes. The precedence implies 2-3 cannot start before 1-2 completes. Activity 1-2 is called the **predecessor** and 2-3 the **successor.**

We let event 1 denote the start of the project; it is shared by all activities that do not have predecessors. As an example, consider the three activities that have no predecessor events shown in Figure 9-5. Because these activities do not have predecessors, they could all start immediately and be in process simultaneously. However, we are not obligated to make it so; the scheduling phase, which we discuss later, determines when activities actually start.

Similarly, all activities with no successors share an ending event, say n, which represents the project completion. This situation is represented by Figure 9-6. As with start times, sharing a completion event does not imply all of these activities complete at the same time.

Now consider two or more activities with no precedence relationship among them, but which must be preceded by a common activity. We can again combine the ending event of the predecessor with the starting event of all successors. Such a situation is depicted in Figure 9-7. Any node having more than one arc leaving it is called a **burst event.** This includes event 6 in Figure 9-7 and the project start event, 1, of Figure 9-5. As we previously noted, none of the successor activities may start before the predecessor completes, but it is not necessary for any of them to start exactly at that time, nor for any of the successors to begin simultaneously.

If there are several activities with no precedence between them, but all precede another activity, we can represent them as in Figure 9-8. An event with more than one arc entering it is called a **merge event.** Event 8 of Figure 9-8 is typical, but the completion event is also a merge event. Again, note that 8-9 cannot start before 5-8, 6-8, and 7-8 are all finished, but it does not have to start immediately when they are done, nor do the three predecessor activities need to complete at the same time.

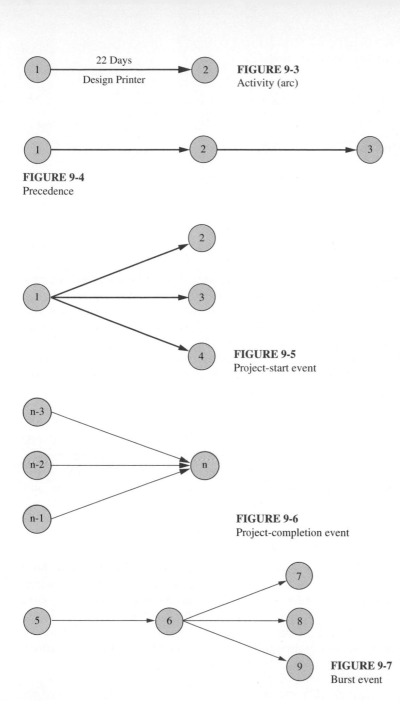

FIGURE 9-3
Activity (arc)

22 Days
Design Printer

FIGURE 9-4
Precedence

FIGURE 9-5
Project-start event

FIGURE 9-6
Project-completion event

FIGURE 9-7
Burst event

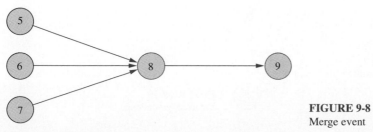

FIGURE 9-8
Merge event

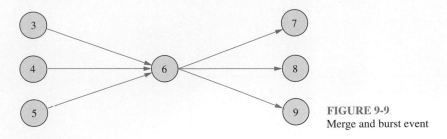

FIGURE 9-9
Merge and burst event

It is possible for an event to be both a burst event and a merge event. An example is event 6 of Figure 9-9.

A project is represented by a collection of nodes and arcs. This graphical representation is called a **network.** The convention we use is called an activity-on-arrow network. Other representations are possible. Each event should have a unique number to avoid confusion. Numbers are usually assigned after the network has been developed. We number events so each activity has a smaller number for its starting event than its ending event. If this cannot be done, there must be a cycle in the network, which is impossible for a real project. Furthermore, we require each activity to have a unique pair of starting and ending events; i.e., two arcs cannot start and end at the same nodes. This allows us to specify an activity uniquely by its corresponding events.

Now consider a project with four activities called A, B, C, and D. Suppose A precedes both C and D, and B precedes D. Drawing this network is much more difficult. The network in Figure 9-10 implies B precedes C, which is wrong. To have a correct representation, we must add a dummy arc. A dummy arc does not represent an actual activity but maintains the logic of the network. Dummies are usually represented by dashed arcs, have no duration, and require no resources. Figure 9-11 gives a correct network representation of this situation.

2.4 Estimating Activity Durations

Once a rough network for the entire project has been developed, we need to determine how long it takes to do each activity. In doing so, we should get as accurate an estimate as possible within the scope of our study. First we must choose a time unit; it could be minutes, hours, days, weeks, or even fortnights. The basic unit should reflect the level of detail of the job at hand. It would be inappropriate to use minutes for building a house—days or even weeks might be more appropriate. If our basic time unit is days, we need not estimate durations

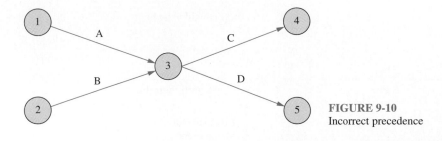

FIGURE 9-10
Incorrect precedence

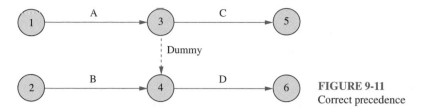

FIGURE 9-11
Correct precedence

more finely than in whole days. If more precision is needed, usually only for short-duration projects, our basic time unit should be changed to half-days or hours.

Typically, a meeting of all concerned parties is called to estimate the **duration** of each activity. An activity should be selected at random and briefly discussed. The time estimate should be made independently of all other activities, and it should be assumed that "normal" effort will be used to perform the activity in question. Furthermore, unusual occurrences such as strikes or accidents should not be considered. Obviously, the person responsible for the activity should have the best idea of how long it should take. Unfortunately, this person may be biased and might give an estimate that is longer than the task is expected to take so he or she will look good upon early completion. Since there is no way we know to completely remove bias, we must live with the possibility of it. Other members of the team can also estimate the duration, and if the results are considerably different, a group discussion can be used to resolve the estimate. However, in the final analysis, the "expert" should carry the most weight in the decision. Also, it is reasonable that estimates should be more accurate for smaller tasks. For example, Lynn's estimate of the time to get the printer to market would likely be less accurate than her estimate of the time to prepare its production drawings.

We must be careful when dealing with time. Suppose we are dealing with a five-day workweek, and our time unit is days. There may be activities that need "natural" time to complete, and this time could be weekends. One example is the curing process for concrete. If we pour concrete on Friday, it dries on Saturday and Sunday even if we are not working. With a little forethought, work-time-versus-calendar-time problems can be handled.

After estimating the duration of each activity, the resource requirements, including costs, for each activity should be handled in the same way.

This is also the time to refine the network. For example, if some activity can be done in less than one time unit, perhaps it should be combined with one or more other activities. If two activities occur in series, with no other precedence before the second in the series, it may be possible to combine these activities into one activity. Of course, this should not be done if one or both of the activities need to "stand out" for any reason.

Example 9-1. Planning for the LJ9000. After carefully considering her task, Lynn divides the LJ9000 project into two subprojects. The first deals with all activities necessary for production of an approved prototype. The second subproject deals with initial production and marketing of the printer. We discuss her approach for the first subproject.

After consulting with other members of the project team, Lynn defines a project master plan, using only major activities. The major activities, along with their duration and precedence relationships, are given in Table 9-3. Using this information, Lynn developed the project network given in Figure 9-12.

TABLE 9-3
LJ9000 printer project data

Activity	Description	Time (weeks)	Precedes
A	Printer specifications	2	B, C
B	Budget and quality needs	3	D, E
C	Printer design	5	F, G
D	License forms preparation	4	H
E	Budget approval	1	I
F	Prototype construction	6	I
G	Package design	2	J
H	License approval	8	—
I	Prototype testing	7	—
J	Package construction	4	—

SECTION 2   PROBLEMS

9.7. Define preparing a meal as a project. Develop a network, define precedence, and estimate durations for each activity.

9.8. Define changing a tire as a project. Develop a network, define precedence, and estimate durations for each activity.

9.9. Draw the following project networks. Activities are denoted by letters and A $\longrightarrow$ B means that activity B cannot start before activity A is complete.

(a) A $\longrightarrow$ C   B $\longrightarrow$ C   A $\longrightarrow$ D

(b) A $\longrightarrow$ B   A $\longrightarrow$ C   A $\longrightarrow$ D   B $\longrightarrow$ E   C $\longrightarrow$ E   D $\longrightarrow$ E

(c) A $\longrightarrow$ B   A $\longrightarrow$ C   B $\longrightarrow$ D   B $\longrightarrow$ E   C $\longrightarrow$ E   D $\longrightarrow$ F   E $\longrightarrow$ F

(d) A $\longrightarrow$ C   A $\longrightarrow$ E   B $\longrightarrow$ D   C $\longrightarrow$ G   D $\longrightarrow$ F   E $\longrightarrow$ F   E $\longrightarrow$ G

3   SCHEDULING

Once we have determined our network, we would like to calculate times when things might take place, the most important being the project's completion. For each activity, we calculate the earliest time it can start and finish, as well as the latest time it can start and finish. For each event, we also calculate an earliest and latest time for its occurrence. This is done in two stages, a forward pass and a backward pass through the network. The forward pass is a sequence of calculations that begins with the project start event and determines the earliest time the project can be completed. In doing so, it assigns the earliest possible start and completion time to each activity. The backward pass is the reverse of the forward pass. It assigns a desired completion time to the ending event and calculates the latest start and completion time for each activity so the project will be completed by the desired time.

Let

$$i\text{-}j = \text{an activity of the project}$$
$$d_{i\text{-}j} = \text{the duration of activity } i\text{-}j$$
$$E_i = \text{the \textbf{earliest time} event } i \text{ can occur}$$
$$ES_{i\text{-}j} = \text{the \textbf{earliest start time} of activity } i\text{-}j$$
$$EF_{i\text{-}j} = \text{its \textbf{earliest finish time}}$$

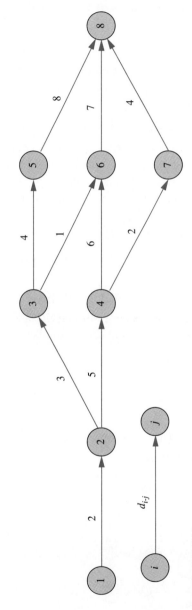

FIGURE 9-12
LJ9000 printer project network

$$LS_{i-j} = \text{the \textbf{latest start time} of activity } i\text{-}j$$
$$LF_{i-j} = \text{the \textbf{latest finish time} of activity } i\text{-}j$$
$$L_i = \text{the \textbf{latest event time}}$$

We assume event 1 is the starting event and event n is the ending event.

3.1   Forward Pass

The purpose of the **forward pass** is to compute the earliest start and finish time for each activity in the project. If we know the earliest start time for an activity, its earliest finish time is the earliest start time plus its duration, i.e.,

$$EF_{i-j} = ES_{i-j} + d_{i-j}$$

(see Figure 9-13). To get earliest start times for activities and earliest event times requires a little thought. We assume an activity starts as soon as all its immediate predecessors are completed. If an activity, say k-j, has only one predecessor, say i-k, its starting event, k, is not a merge event. Its earliest event occurrence is the same as the earliest finish of the predecessor activity, i.e.,

$$E_k = EF_{i-k}$$

This is also the earliest start time of all activities for which this event represents the start event,

$$ES_{k-l} = E_k \qquad \text{for all activities } k\text{-}l$$

Merge events have more than one predecessor activity and cannot take place until all predecessors have completed. The earliest event time is the largest finish time of any activity with this event as the ending event:

$$E_k = \max_{\text{all } i\text{-}k} EF_{i-k}$$

Again, the earliest start of all activities with this event as the starting event is the earliest event time,

$$ES_{k-l} = E_k \qquad \text{for all activities } k\text{-}l$$

This is shown in Figure 9-14. Burst events play no specific role in the forward pass.

Figure 9-15 presents a formal procedure for the forward pass. Assume all nodes are ordered so if i-j is an activity in the network, $i < j$. An example of the forward pass follows.

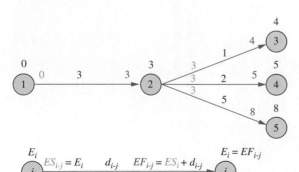

FIGURE 9-13
Forward pass (no merge event)

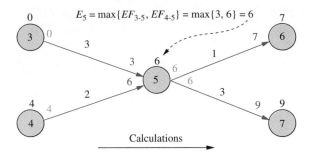

$$E_5 = \max\{EF_{3\text{-}5}, EF_{4\text{-}5}\} = \max\{3, 6\} = 6$$

FIGURE 9-14
Forward pass for a merge event

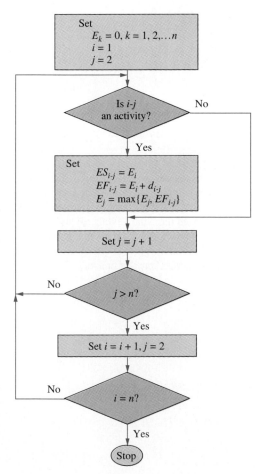

FIGURE 9-15
Forward pass algorithm

Example 9-2. Forward pass for the LJ9000 project. We perform forward pass calculations on the LJ9000 printer project. First, the algorithm sets $E_i = 0$, $i = 1, 2, \ldots, 8$, and $ES_{i\text{-}j} = EF_{i\text{-}j} = 0$ for all arcs in the project. The first arc examined is 1-2:

$$ES_{1\text{-}2} = E_1 = 0$$

$$EF_{1\text{-}2} = ES_{1\text{-}2} + d_{1\text{-}2} = 0 + 2 = 2$$

$$E_2 = \max\{E_2, EF_{1\text{-}2}\} = \max\{0, 2\} = 2$$

These calculations are given in the first row of Table 9-4. Each activity is listed first, followed by the current value of its starting event. This becomes the earliest start time for the activity, which is given in the next column. The duration is given next and added to the start time to get the earliest finish time for the activity. Finally, the earliest event time for the activity's ending event is replaced by the activity's earliest finish time if it is greater than its current earliest finish time. To show calculations for a burst event, skip to activity 3-6:

$$ES_{3\text{-}6} = E_3 = 5 \qquad \text{from the calculations of 2-3}$$

$$EF_{3\text{-}6} = ES_{3\text{-}6} + d_{3\text{-}6} = 5 + 1 = 6$$

$$E_6 = \max\{E_6, EF_{3\text{-}6}\} = \max\{0, 6\} = 6$$

and for 4-6 we have

$$ES_{4\text{-}6} = E_4 = 7 \qquad \text{from the calculations of 2-4}$$

$$EF_{4\text{-}6} = ES_{4\text{-}6} + d_{4\text{-}6} = 7 + 6 = 13$$

$$E_6 = \max\{E_6, EF_{4\text{-}6}\} = \max\{6, 13\} = 13$$

Only these calculations are shown. The remainder are given in Table 9-4. The forward pass calculations are also given on the network of Figure 9-16. Notice that the forward pass assigns an earliest start time of zero to the "start" event and works toward the "end" event, always starting activities as early as possible. When we are through with the forward pass, E_n is the earliest time at which the project can be completed. Unless we can change the duration of one or more critical activities (see Section 3.3) or the precedence structure, the LJ9000 project can be completed no earlier than $E_8 = 20$ weeks.

TABLE 9-4
LJ9000 forward pass calculations

$i\text{-}j$	E_i	$ES_{i\text{-}j}$	$d_{i\text{-}j}$	$EF_{i\text{-}j}$	E_j
1-2	0	0	2	2	$\max\{0, 2\} = 2$
2-3	2	2	3	5	$\max\{0, 5\} = 5$
2-4	2	2	5	7	$\max\{0, 7\} = 7$
3-5	5	5	4	9	$\max\{0, 9\} = 9$
3-6	5	5	1	6	$\max\{0, 6\} = 6$
4-6	7	7	6	13	$\max\{6, 13\} = 13$
4-7	7	7	2	9	$\max\{0, 9\} = 9$
5-8	9	9	8	17	$\max\{0, 17\} = 17$
6-8	13	13	7	20	$\max\{17, 20\} = 20$
7-8	9	9	4	13	$\max\{20, 13\} = 20$

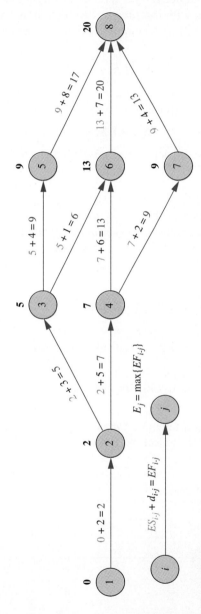

FIGURE 9-16
Forward pass: LJ9000 project

3.2 Backward Pass

The purpose of the **backward pass** is to calculate the latest allowable start and finish times for each activity so the project is completed by a specified time. It is the reverse of the forward pass. The backward pass begins with the project completion and works toward the project start. If we know the latest finish time for an activity, its latest start time is the latest finish time minus its duration, i.e.,

$$LS_{i-j} = LF_{i-j} - d_{i-j}$$

If an activity has only one successor (i.e., it is not a burst event), the latest event occurrence equals the latest start of the successor activity,

$$L_k = LS_{k-j}$$

This is also the latest finish time of all activities for which this event represents the completion event, i.e.,

$$LF_{i-k} = L_k \qquad \text{for all } i\text{-}k$$

Figure 9-17 is an example of this situation.

Burst events have more than one successor activity, and therefore the latest event occurrence cannot take place until all successors have started. In this case, the latest event time is the smallest latest start time of any activity with this event as the starting event:

$$L_k = \min_{\text{all } k\text{-}j} LS_{k-j}$$

Again, the latest finish of all activities with this event as the ending event is the latest event time.

$$LF_{i-k} = L_k \qquad \text{for all activities } i\text{-}k$$

This is shown in Figure 9-18. Merge events play no specific role in the backward pass. Formally, the backward pass algorithm, with the same assumptions as before, is depicted in Figure 9-19.

> **Example 9-3. Backward pass for the LJ9000 project.** Now Lynn is ready to do the backward pass for the LJ9000 printer project. We do the backward pass with the latest event time for

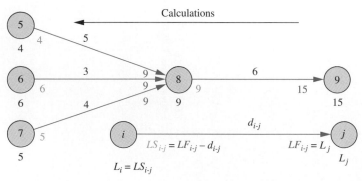

FIGURE 9-17
Backward pass: no burst event

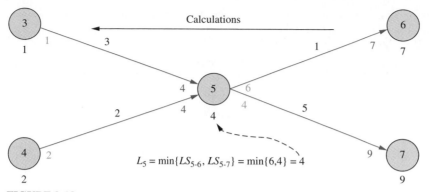

$$L_5 = \min\{LS_{5\text{-}6}, LS_{5\text{-}7}\} = \min\{6,4\} = 4$$

FIGURE 9-18
Backward pass: burst event

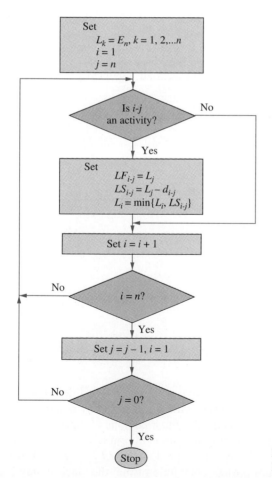

FIGURE 9-19
Backward pass algorithm

the project completion equal to the earliest completion time: set $L_k = E_8 = 20$ for all k. The first activity examined by the algorithm is 5-8:

$$LF_{5\text{-}8} = L_8 = 20$$
$$LS_{5\text{-}8} = LF_{5\text{-}8} - d_{5\text{-}8} = 20 - 8 = 12$$
$$L_5 = \min\{L_5, LS_{5\text{-}8}\} = \min\{20, 12\} = 12$$

Again we show selected calculations; Table 9-5 contains the full calculations. Moving to activity 4-7 we have

$$LF_{4\text{-}7} = L_7 = 16$$
$$LS_{4\text{-}7} = LF_{4\text{-}7} - d_{4\text{-}7} = 16 - 2 = 14$$
$$L_4 = \min\{L_4, LS_{4\text{-}7}\} = \min\{20, 14\} = 14$$

and for 4-6:

$$LF_{4\text{-}6} = L_6 = 13$$
$$LS_{4\text{-}6} = LF_{4\text{-}6} - d_{4\text{-}6} = 13 - 6 = 7$$
$$L_4 = \min\{L_4, LS_{4\text{-}6}\} = \min\{12, 7\} = 7.$$

The late start for activity 1-2 is zero, and for the starting event (event 1) the latest event time is zero. This occurs because we used the earliest completion time (20) for the project's latest completion time. If we had used another value, this would not have happened.

These calculations can be easily carried out on the network itself. Figure 9-20 shows the network and associated values for the LJ9000 project.

TABLE 9-5
LJ9000 backward pass calculations

i-j	L_j	$LF_{i\text{-}j}$	$d_{i\text{-}j}$	$LS_{i\text{-}j}$	L_i
5-8	20	20	8	12	$\min\{20, 12\} = 12$
6-8	20	20	7	13	$\min\{20, 13\} = 13$
7-8	20	20	4	16	$\min\{20, 16\} = 16$
4-7	16	16	2	14	$\min\{20, 14\} = 14$
3-6	13	13	1	12	$\min\{20, 12\} = 12$
4-6	13	13	6	7	$\min\{12, 7\} = 7$
3-5	12	12	4	8	$\min\{20, 8\} = 8$
2-4	7	7	5	2	$\min\{20, 2\} = 2$
2-3	8	8	3	5	$\min\{2, 5\} = 2$
1-2	2	2	2	0	$\min\{20, 0\} = 0$

3.3 Critical Path and Critical Activities

Once the forward and backward passes have been completed, we know a good deal about potential project timing. We know how soon we can complete the project, and by combining information from each pass we can determine which activities must be done at their earliest times and which ones could be delayed without affecting the project completion. First, we define the **slack** of activity i-j to be $S_{i\text{-}j} = LS_{i\text{-}j} - ES_{i\text{-}j}$ (or equivalently, $LF_{i\text{-}j} - EF_{i\text{-}j}$). If we started the backward pass with the minimum project completion time, the slack is how much we can delay activity i-j without delaying the entire project. If an activity with zero

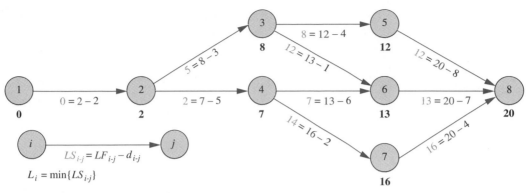

FIGURE 9-20
LJ9000 backward pass

slack is not started and completed at the earliest time, the project is delayed. This is called a **critical activity.**

Consider a path from 1 (the project start) to n (the project finish) formed by the activities $1\text{-}i, i\text{-}j, \ldots, l\text{-}k$, and $k\text{-}n$. There are many such paths in a typical network. If we set $L_n = E_n$, there is at least one path from 1 to n that has zero slack for every activity on the path. We call this path the **critical path,** because all activities on the path are critical activities. This gives rise to the traditional name for the procedure the **critical path method** or CPM (Kelley and Walker, 1959). Delaying any activity on the critical path will delay the project. Each activity on the critical path can be regarded as a bottleneck activity.

There may be several paths with all activities having zero slack and, hence, several critical paths. Also, different paths may have some activities in common and then diverge, have different activities and then converge to share activities in the paths, or have a combination of these.

Zero slack is easily interpreted, but be careful with positive slack. You might think an activity with $S_{i\text{-}j} = 2$ could be delayed by two time units without affecting the completion of the entire project, and in a limited sense you would be correct. You can delay activity $i\text{-}j$ by two time units and not delay the project *if* no other activities are delayed. That is, the slack of an activity is valid only if no other activities are delayed. If more than one activity is delayed, the project completion may be affected even if no single activity is delayed more than its slack. We return to the LJ9000 project to examine this issue.

> **Example 9-4. Critical path for the LJ9000 project.** Figure 9-21 gives the network for the LJ9000 project. Slack for each activity is calculated from late and early start times. The critical path, denoted by crosshatched arcs, is 1-2, 2-4, 4-6, and 6-8. Note the slack is 3 on each of the arcs 2-3, 3-5, and 5-8. Suppose we delay each of these activities by two time units; the project will then be delayed by three time units. From this example we see that the slack in the path matters more than the slack of an individual activity. To better understand this, note that delaying 2-3 by one time unit is equivalent to adding 1 to $d_{1\text{-}2}$. Recalculating with the new duration gives slack of 2 on 3-5 and 5-6. Other types of slack can be defined, but for brevity we omit them.

Obviously, activities on a critical path should be carefully managed, because they can delay the entire project. You might think noncritical activities can be ignored, but this is not true. If an activity has little slack, slippage in the time to do it or other activities in a common path can change the critical path. In this vein, we loosely define near-critical activities

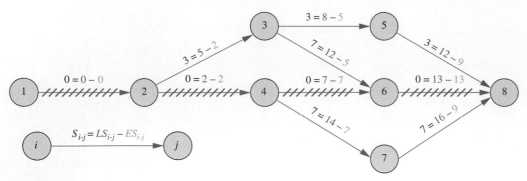

FIGURE 9-21
LJ9000 critical path

as those that have little slack, where little depends on the particular situation. While all activities should be managed carefully, critical and near-critical activities deserve special attention.

In the backward pass calculation, we set $L_n = E_n$. This was, in a sense, an arbitrary decision. We could set $L_n = 0$, but then all latest start and finish times would be negative. Some of them are negative if $L_n < E_n$; this occurs if the due date is sooner than the earliest project completion date. Also, slack can be negative. Setting the late project completion to the early project completion results in the slack of critical activities being zero. If the project has a due date larger than the earliest completion time, we could set the late completion time to this value and do the backward pass. This gives the late start and finish times to finish the project at the desired time. No activity has zero slack, so there is no critical path as previously defined. However, one or more paths have all activities with minimum slack. The minimum slack is equal to the difference of late and early project completion times. We call such a path the minimum slack path; it corresponds to the critical path when we set $L_n = E_n$.

To find near-critical activities, set $L_n = E_n - 1$ and redo the critical path calculations. All critical activities now have slack of -1, and activities with slack of zero are called near-critical. Any path formed by these near-critical paths is called the first near-critical path. There may be no activities with zero slack, so we set $L_n = E_n - 2$, and so on, until we find the first near-critical path. By continuing to reduce L_n, we can determine the second and later near-critical paths.

After the critical path is determined, we may wish to obtain more accurate estimates of the duration of critical and near-critical activities. Activities with large slack are unlikely to affect project duration, so their initial estimates are unlikely to need refinement. If we are confident in our initial estimates of critical activities, let them stay as-is, otherwise more effort on their estimates is warranted.

3.4   Scheduling Activities

Once the backward and forward passes have been completed, we begin scheduling the activities. Scheduling implies assigning a start time to each activity; this assignment is called a **schedule.** For logical reasons, an activity cannot start before its earliest start time, and if we wish the project to finish by L_n, it cannot start after its latest start time. Thus, the assigned start time should be between the earliest and latest start time for that activity. There are two schedules that are often discussed in project management. The first is the **early start schedule,** which has all activities starting as soon as possible. The second is the **late start schedule,** which assigns the latest possible start to all activities.

Many other schedules are possible. Under resource and budget restrictions, neither the early nor late start schedule may be desirable or even possible. However, we now consider only early and late start schedules.

> **Example 9-5. Early and late start LJ9000 schedules.** To construct the early (or late) start schedule for the LJ9000 project, simply start each activity as soon (or as late) as possible. To illustrate, we display each schedule via a **time-scaled network,** which is similar to a Gantt Chart. The horizontal axis is time, running from 0 to E_n. Activities are drawn horizontally with their length equal to their duration. Usually, the critical path is centered vertically with critical activities adjacent. Other paths are represented on different vertical levels with horizontal lines showing precedence. Slack is shown as dashed lines. Figure 9-22 has the early start (ES) schedule at the top and the late start (LS) schedule at the bottom.
>
> In the ES schedule, the critical path is 1-2-4-6-8, as represented by the solid lines. Activity 2-3 starts at time 2, and since it is preceded by 1-2, a dashed vertical line goes from node 2 to the start of 2-3. Activity 3-6 starts at time 5 and ends at time 6. Its slack of 7 units is represented by the horizontal dashed line. The LS schedule is interpreted similarly.

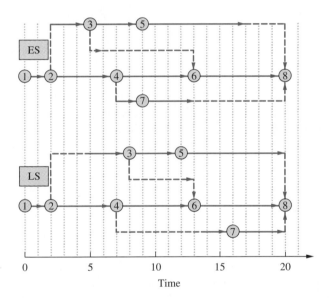

FIGURE 9-22
Early and late start schedules for the LJ9000

3.5 Accelerating the Project

Time to complete the project is critical, particularly in product development projects. If the time-to-market of a product is too great, a competitor may capture the market, or demand for the product can evaporate. Ulrich and Eppinger (1995) give tips for accelerating a project; they are divided into approaches for the project and approaches for critical activities.

For the entire project:

- Start the project early. Often, the urgency to complete a project is not present at the beginning of the project. However, time saved in starting the project translates into quicker completion.

- Manage the project scope. Once the project mission is established, keep to it. Do not let add-ons or enhancements to the project cause delay. A late project, even though elegant, is still late.
- Facilitate information sharing. Ensure that all team members are aware of the status of activities.

Activities on the critical path can be expedited to decrease project completion time. As critical activities are compressed, other paths may become critical. Some guidelines are:

- Complete critical activities more quickly. Focusing on an activity may be enough to ensure completing it early. Making sure resources are available for critical activities, or even adding resources, can reduce an activity's duration. We examine this more fully in Sections 6 and 7.
- Eliminate some critical activities entirely. By redesigning a product or process, a critical activity may be eliminated, thus reducing completion time.
- Eliminate waiting delays for critical activities. Ensure that all resources are available for critical activities. Try to simplify or complete in advance paperwork for these activities.
- Overlap critical activities. It may be possible to start a following critical activity before the first one is completed. An example might be pouring a concrete floor for a large shopping mall. Waiting until the entire floor is poured may not be necessary; after a portion is poured, placing wall studs could begin while the remainder of the floor is poured.
- Pipeline large tasks. Similar to overlapping, pipelining breaks a large task into smaller, sequential tasks. Finding and qualifying many vendors can be done one part or component at a time when a partial bill of materials is completed.
- Outsource or subcontract activities. Although this may be expensive, completing a project early may be worth it.

These guidelines are consistent with the ideas of concurrent engineering (Chapter 2) and set-up reduction (Chapter 10) and are discussed more fully there.

SECTION 3   PROBLEMS

9.10. What is the purpose of the forward pass calculations?

9.11. What role does a burst event play in the forward pass calculations? A merge event?

9.12. Given the accompanying network, use the forward pass calculations to determine the project length if the project starts at time zero. All times are in days.

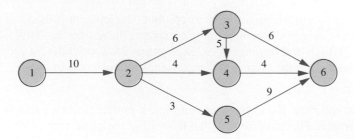

9.13. Given the accompanying network, use the forward pass calculations to determine the project length if the project starts at time zero. All times are in weeks.

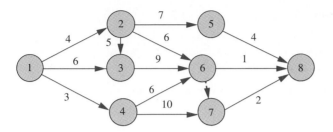

9.14. What is the purpose of backward pass calculations?

9.15. What role does a burst event play in the backward pass calculations? A merge event?

9.16. Perform backward pass calculations on Problem 9.12.

(a) Assume the project needs to be completed as soon as possible.

(b) Assume the project needs to be completed in 30 days.

9.17. Perform backward pass calculations on Problem 9.13.

(a) Assume the project needs to be completed as soon as possible.

(b) Assume the project needs to be completed in 20 weeks.

9.18. Define critical path. What are critical activities?

9.19. Why is it important to identify critical activities and a critical path?

9.20. What is slack? Is slack always zero for some activity? Explain.

9.21. Determine a critical path for Problem 9.12.

9.22. Determine a critical path for Problem 9.13.

9.23. Construct a Gantt Chart for the late start schedule for Problem 9.13.

9.24. Construct both early and late start schedules for Problem 9.12. Draw them on a time-scaled Gantt Chart.

9.25. A maintenance project consists of 10 activities labeled A, B, ..., J. The durations (in days) and precedence for the activities are given below.

Activity	Duration	Precedes
A	7	B, C
B	2	D, F
C	4	E, G
D	3	H
E	5	I
F	6	I
G	1	J
H	5	—
I	9	—
J	8	—

(a) Develop the project network.

(b) Do forward and backward calculations.

(c) What is the slack for activities D, F, and J?

(d) Find all equal slack paths.

(e) Find a critical path and critical activities.

(f) Find the second critical path.

(g) Suppose B takes six days instead of three. What change in project completion occurs?

9.26. Consider the project network depicted in the accompanying figure.

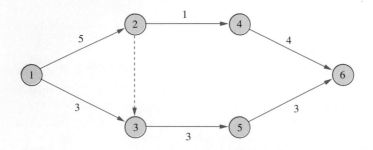

(a) Develop and solve a linear programming model to find the critical path and slack for each activity.

(b) Formulate the dual and interpret it with respect to critical path analysis.

4   PROJECT CONTROL

Once a project is planned and scheduled, the real work has only just begun; now we must control the project. The three characteristics we control are the basics of a successful production system—time, cost, and quality. That is, we must ensure that the project is finished on time, within its budget, and of required quality. To do this we first set standards for time, cost, and quality. These are done through the scheduling, budgeting, and technical specifications of the project. Then we must have measurement and reporting systems to monitor what actually happens with the project. We can then compare actual results versus planned specifications and evaluate the difference. Major deviations are reported to the people responsible for rectifying the discrepancies. Trends can be evaluated and potential trouble spots identified. These can be discussed and corrective action planned and implemented.

4.1   Schedule Control

Schedule control begins with updating the network. The primary function of updating the schedule is to determine the actual duration of each completed or partially completed activity. If an activity takes less time than anticipated, succeeding activities may begin earlier than planned. Conversely, if an activity takes more time than expected, it may delay the start of other activities. Periodically, we replace the calculated completion times of all completed activities with their actual completion times in the network. Partially completed tasks can have their durations revised to reflect the progress to date. We can also add unexpected activities

TABLE 9-6
LJ9000 update data

i-j	$d_{i\text{-}j}$	$LS_{i\text{-}j}$	$AS_{i\text{-}j}$	$AF_{i\text{-}j}$	$Ad_{i\text{-}j}$
1-2	2	0	0	2	2
2-3	3	5	6	3	
2-4	5	2	2	9	7
3-5	4	8	10	—	—
3-6	1	12	—	—	—
4-6	6	7	9	—	—

or precedence relations or delete unnecessary ones. Past performance on some activities may also allow us to develop better estimates of activities of a similar nature that are yet to be done in the project. The frequency of updating depends on the purpose of the project.

After the network is updated, the forward pass is redone to determine changes, if any, to the critical path. Negative slack may occur here, which implies the project is late. Thus, we must expedite activities on the critical path to get back on schedule. One way to do this is by eliminating activities, possibly by subcontracting them out. Another way is to reduce the duration of the activity, either by overtime or additional resources.

Schedule updates are often depicted graphically. Example 9-6 gives an update for the LJ9000 project.

> **Example 9-6. Update for the LJ9000 project.** Lynn reviewed the LJ9000 project after 10 weeks. Table 9-6 gives the status of the project at this point. $AS_{i\text{-}j}$ is the actual start time of activity i-j if it has started. $AF_{i\text{-}j}$ and $Ad_{i\text{-}j}$ are the actual finish time and duration of any activity that has completed. Activities that have not started are not given in the table, since we have no update information about them.
>
> Blue table entries denote deviations from the original plan. Activities 2-3, 3-5, and 4-6 started later than planned, and activity 2-4 had a longer duration than planned. Using these revised data, another forward pass is performed. We do not need to include completed activities. Unless we change the latest project completion time, the backward pass gives the same latest finishes and starts, so it is not needed. The updated network is shown in Figure 9-23.
>
> Several activities in Figure 9-23 have negative slack, for example, 4-6 and 3-5, which is caused by the variation from the original plan. The smallest slack is -2, so unless remedial action is taken, the project will complete two weeks after the planned completion time. Note that there are now two critical paths, 3-5-8 and 4-6-8.

4.2 Cost Control

We have been primarily concerned with time as a major issue in project management. We should also address the issue of cost. Cost is important in planning, scheduling, and implementation. First, we must determine the cost of each activity, usually at the same time and in the same way we determine activity durations. Next, in the scheduling phase we might wish to have costs occur in certain ways. For example, we might want costs to be uniform throughout the life of the project, or maybe we would like to have all costs occur as late as possible. Finally, we use costs as a control mechanism. We compare what we planned with what actually happened; if costs are higher than planned, we find out why and, if possible, take corrective action, or if they are lower, we find out why and try to continue the good results.

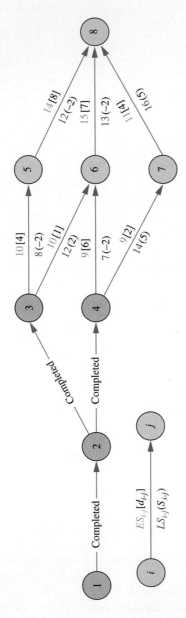

FIGURE 9-23
Updated network for the LJ9000 project

There are several types of costs. Some can easily be tied to a particular activity. These are called direct costs and might include labor, materials, subcontracting, or equipment used only on that activity. Indirect or overhead costs cannot be directly tied to an activity.

Traditional accounting structures are not very good for project costing, since they are oriented toward functional organizations. One way to account for project costs is the C/SCS cost/schedule control system (USAFSC, 1976), which is similar to a matrix management approach. The project is divided into smaller parts called **work packages** or **work breakdown structures,** and costs are allocated to them.

For small projects, a work package can be one activity, but for large projects a work package might consist of many activities. If we define the project on several levels, a work package consists of a group of activities on the lowest level. These activities require a common skill, for example, all activities required to develop a certain component.

A work package should represent work at the level it is performed. It should have a scheduled start and end, be clearly distinguishable from other work packages, have a well-defined budget, and be assignable to a single organizational element. This ensures the right person has responsibility and authority over the work package. As in matrix management, this accounting scheme often cuts across functional lines.

Example 9-7. Work breakdown structure. The Electric Mobile Systems Company (EMS) is developing an electric vehicle for city travel. The company uses project management to plan, schedule, and control the project. Figure 9-24 shows part of their work breakdown structure.

Only one breakdown per level is shown. The work breakdown structure ends at level 3. For each level 3 entry, a work package is developed. This work package is usually a project itself, with its own network, resources, and costs.

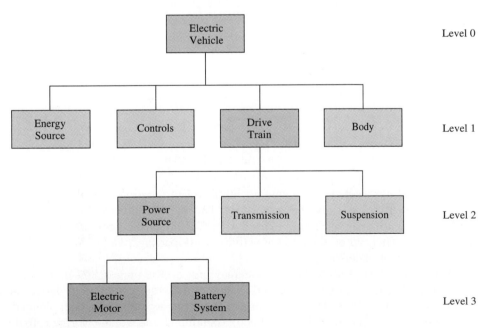

FIGURE 9-24
EMS work breakdown structure

4.2.1   PLANNING AND SCHEDULING COSTS. When planning the project, there is some control over when money is spent. Let c_{i-j} be the cost per unit time associated with activity i-j, and assume the cost occurs at a constant rate throughout the activity duration. Thus if the cost to do activity i-j is \$100, and its duration is 10 days, we expect to spend \$10 each day the activity is in progress. The actual start time of all activities determines the timing of expenditures. These costs can be plotted over time, as we see in the next example.

> **Example 9-8. Cumulative cost curve for ES and LS schedule.** Consider the LJ9000 project. Data for each activity, including costs (in thousands), are given in Table 9-7. Letting all activities start at their early start, we can plot cumulative cost versus time. For each time period, sum the per-time costs of all activities in progress and add to it the sums for all earlier time periods. This gives a curve that spends the money as soon as possible.
>
> Starting all activities as late as possible gives a different curve. These plots are depicted in Figure 9-25. No matter which schedule is used, the total cost is \$341,000. The area between these curves represents all possible timings of expenditures for schedules that complete the project as soon as possible. By allowing activities to start between their early and late start times, a variety of schedules can be constructed with different expenditures over time. However, it should be noted that the total expenditure over the entire project is constant, and we are controlling the timing of these expenditures, which affects present worth of the project. More formal methods of changing the timing can be implemented by treating cost as a fixed resource and using techniques for scheduling under resource constraints.

TABLE 9-7
LJ9000 cost control data

i-j	d_{i-j}	ES_{i-j}	LS_{i-j}	Cost	Cost per week
1-2	2	0	0	10	5
2-3	3	2	5	9	3
2-4	5	2	2	50	10
3-5	4	5	8	4	1
3-6	1	5	12	1	1
4-6	6	7	7	102	17
4-7	2	7	14	20	10
5-8	8	9	12	0	0
6-8	7	13	13	105	15
7-8	4	9	16	40	10

4.2.2   CONTROL. The project manager must control project duration and costs to effectively manage a project. Specifically, the actual cost of work done must be compared with the expected cost of work completed, and expected work done must be compared with actual work completed. This can be done at the activity, work package, and project levels to determine cost overrun or underrun.

Comparing actual costs with budgeted costs may give a false impression. If spending is less than budgeted, but the project is behind schedule, the project may be in danger of a budget overrun. This is because less work has actually been accomplished than planned. Thus, we must take into account actual and planned expenditures and work performed. To do so, we use the Cost/Schedule Control System Criteria (C/SCSC) developed for the U.S. Air Force (USAFSC, 1976).

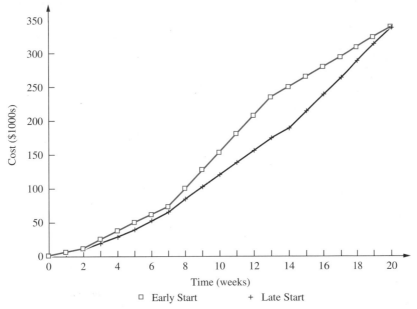

FIGURE 9-25

Cumulative cost usage for early and late start schedule

The **actual cost of work performed** (ACWP) is the money actually spent to accomplish the work that has been done. The **budgeted cost of work performed** (BCWP) is the expected cost of the actual work done at this time. **Budgeted cost of work scheduled** (BCWS) is the expected cost of the work scheduled to be done at this time. BCWS is calculated as in Figure 9-25 for a particular schedule. BCWP is calculated similarly but only for those activities completed or in progress. Compute ACWP the same way, but use the actual instead of projected costs.

Figure 9-26 is a graph of BCWP, ACWP, and BCWS for the first 10 weeks of a project. In the graph, the actual costs (ACWP) exceed the budgeted costs for the work performed (BCWP), so the project is apparently over budget. The difference between BCWP and ACWP is called the cost variance, defined as

$$V^C = \text{BCWP} - \text{ACWP}$$

This is the distance between the BCWP and ACWP lines in Figure 9-26. If $V^C > 0$ (BCWP > ACWP), budgeted cost is greater than actual cost, so we have spent less than anticipated. A negative V^C (BCWP < ACWP) means we are over budget at this time. At week 10, $V^C = \$92,000$ ($\$140,000 - \$48,000$), apparently a significant cost overrun.

However, if more work than planned has been completed, we would expect actual expenditures to be higher. By looking at the budgeted cost of work performed, we see this is not the case. In fact, since the BCWP line is below the BCWS line, we have done less work than planned. Similarly, we can define the schedule variance as

$$V^S = \text{BCWP} - \text{BCWS}$$

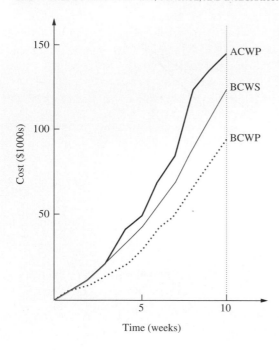

FIGURE 9-26
Updated cost of work performed and scheduled

Time (weeks)

Although V^S is in units of dollars, it measures progress, since it compares budgeted performance versus actual performance. V^S is the distance between BCWP and BCWS in the graph. If $V^S > 0$ (BCWP > BCWS), the "value" of work accomplished is larger than the budget for doing that work. If V^S is negative, we have done less than expected for the money spent. For the project referred to in Figure 9-26, we have $V^S = \$92,000 - \$122,000 = -\$30,000$. This indicates a schedule overrun. Both variances are negative, so the project is both behind schedule and over budget.

These techniques can be used to give a good picture of the project's progress at any point in time. Variations on these measures exist, for example, percentages of the variances. For more detail, see one of the many books on project management. With a little effort, they can be used to extrapolate future events. This can prove invaluable for the project manager.

By now we are familiar with the three major phases of project management—planning, scheduling, and control. Box 9-1 tells the story of using project management at 3M Health Care.

BOX 9-1: USING PROJECT MANAGEMENT AT 3M HEALTH CARE

Medicine, like computing, has come a long way in the past few years. Advances in both technique and equipment mean that people who not long ago may have been confined to home are now able to lead active lives. In many cases this has been made possible by the use of orthopedic prosthesis—artificial joints and sockets which replace originals that have been worn out by time or degenerative disease.

3M Health Care Ltd. has been manufacturing orthopedic implants since 1984. Dr. Phillip Shelley, Technical Manager, began by appraising project management systems

BOX 9-1 (*continued*)

with which he could *"do something a little unconventional."* A bio-medical engineer by training and a software writer by inclination, Shelley was looking for a fast, dynamic system to schedule the entire operation, from the moment the base titanium blocks reached the factory, to the moment they left in the form of joint replacements.

The vision held by Shelley and his colleagues was finite resource scheduling, where every individual in the company would have control over their part of the operation. Crucial information on the machine productivity and production lines would be current and instantly accessible. Production runs could be monitored from start to finish, from any terminal on the site. Open Plan, a project management software package, was selected for this operation and introduced to the plant in 1991.

With 3M's Health Care Ltd.'s focus on design and manufacturing, the greatest impact was felt in production and resource management. Within one year, the company was completing almost 100% of daily scheduled work, where previously it had only achieved around 84%. Schedules were being developed up to two months in advance. Overall output increased by 22% and the company is confident of continuing its record growth.

Source: "3M Health Care Boosts Output 22%," *WST News*, Welcom Software, 1995. Used by permission.

SECTION 4 PROBLEMS

9.27. What is the primary purpose of control?

9.28. What is a work breakdown structure (WBS)? Why is it used? Which organizational structure is it most like?

9.29. Consider a project to build a new production facility for a manufacturer. Give a WBS for this project.

9.30. Consider Problem 9.12. The cost for each activity is given in the accompanying table. Develop cumulative cost usage curves for the early start and late start schedules.

Activity	Cost
1-2	5,000
2-3	12,000
2-4	1,000
2-5	500
3-4	2,000
3-6	1,200
4-6	600
5-6	3,000

9.31. After 15 days, the activities 1-2, 2-3, and 2-5 of Problem 9.12 have been completed. Activities 3-4 and 5-9 can start immediately. As a result of problems, activity 2-4 still needs one more day to complete. Construct an updated network for the project.

9.32. After 15 days, $17,000 has been spent on the project of Problem 9.31. Using the data given in previous problems, develop plots of the updated cost of work performed and scheduled. How do you feel about the project?

9.33. Consider Problem 9.25. The cost for each activity is given in the accompanying table. Develop cumulative cost usage curves for the early start and late start schedules.

Activity	Cost (dollars)
A	10,000
B	15,000
C	100,000
D	20,000
E	5,000
F	6,000
G	30,000
H	16,000
I	28,000
J	20,000

9.34. After 10 days, the activities A, B, C, and E of the maintenance project (Problem 9.25) have been completed. In addition, D has two more days of work to be done, and F has three more days. Because of a delivery failure, G cannot start for at least two more days. Construct an updated network for the project.

9.35. After 10 days, $157,000 has been spent on the maintenance project. Using the data given in previous problems, develop plots of the updated cost of work performed and scheduled. How do you feel about the project?

5   PERT APPROACH TO PROJECT MANAGEMENT

Often, the assumption that we can give a single estimate for the duration of an activity is unreasonable. If so, to account for uncertainty in the duration we assume it is a random variable following some distribution. Scheduling and control proceed in exactly the same manner as CPM. However, instead of giving the project completion date, we specify an expected project completion date or the probability the project is completed by a certain date. This probabilistic approach to project management is called **PERT,** which stands for **Program Evaluation and Review Technique** (Malcolm et al., 1959). Unfortunately, PERT requires certain assumptions, which do not always hold.

There are many reasons why we might not want to specify a single duration for an activity. Because projects typically deal with nonrepetitive activities, we may have never done the activity before and may be very unsure of how long it will take. If it involves research and development, as would be the case in introducing a new product, it is difficult to foresee all possible problems. In construction projects, weather is a prime factor in how long certain activities take, and weather is very uncertain. As a result, even if we could do the same activity a number of times, the time to do it would likely vary each time. Thus, activity durations could be considered random variables.

5.1   Distribution of Activity Duration

As a random variable, the duration follows some probability distribution having certain parameters. The parameters used in PERT calculations are the mean and variance or standard deviation. Typically, both the distribution and the parameters are unknown, but we may be able to estimate them.

If nothing is known about the underlying distribution, the uniform distribution may be appropriate. Rather than estimate the mean and variance, which have little intuitive meaning for many people, we estimate the range $[a, b]$ of the distribution and calculate the mean and variance. The **optimistic estimate** a is how long the activity should take if everything goes as well as possible. If we could do the activity 100 times, it should be done this quickly only once. Conversely, the **pessimistic estimate** b is the amount of time required to do the activity when things go about as badly as one could reasonably expect. Again, it should happen only once in 100 times. Estimating these times is similar to estimating the single duration. That is, they should be made independently by people who understand the activity. Also, extremely rare occurrences such as fire and earthquakes should not be considered even in the pessimistic time estimate. With a uniform distribution, any value between the optimistic and pessimistic values is equally likely. The mean of a uniform distribution on the interval $[a, b]$ is

$$\mu = (a + b)/2$$

and its variance is

$$\sigma^2 = (b - a)^2/12$$

If all values between the optimistic and pessimistic times are not equally likely, the uniform distribution should not be used. A standard distribution, such as the normal, could be used, but in practice distributions of activity durations are usually not symmetrical. The triangular distribution is a skewed distribution. Again, rather than estimate the mean and variance, we can use estimates of the optimistic and pessimistic times along with m, the **most likely time,** to calculate the mean and variance. The most likely time is the duration an activity takes most often if we repeat it many times. The most likely estimate is equivalent to the mode of the distribution. From these three estimates we can determine the mean and variance for a triangular distribution with mode equal to m. The mean is given by

$$\mu = (a + m + b)/3$$

and the variance is

$$\sigma^2 = (a^2 + b^2 + m^2 - ab - am - bm)/18$$

The beta distribution has historically been used in PERT. By judicious choice of parameters, the beta distribution can assume a variety of shapes. Many of the standard distributions, such as the normal and uniform, are special cases of the beta distribution. The parameters of the beta distribution are the mean μ, variance σ^2, and two shape parameters k_1 and k_2. If $k_1 = k_2$, the distribution is symmetric and the mean and mode are equal. If $k_1 = k_2 = 1$, the beta distribution is equivalent to a uniform distribution; as the parameters increase, the beta distribution becomes more rounded with a relatively higher midpoint. For $k_1 = k_2 = 5$, it looks like a normal distribution. If the two shape parameters are unequal, the distribution is skewed, and by reversing the values of the shape parameters, the mirror image is obtained. If $k_1 < k_2$, the distribution is skewed to the left; i.e., the mode is closer to a than b, while $k_1 > k_2$ moves it to the other side. If $k_1 = 2$ and $k_2 = 1$ ($k_1 = 1$ and $k_2 = 2$), the beta distribution is equivalent to a right (left) triangle. A right triangle is simply a straight line from a maximum value at a to zero at b. If both k_1 and k_2 are less than 1, the beta distribution is U-shaped.

Estimating the mean, variance, and shape parameters for each activity is difficult. We can use estimates of a, b, m, and μ to calculate the beta shape parameters. They are

$$k_1 = \frac{(\mu - a)(2m - a - b)}{(m - \mu)(b - a)}$$

and

$$k_2 = \frac{(b - \mu)}{(\mu - a)} k_1$$

The variance is

$$\sigma^2 = \frac{k_1 k_2}{(k_1 + k_2)^2 (k_1 + k_2 + 1)}$$

This requires an estimate of the mean, which may be difficult since historical data are probably not available. The originators of PERT used a three-estimate approach using a, b, and m only and estimating the mean activity duration by

$$\mu = \frac{a + 4m + b}{6}$$

and the variance by

$$\sigma^2 = \frac{(b - a)^2}{36}.$$

This works, but restricts the shape of the resulting beta distribution. In fact the values of the shape parameters are either $k_1 = 3 + \sqrt{2}$, $k_2 = 3 - \sqrt{2}$, $k_1 = 3 - \sqrt{2}$, $k_2 = 3 + \sqrt{2}$ or $k_1 = 4$, $k_2 = 0$. For these cases, the actual mode may not be equal to m, because the three parameters were used to calculate two unknowns. The interested reader can obtain details in Elmaghraby (1977).

Figure 9-27 shows uniform, triangular, and beta distributions with the same range and equal mode for the triangular and beta. A little algebra shows the beta mean is closer to its mode than the triangular distribution's. Also, the variance is smaller for the beta than the triangular, which in turn has smaller variance than the uniform distribution. Since the PERT calculations only deal with mean and variance, use beta when a smaller variance is warranted.

5.2 Probabilistic Analysis of Project Completion Time

Because the activity durations are random variables, the project completion time, which is the sum of the activity times for activities on the critical path, is also a random variable. As such, it has some distribution with a mean and variance. The **central limit theorem** states that, as the number of independently distributed random variables approaches infinity, their sum follows a normal distribution with mean and variance equal to the sum of the individual means and variances. Thus the distribution of the project length is often assumed to be normal with mean and variance equal to the sum of means and variances of the individual activities. This assumption is reasonable if the distributions of activity durations are independent, each duration is negligible compared to the sum, and the number of activities on the critical path is large enough. For a complete discussion of the central limit theorem, see Hines and Montgomery (1990).

Given a normal distribution with its mean and variance for the project duration, we can make probabilistic statements about it. For example, we can find the probability that

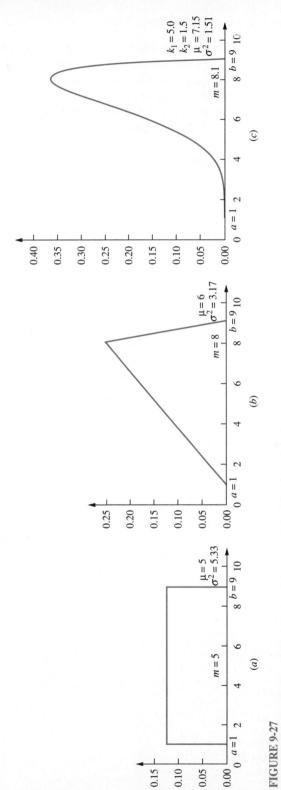

FIGURE 9-27
Some possible distributions for activity durations: (a) uniform, (b) triangular, (c) beta

the project will take longer than a certain number of days, or the probability that it will be completed by some deadline. Similarly, we can determine the date by which we are 90 percent sure the project is completed. Of course, we are not restricted to statements about the project length; we could make similar statements about any event, including milestones. We could also provide confidence intervals on these times. See Section 5.3 for a discussion of limitations to this approach. We now illustrate PERT with an example.

Example 9-9. LJ9000 PERT model. We again look at the LJ9000 printer project. Lynn has evaluated every activity and determined the optimistic, most likely, and pessimistic estimates for each. These data are used to calculate the mean and variance with the three-estimate beta approach. Results are given in Table 9-8.

To get the mean of 1-2, we set

$$\mu = (a + 4m + b)/6 = (1 + 4 \times 2 + 4)/6 = 2.17$$

and $$\sigma^2 = (b - a)^2/36 = (4 - 1)^2/36 = 0.25$$

The remainder of the activities are calculated and given in Table 9-8.

We wish to examine the duration of the project given the distributions on each activity. The CPM calculations are redone using the mean durations. The results are given in Table 9-9. Note that activities are ordered by slack, and critical activities appear first. For each activity, the early and late start and finish times based on the expected time are given along with the variance.

The critical path is 1-2, 2-4, 4-6, and 6-8 and, from the central limit theorem, the expected length is

$$\mu = 2.17 + 5.17 + 6.67 + 7.33 = 21.33 \text{ weeks}$$

The variance for the path is the sum of the variances, or

$$\sigma^2 = 0.25 + 1.36 + 1.77 + 0.44 = 3.82$$

Note that the mean time for the activities are different from the deterministic times, causing the critical path length to change.

From the normality assumption, we can use the mean and standard deviation of the path to compute the expected project completion time and the probability the project will be finished in a given number of weeks. The probability the project will be completed in T weeks is

TABLE 9-8
LJ9000 duration data

i-j	a	m	b	μ	σ^2
1-2	1	2	4	2.17	0.25
2-3	1	3	5	3.00	0.44
2-4	2	5	9	5.17	1.36
3-5	3	4	5	4.00	0.11
3-6	1	1	1	1.00	0.00
4-6	4	6	12	6.67	1.77
4-7	2	2	3	2.17	0.03
5-8	4	8	14	8.33	2.78
6-8	6	7	10	7.33	0.44
7-8	2	4	6	4.00	0.44

TABLE 9-9
LJ9000 CPM calculations using probabilistic data

i-j	$\mu_{i\text{-}j}$	$\sigma_{i\text{-}j}$	$ES_{i\text{-}j}$	$LS_{i\text{-}j}$	$EF_{i\text{-}j}$	$LF_{i\text{-}j}$	$S_{i\text{-}j}$
1-2	2.17	0.50	0.00	0.00	2.17	2.17	0.00
2-4	5.17	1.17	2.17	2.17	7.33	7.33	0.00
4-6	6.67	1.33	7.33	7.33	14.00	14.00	0.00
6-8	7.33	0.67	14.00	14.00	21.33	21.33	0.00
2-3	3.00	0.67	2.17	6.00	5.17	9.00	3.83
3-5	4.00	0.33	5.17	9.00	9.17	13.00	3.83
5-8	8.33	1.67	9.17	13.00	17.50	21.33	3.83
3-6	1.00	0.00	5.17	13.00	6.17	14.00	7.83
4-7	2.17	0.17	7.33	15.17	9.50	17.33	7.83
7-8	4.00	0.67	9.50	17.33	13.50	21.33	7.83

$$P\{E_8 \le T\} = P\left\{ z \le \frac{(T - \mu)}{\sigma} \right\}$$

For example, using Table A-1, the probability the project will be completed in 20 weeks is

$$P\{E_8 \le 20\} = P\left\{ z \le \frac{(20 - 21.33)}{1.95} \right\} = P\{z \le -0.68\} = 0.25$$

An instructive way to view the project completion time is by constructing a graph of the time versus the cumulative probability of completion. Figure 9-28 shows the time of completion of the LJ9000 printer versus the cumulative percentage of completion. These values are obtained

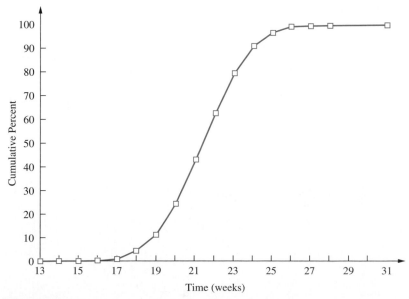

FIGURE 9-28
Probability versus time of LJ9000 project completion

using the same approach as the probability of finishing in 20 weeks. This plot gives a better perspective on the likelihood of finishing the project in a specified amount of time. For example, finishing in 25 weeks seems highly likely, whereas finishing in less than 18 weeks seems very unlikely.

5.3   PERT Limitations

We must be wary of results obtained via PERT. Although the assumptions required to invoke the central limit theorem do not strictly hold in many cases, the theorem is fairly robust and should not cause too much error. If there is a single critical path, the variance of the path is small, and no other path with large variance is close in length, again, the results should be accurate.

However, if there are several paths with lengths close to the mean of the critical path, we should be careful, particularly if one or more of them has a large variance. The project length is actually the length of the longest path, so the true distribution of the project length is actually the maximum of several random variables, one for each path in the network. The maximum of several normal variables does not follow a normal distribution, which may create a problem. The calculations proposed for PERT actually tend to underestimate the project length and overestimate the probability of completing the project by a particular time.

This is usually called the merge-event bias problem. For most projects it is not a serious problem, because extreme accuracy is not required. Using the three-estimate approach to the beta distribution can magnify the problem. For details on how to rectify this problem, see Elmaghraby (1977). An alternative to PERT is simulating the project network for various realizations of the durations and developing an empirical distribution of project completion time.

SECTION 5   PROBLEMS

9.36. Explain the difference between PERT and CPM.

9.37. Why is the beta distribution commonly used in PERT calculations? How does using a triangular distribution differ? A uniform distribution?

9.38. What assumptions are needed to use PERT? What limitations do they cause?

9.39. A project is composed of seven activities labeled A, B, ..., G. Precedence and estimates of optimistic, most likely, and pessimistic durations are presented in the accompanying table.

		Duration (weeks)		
Activity	**Precedes**	**Optimistic**	**Most likely**	**Pessimistic**
A	D	1	1	7
B	E	1	4	7
C	F	2	2	8
D	G	1	1	1
E	G	2	5	14
F	—	2	5	8
G	—	3	6	15

(a) Draw the project network.

(b) Using the beta distribution, find the expected duration and variance of each activity.

(c) Perform forward and backward pass computations for the project.

(d) What is the expected project duration and its variance?

(e) Find the total slack of each activity.

(f) Find the probability the project will be completed
   (i) Three weeks earlier than the expected completion.
   (ii) Three weeks later than the expected completion.

(g) The project was promised to the customer in 18 weeks. What is the probability it will be tardy?

(h) What project completion has a 90 percent chance of being achieved?

(i) What is the probability that activity D completes by time 4?

(j) What effect would assuming a triangular distribution have on expected project completion and variance?

(k) Develop a plot of probability versus project completion time.

9.40. A project is composed of four activities labeled A, B, C, and D. Precedence and estimates of optimistic, most likely, and pessimistic durations are presented in the accompanying table.

Activity	Precedes	Duration (days)		
		Optimistic	Most likely	Pessimistic
A	C	10	10	10
B	D	1	9	11
C	—	10	10	10
D	—	1	9	11

(a) Draw the project network.

(b) Using the beta distribution, find the expected duration and variance of each activity.

(c) Perform forward and backward pass computations for the project.

(d) What is the expected project duration and its variance?

(e) Do you think the PERT assumptions are reasonable for this project? Explain.

(f) What effect would using a triangular distribution have on expected project completion and variance? What about the PERT assumptions?

9.41. A single activity has expected duration μ and range (b-a). This activity is composed of three sequential subactivities in sequence, each with expected duration $\mu/3$. The total range remains (b-a). What is the estimate of variance for completing the activity if it is treated as one activity versus splitting it into three activities? What assumptions did you make? What implications does this have for PERT?

6 LIMITED RESOURCES

Until now, we have ignored any resources that might be required to carry out the activity. This is often unrealistic. For example, in designing a printer, some activities require an electronics engineer, and in building a house, certain activities require one or more carpenters. We classify resources as either renewable or nonrenewable. People are good examples of **renewable resources;** a person who works today is available to work tomorrow. Material is a **nonrenewable resource.** In building a house, if you drive some nails today, the same ones cannot be used later. We focus on renewable resources, since materials can usually be procured in the proper quantities and provided at the right time. Estimating resource usage for each activity is similar to estimating durations. For ease of discussion, we consider a single renewable resource.

If we have an unlimited amount of a resource, its only impact is to add complexity in the planning, monitoring, and control of the project. However, if the resource is limited it has greater impact. CPM assumes two activities can take place simultaneously as long as precedence is followed. With resource limitations this may no longer be true. If two activities require more total resources than are available, the activities cannot occur together, and one of them must be delayed. The delay may be long enough to cause the entire project to be delayed. Thus, a schedule that satisfies limited resource restrictions may have different slack and critical path than the same project that ignores the resources. This can also result in nonunique early and late start schedules.

When resources are limited, we may face two different goals. The most frequently encountered situation has a specified amount of the resource available throughout the project. Here, we would like to finish the project as quickly as possible while never using more of the resource than we have available. This is usually called a **resource-constrained** problem. An example would be in developing a software package, in which each activity requires a specified number of programmers, and there are a fixed number of programmers available, shared by all activities.

The second situation involves an unlimited supply of the resource, but we wish to use the same amount all the time. This is called **resource leveling.** While building a house, day laborers (unskilled workers who are easily hired) are needed. Rather than schedule the work so that one day 100 workers are needed and the next day 20, it would be better if the same number were used each day. This principle also applies to nonrenewable resources; e.g., it may be desirable to procure materials at a steady rate.

Both problems are *NP-hard* (see Box 8-1) and extremely difficult to solve optimally. A guaranteed "best" solution for either apparently requires some form of totally enumerating all the possible solutions, and only small problems can be solved optimally. Although there are clever enumeration schemes (e.g., branch and bound and dynamic programming), getting an optimal answer for problems with 100 activities and five resources might take centuries on the fastest computer available today. Therefore, we compromise and settle for a good solution rather than try to get the best answer. We do this using heuristic procedures, which do not guarantee optimal solutions but are easy to implement and often give close-to-optimal solutions.

6.1   Graphic Approaches

For rough planning, graphic approaches are all that are needed. The most widely used tool for resource consideration is the **resource profile,** sometimes called a **load profile** or **skyline graph.** A simple plot of resource usage versus time for a particular schedule, it is a convenient way to see when resources are overused or underused. A simple example illustrates the resource profile.

TABLE 9-10
Electronic engineers needed for the LJ9000

i-j	1-2	2-3	2-4	3-5	3-6	4-6	4-7	5-8	6-8	7-8
EE	2	1	2	1	0	3	1	0	3	0

Example 9-10. Resource profile for the LJ9000. The LJ9000 project requires electronics engineers for some activities. Four have been assigned to the project, and Lynn would like to see if the project can be completed in 20 weeks with the four engineers or if she needs more. Table 9-10 gives the number of electronics engineers needed for each activity.

Given a schedule, compute the number of electronics engineers needed at any point in time. This is the sum of all engineers used by activities in progress at a given time. For example, in the early start schedule (see Figure 9-29), activity 1-2 is the only ongoing activity from time zero through the end of week 1, so two electronics engineers are needed during this time. Because activities 2-3 and 2-4 both start at week 2, we need to have electronics engineers for both; i.e., $1 + 2 = 3$ are used from the beginning of week 2 until the beginning of week 5, at which time 2-3 completes. Continuing in this manner, we can determine the number of electronics engineers needed for each week of the early start schedule. We can then plot the number versus time; see Figure 9-29(a).

In the figure, each rectangle represents an activity. Its height represents the number of engineers needed for the activity and its length the time required to do it. Activities not using electronic engineers are omitted. When possible, we represent one activity with one box; activity 3-5 must be split into two boxes unless activity 4-6 is split. The dashed line at 4 engineers designates the number available for the project. If the schedule needs more, the graph is higher than the dashed line. This happens for weeks 7 and 8, when five engineers are needed. The early start schedule is resource infeasible.

Creating a resource-feasible schedule for the LJ9000 project is easy; just delay activity 4-7. Activity 4-7 precedes 7-8, both have slack, and 7-8 does not need the resource, so a delay seems possible. In fact, the late start schedule, given in Figure 9-29(b), is resource feasible. Constructing a resource-feasible schedule is not generally an easy task.

A different way to examine resource requirements is the **cumulative resource requirement plot,** which graphs cumulative resource usage versus time. Cumulative resource usage is the sum of the resource usage in the profile from the beginning of the project until the current time. Figure 9-30 is a plot of the cumulative resource requirements of the number of electronics engineers required on the LJ9000 project for both early and late start schedules. The cumulative total of 62 electronics engineers is needed by any schedule. For this example, the schedules are identical for the first two and last four weeks. For any schedule, the actual cumulative resource usage should lie between these two curves. If not, the project is ahead or behind schedule, or resource usage was incorrectly estimated. If actual usage is above the early start curve, either the project is ahead of schedule, or requirements were underestimated. Actual usage below the late start curve implies the opposite.

Another useful planning tool is the **criticality index** (CI), which is the ratio of average per-unit time resource requirement divided by per-unit time resource availability. The average usage is calculated from the cumulative resource data; we divide the cumulative total resource requirement by the project length. For the LJ9000 example, the total requirement is 62 and the project length is 20 weeks, so the average weekly usage is 3.1 electronics engineers.

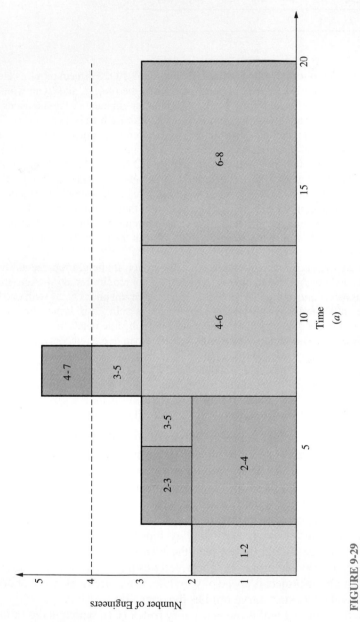

FIGURE 9-29
Resource profile for the LJ9000 project: (a) early start schedule

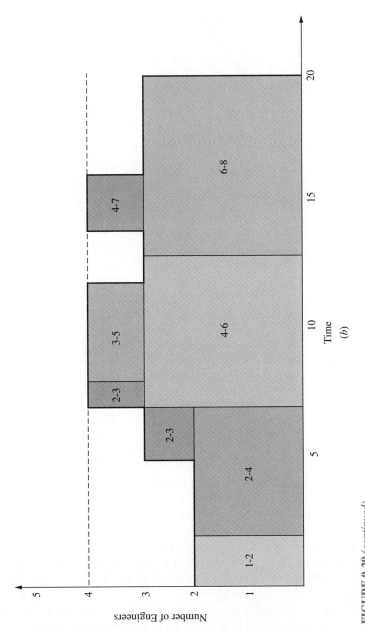

FIGURE 9-29 (*continued*)
Resource profile for the LJ9000 project: (b) late start schedule

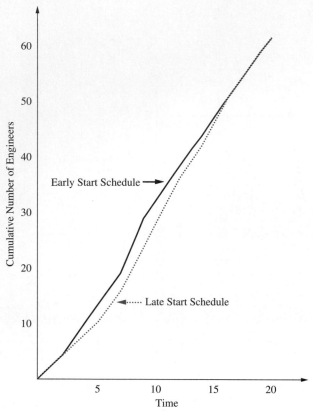

FIGURE 9-30
Cumulative resource profile

If we have 4 engineers available each week, then

$$CI = 3.1/4 = 0.775 \qquad \text{or} \qquad 77.5 \text{ percent}$$

CI is the average utilization of the resource if we use the same amount each time period. If we use exactly 3.1 electronics engineers each week, we can do the project in 20 weeks. Since we have four electronic engineers available, we can use more than the average for some periods and, theoretically, complete the project on time.

    If CI < 1, it may be possible to complete the project on time. The precedence structure may force resource usage in some period to be less than average, so even if CI < 1, on-time completion may be impossible. The smaller CI, the more likely, on average, the project can be completed on time.

    If CI = 1, we must use exactly the resources available each period for the project to finish on time, i.e., perfect utilization. If precedence or activity requirements force us to use more or less in one period, the project will be delayed.

    If CI > 1, the project must take longer. In fact, it must take at least (CI − 1) × 100 per cent longer. This assumes perfect utilization of the available resource; if perfect utilization is impossible, the project will be delayed even more. If we only have three electronic engineers available, $CI = 3.1/3 = 1.03$, and the project must take at least $(1.03 - 1) \times 100 = 3$ percent longer, or 20.6 weeks.

When the criticality index is small, say less than 0.65, resource limitations should not cause much problem. However, larger values indicate care should be taken in scheduling the activities so resources are utilized as well as possible. Heuristics for scheduling with limited resources can be helpful.

6.2 Fixed Resource Limits

When scheduling with limited resources, the objective is typically to minimize the project duration without exceeding resource availability in any time period. First we define notation. Let

$$A = \text{the set of all activities in the network}$$
$$RR_{i\text{-}j} = \text{the resource requirement of activity } i\text{-}j, \text{ which is needed constantly throughout}$$
$$\text{the duration of the activity}$$
$$RA_t = \text{the amount of resource available at time } t$$
$$u_{i\text{-}j} = \text{some measure of urgency or priority of activity } i\text{-}j$$
$$t \text{ and } T = \text{time counters}$$
$$U = \text{the set of unscheduled activities}$$
$$SA_T = \text{the set of all activities that could start at time } T$$
$$SS_{i\text{-}j} = \text{the scheduled start time of activity } i\text{-}j$$
$$SF_{i\text{-}j} = \text{the scheduled finish time of activity } i\text{-}j$$

For a resource feasible schedule to exist, $RR_{i\text{-}j} \leq RA_t$ for every activity $i\text{-}j$ and every time t.

Our approach is to construct a schedule that satisfies the resource limits. Figure 9-31 is a flowchart of such an algorithm. Initially, set the current time $T = 0$ and all scheduled finish times to infinity. Let the unscheduled jobs be all activities in the network. SA_T is the set of schedulable activities at time T. To be a member of the set the activity must be unscheduled. Furthermore, all its predecessors must be completed at time T, so their scheduled finish must be less than or equal to T. (Node 1 is the start node, so activity 1-j has no predecessors; i.e., activity k-1 does not exist and hence satisfies this condition.) Finally, the resource available in each time unit from T until the completion of $i\text{-}j$ must be sufficient to do $i\text{-}j$. If these conditions are met, the activity is included in the schedulable activity set.

If no activities are in the schedulable set, increment T and form the schedulable set for the new time; continue until a time is reached with at least one activity in the schedulable set. Choose $i\text{-}j$, the most urgent activity in the schedulable activity set. There are many measures for urgency, for example, slack and early start time.

Schedule activity $i\text{-}j$ to start at time T and finish at time $T + d_{i\text{-}j}$. For each time period the activity is in process, reduce the resource available by the amount used by the activity. Remove $i\text{-}j$ from the unscheduled set.

If the unscheduled set has no more activities in it, we are finished. The project completion time is the largest scheduled finish time for an activity. If more activities need to be scheduled, the schedulable activity set is updated. It can change because resource use

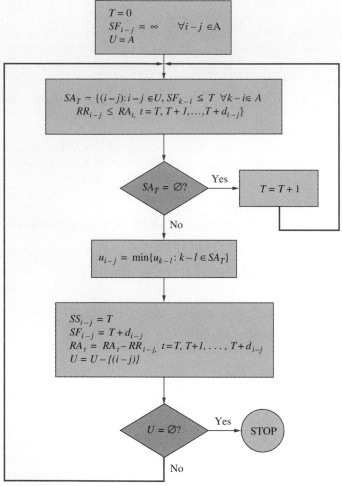

FIGURE 9-31
Heuristic algorithm for resource-constrained projects

increased by an activity completing or decreased by scheduling an activity or a predecessor job completing.

The key to this procedure is the choice of which activity to schedule next. If only one activity is eligible, then we schedule it. If several are available, our choice affects the schedule generated. There are many rules for choosing activities. Empirical studies indicate that smallest slack first or smallest latest finish time first usually give shorter project completions. We demonstrate the procedure with an example.

Example 9-11. Heuristic Schedule for the LJ9000. After looking at the electronics engineer's resource profile for early and late start schedules, Lynn wonders how long the project will be delayed if only three electronics engineers are available. The criticality index of 3.1 indicates the project cannot be done in 20 weeks with only three electronics engineers, but she would like

TABLE 9-11
LJ9000 duration and resource data

i-j	1-2	2-3	2-4	3-5	3-6	4-6	4-7	5-8	6-8	7-8
$d_{i\text{-}j}$	2	3	5	4	1	6	2	8	7	4
$RR_{i\text{-}j}$	2	1	2	1	0	3	1	0	3	0

to know how much longer it will take. To find out, she uses the resource-constraint heuristic. As the measure of urgency, she uses the early start, breaking ties by smallest slack activity. For convenience, the activities, duration, and resource requirements are given in Table 9-11. Activities 3-6, 5-8, and 7-8 do not require electronics engineers, so they can be scheduled independently of the other activities. We wish to construct a resource constrained schedule that completes as soon as possible.

We start by setting $T = 0$, $SF_{i\text{-}j} = \infty$ for all activities i-j and $U = \{1\text{-}2, 2\text{-}3, 2\text{-}4, 3\text{-}5, 4\text{-}7, 4\text{-}6, 6\text{-}8\}$. The resource available, RA_T, is 3 for all time periods. Now determine SA_0.

All activities in U are possible members of SA_0. Activity 1-2 has no uncompleted predecessors, so it could start now. There is more available resource than the resource requirement of 1-2 ($RR_{1\text{-}2} = 2 \leq 3 = RA_0 = RA_1$), so 1-2 is the only schedulable activity; $SA_0 = \{1\text{-}2\}$. Since SA_0 is not empty, we schedule an activity. Because there is only one activity in SA_0, we schedule it. Let

$$SS_{1\text{-}2} = T = 0$$

$$SF_{1\text{-}2} = T + d_{1\text{-}2} = 0 + 2 = 2$$

$$RA_0 = RA_0 - RR_{1\text{-}2} = 3 - 2 = 1$$

$$RA_1 = RA_1 - RR_{1\text{-}2} = 3 - 2 = 1$$

$$U = U - \{1\text{-}2\} = \{2\text{-}3, 2\text{-}4, 3\text{-}5, 4\text{-}7, 4\text{-}6, 6\text{-}8\}$$

There are activities in U, so we determine a new SA_0.

No activity in U has its predecessors completed, so $SA_0 = \emptyset$. Set $T = T + 1 = 1$ and determine SA_1. Again, $SA_1 = \emptyset$, so set $T = T + 1 = 2$. At $T = 2$, 1-2 completes, and now activities 2-3 and 2-4 have their predecessor completed:

$$SF_{1\text{-}2} = 2 \leq 2 = T$$

Furthermore,

$$RR_{2\text{-}3} = 1 \leq 3 = RA_2 = RA_3 = RA_4$$

implies there is enough resource available to schedule 2-3, so it is in the schedulable set. Similarly, 2-4 also is schedulable so $SA_2 = \{2\text{-}3, 2\text{-}4\}$.

Since $SA_2 \neq \emptyset$, we schedule an activity. There is more than one in the set, so we choose the most urgent one. Urgency is defined as early start, and from the CPM calculations we have $ES_{2\text{-}3} = ES_{2\text{-}4} = 2$; we break the tie by least slack. Again, from the CPM calculations, we have $S_{2\text{-}3} = 3$ and $S_{2\text{-}4} = 0$, so we schedule activity 2-4. To schedule activity 2-4, set

$$SS_{2\text{-}4} = T = 2$$

$$SF_{2\text{-}4} = T + d_{2\text{-}4} = 2 + 5 = 7$$

TABLE 9-12

Heuristic algorithm summary for the LJ9000 project

T	RA_T	U	SA_T	i-j	$SS_{i\text{-}j}$	$SF_{i\text{-}j}$	RR_T	RA_T
0	3	1-2, 2-3, 2-4, 3-5, 4-7, 4-6, 6-8	1-2	1-2	0	2	2	1
1	1	2-3, 2-4, 3-5, 4-7, 4-6, 6-8	∅					1
2	3	2-3, 2-4, 3-5, 4-7, 4-6, 6-8	2-3,2-4	2-4	2	7	2	1
2	1	2-3, 3-5, 4-7, 4-6, 6-8	2-3	2-3	2	5	1	0
3	0	3-5, 4-7, 4-6, 6-8	∅					0
4	0	3-5, 4-7, 4-6, 6-8	∅					0
5	1	3-5, 4-7, 4-6, 6-8	3-5	3-5	5	9	1	0
6	0	4-7, 4-6, 6-8	∅					0
7	2	4-7, 4-6, 6-8	4-7	4-7	7	9	1	1
8	1	4-6, 6-8	∅					1
9	3	4-6, 6-8	4-6	4-6	9	15	3	0
10	0	6-8	∅					0
11	0	6-8	∅					0
12	0	6-8	∅					0
13	0	6-8	∅					0
14	0	6-8	∅					0
15	3	6-8	6-8	6-8	15	22	3	0
15	0	∅						0

$$RA_2 = RA_2 - RR_{2\text{-}4} = 3 - 2 = 1$$
$$RA_3 = RA_3 - RR_{2\text{-}4} = 3 - 2 = 1$$
$$RA_4 = RA_4 - RR_{2\text{-}4} = 3 - 2 = 1$$
$$RA_5 = RA_5 - RR_{2\text{-}4} = 3 - 2 = 1$$
$$RA_6 = RA_6 - RR_{2\text{-}4} = 3 - 2 = 1$$
$$U = U - \{2\text{-}4\} = \{2\text{-}3, 3\text{-}5, 4\text{-}7, 4\text{-}6, 6\text{-}8\}$$

Since there are activities in U, we determine a new SA_2. The remainder of the calculations are summarized in Table 9-12. The schedule generated is shown in Figure 9-32. The project completion time increases to 22 weeks when only three electronic engineers are available.

It may be worthwhile to generate several schedules using different rules. Although the slack and late finish rules typically work best, other rules may produce better schedules for some problems. Because the procedure is relatively easy to implement on a computer, a variety of rules could be used and the best schedule from all attempts implemented. Other

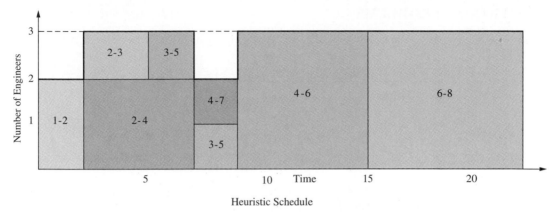

FIGURE 9-32
Resource profile for the heuristic schedule

rules to consider are to choose the activity with the smallest resource usage, smallest duration, longest duration, or most successor activities. For a detailed description of other rules and approaches, see Olaguibel and Goerlich (1989).

6.3 Other Issues

In resource leveling situations, the objective is to smooth resource usage over the life of the project. Noncritical activities can start at any time between their earliest start and latest start without affecting project completion. Thus, the general strategy is to shift the start times of noncritical activities within this range so resource usage is more evenly distributed. For smaller projects, this can be done by trial and error visually, using resource profiles or Gantt Charts. For larger projects, a more formal method is required; see Slowinski and Weglarz (1989) or Morton and Pentico (1993).

Our discussion has assumed there is only one resource required by the activities. More often there are multiple resources and both requirement and availability can vary over time. Conceptually, this causes no problems, as the approaches are still valid. However, we must check the availability of all resources required by the activity. This certainly adds complexity to the problem. Typically, the solutions produced by the heuristics are not as good when there are more resources to consider.

Often, several projects are in progress at the same time. These projects may be treated independently unless they share resources. Again, this poses no conceptual problems, but does require care in selecting which activity to schedule next. For example, choosing the activity with the largest slack may no longer be sufficient, since the slack of activities from different projects may not be totally comparable.

Many general-purpose heuristic algorithms, such as simulated annealing and genetic algorithms have been adapted for resource-constrained project scheduling. Slowinski and Weglarz (1989) provide a summary of some results, and many others can be found in the literature.

SECTION 6   PROBLEMS

9.42. Use the times and resource requirements in the accompanying table on the network of Problem 9.12.

Activity	Time	Resource	Activity	Time	Resource
1-2	6	6	3-4	3	3
2-3	3	2	3-6	4	2
2-4	2	3	4-6	3	2
2-5	2	2	5-6	7	2

(a) What is the criticality index for this problem?

(b) Draw a resource profile for the early start schedule.

(c) Give a resource-feasible schedule and its profile, given that there are six units of resource available at all times.

(d) Use the dispatch heuristic to generate a good resource-feasible schedule. Illustrate its resource profile.

9.43. Consider Problem 9.25. The number of mechanics needed for each activity is given in the accompanying table.

Activity	Mechanics
A	5
B	5
C	4
D	6
E	2
F	3
G	1
H	4
I	7
J	4

(a) What is the criticality index for this problem?

(b) Draw a resource profile for the early start schedule.

(c) If there are 10 mechanics available, give a resource-feasible schedule and its profile.

(d) Use the dispatch heuristic to generate a good resource-feasible schedule. Illustrate its resource profile.

(e) Discuss the pros and cons of using 8, 10, or 12 mechanics. Be as specific as possible.

7   TIME/COST TRADE-OFFS

In earlier sections, we assumed that the time to do an activity was not controllable. However, it may be possible to reduce this time by increasing the effort put into it. For example, in designing a new printer, we may estimate it will take 12 days for the initial design. This time may be based on one engineer doing all of the preliminary design work. If two design engineers are assigned to the task instead of one, maybe the task could be finished in eight days. Of course, adding another engineer will increase the cost substantially. The general idea behind time/cost trade-offs is to reduce the time to do an activity (and, it is hoped, the project) by increasing the effort expended on it, resulting in increased costs.

7.1 Crash and Normal Times

Define the **normal time** to be the time to do an activity under normal conditions and the **normal cost** its associated cost. The **crash time** and **crash cost** are the time and cost to do the activity as quickly as possible. Denote the normal and crash times and costs for activity $i\text{-}j$ by $d_{i\text{-}j}^n$, $d_{i\text{-}j}^c$ and $c_{i\text{-}j}^n$, $c_{i\text{-}j}^c$, respectively. We assume the activity can be completed in any time between the crash and normal times, with proportional associated cost. Figure 9-33 depicts the relationship between time and cost for a typical activity. Although we assume a linear relationship, the approach is valid even if the cost/time function varies in other ways, for example, in discrete steps (see Moder et al., 1983). For simplicity, we only work with linear relationships.

There are two common reasons to reduce the time for an activity. The first is that the project is behind schedule and we must complete it on time; here we wish to do so as cheaply as possible. The second reason is that we might save money by completing the project earlier. Some costs are direct costs attributable to each activity, including the cost to shorten its duration. Other costs are indirect and relate to the overall project rather than to a specific task. Indirect costs include administrative and overhead costs, such as salary of the project manager, opportunity cost, and penalty cost. An example of opportunity costs would be the lost profit a company experiences as a result of the delay in getting a new product to market. Penalty costs, usually contractual, are payments made for being late; construction projects quite often specify a penalty for each day the project runs beyond a specified date. For simplicity, we assume indirect costs are constant, say K, per time period. Thus if the project

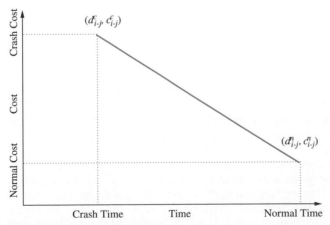

FIGURE 9-33
Typical time/cost relationship for an activity

takes T weeks, the total indirect costs are $T \times K$. By increasing direct cost, we may be able to decrease indirect cost. We next discuss a heuristic procedure to trade off direct costs with indirect costs.

7.2 Heuristic Crashing Procedure

It is easy to compute the total cost when all activities are done in their normal times. We can find the critical path, and T^n, the normal project length. The total direct cost is the sum of the normal costs for all activities, and the total indirect cost is $T^n \times K$. Denote the total normal cost by C^n.

Simply replacing the normal times and costs with crash times and costs and redoing the previous calculations might give the crash time T^c and cost C^c for the project. This is true for the time, but if any noncritical activity has been crashed, we could increase its time, thereby reducing cost, without affecting T^c. Thus, simply doing everything in crash time may not result in the best solution.

One approach to the time/cost trade-off problem is to start with the normal solution and reduce the project length one period at a time in the cheapest way. Given the normal solution, reducing the time of a noncritical activity does not reduce the project length, and hence is a wasted cost. So we want to start by reducing the time of some critical activity, but which one should we reduce? It seems reasonable to choose the activity with the smallest cost per unit time. Let

$$k_{i-j} = \frac{(c_{i-j}^c - c_{i-j}^n)}{(d_{i-j}^n - d_{i-j}^c)}.$$

be the per unit cost of reducing the duration of activity i-j. This is the **crashing cost** of activity i-j and is the slope of the cost curve in Figure 9-33. The duration of the activity on the critical path with smallest crashing cost, k_{i-j}, should be reduced by one unit. This increases the total direct cost by k_{i-j} and reduces the total indirect cost by K while reducing the project completion time by one time unit. We then repeat the process.

This simple idea is easy to implement as long as there is a single critical path. At some point, more than one path likely becomes critical, and reducing the duration of a single activity on one of the critical paths does not reduce the project length. Suppose there are two critical paths; if an activity is common to both, reducing its duration reduces the project length. If there is no common activity, two activities, one on each path, are reduced simultaneously. Choosing the activity on each path with smallest crashing cost and reducing each of them one unit results in a decrease in project length of one unit, decreasing indirect cost by K and increasing direct cost by the sum of the two crashing costs for the chosen activities. Even if there is an activity common to both critical paths, it is cheaper to reduce both activities if the sum of their crashing costs is smaller than the crashing cost of the common activity.

Example 9-12. Heuristic time/cost trade-off. Table 9-13 contains the LJ9000 data with normal times and costs as previously given and crash times and cost included. Times are in weeks and costs in thousands of dollars. The crashing cost k_{i-j} for each activity and the most an event duration can be reduced are computed and included in the table. Recall the critical path for normal times is 1-2, 2-4, 4-6, and 6-8 with length 20 weeks. Using the heuristic of picking the smallest k_{i-j} on the critical path, we reduce the duration of activity 1-2 by one time unit, reducing the

TABLE 9-13
Normal and crash times/costs for the LJ9000 project

i-j	$d_{i\text{-}j}^n$	$d_{i\text{-}j}^e$	$c_{i\text{-}j}^n$	$c_{i\text{-}j}^e$	$k_{i\text{-}j}$	$d_{i\text{-}j}^n - d_{i\text{-}j}^e$
1-2	2	1	5	12	7.00	1
2-3	3	1	3	11	4.00	2
2-4	5	2	10	45	11.67	3
3-5	4	2	1	5	2.00	2
3-6	1	1	1	1	none	0
4-6	6	3	17	42	8.33	3
4-7	2	1	10	25	15.00	1
5-8	8	3	0	8	1.60	5
6-8	7	3	15	72	14.25	4
7-8	4	2	10	32	11.00	2

project completion time to 19 weeks while increasing direct cost by $7000. To further reduce the completion time, we must reduce a different activity, since 1-2 can only be crashed one week. The next smallest $k_{i\text{-}j}$ on the critical path is 8.33 for activity 4-6, so it is crashed one week.

As you might have noticed, when there are more than two critical paths, the situation becomes complicated. The combinations of common versus independent activities make it difficult to choose activities to crash. Also, crashing an activity may reduce another path that was critical, so we can now lengthen some other activity on the previously critical path without increasing the project length. This approach is a heuristic procedure. Fortunately, under some reasonable assumptions, a linear programming approach guarantees an optimal solution.

7.3 Linear Programming Approach to Time/Cost Trade-Offs

In order to model the time/cost trade-off problem as a linear program, we assume all crashing costs are linear, and the indirect costs are constant per time unit. Our objective is to minimize total cost, which is the sum of crashing costs and indirect costs. The normal cost for completing the project is not controllable, so we need only worry about the crashing costs. Let

$y_{i\text{-}j}$ = the number of time units activity i-j is crashed
A = the set of all activities in the network

Recall that E_n is the earliest event time of event n, where event n corresponds to the end of the entire project. Now we can define our objective function mathematically as

$$\text{Minimize} \sum_{i\text{-}j \in A} k_{i\text{-}j} y_{i\text{-}j} + KE_n$$

To ensure precedence is followed, we relate events that correspond to the beginning and end of activities. That is, if i-j belongs to A, then the event time of j, E_j, must be no smaller than the event time of i, E_i, plus the actual duration of activity i-j. The actual duration of i-j

is its normal duration, $d_{i\text{-}j}^n$, minus how much it has been crashed, $y_{i\text{-}j}$. There is a constraint of this type for every activity in the network. Mathematically, we have

$$E_j \geq E_i + (d_{i\text{-}j}^n - y_{i\text{-}j}) \qquad \forall\, i\text{-}j \in A$$

Let $E_1 = 0$, and remove it from the formulation.

Now we ensure we do not "overcrash" an activity. An activity can be crashed no more than the difference between its normal and crash times. Also, the amount crashed cannot be negative. This can be modeled mathematically by

$$0 \leq y_{i\text{-}j} \leq (d_{ij}^n - d_{ij}^c) \qquad \forall\, i\text{-}j \in A$$

Putting these together gives the following linear program

$$\text{Minimize } \sum_{i\text{-}j \in A} k_{i\text{-}j} y_{i\text{-}j} + K E_n$$

subject to

$$E_j - E_i + y_{i\text{-}j} \geq d_{i\text{-}j}^n \qquad \forall\, i\text{-}j \in A$$
$$0 \leq y_{i\text{-}j} \leq (d_{i\text{-}j}^n - d_{i\text{-}j}^c) \qquad \forall\, i\text{-}j \in A$$
$$E_i \geq 0, \quad i = 1, 2, \ldots, n$$

We illustrate the linear programming approach by continuing Example 9-12 in the following example.

Example 9-13. LP time/cost trade-off. Using the data of Table 9-13, we construct a linear programming model to determine the optimal project length given a $10,000 per week indirect cost. This cost is a result of administrative cost, cost of capital, and lost opportunity for not having the printer on the market. The set of activities for the project is

$$A = \{1\text{-}2, 2\text{-}3, 2\text{-}4, 3\text{-}5, 3\text{-}6, 4\text{-}6, 4\text{-}7, 5\text{-}8, 6\text{-}8, 7\text{-}8\}$$

The linear program is

$$\text{Minimize } 7y_{1\text{-}2} + 4y_{2\text{-}3} + 11.67y_{2\text{-}4} + 2y_{3\text{-}5} + 8.33y_{4\text{-}6} + 15y_{4\text{-}7}$$
$$+ 1.6y_{5\text{-}8} + 14.5y_{6\text{-}8} + 11y_{7\text{-}8} + 10E_8$$

subject to

$$
\begin{array}{llll}
E_2 + y_{1\text{-}2} \geq 2 & \quad E_2 \geq 0 & \quad 0 \leq y_{1\text{-}2} \leq 1 \\
E_3 - E_2 + y_{2\text{-}3} \geq 3 & \quad E_3 \geq 0 & \quad 0 \leq y_{2\text{-}3} \leq 2 \\
E_4 - E_2 + y_{2\text{-}4} \geq 5 & \quad E_4 \geq 0 & \quad 0 \leq y_{2\text{-}4} \leq 3 \\
E_5 - E_3 + y_{3\text{-}5} \geq 4 & \quad E_5 \geq 0 & \quad 0 \leq y_{3\text{-}5} \leq 2 \\
E_6 - E_3 \phantom{+ y_{3\text{-}5}} \geq 1 & \quad E_6 \geq 0 & \\
E_6 - E_4 + y_{4\text{-}6} \geq 6 & & \quad 0 \leq y_{4\text{-}6} \leq 3 \\
E_7 - E_4 + y_{4\text{-}7} \geq 2 & \quad E_7 \geq 0 & \quad 0 \leq y_{4\text{-}7} \leq 1 \\
\end{array}
$$

$$E_8 - E_5 + y_{5\text{-}8} \geq 8 \qquad E_8 \geq 0 \qquad 0 \leq y_{5\text{-}8} \leq 5$$
$$E_8 - E_6 + y_{6\text{-}8} \geq 7 \qquad\qquad\qquad 0 \leq y_{6\text{-}8} \leq 4$$
$$E_8 - E_7 + y_{7\text{-}8} \geq 4 \qquad\qquad\qquad 0 \leq y_{7\text{-}8} \leq 2$$

There is no $y_{3\text{-}6}$, because that activity cannot be crashed.

Solving this with a suitable LP code, we get $y_{1\text{-}2} = 1$, $y_{4\text{-}6} = 3$ and $E_8 = 16$, with a cost of \$191,990. This cost considers only crashing and indirect cost, so to get the total cost of the project we must add the \$72,000 in normal costs of the activities, giving a total cost of \$263,990.

Although the optimal solution is important, there are often considerations not accounted for in the model. Then, it is nice to actually "see" the potential trade-offs. To do this, we can set $E_n = T^n - 1$ and solve the LP model. Repeat for successively smaller values of E_n until we reach the crash time. We can then plot the direct, indirect, and sum of the two to get the total cost curve. The curve for the LJ9000 project is given in Figure 9-34. A project length of 16 is the lowest point on the total cost curve.

If the direct cost/period is unknown or does not exist, this approach can still be used. Compute the direct cost of completing the project for every time unit between T^c and T^n as above, but set $K = 0$. A plot of direct costs of the LJ9000 project versus time is given in Figure 9-35; it is just Figure 9-34 with the indirect and total cost curves omitted. It readily shows the impact on direct cost of decreasing the project length. The project manager can then weigh the pros and cons of various options and make a final decision.

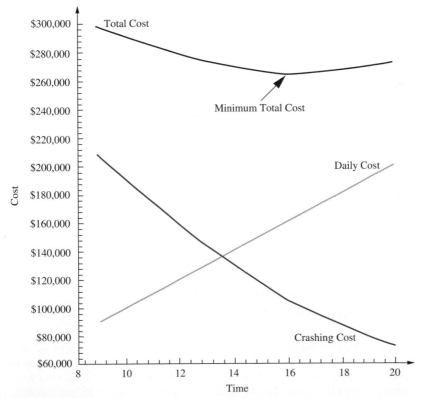

FIGURE 9-34
LJ9000 cost versus time

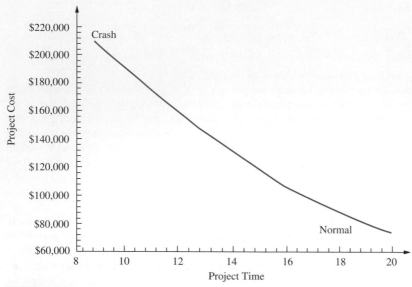

FIGURE 9-35
Time/cost trade-off graph

SECTION 7   PROBLEMS

9.44. Consider Problem 9.12 with the following data on crashing the project:

| | **Normal** | | **Crash** | |
Activity	Time (hours)	Cost (dollars)	Time (hours)	Cost (dollars)
1-2	10	5,000	6	7,000
2-3	6	12,000	3	16,500
2-4	4	1,000	2	2,600
2-5	3	500	2	600
3-4	5	2,000	3	3,200
3-6	6	1,200	4	1,800
4-6	4	500	3	1,500
5-6	9	3,000	7	3,600

(a) Find the normal time to complete the project.

(b) What is the fastest time to complete the project?

(c) Develop a time/cost trade-off curve for the project duration.

(d) Knowing nothing about the project's fixed cost, draw a Gantt Chart of the schedule you would recommend.

9.45. A construction contractor for the state highway department is building a bridge over a road. It is made of prestressed concrete beams. After the foundations are constructed, the beams are placed over the highway. For safety and convenience, the road spanned by the bridge will be closed and traffic rerouted during beam placement. By adding more people and equipment, each activity during the time the road is closed can be speeded up. Lisa, the project manager, has put together the following data:

Description	Precedes	Normal		Crash	
		Time (hours)	Cost (dollars)	Time (hours)	Cost (dollars)
A: Drain water	D	9	110	6	170
B: Prepare bolts	E	8	150	6	200
C: Place beams	F	15	250	10	400
D: Test	F	5	80	3	100
E: Anchor beams	F	10	90	6	150
F: Finish up	—	2	110	1	150

(a) Find the normal time to place the beams.

(b) What is the fastest time to place the beams?

(c) Develop a time/cost trade-off curve for the project duration.

(d) If fixed costs are $60 per hour, what is the least-cost project duration? Construct a Gantt Chart showing the best schedule.

9.46. Give an approach to the time/cost trade-off problem if crashing costs are not linear.

9.47. How can project planning, scheduling, and control be used to speed up product time-to-market? (*Hint:* Think about doing away with activities, compressing them, and breaking down precedence structure as much as possible.)

8   COMPUTER SOFTWARE

Except for back-of-the-envelope studies, a computer is needed for project planning, scheduling, and control. A computer is great for the mundane calculation of early and late start times, slack, and critical paths. It is helpful in cost analysis, resource allocation, and time/cost trade-offs. More importantly, it provides timely data for updates and is useful for "what if" analyses.

If you decide to use a computer, there are many software packages available. The first decision is whether to buy software for a microcomputer or purchase or lease software for a minicomputer or a mainframe. At one time, larger projects could only be handled by mainframe computers, but this is no longer true. Costs for microcomputer packages range from free (public domain) to $50,000 for the fancier versions. Minicomputer and mainframe packages cost from $5000 to several hundred thousand dollars. Many $500 packages for microcomputers do a good job of the basic scheduling functions. Adding cost and resource control increases the cost. Crashing capabilities are found in the more sophisticated packages. A few do resource leveling and allocation, but may only use simple dispatch heuristics.

Because the software industry is changing rapidly, we do not mention specific packages. Periodically, listings and comparisons of available software packages for project planning, scheduling, and control are published. Examples include Wortman (1989), Yahdav (1992), Bloom (1993), and "Project Management Software Buyer's Guide" (1995). For a detailed discussion of selecting project management software, see Kezsbom et al. (1989).

Several journals have columns that evaluate specific project planning, scheduling and control packages. These include *Cost Engineering, Project Management Journal, Byte, PC Magazine,* and *PC World.* Typical examples are referenced in Section 11. Some packages are so widespread that books have been written about them, e.g., Day (1995).

For simpler projects, "academic" software may be sufficient. Again, there are a variety of packages available, including Chang (1995) and Emmons et al. (1989).

9 EVOLUTION

The Egyptians used the concepts of planning, organization, and control over 6000 years ago; some form of project planning, scheduling, and control was probably used on the pyramids. It was not until the mid-1950s that the procedure was formalized. There are, however, two precursors we must mention. The Gantt Chart (1911) contains the fundamental scheduling ideas of project planning, scheduling, and control. Karol Adamiecki, a Polish scientist, developed the Harmonygraph in 1931, a Gantt Chart designed specifically for project scheduling. Activities were ordered by precedence and started as soon as possible, i.e., a forward pass. Since activities were represented by sliding tabs, updating and rescheduling were easily carried out. His discovery was not well known and soon faded.

In the mid-1950s, three groups independently developed project planning, scheduling, and control as we know it today. The Operational Research Section of the British Central Electricity Generating Board wanted to reduce the time to overhaul a generating plant. By 1957 they had a developed a methodology to identify the critical path. The time to overhaul a plant was eventually reduced by more than 40 percent (Lockyer, 1969).

During the same period, a team composed of employees of Lockheed Aircraft Corporation; Booz, Allen, and Hamilton Consultants; and the U.S. Navy worked to cut costs and reduce completion time on government projects. Their methodology, called PERT, was reported by Malcolm et al. (1959). The Polaris Weapon System was planned, scheduled, and controlled using PERT, and was completed ahead of schedule and under budget.

Another collaboration, joining the Du Pont company and Remington Rand Univac, produced CPM (Walker and Sayer, 1959). They were also trying to reduce the time spent on plant overhaul, maintenance, and construction. This group introduced the basic time/cost model (Kelley and Walker, 1959; Kelley, 1961).

The success of these methods led to government standards for controlling costs of projects they funded (DOD and NASA Guide, 1962). Research into resource levelling (Burgess and Killebrew, 1962) and heuristics for resource-constrained models (Weist, 1964, 1967) began. In 1964, Moder and Phillips published the first edition of their classic book, *Project Management with CPM, PERT and Precedence Diagramming* (updated in Moder et al., 1983).

The late 1960s and early 1970s saw commercial software packages developed for mainframe computers. These were very expensive and difficult to use. Input (and sometimes output) data were on punched cards, and often it would take eight or more hours of computer time just to update a large project. The government pushed continued use of the systems (USAFSC, 1976). Research on probability estimates, resource-constrained scheduling heuristics, and different measures of performance was undertaken, but the fundamentals of project planning, scheduling, and control were firmly established. The first rigorous text on the subject was written by Elmaghraby in 1977.

The proliferation of the personal computer has been the dominant factor in project planning, scheduling, and control for the last 15 years. Many user-friendly software packages have been developed and are available for reasonable prices. Such technology has put great power on the desk of nearly every manager and analyst. Research continues in the same areas: limited resources (Olaguibel and Goerlich, 1989; Oguz and Bala, 1994); new measures of performance such as lateness costs (Kim, 1993), early/tardy penalties (Padman and Smith-Daniels, 1993), and multiple objectives (Davis et al., 1992; Slowinski et al., 1994);

probabilistic issues (Gong and Hugsted, 1993; Keefer and Verdini, 1993); and new solution techniques (Icmeli and Erenguc, 1994). Several books, such as Slowinski and Weglarz (1989), Morton and Pentico (1993), and Sprecher (1994) delve deeply into particular aspects of project planning, scheduling, and control. Others, e.g., Badiru (1994), Cleland (1994), and Kezsbom et al. (1989), provide comprehensive introductory texts.

10 SUMMARY

This chapter discusses projects, a set of interrelated activities that must be completed to achieve a goal. Projects can be developing a new product or system, performing maintenance on existing equipment, installing new equipment, or constructing a plant. The major elements are planning, scheduling, and control.

Planning occurs both before and during execution of the project. Choosing a project manager and team are part of planning. Organizational structure can be either project, staff, or matrix. Another part of planning is defining the project. This includes activity definition and estimating activity durations, costs, and resource requirements. Activity precedence must be determined and the final network specified.

Scheduling consists of assigning start times for every activity. The calculations required consist of a forward pass to get earliest times and a backward pass for latest times. Critical activities and the critical path are identified as activities that warrant close attention. Early and late start schedules are also defined.

Once a project is under way, it must be controlled. As activities progress, the estimates of time, money, and resources are updated. The project is rescheduled to account for actual occurrences. To control resources, the project is divided into workpackages or work breakdown structures. Variances between actual and scheduled resource usage identify trouble spots in the project. Although time and money are the most commonly tracked resources, any resource could be controlled this way.

To take uncertainty of activity duration into account, PERT is introduced. Each activity duration is assumed to follow a probability distribution; uniform, triangular, and beta distributions are discussed. The critical path, using expected durations, is found in the standard way. Then a probabilistic analysis of project completion time can be carried out by appealing to the central limit theorem. Assumptions required for this approach may not always be valid, leading to limitations of the PERT approach.

Another extension of basic project calculations is to include limited resources, which can cause project delays. It can be very difficult to find resource-feasible solutions to these problems. Graphs showing resource profiles are helpful in scheduling projects. The criticality index indicates how important effective use of a particular resource is. A simple dispatch heuristic for fixed resources is presented. Other variations, such as resource leveling, multiple resources, and multiple projects are briefly mentioned.

If increased resources can decrease the time to perform an activity, we have a time/cost trade-off. We might be willing to pay more money to reduce the duration of an activity if it reduces indirect project cost or gets the project done earlier. We define normal and crash times and cost and assume a linear relationship between time and cost. A simple cost/unit time heuristic is presented. For larger problems, the number and combinations of critical and near-critical activities make the simple heuristic impractical. A linear programming model, which optimizes total cost for a given indirect cost is presented. Its solution provides a time/cost trade-off graph.

Finally, we briefly discuss software and the evolution of project planning.

MINICASE: FASTRAK TIRE MANUFACTURERS

The recent popularity of FasTrak tires has resulted in increased sales to the point that FasTrak cannot produce enough. Carmen, a manufacturing engineer, proposed adding a cooling station after curing, which should reduce the time to make a tire by 15 percent, thus adding capacity. Jose, the plant manager, has agreed to her idea. She must now plan the tread tube cooling project.

The project begins with preliminary design and layout, which takes 20 days. After completing this, the three subsystems—structural, thermal, and drive—can be designed. It is estimated it will take 30, 14, and 5 days, respectively, to design them. Once structural design is completed, the cooling tank can be designed in 20 days and the structural material ordered, which will take 30 days. The cooling tank is purchased and requires 50 days for delivery. When structural materials arrive, the structure can be built, requiring 15 days; then it is painted in 5 days. Installing the tank on the painted structure takes 10 days. The complete thermal system will be purchased and will be delivered 40 days from placing the order. It will take 20 days to install the thermal system, which must be done before the structure is painted. The drive design requires a complete set of electrical drawings, which takes 5 days. This will specify electrical parts to order, with a 40 day delivery. The drive components are ordered (20 day delivery) and installation of the drive unit takes 3 days and can only be done after the tank is mounted on the structure. The electrical system must be installed (7 days) after the tank but before the drive system. A recirculating pipe must be added after the tank is installed; it will require 5 days. Finally, the electrical system is hooked up (1 day) and the system tested for 2 days. It is then released to production.

All activities done in-house use a combination of engineers (E), mechanics (M), and laborers (L). Structural design, drive design, thermal design, tank design, electrical drawings, structure construction, thermal system installation, drive system installation, electrical system installation, electric hookup, and system testing all require an engineer. Thermal system installation, drive system installation, electrical system installation, tank installation, electric hookup, and system testing require mechanics. Structure construction, structure painting, thermal system installation, drive system installation, electrical system installation, tank installation, circulating pipe installation, electric hookup, and system testing require laborers. All times given above assume one engineer, two mechanics, and a labor crew. There are two engineers, six mechanics, and four labor crews available to the project.

Times were estimated as closely as possible, but Carmen feels they could range from 5 percent shorter to 10 percent longer. The time for delivery of parts and subsystems was quoted by the suppliers. The time to deliver any order can be reduced 25 percent by paying a $10,000 premium. Two engineers, two mechanics, and three crews can be reassigned from other duties to decrease the time to carry out a task. Doubling the manpower cuts the time to do an activity in half. However, assigning more than double manpower does not make it significantly shorter than doubling. A reassigned engineer costs the company $500 per day in lost opportunity for other tasks. Mechanics cost $200 per day and a crew $400 per day. If a task requires more than one skill, all must be increased to reduce the time. Each day the cooler is not running costs the company $10,000 in lost sales. Help Carmen plan this project.

11 REFERENCES

Badiru, A. B., *Comprehensive Project Management: Integrating Optimization Models, Management Practices, and Computers,* Prentice Hall, Englewood Cliffs, NJ, 1994.

Bloom, R., "Software for Project Management," *Transportation & Distribution,* 34, 33–34, 1993.

Burgess, A. R. and Killebrew, J. B., "Variation in Activity Level on a Cyclic Arrow Diagram," *Journal of Industrial Engineering,* 13, 76–83, 1962.

Chang, Y. L., *QS: Quantitative Systems Version 3.0,* Prentice Hall, Englewood Cliffs, NJ, 1995.

Cleland, D. I., *Project Management: Strategic Design and Implementation,* The McGraw-Hill Companies, Inc., New York, 1994.

Davis, K. R., Stam, A., and Grzybowski, R. A., "Resource Constrained Project Scheduling with Multiple Objectives: A Decision Support Approach," *Computers & Operations Research,* 19, 657–669, 1992.

Day, P. J., *Microsoft Project 4.0 for Windows and the Macintosh: Setting Project Management Standards,* Van Nostrand Reinhold, New York, 1995.

DOD and NASA Guide, PERT Cost Systems Design, Catalog D1-6/2:P94, U.S. Government Printing Office, Washington, DC, 1962.

Elmaghraby, S. E., *Activity Networks,* John Wiley & Sons, New York, 1977.

Emmons, H., Flowers, A. D., Khot, C. M., and Mathur, K., *STORM: Quantitative Modeling for Decision Support,* Holden-Day, Oakland, CA, 1989.

Gantt, H. L., ed., *How Scientific Management Is Applied,* Hive Publishing Company, Easton, PA, 1911.

Gong, D. and Hugsted, R., "Time-Uncertainty Analysis in Project Networks with a New Merge-Event Time-Estimation Technique," *International Journal of Project Management,* 11, 165–174, 1993.

Hines, W. W. and Montgomery, D. C., *Probability and Statistics in Engineering and Management Science,* John Wiley & Sons, New York, 1990.

Icmeli, O. and Erenguc, S. S., "A Tabu Search Procedure for the Resource Constrained Project Scheduling Problem with Discounted Cash Flows," *Computers & Operations Research,* 21, 841–853, 1994.

Keefer, D. L. and Verdini, W. A., "Better Estimation of PERT Activity Time Parameters," *Management Science,* 39, 1086–1091, 1993.

Kelley, J. E., "Critical Path Planning and Scheduling: Mathematical Basis," *Operations Research,* 9, 296–320, 1961.

Kelley, J. E. and M. R. Walker, "Critical Path Planning and Scheduling," *Proceedings, Eastern Joint Computer Conference,* 160–173, 1959.

Kezsbom, D. S., Schilling, D. L., and Edward, K. A., *Dynamic Project Management: A Practical Guide for Managers and Engineers,* John Wiley & Sons, New York, 1989.

Kim, S.-Y. and Leachman, R. C., Multi-Project Scheduling with Explicit Lateness Costs," *IIE Transactions,* 25, 34–44, 1993.

Lockyer, K. G., *Introduction to Critical Path Analysis,* Pitman Publishing Company, London, UK, 1969.

Malcolm, D. G., Roseboom, J. H., Clark, C. E., and Fazar, W., "Applications of a Technique for R & D Program Evaluation (PERT)," *Operations Research,* 7, 646–669, 1959.

Moder, J. J., Phillips, C. R., and Davis, E. W., *Project Management with CPM, PERT and Precedence Diagramming,* Van Nostrand Reinhold Company, New York, 1983.

Morton, T. E. and Pentico, D. W., *Heuristic Scheduling Systems,* John Wiley & Sons, New York, 1993.

Oguz, O. and Bala, H., "A Comparative Study of Computational Procedures for the Resource Constrained Project Scheduling Problem," *European Journal of Operational Research,* 72, 406–416, 1994.

Olaguibel, R. A.-V., and Goerlich, J. M. T., "Heuristic Algorithms for Resource-Constrained Project Scheduling: A Review and an Empirical Analysis," in *Advances in Project Scheduling,* Slowinski, R. and Weglarz, J., eds., Elsevier, Amsterdam, 1989.

Padman, R. and Smith-Daniels, D. E., "Early-Tardy Cost Trade-Offs in Resource Constrained Projects with Cash Flows: An Optimization-Guided Heuristic Approach," *European Journal of Operational Research,* 64, 295–311, 1993.

"Project Management Software Buyer's Guide," *Industrial Engineering,* March 1995, pp. 36–37.

Slowinski, R., Soniewicki, B., and Weglarz, J., "DSS for Multiobjective Project Scheduling," *European Journal of Operational Research,* 79, 220–229, 1994.

Slowinski, R. and Weglarz, J., eds., *Advances in Project Scheduling,* Elsevier, Amsterdam, 1989.

Sprecher, A., *Resource-Constrained Project Scheduling: Exact Methods for the Multi-Mode Case,* Springer-Verlag, New York, 1994.

U.S. Air Force Systems Command, *Cost/Schedule Control Systems Criteria, Joint Implementation Guide,* U.S. Government Printing Office, Washington, DC, 1976.

Ulrich, K. T. and Eppinger, S. D., *Product Design and Development,* The McGraw-Hill Companies, Inc., New York, 1995.

Walker, M. R. and Sayer, J. S., "Project Planning and Scheduling," Report 6959, E. I. du Pont de Nemours and Co., Wilmington, DE, 1959.

Weist, J. D., "Some Properties of Schedules for Large Projects with Limited Resources," *Operations Research,* 12, 395–418, 1964.

Weist, J. D., "Heuristic Model for Scheduling Large Projects with Limited Resources,"*Management Science,* 13, B359–B377, 1967.

Wortman, L. A., "Marketing Software Review: Project Management Made Easy," *Business Marketing,* 74, 20–24, 1989.

Yahdav, D., "Tracking the Elusive Project," *Byte,* 17, 119–122, 1992.

CHAPTER
10

INTEGRATED PRODUCTION PLANNING AND CONTROL

1 INTRODUCTION

Louisa is the production manager of a small pharmaceuticals company that has about 300 employees and annual sales of about $45 million and manufactures generic solid pills, tablets, lozenges, and other drugs. The company is family owned and has been in business for over fifty years.

Over the years, the company computerized its production, acquiring several tools to assist in planning and control. The company purchased a material-requirements planning software package to generate master production schedules and purchase orders and to track inventory. Since the bill of material is simple, they feel a relatively simple package is sufficient. Later, a forecasting system to assist the marketing department and costing software were also introduced. Product quality is tracked via a computerized quality control system.

Initially, Louisa felt these systems gave her the latitude to manage production properly. However, in the last few years things have changed. The generic drug market has undergone major changes and competition is fierce, which has generated pressure on Louisa to drastically cut production lead time and cost. She discovered the company's systems did not respond well to the new environment. She felt her major problem was that the different systems were uncoordinated, each using its own data base. Furthermore, their response time was too slow, and because production lots had to move faster on the production floor, control became more difficult. She also wondered if the new environment required changes in the way production interacts with other functions of the organization.

Louisa's problems are common to many industrial organizations. The answer to this class of problems is integration in general and integrated production planning and control in particular.

The thrust of this chapter is integrated production planning and control. However, we first focus on three related issues: interaction of production with the rest of the organization, control, and interplant integration.

2   INTEGRATION RELATED ISSUES

2.1   Production and The Organization

Production is one component in the manufacturing organization. As such, it interacts with the rest of the organization; i.e., decisions made there affect production, and vice versa. There is nothing new in this statement—it was also true in the era of production-driven systems. What is different is the way this interaction takes place in the era of market-driven systems, where integration is a prime mover. In Chapter 2 we discussed two major characteristics of integration, barrier removal within the organization and information integration. We further elaborate on these two issues.

Functional organization tends to create barriers; the underlying assumption is that differentiation is the key to efficiency and control. A different organizational approach is emerging as part of the market-driven era—that of process-based organization.

The primary assumption of process-based organization is that integration optimizes across the enterprise. A forerunner of the process organization is the multifunctional team approach. (Chapter 2).

So what is a process organization, and how does it integrate production? Processes occur in a nested three-level hierarchy.[1]

Level 1   "Operational processes...directly create value for customers...and other stakeholders of an enterprise." Manufacturing belongs to this level, along with product development, customer service, and other value-adding processes.

Level 2   "Strategic planning and controlling processes...provide resources or effect improvement in operational processes." This includes all short- and intermediate-term decisions needed to steer level 1 processes. Examples are allocating resources to processes, developing measures, financing capital investment, and capacity expansion.

Level 3   "Guiding and steering processes create the purpose, vision, and character of the organization." These include setting objectives and managing organizational change.

Production, which is part of level 1, needs both lateral and vertical integration—lateral integration within the level with functions such as product development and marketing and vertical integration with upper-level processes such as resource allocation and change.

A process-based organization, by implication, adopts the *fallen barriers syndrome*. This means a major change in culture (level 3) and organizational processes. We already mentioned teamwork, and we now elaborate on the subject of information integration.

We use an example to discuss this issue (Erens and Hegge, 1994). To focus the discussion, we show information integration in level 1, between production and sales. This integration is achieved through a common data base and information flow.

---

[1]From Jean-Phillippe Deschamps and R. Ranganath Nayak, *Product Juggernauts: How Companies Mobilize to Generate a Stream of Market Winners.* Boston: Harvard Business School Press, 1995, 384–385.

Medicom is one of the largest manufacturers of X-ray equipment for doctors and hospitals. Most medical systems are offered to the market in thousands of variants. Since lead time varies from one to six months, it permits Medicom to assemble product variants in three different modes: make-to-stock of system (end product), make-to-stock of components (subassemblies), or assemble-to-order. This is possible because Medicom's product variety has an hourglass shape (see Chapter 7).

In Figure 10-1 we show how information integrates customer sales and manufacturing. Information is exchanged on different business levels, i.e., design, production planning, marketing communication, order information, and operations. The primary process shows the material flow from manufacturing to assembly, packing, distribution, and installation, which are done in different geographical locations. All this activity is controlled by the MRP system (right-hand side of Figure 10-1). It also integrates order flow and production planning, and part of its data base, the bill of material, serves the marketing communication. This is an example of information integration between level 1 and level 2.

The production control situation is determined by the penetration extent of a customer order (and its identification) into the manufacturing organization (level 1). In situations in which end products are made to stock or assembled to order at the customer's site, the order identification is known only by the sales organization in direct contact with the customer. If products are assembled to order, the order identification will be known in final assembly. Thus, the production control system should be able to handle three different control modes; make-to-stock of systems, make-to-stock of components, and assemble-to-order. This is an example of lateral integration. We next focus on the issue of control.

2.2 Control Architecture

Enterprise integration is both a strategy and technology. The strategy is integrating strategic, tactical, and day-to-day decisions. This is supported by a technology that allows implementing an efficient, timely information flow. The core of this technology is control architecture. There are a number of alternatives for control architecture, and we discuss them in this section.

Architecture is generally defined as the structure that makes systems from components. Consequently, control architecture makes a control system from control components. Thus, for example, control architecture of an advanced production system directs processing and handling activities that transform raw material into finished goods. Therefore, it is required that the control architecture embodies many *decision-making* responsibilities, such as resource allocation, part scheduling, and part routing.

The control architecture allocates these decision-making responsibilities. In addition, it defines the interrelationship between the control components, setting the mechanisms for coordinating the execution of the decisions.

We consider, for example, a flexible manufacturing system. The control architecture will specify a part to be loaded next into the system. Another control component may be responsible for the routing of the part. The architecture would also define the interaction between these two control components. As a consequence, we get a coordinated activity of loading and routing new parts. Further extensions to this control architecture could create a complete control system for flexible manufacturing (Dilts et al., 1991).

The preceding allocation of decision making is not the only one possible. A different allocation may be more or less effective. We make two observations: The control architecture

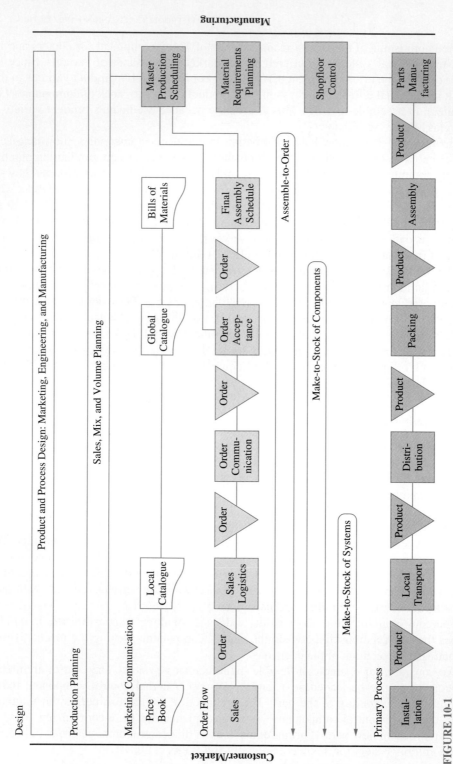

FIGURE 10-1
Integrating customers and manufacturing (Reprinted from Erens and Hegge (1994) with kind permission of Elsevier Science–NL, Sara Burgerhartstraat 25, 1055 KV, Amsterdam, The Netherlands)

determines the control system effectiveness, and there may be more than one design of a control architecture.

It is common to identify four basic designs of control architecture (Dilts et al., 1991), namely, centralized, proper hierarchical, modified hierarchical, and heterarchical (Figure 10-2). These designs show a trend toward increasingly distributed control. However, each design contains all the control responsibilities that need to be executed. Customarily, they are divided into three hierarchical levels: production floor, cell, and machine levels (Figure 10-3). Production floor level deals with master production scheduling: a routing among cells and global resource allocation to meet production requirements, total inventory management, etc. Cell level is concerned with process planning, scheduling, and work in process within the cell. Machine level concentrates on execution of real-time part operations of two types, changes in the part and material handling. Generally, as we descend through the control levels, the level of detail increases and the time period considered decreases.

The **centralized design,** sometimes called total integration, is built around a central computer that performs all planning and information processing functions. It has one global data base. Production-floor and cell-level controls are performed by the central computer, and machine-level control is executed by simple (nonintelligent) controllers dispersed around the production floor.

Centralized architecture is becoming less and less common; however, it has some advantages; for example, one information source and fewer computers are required. Its major drawbacks are slower response speed and a complex manufacturing environment that makes it almost impossible to implement in large-scale production systems.

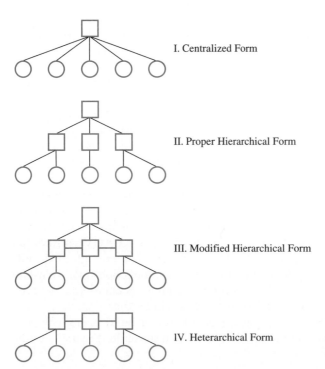

I. Centralized Form

II. Proper Hierarchical Form

III. Modified Hierarchical Form

IV. Heterarchical Form

FIGURE 10-2
Four basic forms of control architectures (from Dilts, Boyd, and Whorms (1991), reprinted from the *Journal of Manufacturing Systems,* by permission of the Society of Manufacturing Engineers)

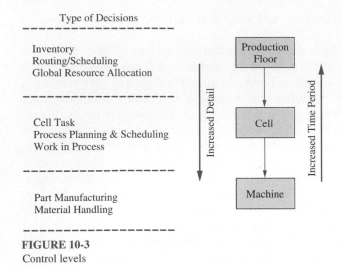

FIGURE 10-3
Control levels

Proper hierarchical design is based on a concept of levels of control, where several control components are arranged in a tree structure. All activities of a lower level ("slave") are dictated by an upper level ("master"). This *master-slave* configuration is typical of this design. At the top of the hierarchy there is a high level computer, and implementing control in other levels is done by using a variety of computing technology. Control decisions flow from the top down, and status reports flow from the bottom up. Each level maintains its own data base. This offers a simple, consistent structure that can manage complex manufacturing systems. It can be gradually implemented, with reduced software development time. Because of the master-slave relationship, response time is faster. Some of the disadvantages are computational limitations of local controllers, unreliable interlevel communication links, difficulty in making future unforeseen modifications, and the fact that a crash at some level can cause the entire system below to come to a halt.

Modified hierarchical design was introduced to overcome some of the drawbacks of the previous design. It shares many of its characteristics; however, subordinates (slaves) have more autonomy with respect to higher levels. One feature of such autonomy is the ability to interact with other subordinates. Local area network (LAN) technology and the availability of inexpensive computing power made this design viable.

In Figure 10-4 we show a possible generic implementation of this control architecture, as part of a flexible manufacturing system (FMS). A similar architecture was used by the General Motors assembly plant in Oshawa, Ontario, Canada (Bookbinder and Kotwa, 1987) in their body framing subsystem. They had a fleet of about 60 AGV carriers (an AGV—automated guide vehicle—is an independently operated, computer-controlled, self-propelled vehicle that is guided along a defined pathway in the production floor), close to 90 robots, and 10 work cells. The flow of AGVs and robot operations is controlled by seven intelligent programmable logic controllers (PLCs) that operate under directions from a supervisory microcomputer responsible for keeping the data base for build operations. The plant's mainframe is in charge of scheduling and issues short-term build directions to the microcomputer.

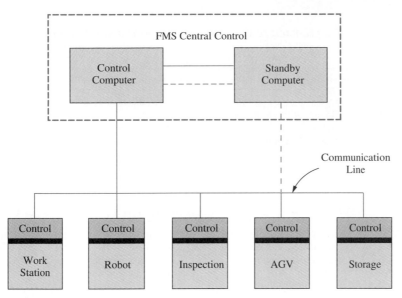

FIGURE 10-4
FMS control architecture

Among the advantages of this design are faster response of the supervisory computer and capability of handling crash situations. The down side includes complication of the control system design and connecting problems with the peer-to-peer communication.

Heterarchical design features distributed locally autonomous control components that communicate with other components *without* the master-slave relationship. These control components have information encapsulated into them, and modularity is emphasized. These control systems function as independent cooperating processes without centralized or explicit direct control. Control decisions are reached through "mutual agreement" and information is exchanged freely. The advantage is that quick response, flexibility, and robustness can be achieved. However, massive communication flow and myopic decisions may hamper the system. This type of control architecture is still very much a research issue, and only a limited number of applications exist. In Table 10-1, we summarize the four control architecture characteristics.

2.3   Interplant Integration

The pressures put on industrial organizations by the market created the need to push integration beyond the boundaries of a specific facility. This change is taking place in three major forms: different locations within the same organization, between the organization and its subsidiaries, and between the organization and external agents (suppliers and customers). The common denominator to all these forms is that their control systems communicate with each other. This is achieved through computer-to-computer exchange of inter- and intracompany business and technical data. The technology that implements this integration is known as electronic data interchange (EDI).

TABLE 10-1

Summary of control architecture characteristics, advantages, and disadvantages

Centralized		
Characteristics	**Advantages**	**Disadvantages**
• Single mainframe computer • All control decisions made at a single location • Global data base records all system activities	• Access to global information • Global optimization possible • Single source for system status information	• Slow and inconsistent speed of response • Reliance on single control unit • Difficult to modify control software

Proper Hierarchical		
Characteristics	**Advantages**	**Disadvantages**
• Multiple, variety of computers • Rigid master-slave relationships between decision-making levels • Supervisor coordinates all activities of subordinates • Aggregated data bases at each level	• Gradual implementation, redundancy, and reduced software development problems • Incremental addition of control possible • Possibility of adaptive behaviors • Allowance for differing time scales • Fast response times	• Computational limitations of local controllers • Increased number of interlevel communication links • Difficulties with dealing with dynamic adaptive control • Difficulty of making future unforseen modifications

Modified Hierarchical		
Characteristics	**Advantages**	**Disadvantages**
• Multiple, variety of computers • Loose master-slave relationships between decision-making levels • Supervisor initiates sequence of activities in subordinates • Subordinates cooperate to complete sequence	• All the advantages of proper hierarchical control • Ability of local systems to have local autonomy • Ability to off-load some linkage tasks to local controllers	• Most of the disadvantages of the proper hierarchical form • Conectivity problems • Limitations of low-level controllers • Increased difficulty of control system design

Heterarchical		
Characteristics	**Advantages**	**Disadvantages**
• Multiple, but less variety, computers • No master-slave relationships • Full local autonomy • Distributed decision making for activity coordination • Local data bases only	• Full local autonomy • Reduced software complexity • Implicit fault-tolerance • Ease of reconfigurability and adaptability • Faster diffusion of information	• Primarily due to technical limits of controllers • No standards for communications, protocols, or operating systems • High likelihood of only local optimization • Requires a high network capacity • Lack of availability of software

Source: Dilts, Boyd, and Whorms (1991), reprinted from the *Journal of Manufacturing Systems,* by permission of the Society of Manufacturing Engineers.

Within the same organization there may be a link that connects a number of functions located in different geographical locations sometimes around the globe. Product development may be in one country, marketing in another, and the production facility in yet a different country. (The Medicom Company described earlier is an example of such an organization.) Headquarters may allocate production orders to subsidiary production facilities in different countries based on available capacity, checked through EDI. It is therefore becoming more common that throughout a manufacturing organization, including its subsidiaries, the same software is used.

Data links between a company and its vendors are also becoming common. Not only data on orders and shipping details flow back and forth, but vendors that have long-term supply contracts with the company can access its inventory file and replenish it whenever necessary. Advantages are clear: Lead time is reduced, and postal costs and process delays are removed.

Computer communication with customers is also gaining popularity. For example, accessing the customer's computer aided design (CAD) software enables obtaining up-to-date product specifications and manufacturing the product accordingly.

Data links between the producer and its suppliers and customers provide one example of the increased scope of the business in the era of market-driven systems (Chapter 2, Figure 2-4). This increased level of integration should not be surprising in times where the World Wide Web is becoming commonplace.

2.3.1 INTEGRATED PRODUCTION PLANNING AND CONTROL. The new trend in production systems design is integrated production systems, which can be achieved through three major design approaches: cellular manufacturing, flexible manufacturing, and computer integrated manufacturing. It is only natural that a different production system will need a different approach to production planning and control. Since an integrated production system has a broader scope, so should its production planning and control (PPC) system. The difference between traditional PPC and integrated PPC is not limited to scope. Traditional PPC was regarded as no more than a production tool. Integrated PPC is much more than that. It is an embracing concept, with an underlying philosophy driving it and a set of tools to implement it. Most of the tools are computer based. On the face of it, the integrated production systems process and the integrated PPC process were totally disconnected. In retrospect, if one tries to philosophize about it, the two processes are closely related: Without integrated production systems there would have been no need for integrated PPC, and without integrated PPC, integrated production systems could achieve only limited objectives.

There are three major approaches to integrated PPC: push systems, pull systems, and bottleneck systems. Ironically, they all started as production tools and later evolved into PPC systems. The forerunner of push systems was a tool called material requirements planning (MRP), developed in 1974 by Joseph Orlicky of IBM. The forerunner of pull systems was the *kanban* system introduced in the late 1960s at Toyota by Taichi Ohno. The origin of bottleneck systems can be attributed to Eli Goldratt, an Israeli physicist, who introduced Optimized Technology (OPT) in the mid 1970s. Furthermore, the three approaches really represent global integration. Push systems originated in the United States, pull systems in Japan, and bottleneck systems in Israel, a three-continent integration. These three approaches are presented in detail in the next sections.

SECTION 2 PROBLEMS

10.1. What are the two major characteristics of integration?

10.2. What is the difference between lateral and vertical integration?

10.3. Give three examples of information flow and links for each of the following departments:

>   Sales–Manufacturing
>   Customer service–Manufacturing
>   Customer service–Sales
>   Quality control–Manufacturing
>   Manufacturing–Costing

10.4. Define the "fallen barriers syndrome."

10.5. Define "control architecture."

10.6. What are the basic forms of control architecture?

10.7. What are the advantages and disadvantages of each control form?

10.8. Classify the following operations to the appropriate control levels (production-floor, cell, machine):

>   Order release to production
>   Material handling within cells
>   Parts sequencing
>   Tool changeover
>   Part loading to machines

10.9. Analyze the following two control schemes:

(a) Routing is fixed and production sequence is known in advance. There are identical machines of the same type, and in real time a part is assigned to a machine with the shortest queue.

(b) Routing is dynamic, and the sequence of operation can be changed. Parts are assigned to machines according to queue length, order due dates, and the amount already produced.

What type of control architecture is suitable for each scenario? Why? What is the trade-off for using each control architecture? Why?

10.10. Citrus Ltd. is a manufacturer of concentrated juice and fruit extracts. Tough competition and market structure change generated pressure on the management to reduce costs. After reviewing several alternatives, management identified the raw-material warehouse as a significant source of none-value-added costs. Raw material is stored in barrels, and four barrels are stacked on a pallet. Forklifts are used to transport pallets to the proper destination. The warehouse is refrigerated to -18 degrees centigrade. An external consultant made the following observations:

- Storage and retrieval requests from the warehouse are handled manually. There is no computer-controlled location management system.
- Production schedules are transferred to the warehouse only two days in advance. Therefore, it is not possible to optimize storage and retrieval requests.
- Raw material is stored in other locations (rented), where the local warehouse utilization is less than 80 percent.
- Fast-moving items are sometimes stored in external locations.
- Shipments of imported raw material are not known in advance. It is then not possible to optimize storage requests.

- Lot tractability cannot be implemented, because there is no documentation of raw material assignment to production lots.
- Quality control tests are performed randomly on stored raw material. It is hard to find the required lots, which in turn causes waste of time and resources.

Answer the following questions:

(a) Classify these observations to symptoms and problems.
(b) Which problems are local to the warehouse and which are not? What is your conclusion?
(c) How can information integration solve (if it can at all!) these problems? Give examples.

3 PUSH SYSTEMS

3.1 Philosophy

Push systems have a technical component as well as an underlying managerial concept. The technical component deals with the way jobs are released into the production system and their flow through the system. As such, it can be viewed as a material-control tool, as described in Figure 10-5.

A due date for each job is determined, either from marketing or its following operation. Jobs are released on a start date, which is the due date minus a lead time. We emphasize that lead time is a deterministic planning parameter. Flow time is the actual time it takes the material to traverse the production system. It is variable, and we would like to reduce its variability as much as possible. Once released, the job flows from operation to operation through the production system regardless of what happens downstream. Hence the term **push** for this method; jobs are pushed through the production system. Another name for push systems is **schedule based systems,** since the schedule pushes the production.

The managerial concept underlying push systems is **central planning.** Decisions on how production orders will be processed are made centrally. These decisions are then pushed to lower levels of the organization; they must comply with the centrally generated schedule.

3.2 MRP II Systems

The terms *MRP II system* and *push system* are often used interchangeably. In concept, MRP II (like other integrated PPC methods) represents a striving toward manufacturing excellence.

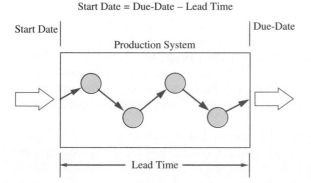

FIGURE 10-5
Push systems (backward scheduling)

More specifically, MRP II can be viewed as a method for the effective planning of all resources of a manufacturing organization. A formal definition is, MRP II *is a computer based planning, scheduling, and control system. It gives management a tool to plan and control its manufacturing activities and supporting operations, obtaining a higher level of customer service while reducing costs.* MRP II is an outgrowth of MRP. Initially, MRP was a computerized tool for scheduling and ordering materials. Later, it was used for replanning by updating due dates for shop orders, resulting in improved vendor and shop floor performance. Attempts to improve production planning, master production scheduling (MPS), and demand forecasting followed. With better MPS incorporated into MRP, it became a closed-loop MRP system. The next phase was improving capacity planning at various levels and adding simulation capabilities. This made it possible to generate financial plans based on the MRP planning process. Thus, MRP became a company-wide system, dealing with planning and controlling operations rather than just a tool for scheduling the flow of materials.

Wight (1984) proposed calling the new system manufacturing resource planning, with the acronym MRP II. The II was necessary to distinguish it from materials requirements planning (MRP). This name stuck since it emphasized the larger scope yet showed its MRP heritage. Figure 10-6 shows a closed-loop MRP II system. It is a much broader system than MRP. We discuss it further in the following section.

3.3   System Components

An MRP II system can be viewed as having three major components: management planning, operations planning, and operations execution. Upper management is responsible for management planning, staff units handle operations planning, and manufacturing personnel handle execution. Each major component has checkpoints to provide feedback information. The feedback determines the adequacy of overall resources, completeness of operations planning, and conformance of execution to plans and allows management to respond to changing conditions.

The company strategy is the basis for the activities of the upper management component of MRP II. Strategy is translated into business objectives for the current year. This, in turn, becomes input to the process of sales planning, in which, sales by product quantity and dollar volume are planned. Production planning, basically a delivery plan for manufacturing, follows. The production plan implies a commitment by every function of the organization to adhere to it.

The second component, operation planning, is the MRP function, previously discussed in detail. The output is an order release schedule for the execution component.

The execution section is where the real action takes place, i.e., where the product is manufactured. Raw material is purchased, material flow and production equipment are controlled, quality is assured, labor hours are tracked, etc. Problems on the production floor are fed back to the MRP component. Performance evaluation provides feedback to business planning for corrective action.

The MRP II model presented is general in nature. It can include more or fewer components than those shown (see Section 3.4). However, the MRP module is required; it is the engine that drives the whole system. So, MRP has not lost its role with the advent of MRP II.

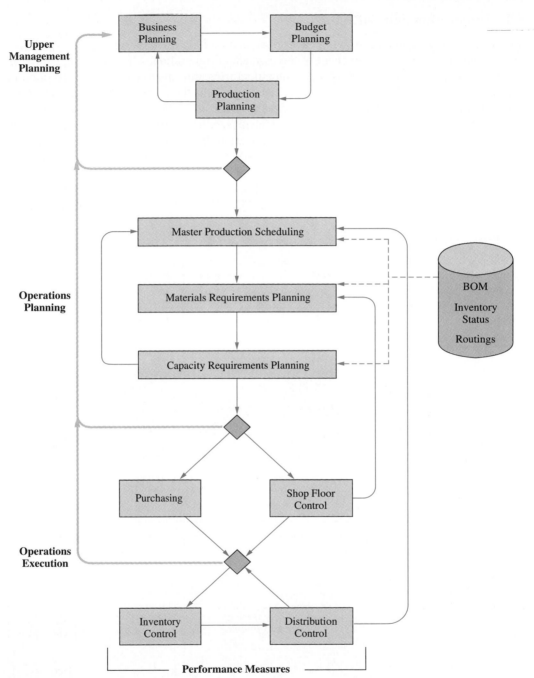

FIGURE 10-6
Functions and feedback loops in a closed-loop MRP II system (Riggs, copyright © 1987. Reprinted with permission of John Wiley & Sons, Inc.)

3.4 Integration and Software

We discuss integration and software under one heading for a good reason. Recall that information integration is one component of the essence of integration. MRP II, by its nature, is an information system (or even better, a manufacturing information system). Furthermore, because of the way MRP II systems were developed and the technical hardware and software limitations that existed during their development, an MRP II system actually consists of a number of separate modules that are interfaced (see Figure 10-6). Each module performs a different function or activity within the organization. Information integration is obviously embedded in the structure of MRP II. As such, MRP II can serve as a major aid in breaking the functional barriers within the organization.

Software is the heart of MRP II. Information integration occurs through the software. Therefore, software and integration are twins in MRP II. The breadth of integration depends

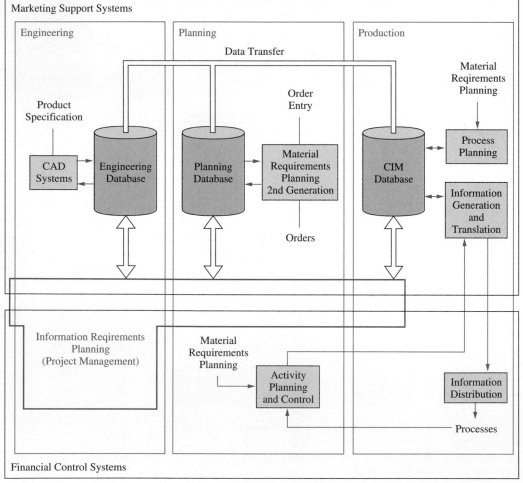

FIGURE 10-7
Generic CIM model (From Bolay et al. (1991), reprinted by permission of Alcatel Telephone, France)

on the number of modules used. For example, NVision, a start-up company in high definition television, reports initially using MRP II with more than 18 integrated modules (Jasany, 1991). The modules are accounts payable, accounts receivable, bank reconciliation, general ledger, inventory control, purchase order, bill of material, estimating, factory documentation, net requirements (requirement planning, capacity planning, resource planning, and job scheduling), work in progress, lot traceability, and job cost. This is an impressive array of activities integrated through MRP II.

There is another aspect of the MRP II role as an information integrator. It opens up opportunities for much broader integration within the manufacturing organization. For example, Alcatel, a multibillion-dollar French telecommunications manufacturer, reports using MRP II as a major constituent in achieving CIM (Bolay et al., 1989). The company's generic model for computer integrated manufacturing is shown in Figure 10-7. Whether CIM can be achieved or not remains to be seen. The important point is that MRP II can interface with other systems, such as computer aided design and manufacturing, quality control, and maintenance, yielding a higher degree of integration.

Sometimes the integration power of MRP II goes beyond company boundaries. Nissan has an MRP II system in place that provides hourly schedules to a number of its vendors. Its car seat supplier, for example, has its MRP II system linked with Nissan's ("Dialogues," 1987).

As previously discussed, software is the heart of MRP II. There are over 200 turnkey software packages commercially available. These run on mainframes, minicomputers, microcomputers, and individual workstations. Most of the software packages are designed for generic industrial applications. However, industry-specific packages are appearing as many industries have specific needs in MRP II. Pharmaceuticals companies have traceability requirements, aerospace industries must be able to comply with regulatory requirements, and plastic manufacturers need to keep track of complex materials formulations. Reprogramming a generic package to suit specific needs should be avoided if possible. It may create bugs, and introducing any updated version of the generic package will be a problem. The rule of thumb is, it is better to have a 100 percent working package meeting 90 percent of your requirements than to have a nonworking package meeting 100 percent of your requirements. Examples of common commercial software available are CONTROL (CINCOM) and AMAPS (Dun & Bradstreet) for mainframe computers, MAPICS XA (Marcam Corp.) for minicomputers, and very many for workstations and microcomputers. For a complete list, see "Buyer's Guide" (1995). Box 10-1 is an example of a typical microcomputer package.

BOX 10-1: MRP II PC SOFTWARE (*Manufacturing Engineer Software, 1990*)

MANUFACTURING PM™

HARDWARE SUPORTED:
  IBM AS/400, System/36, PS/2 Series; MS-DOS-based Hardware
OPERATING SYSTEMS:
  OS/400, SSP, OS/2, MS-DOS
SOURCE LANGUAGES:
  RPG II/III/400

BOX 10-1 (*continued*)

NUMBER OF CLIENTS/USERS:
  250
DESCRIPTION:
  Manufacturing PM is an online, integrated closed loop manufacturing system which includes: Customer Order Management; Product Data Base; Shop Floor and Inventory Control; Purchasing; Shop and Inventory Costing; Master Production Scheduling; Material Requirements Planning; Capacity Requirements Planning; Standard Product Costing; Stock Locator; Accounts Payable; General Ledger; and Accounts Receivable. Also included is full Help Text, online documentation, Alpha Search capabilities, plus an online disk requirements generator. A demo kit which features sample source code and full object code is available.

Source: Institute of Industrial Engineers, 25 Technology Park/Atlanta, Norcross, GA 30092, Copyright ©1990. Reprinted with permission.

MRP II software is constantly changing. Recent attempts to rename it without changing its nature have received lukewarm acceptance. Two of the more common renaming attempts are ERP and COMMS (Turbide, 1995).

ERP stands for enterprise resource planning; the name seeks to describe the next generation of MRP II systems. The system definition includes functionality plus new applications such as maintenance, quality, field service, marketing support, and a number of technology requirements like product configuration and engineering change control. One such software package that is gaining foothold is TRITON (Baan Intl.).

COMMS stands for customer-oriented manufacturing management systems. Its definition is similar to ERP's. It is broken down into three levels: planning, execution, and control. The execution layer falls under the heading of *manufacturing execution systems* and includes plant scheduling, quality, and material handling.

These two new systems should be looked upon as milestones on the development path of MRP II. Applications will become richer, adding more areas of the business. The need for wider scope of the business will generate stronger distribution management capabilities, electronic data interchange (EDI) and coordinated multiplant, multilocation management.

The cost of an MRP II package can start at a few hundred dollars for simple microcomputer software and can grow to several hundred thousand dollars for mainframe systems. The modularity feature of MRP II enables purchasing modules required immediately and adding more later. However, a cautionary note is in order: The cost of the package, especially for minicomputers and mainframes, does not represent the total investment in installing an MRP II system. There are hidden costs that are sometimes greater than the software purchase cost. They fall generally into three categories (Bolay et al., 1989):

- Reprogramming costs: Customizing a generic package, although not recommended, is sometimes done.
- Interfacing costs: The MRP II software may have to interface with existing modules or databases. This may represent substantial cost.

- Training costs: Introducing an MRP II system requires a lot of training. For example, ALCATEL Corporation reports that introducing MRP II in its Norway subsidiary required training more than 400 people at a substantial cost.

Because installing an MRP II system can be a major strategic move, as well as a major investment, Box 10-2 gives some tips from experts.

BOX 10-2: BUYING MRP II SOFTWARE: SOME TIPS FROM THE EXPERTS (Kreisher, 1988)

Software for MRP II will affect every phase of your manufacturing business, so you'd better be prepared to do your homework. This sounds like common sense, but most software suppliers that we spoke with said this can't be emphasized enough. Installed prices for turnkey systems, start at $50,000, and costs in the millions are common. So it's easy to see why a little thought is required before you leap.

Here's a list of things to consider before investing in a system. These recommendations have been gleaned from processors currently using MRP II systems, software suppliers, and independent consultants that have worked on installations in the plastics processing.

1. **Get Organized:** *You should first decide on which person, or group of people, will be responsible for system installation. The key here is to eliminate duplication of effort, a common and costly mistake. Most experts feel that it is best to establish a committee that includes personnel from every manufacturing area that will be affected. This includes personnel from the inventory control department, purchasing, quality control, and, of course, production. The experts also agree that it was a good idea to select a "point person" to lead the committee, and that this position was probably best filled by a production person.*

2. **Get a Consultant:** *For companies not large enough to devote a significant number of personnel to the task, both suppliers and users felt it was a good idea to enlist the help of a consultant. This can eliminate a lot of the busy work, give you an immediate idea of the costs, and get you started a lot more quickly.*

3. **Talk to Other Users:** *Virtually any reputable software supplier will put you in contact with plastics processors that are currently using its MRP II system. Again, this will give you an immediate idea of what you're up against, and you are sure to go back to suppliers with a whole new list of questions.*

4. **Ask About System Upgrades:** *There's almost nothing so fear-provoking as the thought that your system may become obsolete before it's up and working. Asking some questions about system upgrades will settle the issue. Most suppliers upgrade their systems periodically, and they will have a procedure spelled out in their purchase contract for supplying these upgrades to you. There may be a price attached.*

5. **Ask About Training:** *Most suppliers will provide training to some users at their facility, but it is unlikely that they will provide training to more than 10 users. Be prepared to have one individual become completely familiar with the system, so that he or she can train others. Or, perhaps the supplier will provide the extra training at*

BOX 10-2 (*continued*)

your own facility. Training is your chance to be creative: one processor, Gel Inc., in Livonia, Mich., uses the local public school system to train employees basic computer literacy as well as statistical analysis.

6. **Look for Flexibility:** *The things you need from MRP II may change. Look for a system that can grow with your operation. This goes for software and hardware. You may not want to invest in a complete system right away, so find a software package that is totally modular. This way you can expand the system without sacrificing performance. Also, find a software package that can be taken from microcomputers to minicomputers to mainframes without expensive reprogramming.*

7. **Get the Source Code:** *The source code to a computer software program is the list of instructions to the computer that makes the software operate. Without it, upgrading your system is impossible. In the unlikely event that your supplier goes out of business, you will need the source code to upgrade the system yourself, although this will be admittedly difficult, even with the code. Virtually all reputable suppliers have some means of supplying the source code in the case of such an emergency. This is usually accomplished by putting the code into an escrow account.*

Source: Reprinted with permission of *Plastics Technology,* July 1988.

3.5 Industrial Applications

There are numerous industrial applications of MRP II systems—too many to list here. We will give guidelines for implementation, one example application, and field results of using MRP II systems.

There are many guidelines presented in the literature for successful MRP II implementation. One common denominator is the need for upper management commitment. Introducing MRP II into an organization is a major change, and for it to succeed, management has to back it up fully. Beyond commitment there are different ways to achieve successful implementation. In Box 10-3, we present one that worked well for the Raymond Corporation, a manufacturer of material handling equipment and systems since 1920. Note the cross-functional team approach implied by this procedure. Box 10-4 contains a discussion of the use of MRP II at Huck Manufacturing.

BOX 10-3: MRP II AT THE RAYMOND COMPANY
(Quinlan, 1989)

DOING IT THE RIGHT WAY

- *Form a management project team to attack the problems. Include top people from every major function in the company.*
- *Get outside consulting help. Also, visit and observe companies that have gone through the same experience.*
- *Fix responsibility for progress, and set up procedures to measure performance.*

BOX 10-3 (*continued*)

- *Create a team spirit; do away with "foxhole mentality." Get shop and office people communicating with each other.*
- *Record and analyze cost-benefits as the program progresses. If a given procedure isn't creating benefits, drop it and try something else. Don't collect data for data's sake.*
- *Clean up databases, especially those for labor costs, bills of material, and inventories. The best, most expensive computer system will spew out only garbage if it's fed stale, inaccurate, incomplete data.*
- *Finally—it should be the last step—evaluate half a dozen computer hardware/software systems. The MRP II software should fit about 90 percent of your identified needs.*

"Most critical to your success," Stickler, the production manager, stresses, "is a willingness to change. If you're not willing to change, you'll only waste time and money. No computer system can solve your problems all by itself."

Source: Tooling and Production Magazine, October 1989. Reprinted with permission.

BOX 10-4: MRP II AT HUCK MANUFACTURING
("Technology Update," 1989)

MRP II UPS HUCK'S PROFITS

Huck Mfg Co, Irvine, CA, makes fasteners and fastener installation equipment for aerospace, automotive, railroad, and other industries using fabricated metal parts in their equipment. The company operates plants in the US, Canada, France, and the UK, and distributes worldwide.

In 1984, Huck decided to decentralize major business computer operations for its two fastener divisions and its equipment division. Primary goals were to reduce inventories and boost efficiency in manufacturing.

While shopping for a system, Huck kept three criteria in mind:

1. *The software would run in a decentralized mode. Each plant location would have its own copy of the software and its own main computer.*
2. *The software would be flexible enough to support diferences in business operations between the locations.*
3. *The computer system would be designed around the concepts of MRP II.*

First, five software vendors made one-day presentations to Huck's management. From those five, two were selected for in-depth evaluations. The system selected is MANMAN MRP II from ASK Computer Systems Inc, Mountain View, CA. Huck chose Hewlett-Packard equipment for the operating platforms.

During the evaluation process, Huck formed a steering committee that would oversee installation of MRP II at each of the three divisions. Training and education were given high priority.

BOX 10-4 (*continued*)

As it turned out, the most successful implementation occurred in the company's Industrial Fastener Div plant in Waco, TX. There project managers incorporated adoption of MRP II into daily routines.

"At Waco, sales have more than doubled since the MRP II system went into operation," reports Harold Borne, Huck's corporate MIS manager. "Nonetheless, the division has not had to increase its administrative staff by any significant amount."

Moreover, major improvements have been realized in on-time shipments and inventory turns. Accuracies of inventory counts, master production scheduling, material requirements planning, and bills of material have all improved substantially.

Accuracy of inventory counts is now up to a level where the division has been able to replace an annual physical inventory with a cycle-counting system. Further, profit margins have risen significantly since MRP II was implemented.

"We wouldn't have been able to sustain a doubling of business in Waco, had our MRP II system not been implemented," Borne concludes.

Source: *Tooling and Production Magazine*, October 1989. Reprinted with permission.

MRP II systems have been in use for some years now; there have been successes and failures. Success or failure depends on the manufacturing environment within which the system operates. A survey conducted by Business Education Associates ("News and Trends," 1988) showed that of the 400 companies that responded, 53 percent said they have been successful with MRP II. Within this group, the benefits of MRP II after one year were distributed as shown in Figure 10-8. As a specific example of MRP II benefits, Alcatel Corporation reports the following:

Order batch size:	40 percent reduction
Total lead time:	50 percent reduction
Inventory:	60 percent reduction
Work in process:	75 percent reduction
Delivery dates:	98 percent on time

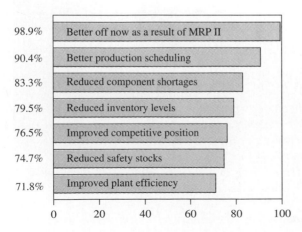

FIGURE 10-8
MRP II benefits ("News and Trends," 1988) (reprinted with permission of *Modern Materials Handling Magazine,* April, 1988, copyright © 1988 by Cahners Publishing Company)

One thing is certain; MRP II is a strong contender for the integrated PPC integrated production systems.

SECTION 3 PROBLEMS

10.11. What is the trigger for releasing orders to production in a push system?

10.12. Define the term *lead time*. What is the relationship between flowtime and lead time?

10.13. The actual time that a job spends in the shop floor was sampled six times. The results were (in days): 5, 6, 7, 5, 6, and 5. What would be a reasonable setting for the manufacturing lead time? What are the various considerations for setting the lead time in this case?

10.14. A major assumption behind the MRP principal is that the lead time is fixed. What are the implications of a nonconstant lead time (because of machine failures, process variability, etc.)?

10.15. Analyze the following scenario: Lead times are often set to be slightly longer than needed. This is done in order to compensate for unexpected events and to avoid shortages. As a result, jobs tend to spend more time on the shop floor, blocking it, and determining the appropriate lead time becomes even harder. When the shop floor is blocked, lead times are set to be even larger, because there is no way to know what is the real lead time.

    (a) What is the relationship between lead time and work in process?

    (b) What causes the lead time to finally stabilize?

    (c) What are the possible causes for this problem?

    (d) Is there a way to avoid this vicious circle?

10.16. What is the difference between MRP II and MRP?

10.17. What are the direct and indirect costs of installing an MRP II system?

10.18. The key concept behind push systems is central planning. Explain why.

10.19. What are the types of feedback an MRP II system needs in order to operate?

10.20. What aspects of a manufacturing organization are integrated through the use of an MRP II system?

10.21. What aspects of a manufacturing system are expected to improve as a result of an MRP II installation?

4   PULL SYSTEMS

4.1   Philosophy

Like push systems, pull systems have a technical component and a managerial concept. The technical component is an outgrowth of a production control technique developed at the Toyota Motor Company in Japan in the early 1960s. Its origin is generally attributed to Ohno and Shingo, both with Toyota at that time. The technique became known as the *Toyota production system.* The goal is to provide a simple production control technique that reduces lead time and work in process (WIP). **Kanban,** the Japanese word for **card,** is the tool originally used to achieve these objectives. This approach enhanced Toyota's ability to meet customers' demand for different car models with minimum delay, i.e., with maximum flexibility.

    There is a subtle difference between push systems and pull systems. A push system controls work release orders, whereas a pull system controls the shop floor. To be more specific, push systems control throughput (by controlling work release) and measure WIP, whereas pull systems control WIP and measure throughput (Spearman, 1992).

    As time passed, the **pull** technique evolved into a much broader managerial concept. It is often called the just-in-time (JIT) or integrated JIT system. This is no longer a "production

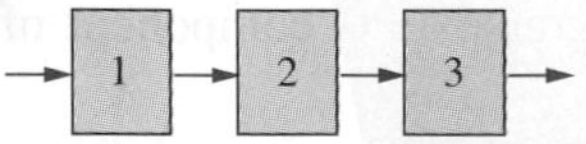

FIGURE 10-9
Sequential interdependence

system to produce the kind of units needed, at the time needed and in the quantities needed" (Monden, 1981), but rather a more embracing concept. It encompasses not only the production systems but suppliers and customers along with controlling quality and work flow. The scope is expanded to include eliminating waste in every shape and form (inventory, bad products, long delivery times, late deliveries, and more). This makes integrated JIT part of a corporate business strategy as well as an integrated PPC tool.

To clarify some terminology, *pull* is a material-flow governing principle. *Kanban* is one manual method to implement a pull system. JIT refers to the whole system, material-flow control and management philosophy. However, in industry JIT may sometimes mean nothing more than another name for a *kanban* system.

4.2 The Pull Principle

Pull systems have been around for many years, and many definitions of *pull* have emerged. The one we believe captures the true spirit of the pull concept is **management of interdependence.** A distinguishing characteristic of a pull system is its approach to dealing with interdependence, particularly in manufacturing operations (Arogyaswamy and Simmons, 1991).

In order to manufacture a product, the job is divided into individual tasks, typically manufacturing or assembly processes. These tasks are interdependent and should be coordinated. Thompson[2] defines a number of interdependency types, two of which, sequential and reciprocal, are relevant to the production floor.

Sequential interdependence is shown in Figure 10-9. Each operation's output is dependent on input from one (or more) preceding operations; i.e., operation 2 is dependent on material flowing from operation 1, and operation 3 is dependent on operation 2. Shutting down operation 1 affects all downstream operations. However, if operation 3 is shut down, none of the upstream operations will be affected; they will continue processing the material, creating in-process inventory until buffers are full. To reduce the interdependence between downstream and upstream operations and to maintain the output of the production line, it is common to introduce buffers between the operations (Figure 10-10). These buffers decouple operations and eliminate the interdependency unless the buffer is emptied when a shutdown occurs upstream. However, if a failure occurs in operation 2, operation 1 is insensitive to that and will keep processing and increasing inventory in the buffer following it.

Reciprocal interdependence is shown in Figure 10-11. It is reciprocal because there is a two-way relationship between operations 1 and 2 and operations 2 and 3. In this relationship, each operation affects and is affected by one or more other operations, requiring mutual

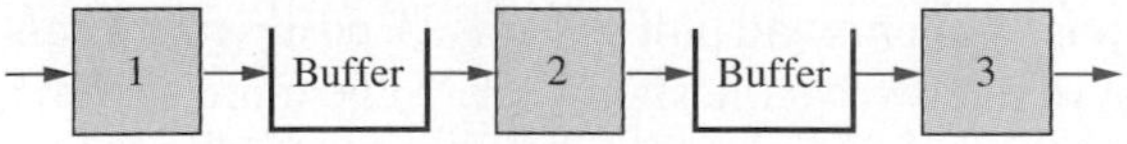

FIGURE 10-10
Operations decoupling

[2]Adapted from Thompson (1967), reproduced with permission of the McGraw-Hill Companies, Inc.

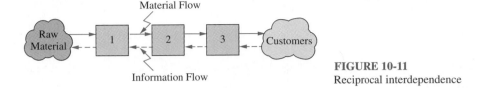

FIGURE 10-11
Reciprocal interdependence

adjustment for their coordination (Thompson, 1967). A shutdown of an upstream operation will affect downstream operations, and vice versa.

The two-way relationship shown in Figure 10-11 can be material flow downstream and information flow upstream. Thus, operation 2 is dependent on operation 1 for **material,** whereas operation 1 is dependent on operation 2 for **information.** In this system, a shutdown of operation 3 will affect operation 2 because of the information flow. In the same way, operation 2 will not start unless it gets an information signal from operation 3 that a product has been withdrawn from the last station. This information will flow upstream and trigger release of raw material to operation 1.

Reciprocal interdependence is the basic principle governing the pull system. Material flows downstream and information flows upstream. A signal from an operation downstream to its preceding operation upstream calls for the required quantity of an item. A pull system transforms a sequential interdependent system to a reciprocal interdependent system. This principle is similar to the one used by American supermarkets; products are pulled onto the shelves according to the demand rate. As a matter of fact, Ohno cites the American supermarket system as the inspiration for the pull system installed at Toyota. The application of the pull principle is commonly known as a JIT system. We discuss it next.

4.3   JIT Systems

JIT systems combine both the production-control component and a management philosophy. Four basic tenets are required for the success of a JIT system (Golhar and Stam, 1991):

- Elimination of waste
- Employee involvement in decision making
- Supplier participation
- Total quality control

Waste is closely related to cost-adding processes (Chapter 2). Of all types of waste, inventory has attracted the most attention. The claim is that excess inventory covers other types of wastes. Reducing inventory, a JIT objective, uncovers these problems. To amplify the issue, a rocks-and-river analogy is often used (Figure 10-12). Rocks are problems, and the river represents the material flowing through the plant. The river level is equated to WIP. When the river level is high, problems are covered. Lowering the river level exposes the problems, the first step required to solve them.

Employee involvement as part of the JIT philosophy is in line with the culture of market-driven systems. In a JIT system this is achieved through teamwork and employee empowerment. Each employee is given more responsibility for the production process. A typical example is responsibility for quality. Its extreme expression is that every employee can stop the whole production line if quality is not satisfactory. This is known as *Jidoka* in the Japanese terminology.

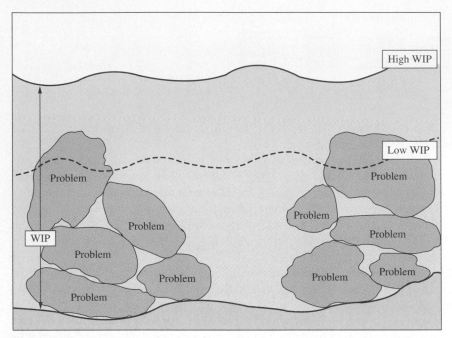

FIGURE 10-12
Rocks-and-river analogy

Supplier participation indicates a different working relationship with the suppliers. Instead of being looked upon as adversaries, suppliers are regarded as partners. The tendency is to reduce the number of suppliers and establish long-term associations with them. This process is also part of the TQM approach, which was discussed in Chapter 2. Its impact is greater when implemented as part of the JIT philosophy.

4.4 *Kanban* Systems

In Japanese, *kanban* means *card* or *visible record.* In a broader sense, it is a communication signal from a consumer (such as a downstream process) to a producer (such as an upstream process). As such, it is a manual information system to control production, material transportation, and inventory. There are different types of *kanban,* but two are most common, production *kanbans* (P-*kanbans*) and transportation *kanbans* (T-*kanbans*). As the name implies, a P-*kanban* authorizes a process to produce a fixed amount of product. A T-*kanban* authorizes transporting a fixed amount of product downstream. The amount of material specified by the P-*kanban* and the T-*kanban* are not necessarily equal. Examples of typical P-*kanbans* and T-*kanbans* are shown in Figure 10-13.

When both *kanbans* are used, we have a dual-card system. Sometimes the production ordering and transportation functions are combined, resulting in a single-card system.

4.4.1 DUAL-CARD SYSTEM. A dual-card system is shown in Figure 10-14. Upstream workcenter $(i - 1)$ supplies downstream workcenter i. Each workcenter has five components:

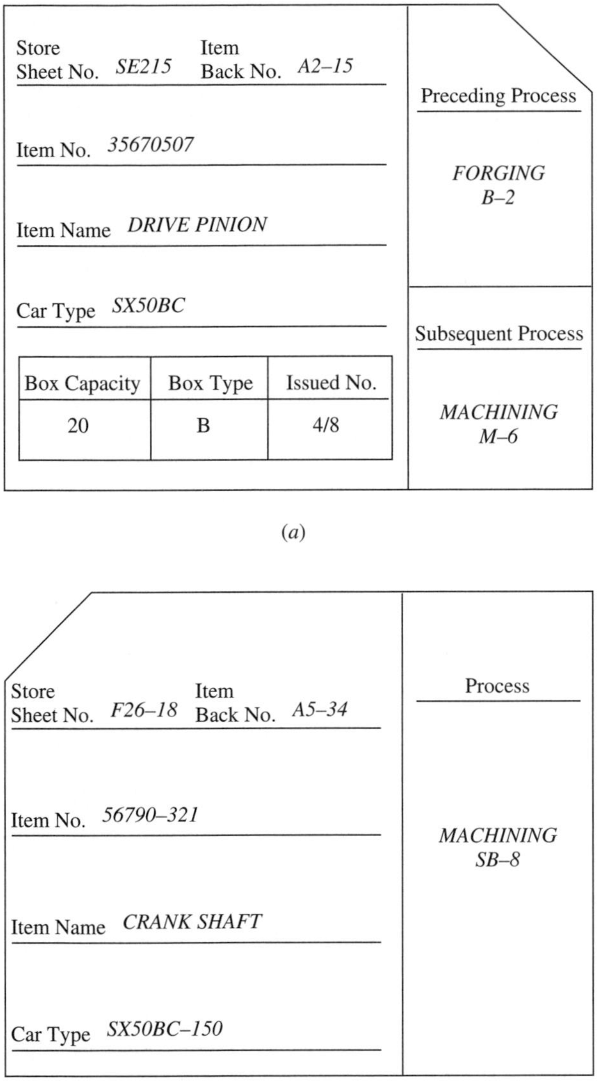

Store Sheet No. *SE215*	Item Back No. *A2–15*		Preceding Process
Item No. *35670507*			FORGING B–2
Item Name *DRIVE PINION*			
Car Type *SX50BC*			Subsequent Process
Box Capacity	Box Type	Issued No.	MACHINING M–6
20	B	4/8	

(a)

Store Sheet No. *F26–18*	Item Back No. *A5–34*	Process
Item No. *56790–321*		MACHINING SB–8
Item Name *CRANK SHAFT*		
Car Type *SX50BC–150*		

(b)

FIGURE 10-13
Two types of *kanban*: (a) T-*kanban*, (b) P-*kanban* (Monden (1993) with the permission of the Institute of Industrial Engineers, 25 Technology Park/Atlanta, Norcross, GA 30092, copyright © 1993)

- Production cell, where the conversion process takes place
- Input store (A)
- Output store (B)
- P-*kanban* post (C)
- T-*kanban* post (D)

The system has two control loops, a P-loop to control cell operation and a T-loop to control material transfer between workcenters. Parts are stored in containers. Each container holds a fixed amount of product that a P-*kanban* authorizes to produce, or a T-*kanban* authorizes to move. Each container in the input store (A) has a T-*kanban* attached. Similarly, each container

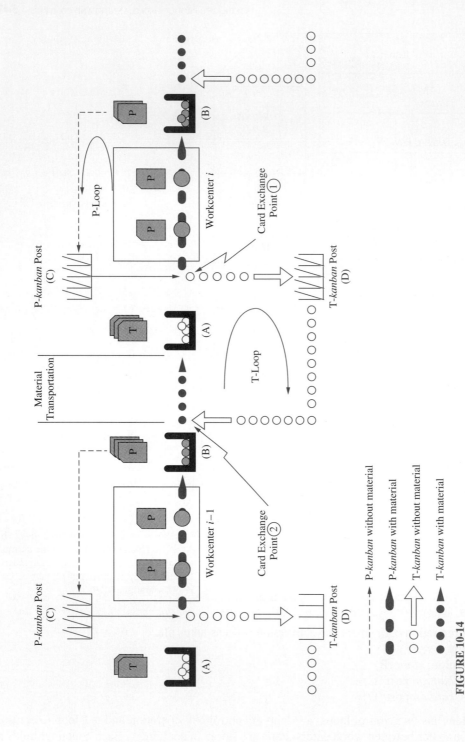

FIGURE 10-14
A dual-card *kanban* system

in the output store (B) has a P-*kanban* attached. To understand how the system operates, we discuss each loop separately.

P-loop. When a predetermined number (batch) of P-*kanbans* is accumulated at the P-*kanban* post (C) of workcenter *i*, it signals workcenter *i* to produce a batch. P-*kanbans* are removed from the post to the card exchange point (1) at the input store (A). There, the T-*kanban* is removed from each container and replaced by a P-*kanban*. The T-*kanbans* are placed in the T-*kanban* post (D). The number of containers in this exchange is equal to the number of P-*kanbans* on the post. Production starts and each container has its P-*kanban* attached. Upon completion, the finished batch is placed in output store (B) with the P-cards still attached. When a container is removed from the output store (B), its P-*kanban* is detached and again placed on the P-*kanban* post (C). The P-*kanban* post makes the *kanbans* visible and shows the queue of work to be performed in the cell.

T-loop. When a predetermined number of T-*kanbans* is accumulated, they are removed from the T-*kanban* post (D) of workcenter *i* and taken to the card exchange point (2) of workcenter $(i-1)$. The P-*kanbans* are removed from each box and replaced by T-*kanbans*. The P-*kanbans* are put on the P-*kanban* post of workcenter $(i-1)$ and the containers with a T-*kanban* are transported to the input store (A) of workcenter *i*. The quantity trigger for T-*kanban* removal is sometimes replaced by a time trigger where T-*kanban* pickup is performed at fixed time intervals.

This discussion of the P-loop and the T-loop demonstrates how the reciprocal interdependence of a pull system works.

There are three major guidelines for *kanban* systems: there is no material container in the system without a *kanban* attached to it, only a P-*kanban* authorizes production, and only a T-*kanban* authorizes transportation. These guidelines force all workcenters to be nearly synchronized. Suppose a breakdown occurs at station *i*. All workcenters downstream will run out of material to work on. All stations upstream will run out of posted P-*kanbans* to authorize production, because T-*kanbans* will not flow upstream to release P-*kanbans*. This results in an almost-synchronized production line. The speed at which interruptions travel along the line depends on the number of *kanbans*. Because there is no material without a *kanban* attached to it, the number of *kanbans* controls the level of inventory in the system.

Kanban systems work best when *demand is level* and waste is minimized. Specifically, when set-up times are small (discussed later), equipment is reliable, and defective products are never transported to a downstream workcenter.

To avoid transfer of defective products, Toyota developed methods and devices for automatic control of defects. It is called *Jidoka* in Japanese, and the English term is **autonomation** (not to be confused with automation). Although autonomation has to do with some type of automation, it can be used in conjunction with manual operations as well. In either case, it is mainly a technique to detect defects and a mechanism to stop production when abnormalities occur.

4.4.2 SINGLE-CARD SYSTEMS. In some cases, it is sufficient to use a single card. Simplicity is gained at the cost of losing some control. Transportation of material is still controlled by T-*kanbans,* but there are no P-*kanbans*. Instead, parts are produced according to a daily schedule and are moved downstream by T-*kanbans*.

In a sense, the single-card system is a combination of push control for production (i.e., producing to a schedule) combined with pull control for deliveries. Inventory will probably be higher in this system because of the schedule-driven production. Single-card systems operate well when production lead time is short and it is possible to create a detailed production schedule. The concept behind the single-card system is similar to the classic two-bin inventory control policy.

An important derivative of the single-card system is the *kanban* square, first introduced in Chapter 2 (Figure 2-8). It acts as a T-*kanban;* when empty, it signals the upstream operation to start production and provide another unit to fill the square. This type of system is sometimes called an *overlapped system,* in contrast to a card system, which is sometimes called a *linked system.* The overlapped system is used when workstations are close together. Visual inspection triggers the replenishment decision. For more on single-card systems, see Schoenberger (1983).

4.4.3 *KANBAN* SYSTEM CHARACTERISTICS.

A *kanban* system is not for everybody. It works best when flow is uniform and the product mix is highly stable. An implied assumption in a *kanban* system is that set-up operations are short at every workcenter. This is required so that every workcenter can switch production of parts as frequently as needed to meet changes in demand specified by the P-*kanbans*.

When there is uniform flow, the *kanban* system operates like a bucket brigade. Everyone in the chain spends about the same amount of time passing the bucket, and no inventory of buckets is needed. If output slows down, the whole chain slows down, and if it speeds up, the chain will speed up. The maximum speed is constrained by the slowest bucket passer and, for most JIT systems, is designed so that it will be less than maximum demand. Variability disrupts a *kanban* system. Extra cards (or containers) must be introduced to avoid backorders.

Finally, *kanban* does not work well in systems with many active stock numbers. The large number of *kanbans* required will increase inventories, and they will be difficult to control since a manual information system is used.

Pull control can be implemented in ways other than *kanban*. For example, the containers themselves may replace the P-*kanban*. T-*kanbans* can be replaced by electronic communications or a light signal to indicate the need for more material.

4.5 JIT Models

There is a vast body of literature describing different aspects of the JIT system. Some studies are empirical, some use simulation, and others use quantitative models. We present models for four aspects of JIT; three relate to the *kanban* system, and one relates to the JIT system itself. They are sequencing mixed-model pull systems, number of *kanbans* required, time-based material flow in a *kanban* system, and, discussed in Section 4.7, the economics of set-up reduction.

4.5.1 SEQUENCING MIXED-MODEL PULL PRODUCTION SYSTEMS.

Modern manufacturers often produce several similar, but not identical, items on the same line. An example is an automobile manufacturer that produces both three- and four-speed automatic transmissions and four- and five-speed manual transmissions on the same production line. Since the line is designed with zero set-up times, a five-speed manual transmission may be followed by a three-speed automatic, rather than producing all of one type together. This is an integral part of the "Toyota Production System."

The two major goals of the system are **balancing the line** and ensuring a **constant rate of usage** of parts for the different products. Balancing the line is a design problem. Assuming the line is balanced with cycle time CT, the line will complete one job every CT time units. The throughput time for each job will be $m(CT)$, where m is the number of stations in the line. The sequence of products made greatly affects the rate of usage of the parts.

Monden (1993), describes the "goal-chasing algorithm" Toyota uses to try to determine the multiproduct sequence that maintains the most nearly constant rate of usage of every component part. Define one time unit to be mCT; actually, it takes mCT to produce a unit, but because they overlap, a unit is completed every CT time units. We will ignore the time of overlap in the discussion. Let

n = the number of different products to be made

D_i = the integral number of units demanded over the scheduling horizon for product i, $i = 1, 2, \ldots, n$

$T = D_1 + D_2 + \cdots + D_n$ be the total number of units of all products to be made

T is also the time, in "units," to produce all items. If the goal is to schedule a constant rate of production of each product, the ideal production rate for product i at time t is given by

$$tD_i / \sum_{k=1}^{t} D_k$$

We wish to have the actual production rate for each product closely approximate the ideal rate at each stage. Let x_{it} be the cumulative number of units of product i produced up to and including time unit t. This leads to the following mathematical objective function:

$$\text{Minimize} \sum_{t=1}^{T} \sum_{i=1}^{n} \left(x_{it} - \left(tD_i / \sum_{k=1}^{t} D_k \right) \right)^2$$

Solving the scheduling problem for this objective is difficult. For complete details, see Monden (1993) or Miltenburg (1989).

Alternatively, the goal of scheduling a constant rate of production of each product can be achieved by maintaining a constant interval between the completion of each unit of product i. This suggests that each job has an ideal completion time, so we assign a due date to each job that reflects this ideal completion time. We propose to minimize the deviation (absolute or squared) between the due dates and the actual completion times. This will penalize a job for being completed early as well as late.

We must make D_i units of product i over the time horizon $T = \sum_{i=1}^{n} D_i$, so a constant production rate would be to complete one unit of product i every T/D_i cycles. If $T = 10$ and $D_1 = 1$, we would like to complete one unit every 10 cycles. Assuming the schedule will repeat, this is done by completing the unit at time 5; in the next cycle it will complete at time 15, 10 cycles apart. If $D_1 = 2$, we would like to complete a unit every five cycles, so there should be five cycles between the due dates of the first and second units of product 1. If the schedule is repeated, there should also be five cycles between the last unit in the first schedule and the first unit in the second. Setting the due date of the first unit at 2.5 and the second at 7.5 will provide exactly five cycles between each unit no matter how many times the sequence repeats. For product i, let

j be the index for each unit of product i ($j = 1, 2, \ldots, D_i$)

d_{ij} be its ideal completion, or due date.

The due date for the first job (unit) of product i is

$$d_{i1} = T/(2D_i)$$

and the ideal completion time for the second job (unit) of product i is

$$d_{i2} = d_{i1} + T/D_i$$
$$= 3T/(2D_i)$$

In general, the due date for job j of product i is

$$d_{ij} = (j - 1/2)T/D_i$$

These ideal completion times simply spread out production as much as possible, presuming there was (and will be) production of essentially the same products before (and after) time T.

The objective is to minimize the total deviation (absolute or squared) between the due dates and the actual completion times. Let t_{ij} denote the completion time of job j of product type i. Using the deviation-squared objective function, the problem is to sequence the unit processing time jobs with given due dates to

$$\text{Minimize} \sum_{i=1}^{n} \sum_{j=1}^{D_i} (t_{ij} - d_{ij})^2$$

This problem is easily solved by sequencing the jobs according to earliest due date (EDD) first. While the EDD sequence minimizes the deviation from the due dates, there is no guarantee that it produces optimal sequences for the cumulative production measure. Given the way due dates are generated, there are often ties in the EDD sequence; to accommodate the cumulative-production objective function, we break ties by giving preference to the job whose product has the largest demand.

Inman and Bulfin (1991) show that, on average, the EDD approach takes little time for large problems and gives slightly better sequences for the cumulative objective than Miltenburg's (1989) heuristic.

> **Example 10-1. Mixed-model scheduling.** A mixed-model production line makes three different shortwave radios. Demand for the next week is 600 basic, 600 intermediate, and 100 advanced radios. How should they be sequenced to smooth part usage? (The numbers for this example are from Miltenburg (1989).)
>
> *Solution.* First, this problem can be reduced to repeating sequences with 6, 6, and 1 of each type radio one hundred times, so we have $n = 3$, $D_1 = 6$, $D_2 = 6$, $D_3 = 1$, and $T = 13$. Table 10-2 gives the due dates for each unit of each radio.
> Ordering these jobs according to EDD results in the schedule I-B-I-B-I-B-A-B-I-B-I-B-I, which is the optimal sequence for both objectives. This schedule would repeat 100 times. Figure 10-15 is a Gantt Chart for the first two repetitions.

4.5.2 NUMBER OF *KANBANS* REQUIRED. There are a number of methods to determine how many *kanbans* are needed. We present the original method used by Toyota to set the number of *kanbans* (Monden, 1993). This method is still in common use today. Let

TABLE 10-2
Due-date calculation for radios

Product (i)	Unit (j)	d_{ij}	c_{ij}
Basic (B)	1	13/12 = 1.08	1
	2	39/12 = 3.25	3
	3	65/12 = 5.42	5
	4	91/12 = 7.58	8
	5	117/12 = 9.75	10
	6	143/12 = 11.92	12
Intermediate (I)	1	13/12 = 1.08	2
	2	39/12 = 3.25	4
	3	65/12 = 5.42	6
	4	91/12 = 7.58	9
	5	117/12 = 9.75	11
	6	143/12 = 11.92	13
Advanced (A)	1	13/2 = 6.50	7

c_{ij} = completion time

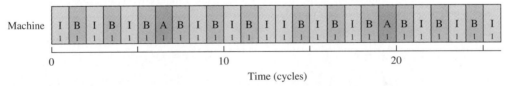

Machine
I B I B I B A B I B I B I I B I B I B A B I B I B I
0
10
20
Time (cycles)

FIGURE 10-15
EDD Mixed-model production schedule

n = number of P- and T-*kanban* sets for a given part
D = demand per unit time, usually a day (D is taken as the leveled demand)
L = average lead time for the *kanban,* in decimal fraction of a day
t_p = average processing time per container, in decimal fraction of a day
t_w = average waiting during the production process plus transportation time per container, in decimal fraction of a day
C = container capacity, in units of products (not more than 10 percent of daily demand)
α = a safety coefficient (not over 10 percent)

Then

$$L = t_p + t_w$$

and

$$n = \frac{DL(1+\alpha)}{C}$$

The numerator represents average demand during lead time plus a safety stock.

The average lead time for P-*kanbans* depends on both the actual manufacturing time and the time spent in the *kanban* queue at the production *kanban* post. For transportation *kanbans*, L is the time that elapses between a T-*kanban* being placed on the T-*kanban* post and its return to the input store. Thus, L is determined by the frequency of pickups and transportation time.

Toyota's practice is to leave the value of n relatively fixed in spite of variations in D. Thus, when D increases, the lead time L must be decreased. If this cannot be achieved through improvement processes, overtime will result. Overtime is waste—something that should be eliminated. Increasing the number of *kanbans* is an alternative, but it will increase WIP, another type of waste. Therefore, α is viewed by management as an indicator of the shop's improvement capability. A smaller α implies a better shop operation. Reduction in WIP can be achieved by reducing α or L.

In the following example, we show how to determine the number of *kanbans*.

Example 10-2. Calculating the number of *kanbans*. The Chipcard Company is a small manufacturer of printed circuit boards (PCBs) for the electronics industry. One phase of the manufacturing process is performed sequentially in a cell with three machines. The three machines perform radial component insertion, axial component insertion, and odd-form component insertion. When the PCB leaves the cell, it moves to a wave soldering machine.

The daily demand for PCBs is 900 units. They are moved between machines in small containers; each holds 15 PCBs. A container spends 0.05 days in processing and 0.12 days in waiting and transportation during the manufacturing cycle. Management policy is to have safety stock equal to 8 percent of lead time demand; i.e., $\alpha = .08$.

Given the above data, the number of *kanban* sets required is

$$n = \frac{900 \times (0.05 + 0.12) \times 1.08}{15} \approx 11$$

Using 11 *kanban* sets, the number of P-*kanbans* is

$$\frac{900 \times 0.12 \times 1.08}{15} \approx 8$$

while the number of T-*kanbans* is

$$\frac{900 \times 0.05 \times 1.08}{15} \approx 3$$

The maximum WIP is 165 boards (11 containers times 15 boards per container).

After an improvement process, total lead time was cut by 20 percent to 0.136 days per container. As a result, the number of *kanbans* required was reduced to

$$\frac{900 \times 0.136 \times 1.08}{15} \approx 9$$

with a corresponding decrease of in-process inventory to 135.

4.5.3   TIME-BASED MATERIAL FLOW. A time-based material flow model of a *kanban* system is presented in Buzacott and Shanthikumar (1993). Their model is actually a generic model for material flow through cells in series as described in Figure 10-14. The model provides a time-based analysis of events such as raw material arrival time and time at which a P-*kanban* is generated. One of the model findings relates to work in process. Placing more initial inventory at later stages of the system provides better service to customer demands. If the product's value added at intermediate stages is negligible, then it is optimal to have all inventory at the final stage.

A common approach to JIT modeling is closed-loop queuing networks (see Graves et al., 1993, for a good review of such models). For most practical applications, queuing models become too cumbersome to solve, and simulation is used instead. Either general purpose simulation packages (e.g., GPSS, SIMAN, and SLAM) or more production-floor oriented packages (e.g., CINEMA, XCELL, and WITNESS) can be used. Many of the simulation packages have color graphics capability, which enhances the analysis. In addition, it is an important aid in conveying the analysis to management.

4.6 CONWIP Models

CONWIP stands for *constant work in process*. This is an approach to pull systems introduced by Spearman et al. (1990). *Kanban* systems work best with uniform flow, a highly stable to develop a system that possesses the benefits of a pull system but can be used in a wider variety of manufacturing environments.

To describe CONWIP, we assume a single production line where parts are moved in containers, and each container holds roughly the same amount of "work content." This ensures that the processing time at each workstation, including a bottleneck, will be about the same. A CONWIP system and a standard *kanban* system are shown in Figure 10-16. Like *kanban*, CONWIP relies on an information signal—either cards, electronic, or the containers themselves. The card is attached to a container at the beginning of the line and travels with it until the end of the line. At that point, the card is removed from the container and returned

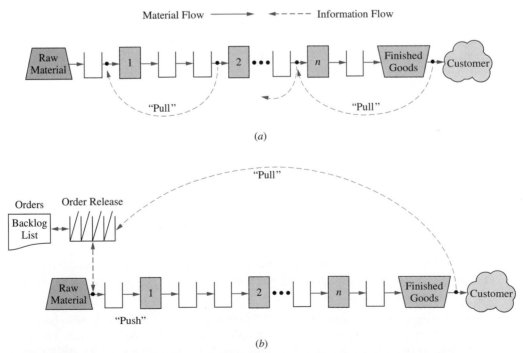

FIGURE 10-16
Comparison of (a) *kanban* and (b) CONWIP systems

to a card queue at the beginning of the line. Eventually, the card will leave the queue (also called a *backlog list*) and be attached to another container of parts in order to traverse the production line again.

In a *kanban* system, a T-*kanban* traverses a loop to the next workcenter downstream and back. In a CONWIP system, the card traverses a circuit that includes the whole production line. Furthermore, in a *kanban* system, each P-*kanban* signals production of a specific product. In a CONWIP line, production cards are assigned to the line rather than a specific product. Part numbers are assigned to the cards at the beginning of the production line. CONWIP systems are similar to single-card systems, since they use a schedule and a T-*kanban*.

The part numbers are taken from a backlog list. The backlog list is generated from a master production schedule or firm orders that are added to the list as they are received. The backlog list dictates what goes into the line, and the card decides when. Only when a card is available will a container enter the line. It will signal production of the first part number on the backlog list that has raw materials available. Note that if no card is available, no container enters the line even if the first workcenter is idle.

CONWIP is a hybrid of push and pull systems. A push system initiates production in anticipation of future demand; for CONWIP the backlog list, based on the MPS, carries out this function. Pull systems respond to present demand, in a fashion similar to the CONWIP card system. Another difference between CONWIP and push is the built-in feedback system (true for all pull systems).

Spearman and Zanzanis (1992) give the following differences between "pure *kanban*" and CONWIP systems:

- CONWIP uses a backlog list to dictate the part number sequence.
- In CONWIP, cards are associated with all parts produced on a line rather than individual part numbers.
- In CONWIP, jobs are pushed between workstations in series once they have been authorized by a card to start at the beginning of the line.

It is claimed that CONWIP, because of its card-per-line approach, better handles production lines that produce many parts. The backlog list copes with fluctuating demand and longer set-ups, as there is explicit control of which parts are produced and in what sequence. Some theoretical analysis shows that CONWIP will result in lower WIP levels than a *kanban* system with the same throughput (Spearman and Zanzanis, 1992). Finally, it is estimated that the most favorable case for applying CONWIP is the one in which a company attempts to operate its production lines near capacity.

To enhance the CONWIP model discussion, we present two models, CONWIP control and CONWIP performance evaluation.

4.6.1 CONTROLLING CONWIP–BASED PRODUCTION. Like any other production control method, there are important operating parameters that must be determined in order to implement this control method. Let

n = The card or container count. In a CONWIP-controlled line, the WIP is bounded, and usually the line operates with the maximum level of WIP possible. This is an important issue, since the robust flow time that characterizes a CONWIP system is related to WIP. Using Little's Law,

$$\text{Flowtime} = \frac{\text{WIP}}{\text{Input rate}}$$

The input rate is of course equal to the output rate. For a given input rate and a fixed level of WIP, the flowtime approximation is very robust.

As in any other production control system, changing the value of these parameters involves trade-offs. Increasing the card count would increase the flowtime (inventories) and service level at the same time. We next show how the card count n can be determined, modifying a method described by Hopp and Spearman (1991).

We consider the same CONWIP line configuration depicted in Figure 10-16. We also assume

- Infinite demand, which implies maximum level of WIP, and the line is working all the time.
- Processing times are fixed. This is a reasonable assumption, since in a highly automated production environment, process variability is very small.
- A single item is being produced.

The question is, how much WIP is really needed?

Let

$m = $ Number of machines
$n = $ The card (container) count
$t_i = $ Processing time on machine i, $i = 1, 2, \ldots, m$
$t_{BN} = $ Processing time on the bottleneck machine, $t_{BN} = \max_{i=1,m} t_i$

We would like the bottleneck machine to work all the time. Since the system is deterministic, queues can only occur before the bottleneck machine. If a certain container leaves the bottleneck machine, the time it takes for it to return to the bottleneck is the sum of the processing times on all other nonbottleneck machines. This is

$$\sum_{i=1}^{m} t_i - t_{BN}$$

During this time, the bottleneck must process all other $(n-1)$ containers, assuming there are n containers in the system (the card count). This time is equal to

$$(n-1)t_{BN}$$

If the bottleneck processes the container under consideration and works all the time, the time it takes for a container to reach the bottleneck must be less than or equal to the time it takes for the bottleneck to process all other $n - 1$ containers. In other words,

$$(n-1)t_{BN} \geq \sum_{i=1}^{m} t_i - t_{BN}$$

or

$$n = \sum_{i=1}^{m} t_i / t_{BN}$$

In practice, the number of containers is an integer. In order that the bottleneck would work all the time, the container-count n must be rounded to the closest integer larger than n. In this case some queue would form in front of the bottleneck machine.

4.6.2 EVALUATING PERFORMANCE OF CONWIP CONTROL. An important issue in CONWIP system implementation is performance evaluation. The approach of pull systems is, "Set WIP and measure throughput," and CONWIP is no exception. For planning, the operational performance measures must be determined. A common measure is mean throughput, because it allows us to calculate completion times and set realistic due dates. CONWIP is a closed production system: When a container reaches the end of the line, the finished goods are removed and the container is sent to the beginning of the line. By Little's Law, when selecting a WIP level there is a trade-off between flowtime and throughput. Setting a high level of WIP results in a higher throughput for a given flowtime. A low level of WIP results in lower throughput for a given flowtime. As noted, CONWIP is a closed production system and can be described in terms of a closed queueing network. There are many robust analytical models and approximations for performance evaluation of closed queueing networks. We give a simple algorithm, called mean value analysis (MVA) first introduced by Reiser and Lavenberg (1980). Let

i = index of workstations ($i = 1, 2, \ldots, m$)

l = number of containers ($l = 1, 2, \ldots, n$)

$W(l)$ = system relative throughput as a function of the number of containers l ($0 < W(l) \leq 1$)

$N_i(l)$ = number of containers at workstation i as a function of the number of containers l

$F_i(l)$ = flowtime at workstation i as a function of the number of containers l

μ_i = average processing rate at workstation i

$N_i(l)$ and $F_i(l)$ are actually random variables. Therefore, computations are performed on expected values. Assuming a single product line,

1. Set $E[N_i(0)] = 0, i = 1, 2, \ldots, m$.

2. For $l = 1, 2, \ldots, n$, calculate

$$E[F_i(l)] = \frac{E[N_i(l - 1)] + 1}{\mu_i} \qquad i = 1, 2, ..., m$$

$$W(l) = l / \sum_{i=0}^{m} \{E[F_i(l)]\}$$

$$E[N_i(l)] = W(l)E[F_i(l)] \qquad i = 1, 2, ..., m$$

3. Stop.

MVA is theoretically correct only for exponentially distributed processing times.

> **Example 10-3. Baer FAX assembly.** Baer, Inc., has a CONWIP-controlled assembly line for FAX machines with five stations, 1, 2, 3, 4, and 5. The process is sequential, with FAX machines arriving one at a time by conveyor. Times at each station are exponential with means

TABLE 10-3
CONWIP performance evaluation

	$N_1(l)$	$N_2(l)$	$N_3(l)$	$N_4(l)$	$N_5(l)$	$F_1(l)$	$F_2(l)$	$F_3(l)$	$F_4(l)$	$F_5(l)$	$W(l)$
$l = 1$	0.25	0.19	0.19	0.19	0.19	1	0.77	0.77	0.77	0.77	0.25
$l = 2$	0.51	0.37	0.37	0.37	0.37	1.25	0.91	0.91	0.91	0.91	0.41
$l = 3$	0.79	0.55	0.55	0.55	0.55	1.51	1.06	1.06	1.06	1.06	0.52
$l = 4$	1.09	0.73	0.73	0.73	0.73	1.79	1.19	1.19	1.19	1.19	0.61
$l = 5$	1.41	0.90	0.90	0.90	0.90	2.09	1.33	1.33	1.33	1.33	0.68
$l = 6$	1.75	1.06	1.06	1.06	1.06	2.41	1.46	1.46	1.46	1.46	0.73
$l = 7$	2.12	1.22	1.22	1.22	1.22	2.75	1.59	1.59	1.59	1.59	0.77
$l = 8$	2.51	1.37	1.37	1.37	1.37	3.12	1.71	1.71	1.71	1.71	0.80

$$\mu_1 = 1.0 \text{ units per minute and}$$
$$\mu_i = 1.3 \text{ units per minute } (i = 2, 3, 4, 5)$$

Move times are negligible. Station 1 is the bottleneck.

We first estimate the minimum number of containers needed for the bottleneck to work all the time. We have $t_1 = 1/1$ minute per unit and $t_i = 1/1.3$ minutes per unit for $i = 2, 3, 4, 5$. Then

$$n = \sum_{i=1}^{5} t_i/t_1 = 4.07 \quad \longrightarrow \quad 5 \text{ containers}$$

Using a spreadsheet, we evaluate the performance with the MVA algorithm. The results are shown in Table 10-3.

With five containers, the expected number of containers at the bottleneck (workstation 1) is more than 1. However, throughput at this stage is below the theoretical throughput. As the number of containers increases, the expected flowtime and throughput also increase. Thus, for eight containers the assembly line reaches 80 percent of its theoretical output.

Throughput will reach the theoretical value of 1 only when queue sizes are unrestricted; i.e., the number of containers reaches infinity. There is a clear trade-off between system throughput and expected flowtime. Figure 10-17 describes the relationship between the number of containers and the resulting throughput. Note (Table 10-3) that queues form also in front of nonbottleneck machines.

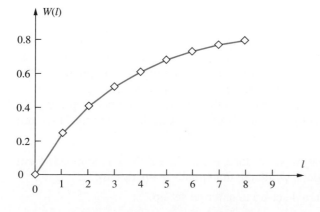

FIGURE 10-17
CONWIP throughput

4.7   Set-Up Reduction

Set-up reduction is one element that indicates whether an organization has a market-driven production culture. Why is this so? We again quote the original objective of the Toyota Production System: "a production system to produce the kind of units needed, at the time needed and in the quantities needed" (Monden, 1993). Set-up reduction shortens lead time and thus supports the "at the time needed" component of this objective. It also enables economic production of small batches, and as such supports the "in the quantities needed" component. In short, set-up reduction adds flexibility to the system—we can economically manufacture many different products ("the kind of units needed") and still maintain short delivery times.

Why would set-up reduction enable economic production of small batches? To answer this question, we revisit the EOQ formula discussed in Chapter 5. We discuss EOQ rather than EPQ, the optimum production quantity, for mathematical convenience; however, the argument holds for EPQ as well. Recall that the optimal economic order quantity Q is given by

$$Q^* = \sqrt{(2AD)/(ic)}$$

where D is the rate of annual demand, ic is the holding cost per unit per unit time, and A is the set-up cost. The set-up cost is proportional to the length of time required for the set-up operation.

For decades, A was taken to be a fixed system parameter, as were holding cost i and unit cost c. Thus, D primarily determined the size of the optimal order quantity; a higher D meant a higher Q and vice versa. Only when market pressure mounted and production flexibility became an imperative was the EOQ equation reexamined and efforts to reduce A initiated. The reasons for such efforts are shown in Figure 10-18.

For the same D and ic, reducing A to $A'(A' < A)$ substantially decreases the total cost and the corresponding order quantity. Although this is a simple concept, it was ignored for many years, because there was no incentive to question it. One of the early examples (1970) of set-up reduction was recorded at Toyota: Set-up time of an 800-ton punch press for the hood and fender was reduced from a number of hours to three minutes!

Set-up reduction requires engineering ingenuity. It may also require additional investment in new equipment, different manufacturing processes, engineering effort, and more. We next present some design principles to achieve set-up reduction, followed by the economics of set-up reduction.

4.7.1   DESIGN PRINCIPLES. A more precise definition of set-up is in order. Set-up (changeover) time can be defined as the time from the last good part of the previous set-up to the first acceptable part in the new set-up. It includes preparing the equipment for the new product and test runs and adjustments until the desired quality is achieved.

Set-up reduction requires a systematic approach that follows a number of principles. These principles were first documented by Shingo (1981) and were later refined. There are basically five steps (Suzaki, 1987).

1. Separate **internal set-up** (work that must be done while the machine is stopped) from **external set-up** (work that can be done while the machine is in operation).

2. As much as possible, transform internal set-up to external set-up.

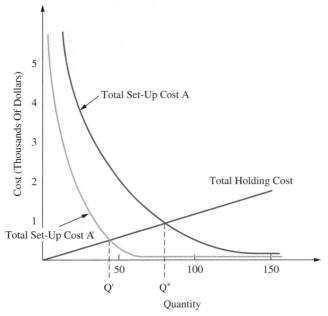

FIGURE 10-18
Effect of reducing set-up

3. Reduce internal set-up by eliminating adjustments, simplifying attachments and detachments, adding a person for additional help, etc.

4. Reduce total time for both internal and external set-up.

5. If possible, eliminate set-up altogether.

Often, in order to achieve best results in set-up reduction, certain design modifications have to be made in the product itself. Figure 10-19 demonstrates some of the ideas of set-up reduction; most of the internal set-up has been transformed to external set-up, and the remaining internal set-up has been simplified.

Set-up reduction implementation. To achieve set-up reduction, a cross-functional team is used, a proven approach in production systems. The team members typically include design and manufacturing engineers, shop-floor personnel, technicians, quality control people, etc. The key is that set-up reduction is a project and therefore should be organized as such.

Results of set-up reduction projects. Results of set-up reduction are well publicized and documented. For example, Figure 10-20 shows the results of set-up reduction at a west-coast household-goods manufacturer (Suzaki, 1987). Initial efforts reduced set-up time by 36 percent. Separating internal and external set-up took about six months and shortened set-up time to about 14 percent of its initial value.

4.7.2 ECONOMICS OF SET-UP REDUCTION. We previously presented set-up reduction in the context of increasing the flexibility of the production system. Flexibility is not the only advantage of set-up reduction. Reduced inventory, improved quality, and increased effective capacity are additional benefits.

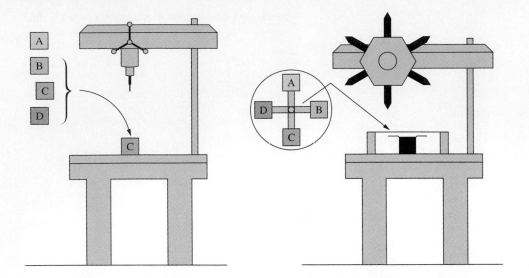

Typically, a machine that has four jobs with four different fixtures or jigs would need four different set-ups, each consisting of changing fixtures and aligning the cutting tool with the workpiece.

With redesign, the four fixtures are mounted on a turntable and quickly aligned and locked into position. A turret replaces the spindle and an automatic down-feeding device replaces the handwheel.

FIGURE 10-19

Set-up reduction (Black (1991) Copyright © 1991, reproduced with permission of the McGraw-Hill Companies, Inc.)

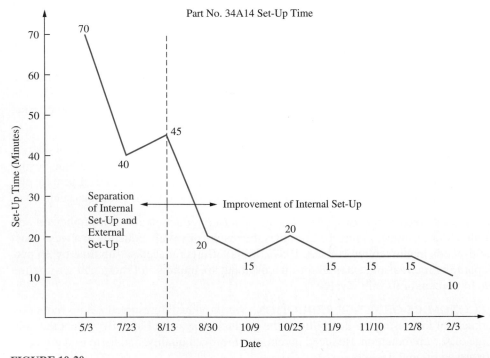

FIGURE 10-20

Benefits of set-up reduction over time (Suzaki (1987), reprinted with the permission of The Free Press, a division of Simon & Schuster, copyright © 1987)

Set-up reduction requires investment. Its economic viability depends upon the economic value of the benefits obtained. The most straightforward economic benefit to evaluate is that of reduced inventory-holding cost. We present a model to analyze the advantage of set-up reduction as related to inventory-holding cost. In principle, the same approach can be used for the other benefits, but their economic equivalence is not as simple to evaluate.

The problem we face is determining how much we should invest in reducing set-up time (or, equivalently, set-up cost). This is basically a trade-off between the cost of two investments, inventory investment and investment in set-up reduction. We can model this situation by extending the EOQ model to include a set-up reduction cost in addition to set-up cost and inventory-holding cost. In formulating this model, we follow the procedure suggested by Porteus.[3]

The basic cost equation presented for the EOQ model was

$$K(Q) = \frac{AD}{Q} + ic\frac{Q}{2}$$

where $K(Q)$ = average total annual cost
D = deterministic continuous annual demand (units per year)
c = unit cost
i = annual cost of capital
A = set-up cost

The economic order quantity is

$$Q^* = \sqrt{(2AD)/(ic)}$$

As previously noted, reducing A will reduce Q^*.

Suppose that $f(A)$ is the investment required to reduce the set-up cost to a level A. The annual cost of this investment is $if(A)$, where i is the annual capital cost. The average annual total cost as a function of A and Q is

$$K(Q, A) = \frac{AD}{Q} + ic\frac{Q}{2} + if(A)$$

We wish to find values of Q and A that minimize $K(Q, A)$.

The function $f(A)$ can take on different forms. One possible approach is to assume it is linear, i.e.,

$$f(A) = v(A_0 - A)$$

where A_0 is the initial (current) set-up cost and A is an arbitrary set-up cost. A logarithmic form of $f(A)$ was suggested by Porteus (1985). Let

$$f(A) = a - v \times \ln(A) \qquad 0 < A < A_0$$

where a and v are given positive constants, and, as before, A_0 is the original set-up cost. For this function, it takes a fixed investment to reduce the set-up by a fixed percentage.

---

[3]Reprinted by permission, Porteus (1985), Institute of Management Science (currently INFORMS), 2 Charles St., Suite 300, Providence, RI 02904.

Suppose θ is the fixed investment required to reduce set-up cost by 10 percent. If we assume $f(A_0) = 0$, we obtain

$$f(A_0) = a - v \times \ln(A_0) = 0$$

or

$$a = v \times \ln(A_0)$$

We also know that

$$f(0.9A_0) = a - v \times \ln(0.9A_0) = \theta$$

Manipulating these two equations, we find that

$$v = \frac{\theta}{\ln(1/0.9)} = 9.5\theta$$

i.e., v is proportional to θ, and v is the cost of reducing the set-up cost by about 63 percent.

We can now write $f(A)$ as

$$f(A) = v[\ln(A_0) - \ln(A)]$$

which is depicted in Figure 10-21. Substituting for $f(A)$ in the average annual cost equation, we obtain

$$K(Q, A) = \frac{AD}{Q} + ic\frac{Q}{2} + i \times v[\ln(A_0) - \ln(A)]$$

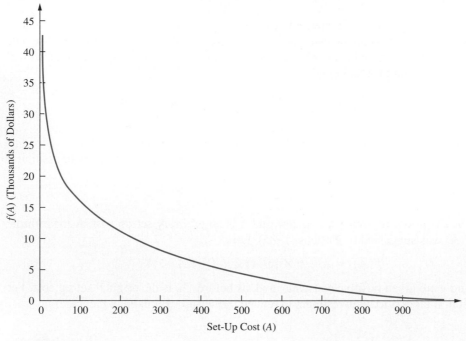

FIGURE 10-21
Plot of A versus $f(A)$

$K(Q, A)$ is strictly convex on $[0, A_0]$, and it has a unique minimum (Porteus, 1985). To find the minimum, we take partial derivatives, set them to zero, and solve the two equations in the unknowns Q and A. The result is

$$A^* = \frac{2i^2v^2}{Dic}$$

and

$$Q^* = \frac{2vi}{ic}$$

If A^* is greater than A_0, the current set-up procedure is better. Therefore, our true minimum is given by

$$A^* = \min[A_0, (2i^2v^2)/(Dic)]$$

and

$$Q^* = \min[\sqrt{(2AD/ic)}, (2vi/ic)]$$

Example 10-4. Set-up reduction at Plasto. The Plasto Company has a line of plastic products. One of its products is a plastic housing for commercial videotapes. It is manufactured in an injection molding machine. Polymer is pressed into a metal die at high pressure and elevated temperature. A die can weigh up to two thousand pounds, and set-up time is about five hours when the machine is idle.

As part of a continuous improvement program, Plasto started a waste reduction drive, including set-up reduction. A study of the set-up activity revealed that the set-up process has two distinct phases. The first is mounting the die on the machine, which takes about two hours. The other phase is preheating the new material to the required process temperature and humidity. If preheating is transformed into external set-up, set-up time could be reduced substantially. A number of technical alternatives exist; the more they cost, the more they reduce preheating time. Economic analysis should be used to find out how much should be invested in external preheating.

In studying the data for this analysis, it was found that reducing set-up cost follows a logarithmic function. A 10 percent reduction in set-up cost requires an investment of $700 ($\theta$). Further, we find that annual demand (D) is 1000 units per year, annual cost of capital (i) is 20 percent per year, the unit cost (c) is $50, and the current set-up cost (A_0) is $1000 per set-up.

Solution. We first find the value of v, which is

$$v = 9.5\theta = \$6650$$

Using the equations for A^* and Q^*, we have

$$A^* = \min[A_0, (2i^2v^2)/(Dic)] = \min(1000, 354) = \$354$$

and

$$Q^* = \min\left[\sqrt{(2AD/ic)}, (2vi/ic)\right] = \min(447, 266) = 266$$

Therefore, the set-up cost is reduced to $354, and order quantity is reduced to 266; the required investment is

$$f(A) = v[\ln(A_0) - \ln(A)] = 6550[\ln(1000) - \ln(354)] = \$6746$$

This $f(A)$ was plotted in Figure 10-21.

The average annual cost before set-up reduction is

$$K(Q) = \frac{AD}{Q} + ic\frac{Q}{2} = \frac{1000 \times 1000}{447} + 0.2 \times 50\frac{447}{2} \approx \$4472$$

and the average annual cost after set-up reduction is

$$K(Q, A) = \frac{AD}{Q} + ic\frac{Q}{2} + iv[\ln(A_0) - \ln(A)]$$

$$= \frac{354 \times 1000}{266} + 10\frac{266}{2} + 0.2 \times 6650[\ln(1000) - \ln(354)] \approx \$4009$$

This results in an annual cost saving of $463.

Comment. The reduced set-up time caused a reduction in production quantity, which adds flexibility to the production line. However, investment of $6746, resulting in annual savings of $463, is not very attractive as such if funds are limited. But, if we consider that the preheating device can reduce set-up cost for other products manufactured on the same machine, this investment becomes worthwhile. Furthermore, the reduction in cycle time and increase in flexibility provided by the set-up reduction are significant advantages not taken into account by the cost function.

4.8   Software

Software for pull systems centers mainly around shop-floor control and is usually called JIT software even though it only handles the technical component of JIT. Pull systems were first implemented as manual *kanban* systems, so software for JIT was developed slowly. Because of the myopic planning of JIT (see Section 7), JIT software is often an add-on to MRP II, substituting for the shop-floor control module. The advantage is that we obtain a strong scheduler that synchronizes the use of capacity. The outcome of such a merger is a hybrid system called JIT-MRP (or JIT-MRP II). Most of the current commercial MRP II software has an accompanying JIT component. When JIT software is used, the manual *kanban* can be eliminated and an electronic *kanban* can be used to trigger the start of production or move material.

More recently, JIT software, per se, emerged. It performs functions of order entry, scheduling, and pull control. The price range is $1000 to $50,000. Comprehensive lists are given by Krepchin (1988) and "Buyer's Guide" (1995). Manufacturing software is still evolving to meet JIT needs.

4.9   Industrial Applications

There are numerous applications of pull systems since their introduction into western industries in the early 1970s. There are also abundant field data to map the general experience with JIT implementation. We discuss two applications and two surveys.

The first application we discuss is Harley Davidson (Reid, 1990), the famous motorcycle company. It was almost wiped out by Japanese competition (from Honda and Yamaha) during the 1970s; in 1973 Harley Davidson (H-D) had a 75 percent share of the superheavyweight motorcycle market, but its share fell to less than 25 percent at the end of the decade. During the late 1970s and early 1980s, the company implemented a rigorous recovery plan. One of its major components was JIT, both as a philosophy and a technique. H-D called its version of JIT the *material as needed* program. From producing in large batches and long production runs, H-D switched to what it called the "jelly beans" system. The assembly line would make every model, in different colors, every day. Other components of JIT that were implemented included waste reduction (set-up reduction and improved quality) and employee involvement. Cellular manufacturing systems were used to arrange the production facilities.

The results of the H-D recovery plan were astounding. From being in the red, the company moved to the black. Market share toward the end of the 1980s increased to over 50 percent. The H-D story is one of the highlights of JIT implementation in America. If there were an integrated PPC hall of fame, H-D would be enshrined.

The second application we examine concerns a small company, Strat Industries, in Australia (Sohal and Naylor, 1992). The company employs 50 people and specializes in design, manufacture, and assembly of climate control units for ducted applications in domestic and industrial environments. Strat Industries had a quality and price advantage over its competitors, but had long lead times that caused lost sales. The company produced the same product continuously for a week. At the end of the week, it changed over to build a different product the following week. To reduce lead time, the company decided to use the JIT manufacturing philosophy. In doing so, mixed-model assembly was feasible, and they sequenced models to meet customer requirements.

The investment in implementing JIT was minimal, as a manual *kanban* system was employed. Lead time was reduced from 10 days to three days, which increased sales and profits by 30 percent. Inventory was reduced by 60 percent, and work in process went down to 40 working hours. Mixed-model assembly has allowed flexibility in scheduling and production. At the time this report was published, improvement efforts were continuing (*kaizen*).

This shows that JIT is appropriate for the small company, and its implementation does not strain capital resources. From the reported figures, return on investment should have been tremendous.

Crawford et al. (1988) report the results of a survey of early implementors of the JIT philosophy in the United States. The survey identified implementation and operating problems. There were 39 respondents to the survey; all were in the process of implementing JIT. Most of the companies surveyed are in the automotive and electronics industries, employing between 60 and 10,000 people. Some of the JIT benefits reported by the survey are an average of 41 percent reduction in inventory, 40 percent reduction in lead time, 26 percent increase in product quality, an average of 30 percent reduction in warehouse space, and an average increase of 54 percent in profit margin. This is a substantial increase in competitive position for the companies. The report also identified implementation problems (such as resistance to change and lack of management commitment) and some operating problems (such as poor quality, data accuracy, and performance measurement).

A survey by White (1993) sampled 1035 organizations in the United States that adopted JIT. Over 80 percent of the organizations report implementing set-up reduction, multifunction employees, and total quality control. A majority of the respondents (86.4 percent) indicated JIT provided an overall net benefit for their organizations. Throughput time is reported to decrease an average of 60 percent, and organizations employing repetitive manufacturing processes have typically implemented the JIT practices more often.

The conclusion of the two surveys is that JIT practices are well entrenched in American industry.

SECTION 4 PROBLEMS

10.22. What is the trigger for starting production at a certain workstation in a pull system?

10.23. Describe the impact of buffers on the performance of a pull system. How can the size of these buffers be determined?

10.24. Explain how the following terms are related to the success of a JIT implementation:

- Elimination of waste
- Employee involvement in decision making
- Supplier participation
- Total quality control

10.25. The following elements can be described as "rocks" (see Figure 10-12):

- Unreliable machines
- Poor quality
- Fluctuating demand
- Long lead times
- Long suppliers' lead times

For each element, explain why WIP is analogous to the "water covering the rocks." How can reducing WIP reveal these problems?

10.26. What is wrong with having high levels of WIP? Is it possible to operate a manufacturing system with almost no WIP at all? Why?

10.27. Total WIP in a *kanban* system is bounded. Why?

10.28. Explain why the following conditions must be met in order to successfully implement a *kanban* system:

- Small fluctuations in demand
- Very small or no set-up
- High quality

10.29. What is the difference between a single-card *kanban* method and a dual-card one?

10.30. What elements of control are lost when single-card *kanban* is used instead of dual-card?

10.31. Reduction in WIP can be achieved by reducing α, C, or L. What would be the implications of reducing C (container capacity) to the bare minimum?

10.32. Gear, Inc., makes automobile transmissions. They assemble four transmissions on the same line with no set-ups. These are a four-speed automatic (A4), an automatic with overdrive (AO), a four-speed regular (R4), and a five-speed regular (R5) transmission. Demand for next week is projected to be 150, 300, 250, and 400 for the A4, AO, R4, and R5, respectively. Give a sequence that will provide smooth flow for the assembly line.

10.33. MaTell makes three products on a single production line: a desk phone (D), a wall phone (W), and an answering machine (A). They have converted this line to a true JIT line, making one product at a time with no set-ups for different products. For the next month, demand for all three products will be stable and is 675, 525, and 350 for D, W, and A, respectively. What product sequence would you recommend?

10.34. Discuss the pros and cons of the due date formulation and the Monden formulation for the mixed-model sequencing problem.

10.35. Prove that the EDD sequence minimizes the squared deviation from the ideal due dates for the mixed-model sequencing problem.

10.36. Let $D = 300$ units per day, $t_w = 0.78$ days, and $t_p = 0.11$ days. Container size is 15 units, and $\alpha = 0.06$. It is known that a unit of WIP costs $2 per day. It is possible to reduce t_w by 0.08 to 0.7 days, and it would cost $2500. What is the payback period?

10.37. It is estimated that demand would grow to 330 units per day in the following year. In this case, the decision is to increase the number of *kanbans* and not to introduce overtime. What would the payback period be then?

10.38. What is the trigger for releasing jobs into production in a CONWIP-based manufacturing line?

10.39. What is the role of the backlog list in a CONWIP system?

10.40. What are the benefits of a CONWIP-controlled system in a mixed-model manufacturing environment?

10.41. The flowtime in a CONWIP system is shown to be fairly robust. Explain why. (*Hint:* Use Little's Law)

10.42. In a CONWIP system, the containers are not part-number specific, in contrast to a *kanban* system. What are the implications of this difference? Explain in detail.

10.43. WIP in a CONWIP system is not maintained per part number. How does this affect the service level (in terms of the probability of a customer arriving and the item is available)?

10.44. CONWIP is considered applicable to production environments characterized by longer set-ups and fluctuating demand. Why?

10.45. An important benefit of CONWIP is the low variability of the flowtime. Why is it so important?

10.46. CONWIP lines are characterized by less WIP compared to similar *kanban* based lines in a mixed-model production environment. Why?

10.47. CONWIP is considered to be a self-regulating system. Why?

10.48. Show that in a CONWIP system, a container arriving at the bottleneck machine must wait $(\|n\| - n)t_{BN}$ units of time, where $\|n\|$ is the smallest integer greater than or equal to n.

10.49. What is the difference between internal and external set-up?

10.50. What are the steps to follow in order to reduce set-up?

10.51. Let $D = 100$ units per day, set-up costs be $20 per batch, and holding cost of a part per day be $2.

    (a) What is the optimal batch size?

    (b) What is the total cost per day?

    (c) What would be the total cost if the set-up cost drops by 15 percent?

    (d) What would be the total cost if the holding cost drops by 15 percent? What is your conclusion?

10.52. Let D be the total demand per day, A be the set-up cost per day, c be the cost of each part, and i be the interest rate. As a result of an improvement process, it is possible to reduce the set-up cost by 10 percent. However, this would cause an increase of g dollars in the price of each part. What must the critical value of g as a function of c be for the improvement process to be worthwhile?

10.53. A logarithmic function is more suitable for describing the set-up reduction cost function. Explain why.

10.54. For the set-up reduction cost function $f(A) = a - v \cdot \ln(A)$, show that v is the cost for reducing the set-up cost by 63 percent.

10.55. For the total cost function

$$K(Q, A) = \frac{AD}{Q} + ic\frac{Q}{2} + iv[\ln(A_0) - \ln(A)]$$

show that

$$A^* = \min\left\{A_0, \frac{2i^2v^2}{icD}\right\}$$

and

$$Q^* = \min\{\sqrt{(2AD/ic)}, (2iv/ic)\}$$

5 BOTTLENECK SYSTEMS

5.1 Philosophy

By now, a standard structure for integrated PPC, a technical component, and a managerial concept should be obvious. Bottleneck systems are no different. We present here one of the better known approaches, although others exist, too. The technical component of this approach is a **bottleneck** scheduler known as *optimized production technology* (OPT). The managerial concept is called the theory of constraints (TOC).

The underlying philosophy of both OPT and TOC is a goal—as a matter of fact *the goal:* "Make money in the present as well as in the future" (Goldratt and Cox, 1986). The strength of TOC is that a simple, straightforward goal is a consistent and forceful guideline to develop its concepts and tools. Furthermore, to accomplish the goal, the company must simultaneously increase throughput, reduce inventory, and cut operating expenses. These points are beyond argument. TOC, along with OPT, was developed to achieve this goal.

The OPT scheduling system was developed in Israel during the early 1970s by Eliyahu Goldratt. The story is that Goldratt, an Israeli physicist, first became involved with production systems when he helped a friend who owned a plant that made chicken coops. In 1979 Goldratt introduced OPT in the United States and started Creative Output, Inc. (COI), to market it. Developing OPT, and later TOC, was almost solely the work of Goldratt.

The premise of OPT is that production bottlenecks are the basis for scheduling and capacity planning. Resources are classified as either bottleneck or nonbottleneck. Bottleneck resources are scheduled to maximum utilization, and nonbottlenecks are scheduled to serve bottlenecks. That means that in some cases nonbottlenecks could be idle. The objective of maximum efficiency for every machine no longer holds. OPT is essentially a software system, but applying some of its principles does not necessarily require software.

In the mid-1980s OPT matured into a more comprehensive management philosophy. In Goldratt's (1988) own words

> Probably the most important result was the formulation of what I consider an overall theory of running an organization. I call it the Theory of Constraints and I regard everything I have done before as just a mere derivative of this theory.

The basis of TOC is his definition of constraint: "anything that limits a system from achieving higher performance in attaining its goal." TOC is a way to cope with the system constraints. The influence of OPT is clear; after all, a bottleneck is one type of constraint on the production floor, and OPT is a method of coping with this constraint. More detailed discussions of OPT and TOC follow.

5.2 The Bottleneck Principles—OPT

Bottleneck is a term we encounter frequently. A bridge can be a traffic bottleneck, a telephone line can be a communication bottleneck, and a checkout counter in a grocery store can be a people bottleneck. A bottleneck is associated with a stream of events. It is the component in the stream that allows, for one reason or another, fewer events to go through it than the rest of the components.

OPT makes a distinction between two types of constraints, bottleneck and capacity constrained resource. Bottleneck applies to the case in which the resource's capacity is less than or equal to the market demand; i.e., a bottleneck is a resource that constrains throughput.

TABLE 10-4
OPT rules

1	Balance flow, not capacity.
2	Constraints determine nonbottleneck utilization.
3	Utilization and activation of a resource are not synonymous.
4	An hour lost at a bottleneck is an hour lost for the total system.
5	An hour saved at a nonbottleneck is a mirage.
6	Bottlenecks govern both throughput and inventory in the system.
7	The transfer batch may not, and many times should not, be equal to the process batch.
8	The process batch should be variable, not fixed.
9	Schedules should be established by looking at all of the constraints. Lead times are the result of a schedule and cannot be predetermined.

Source: Jacobs (1984), reprinted with the permission of the Institute of Industrial Engineers, 25 Technology Park/Atlanta, Norcross, GA 30892, copyright © 1984

A **capacity constrained resource** is a resource that has become a bottleneck as a result of inefficient utilization. For simplicity, we will only use the term bottleneck.

OPT is not the first method that identified and treated bottlenecks. In project scheduling, a critical path is identified. Obviously, each activity on the critical path is a bottleneck activity. Furthermore, any delay of a critical activity will delay the project completion time. On the other hand, to shorten the project duration, we must shorten the duration of at least one bottleneck activity. These concepts are incorporated into the OPT rules. Formulated to achieve maximum utilization of the bottleneck, the OPT rules are listed in Table 10-4.

The influence of critical path concepts can be seen in some of the rules. Rule 7 is probably the most revolutionary. In MRP, all lot sizing techniques assume equal size for both the transfer and the process batch. OPT also differs from MRP by not using predetermined lead times (rule 9). We elaborate on the OPT rules through the following examples.

Example 10-5. OPT Rules. This example elaborates on OPT rules 2, 3, 4, and 5. Consider a job shop that has a lathe (L), one mill (M), and drill (D) (see Figure 10-22). Two products are assembled. Product A is assembled from two drilled components and two components cut by a lathe. Product B is assembled from one milled component and one cut by a lathe. The production sequence is

$$D + L \longrightarrow A$$
$$M + L \longrightarrow B$$

Thus, L is a common resource for both. The shop has two drills and one lathe and mill, and operates three shifts per day (1440 minutes). Demand is 500 units per day of A and 50 units per day of B. The following chart describes the shop load:

	Unit processing time		Units required per assembly		Total processing time			Available	Utilization
	A	**B**	**A**	**B**	**A**	**B**	**Total**		
Assembly	2	4	1	1	600	200	800	1440	55.65%
Drill	4	0	2	0	2400	0	2400	2880	83.33%
Lathe	3	3	2	1	1800	150	1950	1440	135.42%
Mill	0	10	0	2	0	1000	1000	1440	69.44%

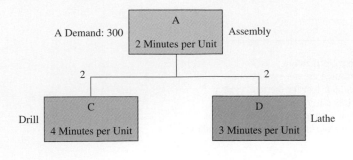

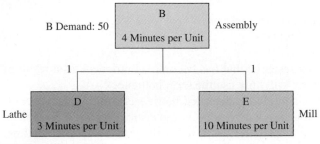

FIGURE 10-22
OPT example

The lathe is the bottleneck resource, and the daily demand cannot be met. The shop can make 215 A and 50 B (verify!). Lathe utilization will be 100 percent, and utilization of the other machines will decrease (rule 2). Obviously, activation of the resources can be at different utilization levels (rule 3). Since the lathe operates now at full capacity, any time lost there will decrease the throughput of the shop (rule 4). Similarly, trying to operate the nonbottleneck operations more efficiently will not contribute anything to throughput (rule 5).

Example 10-6. OPT rule 7. In this example we demonstrate rule 7. Consider the following production process: three operations in sequence, each taking one minute per unit. In the first case, the process batch of 10 is equal to the transfer batch. In the second case, the process batch is 10, but the transfer batch is 5. The production lead time for the two policies is shown in the Gantt Charts of Figure 10-23. By making the transfer batch smaller than the production batch, production lead time has been reduced from 30 minutes to 20 minutes.

5.3 Theory of Constraints (TOC)

The theory of constraints is an outgrowth and enhancement of OPT. Other names for TOC are *OPT* **thoughtware**, **synchronous production**, and **synchronized manufacturing**, with the latter two still sometimes used. TOC can be regarded as a management philosophy built upon a number of guidelines and designed to create a process of ongoing improvement.

The basic premise of TOC is that a system's outputs are determined by its constraints. The definition of constraint suggests that TOC has a wider application than just production planning and control. It identifies the following three broad categories of constraints:

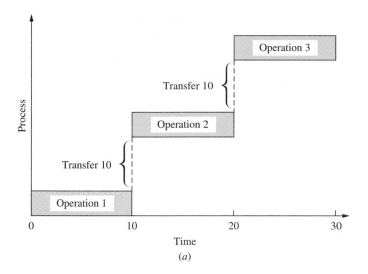

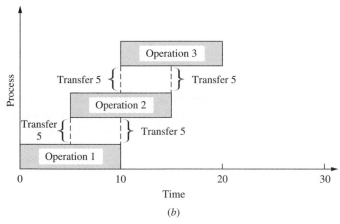

FIGURE 10-23
Gantt Charts for equal and unequal process and transfer batches: (a) process
batch = 10, transfer batch = 10; (b) process batch = 10, transfer
batch = 5

- **Internal resource constraint**—This is the classic bottleneck: a machine, worker, or even a tool.
- **Market constraint**—The market demand is less than the production capacity. In this case the market dictates the pace of production.
- **Policy constraint**—A policy dictates the rate of production (e.g., a policy of not working overtime).

TOC focuses on the role constraints play in systems in order to improve system performance toward the goal. To assess the improvement, two types of performance measures are proposed: financial measures and operational measures. The financial measures used are classic: net profit, return on investment, and cash flow. The following new operational measurements are suggested:

- **Throughput**—This is the rate at which *money* is generated by the system through sales. Unsold product is not throughput.
- **Inventory**—This is money that the system has invested in purchasing things it intends to sell; it measures inventory in terms of material cost only, without accounting for labor and overhead.
- **Operating expenses**—This is the money that the system spends in order to turn inventory into throughput, including all labor, overhead, and other expenses.

Note that efficiency measures, such as resource utilization, are *not* part of the operational measurements.

For continuous improvement, Goldratt developed the five steps of TOC:

1. Identify the system's constraint.
2. Decide how to exploit the system's constraint.
3. Subordinate everything else to the decision made in step 2.
4. Elevate the system's constraint. The term *elevate* means to make it possible to achieve a higher performance relative to the goal.
5. If in the previous steps a constraint has been broken, go back to step 1. Do not let inertia become the constraint.

TOC suggests a number of specific techniques to aid in the implementation of the five steps. These techniques include effect-cause-effect analysis, evaporating clouds, buffer management, and **drum-buffer-rope.** We discuss drum-buffer-rope techniques later. For details of the other techniques, see Fogarty et al. (1991).

To obtain a better understanding of the five TOC steps, we use Example 10-7. This example was developed by Luebbe and Finch[4] from a previous problem discussed by Goldratt. The novelty of this example is that it goes through TOC using a linear programming approach.

> **Example 10-7. TOC Steps.** Consider the production process described in Figure 10-24. Two products, *P* and *Q*, are manufactured; weekly demand is 100 units for *P* and 50 units for *Q*. The selling price for *P* and *Q*, respectively, is $90 and $100. There are four workcenters: *A, B, C,* and *D*. Each center has one machine that can operate up to 2400 minutes per week. Three types of raw material are required. Raw materials costs and the routings and processing times at each workcenter are shown in Figure 10-24.
>
> In line with the goal of making money, the most profitable product mix will be determined, following the five TOC steps.
>
> **Step 1. Identify the system's constraints.** To identify the system's constraints, the weekly load on each machine is evaluated (see Table 10-5), and a capacity resource profile is generated. The obvious bottleneck is workcenter B. In order to satisfy the market demand for P and Q, it should have an additional 25 percent capacity.

---

[4] Adapted from Luebbe and Finch (1992), with kind permission of Taylor & Francis.

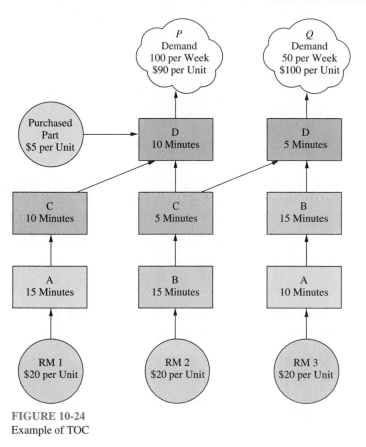

FIGURE 10-24
Example of TOC

TABLE 10-5
Weekly load

Resource	Minutes per week		Process load per week	Available time per week	Percentage load per week
	P	*Q*			
A	1500	500	2000	2400	83.
B	1500	1300	3000	2400	125
C	1500	250	1750	2400	73
D	1000	250	1250	2400	52

TABLE 10-6

Contribution

Product	P	Q
Selling price (dollars)	90	100
Material cost (dollars)	45	40
Contribution (dollars)	45	60
Time (resource B in minutes)	15	30
Dollars per constraint minute	3	2

Linear programming can also be used to show that B is the bottleneck. In the spirit of the goal of making money, we use profit maximization for the LP objective function. We will use the contribution, given in Table 10-6, to represent the profit per unit.

The objective function is maximize$(45P + 60Q)$. The constraints are the capacities of the four machines and the market demand for each product. The complete LP formulation is:

$$\text{Maximum } (45P + 60Q)$$

S. T.

$$15P + 10Q + S_1 = 2400 \qquad \text{(Resource A)}$$

$$15P + 30Q + S_2 = 2400 \qquad \text{(Resource B)}$$

$$15P + 5Q + S_3 = 2400 \qquad \text{(Resource C)}$$

$$10P + 5Q + S_4 = 2400 \qquad \text{(Resource D)}$$

$$P + S_5 = 100 \qquad \text{(Demand for P)}$$

$$Q + S_6 = 50 \qquad \text{(Demand for Q)}$$

$$P, Q, S_i \geq 0$$

where the S_i are slack variables.

The solution yields $P = 100, Q = 30, S_1 = 600, S_2 = 0, S_3 = 750, S_4 = 1250, S_5 = 0$, and $S_6 = 20$. $S_2 = 0$ indicates that resource B is a binding constraint, or the bottleneck. $S_5 = 0$ means that market demand for product P has been met. $S_6 = 20$ means that, because of the bottleneck, market demand for product Q is not met by 20 units.

Step 2. Decide how to exploit the system's constraint. TOC is based on the premise that the performance of a system is determined by its constraints. TOC focuses on maximizing the use of the constraints in relation to the goal (i.e., make money). Exploiting B means maximizing the return per unit of B consumed. In Table 10-6 we compute the contribution per constraint minute, which yields $3.00 for P and $2.00 for Q. It is more profitable to produce as much as possible of P (i.e., 100 units) before we produce Q. The 100 P units consume 1500 constraint minutes, leaving only 900 minutes for Q, which is equivalent to 30 units of Q. We can see that in this case the rule of exploiting the constraint gives the same solution as the LP model.

Step 3. Subordinate everything else to step 2. This step is intended to make sure that exploiting the constraint will guide all other decisions: raw material purchase, scheduling workcenters, etc. We want to keep the constraint busy while maintaining "good value" for the operational measures mentioned before. The TOC technique used to exploit the constraint is drum-buffer-rope (DBR), which we discuss later.

Step 4. Elevate the system's constraint. Every effort is made at this step to achieve higher performance of the constraint relative to the goal: reduction of set-up time, preventive maintenance, etc., to mention a few possibilities. A different approach is, if possible, to move jobs with the least profit per constraint minute away from the bottleneck to other machines. Thus, in our example, if demand for product P were to increase to 150 units per week, one way to cope with the additional demand would be to switch product Q to other resources. Product Q has a lower profit per constraint minute. By shifting work from the constraint to a nonconstraint, the revenue generated by the shop is increased, with little or no increase in operating expenses.

Step 5. If a constraint is broken, go to step 1. Suppose that market demand for products P and Q has increased to 132 and 66, respectively. Also, through engineering improvements, processing times on resource B were reduced to one third of their original value. It is easy to verify that the capacity resource profile is

Percentage load per week	
Resource A	110.00
Resource B	55.00
Resource C	96.25
Resource D	68.75

Resource A is now the constraint, and the previous constraint (resource B) has been broken. The process returns to step 1. Without this step, we might continue scheduling production as if the system constraint is still resource B, which would terminate the improvement process, and inertia would set in.

5.4 DBR Technique

Drum-buffer-rope (DBR) is a production control technique to implement the exploiting, subordinating, and elevating steps of TOC. If the system has a bottleneck, it becomes a natural control point. Its production rate controls the pace of the system. In other words, the bottleneck strikes the beat that drives the system, and hence the name **drum** for this control point. The reason for using the bottleneck as a control point is to guarantee that upstream operations produce enough to create inventory before the bottleneck so it does not starve. This is in line with rule 6 of OPT: "Bottlenecks govern both throughput and inventory in the system."

The most important feature of DBR is that a process batch is not necessarily equal to a transfer batch (rule 7). We now present a precise definition of both terms:

A **process batch** is the number of units produced between two consecutive set-ups. A **transfer batch** is the number of units transported between two adjacent workstations. In many manufacturing systems, the process batch and transfer batch are the same.

The transfer batch focuses on the *part*. The process batch focuses on the *process*. Consider, for example, an assembly line: By our previous definitions, the process batch is infinite, but the transfer batch is *one!*

The DBR technique is basically a feedback system. Figure 10-25 depicts its operation. The production line shown in Figure 10-25 has one bottleneck operation (BN), with a **buffer** placed before it. The purpose of the buffer is to protect the bottleneck from fluctuations and variations in the feeding rate to the bottleneck (i.e., exploit the constraint).

The buffer size is measured in standard time, the time required by the bottleneck to process all items in the buffer. The buffer is connected to the raw material dispatching point at the head of the production line via a feedback loop called a **rope.** This feedback loop communicates the bottleneck production back to the raw material dispatching point. The dispatching point will release only that amount and thus will keep the buffer inventory built

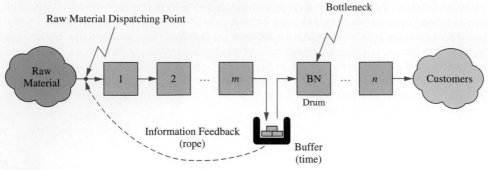

FIGURE 10-25
DBR technique

up. The suggested buffer size is 1/4 of the total actual lead time of the system. Thus, if it takes eight hours to get from the dispatching point to the end of the line, the buffer size should be set to two hours. If everything works as planned, the feedback loop will dictate the dispatching pace, and the buffer size will not change. However, if the buffer size falls below its recommended size, corrective action will have to be taken to expedite material and determine and correct the cause of the delay.

There is no theoretical basis for the suggested buffer size. The best way to set the buffer size is by experimentation. Start with an ample level of the buffer, check the range of buffer variations, and reduce it if possible.

If the bottleneck is actually a capacity-constrained resource (CCR), DBR suggests adding a finished-goods buffer at the end of the line. This is shown in Figure 10-26. In this

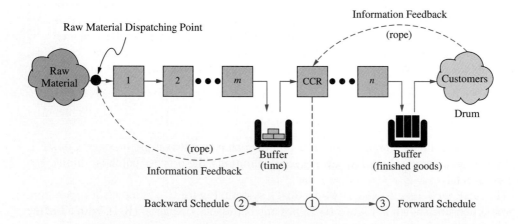

Scheduling Procedure:
(1) Schedule CCR.
(2) Backward schedule to raw material dispatching point.
(3) Forward schedule to finished goods buffer.

FIGURE 10-26
DBR with two feedback loops

case the drum is the market, and there is another feedback information loop to the CCR. The time buffer protects throughput, and the finished-goods inventory protects the market; when there is market demand, finished-goods will be available. Here, the market is the drum, and the rope to CCR sets the pace of production.

DBR scheduling starts by scheduling the bottleneck (constraint). Operations are then scheduled backward from the bottleneck to the raw material dispatching point, and then forward to shipping. The forward schedule provides estimates for customers' deliveries. Thus, DBR can be regarded as a combination of both push and pull. The dispatching of materials is governed by pull, and from there on it is pushed.

To conclude, there are four steps in DBR scheduling: identifying constraint, scheduling constraint, deciding on constraint buffer size, and deciding on the shipping buffer size.

The more bottlenecks we have in a system, the more difficult DBR scheduling becomes. Practice shows that there are usually not very many bottlenecks in actual production and assembly lines. A good ballpark figure is five or six. Furthermore, these constraints rarely interact. Even so, scheduling five constraints (and the rest of the system) is quite an effort. That is where the software system plays a role.

5.5   Bottleneck Scheduling

We know the bottleneck is important; the bottleneck machine should drive the schedule for the whole shop. We now present one method for bottleneck scheduling.

If we can schedule the bottleneck machine effectively, the other machines can be made to comply to this schedule. Machines after the bottleneck (downstream) are forward scheduled, e.g., by dispatch rules. Those before the bottleneck (upstream) are scheduled backward using due dates, as in MRP. We discuss a simple version of a bottleneck algorithm. For more complex versions, see Adams et al. (1988) and Morton and Pentico (1993).

5.5.1   FINDING THE BOTTLENECK MACHINE. In a manufacturing plant, finding the bottleneck is often easy; walk out on the floor and piles of WIP are stacked up in front of the bottleneck. Another approach is to estimate the work load on each machine. A simple estimate is to sum the processing times of all jobs on each machine to get the total work done by the machine. Dividing by the scheduling horizon converts it to a percentage. Thus, if machine 1 has 34 hours of jobs to be processed in a 40 hour week, its work load is $(34/40) \times 100 = 85$ percent. The machine with the highest work-load percentage would likely be the bottleneck.

5.5.2   SCHEDULING THE BOTTLENECK MACHINE. Denote the bottleneck machine by b, and let $j(b)$ be the operation of job i done on b. We know the processing time of job i on machine b is $p_{ij(b)}$; for convenience, let $p'_i = p_{ij(b)}$. We also need to worry about what happens to i upstream and downstream of machine b. Let the bottleneck release time for job i, r_i^b, be the time job i arrives at machine b. It is the release time of job i plus the time it takes job i to get to the bottleneck machine; this includes processing and wait times for previous operations on upstream machines. Initially, we assume that there is no waiting, so we have

$$r_i^b = r_i + \sum_{l=1}^{j(b)-1} p_{il}$$

We could include estimates of waiting times from historical data or queueing results in the equation. We also need to define a bottleneck due date for job i, d_i^b, that reflects when the operation on the bottleneck should be completed. To complete job i by its due date, it must be finished on the bottleneck by a time at least the sum of the downstream operations processing times before the due date. This again assumes there is no wait downstream. Mathematically, we have

$$d_i^b = d_i - \sum_{l=j(b)+1}^{m} p_{il}$$

Now schedule the bottleneck as a single machine with nonzero release times. This is an *NP-hard* problem, so we use a dispatch heuristic (Chapter 8). The priority rule depends on the performance measure for the job shop. Carlier (1982) presents a very fast branch-and-bound algorithm that can be used if better solutions are needed. Let U be the set of unscheduled jobs and t be the current time. The procedure is

Step 0. Set $U = \{1, 2, \ldots, n\}$; $p_i' = p_{ij(b)}$; $i = 1, 2, \ldots, n$; and $t = \min_{i \in U} r_i^b$.

Step 1. Let $S = \{i \mid r_i^b \le t, i \in U\}$ be the available jobs. Schedule job i^* on b, where i^* has the best priority among jobs in S.

Step 2. Set $U \longleftarrow U - \{i^*\}$. If $U = \varnothing$, stop; all jobs have been scheduled. Otherwise, set $t = \max\{\min_{i \in U} r_i^b, t + p_{i*}'\}$ and go to step 1.

There are several priority rules that could be used in the algorithm. If the measure is makespan ($C_{\max}$), choose the available job with the most work remaining, which is equivalent to LPT. For flowtime, choose the job with the least work remaining. To minimize maximum tardiness ($T_{\max}$), choose the job with the smallest bottleneck due date. The R&M priority (see Chapter 8) using bottleneck due date and remaining processing time is a good rule for total tardiness.

The algorithm produces a schedule of jobs on the bottleneck machine. Now we convert it into a schedule for the entire job shop.

5.5.3 UPSTREAM AND DOWNSTREAM SCHEDULES. Upstream and downstream are misnomers in a job shop, because some jobs may use a machine before the bottleneck and others may use the same machine after the bottleneck. The completion time of a job on the bottleneck determines the arrival time for its operation immediately after the bottleneck. Similarly, the start time of a job on the bottleneck gives the due date for the operation immediately preceding the bottleneck. Release times and due dates are determined for jobs on a particular machine from the bottleneck schedule. Then each machine is scheduled as a one-machine problem.

Consider a particular machine. If an operation of a job precedes the bottleneck, the goal is to have the operation completed by its due date so it will arrive at the bottleneck before its scheduled start time there. Since the job may have other operations preceding this one, the goal is to schedule it to finish as late as possible and still arrive on time at the bottleneck. Thus, we try to complete it at its due date. This is backward scheduling. On the other hand, operations after the bottleneck may have other operations following, so we wish to start them as soon as possible to give them time to complete. This is forward scheduling. To schedule the machine, choose the job with the best priority. If its operation on this machine comes before the bottleneck, schedule it to complete as late as possible. If its operation follows the bottleneck, schedule it to start as soon as possible. Keep choosing jobs by priority until they are all scheduled. Then, schedule the other machines.

When all machines have been scheduled independently, a sequence of jobs on each machine results. A dispatch procedure constructs a feasible job-shop schedule. By not allowing a job to enter the available set until both its predecessor operation and all jobs preceding it in the machine sequence have been completed, a complete schedule is easily generated.

If the bottleneck machine is a strong bottleneck, in the sense that it dominates the rest, the remaining machines should have sufficient capacity to do the jobs at the time required to satisfy the bottleneck schedule. If not, the schedule will indicate waiting times in the shop, and they can be used to modify the bottleneck release times and due dates. The entire procedure is repeated until a good schedule for the shop is generated. We illustrate the bottleneck heuristic with an example.

Example 10-8. Bottleneck schedule for Quick Closures. Consider the Quick Closures problem of Chapter 8 (Example 8-20). Table 10-7 restructures the data so that the processing times given are for the particular job/machine pair rather than by operation. Because we deal with one machine at a time, we will omit the use of a superscript denoting the machine on realease time and due dates.

Solution. We sum the times for each job and each machine. Job sums consist of the total amount of processing that must be done on that job. If no waiting occurs, the job will be completed in that time. From Table 10-7 we see that job 4 takes 34 minutes of processing; hence, the makespan must be at least 34 minutes. From the machine sums, machine 3 must be processing for at least 44 minutes, so a better lower bound on makespan is 44. Machine 3 appears to be the bottleneck machine. If idle time occurs on machine 3, makespan will increase. We begin the procedure assuming makespan will be 44.

Using machine 3 as the bottleneck, we construct due dates and release times for a single machine problem; processing times are the processing times of machine 3. The routing for job 1 is 1-2-3-4, so it is processed on machine 3 after processing on machines 1 and 2. The earliest that job 1 could be processed at machine 3 is $p_{11} + p_{12} = 6 + 8 = 14$, so the release time for job 1 on machine 3 will be $r_1 = 14$. Similarly, if job 1 is to be completed by time 44, its last operation (on machine 4) must be completed by time 44. Since $p_{14} = 5$ minutes, the previous operation must be finished by time $44 - 5 = 39$, so $d_1 = 39$. Job 6 has route 3-1-2-4 so its first operation is on machine 3, i.e. its release time is zero. Its due date is the estimate for makespan minus the processing time of all operations of job 6 that follow the operation on machine 3; $d_6 = 44 - 2 - 4 - 5 = 33$. Data for the remainder of the jobs on machine 3 are given in Table 10-9.

TABLE 10-7
Quick Closures: Times by machine

Job	Machine 1	Machine 2	Machine 3	Machine 4	Sum
1	6	8	13	5	32
2	4	1	4	3	12
3	6	8	4	3	21
4	10	5	15	4	34
5	3	4	4	6	17
6	2	4	4	5	15
Sum	31	30	44	26	

TABLE 10-8
Quick Closures machine 3 data

Job i	1	2	3	4	5	6
r_i	14	5	17	15	13	0
d_i	39	41	44	40	44	33
p_i'	13	4	4	15	4	4

TABLE 10-9
Scheduling machine 3 (the bottleneck)

t	U	$[s, c]$
0	**6**	[0, 4]
5	**2**	[5, 9]
13	**5**	[13, 17]
17	**1**, 3, 4	[17, 30]
30	**3**, 4	[30, 45]
45	**3**	[45, 49]

We solve the one-machine problem. Let the available jobs be those with release times as large as the current time. Schedule the available job with the smallest due date to start as soon as possible. Initially, set $t = 0$; $r_6 = 0$, so job 6 is the only available job. Schedule it to start at time 0; since $p_6' = 4$, it will complete at time 4. Now advance t to 4 and repeat.

The remaining jobs are scheduled, with the details given in Table 10-9. Column t gives the current time, U gives the set of available jobs with the one scheduled given in boldface, and $[s, c]$ gives the start and completion time of the scheduled job. The next row starts with t equal to the completion time of the job previously scheduled. When $t = 17$, jobs 1, 3, and 4 can be scheduled. Job 1 has the smallest due date, so it is scheduled next.

The sequence of jobs for machine 3 is 6-2-5-1-4-3 with $C_{\max} = 49$. The schedule is given in Figure 10-27. The estimate of makespan for the Quick Closures job-shop problem is now 49.

Now we schedule the other machines to adhere to the schedule at the bottleneck, on machine 3. For a particular machine, say machine 1, some jobs will have operations processed on the machine before the bottleneck and others after. Jobs 1, 2, 3, 4, and 5 have operations on machine 1 that come before the bottleneck, whereas job 6 is processed on machine 1 after the bottleneck. Jobs with operations before machine 1 will have release times determined by the earliest time they could get to machine 1; these are calculated in the same manner as the bottleneck. (Again, we assume no waiting except idle time scheduled on the bottleneck.) As examples, $r_1 = 0$ for machine 1, since it is its first operation, while machine 1 is the third operation for job 3, following operations on machines 4 and 2, so $r_3 = p_{31} + p_{32} = 3 + 8 = 11$. Due dates for an operation preceding the bottleneck are determined by that job's start time on the bottleneck. Job 1 is scheduled to start on machine 3 at time 17. To do so, it must be finished on machine 1 and complete processing on the intervening machine (2) at time 17. Its due date must be $d_1 = 17 - p_{12} = 17 - 8 = 11$.

An operation is processed on machine 1 after the bottleneck has its release time on machine 1, determined by its completion time on the bottleneck plus any intervening processing times.

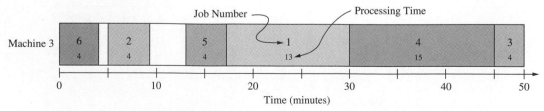

FIGURE 10-27
Gantt Chart for the machine 3 (bottleneck) schedule

TABLE 10-10
Quick Closures machine 1 data

Job i	1^b	2^b	3^b	4^b	5^b	6^f
r_i	0	0	11	5	0	4
d_i	11	4	45	30	3	40
p_i'	6	4	6	10	3	2

b = backward schedule

f = forward schedule

TABLE 10-11
Machine 1 schedule calculations

t	U	$[s, c]$
0	1, 2, **5**	[0, 3]
3	1, **2**	[3, 7]
7	**1**, 4, 6	[7, 13]
13	3, **4**, 6	[20, 30]
13	3, **6**	[13, 15]
15	**3**	[39, 45]

Job 6 has its first operation on the bottleneck, which completes at time 4. Its second operation is on machine 1, so it can arrive at machine 1 immediately upon completion, so $r_6 = 4$. Its due date is the makespan estimate minus processing time after machine 1, or $d_6 = 49 - p_{63} - p_{64} = 49 - 4 - 5 = 40$. Other release times and due dates for machine 1 are given in Table 10-10.

To schedule machine 1, we use a procedure similar to scheduling the bottleneck. From jobs that can be scheduled now, choose the one with the smallest due date. Backward schedule any job with an operation on machine 1 that comes before its operation on machine 3 and forward schedule the others.

To backward schedule a job, schedule it to complete as late as possible and be on time, since there may be other operations of the same job to be done before it. Ideally, it should complete at its due date, but if there is no idle period as long as the processing time of the operation ending at the due date, the job must be scheduled elsewhere. First try to create enough idle time by starting previously scheduled jobs earlier without violating their release times, or by delaying the start of a previously scheduled job without violating its due date. If successful, an idle period is created in which the current job can be scheduled. If this is not possible, schedule the job so that its tardiness is as small as possible. The tardiness of a job is the increase in makespan, because the due dates are based on an estimate of makespan.

A forward-scheduled job should start as soon as possible, since it may have operations that must follow it. If possible, start it at its release time. If not, it must be delayed.

For machine 1, jobs 1, 2, and 5 have release times of zero. Since job 5 has the smallest due date, it is chosen. It should be backward scheduled, denoted by the superscript b in Table 10-10, so schedule it to complete at its due date (time 3) so it will start at time 0. Advance t to 3, and job 2 is scheduled next.

Table 10-11 gives the schedule information for machine 1. The actual schedule is not needed, just the sequence, which is 5-2-1-6-4-3. This is not necessarily the order jobs were chosen; rather, t is determined by the start or completion time of each job.

We must repeat this procedure for machines 2 and 4. The data for these machines are given in Table 10-12.

TABLE 10-12
Data to schedule machines 2 and 4

	Machine 2							Machine 4					
Job i	1^b	2^b	3^b	4^b	5^b	6^f	Job i	1^f	2^f	3^b	4^f	5^b	6^f
r_i	6	4	3	0	3	6	r_i	30	9	0	45	7	10
d_i	17	9	39	20	7	44	d_i	49	49	31	49	13	49
p_i'	8	1	8	5	4	4	p_i'	5	3	3	4	6	5

TABLE 10-13
Schedule calculations for machines 2 and 4

	Machine 2*			Machine 4	
t	U	$[s, c]$	t	U	$[s, c]$
0	**4**	[15, 20]	0	**3**	[29, 31]
3	3, **5**	[3, 7]	7	**5**	[7, 13]
7	1, **2**, 3, 6	[8, 9]	9	**2**	[9, 12]
8	**1**, 3, 6	[13, 21]*	12	**6**	[12, 17]
8	**3**, 6	[31, 39]	30	**1**	[31, 36]
8	**6**	[21, 25]	45	**4**	[45, 49]

*Jobs 2 and 4 were moved to [7, 8] and [8, 13] on machine 2 to reduce the tardiness of job 1.

We schedule the machines in the same way as machine 1. Machine 2 requires a move of previously scheduled jobs. Job 1 should be scheduled to complete at time 17, but job 4 is in process from [15, 20]. There are not 8 (p'_1) idle time units available to insert 1 before 4. Thus, we move jobs 2 and 4 back to make job 1 complete close to its due date. Table 10-13 gives the scheduling calculations.

The sequences for machines 2 and 4 are 5-2-4-1-6-3 and 5-2-6-3-1-4, respectively. At this point, the machine that determines makespan could be designated as the bottleneck and the procedure repeated. However, we will not do another iteration, but schedule the jobs based on the sequence for each machine.

To get the job-shop schedule, we use a dispatch procedure that maintains the sequence of each job on each machine. No priority is needed, since an operation will not be ready to schedule until its previous operation has completed on another machine, *and* the operation of the job immediately preceding it on this machine has completed. For example, job 6 has its first operation on machine 4, but the sequence for machine 4 is 5-2-6-3-1-4, so it will not be allowed to start until job 2 is completed on machine 4. The Gantt Chart for the final schedule is given in Figure 10-28.

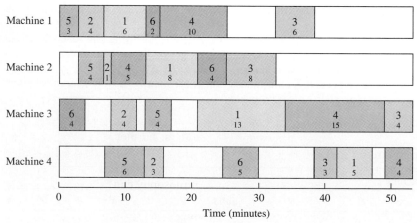

FIGURE 10-28
Gantt Chart for the bottleneck heuristic schedule

Makespan for this schedule is 53, lower than the makespan found in machines 3 and 4. Another machine could be selected as the bottleneck or wait times included in the release times and due dates of machine 3 and the procedure repeated. The solution seems good enough, so we stop. Several operations could be moved without affecting makespan. Job 6 could be started at time 0 or job 1 could be moved before job 3 on machine 4. None of these moves will decrease makespan. A secondary objective (e.g., flowtime) could be improved by these moves.

The bottleneck idea can be implemented in other ways. For different measures, priorities other than due dates would be appropriate. A more complicated implementation of the bottleneck approach can be found in Adams et al. (1988).

5.6 Software

The OPT software package supports bottleneck scheduling. Simple applications of bottleneck scheduling could be performed by spreadsheet methods. The OPT flowchart is shown in Figure 10-29 (Meleton, 1986). The four major modules in the OPT software are

Buildnet module An MRP II data base is used to construct a consolidated network for each end product. This data base includes bill of material, routings, inventories, workcenters, market requirements, and other data. Constructing the end-product data network is the most time-consuming element of OPT.

Serve module The serve module calculates a load profile and average utilization for each resource.

Split module This module divides the network into two areas, critical and noncritical resources. It also allocates time buffers at the appropriate places.

OPT module OPT is a finite forward scheduler (i.e., bottlenecks are scheduled first) that "beats the drum" of the bottleneck. By using a good heuristic, a realistic (i.e., one that considers the constraints) master production schedule is generated. This includes a work schedule report, a load profile for each bottleneck (or CCR), and a forecast of order completion.

If we examine the OPT flowchart, *serve* is to schedule noncritical resources after critical resources are scheduled. In this phase *serve* operates as an infinite backward scheduler that schedules backwards from the master production demands. This ensures that the operations feeding the buffers are completed on time. *Serve* also establishes the feedback loop (rope) to the raw material dispatching point dictating the earliest allowed material release. Table 10-14 shows an example OPT resource utilization report and shipping dates report.

The OPT software also has simulation capabilities. It can simulate different scheduling scenarios and compare the results based on the TOC operational performance measures.

OPT software sells for hundreds of thousands of dollars. Furthermore, at least in the past, the software was not sold unless the company was willing to adapt to the TOC philosophy and its performance measurements. It is not surprising that only big companies could afford the OPT software. However, OPT rules and TOC philosophy can be implemented by any company.

The original OPT software is not the only package now available for bottleneck systems. Other packages that claim to perform similar functions to OPT are MOOPI (Berclain) and PRIORITY (Eshbel).

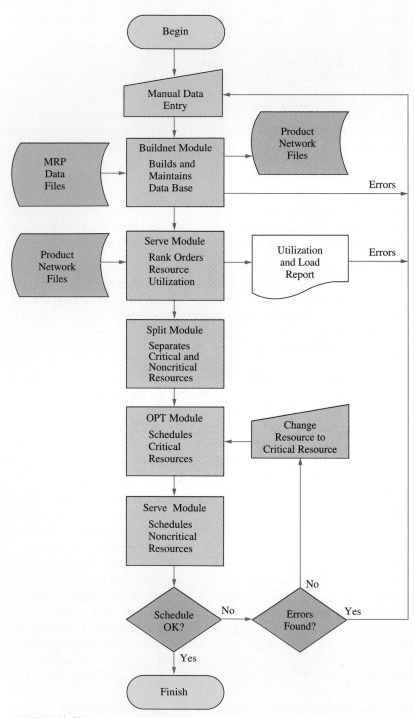

FIGURE 10-29
OPT flowchart (reprinted from Meleton (1986) with permission of the American Production and Inventory Control Society, Falls Church, Virginia)

TABLE 10-14
Example of OPT output

Final run quarterly utilization forecast starting 10/01/99
(with overtime)

Resource	Average	Potential	10/01 week 1	10/08 week 2	10/15 week 3	10/22 week 4	10/29 week 5	11/05 week 6	11/12 week 7	11/19 week 8
Extrusion	94	100	97	100	100	100	100	100	100	100

| Station (Hula-Hoop) | Total | Final run ship dates | | | | | | | | |
		10/29	11/05	11/12	11/19	11/26	12/03	12/10	12/17	12/24
+41026/BLU	5500	—	—	—	—	—	—	—	—	—
+41026/RED	3000	—	—	—	—	—	—	—	—	—
+41102/GRN	8000	1280	1689	—	—	—	—	—	—	—
+41130/BLU	5500	790	—	—	—	—	—	—	—	—
+41130/RED	3000	—	—	—	—	—	—	—	—	—
+41207/GRN	8000	896	1152	1792	1536	1010	—	—	—	—
+41228/BLU	5500	—	103	768	256	768	1792	1813	—	—
+41228/GRN	8000	—	—	—	—	654	1536	2048	3584	—
+41228/RED	3000	362	512	768	384	640	334	—	—	178

Source: Reprinted from Lundrigan (1986) with permission of the American Production and Inventory Control Society, Falls Church, Virginia

5.7   Industrial Applications

Compared to MRP II and JIT, bottleneck scheduling is a relatively new approach, and few well documented implementation cases appear in the literature. An early implementation at General Electric is reported by Johnson (1986); two applications, one at General Motors and one at AT&T, are summarized by Fogarty (1991); and Beckett and Dang (1992) describe implementation at Pratt & Whitney Canada.

General Electric implemented OPT at 20 plants. The results at its Aircraft Engine Business Group in Wilmington, North Carolina, indicate that its production cycles are 40 percent shorter than those of comparable facilities. Furthermore, inventory was cut by $30 million in one year.

General Motors's trim plant at Windsor, Ontario, has implemented *"synchronous manufacturing,"* which is a hybrid TOC/JIT concept. The implementation began in 1986. In 1988, the plant had achieved about 50 inventory turns per year, up from 17 when it started. Lead time was reduced by 94 percent, annual cost was reduced by $23 million, and output was increased by about 17 percent.

An interesting insight into the mechanics of TOC is seen in these results (Fogarty, 1991). Whereas lead time was reduced by 94 percent, inventory was reduced by only 68 percent. Usually, when JIT is first implemented, those two percentages are similar. The reason for the difference is that, in TOC the transfer batch is different from the process batch (Section 5.4), and in JIT they are equal.

AT&T's microelectronic division's Reading, Pennsylvania, plant implemented what it calls *"common sense manufacturing."* This approach also appears to be a merger of TOC and JIT concepts. It reports 50 percent reduction in inventory, a 70 percent reduction in lead time, and a fivefold increase in inventory turnover, but a 60 percent increase in rework. All in all, the plant was very satisfied with the results.

Pratt & Whitney Canada reports short-term results of what it labeled "synchronous manufacturing," another combination of TOC and JIT philosophies. Its stated goal is to achieve cultural changes throughout the organization. Specific objectives are cutting lead time and inventory by 50 percent while increasing on-time deliveries to 100 percent. Between September 1990 and June 1991, on-time deliveries were increased by 50 percent, and inventory and lead times were cut by 25 percent and 38 percent, respectively. In conjunction with applying synchronous manufacturing techniques, P&W reports a massive education program to move away from an efficiency culture to a customer-satisfaction culture.

Implementation of TOC/OPT has its downside too. One example is a semiconductor manufacturer using the theory of constraints to manage its production flow. Whereas production workers and supervisors dreaded being labeled the bottleneck because of the unwanted attention and pressure the label brought, the affiliated engineers felt otherwise. The label of bottleneck was the only way they could get their projects and experiments supported by management. The result was not the most desirable of manufacturing environments.

5.8   Epilogue

Since its inception, OPT/TOC has been a controversial subject. Although this controversy has mellowed in recent years, the *"rave to rage"* gap is still immense. Some consider it the savior of American manufacturing. Others acknowledge its visibility but retort, "This achievement is remarkable for a system developed in the late 1970s by a physicist that has yet to produce its first unqualified success story" (Baudin, 1990). As in many other cases of this nature, we believe that the truth lies somewhere in between.

The reason for the controversy may be caused by the way OPT/TOC was introduced. From the beginning, OPT was developed as a product to be sold, in contrast to MRP II and JIT, which originally were for in-house use. By not revealing how OPT's "secret algorithm" works, its designer ensured it would be shrouded in mystery. Very aggressive marketing by Goldratt approached the level of a missionary's zeal. This approach infuriated some and converted others. "In a new, relatively naive market such as the market for production control systems, a little mystery and a lot of promises go a long way" (Bylinksy, 1983). So maybe the OPT/TOC folks practiced what they preached; they exploited the market constraint!

In the final analysis, these arguments are not important. The crucial issue is whether OPT/TOC makes a contribution to production control and manufacturing thinking. Bottlenecks were not first identified by OPT/TOC, but OPT put the focus on them and developed methods to exploit them. From a mere scheduling tool, OPT developed into a total production philosophy. OPT/TOC is making its mark in industry and as such shares the stage with MRP II and JIT. Are they different? We discuss this in Section 7.

SECTION 5 PROBLEMS

10.56. What are the three categories of constraints?

10.57. What measures of performance are used to assess the improvement of a system?

10.58. Consider the following production process:

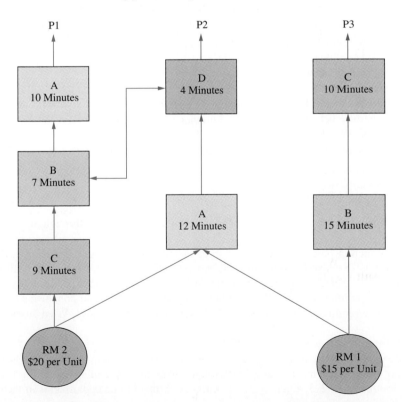

The following data are also available:

Product	Weekly demand	Price (dollars per unit)
P1	120	50
P2	150	100
P3	100	90

Resource availability is the following:

Resource	Availability (minutes per week)
A	1000
B	2000
C	1000
D	1500

(a) Is it possible to meet all the demand? What is the system's constraint?

(b) Restate the problem as an LP model. What is the optimal mix of products with the current capacity constraints?

(c) Assuming there are no capacity constraints, what is the system's constraint?

(d) How much money did the company lose as a result of the inability to meet the demand?

(e) What is the system's constraint and the optimal product mix, assuming that raw material 2 (RM 2) cannot be purchased in quantities greater than 250.

10.59. What is the trigger for releasing orders into production in a DBR-controlled system?

10.60. An important assumption of the DBR method is that the bottleneck's location is fixed (the bottleneck is static, not dynamic). What are the possible causes of a dynamic bottleneck? Is the DBR method applicable in this situation? Explain why.

10.61. The time buffer in a DBR-controlled system is usually set to be 1/4 of the total lead time. Describe the different considerations for setting the time higher and lower than this initial setting.

10.62. What is the difference between MRP data requirements and bottleneck-based control-systems data requirements? Why?

10.63. Consider the following three serial manufacturing-line configurations:

- No buffers between workstations
- Limited buffers between workstations
- Unlimited buffers between workstations

Describe the blocking and starvation effects and the impact they have on throughput and flow-time.

10.64. Consider a production process consisting of three operations in a sequence, each taking one minute per unit. For technological reasons, the process batch is equal to 10 units. For different values of the transfer batch, ranging from 1 unit to 10 units, calculate the resulting lead time. Draw a graph of the relation versus the calculated lead time. What is your conclusion?

10.65. Compare the data required to operate an MRP II system and OPT control. What is your conclusion?

10.66. What is the difference between OPT and TOC?

10.67. AllWood is a make-to-order shop that produces several styles of kitchen cabinets. As the name implies, their products are made wholly from wood. There are outstanding orders for 5 styles, which are designated 1, 2, 3, 4, and 5. All cabinets go through three departments in the same order: cutting (C), assembly (A), and finishing (F). Processing times for each style are given in the accompanying table. As soon as all are completed, they will be put on a truck and shipped to the customers. Schedule the shop so the truck leaves as soon as possible.

	Processing times (hours)		
Style	C	A	F
1	3	12	6
2	10	21	9
3	6	12	1
4	4	18	13
5	6	5	8

10.68. Woody Doer, the foreman at AllWood, claims customers should be considered when scheduling the shop. The order for style 1 is from AllWood's best customer, who would like to have its cabinets no later than one week from now. Styles 2 and 3 are for customers who occasionally place small orders and want their cabinets in 10 days. Style 4 is a first-time order from a large contractor who could potentially buy many cabinets from AllWood; this customer wants its cabinets as quickly as possible. Style 5 is an order from a local contracting firm that places small orders monthly; it needs its cabinets in six days. What schedule would you recommend for AllWood now?

10.69. A job shop has orders for four jobs, 1, 2, 3, and 4. Each job requires the same three machines, A, B, and C. Processing time and routing for these jobs are in the accompanying table. Schedule the shop to complete all jobs as quickly as possible.

	Processing times (minutes)			Operation routing		
Job	A	B	C	1	2	3
1	3	5	6	A	B	C
2	2	2	4	C	B	A
3	1	8	2	B	A	C
4	8	7	2	B	C	A

10.70. Suppose the four jobs in Problem 10.69 are very expensive. What schedule would you recommend? State all assumptions you made.

6   HYBRID PUSH-PULL SYSTEMS

As noted, "pure" push or pull production control systems have drawbacks. Even if a production control architecture is suitable for a certain manufacturing environment, weaknesses still exist. A CONWIP-based control system, which is actually a hybrid of push and pull (pull at the first workstation and push thereafter), is not without drawbacks; CONWIP uses a single card or container for a variety of parts. Therefore, the "safety" stock is relatively low and does not guarantee quick response for customer demands. On one hand, the need for small set-up times is less significant in CONWIP compared to pure pull, thus making it more general, but on the other hand, uniform flow must be preserved if the service level is to be kept at a reasonable level (because of the relatively low safety stock). Set-up times must be kept small

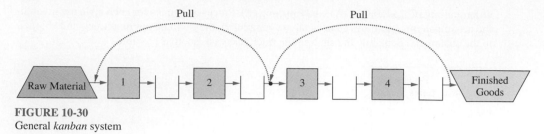

FIGURE 10-30
General *kanban* system

enough to enable continuous flow. With respect to CONWIP system optimization, it is important to note that the WIP can only be changed and controlled on a container basis. Container size is the smallest element of WIP that can be controlled. OPT is also a hybrid system: Pull before the bottleneck and push after. In a mixed-model environment the bottleneck may be shifting from one workstation to another, and it is difficult to handle dynamic bottlenecks in OPT. OPT also needs very accurate data regarding the bottleneck.

Several models were developed to improve the performance of pure push or pull systems and to address the problems in hybrid models like CONWIP. One of these models is called **general *kanban*** and was proposed by Tayur (1992). In principle, *general kanban* is a series of CONWIP-controlled segments linked together in series. Work is pulled between each segment and pushed within segments. Each segment operates like a regular CONWIP line. The production control system topology is illustrated in Figure 10-30.

The *general kanban* system can also be viewed as a series of manufacturing cells linked together. Each cell consists of one or more machines. If the whole manufacturing system is a single cell, the resulting architecture is CONWIP. If all cells consist of a single machine, the resulting architecture is a traditional *kanban* pull.

In a *kanban*-controlled system, there are buffers in every workstation in the form of *kanban* cards. Actually, buffers are needed only in front of the bottleneck, and thus a *kanban*-controlled system operates in a higher-than-necessary level of WIP. In a CONWIP-controlled system, containers accumulate naturally in front of the bottleneck, and a system of this kind can produce the same throughput as a *kanban* system but with a lower level of WIP. When the system is stochastic, this distinction between *kanban* and CONWIP introduces a problem: Bottleneck shifts may cause starvation, because it takes time for WIP to accumulate in front of the new bottleneck. Therefore, in a scenario of this kind, CONWIP needs more WIP to compensate for bottleneck shifts. *General kanban* performs better in situations like these, as showed by simulations. The theoretical work by Tayur (1992) is only for a single product, and therefore, the issue of part-number-specific containers or cards is irrelevant. *General kanban* and its characteristics are the subject of ongoing research, e.g., Hodgson and Wang (1991) and Chang and Yih (1994).

7   COMPARISON

7.1   Push, Pull, and Bottlenecks

Comparing the three approaches can be very complex. To avoid that, we structured this section as follows: We first recap each one of the three approaches, then make a "two-way" comparison, and finally compare all three. Recall that all of them started with a technical component and developed an embracing managerial philosophy.

Push systems started as a material-planning technique and grew into a management and operations planning and execution system. A push system generates an MPS, "explodes" the final product into its parts, orders their delivery to the production floor, and checks and adjusts inventory.

MRP II is a centralized planning concept, with a broad data base to support it. As such, MRP II is a strong tool for planning production and materials. Its data base makes MRP II a good tool for functional integration and data management. Its planning mode is probably the most adequate to deal with dynamic environments, such as job-shop manufacturing.

MRP II has three distinct weaknesses: It assumes infinite capacity; it requires relatively complete and accurate data on all production-floor events; and it assumes fixed lead times, which makes it weak in timing. To alleviate the infinite-capacity assumption, MRP II uses the rough-cut-capacity planning module. This is definitely an approximation and is seldom a good solution. The finite-capacity issue is experiencing a research resurgence, so we should expect to see new developments in this area in the coming years.

Fixed lead time is a major shortcoming of push systems. Lead times vary according to the degree of production-floor loading. The fallacy of MRP II is that its releases produce the very conditions that determine lead times, but these lead times are taken as known and fixed in making the releases (Karmarkar, 1989). In addition, both manufacturing and supply lead times fluctuate in the real world. A fixed lead time will be set high enough to cover all contingencies and will result in excessive inventories.

Remedies exist to overcome the lead time and timing weaknesses of MRP II. The crudest is the "hot list," a list of overdue or about-to-be-overdue parts. Hot lists are informal methods and therefore not well documented. More formal methods are order release methods (X-Flo), scheduling techniques (Class, MIMI), or simulation (Factor). A more rigorous approach is through hybrid systems, which we discuss later.

Pull systems started as a production-control technique, *kanban,* and grew into a production management philosophy, JIT. Its governing principles are lead-time management and elimination of waste in all aspects of manufacturing. The driving force in JIT is the on-time delivery of material to any conversion process.

The major advantages of pull systems are shorter lead times, which add flexibility to the production line to respond to changes in demand; inventory reduction and elimination of other types of waste (scrap and rework, floor utilization, etc.); and capacity considerations, which are embedded in the two-way pull-systems schedule operations. The *kanban* system is an inexpensive means of implementing the pull system. The fact that computerization may or may not be used makes it possible to implement pull systems in small manufacturing organizations.

Pull systems suffer from three major drawbacks:

- They are myopic. They do not recognize future events and therefore do not plan well.
- Pull systems are reactive. They do not operate well in cases where great variations exist. Therefore, uniform production flow is required for good implementation.
- Pull systems cannot perform lot tracking (i.e., they cannot peg lots to specific customers).

Nevertheless, both the techniques and philosophy of pull systems are well established in western industries.

Bottleneck systems are a relatively new arrival in the field of integrated production systems. They started as a bottleneck scheduler (OPT) and evolved into a broad management philosophy (TOC). The driving force behind both OPT and TOC is constraint exploitation. TOC's major contribution is focusing on constraints and promoting the concept of effectiveness versus efficiency (i.e., low machine utilization or labor idle time are not necessarily evil). Neither idea is new, but OPT/TOC enhanced the tools to implement them.

The major advantages of bottleneck systems are dealing with finite capacity, allowing lot splitting, and requiring data integrity only for the bottlenecks. OPT is definitely a very strong production-floor scheduler.

Bottleneck systems are not without flaws. They are sensitive to a number of parameters, such as the number of bottleneck resources, the total number of workcenters, and the complexity of the product structure. OPT is particularly useful in nonrepetitive manufacturing, such as bona fide job shops. Its performance decreases substantially in dynamic bottleneck situations. When the bottleneck shifts from one machine to another, it is called a dynamic bottleneck. Dynamic bottlenecks are caused by changes in product mix or stochastic variations. A field survey of OPT software users (Fry et al., 1992) identified five major weaknesses in the software packages:

- Not user friendly
- Requires extremely accurate and timely feedback
- Overly sophisticated
- Prohibitive maintenance cost
- Nonintuitive results

Total implementation of OPT/TOC requires major organizational changes, which make it both costly and difficult. Furthermore, some of the operational measures suggested by TOC are still controversial, which inhibits their implementation.

There is a basic difference between *push* and *pull systems*. Push systems initiate production in anticipation of future demand, whereas pull systems initiate production as a reaction to present demand (Karmarkar, 1989). Push systems are better for planning, but pull systems are better for scheduling production-floor activities.

However, pull and push systems are not mutually exclusive and do not necessarily conflict with each other. The line between the two is not as sharp as many tend to believe. Furthermore, both can coexist by constructing a hybrid system that builds upon their respective strengths. Indeed, many advanced manufacturing companies practice this hybrid approach. They use a *kanban* or similar system along with a time-tested push "workhorse" such as MRP II.

Hybrid systems should be implemented differently in different situations. For example, in a uniform-flow manufacturing environment, MRP II performs material planning, and a pull method controls the production floor. In repetitive-batch manufacturing with relatively stable lead times, order release can be performed by either MRP II or pull, but material planning should be performed by MRP II. Finally, in a dynamic environment like a job shop, MRP II is invaluable both for planning and, by default, for order release; the maze of material flow is too complex for pull. These hybrid systems have been called *JIT-MRP,* **synchro MRP,** and **rate-based MRP II,** among others.

Push systems and *bottleneck systems* seem to be at odds with each other. In fact, OPT was developed to replace MRP II. Both have strengths and weaknesses, but one fact stands out: There are many more MRP II users than OPT users. This is obvious, because there are about 200 software vendors for MRP II and its derivatives, and there are only a few vendors for bottleneck software.

OPT uses most of the data required for MRP II but processes it in a different way. Therefore, in an organization that uses closed-loop MRP II, the basic data required for OPT and understanding of feedback are already there. The data-integrity requirement for both systems is different. One should take with a grain of salt the claim that OPT needs less-accurate data than MRP II. OPT needs less accuracy for nonbottleneck centers but requires greater accuracy for bottleneck data.

MRP II is transparent to the user. OPT is not always understood by the user, and the black-box syndrome is still there, although it is slowly disappearing. In MRP II, order release is the drum, but OPT can place the drum anywhere. Given that OPT considers finite capacity, it produces more realistic schedules than MRP II.

There is a similarity between the two approaches in requirements for product and process data and managerial commitment. Therefore, both require substantial effort for implementation, particularly in training, education, and instruction. Finally, push systems use a central planning philosophy, whereas bottleneck systems center on constraint exploitation.

Pull systems and *bottleneck systems* have a number of common features. Both are finite-capacity schedulers, and both have overcome MRP II's batch-size problem. Their data integrity requirements are less, whereas JIT's need for data accuracy is almost zero. Both approaches promote set-up reduction; OPT requires set-up reduction only for bottlenecks, whereas JIT requires it for all workcenters. Both pull systems and bottleneck systems share the effectiveness philosophy in their own way. JIT drives for waste elimination, whereas TOC emphasizes constraint exploitation.

OPT does not suffer the planning myopia of JIT. On the other hand, JIT implementation does not necessarily require computerization. Pull systems often require reorganization of the production floor, whereas bottleneck systems do not. Also, pull systems generate schedules faster than OPT, but OPT gives a more complete schedule.

Push, pull, and *bottleneck systems* share a number of characteristics. In one way or another, they all require a change in the organizational culture with relatively high effort in education and training. All need to have management committed to the change process. None of their technical components is best for all production environments and all problems.

To obtain a better feel for this last statement, Table 10-15 compares the three approaches on the basis of integrated PPC function and manufacturing system. Each element of the table contains what we believe is the best approach. If there is no clear winner, two approaches are given. In examining the table, one conclusion stands out: For *all* functions and *all* environments, the best approach is the hybrid one. However, since no commercial product exists, it is more difficult to implement hybrid systems.

7.2 Looking Ahead

Integrated production systems are always in a state of technological change. The manufacturing management tools that support them must keep changing too. Therefore, we do not believe that there is a quick fix to integrated production systems problems. There is no panacea; no single method will fit all manufacturing environments. So where do we go from here? We

TABLE 10-15
Functional application of integrated PPC systems

Flow-time variation	Type of system	Integrated PPC Function			
		MPS	Material planning	Order release	Shop floor
Low	Continuous flow	MRP II	MRP II	JIT	JIT
	Flow shop	MRP II	MRP II	MRP II or JIT	JIT
	Job shop	MRP II	MRP II	MRP II	OPT
High	Make-to-order	MRP II or OPT	MRP II or OPT	OPT	OPT

Source: Adapted from Karmarkar (1989), reprinted by permission of Harvard Business Review. Copyright © 1989 by the President and Fellows of Harvard College. All rights reserved.

believe there are three trends associated with three different parties: system developers, system users, and adopting organizations.

System developers will make an effort to overcome the flaws of each system. One approach, occurring now, employs hybrid systems. Another approach involves improving the system itself. Thus, we see the beginnings of MRP II software with a finite-capacity scheduler and some relaxation of the fixed lead time assumption. One such entry in the field is a software product called *Ashbel.* Bottleneck systems also have a new product called *Disaster* that supposedly solves the dynamic bottleneck issue. More research definitely is needed to improve these systems.

By *system users* we mean those professionals within the organization who will use and service the system. This group is instrumental in the system selection process. As the system users become more professionally sophisticated, there will be a better understanding of the nature of integrated PPC systems. Specifically, understanding that no one size fits all will be more common. The result will be a more careful selection process matching the need and environment with the capabilities of the tool.

For the *adopting organization,* selecting a certain approach must be in concert with the management philosophy. With many organizations undergoing cultural change (TQM, "re-engineering," *kaizen,* etc.), we believe it will be easier to adapt to the management philosophies of each integrated production planning and control system. As a matter of fact, this trend will probably bring the three philosophies closer together. Indeed, it is not a "pie in the sky" anymore. The *Wall Street Journal* (Naj, 1996) reports about the new craze from software in manufacturing: speed. It is a simulation-based software that simulates the supply chain in detail, considering many issues we discussed: MRP, inventory, bottleneck scheduling, finite capacity, fast response time, etc. These software systems can tell you almost instantly whether an order can be delivered on time. If the answer is no, the software will tell you what changes should be made to make the delivery possible. It seems to be the beginning of the next era in manufacturing software, the one beyond MRP II and ERP.

SECTION 7 PROBLEMS

10.71. What are the main differences between push and pull systems?

10.72. What are the drawbacks of pull, push, and bottleneck?

10.73. Can a JIT pull approach be used for material planning? Why?

10.74. Discuss why JIT control is for a make-to-order production environment.

10.75. Can the same performance measures be used for comparing push and pull systems? Why?

10.76. Compare the data requirements for MRP II, OPT, and *kanban* that are needed to control a manufacturing system (processing times, bill of material, demand, etc.). What is your conclusion?

10.77. What is the difference between the Drum-Buffer-Rope approach and CONWIP?

10.78. There are two alternative ways of releasing orders into production:

(a) Release rate is equal to available capacity.

(b) Release rate is equal to the rate the finished goods are leaving the system.

Is there a difference between these alternatives? Describe the effect these release policies have on WIP.

8   EVOLUTION

Each of the three integrated production planning and control methods evolved along a different path. We will discuss each one separately and then give a combined discussion.

The origin of *push* systems can be traced back to the early 1970s, when books on material-requirements planning were first published. The first book, by Plossl and Wight (1971) was followed by New (1974). The book by Orlicky (1975) is probably the most well-known work on MRP. Until that time, reorder point (ROP) systems were used in industry, even though they are not adequate for dependent demand systems. The need to handle dependent demand was there, and the emergence of the computer made it possible to respond to that need. It is believed that the first use of computerized MRP systems occurred around 1970.

Expanding MRP to include other components of the production system was a natural outgrowth. MRP was no longer adequate to describe the new system; MRP II was probably first proposed by Wight (1984a, b). This name represents the wider scope of planning and monitoring the resources of a manufacturing organization, including manufacturing, finance, marketing, and engineering.

It is customary to trace the beginning of pull systems to Toyota in the early 1970s. However, we believe that its roots lie in the Henry Ford era. Ford (1924) said

We have found that in buying materials it is not worthwhile to buy for other than immediate needs . . . . If transportation were perfect and an even flow of material could be assured it would not be necessary to carry any stock whatsoever.

Toyota started experimenting with *pull* ideas in the early 1950s, and by the early 1970s it was in use throughout the company. Two people are primarily responsible for JIT within Toyota, Ohno (1982) and Shingo (1981). Initially, this approach was confined to the Toyota Company. After the oil crisis of 1973, many Japanese companies were economically troubled while Toyota remained stable. This caused other companies to copy the Toyota system, and it spread through Japan. Other companies refined both the technical component and managerial philosophy of JIT. In the late 1970s, elements of JIT started migrating to other parts

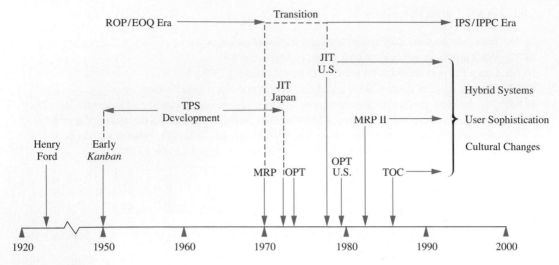

Key:
  ROP = Reorder Point
  IPS   = Integrated Production Systems
  IPPC = Integrated Production Planning and Control
  TPS = Toyota Production Systems

FIGURE 10-31
Evolution of integrated PPC

of the world. Because of poor economic performance by many western companies and the good track record of JIT in Japan, pull systems obtained broad acceptance. Some of the early adopters in the United States were Harley Davidson, Goodyear, and General Electric. Today, pull concepts are part of the corporate culture in many American and European companies.

Early experiments with *bottleneck* scheduling started in Israel in the mid-1970s. OPT gained a foothold in the American market in 1979. Realizing that computerized shop-floor scheduling is just one issue in the broader problem of successfully running a manufacturing organization, Goldratt developed the managerial philosophy, TOC, in the early 1980s. It gradually spread to all parts of the world.

OPT/TOC did not have an easy ride trying to capture its niche in the integrated production-systems market. Furthermore, it created some controversy because of both its concepts and its aggressive marketing approach. Nevertheless, OPT/TOC has earned its place among the leading methods in integrated production systems.

Figure 10-31 is a time scale showing the evolution of integrated PPC methods and management philosophies. Integrated PPC tools dominated the 1970s, and the 1980s was the decade of management philosophy.

9   SUMMARY

In this chapter we focus on integration, a global approach to production planning and control. Integration is used to describe both a concept and a technique, and we examine both aspects in the production planning and control domain.

We start by examining integration-related issues. The interaction of the production function with the rest of the organization is discussed first and includes the concept of process-based organization, one that emerges in the era of market-driven systems. This discussion is enhanced by presenting real-world examples of the production function within a multi-plant, multi-location organization.

The next integration-related issue is control architecture. Four basic designs that embody decision-making responsibilities are treated: centralized, proper hierarchical, modified hierarchical, and heterarchical, and three control levels are related: production-floor, cell, and machine.

The last issue in this category is interplant integration—within the same organization and with suppliers and customers—through the use of electronic data interchange.

Traditional production planning and control is no more than a production tool. Integrated PPC is much more than that; it is an embracing concept that has a philosophy driving it and a set of tools to implement it. The three major approaches to integrated PPC are push systems, pull systems, and bottleneck systems. All three systems have a technical component and an underlying managerial concept.

Push systems are schedule-based systems with a central-planning managerial concept. Push systems are implemented through MRP II. MRP II can be viewed as a method for the effective planning of all resources of a manufacturing organization. It is an outgrowth of MRP, and can be viewed as having three major components: upper management planning, operations planning, and operations execution. MRP II, by its nature, is a manufacturing information system where integration is embedded in its structure. As such, MRP II can serve as a major aid in breaking the functional barriers within the organization. MRP II is a widely used approach, with more than 200 turnkey software packages currently available.

Initially, pull systems were defined as production systems to produce the kind of unit needed at the time needed and in the quantities needed. It grew from a production control technique, *kanban,* to a production management philosophy. It adds both suppliers and customers to the production system. The scope is expanded from controlling flow and WIP to controlling flow and eliminating waste.

The pull concept is management of reciprocal interdependence. We discuss the four basic tenets of JIT philosophy, leading us to discuss the mechanics of *kanban* systems. A detailed analysis of the dual-card system is shown, followed by the five "Monden rules" for implementing a *kanban* system. A model for evaluating the number of *kanbans* is presented, followed by a discussion of a single-card system, whose most common implementation is the *kanban* square. The quantitative modeling approaches to pull systems are discussed next, including sequencing mixed-model pull systems, number of *kanbans,* and time-based material flow. CONWIP is an emerging variation of JIT with some interesting merits. To enhance the CONWIP discussion, two models are presented, CONWIP control and CONWIP performance evaluation. Set-up reduction is a key element in pull systems; we therefore devote a section highlighting its importance, methods to achieve it, and an economic model to evaluate it.

The premise underlying bottleneck systems is that production bottlenecks are the basis for scheduling and capacity planning. The scheduling tool is the software package, OPT. The management philosophy is theory of constraints (TOC), and its basic premise is that a system's outputs are determined by its constraints. The underlying objective of TOC is *the goal:* Make money in the present as well as in the future. The nine OPT rules are defined and analyzed, followed by the five TOC steps.

OPT schedules the bottlenecks first, and then operations are scheduled backward and forward from it. DBR is the feedback-planning and control mechanism used by OPT to control the time buffer in front of the bottleneck. One method for bottleneck scheduling is presented.

An overview of the OPT software is introduced, followed by some industrial applications and a discussion of the controversy surrounding TOC.

A comparison of the three major approaches to integrated PPC is presented next. The conclusion is that they share a number of characteristics. None of their technical components is the best for all production environments and all problems. Hybrid systems, which combine elements of the three systems, have the greatest potential for future application. In discussing the evolution of integrated PPC we see that tools dominated the 1970s and management philosophy dominated the 1980s.

MINICASE: T & R ALARMS

T & R is a manufacturer of high-quality alarm systems. One of the production lines consists of six workstations in a series and operates under CONWIP. Assembly times (semiautomatic, mean, and standard deviation in minutes) for a printed circuit board are:

Station	1	2	3	4	5	6
Mean	3	4	3	4	5	3
Standard deviation	0.5	3	1	3	1	1

Assume the demand is infinite, and handling times are negligible. Use simulation when appropriate, and answer the following questions:

1. Identify the bottleneck workstation. Set the card count for this line. What would be the estimated throughput?
2. What is the distribution of WIP as a function of time?
3. In CONWIP, WIP accumulates naturally in front of the bottleneck. How many bottlenecks are there in this situation? Why?
4. Try to identify a situation where a bottleneck is starved. What causes this situation?
5. Use simulation to determine actual line throughput. What causes the difference between your estimate and the results of the simulation?
6. One of the engineers suggests a process improvement, which would reduce processing variability on workstations 2 and 4 to 0.5. What is the distribution of WIP before each workstation as a function of time? What is the line throughput? Try to explain the difference.
7. Is it possible to reduce the card count and achieve the same throughput for this line? What would be the new card count?
8. Assuming a unit of WIP costs $0.1 per day and there are 300 working days in a year, what would be the annual savings as a result of this improvement?

MINICASE: TVG MANUFACTURING

TVG is a small manufacturer of color television sets. The company produces about 300 TV sets a day, mainly for the domestic market. The product family is characterized by various screen sizes: 14″, 16″, 21″, 26″, and 29″. The main departments of TVG are

- Final assembly. Has four assembly lines with nine workstations at each line.
- Subassembly manufacturing. Large components like cathode ray tubes (CRT) are purchased from external sources. Main subassemblies are PCB boards and chassis.
- Warehouse facilities. The warehouse is divided into two sections: finished goods (TV sets ready for shipping) and subassembly components.
- Marketing. This department is responsible for relationships with distributors, advertising, etc.
- Design. This department is responsible for designing new models and improving the existing product family. The company does not perform any kind of research and uses only proven technology.

Company strategy is to sell TV sets at a competitive price. These TV sets do not offer any innovative features, and the design can be characterized as conservative. The structure of the final assembly line is illustrated in the following figure:

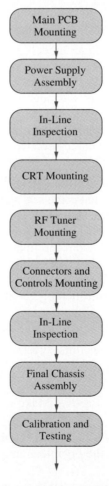

TV sets are transported from one assembly station to another on special-purpose pallets. An operator-controlled asynchronous conveyor (divided into segments) is used as a handling system. When a pallet reaches the end of the line, the finished TV set is removed and taken to the finished-goods storage facility, and the empty pallet is returned to the beginning of the line. An assembly operation at the first station begins only when there is a pallet available. There is room for four TV sets at each workstation. When a set fails one of the in-line inspection tests, the set is taken to a rework area, where technicians fix the problem, and the set is returned to the assembly line. Operation times for each workstation are

Workstation	Time (minutes)
Main PCB mounting	4
Power supply assembly	4
In-line inspection	5
CRT mounting	6
RF tuner mounting	3
Connectors and controls mounting	4
In-line inspection	3
Final chassis assembly	4
Calibration and testing	5

These assembly times are applicable to all models except for the 21″, 26″, and 29″ where CRT mounting takes eight minutes. (The CRT is heavier.)

A few problems emerged last year. Customers were complaining about low quality and unacceptable failure rate. The company warrants the TV sets and had spent a significant amount of money on fixing the problematic sets. TVG market share has dropped by 1.5 percent last year. Distributors were complaining that their orders are not always supplied on time. Some distributors order a few hundred sets two weeks in advance. Company policy is not to make to stock, because of the high cost of components.

An analyst has characterized a few more symptoms of problems:

- Management does not know what is the real status of the shop floor. They know how many sets have reached the finished-goods facility, and what orders were released to production, but have no idea what happens on the shop floor.
- There is insufficient feedback from the final assembly department and the rest of the shop floor. Shop-floor control is not computerized and is performed manually by coordinators and supervisors.
- The flowtime of a set varies considerably. Setting a reasonable lead time for a batch of sets is very difficult.
- Statistics also show that 10 percent of the TV sets need rework during assembly.

Management estimates that unless something drastic is done the company will start losing money in the forthcoming quarters.

Answer the following questions:

1. Categorize the problems described above. Make a clear distinction between symptoms and problems.
2. What aspects of integration are lacking? What should be the type of information integration between departments within the organization and information integration with distributors and suppliers?
3. Try to define what control strategy is suitable for this kind of shop floor. The issues are releasing orders into production (when and in what sequence), triggers for replenishing component buffers in the final assembly, etc.

4. Suggest a strategy for improving the quality of the finished TV sets. Try to draw a checklist of what to look for.

5. What would be the functional requirements for a shop-floor control software system? Define its interface to the material requirement planning software.

6. Assume there is a central data base in the company of all operations, orders, inventories etc. Define the information requirements of each department and management. In other words, what would be the view of each department of this central data base?

7. Define performance measures to evaluate an improvement process.

8. Assume handling times are negligible and all TV sets pass the in-line inspection.

   (a) What is the minimum number of pallets needed for continuous operation of this line?
   (b) What is the theoretical throughput for each mode?
   (c) What is the maximum number of pallets?

10 REFERENCES

Adams, J., Balas, E., and Zawack, D., "The Shifting Bottleneck Procedure for Job Shop Scheduling," *Management Science,* 34, 391–401, 1988.

Aggarwal, S. C., "MRP, JIT, OPT, FMS?" *Harvard Business Review,* 63, 8-16, Sept.–Oct. 1985.

Arogyaswamy, B. and Simmons R. P., "Thriving on Interdependence: The Key to JIT Implementation," *Production and Inventory Management Journal,* 32, 56–60, 1991.

Baudin, M., *Manufacturing Systems Analysis with Application to Production Scheduling,* Prentice Hall, Englewood Cliffs, NJ, 1990.

Beckett, W. K. and Dang, K., "Synchronous Manufacturing, New Methods, New Mind Set," *Journal of Business Strategy,* 12, 53–56, Jan.–Feb 1992.

Bedworth, D. D., Henderson, M. P., and Wolfe, P. M., *Computer Integrated Design and Manufacturing,* The McGraw-Hill Companies, Inc., New York, 1991.

Black J T., *The Design of a Factory with a Future,* The McGraw-Hill Companies, Inc., New York, 1991.

Blackburn, J. D., *Time-Based Competition,* Business One Irwin, Homewood, IL, 1991.

Bookbinder, J. H. and Kotwa, T. R., "Modeling an AGV Automobile Body Framing System," *INTERFACES,* 17, 41–50, 1987.

Bolay, F., Waldraff, A., and White, A., "Manufacturing Planning and Control Systems," *Electrical Communications,* 63, 2, 107–114, 1989.

"Buyer's Guide," *IIE Solutions,* July 1995, pp. 36–39.

Buzacott, J. A. and Shanthikumar, G. J., *Stochastic Models of Manufacturing Systems,* Prentice Hall, Englewood Cliffs, NJ, 1993.

Bylinsky, G., "An Efficiency Guru with a Brown Box," *Fortune,* September 5, 120–132, 1983.

Carlier, J., "The One Machine Sequencing Problem," *European Journal of Operations Research,* 11, 42–47, 1982.

Chang, M. and Yih, Y., "Generic KANBAN Systems for Dynamic Environments," *International Journal of Production Research,* 4, 889–902, 1994.

Cohen, O., "The Drum-Buffer-Rope (DBR) Approach to Logistics" in *Computer Aided Production Management,* A. Rolstadas, ed., Springer-Verlag, New York, 1988.

Crawford, K. M., Blackstone, J. H., and Cox, J. F., "A Study of JIT Implementation and Operating Problems," *International Journal of Production Research,* 26, 1561–1568, 1988.

Deschamps, J. P. and Nayak, P. R., *Product Juggernaughts,* Harvard Business School Press, Boston, 1995.

"Dialogues," *Manufacturing Engineering,* May 1987, p. 30.

Dilts, D. M., Boyd, N. R., and Whorms, H. H., "The Evolution of Control Architectures for Automated Manufacturing Systems," *Journal of Manufacturing Systems,* 10, 79–93, 1991.

Duenys, I., Hopp, W. J., and Spearman, M. L., "Characterizing the Output Process of a CONWIP Line with Deterministic Processing and Random Outages," *Management Science,* 39, 975–988, 1993.

Erens, F. J. and Hegge, H. M. H., "Manufacturing and Sales Coordination for Product Variety," *International Journal of Production Economics,* 37, 83–99, 1994.

Fogarty, D. W., Blackstone, J. H., and Hoffman, T. R., *Production and Inventory Management,* South-Western, Cincinnati, OH, 1991.

Ford, H. and Crowther, S., *My Life and Work,* Heinemann, London, 1924.

Fry, D., Cox, F., and Blackstone J. H., "An Analysis and Discussion of the Optimized Production Technology Software and Its Use," *Production and Operations Management,* 1, 229–242, 1992.

Goldratt, E. M., "Computerized Shop Floor Scheduling," *International Journal of Production Research,* 26, 443–455, 1988.

Goldratt, E. M. and Cox, J., *The Goal: Excellence in Manufacturing,* North River Press, New York, 1984.

Goldratt, E. M. and Cox, J., *The Goal: A Process of Ongoing Improvement,* North River Press, New York, 1986.

Goldratt, E. M. and Fox, R. G., *The Race,* North River Press, New York, 1986.

Golhar, D. Y. and Stam, C. L., "The Just in Time Philosophy: A Literature Review," *International Journal of Production Research,* 29, 657–676, 1991.

Graves, S. C., Rinnooy Kan, A. H. G., and Zipkin, P. H., *Logistics of Production and Inventory,* North Holland, Amsterdam, 1993.

Greenwood, N. R., *Implementing Flexible Manufacturing Systems,* John Wiley & Sons, New York, 1988.

Groover, M. P., *Automation Production Systems and Computer Integrated Manufacturing,* Prentice Hall, Englewood Cliffs, NJ, 1987.

Hodgson, J. and Wang, D. "Optimal Hybrid Push/Pull Control Strategies for a Parallel Multistage System: Part I," *International Journal of Production Research,* 29, 1279–12, 1991.

Hopp, W. J. and Spearman, M. L., "Throughput of a Constant Work in Process Manufacturing Line Subject to Failures," *International Journal of Production Research,* 29, 635–655, 1991.

Inman, R. R. and Bulfin, R. L., "Sequencing JIT Mixed Model Assembly Lines," *Management Science,* 37, 901–904, 1991.

Institute for Defense Analysis, Report R-338, Dec. 1988.

Jacobs, R. F., "OPT Uncovered: Many Production Planning and Scheduling Concepts Can Be Applied without the Software," *Industrial Engineering,* 32–41, Oct. 1984.

Jasany, L. C., "Integrating the Enterprise," *Automation,* 38, 86–88, Dec. 1991.

Johnson, A., "Is Any System Letter Perfect?" *Management Review,* 85, 22–27, Sept. 1986.

Karmarkar, U., "Getting Control of Just in Time," *Harvard Business Review,* 67, 122–131, Sept.-Oct. 1989.

Kearns, D., "Xerox Satisfying Customer Needs with a New Culture," *Management Review,* 78, 61–63, 1989.

Kreisher, K., "MRP II—What It Means to You," *Plastic Technology,* 68, July 1988.

Krepchin, I. R., "How Software Must Change To Meet JIT Demand," *Modern Materials Handling,* 43, 72–74, Dec. 1988.

Luebbe, R. and Finch, B., "Theory of Constraints and Linear Programming: A Comparison," *International Journal of Production Research,* 30, 1471–1478, 1992.

Lundrigan, R., "What Is this Thing Called OPT?" *Production and Inventory Management,* 27, Second Quarter, 2–11, 1986.

Manufacturing Engineering Software, ICP Publications, Indianapolis, IN, 1990.

Meleton, M. P., "OPT—Fantasy or Breakthrough?" *Production and Inventory Management,* 27, Second Quarter, 13–21, 1986.

Miller, R. K. and Walker, T. C., *FMS/CIM Systems Integration Handbook,* Fairman Press, Lilburn, GA, 1990.

Miltenburg, G. J., "Level Schedules for Mixed Model Assembly Lines in Just in Time Production Systems," *Management Science,* 35, 192–207, 1989.

Mitra, A., *Fundamentals of Quality Control and Improvement,* Macmillan, New York, 1993.

Monden, Y., "Adaptable Kanban Systems Helps Toyota Maintain Just in Time Production," *Industrial Engineering,* 13, 5, 28–46, 1981.

Monden, Y., *Toyota Production System,* Industrial Engineering and Management Press, Norcross, GA, 1993.

Morton, T. E. and Pentico, D. W., *Heuristic Scheduling Systems,* John Wiley & Sons, New York, 1993.

Naj, A. M., "Manufacturing Gets a New Craze from Software: Speed," *Wall Street Journal,* Aug. 13, 1996, p. B4.

New, C. *Requirement Planning,* Halstead Press, New York, 1973.

"News and Trends," *Modern Materials Handling,* April 1988, p. 7.

Orlicky, J., *Materials Requirements Planning: The New Way of Life in Production and Inventory Management,* The McGraw-Hill Companies, Inc., New York, 1975.

Plenert, G. and Best, T. D., "MRP, JIT and OPT: What's Best?" *Production and Inventory Management,* 27, Second Quarter, 22–28, 1986.

Plossl, G. W. and Wight, O. W., *Material Requirements Planning by Computer: A Special Report,* American Production and Inventory Control Society, Washington, DC, 1971.

Porteus, E. L., "Investing in Reduced Set-Up in the EOQ Model," *Management Science,* 31, 998–1010, 1985.

Quinlan, J. C., "How MRP II Revived the Raymond Corporation," *Tooling and Production,* 40, 79, 1989.

Reid, C., *Well Made in America: Lessons from Harley Davidson Being the Best,* The McGraw Hill Companies, Inc., New York, 1990.

Reiser, M. and Lavenberg, S., "Mean Value Analysis of Closed Multichain Queueing Networks," *Journal of the Association of Computing Machinery,* 27, 3313–322, 1980.

Riggs, J. L., *Production Systems: Planning, Analysis and Control,* John Wiley & Sons, New York, 1987.

Ronen, B. and Starr, M. K., "Synchronized Manufacturing as in OPT: From Practice to Theory," *Computers in Industrial Engineering,* 18, 585–600, 1990.

Schoenberger, R. J., "Applications of Single Card and Dual Card Kanbans," *INTERFACES,* 13, 4, 56–67, 1983.

Shingo, S., *Study of Toyota Production System from Industrial Engineering Viewpoint,* Productivity Press, Cambridge, MA, 1981.

Sohal, A. S. and Naylor, D., "Implementation of JIT in a Small Manufacturing Firm," *Production and Inventory Management Journal,* 33, First Quarter, 20–25, 1992.

Spearman, M. L., "Customer Service in Pull Production Systems," *Operations Research,* 40, 945–948, 1992.

Spearman, M. L., Woodruff, D., and Hopp, W. J., "CONWIP: A Pull Alternative to Kanban," *International Journal of Production Research,* 28, 879–894, 1990.

Spearman, M. L. and Zanzanis, M. A., "Push and Pull Production Systems: Issues and Comparison," *Operations Research,* 40, 521–532, 1992.

Suzaki, K., *The New Manufacturing Challenge: Techniques for Continuous Improvement,* Collier Macmillan, New York, 1987.

Tayur, "Properties of Serial KANBAN Systems," *Queueing Systems,* 12, 297–318, 1992.

"Technology Update," *Tooling and Production,* 40, 40, 1989.

Thompson, J. D., *Organizations in Action,* The McGraw Hill Companies, Inc., New York, 1967.

Turbide, D. A., "MRP II—Still Number One," *IIE Solutions,* July 1995, pp. 28–31.

Vollman, T. E., "OPT as an Enhancement to MRP II," *Production and Inventory Management,* 27, Second Quarter, 38–47, 1986.

Wallace, T. F., *MRP II: Making It Happen,* Oliver Wight Limited Publications, Essex Junction, VT, 1990.

White, R. E., "An Empirical Assessment of JIT in U. S. Manufacturers," *Production and Inventory Management Journal,* 34, Second Quarter, 38–42, 1993.

Wight, O., *The Executives Guide to Successful MRP II,* Oliver Wight Limited Publications, Essex Junction, VT, 1984a.

Wight, O., *Manufacturing Resource Planning: MRP II,* Oliver Wight Limited Publications, Essex Junction, VT, 1984b.

APPENDIX A

TABLE A-1
Area under the normal curve: $\Phi(z) = \int_{-\infty}^{z} \phi(t)\, dt$

z	0.00	0.01	0.02	0.03	0.04	0.05	0.06	0.07	0.08	0.09
0.0	.5000	.5040	.5080	.5120	.5160	.5199	.5239	.5279	.5319	.5359
0.1	.5398	.5438	.5478	.5517	.5557	.5596	.5636	.5675	.5714	.5753
0.2	.5793	.5832	.5871	.5910	.5948	.5987	.6026	.6064	.6103	.6141
0.3	.6179	.6217	.6255	.6293	.6331	.6368	.6406	.6443	.6480	.6517
0.4	.6554	.6591	.6628	.6664	.6700	.6736	.6772	.6808	.6844	.6879
0.5	.6915	.6950	.6985	.7019	.7054	.7088	.7123	.7157	.7190	.7224
0.6	.7257	.7291	.7324	.7357	.7389	.7422	.7454	.7486	.7517	.7549
0.7	.7580	.7611	.7642	.7673	.7704	.7734	.7764	.7794	.7823	.7852
0.8	.7881	.7910	.7939	.7967	.7995	.8023	.8051	.8079	.8106	.8133
0.9	.8159	.8186	.8212	.8238	.8264	.8289	.8315	.8340	.8365	.8389
1.0	.8413	.8438	.8461	.8485	.8508	.8531	.8554	.8577	.8599	.8621
1.1	.8643	.8665	.8686	.8708	.8729	.8749	.8770	.8790	.8810	.8830
1.2	.8849	.8869	.8888	.8907	.8925	.8944	.8962	.8980	.8997	.9015
1.3	.9032	.9049	.9066	.9082	.9099	.9115	.9131	.9147	.9162	.9177
1.4	.9192	.9207	.9222	.9236	.9251	.9265	.9279	.9292	.9306	.9319
1.5	.9332	.9345	.9357	.9370	.9382	.9394	.9406	.9418	.9429	.9441
1.6	.9452	.9463	.9474	.9484	.9495	.9505	.9515	.9525	.9535	.9545
1.7	.9554	.9564	.9573	.9582	.9591	.9599	.9608	.9616	.9625	.9633
1.8	.9641	.9649	.9656	.9664	.9671	.9678	.9686	.9693	.9699	.9706
1.9	.9713	.9719	.9726	.9732	.9738	.9744	.9750	.9756	.9761	.9767
2.0	.9772	.9778	.9783	.9788	.9793	.9798	.9803	.9808	.9812	.9817
2.1	.9821	.9826	.9830	.9834	.9838	.9842	.9846	.9850	.9854	.9857
2.2	.9861	.9864	.9868	.9871	.9875	.9878	.9881	.9884	.9887	.9890
2.3	.9893	.9896	.9898	.9901	.9904	.9906	.9909	.9911	.9913	.9916
2.4	.9918	.9920	.9922	.9925	.9927	.9929	.9931	.9932	.9934	.9936
2.5	.9938	.9940	.9941	.9943	.9945	.9946	.9948	.9949	.9951	.9952
2.6	.9953	.9955	.9956	.9957	.9959	.9960	.9961	.9962	.9963	.9964
2.7	.9965	.9966	.9967	.9968	.9969	.9970	.9971	.9972	.9973	.9974
2.8	.9974	.9975	.9976	.9977	.9977	.9978	.9979	.9979	.9980	.9981
2.9	.9981	.9982	.9982	.9983	.9984	.9984	.9985	.9985	.9986	.9986
3.0	.9987	.9987	.9987	.9988	.9988	.9989	.9989	.9989	.9990	.9990

Recall:

$$\Phi(-z) = 1 - \Phi(z)$$

$$\text{and}\quad \phi(z) = \frac{1}{\sqrt{2\pi}} e^{-(1/2)z^2}$$

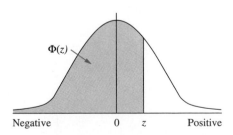

TABLE A-2
Unit normal linear loss integral: $L(z) = \int_z^\infty (t - z)\, \phi(t)\, dt$

z	.00	.01	.02	.03	.04	.05	.06	.07	.08	.09
0.0	.3989	.3940	.3890	.3841	.3793	.3744	.3697	.3649	.3602	.3556
0.1	.3509	.3464	.3418	.3373	.3328	.3284	.3240	.3197	.3154	.3111
0.2	.3069	.3027	.2986	.2944	.2904	.2863	.2824	.2784	.2745	.2706
0.3	.2668	.2630	.2592	.2555	.2518	.2481	.2445	.2409	.2374	.2339
0.4	.2304	.2270	.2236	.2203	.2169	.2137	.2104	.2072	.2040	.2009
0.5	.1978	.1947	.1917	.1887	.1857	.1828	.1799	.1771	.1742	.1714
0.6	.1687	.1659	.1633	.1606	.1580	.1554	.1528	.1503	.1478	.1453
0.7	.1429	.1405	.1381	.1358	.1334	.1312	.1289	.1267	.1245	.1223
0.8	.1202	.1181	.1160	.1140	.1120	.1100	.1080	.1061	.1042	.1023
0.9	.1004	.0986	.0968	.0950	.0933	.0916	.0899	.0882	.0865	.0849
1.0	.0833	.0817	.0802	.0787	.0772	.0757	.0742	.0728	.0714	.0700
1.1	.0686	.0673	.0659	.0646	.0634	.0621	.0609	.0596	.0584	.0573
1.2	.0561	.0550	.0538	.0527	.0517	.0506	.0495	.0485	.0475	.0465
1.3	.0455	.0446	.0436	.0427	.0418	.0409	.0400	.0392	.0383	.0375
1.4	.0367	.0359	.0351	.0343	.0336	.0328	.0321	.0314	.0307	.0300
1.5	.0293	.0286	.0280	.0274	.0267	.0261	.0255	.0249	.0244	.0238
1.6	.0232	.0227	.0222	.0216	.0211	.0206	.0201	.0197	.0192	.0187
1.7	.0183	.0178	.0174	.0170	.0166	.0162	.0158	.0154	.0150	.0146
1.8	.0143	.0139	.0136	.0132	.0129	.0126	.0123	.0119	.0116	.0113
1.9	.0111	.0108	.0105	.0102	.0100	.0097	.0094	.0092	.0090	.0087
2.0	.0085	.0083	.0080	.0078	.0076	.0074	.0072	.0070	.0068	.0066
2.1	.0065	.0063	.0061	.0060	.0058	.0056	.0055	.0053	.0052	.0050
2.2	.0049	.0047	.0046	.0045	.0044	.0042	.0041	.0040	.0039	.0038
2.3	.0037	.0036	.0035	.0034	.0033	.0032	.0031	.0030	.0029	.0028
2.4	.0027	.0026	.0026	.0025	.0024	.0023	.0023	.0022	.0021	.0021
2.5	.0020	.0019	.0019	.0018	.0018	.0017	.0017	.0016	.0016	.0015
2.6	.0015	.0014	.0014	.0013	.0013	.1012	.0012	.0012	.0011	.0011
2.7	.0011	.0010	.0010	.0010	.0009	.0009	.0009	.0008	.0008	.0008
2.8	.0008	.0007	.0007	.0007	.0007	.0006	.0006	.0006	.0006	.0006
2.9	.0005	.0005	.0005	.0005	.0005	.0005	.0004	.0004	.0004	.0004
3.0	.0004	.0004	.0004	.0003	.0003	.0003	.0003	.0003	.0003	.0003

Recall:

$$\phi(t) = \frac{1}{\sqrt{2\pi}} e^{-(1/2)t^2}$$

$$\Phi(z) = \int_{-\infty}^{z} \phi(t)\, dt$$

$$L(-z) = L(z) + z$$

$$L(z) = z\Phi(z) + \phi(z) - z$$

INDEX